BRITANNICA ET AMERICANA
Dritte Folge · Band 36

Herausgegeben von
WOLFRAM R. KELLER
ANDREW JAMES JOHNSTON

TOBIAS GABEL

The Miltonic Sensorium

Sensory Discourse
and Literary Epistemology
in the Writings
of John Milton

Universitätsverlag
WINTER
Heidelberg

Bibliografische Information der Deutschen Nationalbibliothek

Die Deutsche Nationalbibliothek verzeichnet diese Publikation
in der Deutschen Nationalbibliografie;
detaillierte bibliografische Daten sind im Internet
über *http://dnb.d-nb.de* abrufbar.

Zugl.: Gießen; Univ., Diss., 2020

Gedruckt mit Unterstützung
des Förderungsfonds Wissenschaft der VG WORT

UMSCHLAGBILDER

vorn: Eugène Delacroix (1798–1863), *Milton dictant à ses filles son poème épique
«Le paradis perdu»* (1827/28). Kunsthaus Zürich,
Geschenk des Kantons Zürich zum 200-Jahr-Jubiläum
der Zürcher Kunstgesellschaft, 1988.

hinten: Title page illustration (woodcut) from William Parkinson,
*Paradisi in Sole Paradisus Terrestris, Or A Garden of All Sorts of Pleasant Flowers
which Our English Ayre Will Permit to be Noursed Up …*
(London: Tho[mas] Cotes, to be sold by Robert Allot, 1629).

ISBN 978-3-8253-4842-7

Dieses Werk einschließlich aller seiner Teile ist urheberrechtlich geschützt.
Jede Verwertung außerhalb der engen Grenzen des Urheberrechtsgesetzes
ist ohne Zustimmung des Verlages unzulässig und strafbar. Das gilt insbesondere
für Vervielfältigungen, Übersetzungen, Mikroverfilmungen und die Einspeicherung
und Verarbeitung in elektronischen Systemen.
© 2022 Universitätsverlag Winter GmbH Heidelberg
Imprimé en Allemagne · Printed in Germany
Gedruckt auf umweltfreundlichem, chlorfrei gebleichtem
und alterungsbeständigem Papier.

Den Verlag erreichen Sie im Internet unter:
www.winter-verlag.de

*For thus the senses and the intellect
Shall each to each supply a mutual aid,
Invigorate and sharpen and refine
Each other with a power that knows no bound,
And forms and feelings acting thus, and thus
Reacting, they shall each acquire
A living spirit and a character
Till then unfelt, and each be multiplied
With a variety that knows no end.*

WORDSWORTH

Contents

List of Illustrations	vii
Acknowledgements	ix
Prologue: Friedell, Benjamin, Eisenstein, Milton; or, Viewing the Senses through the Lens of History	1
Introduction: Situating Miltonic Sensory Discourse	17
Part One: THE SENSES IN DISCOURSE	
Chapter 1: Milton and the Senses	27
Chapter 2: What Is Sensory Discourse?	51
Part Two: SENSORY DISCOURSE IN MILTON	
Chapter 3: Sensory Discourse in Milton's Latin Elegies (I, V, VII)	113
Chapter 4: Sensory Discourse in Milton's 'Prolusions' (I, II, VI)	169
Chapter 5: Sensory Discourse in the Proems of *Paradise Lost*	251
Conclusion: Trajectories in the Miltonic Sensorium	365
Epilogue: After-Images of the Miltonic Sensorium	371
Bibliography	387
Index	403

List of Illustrations

Figure	Page
1. Francis Bacon, *Instauratio Magna* (1620), title page	55
2. Francis Bacon, *The Advancement of Learning* (1640), title page	56
3. Robert Hooke, *Micrographia* (1665), 'Schem[a] XXXIV': a flea.	77
4. John Parkinson, *Paradisi in Sole Paradisus Terrestris ...* (London, 1629) Various flowers (including '3 *Calendula*. Marigolds.')	183
5. John Bunyan, *The Holy War ...* (1682), frontispiece: 'The Towne of Mansoul'.	313
6. Eugène Delacroix, *Milton Dictating 'Paradise Lost' to His Daughters* (1827/28). Kunsthaus Zürich	377
7. Henry Fuseli, *Milton Dictating to His Daughter* (1793).	379
8. L. Noel after H. Decaisne, *Milton* (1830?).	380

Acknowledgements

This book is a slightly revised version of my doctoral dissertation, submitted to the University of Giessen, Germany, in 2019 and defended on 30 January of the following year.

For his longstanding support – longer, even, than the writing of this study –, I am grateful to Professor Ulrich Horstmann (Marburg), whose openness of mind and ample patience were matched only by a strategically deployed impatience without which I might still now be pondering my notes. For this, as well as for his continuing inspiration towards the literary life, my heartfelt thanks.

To my second advisor, Professor Ingo Berensmeyer (Munich), I hope to have disproved the notion that 'no sound ever comes from the gates of Eden'. I am grateful for his thoughtful comments on my project and his support throughout the dissertation process.

Professors Wolfram R. Keller and Andrew James Johnston (Berlin) kindly accepted my study for publication in the *Britannica et Americana* series, for which I wish to thank them both. My thanks, also, to the editorial team at Universitätsverlag Winter, Dr Andreas Barth and Sarah Bohn. With his inventive cover design, Ralf Stemper once again managed to knock it out of the park (or rather, perhaps, the Garden).

Without the sharp eye and discretion of Francis Ipgrave, whose help in preparing the final version of my manuscript really was invaluable, this book would have been much the poorer. All of my friends and colleagues at the University of Giessen and beyond never failed to lift my spirits throughout the years: I thank you all – and hope we will be able to see more of each other soon.

Finally, I want to thank my wife, Stephanie, who has had to put up with so much in order that I could put this project to rest. Without her steady support and encouragement, who knows whether I would have managed to 'venture down/The dark descent, and up to reascend'? In this book of many careful qualifications, then, nothing will be as true and obvious as its dedication:

Für Steffi.

Heppenheim, 9 December 2021,
on the 413th anniversary of Milton's birth

T. G.

Prologue
Friedell, Benjamin, Eisenstein, Milton; or, Viewing the Senses through the Lens of History

> *The history of the different ways of seeing is the history of the world.*
> Egon Friedell[1]

While Egon Friedell was busy working on *A Cultural History of the Modern Age* in the early 1920s, recent technological developments, leading from photography and recorded sound to the rise of audio-visual media and the advent of the 'talkie' – *The Jazz Singer* was released in 1927, the same year as the German edition of Friedell's book –, had already begun to affect the way contemporaries were thinking about their senses. Cameras, lenses, films, and projectors all provided models to reflect on the difference between *sensation* ('the process by which our sensory receptors and nervous systems receive and represent stimulus energies from our environment') and *perception* ('the process of organizing and interpreting sensory information, enabling us to recognize meaningful objects and events'),[2] just as, two generations before, the camera obscura had provided Karl Marx and Friedrich Engels with a model of what they called 'ideological inversion,' when they argued that, 'if in all ideology men and their circumstances appear upside-down as in a *camera obscura*, this phenomenon arises just as much from their historical life-process as the inversion of objects on the retina does from their physical life-process.'[3] When Marx and Engels published those lines in *The German Ideology* (1846), the earliest processes of monochrome photography were only fifteen years old, and daguerreotype, the first to become widely available, barely ten.[4] Nevertheless, these developments had already begun to affect the way the human sensorium was being conceptualised; witness Marx's much-quoted remark that 'the forming of the

---

[1] Egon Friedell, *A Cultural History of the Modern Age. Vol. 1: Renaissance and Reformation*. With a new introduction by Allan Janik (New Brunswick, N. J.: Transaction Publishers, 2008 [1930, orig. 1927]), 22.
[2] David G. Myers/C. Nathan DeWall, *Psychology*, 12th ed. (New York: Macmillan Worth, 2018), G-9, G-11.
[3] Marx and Engels quoted in Terry Eagleton, *Ideology: An* Introduction (London: Verso, 1991), 71.
[4] While the *camera obscura* and other similar devices, known since antiquity, had become significantly more popular in the seventeenth century, it was their further development in the late eighteenth and early nineteenth centuries which paved the way for photography and film; see Don Gifford, *The Farther Shore: A Cultural History of Perception, 1798–1984* (London: Faber & Faber, 1990), 28–34.

five senses is a labour of the entire history of the world down to the present.'[5] If labour and progress went hand in hand, technological advances in optical technology were sure to contribute to the 'labour' of forming the five senses. From philosophical and socio-political metaphor to artistic appropriation, new sensory technologies stimulated thinking and writing *about* the senses as well as *in terms of* the senses during the long end of the nineteenth and the beginning of the twentieth century.[6] Photography and film, as artistic applications of scientific optics, give us a first impression of how the cultural history of the senses is written, to a considerable extent, by accounting for changes in how they are employed.

Friedell

Egon Friedell, too, was provoked by the (still relatively novel) technology of cameras and lenses into more far-reaching reflections on the functioning of the senses in general, and – as in Marx's bon mot – on their place in history. His claim is comprehensive: *The history of the different ways of seeing is the history of the world.* This should not be taken, however, as a metaphorical expression of *historiographical* relativity – history construed as the history of different outlooks and viewpoints –, or even of the kind of intellectual *Einfühlung* called for by Quentin Skinner, who declared, 'My aspiration is not [...] to enter into the thought-processes of long-dead thinkers; it is simply to use the ordinary techniques of historical enquiry to grasp their concepts, to follow their distinctions, to appreciate their beliefs and, so far as possible, *to see things their way.*'[7] Friedell, for his part, is not using 'history' as shorthand for 'historiography,' and there is nothing metaphorical about his 'history of seeing.' Rather, his 'different ways of seeing' are to be understood in terms of the experiencing body; their place is in history as it unfolds, not in historiography as it is written. It is the problem of sensation and perception itself that he is concerned with. Any abstraction from it, any theorisation of it, be it in the guise of more or less lively metaphor, scientific investigation or artistic representation, must remain grounded in individual experience in history.

When Friedell is considering the ways in which this grounding may occur, this must be considered against the sensory context of his time, which combined a profound epistemological insecurity[8] with the dual sensory revolution of film and recorded sound, soon to be amalgamated into talking film. Like photography in the half-century before, both of these technologies provided the means for 'fixing' a certain sense impression

---

[5] Marx quoted in Robert Jütte, *A History of the Senses: From Antiquity to Cyberspace*, trans. J. Lynn (Cambridge: Polity, 2005 [2000]), 8.

[6] While I restrict my brief survey to 'writers' in the broad sense of the term, photography and film of course had considerable impact upon other, primarily visual, art forms of the day as well, such as cubist and other avant-garde painting.

[7] Quentin Skinner, 'Introduction: Seeing Things Their Way,' in: Idem, *Visions of Politics, Volume I: Regarding Method* (Cambridge: Cambridge University Press, 2002), 1–7, at 3. Note the double reference to sight – 'visions,' 'regarding' – in the title of Skinner's book.

[8] See Sara Danius, *The Senses of Modernism: Technology, Perception, and Aesthetics* (Ithaca, N. Y.: Cornell University Press, 2002), 56.

and making it available to large audiences and/or spectatorships.[9] They also changed the way in which sight, the most paradigmatic of senses for much of the modern period, was understood and appreciated. Furthermore, they yielded a conceptual framework useful for thinking about the trans-historical communication of sense impressions in a more abstract way: If we had some reels of film from Augustan Rome, or a field recording of the sounds of seventeenth-century London – would that not bring us closer to the sensescapes and the sensoria of those eras?

Significantly, Friedell's own discussion is given, at the outset, not in terms of a technological, but rather in those of a natural history of the senses. Everything about the senses is historically contingent: 'Every age has ... its particular physiology,' Friedell writes, 'and even individual senses of its own, an optic, acoustic, neural character which belongs to it alone.'[10] The problem with this is that it appears to gloss over an important distinction. For Friedell, *sensation* (the immediate, physiological response of the sensory organs to a stimulus) and *perception* (the conscious appreciation of that stimulus as an act of cognition) come to be one and the same thing. Herein, though, lies the danger of a reductive – and misleadingly skewed – biological determinism vis-à-vis the human sensorium, as when he adds that,

> 'Reality' is always and everywhere the same – namely: unknown. But it affects always different sense-nerves, retinae, brain-cells, and ear-drums. This picture of the world [*Bild von der Welt*] undergoes a change with almost every generation. […] If there was a wizard who by his magic could reconstruct for us the retina-image of a forest landscape in the eye of an Athenian of the days of Pericles and then the retina-image of the same landscape in the eye of a crusader of the Middle Ages, the two pictures would be quite dissimilar; and if we then went ourselves to the spot and looked at the forest, we should recognize the one no more than the other in it.[11]

This thought experiment is striking, and we might almost agree with Friedell's view; however, it is important to realise that, while the 'retina-image' of the ancient Athenian or the crusader would – even *ceteris imparibus*, i.e. barring slight disparities on account of corrective lenses, nutrition, etc. – not have been much different from our own, its *cognitive correlate* – what the Athenian *knew* or *thought she knew* she was seeing, and what she was making of that – must have been quite different. While sensation – unaided, again, by technological enhancement – is historically stable below the natural-historical macro-level of evolution, perception is bound up with cultural factors and therefore historically contingent. Since the most fundamental of these factors, certainly,

---

[9] It may not be entirely coincidental that the semantic extension of the term 'sensation' from a narrowly sensory definition to its additional – and now, perhaps, predominant – meaning of 'an event or a person that "creates a sensation"' is dated by the *OED* to the latter half of the nineteenth century (s. v. 'sensation,' 3c). On the nexus between the senses and the sensational, see also John Jervis, *Sensational Subjects: The Dramatization of Experience in the Modern World* (London: Bloomsbury, 2015), 1–13.
[10] Friedell, *Cultural History of the Modern Age*, 22.
[11] Friedell, *Cultural History of the Modern Age*, 23.

is language, Friedell's 'history of the different ways of seeing' would have to be considered a history of communicating (about) sensory experience in order to be at all accessible; however, if these are indeed the lines along which Friedell is thinking, then he does not make this explicit. Tellingly, the 'retina-image' of the past is recreated not by some sort of technician, or even an archaeologist, but by a wizard – perhaps a stand-in for the cultural historian?

In failing to acknowledge the difference between sensation and perception, Friedell misses an opportunity to come to terms with what perplexes him. After all, this difference may be compared to the difference between releasing the shutter of a camera, and looking at – appreciating, even talking about – the finished image. While sensation corresponds to the straightforward physical process of 'capturing' a given frame on the *object* media of film or digital memory (with all the possibilities of interference this suggests), perception presupposes a 'beholding' (or, in any case, receptive) *subject*. When he turns to photography, Friedell actually appears to have a similar distinction in mind:

> Even a photographic camera, reputed the deadest of apparatus, which apparently registers with perfectly mechanical passivity, is affected by our subjectivity. *Even the 'objective' is not objective.* For it is an inexplicable but undeniable fact that, just like a painter, a photographer photographs only himself. If he has the taste of an uneducated, suburban mind, his camera will produce nothing but coarse, vulgar figures; if he has a cultivated mind and an artistic point of view, his pictures will have the superior look of delicate engravings. And that being so, our photographs, like our paintings, will appear to future ages, not as naturalistic reproductions of our outward appearance, but as monstrous caricatures.[12]

If, this time, there appears to be an acknowledgement of the historical contingency of perception, this is undercut by a certain inconsistency. While the second half of Friedell's observation targets *perception* (the indispensable *interpretation* of sensory impressions), the first is concerned with what should properly be considered a mechanised simulacrum of *sensation*. In other words, Friedell again appears to ignore the fact that, in taking a photograph, the 'natural' sequence of events is reversed, and that the perception (of a suitable motif) precedes the pushing of a button that leads to the release of the shutter which, in turn, triggers a process metaphorically comparable, at least, to that of sensation. Judged consistently within the framework of his camera–eye metaphor, then, Friedell is wrong: The objective *is* objective. It is the perceiving subject handling the camera who brings into play their own perspective. It is the proverbial beholder – whether behind the viewfinder or in the darkroom – who turns (mechanised) sensation into structured perception.

When Friedell was writing, the scientific distinction between sensation and perception, which had begun with the advent of empirical psychology in the nineteenth century, was already well established.[13] As a result, the locus of the former had become all

---

[12] Ibid. (emphasis added).
[13] See Edwin G. Boring, *Sensation and Perception in the History of Experimental Psychology* (New York: Appleton-Century-Crofts, 1942), 3–52.

but inaccessible, as sensation itself was representable (and thus itself *perceptible*) only through specialist machinery. Put thus at a remove from the assessment of the perceiving subject, sensation stands, always, in need of 'imaging', 'sonification' or other forms of technological processing.[14] Two basic premises of this book emerge from this differentiation between sensation and perception, as well as from the experimental relativity of the former and the cultural relativity of the latter.

Firstly, neither sensation nor perception are self-evident, whether they are communicated through test readings, philosophical reflection, anatomical illustrations or poetry; they are both equally in need of contextualising interpretation. Put yet another way, both sensation and perception are embedded in the respective practices of their time (In this respect, at least, they may be seen as equivalent, their differences reconciled in a more fundamental understanding of their shared preconditions).

The second premise relates to the validity of applying the sensation–perception divide in a historical perspective. Is there not an anachronism lurking here? It is true that the concept as it now stands was practically unknown to the early modern discussion, for example. Nevertheless, I feel that its wider implications of a fundamental 'madeness' of all conscious perception justifies its consideration, particularly in such cases where scientific explanations of the senses are confronted with more imaginative attempts at coming to terms with them. In any case, a rash conflation of sensation and perception brings with it the greater danger of 'putting the cart before the horse' – or the photographer before their camera.

All things considered, Friedell's two points about sensation as perception (or vice versa) are meaningful in a sense slightly different from the one he had intended: Every age does indeed have 'its particular physiology' as well as 'always different sense-nerves, retinae, brain-cells, and ear-drums', to the effect that the state of scientific knowledge about these components of the human sensory apparatus shifts as physiological research moves into the future. The set of beliefs regarding the sensory organs held by any member of the generations now living in the Western world might, in part, be scientifically naïve, or even wrong – some misconceptions die hard. However, they are clearly not the same as those held by Friedell's paradigmatic Athenian.[15] From the pragmatic point of view adopted in this book, today's retinae are, in point of *cultural* fact, fundamentally different from those of the ancient Greeks – if only because we *call* them 'retinae,' command a wide array of methods for medical intervention and might even, by now, conceive of the mechanisms of sight along the lines of the CCD chip inside a digital camera, rather than as a piece of film waiting to be developed in a darkroom. In terms of their actual physiological make-up, the difference will not be nearly as marked.

If advances in science and technology have not only changed the ways the senses were used in the past, but have also had a profound influence on how they were con-

---

[14] That this is not always easy – and sometimes even questionable – is suggested by Jonathan Sterne and Mitchell Akiyama, 'The Recording That Never Wanted to Be Heard and Other Stories of Sonification,' in: *The Oxford Handbook of Sound Studies*, eds Trevor Pinch and Karin Bijsterveld (New York: Oxford University Press, 2011), 544–560.

[15] See John I. Beare, *Greek Theories of Elementary Cognition from Alcmaeon to Aristotle* (Oxford: Clarendon Press, 2004 [1906]).

ceived of, then why not simply write a technological history of the senses? There are two answers to this question, one extrinsic to science, the other – perhaps less obvious – intrinsic to it. Historically speaking, the scientific exploration and technological modification of the senses has been only one, albeit important, factor in the formation of the human sensorium; others – such as religion, philosophy, or the arts – have largely kept pace. In concert with science and technology, they all establish the *cultural* context in which the sensorium is formed. On the other hand, a concentration on the history of science has, in the past, tended unduly to magnify the *physiological* foundations of perception. In such a perspective, it is tempting to frame accounts of the human sensorium in quasi-evolutionary terms: as accounts of a progressing – 'labour'-intensive, as Marx had it – refinement of the senses, or else as the story of their deterioration at the hands of civilisation. Both of these options flirt with a biologism which is just a little too neat. The formation of the sensorium is the work, not always intentional, of many hands.

This last notion signals a move beyond the narrowly subjective perception of Friedell's lone Athenian, and towards the 'collective subjectivism' of the social and artistic spheres (as does, for that matter, the idea of a sensory *consensus* underlying these reflections so far). In Walter Benjamin's approach to sensory history, developed at much the same time as Friedell's, both of those two dimensions are clearly evident.

Benjamin

Few, if any, contributions to the early-twentieth-century debate about visual perception and its technological challenges are as widely known as Walter Benjamin's essay on 'The Work of Art in the Age of Its Technical Reproducibility,' first published in 1936.[16] While most commentators have focused on the concept of the 'aura' (and its 'decay' at the hands of reproductive technologies such as photography), Benjamin, in fact, also addresses the history of the senses in a narrower sense:[17]

> Just as the entire mode of existence of human collectives changes over long historical periods, so too does their mode of perception. The way in which human

---

[16] Walter Benjamin, 'The Work of Art in the Age of Its Technological Reproducibility: Second Version' [1936], in *The Work of Art in the Age of Its Technological Reproducibility, and Other Writings on Media*, ed. Michael W. Jennings, Brigid Doherty, and Thomas Y. Levin (Cambridge, Mass.: Belknap Press of Harvard University Press, 2008), 19–55.

[17] It seems worth noting in the present context that the primary figurative meaning (2a) listed by the *OED* for 'aura, n.' (originally denoting a gentle/morning breeze) connects the term to olfaction: 'A subtle emanation or exhalation from any substance, e.g. the aroma of blood, the odour of flowers, etc.' Benjamin's own explication integrates a trace of this 'aromatic' dimension of 'aura' into a strikingly multi-sensory image: 'To follow *with the eye* – while *resting on a summer afternoon* – a mountain range on the horizon or a branch that casts its shadow on the beholder *is to breathe the aura* of those mountains, of that branch.' ('The Work of Art,' 23, emphases mine). On comparable multi-sensory settings in Milton, see chapters 3–5 below.

perception is organized – the medium in which it occurs – is conditioned not only by nature but by history.[18]

While Benjamin's overall claim – that human perception is subject to historical change – coincides with both Marx and Friedell's, the thrust of his argument goes against Friedell's regard for the individual. Benjamin's concern, by contrast, is with the human sensory *collective*, with the *social* life of the senses, and it is precisely this which makes him an early exponent of a broadly defined approach to the human sensorium as a wider cultural (rather than a narrowly physiological) entity. At the same time, Benjamin's suggestion of a 'medium' of collective modes of perception contradicts Friedell's notion, implied in his particularising reference to 'sense-nerves, retinae, brain-cells, and ear-drums,' of the intimate immediacy of the sensory-perceptive moment. While Friedell seeks to keep perception close to the perceiving subject, Benjamin pushes it out into the world, and it seems almost as if he had in mind the analogy of sound waves, air, and hearing: Just as these three are tied together in the mechanism of sensation as stimulus, medium, and processing, the process of perception itself – far from taking place in a semantic vacuum or being 'glued' to its object at zero remove – also requires a medium. In a first, general sense, this medium is (sensory) culture.

Benjamin's second postulate is the fundamentally mediated quality not just of sensation, but also of *perception*. This follows from the first, his postulate of sensory communality, which suggests not only the historicity of human perception's 'mode' of self-organisation,[19] but also ascribes the changes it undergoes to 'human collectives.' If perception, conceived of as a historically contingent phenomenon, is indeed a collective enterprise, it must be predicated on *some* medium or media of exchange; otherwise it would be hard to imagine how individual experiences could be shared, compared, or contested. The 'medium' of perception, understood within a larger cultural context, would have to facilitate such exchanges. It would also have to accommodate the various changes which cultures – 'modes of existence', in Benjamin's words – inevitably undergo over time. Arguably, it is *language* which fulfils all of these requirements. As the medium of that 'sensory discourse' in which sense experience is both conveyed and debated (and which I will develop as an analytical category in Chapter 2), language transports explicit and implicit expressions of sensory culture. Situated at the conceptual intersection of individual and collective perception, of language change and cultural context, it caters to the impulse for exchange and debate implicit in Benjamin's observation, and registers the changes that different 'modes of existence' undergo. In another, more restricted and precise sense, then, Benjamin's historically conditioned 'medium in which [human perception] occurs' is the linguistic expression of sensory discourse, the linguistic reflection of the organisational work of the senses.

Benjamin does not stop at his observation about the collective quality of perception, however, and his further remarks point towards another factor with a bearing upon the

---

[18] Benjamin, 'The Work of Art,' 23, emphasis in the original.
[19] This is what Benjamin's reflexive wording suggests in the original German: 'Die Art und Weise, in der die menschliche Sinneswahrnehmung *sich* organisiert – das Medium, in dem sie erfolgt – ist nicht nur natürlich, sondern auch geschichtlich bedingt' (emphasis added), implying a continual feedback loop of perception and sense-formation.

development of sensory discourse: that of a *social conditioning* of the senses. Whereas Friedell remains inconclusive as to the deeper causes of the shifts and changes observable in perception, Benjamin has no qualms about analysing what he identifies as their underlying reasons. For him, this means moving beyond an investigation of 'mere culture' and entering into the realm of social history, and Benjamin is confident that his own vantage point in history will enable him to identify the true (social) nature of the sensory formations of the past. As he explains with reference to debates in late-nineteenth-century art history,

> the era of the migration of peoples, an era which saw the rise of the late-Roman art industry and the Vienna Genesis, developed not only an art different from that of antiquity but also a different perception. The scholars of the Viennese school Riegl and Wickhoff […] were the first to think of using such art to draw conclusions about the organization of perception at the time the art was produced. However far-reaching their insight, it was limited by the fact that these scholars […] did not attempt to show the social upheavals manifested in these changes in perception – and perhaps could not have hoped to do so at that time. Today, the conditions for an analogous insight are more favorable.[20]

The passages quoted contain Benjamin's notion of sensory history as in a nutshell. With striking confidence, he suggests a historical-perceptive consonance, a triad of art, perception, and their shared social foundations. For Benjamin, revolutions are always revolutions of the sensorium, causing artistic conventions to develop and transform in their wake. If, as Marx had it, 'revolutions are the locomotives of history,' art and perception are not exempt from their pull, as Benjamin points out: Their trains of thought and reflection run according to the common schedule.

In that it rests on an essentially Marxist conception of history, Benjamin's analysis is itself a monument to the time during which it was written, and the same could be said of its technological preoccupations. Expressions of a thinking focused on rupture and radical change, both aspects contribute in equal measure to Benjamin's essay, which combines an interest in two recent revolutions – one social, one optical-technological – with questions of societal change and the political instrumentalisation of art. It is no coincidence that Benjamin undertakes his short excursus into sensory history in precisely this context: Sensory history, too, is predestined to trace the fault lines with which he is most concerned.

Benjamin's contribution represents the ambiguous character of sensory discourse, to be explored more fully in a subsequent chapter. He wrote during a moment in history that was distinctly modern and which, in that sense, is still 'of our own time.' However, while we immediately recognise the sensory world of his text, its cameras and photographs and movie screens, its pragmatic thrust is not directed at a twenty-first-century audience. Today, we may take up Benjamin's suggestions and read him as a historian of the senses, or we may historicise his essay, studying it as a chapter in the history of reflective sensory discourse. However, neither of these two approaches, if taken for

---

[20] Benjamin, 'The Work of Art,' 23.

themselves, can do justice to the full complexity of sensory discourse 'in the wild.' This is why the analyses presented below – even though they are, of course, concerned with a time and with beliefs much more remote from our own – aim to recover *both* dimensions of sensory discourse, the expressive and the reflective.

Mann, Eisenstein, Milton

Like a burning glass, periods of technological or social change highlight shifts in the prevailing sensory consensus. They bring into focus the various roles played by sensory perception in the lives of contemporaries – going to see a movie, listening to the radio. They make possible new ways of conceptualising the world – as made up of tiny particles or being in tune with the cosmos. They force received and emerging opinions to enter into debate.

It is perhaps no coincidence that, in their discussion of perception and history, Friedell and Benjamin reference scientific progress and technological innovation side by side with social and economic change: the close interplay of all of these factors has been identified as a defining signature of their age.[21] Today, we encounter the particular flair of this specifically modernist take on sensory culture most often in the work of artists operating in diverse media. Quite possibly we feel that they are still speaking to us. On the other hand, though, their preoccupation with new optical technology, for instance, must clearly be seen in the context of their own time. Witness Thomas Mann's account, in the 'Danse Macabre' chapter of *The Magic Mountain* (1924), of the ostensibly visual – yet, in effect, multi-sensory – experience of going to the movies high up in the Swiss Alps in the years leading up to the Great War:

> Being used to only the purest air, they felt ill at ease in the bad air that weighed heavily in their lungs and clouded their minds in a murky fog, while up ahead on the screen life flickered before their smarting eyes—all sorts of life, chopped up in hurried, diverting scraps that leapt into fidgety action, lingered, and twitched out of sight in alarm, to the accompaniment of trivial music, which offered present rhythms to match vanishing phantoms from the past and which despite limited means ran the gamut of solemnity, pomposity, passion, savagery, and cooing sensuality.[22]

Mann's rather disparaging treatment of the cinematographic sphere – was he, perhaps, just as aware as Benjamin of a possible connection between changes in perception and social upheaval? – is underpinned by references to the visual as well as the non-visual senses, as Mann's movie-goers are not so much titillated as assaulted: the air is bad; it

---

[21] See the concise exposition of the modernist-perceptive complex in Danius, *The Senses of Modernism*, 1–24.

[22] Thomas Mann, *The Magic Mountain*, tr. John E. Woods (New York: Knopf, 1995 [1924]), 310. In another perception-centred chapter, *Fülle des Wohllauts* ('Fullness of Harmony'), Mann has his pure-hearted, foolish protagonist Hans Castorp reflect extensively upon the wonders of the gramophone. For a discussion of Mann's novel in the context of the optical technology of his day, see ch. 2 in Danius, *The Senses of Modernism*.

weighs heavy on their weakened lungs; their eyes hurt; their ears are offended by triviality. Was this all that the new technology had in store? Mann's dwelling on the significance of film as a new visual technology (developed more fully over the course this much longer episode) attests to the ambivalent fascination that film, being both a mode of artistic production and a medium of perception, held for writers of the period. Indeed, the passage quoted may be read as expressing the fear that this new medium of film would create serious competition for literary writing, given that it included modes of representing sensory content which, before, had been thought exclusive to literature. More specifically, Mann's clear *perceptual* framing of an (albeit notional) instance of bodily *sensation* – immediate, unthinking – seems, at the same time as it mocks the new technology, to be an attempt to assert the autonomy of literary discourse. Just like Friedell, one might say, Mann is intent on putting the supposedly 'objective objective' in its place. Evoking how someone felt, presenting what they perceived at a given moment, reflecting on those perceptions and thus adding depth to them: is that not what literature is for?

On the other side of the filmic–literary divide, and only a little later, the Russian director and theoretician of filmic perception, Sergei Eisenstein, put forward his notion of a *Film Sense* as a supplement to, or perhaps even in supersession of, the traditional divided sensorium.[23] Eisenstein was, as his translator notes, very much aware of the 'social function' of film – as of any art – in the context of Soviet cultural politics.[24] At the same time, however, – and his wide-ranging references attest to this – Eisenstein was uniquely aware of the cross-modal interrelations of different media as they developed over time.

Not so much interested in historical contextualisation as in seeking out innovative uses of established aesthetic codes, he finds a prime example of audio-visual montage in that most unlikely of places, considering his avant-garde credentials as a filmmaker: the literature of seventeenth-century England. In the context of adapting the poetic concept of 'enjambement' to the rhythmic disposition of film, Eisenstein comments on the work of various writers, but writes that, 'of course the most interesting poet in this regard is Milton.'[25] '*Paradise Lost* itself,' Eisenstein explains,

> is a first-rate school in which to study montage and audio-visual relationships. [... I doubt] whether many of my British or American colleagues are in the habit of dipping often into *Paradise Lost*, although there is much in it that is very instructive for the film-maker. [...] Studying the pages of [Milton's] poem, and in each individual case analysing the determining qualities and expressive effects of each example, we become extraordinarily enriched in experience of the audio-visual distribution of images in his sound montage.

---

[23] Sergei Eisenstein, *The Film Sense* (London: Faber and Faber, 1968 [1942]). Eisenstein had made his name in the 1920s with the outspokenly revolutionary films *Strike*, *Battleship Potemkin*, and *October* (which recall Benjamin's nexus of film, perceptual change, and political revolution).
[24] Eisenstein, *The Film Sense*, 9.
[25] Eisenstein, *The Film Sense*, 54–58. All subsequent quotations from Eisenstein's book are from these pages (all emphases in the original).

As an example of Milton's proto-filmic visual imagination, Eisenstein cites the following passage, which suggests first a sweeping pan of the flaming horizon, then, as he notes with excitement, 'a cinematographic instruction [...] to *change the camera set-up*: "neerer [sic] view"!':

>   at last
> Far in the horizon to the north appeared
> From skirt to skirt a fiery region, stretched
> In battailous aspèct, and nearer view
> Bristled with upright beams innumerable
> Of rigid spears, and helmets thronged, and shields
> Various ...
> (*PL* 6.78–84)

Since, as Eisenstein notes, 'Milton is particularly fine in battle scenes,' he dedicates the next few pages of his chapter on 'Word and Image' to a discussion of passages from book 6 of *Paradise Lost*, Milton's account of the 'war in heaven,' supplemented with a description of Satan's army taken from the first book of the poem.[26] In analysing these 'scenes' (as he thinks of them), Eisenstein applies a method he had developed in an earlier chapter using the example of Alexander Pushkin's long poem *Poltava*, about the eponymous battle. He breaks Milton's verse down into its constituent lines, which he rearranges 'in accordance with the various compositional set-ups, as a shooting-script, where each number will indicate a new montage-piece, or shot.' Thus, a passage like the following:

I.	The overthrown he raised, and as a herd
II.	Of goats or timorous flock together thronged
III.	Drove them before him thunderstruck, pursued
IV.	With terrors and with furies to the bounds
V.	And crystal wall of heav'n, which op'ning wide,
VI.	Rolled inward, and a spacious gap disclosed
VII.	Into the wasteful deep; ... (*PL* 6.856–862)[27]

is recast, according to Eisenstein's practice of dissolving run-on lines into a sequence of shots, as:

1.	The overthrown he raised, and
2.	as a herd of goats or timorous flock together thronged
3.	drove them before him thunderstruck,
4.	pursued with terrors and with furies to the bounds and crystal wall of heav'n,
5.	which op'ning wide, rolled inward,

---

[26] The passages discussed are *PL* 1.533–553; 6.78–86, 6.231–246, 6.853–866, 871.
[27] The numbering, in this as in the following quotations, is Eisenstein's; the text has been adapted from Alastair Fowler's edition of *Paradise Lost* (as against Eisenstein's old-spelling version).

6.	and a spacious gap disclosed
7.	into the wasteful deep; ...

Eisenstein's admiration for Milton stems from the fact that, even though a re-organisation of the action must break up the original verse, the number of lines in the original and the number of shots in the new 'shooting-script' correspond, despite the difference in visual rhythm. In another, earlier passage, the effect is even more striking. As

	... in strength each armèd hand	
I.	A legion; led in fight, yet leader seemed	
II.	Each warrior single as in chief, expert	
III.	When to advance, or stand, or turn the sway	
IV.	Of battle, open when, and when to close	
V.	The ridges of grim war; ...,	(*PL* 6.231–236)

becomes

1. led in fight, yet leader seemed each warrior single as in chief,
2. expert when to advance,
3. or stand,
4. or turn the sway of battle,
5. open when,
6. and when to close the ridges of grim war; ... ,

one expects the series of very short cuts which opens this sequence to unbalance the correspondence between Milton's poem and Eisenstein's imaginary storyboard.[28] Yet over the course of the passage, which continues for another ten lines, there is a rhythmical alternation of short and long shots, a fluctuation between heavy and subdued fragmentation in both the poem and its appropriation, which nevertheless still results, in the end, in a balance.[29] In reading these lines, Eisenstein argues, the reader's mind is stirred by the offset between the (proto-)visual arrangement of Milton's images and the arrangement of his verse, both typographically on the page and metrically in the (mind's) ear: 'there is built up here a contrapuntal [!] design of non-coincidences between the limits of the representations and the limits of the rhythmical articulations.' As a kind of multi-sensory fugue, the passages from *Paradise Lost* anticipate, in Eisenstein's analysis, potentials of representation usually associated with much later developments, scientific, technological, artistic – and social. At its most fundamental level, he

---

[28] Eisenstein's reflections on *Paradise Lost* had inspired parts of his film *Alexander Nevsky*, with its depiction of the thirteenth-century 'Battle on the Ice'; see Concetta Carestia Greenfield, 'S. M. Eisenstein's *Alexander Nevsky* and John Milton's *Paradise Lost*: A Structural Comparison,' *MQ* 9 (1975), 93–99.

[29] Eisenstein himself is reminded by this effect of another passage in *Paradise Lost*: '... mazes intricate,/Eccentric, intervolved, yet regular,/Then most, when most irregular they seem' (*PL* 5.622–624).

conceives of *Paradise Lost* much as Milton himself had: as a combination of embodied voice and evocative imagery; in any case as eminently geared towards the senses.

Drawing on a work of art quite alien, at first sight, to his own medium of choice – and on a literary text so remote from his own historical environment – Eisenstein's explication of Milton's audio-visual strategy presents an extraordinary bridging of the gap between two widely different sensory cultures, and appears to testify to a fundamental compatibility of sensory discourse throughout history. Seen from the twentieth-century perspective, affinities appeared to be running both ways: In Eisenstein's eyes, *Paradise Lost* possessed considerable sensory-visual appeal because its proto-filmic qualities made it seem ahead of its time. Conversely, however, there is also the high modernist director's appeal to the early modern poem as a model worthy of being emulated in a radically different context: a model which had become so strange, perhaps, that it was now ready to inspire something new.

These reflections are not to deny the pitfalls any such (more or less elective) affinity might conceal. On his cross-medial, transhistorical *tour de force*, Eisenstein is not concerned with the question of what *conditioned* the phenomena he singles out for analysis – a question which is central, however, to the sensory-historical reading of a text as understood in this book. What could it possibly mean, after all, in a discussion of the *historical specificity* of the perceptual codes and tropes deployed in a literary text, to ascribe to that text – with carefree anachronism – operations made possible only by more recent advances in 'sensory technology'?

Perhaps one might argue that to speak of Milton's use of audio-visual 'montage' is precisely that, only a manner of speaking, and a basically 'objective' way of evoking a clearly definable – and historically stable – pattern of sensory perception which just happens to have found its clearest realisation to date in twentieth-century film technology. Quite to the contrary, however, this book argues that any use of sensory discourse – any use of the terminology and tropes associated with sensory perception, its physiological foundations or technological modifications, its merits and discontents –, any *utilisation*, that is, of the descriptive and normative potentials of sensory discourse, is inextricably bound up with the historically specific setting in which it occurs, and to which it owes its particular thrust. As sensory discourse is conditioned by the habits, values, and technical practicalities of its day, it can never fully shed that historical specificity.

At the outset of this study of the senses in Milton, Sergei Eisenstein's enthusiastic appropriation of *Paradise Lost* reminds us of the simple truth that all explicit analysis of earlier cultural formations initiates, at the same time, the implicit analysis of one's own – to be made explicit, perhaps, by later commentators. Nevertheless, a consideration of Eisenstein's place in sensory history brings together all the various strands and layers of that history referred to so far: the arts and the sciences; our present position of taking film for granted; Eisenstein's past position of still finding out what film might be; Milton's past perfect of having commanded, arguably, a proto-cinematographic imaginary.

From Modernity to Early Modernity

This prologue has highlighted a number of distinct contributions to the modernist moment in sensory history. In their various engagements with photography and film, different authors have dealt in different ways with the 'provocation of the objective' and, in a diachronic perspective, with the provocation that is sensory history. While these short glimpses have been, by necessity, both technocentric and focused on vision, they have also afforded the opportunity to consider some aspects of sensory history in a more general sense. Neither Friedell and Benjamin nor Mann and Eisenstein were intending to write histories of photography or film. Rather, it was the photographic and cinematographic reproduction of images which supplied test cases for their respective arguments about the mutability (or, in Eisenstein's case, persistence) of the human sensorium. To illustrate their theses, they simply chose what to them were striking, and, it seems, obvious, instances of culturally mediated sense perception.

Writing during the first quarter of the twentieth century, these writers occupied a vantage point close to our own sensibilities in certain respects; in others, their preoccupations already appear thoroughly historical. Still, they may act as sensory-historical go-betweens on two connected counts: for analysing the visual ways of their time as much as articulating them; and for belonging to our own modern era as much as to the prehistory of the current sensory regime. Once more, it is the eerily, uncannily half-familiar which promises to be the most fruitful in terms of sensory-historical analysis and which will highlight, I believe, the capacity of the approach proposed in this book to recover the nuances of 'lost' ways of looking at the world.

Egon Friedell and Thomas Mann appear to have felt the 'wound of the camera lens'; their attitude towards the new technology is above all one of caution. Whether or not Friedell identified with the elusive 'wizard' to whom he refers is hard to fathom; the cool contempt felt for the cinematographic sphere by that other 'magician,' Mann, is only too palpable.[30] Walter Benjamin, while wary of the consequences of the new technology for established forms of art, acknowledges its potential not only for opening the critic's eyes to aspects of his own culture, but also for helping him contextualise the art and perception of earlier eras as well.

In their different ways, Friedell, Benjamin, and Mann all appear to substantiate the claim that sensory discourse is intimately bound up with its specific locus in cultural history. Sergei Eisenstein, as if to challenge this apparent orthodoxy, points to the possibility of transhistorical dialogue. Today, all their different ideas about the significance and historicity of the human sense apparatus may themselves be subjected to historical analysis. This indicates that the investigation of 'strange' ways of sensing the world need not be restricted to faraway lands, 'exotic' cultures or the remote past: it can start from a minimal difference, and the writers of the early twentieth century have moved well beyond that. In some respects, their views of technology and tacit assumptions about sense perception are still with us in the twenty-first century, making them semi-contemporaries of our own moment in sensory history. In other respects, we have moved on, but their shared implicit premise seems hard to contest: perception, as a function of bodily sensation, is grounded in a physical world doubling, always, as a cultural-historical scene or sensescape. In delineating, first, the interlinked dimensions

---

[30] Among other aspects of Mann's novel, the fact that everything in *The Magic Mountain* is arranged to lead up to the gigantic cataclysm of the First World War – a conflict studied intensely in recent years in terms of its sensory-historical impact – points towards the specific historical locus of that contempt. See, for example, the multi-sensory readings put foward by Julia Encke, *Augenblicke der Gefahr: Der Krieg und die Sinne, 1914–1934* (Munich: Wilhelm Fink, 2006).

of sensory discourse as reflective of that cultural-historical scene, and secondly, some of its manifestations in the writings of John Milton, this book aims to place these writings within their early modern sensory context and, ultimately, shed light on the specific perceptual and affective properties at work in the 'Miltonic sensorium.'

Introduction
Situating Miltonic Sensory Discourse

Milton's World
England, Europe, and Beyond

England around the middle of the seventeenth century was a scarcely less tumultuous place than Eisenstein's Russia. This is true, first of all, in terms of politics, as the civil warfare begun in 1642 culminated in the execution, hitherto unthinkable, of King Charles I in January 1649, followed by the double experiment of the republican Commonwealth and the quasi-monarchical Protectorate. In the heated atmosphere of the civil war years, many thought that the end times were at hand. However, it was also a tumultuous era on a geographically and culturally wider scale, in the nested contexts of European and global developments. Throughout the northern and western parts of Europe, only just beginning to recover from the havoc of the Thirty Years' War, the effects of the Protestant Reformation not so much lasted as continued to unfold, while a marked reaction to new ways of worship was in evidence even in those parts of the continent not conventionally associated with Protestantism. On the global stage, the process could be described as one of bilateral flux. Just as Englishmen (and women) went out into the world, with diverse motivations and strategies – from the group of English settlers known as the Pilgrims landing at Plymouth Rock to Cromwell's capture of Jamaica from the Spanish in 1655 –, the world came back into their ports. From trinkets to luxury items – whether textiles, scents, or spices – the material life-worlds of a broadening segment of the population became markedly more diversified.[1] Exotic fruits such as the pineapple became an obsession among the elites – and among philosophers: if people who *had* tasted the famed pineapple were unable to describe its taste – the *perfect* taste! – to those who had not been so lucky, John Locke and others wondered, how could they place any trust in the capacity of language accurately to convey sensory experience at all? The resulting debate has led Steven Shapin to conclude that 'the taste of a pineapple was perhaps the first truly modern philosophical problem.'[2] Spices, on the other hand, brought together the two unlikely worlds of aromas and – at times strong-armed – diplomacy. It is not at all coincidental that, when young Samuel Pepys, Clerk of the Acts to the restored Charles II's Navy Office, waded through 'whole rooms full' of 'Pepper scattered through every chink,' to the point that he 'trod upon it [and] in cloves and

---

[1] Linda Levy Peck, *Consuming Splendor: Society and Culture in Seventeenth-Century England* (Cambridge: Cambridge University Press, 2005).
[2] See Steven Shapin, *Changing Tastes: How Things Tasted in the Early Modern Period and How They Taste Now* (Uppsala: Uppsalas Universitet, 2011), 24–30, quotation at 29–30; see also Kari O'Connor, *Pineapple: A Global History* (London: Reaktion, 2013), and Sean B. Silver, 'Locke's Pineapple and the History of Taste,' *The Eighteenth Century* 49 (2008): 43–65.

nutmegs, ... walked above the knees,' on Thursday, 16 November 1665, he did so onboard a vessel captured in the on-going maritime war with the Dutch – 'the India shipp,' as Pepys pointedly calls it.[3] In the tumultuous world of seventeenth-century life, high politics and high cuisine might well go together; to the victor the savoury spoils.[4]

Through its sources and interpretive outlook, this study is situated firmly within the context just sketched – as firmly as is possible vis-à-vis a world of upheaval and, at times, drastic change. Its wider concern, one could say, is with those experienced realities of seventeenth-century England, as reflected and transformed in the writings of John Milton. Its particular focal point, on the one hand, is on the account Milton provides of the five human senses, and on the characteristics of the 'Miltonic sensorium.' On the levels of methodology and then of analysis, it focusses is on the notional place where perception and language meet, on the sensory-linguistic nexus of what I will call 'sensory discourse.'

Milton in His World
Poetry, Politics, Experience

Although this book is not intended, primarily, as a biographical study of Milton's writings, a brief review of his life and work will help to establish the perspective taken in later chapters. Born in London in 1608, John Milton was a party to all of the developments outlined above. That England of turmoil and experiment was his England, that Europe of exchange and contention, his Europe; in his *Brief History of Moscovia*, he would more than glance at the sphere of English mercantile expansion 'eastward of Russia as far as Cathay.'[5] His father, John senior, a near-exact contemporary of Shakespeare's, was a self-made scrivener and, turning to music in his free hours, a well-respected composer of madrigals and psalm settings, some of which were published. Milton senior had come to the metropolis from Oxfordshire, reputedly after breaking with his family over the issue of religion (as family tradition had it, the poet's grandfather had disinherited his son after having found him reading an English Bible).[6]

The younger Milton was educated first at St Paul's School and then at Christ's College, Cambridge, where he was subjected (as he himself perceived it) to the still pre-

---

[3] Samuel Pepys, *The Diary of Samuel Pepys*, ed. Robert Latham, vol. 6: 1665 (London: Bell, 1972), 300 (16 November 1665). Ever the enthusiast, Pepys calls this tableau 'as noble a sight as ever I saw in my life.'
[4] Wolfgang Schivelbusch has argued that the role played by spices in mediaeval and early modern long-distance trade could well be compared to that of oil in more recent times – both as regards demand and political implications: *Tastes of Paradise: A Social History of Spices, Stimulants and Intoxicants*, tr. David Jacobson [New York: Vintage, 1993 [1980]), 9. See the Epilogue below for an instance of Miltonic sensory discourse transplanted to the 'Age of Petroleum.'
[5] CPW 8: 473, facsimile of original title page.
[6] Barbara K. Lewalski, *The Life of John Milton: A Critical Biography* (Malden, Mass.: Blackwell, 2000), 2–3.

dominantly scholastic teaching of the day.[7] This resulted, as Barbara Lewalski notes, in 'a lifelong antipathy to the university curriculum, which he blamed for producing ignorant statesmen, ministers, and citizens.'[8] Following his graduation as Master of Arts in 1632, his solidly middle-class background afforded him a seven-year period of 'studious retirement' in the country, where he followed an ambitious reading plan in ancient history, the church fathers, and Renaissance epic, as well as composing his early Latin poetry, *Comus*, and *Lycidas*.[9]

In 1638/39, Milton travelled on the Continent, gaining first-hand experience of European Baroque culture. While France utterly failed to impress him, it was in Italy that he found himself caught between the attractions of the Roman past, scholarly hospitality of the Renaissance humanist kind, and the – to his mind – more repulsive (because more alluring?) aspects of the baroque present.[10] What certainly proved more alluring than repulsive to him were the musical offerings of his stay; after all, music had been a major part of his upbringing in an exceptionally musical household.[11] There are few places one might less expect to encounter the soon-to-be author of anti-prelatical tracts (and, already, author of *Lycidas*) than at a musical entertainment – the performance of a comic opera! – at a Roman cardinal's palazzo –; however, that is exactly where we find him, one evening in February 1639. Recounting in a letter the private audience granted to him by the Cardinal, Francesco Barberini, the next day, Milton – choosing his words carefully, no doubt – praises Barberini as a patron of the arts (not, of course, as a churchman) and remarks on the 'truly Roman magnificence' of the occasion.[12] The magnificence of the Roman present carries as its palimpsest the magnificence of the

---

[7] See William T. Costello, *The Scholastic Curriculum at Early Seventeenth-Century Cambridge* (Cambridge, Mass.: Harvard University Press, 1958), esp. 92–96 on undergraduate teaching of the senses and the faculties of the soul.

[8] Lewalski, *Life*, 28.

[9] The phrase is from a letter to a friend Milton probably wrote from his father's country home at Horton in 1633 (CPW 1: 319). On his reading, see Lewalski, *Life*, 65–6. Milton's *Commonplace Book*, begun during the period of study at Horton, is printed in CPW 1: 344–513.

[10] See Lewalski, *Life*, 108. My stark juxtaposition rather downplays the extent of Milton's appreciation for the Italy of his day, even beyond the circle of friends he made; as one indicator, Italian was to remain the only modern language he used in his own composition; see John K. Hale, *Milton's Languages: The Impact of Multilingualism on Style* (Cambridge: Cambridge University Press, 1997), 7.

[11] Exceptional even by the standards of the early seventeenth-century middle class during 'one of the most remarkable and fruitful periods in English musical history': Peter Le Huray, 'The fair musick that all creatures made,' in: *The Age of Milton: Backgrounds to Seventeenth-Century Literature*, eds C. A. Patrides/Raymond B. Waddington (Manchester: Manchester University Press, 1980), 241–272. See also the reflections on Milton's purchases of music books in Italy by Mortimer H. Frank, 'Milton's Knowledge of Music: Some Speculations,' in: *Milton and the Art of Sacred Song*, eds J. Max Patrick/Roger H. Sundell (Madison, Wisc.: University of Wisconsin Press, 1979), 83–98, and the older, comprehensive study by Sigmund G. Spaeth, *Milton's Knowledge of Music: Its Sources and Its Significance in His Works* (New York: Da Capo Press, 1973 [1913]), esp. 12–27 on Milton as an active musician.

[12] CPW I: 333–6, at 334 ('Letter to Lukas Holste at the Vatican'). Holste was a scholar and papal librarian who had introduced Milton to the Cardinal; see also Lewalski, *Life of John Milton*, 100–1.

'truly Roman' past; on the Counter-Reformation magnificence of the Italian present, Milton maintains a judicious silence.

Another notable exponent of that Italian present, the elderly Galileo Galilei, placed under house arrest by order of the Inquisition, would later turn up as 'the Tuscan artist' in *Paradise Lost*.[13] Whether or not Milton did indeed pay a visit to the captive astronomer – as has been assumed –, the impression Galileo, that major representative of the new science, must have made on him is evident from a number of references and allusions throughout the Miltonic corpus.[14] When, writing in his treatise *Of Education* barely five years later, Milton stresses the instructive value of travelling in one's youth – 'not to learn principles, but to enlarge experience, and make wise observation' –, it is hard not to read this, too, as a piece of experience gained from practice.[15]

When Milton returned to England, he did not leave Europe behind. His activities of the 1640s – including the publication of his multi-lingual 1645 *Poems* – bear ample testimony to this.[16] Throughout the civil war years, Milton engaged in a number of national and international pamphlet controversies on the topics of ecclesiastical, then secular government (against bishops, later against kings), as well as publishing a series of 'divorce tracts,' in which he argued that a marriage of true minds should on no account be impeded by the forced, loveless union of mere bodies. (In the latter he could only hear, with characteristic forcefulness of phrase, mechanical grindings 'in the mill of an undelighted and servil copulation.')[17]

In 1649, the year that began with the execution of Charles I, Milton re-entered the European universe of discourse in a new capacity and in a more consequential way than before. As Latin Secretary to the Commonwealth, and then to Oliver Cromwell's protectorate, he was in charge of defending the English government against the double accusation of regicide and blasphemy. Already blind in one eye at the beginning of his tenure, he was forced to retire from his post in 1652 after the onset of total blindness. As Milton argues in one of the sonnets addressing the failure of his eyes, the affliction, though due to the strain of the political life, had been a sacrifice for the sake of a greater, and more widely effective, cause; he had lost his sight '[i]n liberty's defence, my noble task,/Of which all Europe talks from side to side.'[18]

Arguably, it is at this point that we finally encounter the iconic Milton of later tradition – not the pamphleteer or sonneteer but the blind and self-sufficient epic bard, in-

---

[13] PL 1.288. In a second mention at PL 5.262, Galileo becomes the only contemporary individual identified by name in *Paradise Lost*.
[14] See Mario A. di Cesare (ed.), *Milton in Italy: Contexts, Images, Contradictions* (Binghamton, N.Y.: ACMRS, 1991).
[15] CPW 2: 414.
[16] See Joad Raymond, 'John Milton, European,' in: *The Oxford Handbook of Milton*, eds Nicholas McDowell/Nigel Smith (Oxford: Oxford University Press, 2009), 272–290. The point about *Poems* is made by George Steiner, *After Babel: Aspects of Language and Translation* (Oxford: Oxford University Press, 1977 [1975]), 247–8.
[17] *The Doctrine and Discipline of Divorce* (1643/44); CPW 2: 258.
[18] Sonnet 22: 12.

spired by his muse, ringed only by his daughters and amanuenses.[19] In fact, of course, the world was certainly still with him in the later 1650s and the Restoration 1660s – at times too much so, if we consider his temporary imprisonment during the autumn of 1660, following the return of Charles II.[20] It was in this atmosphere of feeling '[in] darkness, and with dangers compassed round' that he composed the greater part of *Paradise Lost* as well as (probably) *Samson Agonistes* and *Paradise Regained.*[21]

At the time of Milton's death in 1674 – despite all the prophecies and apprehensions of the previous decades, and despite all the actual catastrophes and hardships which had befallen the country, and London in particular – the world had *not* ended, but a very particular historical moment had passed. The larger developments I have outlined continued to unfold. New players, however, had entered the stage.

Milton's World in Milton's Words
The Approach and Structure of This Book

This book is divided into two unequal parts. The first, 'The Senses in Discourse' (Chapters 1 and 2), is concerned with establishing a research framework for the analyses contained in the second part, 'Sensory Discourse in Milton' (Chapters 3, 4, and 5). My prologue was intended to meet readers halfway, to more or less 'split the difference' between our shared present of the 'long twentieth'/twenty-first century and the core period of my study, which is roughly coextensive with the span of Milton's life in the seventeenth; a brief epilogue will take us back beyond the early modern era and return us to our point of origin.

As indicated at the outset, the objective of this book is to delineate the contours of what I have called, for the sake of convenience, 'the Miltonic sensorium.' By this I mean the explicit and implicit account Milton gives of the workings of the five human senses within the sensory sphere, expressed and mediated through the various treatments of this topic across different periods and areas of his writing. Indeed, it is my first contention that *(1) any fundamental characterisation of the Miltonic sensorium should account for both Milton's prose and his poetry*. The first part of Chapter 1 is dedicated to establishing the advisability of such an approach via a paradigmatic analysis of how the senses have traditionally been addressed in discussions of Milton and how they are being addressed in the growing field of research into 'Milton and the senses.' In the second part of Chapter 1, I indicate the wider, 'sensory studies' genealogy (and present-day research context) upon which any discussion of the senses in Milton should rest if it is to reflect the cultural and historical embeddedness of the texts it studies. Next, Chapter 2 elaborates the analytical category of 'sensory discourse.' While this chapter draws eclectically on earlier approaches to metaphor and the historical study of language in use, I also argue that *(2) the discursive parameters distinctive to my period of study necessitate an integrative approach to the senses in language*. In early modern culture, most later disciplinary and other specialised discourses had not yet become

---

[19] The scene has entered the common imaginary not least through its depiction in numerous paintings and engravings, by Fuseli, Delacroix, and others. See the Epilogue below.
[20] Lewalski, *Life of John Milton*, 401–4.
[21] PL 7.27.

distinct – not to mention the emergence of a separate 'aesthetic' discourse of literature.[22] Hence, explicit and implicit, 'illustrative' and 'conceptual' references to sense perception should not be treated as belonging to fundamentally separate spheres (e.g., those of 'science' and 'poetry') but should be seen as expressions of a single discursive formation, to which I refer as 'sensory discourse.' This, I argue, can be delineated by reference to Milton's own understanding of 'discourse,' which carries a distinct notion of embodiment and perceptibility; but it also relates to how the role of the senses in language and the concept of 'discourse' were understood by subsequent writers on the topic.

A subordinate but nonetheless constitutive aspect of sensory discourse as it emerges from these Miltonic and other, early modern and later sources, is its inherent orientation towards the acquisition, communication, and preservation of knowledge. Seen from today's perspective, and taking for granted some version of a qualified empiricism, this might seem obvious. With respect to a period during which the claim of the senses to epistemic worth (or even utility) was far from settled, however, this point deserves attention.[23] As will emerge from the discussion in the second half of this study, the association of sensory discourse with knowledge was valid even in contexts in which sense perception itself was explicitly presented as inadequate for the acquisition of knowledge. Consequently, my contention in the following will be that *(3) Milton's specific engagement in sensory discourse is, to a significant extent, conditioned by the antagonistic demands imposed on the senses by conflicting epistemic categories.* Inasmuch as the linguistic strategies and devices to which Milton resorts in his deployment of sensory discourse are often of a prototypically 'literary' (i.e., non-literal, trope-based) kind, and to the extent that we may – under the discursive conditions of his time – consider *all* of Milton's writing as part of a poetic (not just a pragmatic) endeavour, this inherent orientation of sensory discourse towards knowledge would then contribute to a specific kind of *literary epistemology*.[24]

The second half of this book, 'Sensory Discourse in Milton,' presents case studies of individual but, as I will argue, interrelated instances of sensory discourse in Milton's poetry and prose. Individual chapters will deal with Milton's early Latin elegies (Chapter 3) and his university prose (Chapter 4). The last analytical chapter (Chapter 5) will focus on *Paradise Lost* as the central text of Milton's later writing, and more

---

[22] See Ingo Berensmeyer, *'Angles of Contingency': Literarische Kultur im England des siebzehnten Jahrhunderts* (Tübingen: Niemeyer, 2007), 2–3, 10 (this book is now available in a revised English edition: *Literary Culture in Early Modern England, 1630–1700: Angles of Contingency* [Berlin: De Gruyter, 2020]). For an example of how different disciplinary discourses (in the case under discussion, those of theology and medicine) could interact and combine in early modern *sensory* discourse, see my essay on 'Hierarchies of Vision in John Milton's *Paradise Lost*,' in: Annette Kern-Stähler/Beatrix Busse/Wietse de Boer (eds), *The Five Senses in Medieval and Early Modern England* (Leiden: Brill, 2016), 117– 134, at 120–122.

[23] For a survey of the early modern gradation of epistemic reliability, see Barbara Shapiro, *Probability and Certainty in Seventeenth-Century England: A Study of the Relationships between Natural Science, Religion, History, Law, and Literature* (Princeton, N. J.: Princeton University Press, 1983), 27–37, and esp. the chart at 29.

[24] I borrow this phrase from Berensmeyer, *'Angles of Contingency,'* 115 and passim.

particularly on the four proems to books 1, 3, 7, and 9, which both connect to the sensory discourse of the earlier texts and offer a compressed glimpse of the sensory discourse of Milton's epic. In all of these analyses, my focus is on the significance of the sensory sphere for Milton's argument and/or presentation. Inevitably, many other significant aspects of the texts discussed can only be glanced at – or must even be disregarded completely. All the same, I endeavour to show how a reading for Milton's use of sensory discourse may illuminate distinct thematic complexes only mediately related to the senses themselves.

The texts discussed in the second part of this book – Milton's elegies, prolusions, and proems – have been chosen, firstly, for their relative similarity among themselves. This makes it possible to compare and contrast 'specimens' of sensory discourse in texts with a comparable discursive setting and purpose. At the same time, of course, their respective groups not only differ in generic and discursive character but also mark the extremes, almost, of Milton's writing life; they should thus be expected to reveal some significant differences in Milton's use of sensory discourse across genres as well as over time. The findings of this approach may then serve as a heuristic for further sensory analyses of other of Milton's writings not yet analysed here: his polemical prose; *Comus*; the sonnets; the bulk of *Paradise Lost* as well as *Samson Agonistes* and *Paradise Regained*.

The sample of texts analysed below, while certainly as heterogeneous as it is selective, accords with my proposition that Milton's treatment of the senses across his poetry and prose should be examined more closely in terms of possible *contiguities*; on the other hand, it picks up on the common observation that there are marked and often surprising thematic *continuities* in Milton's views and preoccupations, ranging from the earliest poetry and the commonplace book begun in the mid-1630s to his very last writings. The triad of elegies, prolusions, and proems is thus meant to represent, to the extent practically feasible, not only the range of Milton's writing interests across poetry and prose but also the wide chronological span of his writing, which ranges over almost half a century. Since the elegies and prolusions, at the same time, are among the least considered writings of a much-studied author, I aim to indicate how an understanding of Milton's sensory discourse in these texts may shed light on that in the more canonical ones (such as *Paradise Lost*) and vice versa.

Apart from the generic and chronological grouping of those texts, and apart beyond the productive tension it creates between commensurability and difference, there is a third aspect, I think, which supports this selection of material. This is the common notion that there is a specifically Miltonic language, whether one links this to Milton's penchant for neologism; to his prodigal knowledge of languages other than English; or to the structural peculiarities of his style.[25] The second of these aspects is interrelated with the other two, and it only seems appropriate to include samples from Milton's

---

[25] For a survey, see Thomas N. Corns, 'Milton's English,' in: *A Companion to Milton*, ed. Thomas N. Corns (Malden, Mass.: Blackwell, 2003), 91–106; see also Corns's monographs on *The Development of Milton's Prose Style* (Oxford: Oxford University Press, 1982) and *Milton's Language* (Oxford: Basil Blackwell, 1990). The impact of Milton's multilingualism on his style is treated by Hale, *Milton's Languages*.

Latin poetry (the elegies) and prose (the prolusions), considering the strong presence by volume of Latin-language writings within the Miltonic corpus.[26]

Finally, through the contextualising analyses of the Miltonic sensorium offered in the chapters below – i.e., through analyses of how Milton employed sensory discourse in his writings to specific ends –, I hope to demonstrate the characteristic features of that sensorium, both specific and conventional.[27] The question ultimately raised here is how far *(4) there is an 'eigen-sense' to Milton's engagement in sensory discourse*. By this I mean a conception of the sensorium and its uses (both pre-discursive and discursive) which may be considered characteristic of Milton.[28] Having started from the descriptive presentation of sense perception in Milton, we will then have arrived at an assessment of sensory discourse as a conceptual presence in Milton's writing and thought.

Nevertheless, given the dimensions of the Miltonic corpus as a whole, this book cannot present an exhaustive account; it is not a handbook of the senses in Milton. However, I am confident to have established, through my analyses, a number of reliable conclusions with evident potential for further investigation: If my claims carry any weight, the following reflections on the specifically *Miltonic* sensorium might also provide a model for the tracing of similar effects in the writings of other authors, as well as in early modern culture more generally.

---

[26] In a phrase echoing the mid-twentieth-century debate over Milton's (lack of) 'sensibility' (on which see Chapter 1 below), Douglas Bush even argued that, in Milton's Latin writings, 'the obscurity of a learned language ... encouraged *more spontaneous and sensuous self-revelation* than he allowed himself in his native tongue' (*English Literature in the Earlier Seventeenth Century, 1600–1660*, 2nd, rev. ed. [Oxford: Clarendon, 1962 (1945)], 380, emphasis added).

[27] Of course, what is deemed *conventional* on a synchronic plane may well be regarded as *specific* in a diachronic perspective; conversely, putative diachronic specificities may turn out to be matters of synchronic convention. They may thus, from the point of view of an historically informed analysis, both be considered *characteristic*, either of the writer or the historical moment.

[28] My coinage follows the lead of such terms as 'eigenvalue' or 'eigenfunction,' in which the German loan prefix denotes a quality of 'being peculiar to' or 'being characteristic of' (see *OED*, 'eigen-'); the simultaneous overtones of *Eigensinn* as a proud, even stubborn sense of independence (and independent agency) fit rather well, I think, Milton's image of himself; on this – *and* the necessary qualifications – see Stephen M. Fallon, *Milton's Peculiar Grace: Self-Representation and Authority* (Ithaca, N. Y.: Cornell University Press, 2007).

Part One: THE SENSES IN DISCOURSE

1. Milton and the Senses
Disciplinary and Cross-Disciplinary Lineages

1.1 The Senses in Milton Studies

To approach Milton from a 'sensory angle' is by no means unheard of. Throughout the long reception history of the Miltonic corpus, critics have repeatedly commented on the sensory (or sensuous or sensual) qualities, or lack thereof, observable in Milton's poetry and prose. Indeed, any discussion of the senses in Milton – and of the critical and scholarly traditions dealing with them – may well start from a brief consideration of these three terms: sensory, sensual, and sensuous.

The ambiguities inherent within these adjectives are due to semantic shifts and overlap in both diachronic and synchronic terms, respectively, within 'the very complicated group of words centred on *sense*.'[1] While 'sensory' is generally taken to be (1) the neutral, descriptive term relating to 'the physical process of sensation' or to the senses in general, the *OED* notes that, in this more general meaning, the use of the word 'sensory' was rare before the mid-nineteenth century; the first attestation given is from Walter Charleton's *Physiologia Epicuro-Gassendo-Charltoniana* (1654).[2] 'Sensual,' by contrast, is taken to express (2) a tendentially prescriptive point of view, connoting an all too pronounced indulgence in (the pleasures of) sense perception. While the *OED* treats (2) as the primary meaning of 'sensual,' with (1) as an alternative, the close temporal proximity and uncertainty of the respective first attestations (?1425 and c1443) argue for a fundamental ambiguity.

The case history of 'sensuous' is even more complicated and, at the same time, more Miltonic. Through it, we enter the history of the reception of the Miltonic sensorium proper. After the first two *OED* attestations of 'sensuous,' both from Milton's prose (*Of Reformation*, 1641, and *Of Education*, 1644), which are taken by the editors to carry a neutral meaning, the term is consciously revived in this sense only by Coleridge, in his *Principles of Genial Criticism* of 1814: 'Thus to express in one word what belongs to the senses, or the recipient and more passive faculty of the soul, I have re-introduced the word, *sensuous*, used among many others of our elder writers by Milton.'[3] In the meantime, however, Samuel Johnson had defined 'sensuous' as 'tender, pathetick; full of

---

[1] Raymond Williams, 'Sensibility,' in: Idem, *Keywords: A Vocabulary of Culture and Society* [London: Fontana, 1976], 235–239, at 236. Williams's essay is concerned with the development of 'sensibility' between the two familiar poles of 'being sensible' and 'being sensitive'; its particular focus, of course, is on the eighteenth century, but Williams's treatment of the 'prehistory' of sensibility is relevant to the present study.
[2] *OED*, 'sensory,' adj., 1., 2.
[3] Coleridge cited in *OED* 1a, which also holds that, considering a lack of evidence from earlier sources, 'Coleridge's assertion of more widespread usage in earlier writers is incorrect.'

passion,' which the *OED* argues was due to a misinterpretation of Milton's more neutral usage in *Of Education*.[4] Later, the more neutral 'Coleridgean' and the more subjectively tinted 'Johnsonian' meanings (the latter defined by the *OED* as 'full of tender or passionate feelings') were fused for 'sensuous' to refer, in much subsequent use, to (3) the physically pleasurable aspects of sense perception, without necessary condemnation.[5] In the following, I will take (1) 'sensory' to refer to the senses and sense perception in the most general terms (the 'aisthetic'); (2) 'sensual' to refer to an excessive and/or potentially detrimental enjoyment of sense perception; and (3) 'sensuous' to refer to a conscious or deliberate responsiveness to the gratification of the senses and the pleasure derived from this (the 'aesthetic').[6] This also appears to be the predominant allocation of meanings in current writing, while usage in early modern source materials – with Milton's ambiguous use of 'sensuous' being one example – tends to be less clear-cut.[7]

Following on from Johnson's (arguably mistaken) detection of passionate feelings in Milton's use of 'sensuous,' and Coleridge's reversal of this reading, Walter Bagehot's discussion of Milton in his *Literary Studies* (1859) reveals a further layer of reception history.[8] Typically of his time, perhaps, Bagehot – whose remarks centred on the sensory qualities of *Paradise Lost* – is interested in Milton's sensory 'character' in a very literal sense, as John Leonard points out: '[Bagehot] discerns two opposed characteristics in Milton's style. The first he calls "ancient", "classical", and "simple"; the second, "modern", "romantic", and "lavish". He thinks that most poets must choose between these features, but that [Milton] uniquely combines them.'[9] The image used by Bagehot to express this duality of 'thought' and 'feeling' – as the two characteristics could be defined – bears an obvious relation to the landscape (and sensescape) of Milton's Paradise:

---

[4] Johnson cited in *OED* 2. The relevant passage from *Of Education* runs, 'Logic therefore so much as is usefull, is to be referr'd to this due place withall her well coucht heads and Topics, untill it be time to open her contracted palm into a gracefull and ornate Rhetorick taught out of the rule of *Plato, Aristotle, Phalereus ... To which Poetry would be made* subsequent, or indeed rather *precedent, as being lesse suttle and fine, but more simple, sensuous and passionate*' (CPW 2: 402–3). Quoted by Johnson are the parts italicized after the ellipsis, without specifying his own elision, and with slight orthographical changes: Samuel Johnson, *A dictionary of the English language ...* 2 vols (London: W. Strahan for J. and P. Knapton, 1755), II, 633.
[5] *OED* 3–5.
[6] The three terms could be arranged along two distinct scales: either expressing a gradation from (1) objective-neutral through (3) subjective-positive to (2) subjective-negative meanings; or with (1) holding the middle ground between the two poles of (3) innocent pleasure and (2) lust.
[7] Thus J. M. Evans has remarked about some lines from the late-antique poet, Dracontius, that '[t]here is nothing in the whole literature of the Fall to match this picture of Eve, unashamedly sensuous yet without the slightest hint of sensuality' (*'Paradise Lost' and the Genesis Tradition* [Oxford: Clarendon, 1968], 130).
[8] Bagehot quoted in John Leonard, *Faithful Labourers: A Reception History of 'Paradise Lost,' 1667–1970*, 2 vols (Oxford: Oxford University Press, 2013), I, 128–131.
[9] Leonard, *Faithful Labourers*, I, 128. Contrast Bagehot's conjunction of 'simple' and the attributes 'ancient' and 'classical' with Milton's association of 'simple' with 'sensuous' and 'passionate' in *OE*.

> His poetry in consequence is like an artificial park, green, and soft, and beautiful, yet with outlines bold, distinct, and firm, and the eternal rock ever jutting out; ... In both his character and his poetry there was an ascetic nature in a sheath of poetry.

As Leonard, again, points out, this duality of beauty (softness, poetry) and form (firmness, asceticism) is based in a typology of characters which Bagehot had developed earlier in his essay and in which he distinguished two kinds of 'goodness,' namely 'the sensuous and the ascetic.' Sensuous characters, Bagehot writes, are prone to temptation but, by the same token, they also have 'charm' and 'sensuous sweetness': 'Being sensitive to the world, they sympathize with the world; being familiar with all the moral incidents of life, their goodness has a richness and a complication.' In opposition to this first of the two characters, Bagehot defines 'the ascetic' not so much as a product of conscious renunciation but rather as defined by an innate aversion to the sensuous: 'Some men have by nature what others have to elaborate by effort. Some men have a repulsion from the world.' For Bagehot, Milton 'almost exactly' – but not quite – 'embodied' the character of this 'ascetic, or austere species':

> Milton's austere character is in some sort the more evident, because he possessed in large measure a relieving element, in which those who are eminent in that character are very deficient. *Generally such persons have but obtuse senses.* We are prone to attribute the purity of their conduct to the dullness of their sensations. *Milton had no such obtuseness.* He had every opportunity for knowing the world of eye and ear. You cannot open his works without seeing how much he did know of it. *The austerity of his nature was not caused by the deficiency of his senses*, but by an excess of the warning instinct.[10]

At first glance, this appears to establish an unequivocal correlation, linking the poet's very own sensory receptivity to the expression of 'sensuous sweetness' in his work (here conceived of as 'a relieving element'). In Bagehot's account of how the more sensuous side of Milton's poetry came into being, sense perception is not just an idea, but a physical, physiological, and 'embodied'[11] fact of life and, more to the point, of Milton's life. Milton the man, Bagehot claims, had very keen senses – his eyes and ears were wide open. On reflection, however, things appear rather less clear: what about the poet's blindness? Surely this must be of consequence to an argument grounded – with such emphasis – in the life of the individual? Bagehot's answer – 'He had every opportunity for knowing the world of eye and ear' – contains, in its volte-face from the seeing subject to the objects seen, more than just a partial retraction of the point made in the preceding sentences: the poet had (or 'had had'?) 'every opportunity' – and yet from 1652, at least six years before Milton's work on *Paradise Lost* was begun in earnest, he

---

[10] Bagehot quoted in Leonard, *Faithful Labourers*, I, 130, emphases added.
[11] This is Bagehot's term; Milton's conception would have differed.

had to work from visual memory, or perhaps, some sort of inner vision, unspecified by Bagehot. It is for his readers to 'open his works' and *see* the knowledge they contain.[12]

After this contradictory portrayal of Milton as both more *and* less sensuous than we might think – truly a 'sensuous puritan' –, Bagehot arrives at the conclusion that, while Milton's art may appear 'romantic and modern,' this is by no means its *essence*. 'Milton's sensuous richness,' Leonard glosses Bagehot's verdict, 'is not deep but superficial. ... For Bagehot, Milton's sensual imagination fails to overcome his austerity. The beauty lies on the surface and has shallow roots; the austerity is hard as rock and cold as steel.'[13] The sensuous beauties of Milton's verse lie exposed to the reader's view; but seeing them is knowing what lies beneath.

For all the importance it does ascribe, in the end, to the corporeal senses, Bagehot's paradoxical depiction of the relationship between sensuousness and asceticism in Milton could be said to prefigure the influential account of an alleged 'dissociation of sensibility' in seventeenth-century poetry provided, sixty years later, by T. S. Eliot. In his essay on 'The Metaphysical Poets,' Eliot argues that an earlier unity of feeling and intellectual content in the poetry and drama of the sixteenth and early seventeenth centuries had been 'dissociated' from around the middle third of the seventeenth, with Milton attracting much of the blame.[14] Eliot refers to the ideal compound of both dimensions as 'sensibility';[15] his prime exponent of the earlier, unified sensibility is John Donne.[16] As Eliot contends in a prototypically sensory image, Donne and the other

---

[12] An echo of PL 3.47 (if against the wider context of that passage) might be intended; see Chapter 5.2 below.

[13] Leonard, *Faithful Labourers*, I, 131. I owe the felicitous paradox 'sensuous puritan' to Hannah Disinger Demaray, 'Milton's "Perfect" Paradise and the Landscapes of Italy,' *Milton Quarterly* 8 (1974), 33–41, at 35. In opening his introduction to the first volume of the *Complete Prose Works* of Milton, the general editor Don M. Wolfe argues that 'Puritanism in Milton's day was many things: denial of sensory joys; sober devotion to labor; ... distrust of beauty in color, music, incense; ...' (CPW 1: 2).

[14] T. S. Eliot, 'The Metaphysical Poets' [1921], in: Idem, *Selected Prose*, ed. Frank Kermode (New York: Harcourt Brace Jovanovich, 1988 [1975]), 59–67.

[15] The intricate history of this term has been traced by Williams, 'Sensibility.' In early use (from the 1400s), Williams notes, the term soon came to mean a feeling imparted through the (physical) senses *or* sense perception in general (it is in this sense that Milton speaks of 'the sensible of pain' at PL 2.278). Later came the associations more common today, rationality (being 'sensible') and tender feeling (the lasting legacy of the 'age of sensibility' in the eighteenth century). See also the chapter entitled 'Sense and Sensibility' in William Empson, *The Structure of Complex Words* (Cambridge, Mass.: Harvard University Press, 1989 [1951]), 250–269.

[16] Significantly, however, Eliot specifies the era of unified sensibility as 'the time of Donne or Lord Herbert of Cherbury' ('Metaphysical Poets,' 64). Aubrey, in his 'brief life' of Herbert, does not even mention his poetry (but does quote some lines from Donne, whose close associate Herbert had been). Today Herbert is better remembered as a philosopher and statesman than as a poet. In his *De Veritate* (pr. 1624, 1645), there is an extended theoretical discussion of the external senses, which indicates that, while Eliot might not have observed a 'dissociation' of sensibility in Herbert's poems, there definitively was a marked *differentiation* of sensuous thought and thinking about the senses even before Eliot's terminus post quem; see Edward Lord Herbert of Cherbury, *De Veritate*, ed. Günter Gawlick (Stuttgart: Frommann-Holzboog, 1966), 128–152.

1.1 The Senses in Milton Studies

poets of the metaphysical school had '[felt] their thought as immediately as the odour of a rose.'[17]

To be sure, Eliot's 'sensibility' is not necessarily identical with sensation; he does also talk about 'feeling' in a more general sense. However, his reference to the 'odour of a rose,' as well as his ascription (to Chapman) of 'a direct sensuous apprehension of thought,' appears to suggest that, for Eliot, 'sensibility' as a positive ideal is dependent, to some degree, on sense perception.[18] In discussing his view of the matter, in fact, there is an undeniable temptation to refer to 'perception' as 'sensation' (as I myself have done earlier in this paragraph). One way of framing his notion of a unified sensibility would be to say that it presents perception (in the mind of the ideal poet) *as if it were* pure, unmediated sensation; another would be that it ascribes sensation to the poet and perception to the 'direct sensuous apprehension of thought' expressed in the poem. In my view, Eliot's 'brief exposition of a theory' ('too brief, perhaps', as he readily admits) authorises both interpretations.[19]

The image of the odorous rose, drawing as it does on a longstanding association of (floral) scent and interiority, captures Eliot's concept of the intimate nexus between sensation/perception and reflection.[20] It does not, however, convey his further idea that the earlier poets had 'constantly [been] amalgamating *disparate* experience,' a notion which, in suggesting the primary disparity of perception(s), underlines that moment of agency without which the supposedly unified sensibility of earlier eras could not have *been* unified.[21] As effortless and instinctive as this process might have been (and as arduous as it might have later become), Eliot's acknowledgement of an original (and historically stable) disparity of perception enables him to lay the blame for the alleged failure of the process among later writers with *them* – instead of asking whether it might not have been manners of perception themselves that had changed. In Eliot's treatment, the perception of the poet becomes not just a responsive activity, but a responsible one. 'Sensibility,' which, in earlier centuries, had oscillated between sense perception, thought, and feeling, becomes 'the *apparently* unifying word, and ... [is] transferred from kinds of response to a use equivalent to the formation of a particular mind: a whole activity, a whole way of perceiving and responding, not to be reduced to either "thought" or "feeling".'[22]

One point on which Bagehot and Eliot might be thought *not* to see eye to eye is the question of how Milton's blindness may or may not have had an impact on his general

---

[17] Eliot, 'Metaphysical Poets,' 64. Eliot's remarks in his later essays on Milton, discussed below, also argue the central relevance of sense perception to his idea of sensibility.
[18] Eliot, 'Metaphysical Poets,' 63.
[19] Eliot, 'Metaphysical Poets,' 65.
[20] Longstanding but not ahistorical: see Keith Thomas, *Man and the Natural World: Changing Attitudes in England 1500–1800* (London: Allen Lane, 1983), 223–224; Constance Classen, *Worlds of Sense: Exploring the Senses in History and Across Cultures* (London: Routledge, 1993), 15–36, and esp. Holly Dugan, *The Ephemeral History of Perfume: Scent and Sense in Early Modern England* (Baltimore, Md.: Johns Hopkins University Press, 2011), 42–69. On the significance of the rose in the Miltonic sensorium, see Chapter 2.2 and the Epilogue below.
[21] Eliot, 'Metaphysical Poets,' 64, emphasis added.
[22] Williams, 'Sensibility,' 238, emphasis added.

sensory acuity. Whereas Bagehot offered the conflicted reading outlined above, Eliot declared, in a later essay, that '[t]he most important fact about Milton, for my purpose, is his blindness.'[23] In itself, he argues, this need not have been a problem:

> Had Milton been a man of very keen senses – I mean *all* the five senses – his blindness would not have mattered so much. But for a man whose sensuousness, such as it was, had been withered early by book-learning, and whose gifts were naturally aural, it mattered a great deal. It would seem, indeed, to have helped him to concentrate on what he could do best.[24]

'Such as it was,' Milton's sensorium had actually been *further dulled* by his blindness, with the possible exception of what Eliot refers to, a few pages later, as the resulting 'hypertrophy of [his] auditory imagination,' which had, however, been bolstered 'at the expense of the visual and tactile.'[25] Even where it had 'helped him to concentrate on what he could do best,' then, Milton's blindness had had a detrimental effect on his overall sensory receptivity, according to Eliot.[26] It should be noted that, in contrast to Eliot's faint praise at the outset of his essay, its later restatement betrays a degree of conflict or of double-standards: why not conceptualize the 'hypertrophy' noted as an 'hyperacuity' or even a refinement of the poet's ear? Conversely, and perhaps more importantly: if the aberration might be said only to concern the poet's 'imagination,' why relate it to his actual, bodily blindness? The result of this confusion becomes immediately apparent in Eliot's inference that, through this 'weakening of the visual and tactile,'

> the inner meaning is separated from the surface, and tends to become something occult, or at least without effect upon the reader until fully understood. To extract everything possible from *Paradise Lost*, it would seem necessary to read it in two different ways, first solely for the sound, and second for the sense.[27]

The 'sound' mentioned here has become wholly the sound of the critic himself, reciting – any sense that we might be talking about *a sound Milton might have meant* is lost. Eliot's 'sense' – in the sense of 'meaning' –, if it is Milton's, is not sensory. Whether blindness has much of a bearing on Eliot's assessment must, despite his initial declaration, remain doubtful: '*At no period* is the visual imagination conspicuous in Milton's

---

[23] 23 T. S. Eliot, 'Milton I' [1936], in: Idem, *Selected Prose*, ed. Kermode, 258–264, at 259.
[24] Eliot, 'Milton I,' 259.
[25] Eliot, 'Milton I,' 263. See also Beverley Sherry, 'The Legacy of T. S. Eliot to Milton Studies,' *Literature & Aesthetics* 18 (2008), 135–151.
[26] This, it should be noted, is in clear contrast to the reported experience even of acquired blindness. See for instance the short essay by the scholar and writer, John Hull, 'Rainfall and the Blind Body,' in: *The Book of Touch*, ed. Constance Classen (Oxford: Berg, 2005), 324–327. Hull became blind at roughly the same age as Milton.
[27] Eliot, 'Milton I,' 263.

poetry'.[28] All things considered, and as with his statements in his essay on the 'Metaphysical Poets', Eliot's professed concern with the bodily, sensory sphere appears rather an argumentative pretext for value judgements on a different level, namely the altogether more abstract – or, at least, more impressionistic – plane of individual reception. The obviously sensuous qualities Eliot allows on the side of his ideal of sensibility ('odour of a rose'), he denies, or 'dematerializes,' on the side of blame ('auditory *imagination*'). When Raymond Williams commented on 'the *apparently* unifying word ["sensibility"],' he might be said to have pointed to precisely this disjunction. For his own part, in any case, Eliot concludes that 'I cannot feel that my appreciation of Milton leads anywhere outside of the mazes of sound.'[29]

I would like to suggest that Eliot's judgment of the general sensuous inadequacy of Milton's verse – which is modified slightly, but not fundamentally, by references to the musicality of Milton's language and a more nuanced assessment of his imagery –,[30] itself effected that which it professed merely to observe: a dissociation of the somatic and allied conceptual dimensions of perception (as a bodily process and encoding of shared experience) from a semantic dimension supposedly discontinuous with it ('the ratiocinative, the descriptive,' as Eliot refers to it).[31] Certain resemblances to Eliot's characterization of Milton were present in Bagehot's treatment of similar territory; however, whereas Bagehot had kept the implicit contradictions of his account in suspense – and, more importantly: had kept the senses in play –, Eliot severs this connection by basically denying the frequent references to perception in Milton their corporeal foundation. Even the importance of sound in Milton (which Eliot cannot deny) is traced by him not to the actual ears of the poet (or of anyone, for that matter), but to 'the auditory imagination.' Bagehot, by contrast, had defended Milton against the accusation of sensory 'obtuseness.' The respective arguments of Bagehot and Eliot both draw on certain shared traditions of looking at Milton: this explains their general proximity; with a view to their specific differences, however, it was Eliot's account that would prove the more influential.

In due course, Eliot's comments on Milton's alleged lack of sensuous sensibility – supported prominently by F. R. Leavis, who diagnosed 'a certain sensuous poverty' in Milton's verse, but contradicted early by Eustace Tillyard and later, most notably, by Christopher Ricks – developed into what became known, in Ricks's phrase, as the 'Milton controversy,' a critical and scholarly dispute which spanned the middle decades of

---

[28] Eliot, 'Milton I,' 259, emphasis added. For balancing views, see Roland Mushat Frye, *Milton's Imagery and the Visual Arts: Iconographic Tradition in the Epic Poems* (Princeton, N. J.: Princeton University Press, 1978); Diane McColley, *A Gust for Paradise: Milton's Eden and the Visual Arts* (Urbana, Ill.: University of Illinois Press, 1993); Stephen B. Dobranski, *Milton's Visual Imagination: Imagery in 'Paradise Lost'* (Cambridge: Cambridge University Press, 2016).
[29] Eliot, 'Milton I,' 263. A more positive assessment of Eliot's response to the aural 'physicality' of Milton's verse may be found in Sherry, 'Legacy of T. S. Eliot,' 139–141.
[30] See Lewalski, *Life of Milton*, 546; Sherry, 'Legacy of T. S. Eliot,' 136.
[31] Eliot, 'The Metaphysical Poets,' 65.

the twentieth century shaping both research emphases and syllabi and the discussion of Milton in other contexts.[32]

Taken together, the development traced above – from Johnson's misreading of Milton's use of 'sensuous,' through Coleridge's revival of it (in support, no less, of a more *Genial Criticism*) and Bagehot's sensory character study to Eliot's endeavours to appreciate what sensibility he discerned in Milton's works – could be described as the 'critical tradition' in the study of the Miltonic sensorium.[33] Its exponents were not particularly interested in the senses as the primary human means of discovering the world. Rather, their interest in the senses in Milton was strictly limited to their function as a source of poetic effects, epitomized by that unduly disambiguated term, 'sensuous.' They had no regard for the sensory preconditions of those sensuous effects – either in terms of bodily processes or historically specific formations of concepts –, and this may to help explain their exclusive focus on Milton's poetry.[34] While this critical tradition is, in a limited but undeniable sense, contiguous with the concerns of this study – both draw, for their source material, on the presentation of sense perception in Milton –, it is only so in a *limited* sense: limited to the poetry; limited, mostly, to the implicit treatment of the senses through their objects of perception; limited, not least, by its disregard for the historical and cultural context. Whatever critical insights this approach has generated, its discussion here has served primarily as a negative foil. For the purposes of this book, and in the interest of an adequate contextualization of the Miltonic sensorium in its historical and cultural setting, it is necessary to supplement this approach with impulses from a different source.

In his introduction to the first volume of the Yale edition of Milton's *Complete Prose Works* (published 1953), Don M. Wolfe, the general editor of that edition, ad-

---

[32] The sheer extent of this debate precludes its more detailed discussion in the present context; see Sherry, 'Legacy of T. S. Eliot,' esp. 135–139, the remarks in Corns, *Milton's Language*, 1–9, and the extensive treatment in Leonard, *Faithful Labourers*, I, 169–265. Leavis's initial contribution to the controversy is in 'Milton's Verse' (1933), reprinted as Chapter 2 of *Revaluation* (Harmondsworth: Penguin, 1994 [1936]), 42–61, quotation at 45; E. M. W. Tillyard's reply, in his *Milton* (London: Chatto & Windus, 1961 [1930]); Ricks's, in his *Milton's Grand Style* (Oxford: Clarendon, 1963). Tillyard, interestingly, does not wholly reject Eliot's claims, but argues that Milton's alleged austerity was a conscious and 'not necessarily undesirable' choice: he did not admit just *any* experience to his poetic stock (*Milton*, 356–357). As to possible 'other contexts,' it would be intriguing to consider, for instance, to what extent the sharpening of Milton's image as a political radical in the 1960s and 1970s, promoted among others by Christopher Hill, depended, alongside more obviously ideological factors, on the preceding 'de-sensualization' of the poet.
[33] As opposed to a tradition of 'scholarship.' For an account by a contemporary of Eliot's, see Louis Teeter, 'Scholarship and the Art of Criticism,' *ELH* 5 (1938), 173–194.
[34] Among early critics, I have not come across any extended reflections on the role of the senses in Milton's prose, but of course I cannot claim any finality on this point. One reason for the apparent lack may be that much of the commonly discussed prose (with the notable exceptions of the *Defensio Secunda* and *The Readie and Easie Way*) was composed before the onset of Milton's blindness, thus eliminating one of the 'traditional' reasons for addressing the senses in Milton in the first place; another, that his prose was traditionally read for its content rather than its style. A concise account of the latter is given by Corns, *Development of Milton's Prose Style*.

dresses a contradiction which he observed with regard to Milton's first published tract, *Of Reformation, Touching Church-Discipline in England* (1641):

> Milton opens *Of Reformation* with an arresting comparison of the spirit of primitive Christianity with what he considers the corrupt ceremonies of the Church of England. These he calls 'the new-vomited Paganisme of sensuall Idolatry,' deriding the superstitious dependence on the senses which breeds in the worshipers no quickening of the spirit, but only mechanical motions accompanied by slavish fear. Even the first page of *Of Reformation* thus shows a striking contradiction between Milton the poet and Milton the religious thinker. As a poet Milton was constantly aware of the need of images, of dependence upon the magic of color and sound and touch, of the efficacy of pageantry and music to release the inmost springs of his reader's mind. Master of the classicist art, he understood how to transport his readers into the realm of fantasy through the medium of sensory language. Yet in religious practices he rejected the uses of art.[35]

In analysing Wolfe's characterization of the role played by the senses in Milton, two decisive differences from the 'critical' approach outlined above become immediately apparent. These relate to the respective characterization of Milton's poetry and prose. For the first time in our survey, in fact, the focus is on a passage from Milton's prose. 'Critical' discussion of the senses in Milton had centred on the 'sensuous' aspects of his *poetry* – which might be considered ironic if we remember that the very term 'sensuous' had, initially, been derived from Milton's *prose*. More significantly, however, and more surprisingly, the opposition Wolfe makes out is not actually between Milton the poet and Milton the prose writer, but rather between Milton the poet and Milton the 'religious thinker.' Now, apart from the fact that Milton the poet did regularly double as a religious thinker (poems from all periods of his life attest to this, from the 'Nativity Ode' to Sonnet 19, not to mention the late poems), Wolfe's juxtaposition presents – as in the case of Eliot's pairing 'sensuous apprehension' and 'auditory imagination' – a marked imbalance in the categories of comparison. Indeed, in an argument such as that advanced by Wolfe, with such a clear focus on the *craft* of the poet, the corresponding craft of the *prose writer* might be expected to be the point of comparison; however, this is not the case. Why is this? Was Milton the pamphleteer not 'constantly aware of the need of images, of dependence upon the magic of color and sound and touch'? Is not, in fact, the phrase 'new-vomited Paganisme of sensuall idolatry' a rather striking image and, in its evocation of visceral disgust, an instance of the very 'sensory language' Wolfe disclaims for 'Milton the religious thinker'?

It appears that, while Wolfe acknowledges the presence of a 'sensory language' in Milton, he does not take this to be an essential aspect of his prose, still less of his religious (or other) thought. He finds the reason for this in a supposed lack of imagery and 'art' in Milton's prose. However, in light of later investigations into Milton's prose style, Wolfe's account cannot be maintained. As the findings of Thomas Corns suggest, it is only Milton's *final* tracts which conform to the terse quality often associated with his

---

[35] CPW 1: 109. The passage quoted is on p. 520.

prose writing more generally; this must be seen, though, as the result of 'a radical shift in [Milton's] prose style. The anti-prelatical tracts [of which *Of Reformation* is the first, T. G.] are *luxuriant* ... a sharp contrast with the spareness of the last pamphlets, which are characterized by a lexical sobriety and the use of fewer and terser images ...'[36] Together with the evidence of Milton's phrase, 'new-vomited Paganisme', this presents a first indication that any comprehensive discussion of Milton's use of 'sensory language' will have to account for not only for his poetry but also for his prose.

Nevertheless, Wolfe's reference to 'sensory language' (as opposed to the 'sensuous' language detected by earlier critics) does mark an important shift in the attention given to the Miltonic sensorium, even if, admittedly, he draws less extensive conclusions from the expression than I do. It might even be said, with only apparent paradox, that precisely through Wolfe's more neutral, technical reference to Milton's '*sensory* language,' the whole thematic complex of the senses in Milton is restored to a degree of corporeality which it had come to lack in the wake of the 'Milton Controversy.' This is a decisive step in the direction of the notion of 'sensory discourse' as developed below – although I would argue, above and beyond what Wolfe was prepared to class as 'sensory language,' that, in its clear preoccupation with sensory matters, Milton's explicit reference to 'sensuall Idolatry' (as, in fact, any discussion of idolatry) forms part of the sensory sphere, since it addresses a kind of sensory engagement which is perceived as excessive and reprehensible. In castigating idolatry alone, and 'sensuall Idolatry' at that, Milton was engaging in sensory discourse.

The second, if perhaps less obvious, difference between Wolfe's approach and those discussed earlier is that it takes into consideration the context of the original publication and reception of Milton's pamphlet, and refers to the world outside of the text, its historical and cultural context of origin. If this is only hinted at in Wolfe's remark about 'what [Milton] considers the corrupt ceremonies of the Church of England,' it does still mark a departure from the exclusively text-centred approach exemplified by Eliot. By contrast, in the terms of his time, Wolfe follows the avenue of 'scholarship' (as opposed to that of 'criticism' outlined above). Indeed, the whole Yale edition of the prose, with its historical introductions and meticulous parsing of the various debates in which Milton engaged, was indebted to this particular mode of study. As a mode of interpreting the sensory aspects of Milton's poetry, however, it was, as yet, virtually non-existent.[37] As Louis Teeter had argued in his 1938 essay on 'Scholarship and the Art of Criticism,' the difference between the two approaches should not be seen to 'consist in an antithesis between science and art, but between past and present,' continuing that

> due to the very terms of our existence in a world of change there are two sets of data concerning a past work of literature which one may propose to investigate and formulate: its probable meanings and values to the author and his contemporaries and its possible meanings and values to the present-day reader. The first, if

---

[36] Corns, *Development of Milton's Prose Style*, 101, emphasis added.

[37] See, however, the seminal essay by Marjorie Nicolson, 'Milton and the Telescope,' *ELH* 2 (1935), 1–32. Arguably, Spaeth, *Milton's Knowledge of Music*, as well as Eleanor Gertrude Brown, *Milton's Blindness* (New York: Octagon, 1968 [1934]), could also be counted among the pioneers of a 'scholarly,' i.e., historicizing investigation of the Miltonic sensorium.

1.1 The Senses in Milton Studies

possible, is a problem in reconstruction and quite clearly falls within the province of the literary scholar. The second, if desirable, is a problem in revaluation and belongs to the critic.[38]

It is easy to recognize, in this mid-twentieth-century restatement of the historicist/positivist divide, the approaches to the Miltonic sensorium that we have reviewed thus far: Eliot and others assessing the sensuous *value* of Milton's verse as well as the – at least implicit – commitment to historical *contextualization* expressed by Wolfe, and the Yale edition more generally. In the further course of his essay, Teeter argues that both approaches, the critical and the scholarly, should be combined in an attempt to relate past and present one to another, both in terms of prevailing aesthetic criteria and their wider historical context.[39] In the further development of the ways in which the Miltonic sensorium was studied over the latter half of the twentieth century, precisely such a convergence began to emerge.

The first beginnings of this trend may be observed in Wayne Shumaker's *Unpremeditated Verse: Feeling and Perception in 'Paradise Lost'* (1967).[40] Shumaker, whose whole title seems almost to be directed against Eliot's contention that Milton had lacked both feeling *and* perception, focuses on three kinds of perception in the epic: visual, auditory, and (as he terms it) somatic. Touch, taste, and smell, he argues, 'appear to play a comparatively minor role in literature except on special occasions', such as the banquet scene in *Paradise Regained*.[41] Throughout, Shumaker prefers to refer to 'sensory' perception or imagery, and the more objective quality of the former term is evident when he refers, by contrast, to 'the innocent sensuality of the primeval Garden' or 'the reader who does not shrink from sensuousness in poetry but is willing to expose himself to a bombardment of half-living colors, shapes and feelings.'[42]

When discussion turns to the 'sensory responses' of (twentieth-century) readers, however, it is obvious that Shumaker has not departed from the critical paradigm. In fact, as he had stated at the outset, 'the lack of consistent historical orientation in what follows ... does not imply disesteem of *historical scholarship*. ... [I]t simply happens that ... I have been embarked on a *critical task* which requires a different emphasis.'[43] Nevertheless, there is a marked difference between Shumaker's approach and those earlier ones outlined above, and this rests in his firm emphasis on the cognitive, and

---

[38] Teeter, 'Scholarship and the Art of Criticism,' 173.
[39] Teeter, 'Scholarship and the Art of Criticism,' 192–194.
[40] Wayne Shumaker, *Unpremeditated Verse: Feeling and Perception in 'Paradise Lost'* (Princeton, N. J.: Princeton University Press, 1967).
[41] Shumaker, *Unpremeditated Verse*, viii. The book's main title is taken from the proem to Book 9, PL 9.24, where the reference is to the speaker's 'celestial patroness,' the Muse, 'who deigns/Her nightly visitation unimplored,/And dictates to me slumbering; or inspires/Easy my unpremeditated verse' (21–24). Shumaker takes issue with Eliot on Milton (*Unpremeditated Verse*, 20–1) and Wordsworth (171), but does not enter into a detailed discussion. However, Shumaker's claim that '[Milton] drew no ... distinction between sensory and cortical materials and therefore allowed his feelings to work in full cooperation with his intelligence' (60) reads like a refutation of Eliot phrased in more current, neurophysiological terminology.
[42] Shumaker, *Unpremeditated Verse*, 22, 89.
[43] Shumaker, *Unpremeditated Verse*, ix, emphases added.

thus lastly corporeal, grounding of sensory imagery – 'How can one think "red" without having a glimpse of redness?' – as well as in his regard, belying the professed indifference to historical context cited above, for the contemporary receptive setting of Milton's poetry: 'Contemporary readers would have grasped the meaning at once,' he at one point remarks concerning the sensory implications in Milton's portrayal of Adam and Eve as 'erect and tall/Godlike erect' – a consideration of no relevance at all for Eliot and his followers.[44] Other fields of 'outside reference' in Shumaker include developmental psychology, biology, and ethnology.[45]

In the end, Shumaker speaks for an appreciation of the specific power of poetry to integrate imagery and feeling in a way that is not merely mimetic but effects an 'interpenetration of [sense] datum and significance,' an effect in which 'stimulus and response are registered pretty much together.'[46] While his analysis does not consistently refer to historical context, it suggests that the disjunction between 'critical' and 'scholarly' approaches to the Miltonic sensorium *can* be of an analytic nature if historical or other contextualization is made to highlight the functional principles of the literary text.

Over more recent years, a multitude of contributions, many of them journal articles or book chapters, have grounded their analyses of the senses in Milton in considerations of the historical contexts relevant to them – where 'history' is understood as indicating the full breadth of relevant facets in early modern culture, from theology and philosophy to contemporary medicine and material culture. They have thus given the study of the Miltonic sensorium an altogether more 'scholarly' character, in the sense of the term outlined above, not least because their discussion of Milton has often been in the context of an overarching argument regarding, for example a particular sense in history.[47] Others, such as Donald Friedman, have turned to individual aspects of Milton's oeuvre. In his essay on Milton's masque and 'the truth of the ear,' Friedman relates *Comus* in part to contemporary puritan attitudes toward preaching and, in particular, the *hearing* of sermons. Likewise, Katherine Cox also convincingly links certain aspects of sound in *Paradise Lost* both to Milton's materialism and to the early modern implications of the acoustic terminology Milton employs.[48] Indeed, the relationship between Milton's mate-

---

[44] Shumaker, *Unpremeditated Verse*, 105, 49. The contemporary significance of the passage at PL 4.286–7, Shumaker specifies, would have been that, 'unlike the beasts, man aspires heavenward and raises his eyes instinctively toward his Maker.'
[45] Shumaker, *Unpremeditated Verse*, 4–18.
[46] Shumaker, *Unpremeditated Verse*, 54–4, at 54.
[47] As an example on vision, see the relevant passages on Milton in Berensmeyer, *'Angles of Contigency,'* 115–151; Jane Partner, *Poetry and Vision in Early Modern England* (Cham: Palgrave Macmillan, 2018), 213–258; Erin Webster, *The Curious Eye: Optics and Imaginative Literature in Seventeenth-Century England* (Oxford: Oxford University Press, 2020), esp. 103–162; on smell, Dugan, *Ephemeral History of Perfume*, 170–175; on taste, Denise Gigante, *Taste: A Literary History* (New Haven, Conn.: Yale University Press, 2005), 22–46, as well as Wendy Wall, *Recipes for Thought: Knowledge and Taste in the Early Modern Kitchen* (Philadelphia: University of Pennsylvania Press, 2016), 61–64; on touch, Joe Moshenska, *Feeling Pleasures: The Sense of Touch in Renaissance England* (Oxford: Oxford University Press, 2014), 245–284.
[48] Donald M. Friedman, 'Comus and the Truth of the Ear,' in: *The Muses Common-Weale: Poetry and Politics in the Seventeenth-Century*, eds Claude J. Summers/Ted-Larry Pebworth (Columbia, Mo.: University of Missouri Press, 1988), 119–34, 'not suggesting,' to be sure, 'a simple, direct

rialist monism and his understanding of sense perception has been a minor research focus in its own right.[49]

Significantly, this new kind of attention to the Miltonic sensorium has not been restricted to Milton's poetry. In an early instance, Stanley Fish has called Milton's *The Reason of Church-Government* (1642), in which visual metaphors serve not to persuade but (Fish argues) to blindside the reader into accepting Milton's argument, 'one continuing and elaborate "eye test."'[50] Following the broadly new historicist impetus of analysing different kinds of texts as participating in a shared and common 'circulation of meaning,' Lana Cable has examined the 'sensory or "carnal" dimension' in Milton's polemic language and has argued, beyond a mere acknowledgment of sensory content in Milton's (prose) metaphors, for 'recognizing the *cognitive* worth of language that is otherwise too easily devalued as mere rhetorical flourish.'[51] When Cable notes that the 'richly sensuous metaphoric arguments in [Milton's early polemical tracts] actually feed on and derive their energy from the images of those whom he attacks,' this, while in congruence with the new historicist proposition that 'every act of ... opposition uses the tools it condemns and risks falling prey to the practice it exposes,' goes significantly beyond it:[52] Milton the image-maker, Cable suggests, was dependent on the zeal and imaginative impetus of Milton the image-breaker; the 'carnal rhetoric' of the prose tracts, including where they overlap with what had been considered by Shumaker or earlier critics to be the sensory or sensuous language of the poems, was intimately bound up with the objectives those tracts pursued. In coining the concept of 'creative

---

identification of the masque and the Puritan sermon' (126); Katherine Cox, '"How cam'st thou speakable of mute": Satanic Acoustics in "Paradise Lost",' *Milton Studies* 57 (2016), 233–260. In terms of sensory history, Friedman's topic has more recently been discussed in depth by Arnold Hunt, *The Art of Hearing: English Preachers and Their Audiences, 1590–1640* (Cambridge: Cambridge University Press, 2010).

[49] In addition to Cox, see Lauren Shohet, 'The Fragrance of the Fall,' in: *Milton, Materialism, and Embodiment: One First Matter All*, eds Kevin J. Donovan/Thomas Festa (Pittsburgh, Pa.: Duquesne University Press, 2017), 19–36, and Seth Herbst, 'Sound and Matter: Milton, Music, and Monism,' in: *Milton, Materialism, and Embodiment*, eds Donovan/Festa, 37–55. Fundamental discussions of Milton's monism can be found in Stephen M. Fallon, *Milton Among the Philosophers: Poetry and Materialism in Seventeenth-Century England* (Ithaca, N. Y.: Cornell University Press, 1991), and John H. Rogers, *The Matter of Revolution: Science, Poetry, and Politics in the Age of Milton* (Ithaca, N. Y.: Cornell University Press, 1998 [1996]), 104–180.

[50] Stanley Fish, 'Reasons That Imply Themselves: Imagery, Argument, and the Reader in Milton's *Reason of Church Government*,' in: Earl Miner (ed.), *Seventeenth-Century Imagery: Essays on Uses of Figurative Language from Donne to Farquhar* (Berkeley, Calif.: University of California Press, 1971), 83–102, at 88.

[51] Lana Cable, *Carnal Rhetoric: Milton's Iconoclasm and the Poetics of Desire* (Durham, N.C.: Duke University Press, 1995), 2–3.

[52] Cable, *Carnal Rhetoric*, 6; H. Aram Veeser, 'Introduction,' in: *The New Historicism*, ed. H. Aram Veeser (New York: Routledge, 1989), ix–xvi, at xi. A connected point regarding the 'iconomaniacal' impulse of Milton's iconoclasm is made by Berensmeyer, *'Angles of Contingency,'* 9: 'Die literarische Kultur des 17. Jahrhunderts ist nicht nur rhetorisch, sondern hochgradig visuell und bildhaft bestimmt – mitunter geradezu bildbesessen, selbst da, wo sie sich (wie etwa bei Milton) ikonoklastisch geriert.'

iconoclasm,' Cable captures both the uneasy relation between Milton's making and breaking of imagery and the fraught quality this brings to his sensory or 'carnal' language.[53] Ultimately, Cable argues for an integration of the 'carnal' and the notional in Milton's rhetoric, classing his 'linguistic vehemence as integral to his creativity on a level simultaneously philosophical and sensory.'[54]

While Cable's focus on 'affective stylistics' and nods in the direction of reader-response *criticism* could be seen as traces of earlier traditions of reading the Miltonic sensorium, the fundamental reliance on historical context which underlies her critique of Milton's iconoclastic agency is indicative of the critical – or rather, scholarly – reorientation with which this survey is concerned.[55] In her emphasis on the centrality of carnality in the rhetoric of Milton's prose, Cable is in clear opposition to the 'anti-sensory' assessment of the prose offered by Wolfe in his introduction to the Yale edition of Milton's prose.[56] Wolfe, we remember, had contrasted Milton's (sensory) needs as a poet with those of Milton the (austere) prose writer – however, these two personae were arguably only different names for the *Milton Eikonistes* and *Milton Eikonoklastes* observed by Cable to be active across generic boundaries.[57] From the point of view established in more recent discussion, then, it becomes clear that Milton's iconoclastic rhetoric not only engages the senses *ex negativo* (as I have tentatively suggested above), but that the sensory sphere played a *positive* or, as one could say in view of the arguable materiality of perception in Milton, a *material* role in Milton's prose rhetoric as well.

It is only consistent, then, that the very passage from *Of Reformation* which Wolfe had used to point out the anti-sensory qualities of Milton's prose has more recently been subject to a re-reading along sensory lines. Discussing the tract in the context of Milton's other early prose writings, Elizabeth Skerpan Wheeler highlights the importance of the governing metaphors of the body and, in particular, of the eye and seeing: reformation, in Milton's demonstrably more extensive understanding of the term, comprises a removal of all that is 'bodily forme' with regard to public worship, until the intangible form of true doctrine is reinstated.[58] Again, and in marked contrast to the earlier assessment of the same passage discussed above, Milton's recourse to the senses is seen as integral to his general argument.

---

[53] Cable, *Carnal Rhetoric*, 4. The conflict between iconoclastic and imaginative impulses in English Renaissance poetry had earlier been observed by Ernest B. Gilman, *Iconoclasm and Poetry in the English Reformation: Down Went Dagon* (Chicago: University of Chicago Press, 1986), see esp. 149–178 on *Samson Agonistes*.
[54] Cable, *Carnal Rhetoric*, 6.
[55] Cable speaks of 'the participation of all his [sc. Milton's] writings in *discourses specific to early modernism*' (*Carnal Rhetoric*, 1, emphasis added).
[56] Cable's reading is also in keeping with the findings of Corns, *Development of Milton's Prose Style*, as pointed out above.
[57] As Milton himself might have felt moved to point out, an *eikonistês* is not so much an 'image-maker' but a registrar or an archivist (*LSJ*); still, the idea that Milton's imagery 'registers' and 'archives' significant aspects of the sensory culture of his time resonates with my general argument about the importance of historical context.
[58] Elizabeth Skerpan Wheeler, 'Early Political Prose,' in: *A Companion to Milton*, ed. Thomas N. Corns (Malden, Mass.: Blackwell, 2003), 263–278, at 266–269.

***

In this survey, I have outlined a movement observable from the earliest discussions of the senses in Milton through the 'Milton controversy' over the sensuous qualities of his verse and leading to more recent discussions of the Miltonic sensorium as a historically specific set of preconceptions, valuations, and forms of expression relating to the senses. Three interrelated but distinguishable developments deserve highlighting here:

1. There has been a shift from the evaluative judgment of the sensuous content in Milton (associated with 'criticism') towards an explicative or interpretive tracing of sensory elements in Milton, their respective derivation (from earlier traditions or contemporary context), interrelations (both within Milton's work and in view of other authors), and function (with regard to the particular text under discussion). I have associated this latter approach with the blanket term of 'scholarship'.
2. There has been a tendency to extend the area of reference when discussing the Miltonic sensorium, so as to include Milton's prose. As a result, sensory references in the poetry may shed light on comparable (or contrasting) references in the prose, and vice versa. In general, the earlier notion of Milton's prose as devoid of any sensory interest has been disproved both on quantitative (by Corns) and qualitative grounds (by Cable and others).
3. There has been a renewed emphasis on the corporeal dimension of Milton's portrayal of sense perception, i.e., on the ways his utilization of sensory imagery is grounded in physiological processes of or somatic responses to sense perception. This has come after the attribution to Milton's verse, by Eliot and others, of a characteristic sensory sterility, or a merely conventional use of sensory terminology.

While most of the more recent studies in the Miltonic sensorium have preserved, to a very high degree, the close attention to, and intimate engagement with, the text that was held to be characteristic of the 'critical' approach, their re-orientation towards context is unmistakable. My own approach in this book is indebted, above all, to this more recent scholarship and its historicising approach to textual study. While my (reasonably close) readings of individual passages in the analytical chapters below take some of their cues from the close 'critical' attention of the older approaches, their concern with a (re-)valuation of Milton's 'sensibility' or 'austerity of nature' is not germane to this study. Rather, my aim is to contribute the ongoing (re-)contextualisation of the senses in Milton.

1.2 From 'Historical Psychology' to 'Cognitive Historicism': Research Contexts

In my brief outline of Milton's biography, I began by stressing the more sensuous aspects of the spicy, spectacular world in which Milton lived and wrote. From a consideration of the reception history of the senses in Milton's own work, it appears that the senses played a considerable role in his writing – and that this was recognised, and fought over, in later scholarship. In fact, both of these aspects, the respective role of the senses in the contextual 'life world' and in Milton's world of words, should be seen together. In order to prepare their fusion in the chapters that follow, I would like to indicate the extent and character of my indebtedness to previous research in the field of what more recently has been designated as 'sensory studies,' an area of research which can be traced to much earlier scholarly concerns.

That the sensory aspects of early modern culture have found a growing scholarly interest in recent years is evidenced by a wealth of relevant publications.[59] This has come in the wake of a more general development in which the cultural semantics and pragmatics of the human senses, including social and behavioural aspects of sense perception, have come to the fore. In order to contextualize my own approach, it will be necessary to point out the most important lineages in the development of 'sensory studies' (as this somewhat diffuse field of interest is now known). These derive from social and cultural history; the historical study of literature and the arts; ethnology; and certain applications of neuroscientific findings to language use.

The most directly traceable roots of the current branch of enquiry lie with earlier efforts among French historians of the *Annales* school.[60] Starting from the contention that, as Lucien Febvre put it in 1947, 'a series of fascinating studies could be done on the *sensory underpinnings of thought* in different periods,' these early studies aimed to establish the *mentalités* or the 'historical psychology' of past populations by way of a (primarily social) history of the senses.[61] The questions arising from such work lead towards my own concern, too: Was it possible, Alain Corbin asks in a programmatic essay, 'to discern retrospectively the nature of the presence in the world of people in the past through an analysis of the hierarchy of the senses and the balance established be-

[59] I will not try to provide a comprehensive bibliography here but will rather cite individual contributions below as applicable. For the period at hand, good starting points for further exploration are Simon Smith et al. (eds), *The Senses in Early Modern England, 1558–1660* (Manchester: Manchester University Press, 2015), and *A Cultural History of the Senses in the Renaissance*, ed. Herman Roodenburg (London: Bloomsbury, 2014), the third volume in a six-volume set ranging from antiquity to the modern age (gen. ed. Constance Classen, all London: Bloomsbury, 2014). A concise introduction from a historical perspective is Mark M. Smith, *Sensory History* (Oxford: Berg, 2007). New publications in the field are announced regularly in the 'Books of Note' section at <http://www.sensorystudies.org> (last accessed 18 June 2021).
[60] One alternative genealogy of sensory studies might be constructed by reference to Karl Marx in combination with the Viennese school of art history (Alois Riegl, Franz Wickhoff) via Walter Benjamin's essay on *The Work of Art in the Age of Its Technological Reproducibility*; see the Prologue above, as well as Robert Jütte, *A History of the Senses: From Antiquity to Cyberspace*, tr. James Lynn (Cambridge: Polity, 2005 [1998]), 8–10.
[61] Lucien Febvre, *The Problem of Unbelief in the Sixteenth Century: The Religion of Rabelais*, tr. Beatrice Gottlieb (Cambridge, Mass.: Harvard University Press, 1982 [1947]), 436 (emphasis added), see also 423–454; the 'historical psychology' approach is that of Robert Mandrou, *Introduction to Modern France, 1500–1640: An Essay in Historical Psychology*, tr. R. E. Hallmark (London: Edward Arnold, 1975 [1961]), esp. 49–61. Further landmark studies in this line of enquiry are Alain Corbin, *The Foul and the Fragrant: Odour and the French Social Imagination*, tr. M. L. Kochan (Cambridge, Mass.: Harvard University Press, 1986 [1982]), and idem, *Village Bells: Sound and Meaning in the Nineteenth-Century French Countryside*, tr. Martin Thom (New York: Columbia University Press, 1998 [1994]).

tween them at a particular moment in history and within a given society?' Could historians really '*detect the functions of these hierarchies*, and thus identify the purposes which presided over this organization of the relations between the senses?' As Corbin points out, the reconstruction of past mentalities might turn out to be more complicated than Febvre had hoped: in between the potentially specious definitiveness of normative sources and the possibility of changing 'modalities of attention, thresholds of perception, significance of noises, and configuration of the tolerable and the intolerable,' historians would have to weigh carefully their assessments of past lived experience as communicated through the material at their disposal.[62] The decisive contribution of this first approach lies in its carefully theorized, self-reflexive qualities; its particular relevance for the purposes of this book derive from its – as it were genetic – alertness to the peculiarities of early modern culture, combined with a fundamental openness regarding its application in literary study: 'All of these logics are to be found,' Corbin writes, 'usually with a slight time lag, at the heart of fiction.'[63]

Indeed, a second strand of the sensory studies tradition treats the senses as a complex of (explicit or implicit) *themes* in literature and the visual arts (as opposed to the more technical approach studying the prevailing physiological model at a given point in time). Although studies of this type have been conducted for some time in art history, arguably the most influential book in this category, in the sense that it stimulated a great amount of later research, has proved to be Louise Vinge's *The Five Senses: Studies in a Literary Tradition*, which, despite its title, also considers painting and philosophy.[64] Other early studies of individual senses – almost invariably of a strongly philological character – might be seen not only as precursors of the present-day focus on 'visual culture,' 'auditory culture,' *et cetera*, but also as breaking new ground for later research

---

[62] Alain Corbin, 'A History and Anthropology of the Senses,' in: Idem, *Time, Desire and Horror: Towards a History of the Senses*, tr. Jean Birrell (Cambridge: Polity, 1995 [1991]), 181–195, at 182–83 (emphasis added), 185. Studies whose approach to early modern English sensory culture is broadly compatible with the one outlined here include Bruce R. Smith, *The Acoustic World of Early Modern England: Attending to the O-Factor* (Chicago: University of Chicago Press, 1999), and Emily Cockayne, *Hubbub: Filth, Noise and Stench in England, 1600–1770* (New Haven, Conn.: Yale University Press, 2007); on early American (colonial and indigenous) sensescapes, see Peter Charles Hoffer, *Sensory Worlds in Early America* (Baltimore, Md.: Johns Hopkins University Press, 2003), and Richard Cullen Rath, *How Early America Sounded* (Ithaca, N.Y.: Cornell University Press, 2005).
[63] Corbin, 'History and Anthropology of the Senses,' 188.
[64] Louise Vinge, *The Five Senses: Studies in a Literary Tradition* (Lund: CWK Gleerup, 1975). A further largely literary treatment of the five senses, albeit with glances at pictorial representation, is Frank Kermode's essay on 'The Banquet of Sense,' in: Idem, *Shakespeare, Spenser, Donne: Renaissance Essays* (London: Routledge & Kegan Paul, 1971), 84–115. Apart from these (Vinge focuses on wall paintings and engravings, Kermode refers briefly to the *picturae* of emblems and to other engravings), the pictorial representation of the five senses, often in the form of allegorical cycles, has been discussed in early articles by Hans Kauffmann (publ. 1943; reference given by Vinge, *Five Senses*, 14n16) as well as by Carl Nordenfalk, 'The Five Senses in Late Medieval and Renaissance Art,' *Journal of the Warburg and Courtauld Institutes* 48 (1985), 1–22, and Idem, 'The Five Senses in Flemish Art before 1600,' in: *Netherlandish Mannerism*, ed. Görel Cavalli-Björkmann (Stockholm: Nationalmuseum, 1985), 135–154, all of them with pertinent illustrations.

by surveying and interpreting vast amounts of primary sources.[65] Generally, the lasting value of contributions in this category lies both in their opening up materials in this way and in the fact that – in many cases, with Vinge's book being a prime example – they already consider the integration of their respective subject matter into a wider context: the individual sense within the whole sensorium; individual arts among other forms of artistic expression or modes of thought; the sensory sphere in its relations to the culture at large.

With this I arrive at the current epoch of sensory studies as a self-reflecting, albeit scarcely institutionalized, discipline in the more general domain of cultural studies.[66] Its beginnings might be dated from the publication of two early works by seminal authors in the field, the sociologist David Howes's edited volume *The Varieties of Sensory Experience: A Sourcebook in the Anthropology of the Senses* (1991) and the cultural historian Constance Classen's *Worlds of Sense: Exploring the Senses in History and Across Cultures* (1993).[67] In their respective bodies of work, both authors are clearly indebted to earlier efforts. In fact, it could be said that Howes, particularly in his later work, owes slightly more to the first strand of tradition associated above with the *Annales* school, whereas Classen is closer to the second strand of literary-cultural exploration.[68] However, Howes and Classen not only combine those two strands, but add a third perspective already suggested by the terms 'anthropology' and 'worlds' in the titles cited above: that of cultural anthropology or ethnology. As the various case studies in their books indicate, there is no reason to consider the traditionally prevailing sensory order of Western culture – five senses organized in a hierarchy ranking from vision to touch – as in any way obligatory. Other 'worlds' may be organized quite differently, and with a striking degree of consistency, including with regard to the most personal and fundamental aspects of life and death. Consider Classen's précis of the olfactory worldview (if this term still applies) held by a particular group of Andaman Islanders:

> When an Ongee wishes to refer to himself as 'me,' he puts a finger to the tip of his nose, the organ of smell. This is not only because of the centrality of olfaction in Ongee thought, but also because living beings are thought to be composed of smell. The most concentrated form of odor, according to the Ongee, are bones,

---

[65] See for instance, Gudrun Schleusener-Eichholz, *Das Auge im Mittelalter*, 2 vols (Munich: Wilhelm Fink, 1985), or Günther Wille, *Akroasis: Der akustische Sinnesbereich in der griechischen Literatur bis zum Ende der klassischen Zeit*, 2 vols (Tübingen: Attempto, 2001 [*Habilitation* thesis, Tübingen 1958]).

[66] Understood here in the more *kulturwissenschaftlich* meaning of the term as 'an academic field of study characterized by a multidisciplinary approach ... to the study of ... culture' (adapted from *OED*, 'cultural studies').

[67] David Howes (ed.), *The Varieties of Sensory Experience: A Sourcebook in the Anthropology of the Senses* (Toronto: University of Toronto Press, 1991); Classen, *Worlds of Sense*. Howes's title pays homage to William James's *The Varieties of Religious Experience* (1902), further indicating the breadth of influences at work.

[68] See Howes (ed.), *Empire of the Senses*, 55–58. Classen's interest in the literary sphere is evident in *Worlds of Sense*, esp. 15–36; see also her *The Color of Angels: Cosmology, Gender, and the Aesthetic Imagination* (London: Routledge, 1998).

1.2 From 'Historical Psychology' to 'Cognitive Historicism': Research Contexts 45

believed to be solid smell. ... An inner spirit is said to reside within the bones of living beings. While one is sleeping, this internal spirit gathers all the odors one has scattered during the day and returns them to the body, making continued life possible ... The concern of the Ongees to maintain a healthy state of olfactory equilibrium is expressed in their forms of greeting. The Ongee equivalent of 'how are you?' is *'konyune? onorange-tanka?'*, 'how is your nose?', or literally, 'when/why/where is the nose to be?' ... Death is explained by the Ongee as the loss of one's personal odor.[69]

In the world of the Ongee, it is not sight or even hearing but rather smell which carries fundamental importance when it comes to individuals' perception of the world, of each other, and of themselves. This, the sensory studies approach suggests, should alert us to the relativity of the 'sensory formations' obtaining within our own cultures, past and present.[70]

Here one might detect a certain convergence with the tendency, observable in a previous generation of early-modernists, to draw parallels between their own research and the ethnological practice of the day.[71] Indeed, when Classen outlines the 'thermal order of the cosmos' as it appears to the Tzotzil people of southern Mexico, who hold that 'men ... possess more heat than women, making women symbolically cold by contrast,' this is distinctly reminiscent of early modern humoral theory, according to which men were considered to be hot and dry by nature, whereas women were thought to have a cold and wet constitution.[72] It seems clear that, behind the turn to ethnology in historical sensory studies old and new, lies a fundamental agreement with L. P. Hartley's much-quoted proposition about 'the past' being 'a foreign country; they do things differently there.'[73] The goal of any such approach would then be to elucidate, as far as possible,

---

[69] Classen, *Worlds of Sense*, 126–27. Contrast the final idea cited here with the Western notion of 'closing one's eyes upon the world' in death.

[70] For the notion of 'sensory formations,' see the case studies in David Howes, *Sensual Relations: Engaging the Senses in Culture and Social Theory* (Ann Arbor, Mich.: University of Michigan Press, 2003). Although this is not spelled out by Howes, the concept appears to be modelled on Foucault's notion of 'discursive formations,' with these being 'system[s] of dispersion,' 'regularit[ies]' observable 'between objects, types of statement, concepts, or thematic choices' and actualized in concrete statements; see Michel Foucault, *The Archaeology of Knowledge*, tr. A. M. Sheridan-Smith (London: Routledge, 2002 [1969]), esp. 34–43, quotation at 41.

[71] See, for instance, Keith Thomas, *Religion and the Decline of Magic* (Harmondsworth: Penguin, 1971), 52 and passim; Christopher Hill, *Change and Continuity in Seventeenth-Century England* (London: Weidenfeld and Nicolson, 1974).

[72] Classen, *Worlds of Sense*, 122–126, at 123; Constance Classen, 'The Witch's Senses: Sensory Ideologies and Transgressive Femininities from the Renaissance to Modernity,' in: *Empire of the Senses*, ed. Howes, 70–84, at 72–3. In *Worlds of Sense*, Classen actually speculates that the prevalence of thermal symbolism among the indigenous cultures of Latin America may be due, in part, to the impact of the Spanish Conquest and hence descended from early modern European humoralism; as she points out, however, the indigenous symbolism is 'much more encompassing than that expressed by Western humoral theory, and indeed can vary widely from place to place' (122).

[73] L. P. Hartley, *The Go-Between* (London: Hamilton, 1961), 9. For the related point that an ongoing history of perception also implies a changing perception of history (partly determined in

what 'doing things differently' with the senses had meant at different points in the past. As will become clear in the following, this notion of sensory agency is one I also subscribe to.

In recent years, the sensory studies paradigm has been enriched by new approaches – not genetically related, necessarily, to the tradition outlined so far – which have drawn upon current research in the neurosciences. Such endeavours are being undertaken in historical scholarship, not to mention neurolinguistics.[74] In terms of historical lines of enquiry in literary studies (where the wider approach has been given the common denomination of 'cognitive cultural studies'), this trend has been designated 'cognitive historicism' by some of those involved.[75]

Since the wider field of cognitive cultural studies rests upon the idea that there is a degree of universality in how humans perceive and think (at least on a sub-evolutionary time scale), the result is a certain tension between the wish to historicise on the one hand and, on the other, the intention to identify particular universals of cognition in cultural use, including sense perception, that are valid across history. One way of addressing this issue would be to stress the primacy of cultural factors, and to argue that the processes of cognition are only universal *ceteris paribus*: if two pairs of eyes from different eras are looking at the same thing, this position would hold, they are *not seeing the same thing*.[76] According to the cognitive cultural studies approach, however, this argument would fall short of the complex negotiations between sensation and perception that really shape sensory culture at any given point in time. Rather than pitting cultural relativism against cognitive universalism in a sharp dichotomy, Lisa Zunshine argues, we should consider culture as 'an ongoing interplay – simultaneously a give-and-take and a tug-of-war – between human cognitive architecture and specific historical circumstances.'[77] This would mean that, even at the most fundamental level of individual percepts, the precepts of cultural context come into play. The senses, then, really

---

terms of the senses), see David Lowenthal, *The Past is a Foreign Country: Revisited* (Cambridge: Cambridge University Press, 2015 [1985]), 14.

[74] See, with a focus on the history of religion, Luther H. Martin/Jesper Sørensen (eds), *Past Minds: Studies in Cognitive Historiography* (London: Routledge, 2011), esp. the chapters by Martin (1–10), Wiebe (167–178), and Sørensen (179–196). As one example of how neurolinguistic research may prove relevant to both sensory and literary studies, see Michael L. Slepian/Nalini Ambady, 'Simulating Sensorimotor Metaphors: Novel Metaphors Influence Sensory Judgments,' *Cognition* 130 (2014), 309–314. Significantly, considering the 'ethnological bent' of sensory studies described above, there is a marked concurrence of both neurolinguistic and ethnological interest in the senses in the field of cognitive ethnolinguistics, see, for instance, Ewelina Wnuk/Asifa Majid, 'Revisiting the Limits of Language: The Odor Lexicon of Maniq,' *Cognition* 131 (2014), 125–138; Louise Fryer et al., 'Touching Words Is Not Enough: How Visual Experience Influences Haptic-auditory Associations in the "Bouba-Kiki" Effect,' *Cognition* 132 (2014), 164–173.

[75] See the introduction and essays in Lisa Zunshine (ed.), *Introduction to Cognitive Cultural Studies* (Baltimore, Md.: Johns Hopkins University Press, 2010), 61–150.

[76] See the discussion of a similar point, raised by Egon Friedell, in the Prologue above.

[77] Lisa Zunshine, 'Cognitive Historicism,' in: *Cognitive Cultural Studies*, ed. Zunshine, 61–63, at 61–62.

are formed – but they are formed in history. This may either be said to be setting the Marxian dictum cited in the Prologue – 'the forming of the five senses is a labour of the entire history of the world down to the present' – on its neurological-material feet; or it might be criticized as uncritical for attaching overmuch importance to the often ambiguous findings of neuroscientific imaging.

In any case, the adduction of findings from scientific psychology to the interpretation of literary texts is not an entirely novel phenomenon. As early as 1978, the cognitive psychologist Lawrence E. Marks applied empirical findings from his field to the sensory dimension(s) of literature, and poetry, in particular.[78] What *is* new in this approach – beyond, of course, its access to more recent scientific findings – is that, on the one hand, it is a concerted endeavour from within field of literary-studies, while, on the other, it is aiming to establish certain universals of reception across genres that can be framed in cognitive-scientific terms.

In theory – and for 'cognitive historicism,' in particular – this could mean that 'the universals of human cognitive processing [are considered] as they function in their several [sc. historical, cultural] contexts.'[79] In practice, we might consider how the ways in which certain stimuli are represented by the brain impact upon our actual *perception*, at some level, of imagery in literature, and we would find, for instance, that, while 'auditory images involve many of the same areas of the brain as actual audition,' the actual condition of synaesthesia and what often passes for synaesthetic experience in literature are actually two very different things.[80] Alternatively we might reflect, as Michael W. Clune does, on the possibility that what literature triggers in the brain – via the sensory imaginary – is not so much a mirroring as a complex, and at least partly conscious, transformation of 'normal' perceptual content.[81] Clune, however, argues that a notion of 'science tells us what the brain can do, and the critics show how literature does it' – which is a slightly polemical though not wholly inaccurate rendering of at least some cognitively inspired criticism –[82] does not suffice as a justification for literary study:

---

[78] 'Dimension(s)' captures Marks's main point, expressed in the title of his study: Lawrence E. Marks, *The Unity of the Senses: Interrelations among the Modalities* (New York: Academic Press, 1978). Of particular interest are the chapters on 'Sound Symbolism in Poetry' (193–210) and 'Synesthetic Metaphor in Poetry' (211–255), but there are numerous, incisive references to literary texts throughout the book.

[79] Ellen Spolsky, 'Cognitive Literary Historicism: A Response to Adler and Gross,' *Poetics Today* 24 (2003), 161–183, at 168.

[80] Examples taken from G. Gabrielle Starr, 'Multisensory Imagery,' in *Cognitive Cultural Studies*, ed. Zunshine, 275–291, at 278, 288. This at least complicates the earlier view of Marks, *Unity of the Senses*, e.g. 220–224.

[81] Michael W. Clune, *Writing Against Time* (Stanford, Calif.: Stanford University Press, 2013). Clune's reformulation of the classical/Romantic dichotomy in terms of cognitive science (15–20) answers M.H. Abram's classic *The Mirror and the Lamp: Romantic Theory and the Critical Tradition* (New York: Norton, 1958).

[82] One example would be the strong connection between sense perception and memory (see Starr, 'Multisensory Imagery,' 277), which has long been recognized and theorized in literary study, Proustian or otherwise. (A parallel case could be made, incidentally, regarding sensory-historical study; see, with a focus on how 'the individual's sense of sound' was woven into 'the fabric of the communal sense of past and present' in Tudor times, Daniel Woolf, 'Speech, Text, and Time: The

'literary criticism's best opportunity for creating new knowledge lies not in the description of art's embeddedness in contexts recognizable to historians or sociologists, but in the description of the forces by which art attempts to free itself of such contexts and such recognitions.'[83] Although he focuses on Romantic and post-Romantic texts, it is striking that Clune enlists Milton as a not-so-distant precursor of what he terms 'Romantic virtuality,' by which he means a concern with 'the difference between actual and virtual forms of perception' which, he goes on to write, 'echoes and develops Milton's description of pre- and post-lapsarian sensation in *Paradise Lost*.'[84] This addresses the familiar view of Milton as a romantic *avant la lettre* in neuroscientific terms, while at the same time connecting to the core concern of this book with Milton's view(s) of the human sensorium.

Many of the most engaging new studies in the cultural history of the senses manage to combine two or more of the approaches outlined above. They all take the notion that 'the past is a foreign country' quite seriously, but that does not preclude, of course, the possibility of trying to 'get there' along various paths. In subsequent chapters, I will draw freely on the various findings that these different approaches to the senses in history and literature have yielded thus far, while also aiming to incorporate the caveats already raised.

In bringing these methodological considerations to a conclusion, I would like briefly to address a problem common to all kinds of historicising interpretation (or interpretive historical study), and thus also to historical sensory studies. This might be described as a tension, projected onto historical research, between two kinds of 'making strange.' In the first instance, the supposedly familiar past is strategically 'defamiliarized' in order to emphasize the full extent of its difference from the present. In the second, this defamiliarizing impulse may become excessive, and result in a blanket defamiliarization of things which are perhaps not so unfamiliar after all. Considering this second possibility, it might possible to raise the objection to the sensory studies approach to cultural history that it focuses unduly on historical difference, and that its 'ethnological gaze,' in particular, constructs an unwarranted distance between early modern and later modes of perception. In other words, are we well advised to 'make strange' where defamiliarization results in only apparent difference?

The answer to this first question must rest on our assessment of the extent of cultural-historical change and - for my present purposes - of changes to the common sensorium. However, if we consider the position that (as George Steiner has argued) '[f]undamental breaks in the history of human perception are very rare,'[85] this raises the related questions of (1) what could be said to constitute such a 'break'; and (2) whether, in sensory studies, it really is heavily disruptive breaks that we are looking for, primarily. The very first pineapple grown in a British hothouse could only be tasted by so many people. Some received notions about the workings of the senses died surprisingly slowly. Instead, I would base my argument on the perhaps minute but nevertheless pervasive

Sense of Hearing and the Sense of the Past in Renaissance England,' *Albion* 18 (1986), 159–193, quotation at 181.)
[83] Clune, *Writing Against Time*, 19, 17.
[84] Clune, *Writing Against Time*, 154n20.
[85] George Steiner, *Real Presences* (Chicago: University of Chicago Press, 1991 [1989]), 87.

1.2 From 'Historical Psychology' to 'Cognitive Historicism': Research Contexts

and incrementally momentous changes to habits of perception which did demonstrably occur. Rather than have us look for drastic ruptures alone ('fundamental *breaks*'), the notion of '*fundamental* breaks' (whose geological overtones might match those of 'sensory formations'), should lead us to ground our understanding of the sensorium through history in an incremental build-up of cultural difference over the *longue durée*. In general, as the many instances of unfamiliar (or only superficially familiar) 'senseways' documented in historical research attest, it does indeed seem advisable to suspect strangeness, if only as a first heuristic.[86]

The cultural history of human cognition, then, is only partly one of recognition. It is, for the most part, one of graduated unfamiliarity, to be charted against the full scale of 'change and continuity in seventeenth-century England' (in Christopher Hill's phrase) – or, indeed, in early modern European culture at large. In order to render the methodological reflections and material findings of sensory history applicable to my proposed analysis of Milton's writings – manifestly *textual* objects of study –, I will now turn to an elaboration of the concept of 'sensory discourse,' the central category of that analysis. This, in short, provides the link between the (historically and culturally situated) sensorium and the text, between Milton's world and Milton's words. We know now what the Ongee equivalent of 'how are you?' is. But what might be the early modern, what the Miltonic equivalent of *'konyune? onorange-tanka?'*

---

[86] 'Senseways' is derived from Rath's notion of 'soundways,' meaning the 'paths, trajectories, transformations, mediations, practices, and techniques – in short, the ways – that people employ to interpret and express their attitudes and beliefs about sound' (*How Early America Sounded*, 2).

2. What Is Sensory Discourse?

2.1 Milton's Conception of 'Discourse'

As Milton's Satan departs Hell in book 2 of *Paradise Lost* on his mission to ruin humankind, the fallen angels he leaves behind disperse across the hellscape, seeking entertainment. Some turn to athletics reminiscent of 'the Olympian games or Pythian fields,' others 'sing/With notes angelical to many a harp/Their own heroic deeds,' and others still engage in complex theological reasoning:

> In discourse more sweet
> (For eloquence the soul, song charms the sense)
> Others apart sat on a hill retired,
> In thoughts more elevate, and reasoned high
> Of providence, foreknowledge, will, and fate,
> Fixed fate, free will, foreknowledge absolute,
> And found no end, in wandering mazes lost. (2.530, 547–9, 555–61)

Several aspects of this passage invite comment, and will help prepare the ground for my discussion of 'sensory discourse' in this chapter. As might be expected, I take Milton's use of the term 'discourse' as my starting point. The dominant meaning of 'discourse' in the passage cited appears to be that given by the *OED* as sense 4a: 'the action or process of communicating thought by means of the spoken word ... conversation, talk.'[1] Some of the devils – perhaps those who are less athletically or musically inclined – are making conversation. However, the fact that this meaning only ranks fourth in the *OED*'s sequence of semantic evolution should make us curious as to possible overtones or ambiguities – as should the fact that, for most of the meanings and sub-meanings attested earlier, their first attestations are crowded in a comparatively narrow forty-year interval straddling the middle of the sixteenth century, which suggests an extent of ambiguity in early modern usage. The aspect that all entries share is their reference to reason, or to an ordered process of reasoning (e.g., 'the process or faculty of reasoning; reasoned argument or thought; reason, rationality'). This level of meaning, too, can be shown to be present in Milton's passage.

After all, not only are the devils engaged in discourse explicitly said to '[reason] high'; the passage also suggests a kind of trichotomy ordering the diverse activities they pursue: athletics, song, and reasoning. In the context of Milton's frequently allegorical epic, this trichotomy arguably mirrors the tripartite structure of body (*sōma*), soul (*psuchê*), and intellect/spirit (*noûs/pneûma*) in Platonic or Pauline thought, or of the

---

[1] *OED*, 'discourse, n.'

vegetative, sensitive and rational powers of the organic and the intellective soul in the various interpretations of Aristotle.[2] The physical, bodily exercise of the first group speaks for itself; the affinity of the second with the sensitive soul is quite plausible; the reasoning of the third, as pointed out, is again made explicit.

Indeed, Milton's explicit references to 'soul' and 'sense' might offer further corroboration, since here 'soul' appears to stand, by way of metonymy, for 'intellective soul.' Such a metonymic association appears justified by other references to the rational human soul later in the epic: During the early stages of their conversation in book 5, the archangel Raphael, speaking of the human soul and its tripartite nature, will explain to Adam that 'reason is her being [i.e., her distinctive quality],/Discursive, or intuitive; discourse/Is oftest yours, the latter most is ours [i.e., the angels'],/Differing but in degree, of kind the same' (5.487–90). Thus, discursive reason – reason operating by a kind of 'discourse' – is established as the capstone of human nature, the point of contact between man and the angels.[3] With a view to the passage at hand, again, the successive tiers of the tripartite soul appear associated with the distinct activities of the three groups of fallen angels.

On the other hand, one could state with equal justification that, in Milton's presentation, the three areas of activity – (1) somatic, (2) sensuous, and (3) rational – cohere, or mirror each other: the discourse of reasoning is '*more* sweet' than that of 'song' (i.e., both vocal music and poetry), and is thus characterised as, in its way, sensuous (at least as 'eloquence,' which 'charms' the soul).[4] 'Song,' we understand by the same token, does not exist in a realm entirely separated from that of discourse and reason.[5] Likewise, it is hard to conceive that Milton, in writing of 'Olympian games or Pythian fields,' did

---

[2] For the first, see *Timaeus* 30 and 1 Thess. 5:23, respectively; the origin of the second is in *De anima* 2.2–3/673a; see also the chapters by Katherine Park, 'The Organic Soul' (464–484), and Eckhard Keßler, 'The Intellective Soul' (485–534), in: *The Cambridge History of Renaissance Philosophy*, eds Charles B. Schmitt/Quentin Skinner (Cambridge: Cambridge University Press, 1988).
[3] With reference to Milton's translation of Petrus Ramus's *Dialectic* as the *Art of Logic*, Walter J. Ong has argued that, in redefining logic as 'the art of reasoning well' (*ars bene ratiocinandi*) rather than 'the art of discoursing well' (*ars bene disserendi*, the definition in Ramus's original, drawn from Cicero), 'Milton, even more than Ramus, tends to assign thought not so much to a world of discourse as to the Cartesian monologic or solipsistic universe: "reasoning," unlike discoursing, can be presumed to go on in one's own consciousness independently of overt communication.' ('Logic and Rhetoric,' in: *A Milton Encyclopedia*, ed. William B. Hunter, vol. 5 [Lewisburg, Pa.: Bucknell University Press, 1979], 30–36, at 33.) As the passage from *Paradise Lost* indicates, however, the notion of 'discourse' as a fundamental mode of *thinking* (i.e., ratiocination, whether internal or externalised) was not alien to Milton. The relevant passage of the *Art of Logic* is in CPW 8: 217–8; in his notes ad loc., Ong also observes a 'detachment of thought from discourse' evident in Milton (218n6).
[4] Several passages in his writings suggest that Milton was aware of the double etymology of 'charm' from Latin *carmen*, 'song,' and Old English *cierm*, 'magic spell' (see Fowler *ad PL* 4.642).
[5] This mirrors Milton's view of the human–animal dichotomy: at *PL* 8.373–4, God tells Adam that 'They [sc. the animals] also know,/And reason not contemptibly.' Note that, in this (partial) attribution of reasoning powers to animals, Milton uses the verb cautiously: animals are not *given reason* as humans. On early modern debates about this point – with some authors claiming 'a kind of perception' even in plants –, see Thomas, *Man and the Natural World*, 137, 179.

not also intend a reference to the respective Pindaric victory odes (i.e., *ōdai*, 'songs');[6] in turn, the identification of discursive, rational thought with ancient Greece is a persistent theme throughout Milton's writings.[7] Finally, both the sensuous and rational areas of activity rely on corporeal 'equipment,' linking them to the somatic sphere.

The devils' singing is such that 'the harmony/.../Suspended Hell, and took with ravishment/The thronging audience' (2.552–5): an instance of emphatically embodied sensation (Hell, persistently portrayed in the first two books as a place of continuous torment, is '[s]uspended,' i.e., made temporarily ineffective) as well as embodied perception (of the passion, or emotion, of ravishment). 'Thronging audience' restates both the aural nature of the experience and its embodied materiality, which is a rather ambiguous circumstance. With the lone exception of the Incarnation, after all, in Milton the notion of what could be called 'dynamic embodiment,' i.e., embodiment *as process or event*, carries a strong negative force: thus, in the markedly neo-Platonic context of *Comus*, for instance, there is a constant risk that 'the soul .../Embodies, and imbrutes' (466–7). This is opposed to the notion of the soul's embodiment *as created condition*, which is a feature of Milton's monist-materialist ontology inherited, arguably, from Hebraic psychology.[8]

At the same time, the indisputably *physical* exercise of the first group of devils, who – to give the fuller quotation –

> Part on the plain, or in the air sublime,
> Upon the wing or in swift race contend,
> As at the Olympian games or Pythian fields;
> Part curb their fiery steeds, or shun the goal
> With rapid wheels,   (2.528–532)

gains a perhaps unexpected 'discursivity' if we consider the etymological dimension: 'discourse' is derived from Latin *discursus* (from *dis-currere*), which, the *OED* notes, describes an 'action of running off in different directions, dispersal, action of running

---

[6] From *aeidein*, 'to sing' (*LSJ*). The devils pointedly 'sing ... [t]heir own heroic deeds,' as Pindar sang those of victorious athletes. It might be added that, in having them sing 'to many a harp' (548), Milton expands the Greek notion with the Hebrew one of *samar* ('to sing or play on a stringed instrument'), root of *mismor*, 'a psalm,' and he does so with intent: the fallen angels *should* be psalmodising, but instead they are just 'odising,' in the pagan manner. This certainly should count as another instance of Milton's 'fusing Greek with Hebrew' concepts, observed on several occasions by Hale, *Milton's Languages*.

[7] While a 1620 edition of Pindar long thought to have been Milton's (the 'Harvard Pindar') most likely was not, his familiarity with Pindar's works is beyond doubt, see Jackson Campbell Boswell, *Milton's Library: A Catalogue of the Remains of John Milton's Library and An Annotated Reconstruction of Milton's Library and Ancillary Readings* (New York: Garland Publishing, 1975), 193; Greek philosophy makes an early appearance in *At a Vacation Exercise* (1628?, *SP* 23); the most extended association of ancient Greece and philosophy in Milton's late work is in *PR* 4.236–284 (Satan presents to Jesus 'Athens the eye of Greece' and all her philosophical wonders).

[8] See my reference to the term *nephesh*, 'soul, life-spirit,' in Chapter 5 below. Angels, though free to take any shape they choose, should not be tied to a permanent bodily form (see *PL* 6.351–3).

about, bustling activity.'⁹ That this particular semantic dimension of the term may have been more obvious to Milton's first, intended audience (a possibly rigorous training in Latin aside) is indicated by stress: 'discoùrse,' in all of its eleven occurrences in *Paradise Lost* (of which the one at 2.555 is the first) must, on metrical grounds, be stressed, as is presently the norm in the case of the verb, 'to discourse,' on the ultimate, and not, as in current usage of the noun, on the penultimate syllable , thus arguably reinforcing the root etymon.

This may also be suggested by the fact that John Florio's much-used Italian-English dictionary, first published in 1598, glosses the cognate 'Discórso' (the noun) not only as 'discourse, reason, consideration,' but also, in a separate entry for the participle, as 'discoursed, reasoned, *run too and fro.*'¹⁰ In Milton's time, the latter phrase was prominently associated with the prophetic assurance, given in the Book of Daniel, that, in the end times, 'many shall run to and fro, and knowledge shall be increased.' This became a frequently cited motto around the middle of the seventeenth century, and something of a slogan for the so-called new science; Francis Bacon put a slightly different Latin version (*Multi pertransibunt et augebitur scientia*) on the title pages of his *Great Instauration* (1620) and *Advancement of Learning* (1640), where it is associated with (sea) travel (see Figures 1 and 2).¹¹ Even the frantic activity of those fallen angels not engaging in (discursive) debate should thus still be considered in the wider context associated with the notion of 'discourse.'

---

⁹ *OED*, 'discourse, n.'; with *discursus*, the meaning of 'conversation' is post-classical. Corns, who in general aims to disprove the cliché of Milton's style as more Latin than English, judges that 'Milton ... operated always from a clear awareness of distinctions between English and Latin usage. In poetic discourse a certain Latinizing tendency, though of a rather particular and muted kind, is apparent,' and speaks of Milton's 'clever revitaliz[ation]' of a particular submerged Latin meaning (*Milton's Language*, 96).

¹⁰ [Iohn Florio,] *Queen Anna's New World of Words, or Dictionarie of the Italian and English tongues* ... (Melch. Bradwood for Edw. Blount and William Barrett, 1611), 152, emphasis added. Around the middle of the sixteenth century, 'discourse' was still perceived as an Italian loan word, as is suggested by the first citation for *OED* sense 4a ('the action of communicating thought by means of the spoken word ... In later use also: the written representation of this ...'), from a letter of Bishop Stephen Gardiner: 'The man is wise and of good discourse, as the Italyan sayth.' Given Milton's solid knowledge of Italian, it does not seem a stretch to assume his awareness of the etymological background of 'discourse.' That the term was not wholly assimilated into English at the turn of the seventeenth century is also suggested by its scarcity in the Authorised Version, where it only occurs in Ecclesiasticus, translating either Greek *diêgêsis* or *diêgêma*, 'narrative account.'

¹¹ The passage quoted is in Dan. 12:4. Bacon's version is based on the Vulgate (dating from the late fourth century), which may go some way towards explaining why *discurrere* is not used: it had, by that time, moved further in the semantic direction of 'speech', as opposed to 'movement' (note, however, Thomas Carlyle's double-edged parody of the phrase as 'Multi discurrent et augebitur stultitia!'). The Tremellius–Junius version, Milton's favoured Latin Bible, has 'percurrent multi, & augebitur cognitio.' The Hebrew root *shuwt* present in the original is closer in meaning, in any case, to classical Latin *discurrere*, or indeed *percurrere* (both 'to run to and fro') than it is to *pertransire* ('to go beyond, travel'). On the wide influence of the passage from Daniel, see Richard Popkin, 'The Religious Background of Seventeenth-Century Philosophy,' in: *The Cambridge History of Seventeenth-Century Philosophy*, eds Daniel Garber/Michael Ayers, 2 vols (Cambridge: Cambridge University Press, 2003), I, 393–422, at 395; Mordechai Feingold, '"And Knowledge Shall Be Increased:" Millenarianism and the Advancement of Learning

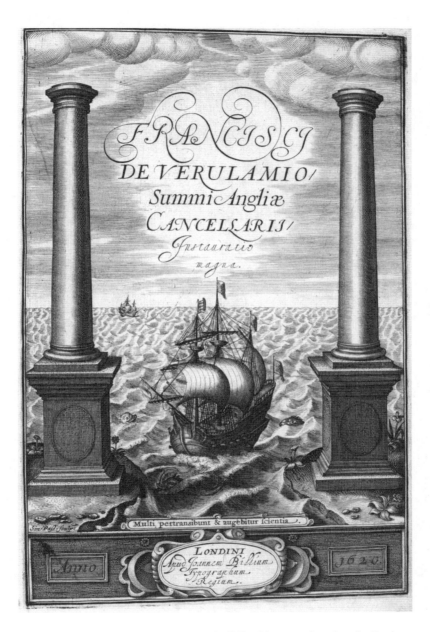

Fig. 1: Francis Bacon, *Instauratio Magna* (1620), title page, bearing the Latin motto 'Multi pertransibunt et augebitur scientia.' (Source: Cabinet Project, Oxford University, <https://www.cabinet.ox.ac>)

Fig. 2: Francis Bacon, *The Advancement of Learning* (1640), title page, bearing the Latin motto 'Multi pertransibunt et augebitur scientia.' (Source: Cabinet Project, Oxford University, <https://www.cabinet.ox.ac>)

2.1 Milton's Conception of 'Discourse'

Having expended some energy establishing a connection between running, various kinds of 'discourse,' and reason in the passage at hand, one crucial question remains: how reasonable is the devils' (verbal) discourse, really? I have offered clues for an intended association of the third group of devils with the domain of reason, intellect, or spirit: in particular, their positioning in opposition to the first two groups, which may plausibly be associated with the body and the (sensitive) soul, respectively; but also the implied contrast between (the rational) 'soul' and 'sense'; and their identification with the established vocabulary of academic theological and philosophical debate, of 'providence, foreknowledge, will, and fate.' What I would like to suggest now is that all of these intricate relations between what the different groups of fallen angels do and how they do it constitute, in effect, a kind of 'red herring', intended to challenge the presumption of the third group.

The most obvious element of that challenge lies in Milton's presentation of the supposedly 'highest' group of fallen angels, depicted as engaging '[i]n thoughts more elevate.' Theirs is indeed a philosophical-theological debate, but it is presented as the cliché of fruitless scholastic discourse-as-verbiage which Milton loved to scorn since his days at Cambridge: they are discussing 'providence, foreknowledge, will, and fate,' then again, 'fixed fate, free will, foreknowledge absolute,' and so on, in endless permutation. Their reason, moreover, is not the 'right reason' given by God but mere reasoning, and Milton's use of 'reason' as a verb is significant here: when the devils '[reason] high,' this is a creative activity in the *worst* possible sense of the term, being 'vain wisdom all, and false philosophy' (2.565).[12]

The association of the devils' activity with the rational soul, while suggested by the structure of the passage at large, is, in the end, also spurious. After all, it is not reason, nor even the words of a rational argument, that '[charms] the soul', but rather 'eloquence.' To be sure, Milton is not denigrating rhetoric itself (rhetoric is not the opposite of virtue); but he is attacking its employment to unfruitful, pernicious ends.[13] Earlier in book 2, Belial (Hebr., 'useless'), one of the more prominent devils, had been characterised by reference to the sophistic strategy of *ton hēttō logon kreittō poiein* – to 'make the weaker *logos* stronger' or, as Milton paraphrases, 'make the worse appear/The better reason' (2.113).[14] It is also said of Belial that 'he seemed/For dignity composed, and

---

Revisited,' *The Seventeenth Century* 28 (2013), 363–393. In the sensorium of the Hebrew Bible, incidentally, 'walking' is not only conceptualised as one of the senses, but is closely associated with both instruction and obedience, see Yael Avrahami, *The Senses of Scripture: Sensory Perception in the Hebrew Bible* (New York: T&T Clark, 2012), 75–79; Avrahami specifically comments on the passage from Daniel at 160–1.

[12] At a later point in the epic, God will instruct Adam that even animals 'reason not contemptibly,' cf. n5 above.

[13] In his *History of Britain*, Milton actually posits a connection between eloquence and virtue: 'For worthy deeds are not often destitute of worthy relaters: as by a certain Fate great Acts and great Eloquence have most commonly gon hand in hand, equalling and honouring each other in the same Ages' (CPW 5: 39–40). See also Nicholas von Maltzahn, *Milton's 'History of Britain': Republican Historiography in the English Revolution* (Oxford: Oxford University Press, 1991), 69.

[14] The principle is attributed to Protagoras by Aristotle, Rhet. 1402a24.

high exploit./But all was false and hollow; though his tongue/Dropped manna, ... [and] he pleased the ear, ...' and later, that he presented 'words clothed in reason's garb' (2.110–3, 226). The synaesthetic association between the proverbial sweetness of the biblical manna – whose 'taste ... was like wafers made with honey' – and aurally pleasing speech is taken up in the 'discourse more sweet' of the present passage.[15] However, that, in the wider poetic universe of *Paradise Lost*, the sensuous quality of 'sweet discourse' is not reprehensible per se, may be inferred from Adam's enthusiastic exclamation, having conversed for a while with Raphael:

> ... while I sit with thee, I seem in heaven,
> And sweeter thy discourse is to my ear
> Than fruits of palm-tree pleasantest to thirst
> And hunger both, from labour, at the hour
> Of sweet repast; they satiate, and soon fill,
> Though pleasant, but thy words, with grace divine
> Imbued, bring to their sweetness no satiety. (*PL* 8.210–6)

The specifically positive, or at least not straightforwardly cloying, sweetness of Raphael's discourse contrasts with that of the devils' 'sweet discourse.' In the present context of *infernal* rhetoric, 'sweet discourse' is used to sugar-coat errors and manifest untruths, and thus to 'make the weaker *logos* stronger.'

Logos itself covers a wide semantic spectrum, ranging from the meanings of 'reason' (themselves multiple) to 'meaning,' 'word,' and the various meanings of 'speech.' It is the same unstable duality of *logos* as (mere) speech and (well-founded) reason – or discourse-as-speech and discourse-of-reason, or dialectical reasoning and monologic reason – which informs the particular thrust of 'eloquence' in the passage at hand. In reality, we are forced to conclude, 'eloquence' charms the 'soul' *just as* – not *whereas* – 'song charms the sense.' The soul in question was the sensitive soul all along; our identification of 'eloquence' with reason, though urged by the composition of the passage, was erroneous. Through an error 'built into' the misleading description of the misled fallen angels, and by allusion to the difference between the sphere of the senses and the realm of the rational mind, the reader has been taught; knowledge, in other words, may have been imparted.

Finally, we may return to the idea of discourse as 'going to and fro.' The debating devils, while 'apart sat on a hill retired,' are not wholly still; after all, they are discoursing. But this, again, is presented in terms of a movement (however futile): they 'found no end, in wandering mazes lost.' Their discourse is moving, but it is not moving forward (or upward), as would be expected of discursive activity in light of other passages in the poem.[16] We should also note that it is not they who are moving *inside of* one or

---

[15] Ex. 16:31.
[16] See, for example 5.468–503. On the wider relevance of conceptual metaphors to sensory discourse, see my discussion in Chapter 2.4 below. A striking parallel to the devils' stunted but endless discourse appears in the quarrel between Adam and Eve immediately after the Fall: 'Thus they in mutual accusation spent/The fruitless hours, but neither self-condemning;/And of their

2.1 Milton's Conception of 'Discourse'

several mazes but that Milton's reference is to 'wandering mazes': they themselves create the mazes in which they entrap themselves, conjuring them up by their endless reasoning.[17] Finally, the devils' faulty mode of discursive movement matches the presentation of their faulty reasoning on a less metaphorical plane. As often in Milton, the criticism of the passage, made explicit only in the final line or even half-line, seems at first to strike wholesale at targets which its author demonstrably did not consider blameworthy in themselves.[18] Ultimately, however, it rests on the specific difference in the case presented: namely, on the devils' *faulty intention* (in singing their own deeds, straying from God, etc.), which is thus highlighted – a procedure typical of Milton's treatment of 'ethical' subjects through apparent contradiction.

Milton does allude to the triad of body, soul, and spirit, he does hint at the tripartite soul, and he does adumbrate a system in which the vegetative, sensitive, and rational/intellective realms are intertwined.[19] At second glance, however, the last of the three categories implied is merely that, an implied category; its reference is empty. Whereas the devils do engage in athletic contests to pass the time (although even the positive association with the Olympic and Pythian games is, strictly speaking, part of an epic simile), and whereas they do sing and experience the visceral sensations associated with this (although the pains of hell are 'suspended' only temporarily and the passion of 'ravishment,' with its overtones of being forced, is a highly ambiguous one), they *do not* actually employ their reason (which, as *recta ratio*, would lead them not into mazes but towards God).

We are looking, therefore, at a doubly conflicted passage: there is the superimposition of a fairly explicit trichotomy (body, soul, and spirit) with its implicit undermining through cross-correlation of its distinct domains; and there is the insecurity about proper behaviour, related to the concept of 'discourse' – and the different ways in which this concept may be understood –, expressed in terms of target-oriented movement or inter-

---

vain contest appeared no end' (9.1187–9), with similar conceptual-metaphoric implications (and a bitter pun on the forbidden fruit).

[17] This figure of thought resembles other references to the devils' punishment as infinite self-entrapment; compare Satan's complaint at *PL* 4.73–75: 'Me miserable, which way shall I fly/Infinite wrath and infinite despair?/*Which way I fly is hell; myself am hell* .../And in the lowest deep, a lower deep/Still threatening to devour me opens wide,/To which the hell I suffer seems a heaven' (emphasis added), the falsification of his earlier boast that 'The mind is its own place, and in itself/Can make a heaven of hell, a hell of heaven' (1.254–5).

[18] Athletic exercise is expressly commended in *Of Education* (see CPW 2: 408–9); 'song,' that is, the sister arts of poetry and music, are addressed as 'Blest pair of Sirens, pledges of Heav'ns joy' in *At a Solemn Musick* (1); abstract reasoning of the good kind is celebrated in the *Art of Logic*, although this includes a strict separation – obviously disregarded by the devils – of logic and theology (see CPW 8: 208).

[19] In the portion of the poem between the passage just discussed and the return of the narrative focus to Satan at 2.629, a fourth party of devils is described (which itself subdivides into four groups). The description of their 'bold adventure to discover wide/That dismal world .../ [with] flying march' – 'roving on/In confused march forlorn,' finding 'no rest' –, does not, I would argue, negate the tripartite structure outlined above, but rather supplements it by developing the theme of restless but ultimately fruitless movement (2.571–4, 614–5, 618). The passage 2.562–569 appears to me to establish a clear division between the former three groups and the exploits of the fourth.

minable erring. In a somatic, sensory-motor way, the corruption of the devils' discourse is apparent from their *persistence in error*;[20] in the more abstract sense of the term 'discourse,' this corruption is expressed through a semantic transmutation of 'reason' into 'mere language.'

***

From the passage at hand, we may derive four interrelated notions of 'discourse': as something that (1) takes place through the medium of language and is (2) connected with reason and knowledge (which may be employed or not, may be increased or not, depending on the quality of the discourse); but which is (3) causally associated with the body and the senses, meaning its operation is embodied; and, ideally, (4) is not static but a kind of directed movement (possibly going 'to and fro,' as in the instructive exchange of two partners in conversation). We will encounter all these aspects again in the subsequent discussion. Most of them can be linked to the etymology and diverse meanings of 'discourse' offered by the *OED*. Only one stands out as determined not so much by the traditional meanings of the term as by Milton's employment of it in his poem: the notion of discourse as charming, sweet and pleasing, as inherently sensuous.

The trouble with discourse, it has been suggested, is precisely what Milton's devils are forced to experience without comprehending: it has no end. In fact, the issue of Milton's complex notion of 'discourse' – sweet but contributive to reason, necessary but not sufficient to salvation, prone to error – will be taken up again below. The purpose of the present chapter is to establish what I call 'sensory discourse' as a category of analysis and lay out the points of departure for the subsequent interpretive chapters.[21] In terms of argumentative structure, then, this chapter forms a connection between the research context outlined in the preceding and the readings of Milton's texts offered in subsequent chapters.

In a first step, I will consider the connection between the senses and language: how precisely may we say the sensorium is verbalised? The sensory-linguistic relation can be considered in two different ways: either, on the most basic level, as inherent to the sensorium (as perception must be verbalised) or as the result of more obviously cultural

---

[20] One instance of 'erring' as an (ultimately etymological) pun, 'to be mistaken' and 'to stray', is at *PL* 6.172–3.

[21] I should point out, perhaps, that a reference to Jean-François Lyotard's use of *discours sensible*, rendered by his translators into English as 'sensory discourse,' is not intended. Interestingly, the term appears to denote, in Lyotard's version, the discursive mode of a kind of transition period roughly equal to early modernity, when, in parallel to the rise of 'the discourse of knowledge,' '[s]ensory reality is no longer "spoken" according to the narrative discourse that recounts the creature's adventure; it does, however, continue to hold a discourse. It is only much later that its intelligibility will become unintelligible, that one will only speak *of it*, that it will, therefore, side entirely with reference.' ('*Veduta* on a Fragment of the "History" of Desire,' in: Idem, *Discourse, Figure*, trs Anthony Hudek/Mary Lydon [Minneapolis, Minn.: University of Minnesota Press, 2011 (1971)], 157–201, at 175–7.) In contrast to this, I intend 'sensory discourse' as a discursive category that is stable inasmuch as it encompasses both: the transmission of experience (to the extent possible) *and* explicit references to perception and its requirements (whereas Lyotard's *discours sensible* appears to be forever slipping away from experience, and towards 'mere' reference).

interference and more or less conscious choices: these are the 'historical' and 'stylistic/poetic' dimensions of sensory language, respectively. Their discussion comes down to the question of how something like a specifically 'sensory language' may be delineated.

A second section considers metaphor, first as a linguistic phenomenon of particular affinity to sense perception – a view dating back to antiquity. However, as will become clear by reference to more recent authors, the significance of metaphor extends beyond the merely linguistic to the cognitive-conceptual sphere. Here, we may both reconnect the discussion to the sensory domain and consider metaphor as shaped, in part, by discourse – understood here as linguistic context.

In a third section, drawing on the understanding of discourse developed by Michel Foucault in *The Archaeology of Knowledge*, I elaborate on this notion of discourse as context. Context (including non-discursive context) thus joins sensory language and the relevant (conceptual) metaphors as an element constitutive of sensory discourse.

In all three sections, sensory language, metaphor, and discourse will emerge as analytical categories inherently involved with questions of knowledge and knowledge making. If what unites them at the outset of this survey is their connection to sense perception, it is their shared commitment to epistemic matters that stand as its conclusion. Throughout, I aim to combine theoretical reflection with illustrative application, returning to the perceived relations between discourse and the senses in Milton and his contemporaries.

2.2 The Senses in Discourse: Perception – Communication – Language

As the advocates of sensory history consistently point out, 'the human sensorium … never exists in a natural state.'[22] How does this relate, though, to the problem of accurately characterising the presence of perception in Milton's early modern discourse? The answer may be derived from a triad suggested by Howes.[23] From the always already *acculturated* quality of the sensorium – as opposed to a persistent association of the senses with nature, whether imagined as 'innocent' or 'savage' – follows its *social* character: the individual sensorium is one among many in a society sharing at least a family resemblance. Human society, in turn, implies communication. It is the place – whether in a traditional-literal or, increasingly, in a notional sense – where 'information, knowledge, or ideas' are communicated or 'made common.'[24]

This, at the latest, is where percepts – the contents of perception – enter the sphere of language. While there remains, and arguably must remain, a certain tension between the contents of the perceptive experience and their communication in language – whether we conceive of this as 'unstated sensibilities' or 'a certain sense of alienation from lived experience' –, language is our foremost, our most readily available avenue of making them *known* to others. As cognitive science and neurolinguistics suggest, we might also be making ourselves *felt*: communication *about* perception is processed by

---

[22] David Howes, 'Introduction: Empires of the Senses,' in: *Empire of the Senses*, ed. Howes, 1–17, at 3.
[23] For the following, see Howes, 'Introduction,' 3–4. Howes is also concerned with 'analysing the social ideologies conveyed through sensory values and practices.'
[24] *OED*, 'communication,' origin and II.5.b.

the human brain in a manner akin to the processing of our own sensations. Barring other means of imitative evocation or imaginative re-creation (e.g., artificial flavourings, painting), which, as a rule, raise greater demands of material, technology, or skill, language, if used 'creatively, critically, and sensitively,' is the primary passage out of our own sensoria into the world – and on into the sensoria of others, whether synchronically or diachronically.[25] While this raises hopes of 'coming to terms' with the problem of perception in language, it also calls for a critical awareness of the necessary mismatch in trying to 'suit the perception to the word.' Yet there appears to be no easy way around the problem: 'It would seem to be the fate of the senses that their astonishing power to reveal and engage should forever be judged and "sentenced" in the court of language.'[26] In cultural terms, the sensorium, for the most part, must exist in a verbalised condition.

These reflections connect to the linguistic concerns of sensory studies as outlined above. Not only do they work towards confirming Alain Corbin's suggestive remark about the affinities between sensory history and literature (literature being a reflective, self-conscious use of language); they also correspond to the linguistic groundwork of cognitive cultural studies. Not least, the ethnographic bend so prominent in sensory studies already brings with it a tendency to adopt a language-centred approach: ethnology, if it is to move beyond mere statistics, is hardly conceivable without language, both in terms of the linguistic proficiency of the researcher in the field and as the medium in which to formulate their descriptive and interpretive findings.[27] While the accessibility of the sensorium to linguistic analysis is thus established, we are, ultimately, thrown back to the question of a specifically sensory language in the early modern cultural setting. An approach to such a language as *substantially* recognizable (i.e., determined by a particular lexis) could begin by exploring either of two avenues: an 'historical' or a 'poetical' one (echoing the 'scholarship'/'criticism' distinction referred to in Chapter 1 above).

---

[25] Howes, 'Introduction,' 4. See also the account of the origin of shared concepts in Zoltán Kövecses, *Where Metaphors Come From: Reconsidering Context in Metaphor* (Oxford: Oxford University Press, 2015), ix–xi.

[26] Howes, 'Introduction,' 4. Arguably, Howes's metaphor relates to the literal implications of what I have called 'critical awareness': language inevitably 'judges' perception, but our best bet in coming to terms with this necessary dilution would be to 'pass judgement,' in turn, upon the various factors implied in the genesis of the perceptual statement in the first place. Howes, too, is careful to note that his argument is not directed against the adequacy of language *per se*, but against *undue* trust in the linguistic paradigm of expressing perceptual content, citing the phenomenologist Michel Serres's concession that 'my own language denies what [it] maintains, namely the emptiness, abstraction and rigor mortis of language.'

[27] Versions of this view are often attributed to Clifford Geertz. Geertz not only stressed, however, that linguistic proficiency is a necessary (not a sufficient) condition of ethnographic activity, but also argued that 'cognition … one assumes … works the same among them [people from other cultures] as it does among us' ('Thick Description: Toward an Interpretive Theory of Culture,' in: Idem, *The Interpretation of Cultures* [New York: Basic Books, 1973], 3–30, at 13). While the proponents of sensory anthropology would certainly agree with the first point, they would not necessarily support the latter (see Howes, *Sensual Relations*, esp. 32–58, and the references given in Chapter 1, n.74 above).

On the historical side, recent decades have seen a strong interest in verbal-conceptual determinants of analysis, whether in the form of conceptual history or, focusing on *parole* rather than *langue*, as the study of 'idioms, rhetorics, ways of talking about politics, distinguishable language games of which each may have its own vocabulary, rules, preconditions, and implications, tone and style.'[28] It is clear that the conceptual-historical study of individual terms has much to offer in the way of contextualising particular references to sense perception in language; however its main focus, by definition, is on an abstract and diachronic, rather than on a synchronic and particularising, plane. As the diachronic variability of some of the most prominent terms from the semantic field of sense perception indicates (conceptual heavyweights such as 'sensibility' or 'taste'), a more 'finely tuned' approach to sensory language will still have to account for individual instances of usage.

Taking a cue from John Pocock's notion of 'idioms' as 'ways of talking about politics,' quoted above, we might ask whether a 'sensory idiom' – delineating, perhaps, 'ways of talking about the senses' – would offer a ready conceptual tool. The trouble with this is that, in Pocock's model, the 'idioms' employed in the political sphere are derived from, and firmly rooted in, readily identifiable source domains: the sphere of law, say, or that of theology.[29] With the senses, I would argue, matters are a little different. Sensory language has no 'home' in the way that legal language is tied to the institutions and practices of the law. In fact, if we were to assign priority to one or another of the various areas in which reference to the sensory sphere is common – poetry, philosophy, the visual arts, music, science, cooking –, this would be highly questionable. References to sense perception in poetry may, on principle, be less reflected than those in philosophy; but since they arguably aim at greater immediacy, it would be absurd to call one more fundamental than the other in the early modern discourse on the senses. If we add to this the propensity of early modern discourses, already noted, for ambiguity and coalescence, it becomes clear that there can be no one 'sensory idiom' in the sense intended by Pocock. In its eclecticism, the language of sense perception would have to be closer in its features to the Pocockian languages of politics – and would, in fact, have to be considered multiple, just as they are.

At this point we are caught in a quandary between the high level of abstraction implicit in conceptual history on the one hand, and a lack of clear discursive orientation on the other (since the source domains of Pocock's 'idioms' could, in a sense not wholly

---

[28] J. G. A. Pocock, 'The Concept of a Language and the *metier d'historien*: Some Considerations on Practice (1987),' in: Idem, *Political Thought and History: Essays on Theory and Method* (Cambridge: Cambridge University Press, 2011), 87–105, at 89.

[29] See J. G. A. Pocock, 'Languages and Their Implications: The Transformation of the Study of Political Thought,' in: Idem, *Politics, Language, and Time: Essays on Political Thought and History* (Chicago: University of Chicago Press, 1989 [1971]), 3–41, esp. 25, on 'idioms': 'The historian's first problem … is to identify the "language" or "vocabulary" with and within which the author operated, and to show how it functioned paradigmatically to prescribe what he might say and how he might say it. This task can be more easily be imagined if we suppose (as was generally the case in the "early-modern" or "late Renaissance period" …) that his society possessed a number of distinguishable idioms, diverse in both their cultural origins and their linguistic functions, with which to discuss questions of politics – theological, legal, humanist and so on.'

dissimilar to Foucault's, be called individual 'discourses' – of law, of medicine, etc.). In this situation, the attempt to reconstruct the particular sensory vocabularies of a given context, or author, or to collect a 'sensory glossary' for a particular era or as a diachronic 'road map' to sensory history may be thought to offer a way forward. Such glossaries on the divergent meanings of past sensory languages have indeed been compiled. Thus, we might learn that early modern authors would be self-consciously reflecting the poverty of their own sensory language vis-à-vis the rich vocabulary for different tastes of wine in classical Latin; that terms like 'ditty' and 'warble' might have historically or technically specific meanings not necessarily associated with them today; or that the words 'spice' and 'spicy' are, ultimately, derived from *specere*, 'to look,' and hence from the visual sphere.[30]

While many such collections of evidence are lacking in immediate interpretive force, their diachronic awareness and their undifferentiated combination of 'experiential' and 'explanatory' (or 'phenomenological' and 'technical') terms relating to sense perception both point to the wide range that any comprehensive account of sensory language in history would have to cover. Furthermore, if there can be no private language in a strict sense, there certainly can be a 'language of one's own' in the sense of observable regularities, consistent peculiarities, and a certain discrepancy from common usage. In this sense, the notion of a 'Miltonic language,' a language of Milton's own, has long been established, and has been studied in various regards.[31] In its more specific form as a gloss on Milton's use of vocabulary in a particular context, however, such reflection inevitably takes on an interpretive character.[32] What we can take away from the idea of a 'sensory glossary,' in general, is that any such collection would have to account for both, references to sensory qualities *and* to the wider sensory sphere, including scholarly, technological, or other cultural preoccupations with the senses. These, we may designate, (1) on a purely linguistic level, as primary and secondary sensory language, and (2) in their wider interrelations with contemporary context, as direct and indirect sensory discourse. For now, however, I will consider 'sensory language' as 'historically idiomatic' in a vaguely – because not easily traceable – Pocockian sense. To consider the supposition that sensory language *does* have a 'home' – in poetry –, we now turn to the notion of poetic language as particularly germane to sense perception.

On the side of poetry, it is tempting to start from a common preconception of poetic or literary language as characterised by a particular affinity to sense perception, and

---

[30] Examples are taken from Steven Shapin's discussion of the 'Galenic vocabulary' of taste in his *Changing Tastes: How Things Tasted in the Early Modern Period and How They Taste Now* (Uppsala: Uppsala Universitet, 2011), 5–7; the musical glossary in Spaeth, *Milton's Knowledge of Music*, 154–174; and the chapter 'Words of Sense' in Classen, *Worlds of Sense*, 50–76.
[31] E.g., with reference to Milton's stylistic development(s) (see Corns, *Development of Milton's Prose Style*; Corns, *Milton's Language*) or his multilingualism (see Hale, *Milton's Languages*).
[32] With a view to sensory vocabulary, in particular, see Paul Hammond, *Milton's Complex Words: Essays on the Conceptual Structure of 'Paradise Lost'* (Oxford: Oxford University Press, 2017), vii; and, in particular, Hammond's contrastive essays on 'dark' and 'light,' 'idol' and 'image,' 'see' and 'seem' in *Paradise Lost*. See also Annabel Patterson's *Milton's Words* (Oxford: Oxford University Press, 2009).

2.2 The Senses in Discourse: Perception – Communication – Language 65

more specifically to the communication of (often pleasant) percepts.[33] General acceptance of the proposition would likely be higher still if we took 'poetic language' to mean 'the language of lyric (or epic) poetry,' and not also that of literary prose. As I have indicated, the sensory dimension of Milton's writing was long seen as a property exclusive to his poetry – if it was acknowledged at all. In distinction to the notion of 'sensory discourse' to be outlined here, we could refer to this kind (or register) of language – allegedly a hallmark of poetic discourse – as a 'sensuous' or, allowing for more subdued instances, a 'sensory mode' or 'language.' Notably, it seems to be the presence of this mode as a subcomponent of poetic language that has accounted, in large part, for the perceived difference between ordinary language and the language of poetry.

One aspect of this sensory mode is the utterly conventional – neither 'romantic' nor 'classical' – notion of poetic language as 'flowery' language in a very literal sense: as the language of nature and natural delights. This register is very much in evidence in the poetry of Milton's youth, where it often combines with the imagery of daybreak, sunrise and fresh beginnings.[34] Thus in the 'Carmina Elegiaca' ('Elegiac Verses,' 1624?), discovered in manuscript only in the 1870s and now dated among Milton's earliest extant poetry, the speaker exhorts an imagined counterpart to rise and – references to 'work' and laziness notwithstanding – enjoy the pleasures of nature:

> Surge, age surge, leves, iam convenit, excute somnos,
> Lux oritur, tepidi fulcra relique tori
> Iam canit excubitor gallus praenuntius ales
> Solis et invigilans ad sua quemque vocat
> Flammiger Eois Titan caput exserit undis
> Et spargit nitidum laeta per arva iubar
> Daulias argutum modulatur ab ilice carmen
> Edit et excultos mitis alauda modos
> Iam rosa fragrantes spirat silvestris odores
> Iam redolent violae luxuriatque seges
> Ecce novo campos Zephyritis gramine vestit
> Fertilis, et vitreo rore madescit humus
> Segnes invenias molli vix talia lecto
> Cum premat imbellis lumina fessa sopor (1–14)

[Get up, come on, get up! It's time! Shake off these worthless slumbers: it's getting light. Come on out from between the posts of that warm bed. The cock's crowing already: the guardsman cock: the bird that forewarns us of sunrise. He's wide awake and calling everyone to work. Fiery Titan is rearing his head above the eastern waves, and flinging bright sunlight over the gay fields. From her oak-tree perch the Daulian bird [i.e., the nightingale] trills a piercing song, and the gentle lark is pouring forth exquisite harmonies. Now the

---

[33] This is something of an oversimplification. For a profound discussion of the complex relationship between the senses, the wider body, and poetic speaking through history, see Susan Stewart, *Poetry and the Fate of the Senses* (Chicago: University of Chicago Press, 2002).
[34] Apart from the lines discussed here, see the discussion of Elegy V (1629) in Chapter 4.2 below; 'Song: On May Morning' (1629); and lines 41–56, 60–63 of *L'Allegro* (1631?).

wild rose breathes out sweet perfumes; now violets scent the air, and the standing corn frisks and dances. Look, fruit-bringing Flora ['Zephyritis,' i.e. Chloris, wife of Zephyr, identified with Flora] is decking out the fields in fresh turf, and watering the ground with dew as bright as glass. You sluggard, you're not likely to find such sights as these in that downy bed of yours, where feeble lethargy closes your eyes.]

In these few lines, it could be argued, all the senses are addressed. 'Bright sunlight' is both the precondition of seeing 'the gay fields' and the determining factor of the speaker's motivation to address his counterpart in the first place; its polar opposite is expressed in the 'wearied eyes' ('lumina fessa') oppressed by an unusually deep sleep.[35] The song of the various birds named (a cock crowing, lark and nightingale singing at once, despite their conventional opposition) characterises the idealised pastoral soundscape representing both sides of the threshold between night and day. The sweet smell of roses and violets excites the nose, while, arguably, the mention of bountiful fields evokes the pleasures of the palate ('*fruit-bringing* Flora' is Carey's telling interpolation). Finally, the contrast between the fresh and dewy turf ('vitreo rore madescit humus') and the warm and downy bed ('tepidi ... tori,' 'molli ... lecto,' where the ultimately metonymic *torus*, 'a swelling, cushion,' also implies softness) relates to the sense of touch. What is remarkable, however, is that the sequence of sense perceptions represented does not coincide with a sensory hierarchy ranging from sight to touch, nor is it wholly arbitrary; rather it reproduces, as J. Martin Evans notes, the natural perceptual sequence of waking up: from hearing the 'sentinel bird' and seeing the sun rise to a first awareness of the smell of flowers, 'one by one the sleeper's senses gradually come back to life.'[36]

As might be expected from such a youthful work – Milton was around sixteen years old when he composed it –, and given the known focus of early modern language-teaching practice on the imitation of 'worthy models,' the 'Elegiac Verses' incorporate a number of stock phrases from classical poetry, several of them relating to the sensory sphere.[37] Intriguingly, the same manuscript leaf on which these lines were preserved also contains, apart from another short piece of verse on the dangers of 'idle slumber,' the earliest known sample of Milton's Latin prose, most likely also a product of his London schooling.[38] This, a short essay now titled 'Theme on Early Rising' and tentatively assigned to the final years of Milton's time at St Paul's School (1623–5?), treads much the same ground as the 'Elegiac Verses.'[39] Illustrating the proverb, 'Mane citus lectum fuge' ('flee your bed early in the morning,' i.e., 'early rising is best'), its borrowing from classical models is even more conspicuous than in the 'Elegiac Verses,'

---

[35] *OLD* 'fessus,' 'sopor.'
[36] J. Martin Evans, *The Miltonic Moment* (Lexington, Ky.: University Press of Kentucky, 1998), 2. I would add to Evans's account of the 'Elegiac Verses' that it is not so much hearing but the immediate tactile experience of the warm bed, which precedes even the perception of the cock crowing, that serves as the baseline of sense perception in the passage.
[37] See the references given in *Variorum* 1: 11, 333–6.
[38] The other verse fragment, consisting of eight lines in the lesser Asclepiad metre, is 'Ignavus satrapam ...' ('Kings should not oversleep'), quotation at 1–2.
[39] CPW 1: 1034–39, an account of the discovery of the three texts and their (reasonably secure) ascription to Milton is at 1034–6.

2.2 The Senses in Discourse: Perception – Communication – Language

with explicit quotations from Theocritus ('There is no need to sleep deeply') and Homer ('Are you asleep, son of the wise Atreus, tamer of horses?/It is not seemly for a councilor to sleep the whole night through').[40] In its sensory passages, the close resemblance between the prose and verse treatments of the theme is unmistakable:

> ... surge igitur, surge deses nec semper teneat te mollis lectus, nescis quot oblectamenta praebet aurora. Oculos delectare cupis? aspice solem purpureo colore orientem, coelum purum, et salubre, herbescentem agrorum viriditatem, florum omnium varietatem. Aures juvare velis? audi argutos auvium concetus et leves apum susurros: naribus placebis? non satiari possis suavitate odorum qui è floribus efflantur. Quod si haec non arrident, rationem salutis tuae aliquantulùm quaeso ducas; quippe summo mane cubitu surgere ad firmam corporis valetudinem non parum conducit studijs verò aptissimum est tunc enim in numerato habes ingenium.

> [Up, then, up, you sluggard, and let not soft sheets [lit., 'a soft bed'] keep you forever. You know not the number of Dawn's delights. Would you feast your eyes? Behold the purple hue of the rising sun, the clear brisk sky, the green growth of the fields, the diversity of all the flowers. Would you give pleasure to your ears? Listen to the melodious harmony of the birds and the soft humming of the bees. Would you satisfy your sense of smell? [lit., 'your nostrils'] You will never tire of the sweet odors flowing from the flowers. If such delights please you not, I beg you to have some consideration for your well-being; for surely rising at daybreak is a great step towards bodily health. it is best for study as well, for then your faculties are readiest ...][41]

In this short passage alone, there are not only, again, several instances of 'sensory borrowing' from classical models,[42] but also a number of thematic and verbal parallels with the account of early morning given in the 'Elegiac Verses.' Again, there is the 'mollis lectus' of the lingering sleeper; again, there is the 'piercing' (*argutus*) song of birds (which is now contrasted, in a Virgilian turn, with the more subdued background hum – 'leves ... sursurros' – of bees); again, there are the pleasures of eyes, ears, and nose. Early rising, finally, renders the prudent reader both healthy and wise: *firma corporis valetudino* as well as successful *studia* will be its result. Milton's addition to the proverbial notion lies in the close connection he establishes between (by all means appreciative) sense perception and correct living. Both texts, prose and verse, associate the sensorium as a whole with day, life, and activity; they oppose it, accordingly, to night, sleep (twin brother of death), and lethargy. The sensuous enjoyment of perception early in the morning, right after sleep, may be said to embody (and evaluate) this opposition.

Another conventional association of the sensuous mode, namely, its close connection with romantic love, is only implied in the 'Elegiac Verses' through their references

---

[40] CPW 1: 1038.
[41] Original from the Columbia edition; translation from CPW 1: 1037.
[42] With almost literal precision, 'florum omnium varietate' and 'suavitate odorum qui è floribus efflantur' can be traced to Seneca (*De senectute*, 15,54; 17,59); 'auvium concentus,' to Virgil (*Georgics* 1,422); see the notes to CPW 1: 1037.

to two (notionally) female figures: Chloris/Flora (introduced, significantly, as 'Zephyritis,' i.e., '*wife* of Zephyr') and the nightingale, itself associated with romantic love. In later poems, this particular aspect is developed more fully.[43] What is already firmly suggested in the lines at hand is a propensity of poetic language to represent sense perceptions, as it were, in multi-sensory clusters. As a tentative interpretation, we may connect this to the fundamental unity of perceptual experience posited by both phenomenology and cognitive psychology.[44] In fact, this 'gregariousness of the senses' in both the 'Elegiac Verses' and the prose 'Theme on Early Rising' might be thought specific to the language of lyric poetry – but it is still equally present in both texts (or may even be more pronounced in the prose theme, as Evans argued).[45]

Such language may be said to be both *highly and complexly* multi-sensory: the first on account of the number of different senses involved; the second, on account of their (at times ambiguous) interrelation, expressed through shared representatives in the text, as in the reference to 'gentle airs' at *PL* 8.515, which may in context be read as 'melodies' or else as – either odorous or tactile – 'breezes'. In contrast to these kinds of multi-sensoriality, I reserve the term 'synaesthesia' proper for the explicit expression of one kind of sense perception in terms of another (as in Bottom's comical 'I see a voice' in *A Midsummer Night's Dream*) or the explicit cross-association of one sensory mode with another, more generally (as in Milton addressing the bishops, in *Lycidas*, as 'Blind mouths!').[46] Yet such distinctions are, to an extent, analytical. In many cases, as in those of the 'Elegiac Verses' and the 'Theme on Early Rising,' we might ask whether the cumulative effect of so many different – and, at times, ambiguously attributed – sense perceptions does not result in a kind of 'sequential' or, indeed, 'cumulative synaesthesia' in the mind of the reader, in much the same way as two musical notes sounding in close temporal proximity may establish a harmonic relationship in the perception of the listener.

The sensory language of Milton's early 'Elegiac Verses' and the 'Theme on Early Rising' can be characterised, then, as tendentially multi-sensory, rather conventional (as

---

[43] See Chapter 3 below. Milton's Sonnet 1 (1629), centred on the nightingale, refers to the 'amorous power' of its (or her) song, before concluding: 'Whether the Muse, or Love call thee his mate,/Both them I serve, and of their train am I' (8, 13–4).

[44] See, again, Marks, *Unity of the Senses*, with its frequent references to lyric poetry, and Starr, 'Multisensory Imagery.'

[45] Evans, *Miltonic Moment*, 133n4: in comparison with the 'Elegiac Verses,' 'the emphasis on the various senses is even more obvious [in the 'Theme on Early Rising'].'

[46] William Shakespeare, *A Midsummer Night's Dream*, 5.1; *Lycidas*, 119: Ruskin saw a sensory-etymological pun here and 'took this as the antithesis of "bishop" (one who sees) and "pastor" (one who feeds)' (Carey ad loc.). In cognitive science, 'synesthesia proper' has been used to refer to the involuntary and simultaneous perception of a stimulus presented to one sense 'as if by one or more other, additional senses' (e.g., a certain taste triggering the impression of dark green), whereas 'cognitive' or 'category synesthesia' refers to the invariable association of certain elements of perception (e.g., individual letter shapes) with a certain 'sensory addition,' e.g. a particular and consistent colour, regardless of the colour of the shape actually presented; Sean Day, 'Some Demographic and Socio-Cultural Aspects of Synesthesia,' in: Lynn C. Robertson/Noam Sagiv (eds), *Synesthesia: Perspectives from Cognitive Neuroscience* (New York: Oxford University Press, 2005), 11–33, at 12.

2.2 The Senses in Discourse: Perception – Communication – Language 69

indicated by heavy borrowing), and cross-generic: it cannot be drawn upon to distinguish, at this point, Milton's poetry from his prose. While the last point, again, points to the necessity of considering the senses in Milton across generic boundaries, the conventionality of Milton's sensory language raises the question of the extent to which his references to the sensory sphere should be considered, primarily, a personal stylistic feature. Despite its appeal to individual and embodied experience, reference to sense perception is just as likely to draw on any number of traditions in the arts, philosophy, the Bible, and other sources. Only in interplay with these may possible 'personal' aspects of sensory discourse be gauged. It would be misguided, I think, to downplay the significance of Milton's blindness, for example, or of his musical training; still, any interpretation drawing on these factors is not exempt from considering their context, such as contemporary attitudes towards blindness or ideas about music.

We have now gained a concept of sensory language in poetry (or prose) as a historically conditioned way of communicating sense experience, often in a multi-sensory and decidedly sensuous form. How would we account, though, for a passage such as the following, from book 5 of *Paradise Lost*? The scene is at the Gate of Heaven, the experiencing subject Raphael, the archangel, who has just been commissioned by the Father to instruct and admonish Adam and Eve:

> From hence no cloud, or, to obstruct his sight,
> Star interposed, however small he sees,
> Not unconformed to other shining globes,
> Earth, and the garden of God, with cedars crowned
> Above all hills. As when by night the glass
> Of Galileo, less assured, observes
> Imagined lands and regions in the moon:
> Or pilot, from amidst the Cyclades
> Delos or Samos first appearing, kens
> A cloudy spot.   (*PL* 5.257–266)

Clearly, the main reference is to vision, although the main point of the first four and a half lines arguably is not to convey an appreciative perception; it does not matter whether Raphael likes what he sees.[47] The point rather is to establish (or perhaps, given their mention in earlier parts of the poem, to underline) two things: the superior vision of angels, further enhanced here by an absence of clouds; and the small size of the earth when scaled against its cosmic background.[48] Both of these aspects of the passage may be historicised: the first by reference not only to angelological (and indeed demonological) debates over the visual powers of spirits, but also through reference to a more general association of angel and eye(-sight);[49] the second, by reference to contemporary

---

[47] The fragmented primal scene of the appreciative kind of looking is contained in the Creation account of *PL* 7: 'God saw that it was good' (309, and passim).

[48] Fowler notes ad loc. that 'from Raphael's startling viewpoint, earth is almost too *small* to be like *other shining globes* (stars).'

[49] On the first point, see Joad Raymond, *Milton's Angels: The Early-Modern Imagination* (Oxford: Oxford University Press, 2010), 291–299; Stuart Clark, *Vanities of the Eye: Vision in Early*

developments in astronomy – and it is this contextual link which motivates the first of two similes in the second half of the passage.[50] Aspiring, in a sense, to the angelic viewpoint (only with the axis of sight reversed), Galileo scrutinises the barren surface of the moon (Raphael had been looking, in particular, at the 'garden of God'). In the confrontation of God-given visual faculty and man-made optical technology, vision itself comes to the fore, but it clearly no longer is the 'feast[ing of the] eyes' we encountered in the 'Theme on Early Rising.'

While a lack of sensuousness need not speak against 'sensory language' as outlined above, there appears to be a further shift of focus if we contrast this passage with the texts discussed earlier: a shift from the awareness of perception to its preconditions and mechanisms; from the self-sufficiency, if not self-predication, of percepts (the smell of roses in the earlier verse arguably has no *direct* reference beyond itself)[51] to their functioning in a wider framework (that of the created world within the poem, that of theoretical knowledge or other preconceptions about the senses as well as contemporary developments in the contextual world surrounding it).[52] Such 'objective,' factual elements as the reference to Galileo may suggest multiple other domains of knowledge beyond their immediate reference (in this case, astronomy). Galileo was a celebrity of his time, and the most frequently mentioned early 'scientist' in English seventeenth-century literature.[53] Yet, his fame (for some, his infamy) rested as much on his conflict with the Roman Church as on his empirical observations, from which of course it could not easily be divorced. It seems unlikely that Milton, whose interest in Galileo and his findings may be gleaned from his frequent references to the astronomer, would have disregarded these contexts. Harinder Singh Marjara has argued that Milton actually presupposes in his readers a solid grasp of what Galileo had found out about the surface of the moon (that it was not perfect, as had been thought), the phases of Venus (which showed that even Venus borrowed its light from the sun), and other celestial phenomena.[54] Even

---

Modern European Culture (Oxford: Oxford University Press, 2009 [2007]), 135; and *PL* 1.59; on the second, *PL* 3.650 and the late-sixteenth-century view of Pierre de la Primaudaye, 'that Angels and the spirits of men, which are spirituall and invisible creatures, are illuminated by the meanes of understanding, with that spirituall and heavenly light whereof God hath made them partakers: as the bodies of living creatures, and chiefly of man are illuminated with the corporall light of the Sunne by meanes of the eyes' (quoted in Clark, *Vanities of the Eye*, 11).

[50] The second, that of the Cycladean pilot, is motivated – apart from its similar relation to human eyesight – by the subsequent description of Raphael in flight as 'sail[ing] between worlds and worlds' (268). I will return to this passage in Chapter 5.3 below.

[51] As an *indirect*, not necessarily intentional point of reference, I would consider any element of the wider cultural tradition regarding flowers, and roses in particular (the 'discourse on roses').

[52] In one statement of this idea, Paul Ricoeur has argued that 'poetic language presents a certain "fusion" between meaning or sense and the senses' and that this, in turn, 'tends to produce an object closed in on itself, in contrast to ordinary language and its thoroughly referential character': Paul Ricoeur, *The Rule of Metaphor: Multi-Disciplinary Studies of the Creation of Meaning in Language*, tr. Robert Czerny (London: Routledge & Kegan Paul, 1978 [1975]), 209.

[53] See Harinder S. Marjara, *Contemplation of Created Things: Science in 'Paradise Lost'* (Toronto: University of Toronto Press, 1992), 59.

[54] See Marjara, *Contemplation of Created Things*, 62; see also Thomas S. Kuhn, *The Copernican Revolution* (Cambridge, Mass.: Harvard University Press, 1976 [1957]), 219–226. I do not agree

apart from their perceived theological implications, these findings were not uncontested. It is thus a whole slice of early modern cultural history in the making that goes into Milton's reference to 'the glass/Of Galileo, less assured' than Raphael's faultless vision.

From this now apparent wider source area of sensory references emerges a need for terminological clarification: if 'sensory language' is equal to the 'flowery language' epitomised by poetry, with its odorous roses and highlighting of sense-percepts, of particular aisthetic qualities and their aesthetic evaluation, the language of 'sensory discourse' may be said to incorporate an additional, wider field of reference, which comprises theoretical concepts and specialist vocabulary referring to the various components of sense perception in a reflected and conscious manner. If Milton's 'Elegiac Verses' were written in the language of sensory discourse, so was Aristotle's *De Anima*. The language of sensory discourse, that is to say, may present as 'flowery language,' or 'botanical language,' or as both at the same time. If sensory ('flowery') language is concerned with the odour of the rose, sensory discourse adds the knowledge and idiom of plant physiology ('pistil,' 'caulome') and taxonomy (*Rosa x damascena*), as well as wider associations (with secrecy, or love, or with Mary, the 'Mystical Rose' of Catholic devotion), which may be expressed metaphorically.[55] As a concept of analysis, then, sensory discourse is the conceptual-linguistic corollary of sensory studies in the fullest sense.

2.3 Sensory Metaphor: Sweetness and Light?

I have referred to the 'language of sensory discourse,' which may seem tautological, and to its 'conceptual-linguistic' quality, which – considering, again, the primarily linguistic notion of 'discourse' established at the outset – may appear gratuitous. Some further considerations will serve to clarify this point. In particular, I would like to take up the notion of metaphor introduced at the end of the previous section. In its conventional associations, metaphor – the identifying expression of one thing in terms of another – is just as closely related to the notion of poetry as are the senses. This is apparent from early on in the tradition. 'It is a great thing, indeed, to make proper use of the poetic forms [*tōn eirêmenōn prepontōs khrêsthai*],' Aristotle remarks, '... But the greatest thing by far is to be a master of metaphor [*to metaphorikon einai*].'[56] The reason for this, according to Aristotle, is that a gift for metaphor indicates an intuitive perception of similarities, an ability that is to be considered 'a token of genius. For the right use of metaphor means an eye for resemblances [*to gar eu metapherein to to homoion theōrein estin*].'[57] Metaphor is not only a hallmark of poetic language; it argues a particular kind

---

with Kuhn's assessment that, in his references to Galileo, Milton was necessarily more focused on 'extrascientific issues' (194–5), if by that we mean Galileo's conflict with the Catholic Church.

[55] For instances of such wider associations of a rose, see the Epilogue below.

[56] *Poetics* 1459a.

[57] Ibid. This gift, Aristotle claims, unites the poet and the (natural) philosopher. Derivations of *theōrein/theōria* into English retained their connection to bodily vision into the early modern period. Thus, Sir Thomas Browne can write (in *Religio Medici*, §44), '... nor can I thinke I have the true Theory of death, when I contemplate a skull, or behold a Skeleton with those vulgar imaginations it casts upon us.' For the Neoplatonist Browne, the 'true Theory' lies *discretely*

of perspicacity, one that is connected to the *perception* – and the notion of *sense* perception is by all means implied – of patterns in the world. The secondary beneficiaries of this kind of genius are those to whom the metaphor is communicated: it is the distinguishing quality of metaphor, and, says Aristotle, the particular virtue of the *best* kinds of metaphor, that it 'sets things before the eyes [*pro ommatōn poiei*].'

That Aristotle's phrases are themselves 'just' sensory metaphors poses no objection, since, on one level, they simply perform that of which they speak; moreover, neuroscientific findings and cognitive metaphor theory (discussed at greater length below) raise serious doubts about whether such a thing – a 'mere sensory metaphor' without cognitive relation to sense perception – can even exist. For the present, then, metaphor may be regarded as a linguistic phenomenon bearing a particular affinity to sense perception. In his discussion of the Aristotelian theory of metaphor, Paul Ricoeur both generalises the Aristotelian notion of 'setting before the eyes' and argues for the centrality of the sensory sphere to metaphorical language:

> How does Aristotle connect this power of 'placing things before our eyes' to the feature of spiritedness, elegance, urbanity? By appealing to the characteristic of all metaphor, which is to point out or show, to 'make visible' [*faire voir*]. And this feature brings us to the heart of the problem of *lexis*, whose function, we said, is to 'make discourse appear to the senses' [*faire paraître le discours*]. 'To place things before the eyes,' then, is not an accessory function of metaphor, but the proper function of the figure of speech.[58]

Ricoeur's reference to 'discourse' finds a close equivalent in Aristotle's reference, quoted above, to *ta eirêmena*, 'poetic forms,' literally 'the things said.' As characterised by Ricoeur, the Aristotelian conception of poetic, metaphorical language is akin to Milton's notion of discourse as traced above, in that it is conceived in terms of an embodied speech; for Aristotle, its appeal to the senses is heightened even further by its evocative qualities, its 'setting things before the eyes.'

Milton, in his Ramist *Art of Logic* (*Artis logicae plenior institutio*, 1672), characterises metaphor as a 'contracted form of similarity … similarity reduced to a single word, where the signs [which indicate 'similar things'] are lacking but nevertheless understood.' Those signs of similarity are 'either nouns such as *resemblance, effigy, image, in the fashion of, after the manner of, like to, the way*; adverbs such as *such as, just as, as if, just as if*; or verbs such as *imitate, refer to*, etc. …'[59] There is a near continuity, then,

---

beyond what is actually seen; in Aristotle, the two, phenomena and forms, are fused. See also Williams, *Keywords*, 266–7.

[58] Ricoeur, *Rule of Metaphor*, 34. Czerny's interpolation, 'to the senses,' is justified by Ricoeur's notion of 'making discourse appear' as invariably taking 'a detour through the sensible' [*un détour sensible*] (143–148, quotation at 146). Returning to this thought in a later chapter, Ricoeur asks, 'Is not the presentation of one thought in terms of another always, in one way or another, to make visible, to show the first in the light of the more vivid appearance of the second? Going further, is it not the property of figure as such to convey visibility [*donner un apparaître*], to make discourse appear? [*faire paraître le discours*]' (193).

[59] CPW 8: 284.

2.3 Sensory Metaphor: Sweetness and Light?

between simile and metaphor: both are instances of similarity, operating at two different (perhaps even several varying) degrees of contraction. At bottom, however, *'nothing similar is identical ... every similarity limps'* – a metaphoric expression, perhaps, of the necessary impairment of all discourse.[60]

Aristotle, too, had also considered the relation between simile – as in Milton's statements about 'similar things' – and metaphor; but, going beyond a gradual association of the two concepts, he had argued that simile was actually subordinate to metaphor: 'similes [*eikones*] also ... are always in a manner approved metaphors; since they always consist of two terms [*ek duoin legontai*], like the proportional metaphor.'[61] Similes are *eikones* – 'images,' apt to be 'put before the eyes' –, and they are always predicated of two things; this allies them to the metaphor proper. Simile differs from metaphor 'only by the addition of a word [*prothesei*]' – namely, a particle of comparison or other indication of similarity –, '*dio hêtton hêdu, hoti makroterōs*': 'wherefore it [simile] is less pleasant [lit., 'sweet'] because it is longer.' The more contracted, the sweeter: thus runs Aristotle's explanation of the evocative – and sensory – appeal of metaphor.

However, metaphor is not only appealing. According to Aristotle, it serves a very important *purpose*, and therein lies another crucial point of contact between the Miltonic notion of discourse and the Aristotelian theory of metaphor: their common connection to knowledge. Starting from the idea that, while 'all words which make us learn something [*poiei hêmin mathêsin*] are most pleasant [*hêdista*, lit. 'most sweet'],' those which we do not know yet, or at least not *in this sense*, hold the most potential, Aristotle argues that 'metaphor ... above all produces this effect [sc. of learning]; for when Homer calls old age stubble, he teaches and informs us [*epoiêsen mathêsin kai gnōsin*] through the genus [i.e., through similarity]; for both [sc. old age and stubble] have lost their bloom.'[62] Metaphor, then, delights *and* teaches, and it does so in ways that are expressed in sensory terms: it 'sets things before the eyes,' thus bringing them to our attention; and it is 'sweetest' when it is contracted and novel. Although there is an initial association of sight and taste with those two distinct aspects, visibility and sweetness ultimately combine in the pleasant teaching function of metaphor, its doubly 'sensible,' epistemogenic potential.

In Milton's metaphorical *practice* – within which, considering the contiguity just outlined, we may include 'metaphors proper' ('Blind mouths!') as well as epic and other similes ('As when by night the glass/Of Galileo ...') –, a strong affinity to the sensory sphere is evident. This comes to the fore, in particular, in the 'extended-substitution imagery' of Milton's early tracts, and the degree of detail these images transport bears comparison with the epic similes of the late poems.[63] Thus, in Milton's

---

[60] CPW 8: 285.
[61] *Rhetoric* 1412b. Strictly speaking, it is only one kind of simile (the lexical kind) that is associated with metaphor; the other – what Aristotle calls *parabolê* – belongs to the domain of 'proof'; see Ricoeur, *Rule of Metaphor*, 25.
[62] *Rhetoric* 1410b.
[63] For the concept of 'extended-substitution imagery,' see Corns, *Development of Milton's Prose Style*, 46–7.

earliest tract, *Of Reformation* (1641), the episcopal system of church governance is compared to a cooking pot of unspecified content, and to drastic effect:

> And it is still *Episcopacie* that before all our eyes worsens and sluggs the most learned, and seeming religious of our *Ministers*, who no sooner advanc't to it, but like a seething pot set to coole, sensibly exhale and reake out the greatest part of that zeale, and those Gifts which were formerly in them, settling in a skinny congealment of ease and sloth at the top: and if they keep their Learning by some potent sway of Nature, 'tis a rare chance; but their *devotion* most commonly comes to that queazy temper of luke-warmnesse, that gives a Vomit to God himselfe[64]

Taken from the hot stove of religious fervour, the soup or stew of faith not only cools but, in doing so, 'sensibly exhale[s] and reake[s] out' most of its zeal. That this is meant as an olfactory image is clear from Milton's reference to the 'sensibl[e]' quality of the process.[65] The resulting, unpalatable conglomerate of tepid devotion is not only revolting to the sight and/or touch ('skinny congealment' – like skin, but not human, hence uncanny and repulsive), but is also, through its 'queazy temper of luke-warmnesse' disgusting in a more literal, gustatory sense. The drastic final effect of this transformation is beyond most traditional piety.[66]

If this simile is 'vivid, sensuous, and naturalistic,' it is clearly a long way from the 'flowery language' with which this survey of the sensory mode in literature started, and hardly conforms to the Aristotelian postulate that a metaphor should be pleasing.[67] It does attest, however, both to the immediate, visceral appeal of sensory language and to the epistemic impact of metaphor.[68] Depending on perspective, this latter may be taken as an Aristotelian imparting of *mathêsis* (making the reader *perceive* that episcopacy is indeed disgusting, thus having them *know* that it is bad); as a quasi-argumentative conveying of embodied knowledge (making the reader *feel* that episcopacy is indeed disgusting and hence bad); or as a (pseudo- or para-argumentative) strategy of sensory diversion: making the reader feel disgusted, tricking them into accepting the proposition that episcopacy is bad.[69]

---

[64] CPW 1: 536–7.
[65] See also *OED*, 'reek, v.1,' esp. senses 4b and 7a ('chiefly ... of a powerful, unpleasant smell,' 'to stink'). Given the context, 'exhale' (*OED*, v.1) may be said to bear similar connotations through its etymological association with (bad) breath and wider implications of unwholesome vapours (on whose thematic relevance in *Paradise Lost* see Marjara, *Contemplation of Created Things*, 178–88).
[66] Even though the source of the image is, of course, biblical: 'I know thy works, that thou art neither cold nor hot: I would thou wert cold or hot. So then because thou art lukewarm, and neither cold nor hot, I will spue thee out of my mouth' (Rev. 3:15–16).
[67] Corns, *Development of Milton's Style*, 53, obviously adopting a broad meaning of 'sensuous.' Corns also points to the detailed, point-by-point quality of the simile; for instance, the most ambitious clerics are implied to 'settle at the top' of the ecclesiastical hierarchy.
[68] Cable, *Carnal Rhetoric*, 3.
[69] Cable, *Carnal Rhetoric*, 64, argues that 'Milton's images lure us into an aesthetic experience that purports to embody moral truth.' See also Cable, *Carnal Rhetoric*, 72. For the view of

2.3 Sensory Metaphor: Sweetness and Light? 75

Excursus: Seventeenth-Century Attacks on Metaphor

While the poetic nature of metaphor remained commonly accepted over time, its claim to epistemic value – as laid out by Aristotle – was not quite as secure. In the early modern period, in particular, there was an intense debate over the uses and abuses of metaphoric speech. This arguably resulted from the combination of two circumstances: on the one hand, there was a strong prevalence of metaphor in the language of many different fields, and this 'language was crucial to ontology, epistemology, and metaphysics'; at the same time, there was a distinct awareness, inherited from the classical rhetorical tradition, that 'metaphor was, technically, an "abuse" of language.'[70] If we combine this with a setting in which 'all speech, poetry included, was assumed to be probatory or disprobatory unless there were positive indications to the contrary,' the relationship between what is (literally) said and what is (metaphorically) meant necessarily becomes a problem.[71] Around the middle of the seventeenth century, then, there were 'strong and profoundly-held reorientations of the distinction [between the literal and figurative use of language], mostly as a result of the conjoined and inseparable revolutions in intellectual history constituted by philosophical rationalism and scientific empiricism.'[72]

Thomas Hobbes, for one, took issue with the often emotional appeal of metaphor; 'reasoning upon [metaphors],' he writes in *Leviathan*, 'is wandering amongst innumerable absurdities; and their end, contention and sedition or contempt.'[73] As Hobbes's phrasing already indicates, however, getting rid of metaphor was not as easy as one might think: his 'wandering' bears an obvious metaphorical relation to the notion of faulty discourse as an 'erring' or 'wandering' as found in *Paradise Lost*. Positions similar to that of Hobbes were held by many of his contemporaries, from proto-scientists like Robert Boyle to philosophers such as John Locke.[74] Many shared Hobbes's con-

---

sensory metaphor in Milton as obfuscatory and downright anti-argumentative, see Fish, 'Reasons That Imply Themselves.'

[70] Earl Miner, 'Preface,' in: Idem (ed.), *Seventeenth-Century Imagery: Essays on Uses of Figurative Language from Donne to Farquhar* (Berkeley, Calif.: University of California Press, 1971), v–xiv, at ix–x.

[71] Ong in his introduction to the *Art of Logic* (CPW 8: 160). Ong points to Milton's notion of 'justify[ing] the ways of God,' and to the 'arguments' prefixed to the individual books of *Paradise Lost* (1674). Milton, he says, saw 'proof' and 'refutation' even in passages we would judge non-polemical or even non-argumentative.

[72] John R. R. Christie, 'Introduction: Rhetoric and Writing in Early Modern Philosophy and Science,' in: Andrew E. Benjamin et al. (eds), *The Figural and the Literal: Problems of Language in the History of Science and Philosophy, 1630–1800* (Manchester: Manchester University Press, 1987), 1–9, at 2.

[73] From pt. 1, ch. 5 ('Of Reason, and Science') of *Leviathan* (Oxford: Clarendon, 1958], 37–38.

[74] On Boyle (who, too, had to realise that he could not dispense with persuasive language altogether), see Jan V. Golinski, 'Robert Boyle: Scepticism and Authority in Seventeenth-Century Chemical Discourse,' in: *The Figural and the Literal*, Benjamin et al. (eds), 58–82, esp. 63–69. Locke's positioning against figurative language in all areas 'where truth and knowledge are concerned' is at the conclusion of Chapter 10 ('Of the Abuse of Words') in Book III of his *Essay Concerning Human Understanding*, ed. Peter H. Nidditch (Oxford: Clarendon, 1979 [1975]), 508.

cerns about the deep rootedness of figurative turns of phrase in the language, though not all struggled as greatly with this as the theologian Samuel Parker, who contended, in an attack on the philosophy and theology of the 'Cambridge Platonists,' that

> all those Theories in Philosophy which are expressed only in metaphorical Termes, are not real Truths, but the meer products of Imagination, dress'd up (like Childrens babies) in a few spangled empty words. ... Thus their wanton and luxuriant fancies climbing up into the Bed of Reason, do not only defile it by unchaste and illegitimate Embraces, but instead of real conceptions and notices of Things, impregnate the mind with nothing but Ayerie and Subventaneous Phantasmes.[75]

It seems unnecessary to point out that here that Parker's attack on metaphors in philosophy is couched in simile, wordplay (his punning on 'conceptions' and 'impregnate'), and elaborate, extended metaphor. This may be considered as typical of a time in which metaphorical discourse reigned supreme, despite all protestations to the contrary; perhaps it is precisely the intensity of the reaction against metaphor which indicates its deep rootedness and lasting currency even in ostensibly 'sober' discourse. As in Robert Hooke's near lyrical description of the 'beauty' of the flea under his microscope – 'all over adorn'd with a curiously polish'd suit of *sable* Armour' – the difference between early modern and present-day classifications of discursive propriety is striking (Fig. 3).[76]

Parker was an early Fellow of the Royal Society (as, of course, was Hooke). It is fitting that what is probably the best-known contribution to the mid-seventeenth-century debate over metaphor is Thomas Sprat's championing of a language of 'primitive purity and shortness' in his 1667 *History of the Royal-Society*. Considering that Sprat was commissioned to write his tract in 1663, barely three years after the Society had been founded, this must be considered a manifesto of its self-perception and projects rather than a retrospective account of its achievements up to that point. In ringing cadences which rather underline just how much work, apparently, still remained yet to be done, Sprat chastises the 'luxury and redundance of *speech*' as well as the 'ill effects of this superfluity of talking [which] have already overwhelm'd most other *Arts* and *Professions*,' and expresses his yearning for a golden age when 'the Ornaments of speaking'

---

[75] Samuel Parker, *A Free and Impartial Censure of the Platonick Philosophie* ... (Oxford: W. Hall for Richard Davis, 1666), 73–7, quotation at 75–6.
[76] Robert Hooke, *Micrographia* ... (London: J. Martyn and J. Allestry, 1665), n. p. ('Observ. LIII. *Of a* Flea.').

2.3 Sensory Metaphor: Sweetness and Light?

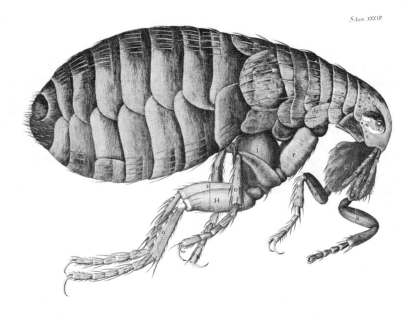

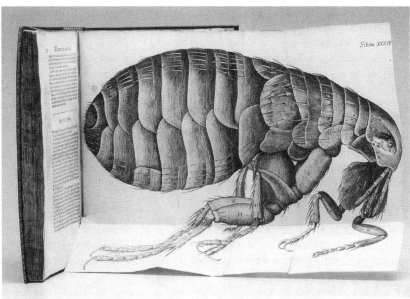

Fig. 3a and 3b: Robert Hooke, *Micrographia* (1665): 'Schem[a] XXXIV': a flea (engraving and fold-out showcasing the magnifying power of Hooke's microscope). Source: National Library of Australia.

were not only in complete accordance with what was proper to the occasion and with common morality, but also contributed to the generation of knowledge about the external world – knowledge which was ultimately derived from the senses:

> They [viz., the 'Ornaments of speaking'] were at first, no doubt, an admirable Instrument in the hands of *Wise Men:* when they were onely employ'd to describe *Goodneß, Honesty, Obedience*; in larger, fairer, and more moving Images: to represent *Truth*, cloth'd with Bodies; and to bring *Knowledge* back again to our very senses, from whence it was at first deriv'd to our understandings. But now they are generally changed to worse uses: They make the *Fancy* disgust the best things, if they come sound, and unadorn'd: they are in open defiance against *Reason*; professing, not to hold much correspondence with that; but with its Slaves, *the Passions:* they give the mind a motion too changeable, and bewitching, to consist with *right practice*. Who can behold, without indignation, how many mists and uncertainties, these specious *Tropes* and *Figures* have brought on our Knowledg? How many rewards, which are due to more profitable, and difficult *Arts*, have been still snatch'd away by the easie vanity of *fine speaking*?[77]

The primal epistemic order that Sprat pines for quite possibly never existed, not even at a time 'when men deliver'd so many *things*, almost in equal number of *words*.' Nevertheless, Sprat's diatribe serves to identify the leading bogeyman of the more radically scientific element within the Royal Society – namely, the poet, with his 'volubility of *Tongue*, which makes so great a noise in the World' – and highlights the regulatory ideal of (scientific) knowledge which its members pledged to pursue instead. Far from preserving or even heightening sensory experience through language (as might be commonly expected of poetry), the injudicious activities of writers throughout the centuries had brought about a progressive clouding and dulling of the senses through language. To counteract this history of dilapidation, Sprat claims, the Royal Society had

> exacted from all their members, a close, naked, natural way of speaking; positive expressions, clear senses; a native easiness: bringing all things as near the Mathematical plainness, as they can: and preferring the language of Artizans, Countrymen, and Merchants, before that, of Wits, or Scholars[78]

Ironically, Sprat's ideal is most neatly expressed, in the above passage, in one of the ambiguities he so deplores: 'clear senses' in language will bring about 'clear senses' in the empirical exploration of the world, which will then feed back into a further clarification of language, and so on, *ad infinitum*.

What emerges from these examples is the view of an era in which – over and above the content-related coalescence of discourses already sketched – there was a marked reliance, on all sides, on metaphorical forms of expression. These had been associated,

---

[77] Thomas Sprat, *The History of the Royal-Society of London, For the Improving of Natural Knowledge* (London: Printed by T. R. for J. Martyn, 1667), 111–2.
[78] Sprat, *History of the Royal-Society*, 112–3.

2.4 Conceptual Metaphor: Discourse and Context

traditionally, with both the senses *and* knowledge; now, however, their (ostensible) detractors – professing to re-evaluate the traditional relationship between metaphorical language and the process of sense perception – denied the claim of metaphor to epistemic value. Or rather, the terms of the contemporary debate *suggest* a profound revaluation (and progressive separation) of such literal/figurative dichotomies as truth/poetry, science/rhetoric, or philosophy/literature. The impression they ultimately leave, however, is that of a metaphorical-discursive continuum spanning domains of knowledge and enquiry which have since separated.

In addressing sensory discourse, then, and thus exploring a domain that is so deeply invested not only in various disciplinary discourses but also in the meta-discourse of metaphor, it seems advisable to heed the suggestion of John Christie, who has written on the paradoxical relationship between literal and non-literal uses of language in early modern discourse, that,

> rather than live uncomfortably within the logic of a paradox which simultaneously insists on the literal/figural distinction, inscribes the essential nature of science and philosophy around the pole of the literal, yet acknowledges the figural in pursuit of the literal, it is sensible instead to entertain the notion that the literal and figural are part of a common linguistic field, and demand a simultaneous investigation[79]

The preceding examination of metaphor has yielded further evidence of the essential interconnectedness of early modern discourses observed earlier. Sensory discourse, as I conceive of it, is transverse to disciplinary or other individual discourses, both in terms of its lexis and its metaphorical means. It is not, however, defined by these two aspects. What remains to be demonstrated is how the lexical and wider linguistic side of sensory discourse – the sensory idiom discussed thus far – may be said to connect to its conceptual substratum. The key to this conceptual dimension of sensory discourse lies in a modified understanding of metaphor.

2.4 Conceptual Metaphor: Discourse and Context

What I have discussed so far under the name of 'metaphor' would, in current linguistic parlance, actually be called 'metaphorical linguistic expressions.'[80] The shift that stands behind this further specification of the term is connected, above all, with the rise of cognitive linguistics and the notion of 'conceptual metaphor.'[81] According to the conventional notion of metaphor, exemplified by the tradition deriving from Aristotle, metaphor is (1) a linguistic phenomenon that is (2) typical of rhetorical and artistic language use, is (3) based on the resemblance of two entities that are compared and identi-

---

[79] Christie, 'Introduction: Rhetoric and Writing,' 4.
[80] See Zoltán Kövecses, *Metaphor: A Practical Introduction* (Oxford: Oxford University Press, ²2010), 4.
[81] This was pioneered by George Lakoff/Mark Johnson, *Metaphors We Live By* (Chicago: University of Chicago Press, 1980).

fied (such as 'when Homer calls old age stubble'), (4) requires particular skill, and (5) is a kind of 'special effect,' nice to have but not essential to any 'regular' use of language.

The new, cognitive-linguistic view of metaphor, by contrast, contends that (1) metaphor is a property of concepts, not of words; (2) its purpose is not merely aesthetic but also, in a sense, epistemic: it is geared towards a better understanding of abstract concepts; (3) it is often *not* based on similarity at all but on correlation; (4) it is used by everybody, all the time, and in everyday life because it is (5) an inevitable process of human thought and reasoning.[82] Relevant related insights concern the embodied, experiential basis of conceptual metaphors and the idea that there is no such thing as a 'dead metaphor': those metaphors that have become inconspicuous in everyday use may exert a particularly strong influence upon the patterning of thought.[83]

The central idea behind this new view, then, is that metaphors in the conventional, older sense are manifestations, in language, of more fundamental *conceptual* metaphors, linking not just words but distinct conceptual domains, which may then be understood in terms of one another. Typically, this means that a more abstract notion from one conceptual domain (the *target*) is expressed, and hence elucidated, in terms of a more concrete notion from a different conceptual domain (the *source*). Additionally, again, in many cases, 'more concrete' may be taken to mean *more readily apparent to the senses*: 'what they [i.e., the basic meanings underlying metaphor] evoke is easier to imagine, see, hear, feel, smell, and taste.'[84] Consequently, the human body is one of the most common source domains, and this is then apparent in the linguistic expression of such metaphors: we refer to 'the *heart* of the problem' or 'the *head* of the department.'[85] On the other side of the metaphorical transfer, mental states and processes (emotions, desires, or thought) are often the target domain, as in 'She is *hungry* for knowledge' or 'I *see* your point.'[86]

Thus, the conceptual metaphor LIFE IS A JOURNEY expresses a more abstract, general notion, which most living people have only experienced in part so far (namely 'life,' the target) in terms of another, which most people have experienced at least once in its entirety, from beginning to end (namely 'a journey,' the source).[87] The notion of 'journey,' part of our lived experience, thus helps us 'come to grips with' the more abstract notion of 'life.'[88] The conceptual metaphor may comprise special cases (LIFE IS A SEA

---

[82] Synopsis adapted from Kövecses, *Metaphor*, ix–x. Kövecses appears to miss the fact that the epistemic value of metaphor has in fact been an (albeit often neglected) aspect of the traditional view, from Aristotle to Ricoeur.

[83] On the importance of the 'experiential basis' and embodiment in conceptual metaphor, see Lakoff/Johnson, *Metaphors We Live By*, 19, Kövecses, *Metaphor*, and the discussion in Kövecses, *Where Metaphors Come From*; on the question of supposedly 'dead' metaphors, see Kövecses, *Metaphor*, xi. Ricoeur, *The Rule of Metaphor*, disagrees on the second point (its original title, pointedly, is *La Métaphore vive*): a 'dead metaphor' has lost the event character Ricoeur deems necessary for the metaphoric communication of meaning.

[84] Kövecses, *Metaphor*, 5.

[85] See Kövecses, *Metaphor*, 18–23, quotations at 18.

[86] See Kövecses, *Metaphor*, 23–8, quotations at 23–4.

[87] I adopt the standard practice of formatting conceptual metaphors in SMALL CAPS.

[88] 'Come to grips with,' incidentally, is an instance of the conceptual metonymy (i.e., both elements are taken from the same conceptual domain) CONTROL IS A TOUCH OF THE HAND, which

JOURNEY, LIFE IS A PILGRIMAGE) or be related to other, similar conceptual metaphors (LOVE IS A JOURNEY, EDUCATION IS A JOURNEY). What they all share is that they find their primary (though not their only) expression in language:[89] thus, we talk about 'getting a head start in life' or 'being at a crossroads in one's life.'

In its most abstract forms, the explanatory source of conceptual metaphor may be something like categories of spatial orientation (MORE IS UP, HAPPY IS UP, CONSCIOUS IS UP). Even such rather abstract cases have been shown to relate to primary (bodily) experience (seeing a material being piled up; bodily postures indicating happiness as opposed to those indicating sadness; standing up waking as opposed to lying down sleeping, etc.). These experiential bases, George Lakoff and Mark Johnson have argued, should, in theory, be accessible to analysis; in fact, they say, 'no metaphor can ever be comprehended or even adequately represented independently of its experiential basis: ... MORE IS UP has a very different kind of experiential basis than HAPPY IS UP or RATIONAL IS UP.'[90] As in the case of less abstract conceptual metaphors, such orientational metaphors need not be expressed in language, as is evident from the conventional (yet ultimately arbitrary) placement of items in a ranked order, top to bottom, or the positioning of athletes at a victory ceremony; in both cases, MORE IS UP or BETTER IS UP is implied.

As may be expected, considering the evident rootedness of conceptual metaphor in bodily experience, many of the examples cited in the literature are connected explicitly to the senses: among the conceptual metaphors and metonymies that have been discussed are such examples as THINKING IS LOOKING, KNOWING IS SEEING; EYES ARE LIMBS, SEEING IS TOUCHING; UNDERSTANDING IS TOUCHING; LUST IS HUNGER, IDEAS ARE FOOD, UNDERSTANDING IS DIGESTING.[91] From this arbitrary selection, three aspects stand out: an obvious preoccupation with epistemic matters; the role played in this by the body/senses; the respective systematic coherence of several metaphors at a time (thus, if thinking is looking, i.e. directing the view, knowing, its result, is seeing, i.e., perceiving something by fixing the previously directed view on something.)[92]

Linguistic metaphor, therefore, forms part of the poetic and other languages referred to above, whereas conceptual metaphor represents the more fundamental stratum of the notions expressed *through* language. While the relationship between conceptual metaphor, (linguistic) 'everyday metaphor,' and (linguistic) poetic or literary metaphor is still being debated, it seems clear that neither creativity nor conventionality in linguistic use can be summarily assigned to one or the other side. In many cases, literary use of metaphor, while often employing its material in new and unusual ways – through an

---

also gives rise to 'being under someone's thumb' and 'gaining the upper hand,' among many others (see Kövecses, *Metaphor*, 171–91, on the relationship between conceptual metaphors and metonymies, and 243–5, discussing THE HAND STANDS FOR CONTROL as one of several conceptual metaphors and metonymies expressed in idioms relating to the hand).

[89] In the two instances mentioned last, consider such concepts or customs as the honeymoon journey, the 'grand tour,' or (considering life more generally) various *rites de passage*, which are all expressive of underlying conceptual metaphors in performative, non-linguistic ways.
[90] Lakoff/Johnson, *Metaphors We Live By*, 19.
[91] Examples taken from Lakoff/Johnson, *Metaphors We Live By*, and Kövecses, *Metaphor*.
[92] On this systematic quality of conceptual metaphors see Lakoff/Johnson, *Metaphors We Live By*, 9.

extension, elaboration, questioning, or combining of existing metaphors –, depends on the conceptual stock common to the language at large, and indeed makes 'heavy use of conventional, everyday metaphors,' on which its creativity to some extent rests.[93] At the same time, everyday (or in any case non-literary) language may employ just the same means to various ends. In the end, there appears to exist a continuum between the two poles of conventionality and creativity, with diverse uses across genres and fields of application positioning themselves along that spectrum.

Three brief examples will serve to illustrate the interplay of conceptual metaphor and sensory language in *Paradise Lost*. After various references to 'the monarchy of God' (verbatim at *PL* 1.42) have established the conceptual metaphor GOD IS A KING, the following passage from the beginning of book 3 takes up that metaphor and combines it with others:

> Now had the Almighty Father from above,
> From the pure empyrean where he sits
> High throned above all heighth, bent down his eye
> His own works and their works at once to view: (3.56–59)

The two conceptual metaphors GOD IS A KING and GOD IS UP are present in the choice of '*High throned*,' while the association of God's vision with his power ('*Almighty* Father ... bent down his *eye* ... to *view*') is conventional in the Hebrew Bible.[94] In fact, *derived* meanings of the eyes or seeing (for instance as references to providence or authority) account for the majority of verses containing references to sight, 'the central sense in biblical perception.' Although the somatic element is often highlighted, even in the figurative cases, literal references to actual acts of perception are, by comparison, less common.[95] This speaks to the strong associative potential of sense perception in biblical language. Since it implies that VISION IS UP, this passage also conforms to the conventional sensory hierarchy dominated by vision; other concrete elaborations and reworkings of this conceptual metaphor in Milton's writing will be discussed below.

Other passages show how Milton might question established conceptual metaphors to reconsider the terms connected to them. Again, knowledge plays a central role here. During Adam's extended colloquy with Raphael which, including the subsidiary narratives embedded within it, spans the better part of books 5 to 8 of *Paradise Lost*, there occurs a moment, early in book 7, when Adam's curiosity and thirst for knowledge – a persistent theme throughout the conversation – once again come to the fore. Raphael's mission, of course, is to admonish Adam and Eve, and to repeat the interdiction not to eat of the forbidden tree of knowledge. This he has already done, after finishing his account of the war in heaven, at the end of book 6. Now, however, Adam repeats his earlier request for instruction, this time with regard to Creation: 'How first began this

---

[93] Kövecses, *Metaphor*, 49–62, quotation at 52. As examples of such reworking: LIFE IS A JOURNEY, yet '"Life," says the dervish, "is a journey, and a short one."/How true! The furthest we ever get/Is five or six feet above the earth,/And the same distance underneath it!' (Kleist, *The Prince of Homburg*, 4.3.1–3); LIFE IS A STORY, but it is 'a tale/Told by an idiot' (*Macbeth*, 5.5.26–7).
[94] On GOD IS UP, see Kövecses, *Metaphor*, 64–5.
[95] See Avrahami, *Senses of Scripture*, 108, 116, quotation at 116.

2.4 Conceptual Metaphor: Discourse and Context

Heaven which we behold/Distant so high, with moving fires adorned/Innumerable …?' (7.86–8). Raphael's answer, while not an outright refusal, urges caution with regard to an undue appetite for knowledge:

> This also thy request, with caution asked,
> Obtain; though to recount almighty works
> What words or tongue of Seraph can suffice,
> Or heart of man suffice to comprehend?
> Yet what thou canst attain, which best may serve
> To glorify the Maker, and infer
> Thee also happier, shall not be withheld
> Thy hearing; such commission from above
> I have received, to answer thy desire
> Of knowledge within bounds; beyond, abstain
> To ask; …
> …
> Enough is left besides to search and know.
> But knowledge is as food, and needs no less
> Her temperance over appetite, to know
> In measure what the mind may well contain;
> Oppresses else with surfeit, and soon turns
> Wisdom to folly, as nourishment to wind. (7.111–30)

The extended comparison in the second half of this passage connects to two aspects of its wider conceptual context. First, it takes up the earlier passage in book 5, already referred to above, in which Milton comments on the 'keen dispatch/Of real hunger' with which the archangel consumes (and 'transubstantiate[s]') the evening meal prepared by Eve. That eating, in this and other similar instances, should be associated with tasting, is made clear by reference to Eve's preparation: 'from *sweet* kernels pressed/She tempers *dulcet* creams' (5.346–7, emphases added), as well as by Raphael's assurance that 'to taste/Think not I shall be nice,' which follows a reference to the 'mellifluous dews' and 'pearly grain' (i.e., manna) of Heaven (5.432–8).

At the same time as referencing his own earlier enjoyment of (and comments about) the act of eating, alongside its subsequent elaboration, Raphael's assertion that 'knowledge is as food' (although technically speaking a simile) realises the conceptual metaphor IDEAS ARE FOOD. As Zoltán Kövecses has suggested, a detailed set of correspondences may be traced to explain the perceived functional similarity between food and ideas, and the structural similarities between the respective activities associated with a number of corresponding stages. These include the acts of (1) cooking/thinking, (2) chewing/considering, (3) swallowing/accepting, (4) digesting/understanding, and (5) nourishment/mental well-being. Each of these may, in turn, give rise to individual linguistic metaphors (e.g., 'Let me stew over this,' 'a half-baked theory,' 'I can't stomach that idea,' etc.).[96] As already indicated, then, IDEAS ARE FOOD forms part of a constella-

---

[96] Kövecses, *Metaphor*, 83–4; see also 6–7 and Lakoff/Johnson, *Metaphors We Live By*, 46–7.

tion of metaphors that also includes LUST IS HUNGER [97] and UNDERSTANDING IS DIGESTING. However, Milton does not simply endorse the metaphor – from Raphael's earlier remarks we know already that the slow ascent toward knowledge may indeed be compared to a process of *digestion* and refinement –; he modifies it to indicate that an intemperate hunger for knowledge may lead not to 'wisdom' but, as the result of epistemic *indigestion,* to 'folly.' That this is the exact opposite of the process of refinement delineated earlier is made clear through the coarse image of flatulence. Knowledge and wisdom may *taste* the same (i.e., first judgment may mistake them), but their proof is in their digestion (the understanding of them), and their right consumption requires a prior grasp of temperance.

In its crass focus on an irregularity of food consumption and digestion, Raphael's image is reminiscent of the 'pot simile' from *Of Reformation,* discussed above.[98] There, episcopacy had 'give[n] a Vomit to God himselfe'; here, an intemperate hunger for knowledge turns 'nourishment to wind.' In both cases, it is a misuse of the God-given means to wisdom (derived from revelation) that is construed as causing a disruption to the cognitive-digestive process. By virtue of conceptual metaphor theory, we can discern the same metaphor, IDEAS ARE FOOD, as operative in both images: the idea of episcopacy and that of human epistemic presumption are both presented as repulsive. The imagery used, if it does not aim at a visceral reaction on the part of the reader, in any case does call attention to the bodily processes of ingestion and (in)digestion as well as to their deeper (i.e., their conceptual-metaphorical) significance in the given context.

Finally, if we recall to mind some other linguistic metaphors addressed earlier in this chapter, it becomes clear that they, too, actually form expressions of underlying conceptual metaphors. Thus, Milton's depiction of the fallen angels debating, 'in wandering mazes lost,' and Hobbes's metaphorical critique of metaphors ('reasoning upon them is wandering amongst innumerable absurdities') both express the conceptual metaphor UNDERSTANDING IS REACHING A GOAL, where the abstract notion of 'understanding' is expressed in terms of a bodily movement through space, and the implied goal is knowledge.[99] Whereas some instances of comparable metaphors may be traced to the equivocal quality of the word 'erring' (i.e., may be characterised as working on a primarily linguistic level), Milton's reference to 'wandering mazes' (as well as his subse-

---

[97] It should be kept in mind that 'the range of early modern passions embraced some that we would not now recognise as passions at all, the *desire for knowledge* being a significant example' (Adrian Johns, *The Nature of the Book: Print and Knowledge in the Making* [Chicago: University of Chicago Press, 1998], 398, emphasis added). At 3.694–8, the archangel Uriel, not recognising Satan in the disguise of a particularly inquisitive young cherub, addresses him: 'Fair angel, thy desire, which tends to know/The works of God, thereby to glorify/The great Work-master, leads to no excess/That reaches blame, but rather merits praise/The more it seems excess …'

[98] On the gradual development of attitudes which makes possible Milton's rhetorical strategy in both passages, see Norbert Elias, *The Civilizing Process: Sociogenetic and Psychogenetic Investigations,* tr. Edmund Jephcott (Oxford: Blackwell, 2000 [1939]), esp. 109–120 ('Changes in Attitudes towards the Natural Functions').

[99] With reference to this and other passages from Milton, we might add UNDERSTANDING IS UP and UNDERSTANDING IS FORWARD, while the fallen angels, paradoxically, remain seated *and* are wandering in mazes, i.e. not even *moving towards* a goal.

quent dramatisation of that image) and Hobbes's reference to 'wandering amongst ... absurdities' are informed wholly by the non-conformity of the action described to the underlying conceptual metaphor UNDERSTANDING IS REACHING A GOAL.[100]

The metaphorical use of sensory language, these examples suggest, will often be reducible to underlying conceptual metaphor. This is due in part to the somatic origin of much conceptual metaphor. In subsequent chapters, further examples of underlying conceptual metaphors connecting individual linguistic metaphorical expressions across Milton's writing life will be discussed. Having now considered the properties of sensory language and the role of metaphor in sensory discourse, it is time to consider another notion of 'discourse' as shaped, also, by its context.

2.5 Metaphor in Context – Metaphor in Discourse

Thus far, we have established a notion of 'sensory discourse' as more than just 'flowery language' (because it also draws on the 'technical' aspects of sense perception), and yet different from any clear-cut 'sensory idiom' (because it cannot be pinpointed to any one area of reference). The foregoing consideration of metaphor has shown how we may account for a focus on knowledge in sensory discourse and, at the same time, reconnect aspects of sensory language that were shared in seventeenth-century poetic, protoscientific, and other discourses which have since separated. Conceptual metaphor theory, in particular, has substantiated the connection between sense perception and language established at the outset of this chapter. There is, however, another aspect of conceptual metaphor theory which has a bearing on how the verbalised sensorium may be addressed: namely, its potential to account for *contextual influences* on discourse. While this facet of conceptual metaphors has only recently come into focus, versions of it were arguably part of conceptual-metaphorical reflection from the outset. Thus, in their discussion of embodied or 'direct physical' experience, Lakoff and Johnson already point out that

> what we call 'direct physical experience' is never merely a matter of having a body of a certain sort; rather, *every* experience takes place within a vast background of cultural presuppositions. It can be misleading, therefore, to speak of direct physical experience as though there were some core of immediate experience which we then 'interpret' in terms of our conceptual system. Cultural as-

---

[100] This becomes even clearer if we consider that the verbal sign 'wandering,' in other contexts, may primarily suit the needs of such conceptual metaphors as LIFE IS A JOURNEY or LIFE IS A PILGRIMAGE. Thus, at the very end of *Paradise Lost*, Adam and Eve are released into history in precisely those terms: 'They, hand in hand, with *wandering* steps and slow,/Through Eden took their solitary way' (12.648–9, emphasis added). In fact, there may be more than a suggestion here of 'wandering' as 'erring' as well, as in 'travelling ... along in an uncertain, or frequently changing direction' (*OED*, 2a). See also Moshe Barasch, *Blindness: The History of a Mental Image in Western Thought* (London: Routledge, 2001), 111–3 on the mediaeval and early modern notion of life as a pilgrimage of uncertain course (discussing Brueghel's *The Blind Leading the Blind* of 1568, in which the depiction of the blind men, Barasch argues, conforms to similar depictions of pilgrims).

> sumptions, values, and attitudes are not a conceptual overlay which we may or may not place upon experience as we choose. It would be more correct to say that all experience is cultural through and through, that we experience our 'world' in such a way that our culture is already present in the very experience itself.[101]

At first glance, this appears to be a linguistic version of David Howes's cultural-anthropological observation that 'the human sensorium ... never exists in a natural state.' What is different in the conceptual-metaphorical approach to the issue, however, is that the different ways in which bodily experience may give rise to a transfer of meaning are also accounted for. It all depends, Lakoff and Johnson continue, upon 'the distinction between an experience and the way we conceptualize it' (which corresponds, roughly, to the distinction between sensation and perception).[102] There is, then, no (1) perception without (2) conceptual framing – which in turn is the precondition for (3) the linguistic expression of individual percepts. In this triad, the linguistic-conceptual tributary of sensory discourse can be summarised. The 'missing leg' of the triangle, namely, the direct relation between perception and linguistic expression, is what is postulated by the notion of a direct transposition of perception into language. In the analysis of conceptual metaphor theory, however, this transposition is always mediated through the inevitable conceptual framework of 'cultural assumptions, values, and attitudes.'

In a further analytical layer to the sensation–perception distinction, then, all perception, at the same time as being moulded by prior experience and subjective association, is shaped and co-determined by cultural influences. It should be stressed, however, that an acknowledgment of different factors of influence upon perception is not meant to render that process reducible in terms of any single one of them, as Lakoff and Johnson also emphasise:

> We are not claiming that physical experience is in any way more basic than other kinds of experience, whether emotional, mental, cultural, or whatever. All of these experiences may be just as basic as physical experiences. Rather, what we are claiming about grounding is that we typically conceptualize the nonphysical *in terms of* the physical – that is, we conceptualize the less clearly delineated in terms of the more clearly delineated.[103]

The way conceptual metaphors are grounded in experience will be influenced by cultural factors, always in the plural; this is one way, Lakoff and Johnson argue, in which cultural background shapes perception.

The importance of context in the study of conceptual metaphors has since been brought out more clearly. Kövecses discusses what he calls 'context-induced creativity' in the use of metaphor as one aspect of how metaphors relate to wider discourse: 'we need to look at entire discourses and study their several creative aspects.'[104] Within such

---

[101] Lakoff/Johnson, *Metaphors We Live By*, 57.
[102] Lakoff/Johnson, *Metaphors We Live By*, 59.
[103] Ibid.
[104] See Kövecses, *Metaphor*, 285–298, quotations at 285, 292.

2.5 Metaphor in Context – Metaphor in Discourse

discourses – Kövecses's basic working definition of 'discourse' is as 'a series of concepts organised in a particular way' and refers, in the first place, to written texts – metaphors provide intratextual coherence.[105] An example given by Kövecses is the leading metaphor of a newspaper article, introduced at its beginning and taken up again at the end; drawing on examples already introduced above, we may point to the various ways in which the metaphor PHYSICAL VISION IS KNOWLEDGE is employed (in the reference to God's all-seeing vision), questioned (Galileo's glass is 'less assured' than angelic vision) and, not uncommonly, ironised in *Paradise Lost*: at 1.59–60, we learn of Satan that 'at once as far as angels ken he views/The dismal situation waste and wild' – yet, as from comparable instances of Satanic 'mere looking' without seeing, no superior insight follows from this comparatively superior vision. The other kind of coherence facilitated by conceptual metaphor, according to Kövecses, obtains *across discourses*, or between texts. Such intertextual coherence may link texts which are reasonably close, historically (as with the instances of IDEAS ARE FOOD referred to above), or it may be 'achieved through inheriting and using a particular conceptual metaphor at different historical periods.' A prime example of this, Kövecses notes, is the way in which 'several biblical metaphors have been recycled over the ages.'[106]

In the end, of course, both kinds of metaphorical coherence (intra- and intertextual) may well be intertwined; one and the same metaphor 'can provide coherence across a variety of discourses, both historically and simultaneously.'[107] In other words: conceptual metaphors may form their own referential networks, both synchronically and diachronically. This does not mean, of course, that the 'conceptualiser' (user of metaphor) is bound by those networks to engage in a particular kind of metaphor use, or even to accept all the aspects a chosen metaphor entails; it does suggest, however, that certain established notions about how a particular idea is to be conceptualised will exert what Kövecses terms the 'pressure of coherence,' i.e., an urge towards a metaphorical usage that is 'in tune' with the various contexts at play in a given discursive situation.[108] In other words, there is both a supra-individual and an individual level to the use of conceptual metaphor, which may lead either to 'the emergence and use of well-worn, conventional metaphorical expressions … [or] may produce genuinely novel or at least unconventional expressions.'[109] Either case, however, is to be defined only as against its context.

Such intra- or cross-discursive context may be supplied in a number of ways. With no claim to completeness, Kövecses identifies five factors here: (1) immediate linguistic context; (2) prior knowledge about any of the major entities participating in discourse (the speaker/conceptualiser, the addressee/conceptualiser, and the topic addressed); (3) the physical setting; (4) the social setting; (5) the immediate cultural context.[110] The last three factors, in particular, may be hard to distinguish in individual cases, as Kövecses readily acknowledges; however, as will become clear below, there is also a considerable

---

[105] Kövecses, *Metaphor*, 292.
[106] Kövecses, *Metaphor*, 285.
[107] Kövecses, *Metaphor*, 286.
[108] Kövecses, *Metaphor*, 298.
[109] See Kövecses, *Metaphor*, 289–91, quotation at 298.
[110] See Kövecses, *Metaphor*, 292–8.

blurring between what might be considered merely 'objective' information about the participants in discursive exchange, on the one hand, and the social or other valuations of the various roles they may claim for themselves or ascribe to each other. For now, it will suffice to point to such instances as Milton's punning and other imagery in his (misguided) attacks on Alexander More (or Morus) in *Defensio Secunda* (1654) and the subsequent *Pro Se Defensio* (1655).

Following upon the earlier *Defensio pro Populo Anglicano* (1651), Milton's 'Defence of the English People' against accusations of regicide raised by the French scholar Claudius Salmasius (Claude de Saumaise), his latter two defences were triggered by the anonymous *Regii Sanguinis Clamor ad Coelum adversus Parricidas Anglicanos* ('The Cry of the Royal Blood against the English Parricides,' 1652), written by the Anglican clergyman and religious controversialist Pierre du Moulin, but mistakenly attributed by Milton to Alexander More, a French Calvinist academic of Scottish origin. In the *Clamor*, the attacker's description of Milton – in words borrowed from Virgil – as 'a monster, dreadful, ugly, huge, deprived of sight' had been harsh, personal, and phrased in sensory language.[111] It had also drawn on an intertextual context via its quotation from the *Aeneid*, in which the blinded cyclops Polyphemus is described as 'horrible, shapeless, huge, bereft of light/sight' ('monstrum horrendum, informe, ingens, cui lumen ademptum,' 3.568).

In his two replies, Milton paid his detractor – in the case of the dedicatory preface, this actually *was* More – back in kind.[112] In the *Pro Se Defensio*, he first accuses More of illicit sexual relations, punning both on the supposed scene of the crime (a garden outside Geneva) and on his opponent's name: 'And it has surely "perished" ..., that paradise of yours, and the fig tree, and the mulberry, and the sycamore [et ficus et morus et sycomorus], by which your iniquity was shadowed as virtuously as it could be ...'[113] The concrete elaboration of the (ironic) metaphor A PLACE OF SENSUAL EXCESS IS A PARADISE depends, if the audience is to fully comprehend Milton's Latin, on some prior knowledge regarding the target of his tract, i.e., the addressee-made-topic. Some pages later, Milton turns to the pastors of the French Protestants at Amsterdam, where More had moved since his alleged misconduct in Geneva, urging them to bar his opponent from all pastoral office: 'Drive far off from the walls of the church this preaching wolf; allow not this goatish voice, so impure with lewdness and adulteries, giving, nay selling, words to the people, and that from a higher place, as he says, to be heard any

---

[111] CPW 4: 587; a variant translation is quoted in Lewalski, *Life of Milton*, 289.
[112] More's authorship of the passage in question is pointed out, helpfully, by William Poole, *Milton and the Making of 'Paradise Lost'* (Cambridge, Mass.: Harvard University Press, 2017), 131. Poole also notes that 'in response to this one passing Virgilian allusion, Milton defiantly stacked up examples of the righteous blind [see CPW 4: 585–87]. ... It is the classic historical sweep of Milton: Greco-Roman republican statesmanship, a crusading doge, two Protestant heroes of the battlefield and of the study, examples enlisted from the Bible itself, and at the end of this righteous tradition, Milton himself.'
[113] CPW 4: 738. Kester Svendsen notes in his commentary to the Yale edition that, apart from the punning on More's name, 'from this point to the end of the paragraph occurs a succession of puns on rhetoric, flowering, and fornication.'

more in the sacred company.'[114] On a conceptual level, this satisfies the two metaphors OBJECTIONABLE PEOPLE ARE ANIMALS and OBJECTIONABLE HUMAN BEHAVIOUR IS ANIMAL BEHAVIOUR.[115] In terms of sensory history, it follows the established trope of certain animals being associated with lust.[116] In a more specific and contextual sense, however, the images are used refer to Alexander More, the lustful *preacher*; hence the highlighting of the 'goatish voice,' hence also, in the present instance, Milton's limiting of his polemic to the two 'vocal' animals, goat and wolf.[117]

In both cases, as in the original attack on Milton in the *Clamor*, the wording and choice of metaphor is affected by a range of contextual relations: to other texts, to established, traditional tropes, to the respective opponent's (supposed) person. Still, the general communicative situation in Milton's polemical prose can be shown to conform to a (notional) exchange of spoken discourse and, again, with an emphasis on the bodily-perceptive component which that entails. In the *Defensio Secunda*, his first reply to the *Regii Sanguinis Clamor*, Milton challenges his adversary:

> But now let us come at last to this creature, whatever he is, who cries out against us: a 'Cry' indeed I hear, not 'of the Royal Blood,' as the title boasts, but of some unknown rascal, for nowhere do I find the crier. You there! Who are you? A man or nobody?[118]

Since Milton had responded to the *Clamor*'s aspersion of Cyclopean blindness barely a page earlier, there seems to be another reference intended here to the story of Odysseus (Ulysses), who had told the drunk Polyphemus that his name was 'Nobody.' 'If I really were the Cyclops,' Milton appears to argue, 'you'd have to be Ulysses. But since your slander was published anonymously, you *really* are nobody.' Here again, then, there is an overlay of synchronic and diachronic, of intra- and intertextual factors in discursive context: Milton's imagery relates to the Homeric and Virgilian epic tradition, to the *Clamor*, and to his own earlier reference to the *Clamor*'s preface which had 'imputed my blindness to me.'[119] At the same time, it portrays his opponent as an interlocutor ('who cries out against us'), and their interaction as a pointedly somatic and sensory event ('a "Cry" indeed I hear'). We have returned, then, to a notion of 'discourse' as, primarily, embodied speech.

---

[114] CPW 4: 761.
[115] See Kövecses, *Metaphor*, 153.
[116] Regarding a similar attack a few pages earlier, Svendsen comments that, 'in comparing More to the goat, the boar, and the wolf, Milton invokes equally well-known emblems of violence and sexual excess' (CPW 4: 751n127). See also Karl P. Wentersdorf, 'The "Rout of Monsters" in Comus,' *MQ* 12 (1978), 119–25, on 'wolf, or bear,/Or ounce, or tiger, hog, or bearded goat' (*Comus*, 70–1) as emblems of lechery. In Milton's prelapsarian Paradise, by contrast, 'sporting the lion ramped, and in his paw/Dandled the kid; bears, tigers, ounces, pards,/Gamboled before them' (*PL* 4.341–3). See also Fowler's note on the 'ox' and 'ape' of *PL* 8.396.
[117] In addition, the image of the preacher-wolf figures prominently elsewhere in Milton's writings (see, for instance, *PL* 4.181–91, *Lycidas* 119–29).
[118] CPW 4: 560.
[119] CPW 4: 559. Strictly speaking, Milton misremembers this point, ascribing the relevant passage to the earlier attack by Salmasius, who had since died.

This not only links up with the previously introduced conception of discourse as essentially embodied; it can also be shown to connect to metaphor theory. In fact, current research in linguistics indicates that the emergence of conceptual metaphors from the 'ad hoc' use of linguistic metaphors in spoken discourse is facilitated by an intermediate level of 'systematic metaphor,' at which both (or all) interlocutors draw on a shared imagery in order to give coherence to their conversation and, at the same time, build rapport.[120] In its last consequence, this means that metaphor at all levels along the spectrum between linguistic implementation and conceptual abstraction is, ultimately, a corollary of discourse as speech. Of course, as the few examples cited already suggest, a shared cultural repository of metaphor might equally well be put to polemical use. Nevertheless, it is Milton and his opponents' all-round reference to a manifestly sensory pool of metaphor which underlines the embodied, notionally vocal quality of their trading barbs. Milton's response to the *Clamor*, the 'Cry' of Charles I's blood denouncing the regicides, itself takes the form of a vociferous challenge: 'You there! Who are you? A man or nobody?'

Milton, too, is crying out, then, but, quite clearly, he is not 'nobody.' As the title page of the *Second Defence* proclaims, this is 'Joannis Miltoni Angli Pro Populo Anglicano Defensio Secunda Contra infamem libellum anonymum …' – as authorial self-assertion goes, 'John Milton, Englishman' and his nameless detractor could not be further apart.[121] What divides them are the different speaking positions they take – which in the case of the anonymous attacker is a position of evasion, and in Milton's, a position of power *ex officio*.[122] Where they meet is in their exchange of notionally vocal, embodied discourse.

This notion of text and discourse as a manifestation of the living, audible voice of a speaking subject is a commonplace of seventeenth-century culture; we find it expressed not least in such pamphlet titles as *A Just Complaint, or Loud Crie, Of All the Well-Affected Subjects* (1643).[123] Unsurprisingly, the idea is common in Milton, also. Here it may be found in the poetry, with a particular focus on 'song,'[124] and it also occurs with striking regularity in Milton's prose as well. Already at the outset of the *Defensio Secunda*, he portrays himself as an orator, standing, bodily, 'on the very threshold of my

---

[120] See Kövecses, *Metaphor*, 300–3.

[121] See the reproduction in CPW 4: 547. For a study of Milton's strategies of authorial self-representation, see Fallon, *Milton's Peculiar Grace*.

[122] Although Milton's ability to act in an official role was now severely impaired by his blindness, he nevertheless kept his post of Secretary for Foreign Tongues with the Protectorate government; see Lewalski, *Life of Milton*, 299–302.

[123] See CPW 2: 28n10.

[124] John Hollander, in his *Vision and Resonance: Two Senses of Poetic Form* (New Haven, Conn.: Yale University Press, 1985 [1975]), has warned of an overhasty identification of poetry and song; but Milton explicitly suggests precisely this identification in a number of places. Thus, explicitly, at *PL* 7.24–5: 'More safe I sing with mortal voice, unchanged/To hoarse or mute, …'. In the proem to book 9 of *Paradise Lost*, there is the intriguing reminder that Raphael's 'discourse' with Adam is, in fact, part of the speaker's epic song: 'No more of *talk* where God or angel guest/With Man [...] / [...] permitting him the while/Venial *discourse* unblamed. I now must change/*Those notes* to tragic; …' (9.1–6, emphasis added).

2.5 Metaphor in Context – Metaphor in Discourse

speech [*in ipso limine orationis*].'[125] In the opening paragraph of *Areopagitica* (1644), written a good ten years earlier, the notionally vocal, yet practically ambivalent quality of the communicative situation is made explicit through references to both, voice and writing: 'They who to States and Governours of the Commonwealth direct their Speech, High Court of Parlament,' Milton opens with a direct address, 'or wanting such accesse in a private condition, write that which they foresee may advance the publick good; I suppose them as at the beginning of no mean endeavour …,' before announcing that 'this whole Discourse propos'd' will be expressive of his love of liberty.[126] A 'Discourse' may be both, of course, a spoken account and its written record, but its domain of origin is that of vocal speech. Liberty, Milton reminds us, is not the same as a complete absence of conflict – 'that let no man in this World expect; but when complaints are *freely heard*, deeply consider'd, and speedily reform'd, then is the utmost bound of civill liberty attain'd, that wise men looke for.'

The grounds of this kind of liberty, then, are free and vocal speech – and free audience. Its nature – in the utterance and hearing of complaints, in the formulation of replies and practical responses – is discursive. Indeed, the very 'Discourse' of *Areopagitica* is an instance of free and vocal speech, just as its author had asked for free audience:

> To which [i.e., the attainable kind of discursive liberty] *if I now manifest by the very sound of this which I shall utter*, that wee are already in good part arriv'd, and yet from such steepe disadvantage of tyranny and superstition grounded into our principles as was beyond the manhood of a *Roman* recovery, it will bee attributed first, as is most due, to the strong assistance of God our deliverer, next to your faithfull guidance and undaunted Wisdome, Lords and Commons of *England*.[127]

If Milton's oratorical posture in these passages can be explained by reference to the ideal role of classical rhetoric, the image of the Greco-Roman rhetor, and the resulting notions of what oratory should be, it clearly owes much of its effect to the repeated evocation of actual, vocal rhetorical performance.[128] Indeed, both aspects, the classical-traditional and the 'audio-suggestive,' merge in Milton's portrayal of how 'Discourse' should perform its work in the commonwealth. Of the two options, audible oratory and writing, it is vocal speech which is the nobler, not only because it conforms to the classical ideal of the orator in the senate but also because it presupposes direct access to the 'States and Governours of the Commonwealth', as well as the authority to take the floor and speak in their presence as an equal. Only those 'wanting such accesse … write.' On a more fundamental level still, speech itself is not fixed as writing is; its free and apparently spontaneous command represents the very discursive liberty that *Areopagitica*

---

[125] CPW 4: 548.
[126] CPW 2: 486–7.
[127] CPW 2: 487, first emphasis added.
[128] This includes the point that, while *Areopagitica* is formally addressed to the Long Parliament, its real (reading) audience was intended to be much wider. See the commentary in CPW 2: 170–8, esp. 172–3.

demands. By emphatically framing his tract as (a) speech in writing, Milton claims the high status and personal virtue associated with the former while availing himself of the advantages of the latter (durability, wide dissemination). The wisest and most honourable thing the recipients of that speech can do is to acknowledge the soundness of the discourse addressed to them (which of course implies no small praise to the orator himself):

> But if from the industry of a life wholly dedicated to studious labours, and those naturall endowments haply not the worst for two and fifty degrees of northern latitude, so much must be derogated, as to count me not equall to any of those who had this priviledge [sc. of addressing popular assemblies], I would obtain to be thought not so inferior, as your selves are superior to the most of them who receiv'd their counsell: and how farre you excell them, be assur'd Lords and Commons, there can no greater testimony appear, then *when your prudent spirit acknowledges and obeyes the voice of reason from what quarter soever it be heard speaking*; …[129]

In discussing the passage from book 2 of *Paradise Lost* at the very outset of this chapter, I established a number of features ascribed there, by Milton, to the notion of 'discourse.' In the opening of *Areopagitica*, also, good discourse is a number of things. It is both sensuous (spoken, audible, and heard) and abstract (as 'a series of concepts organised in a particular way' and put into writing, as 'the voice of reason'); it is potentially beneficial (rational, virtuous, as a means to knowledge) but not infallible (especially up north); its rational perfection is due to 'the strong assistance of God our deliverer,' creator of right reason, but its fallibility is deeply human (i.e., traceable to the individual speaker and his life).[130] Excepting only the etymological reading of 'discourse' as 'going to and fro,' these characterisations correspond to the four features of Miltonic 'discourse' observed above. As will become clear in later discussion, in fact, wherever discourse is addressed explicitly in Milton, it will be discussed, on the whole, in terms of these conflicting, but not necessarily contradictory, ascriptions.

Taken together, Milton's references to the sensuous quality of speech in the passages from *Areopagitica* appear to fluctuate between the notional yet, in a sense, 'literal' vocality of '… if I now manifest by the very sound of this which I shall utter,' on the one hand, and the more obvious metaphorically 'voice of reason' on the other.[131] In this,

---

[129] CPW 2: 489–90, emphasis added. The idea that the English climate was unfavourable to intellectual pursuits is a recurring theme in Milton (see n.14 on this passage and, as one further example, *PL* 9.44–6); in this particular instance, it appears to underline, with conspicuous modesty, the contrast between Milton, the English orator, and his classical counterparts (represented by references to 'the Parlament of *Athens*' and Dion Prusaeus in the lines immediately preceding.

[130] The 'faithfull guidance and undaunted Wisdome' attributed to Parliament also have their origin in God-given faith and *recta ratio*.

[131] Even in this case, however, the perceptual-somatic grounding of the metaphor is reiterated by Milton's reference to its 'speaking' as well as, more subtly, through the sensory etymology of 'obey'/'obedience' from Latin *ob-audire*/*ob-oedientia* (lit. 'to hearken intently'/'listening'). On

they span the entire spectrum of sensory discourse as an expressive linguistic mode. Likewise, in the passages from the *Second Defence*, the sensory imagery used is also conventional (as in the references to Paradise and the myth of Odysseus) yet, in its establishing of contextual relations of a personal and political kind, we re-encounter the potential of sensory metaphor for creative polemical application (as earlier in the pot simile, but now with a clear contextual twist). From this notion of discourse as a linguistic-conceptual compound distinctly shaped by context, it is only a small step to its further reconception as *essentially* contextual.

2.6 Foucauldian Discourse: Discourse as Context

The analytical value of context has been variously discussed, and at length.[132] In the present connection, I am not so much interested in the general meaningfulness of contextual study but rather in the further contextual potential inherent in the notion of discourse, and hence in sensory discourse as the discourse of (and on) the senses. According to one distinction between the 'historical context' and the '(inter-)texture' of a text at hand, the two exist side by side:

> Texts, in other words, appear in two forms: within a historical context variously constituted by a number of extra-textual features; and within a present texture, or inter-text, whose centre-piece is the examined text but which can include elements from the farthest past or near present if their interpretive or analytical presence is necessary or relevant.[133]

In this section I argue for the close interrelation between the two, context and texture, in the realm of sensory discourse.[134] Such an essentially contextual notion of discourse, of particular value to my approach to sensory discourse, is frequently associated with the name of Michel Foucault, whose most extensive elaboration of the term is in his *The Archaeology of Knowledge* (1969). Foucault himself comments on 'the equivocal meaning of the term *discourse*, which I have used and abused in many different senses,' and it lies beyond the scope of this chapter to offer a full reconstruction of those uses and abuses.[135] Neither is Foucault's highly abstract and, at bottom, impersonal conception of discourse fully applicable to the discourse of the senses as I understand it: in this as in other chapters, after all, I refer not only to Milton but also to other individual participants in discourse, significant in themselves as observing and commenting subjects.

---

this and the parallel cases of Greek *hup-akouein* and German *ge-horchen*, with reference to *Paradise Lost*, see Hale, *Milton's Languages*, 133.

[132] For an overview see Peter Burke, 'Context in Context,' *Common Knowledge* 8 (2002), 152–77.

[133] Christie, 'Introduction: Rhetoric and Writing,' 8.

[134] For an alternative formulation of this nexus in terms of a fundamentally discursive and thus non-hierarchical 'contexture' (*Kontextur*) see Berensmeyer, *'Angles of Contingency,'* 45–48.

[135] Michel Foucault, *The Archaeology of Knowledge*, tr. A. M. Sheridan Smith (London: Routledge, 2002 [1969]), 120. Over the course of his writing career, Foucault's notion of 'discourse' changed, implying varying emphases at various times. My references to 'Foucauldian discourse' in the following refer to the conception laid out in *Archaeology of Knowledge*.

However, a brief consideration of Foucault's notion of discourse and its possible implications in an early modern (sensory) context will extend our understanding of 'sensory discourse' beyond the linguistic-conceptual notion outlined above, thus permitting me to account for phenomena in sensory culture not otherwise relatable to my objects of analysis in the writings of Milton.

To begin with, Foucauldian discourse is not wholly divorced from language (and thus the 'classical' notion of the term we have already encountered). 'In the most general and vaguest way,' Foucault writes, 'discourse,' for him also, 'denote[s] a group of verbal performances,' whether by a single subject (as in 'holding a discourse') or in dialogue (as in 'discoursing with somebody'). At the same time, however, Foucault also uses the term to refer to 'a group of acts of formulations, a series of sentences of propositions,' that is, a body of statements of a clearly defined interrelation and content.[136] These statements, he notes, 'belong to a single system of formation; thus I shall be able to speak of clinical discourse, economic discourse, the discourse of natural history, psychiatric discourse ...'[137]

Such individual discourses are expressive of what Foucault calls 'discursive formations,' ensembles of rules and presuppositions obtaining in a particular field: 'the discursive formation is the general enunciative system that governs a group of verbal performances.'[138] It is observed (and described) not as 'a progressively deductive structure, nor as an enormous book that is being gradually and continuously written, nor as the *œuvre* of a collective subject', but rather as an ensemble of regularities, as what Foucault calls a 'system of dispersion.'[139] Conversely, Foucault says, 'we shall call discourse a group of statements in so far as they belong to the same discursive formation,' that is, in so far as they may be described in terms of the same system of regularities.[140] These discursive formations are almost comparable to what are otherwise designated (scientific or other) disciplines; where they differ is in the extent and the quality of the restrictions that go into their demarcation.

Scientific or other disciplines of study are usually demarcated by reference to their objects, theories, and methods. Foucault's first hypothesis, immediately rejected as unsatisfactory, had been that 'statements different in form, and dispersed in time, form a group [i.e., a discourse] if they refer to one and the same object' – however, objects are neither uniform nor stable across time. Rather, Foucault argues, discourses *constitute* their objects.[141] The objects of sensory discourse, naturally, are sense perception and the

---

[136] Regarding his particular notion of the term 'statement,' Foucault explains that 'a statement belongs to a discursive formation as a sentence belongs to a text, and a proposition to a deductive whole' (*Archaeology of Knowledge*, 130). This also indicates how the analysis of a statement in the given sense differs from the interpretation of a sentence in a text: the former has to account for the discursive preconditions of the statement's production.
[137] Foucault, *Archaeology of Knowledge*, 120–1.
[138] Foucault, *Archaeology of Knowledge*, 130.
[139] Foucault, *Archaeology of Knowledge*, 40–1.
[140] Foucault, *Archaeology of Knowledge*, 131. On the sensory-studies term 'sensory formations,' derived from Foucault's notion of the discursive formation, see Chapter 1.2 above.
[141] Foucault, *Archaeology of Knowledge*, 35–6, quotation at 35. Foucault's three other hypotheses – regarding a particular 'style,' a 'system of permanent and coherent concepts,' or an 'identity and

senses as the (bodily and notional) loci of that perception. Culturally, the points of their articulation in seventeenth-century England – instances of what Foucault calls the 'surfaces of their emergence' – may be just what we might expect (e.g., the laboratory, the dissecting room, the artist's workshop), or they may be historically more specific, if only in the sense of being less self-evident from today's point of view.[142]

Another such ordinary 'surface' that keeps recurring in discussions of the early modern sensorium is the marketplace.[143] As the readers of the comprehensive *The merchants Mappe of Commerce* (1638) by the Levant merchant and writer on economic matters Sir Lewes Roberts were told in the margins of a chapter entitled 'Of Commodities in generall used by the way of Merchandize, and of the knowledge thereof,' 'All commodities are known by the senses' – and by *all* the senses:

> all commodities are not learned by one sense alone, though otherwise never so perfect; nor yet by two, but somtimes by three, somtimes by foure, and somtimes by all: and yet this Art [sc. of 'Merchandizing'] is now a dayes come to that heigth, (I may say) to that heigth of cunning, that all these are little enough too.[144]

An intimate knowledge of merchandise gained by experience and through a honing of perception, Roberts argues, is necessary 'now a dayes' more than ever, as luxury items and staple goods of distant, little-known origin are increasingly present in the English marketplace (again, we remember Pepys below deck, wading through heaps of spices). However, this honing of the senses is not just to come to terms with a torrent of unfamiliar goods, or to foster a greater appreciation for quality products – the eighteenth century would see to that development of 'taste.' Rather, Roberts warns buyers, and would-be merchants in particular, to beware, for

> he that is imperfect in any one natural Sense ... must neither be a merchant nor yet addict himself to the knowledge: for any one Sense being either depraved or defective in part or in whole, will force him to commit ... many Errors, and constrain him to take ... (as we say) Chalk for Cheese, or one thing for another ...[145]

The sensory knowledge of merchandise, acquired literally 'at first hand' (as well as through the eye, nose, tongue, or – tapping for consistency – by ear) is meant to protect the unwary and to help regulate economic transactions. Attempts at commercial fraud and deception were a widespread problem, and it was not for nothing that market regu-

---

persistence of themes' characteristic of particular discourses – are equally rejected (36–40). They may be seen as roughly relatable to the theories and methods of a given discipline in the conventional sense.
[142] Foucault, *Archaeology of Knowledge*, 45.
[143] See Evelyn Welch, 'The Senses in the Marketplace: Sensory Knowledge in a Material World,' in: *Cultural History of the Senses in the Renaissance*, ed. Roodenburg, 61–86.
[144] Lewes Roberts, *The Merchants Mappe of Commerce wherein, the universall manner and matter of trade, is compendiously handled* ... (London: Printed by R. O. for Ralph Mabb, 1638), 41.
[145] Roberts, *The Merchants Mappe of Commerce*, 37.

lations stipulated that goods should only be sold during daylight hours.[146] In this era of direct mercantile exchange, commercial deception was most commonly sensory deception, and a trained sensorium could save its possessor a fortune. If knowledge was power – as an often-quoted maxim of the period has it –, it also had its uses in a literal economy of perception. In the seventeenth-century marketplace, where even a scholar as brilliant as Galileo might be tricked into mistaking base metals for silver, this kind of profitable knowledge had to be acquired through the senses.[147]

A more developed and formalised version of the same sensory 'cunning' deemed necessary by Roberts for merchants and customers alike could be seen at work in the case of artisan 'searchers,' guild officials responsible for ensuring compliance with quality standards for a wide range of alimentary merchandise, for materials such as pewter or silk, or, in a particularly consequential case, for medicinal substances. The searchers, too, while over time developing novel experimental approaches to the analysis of materials, grounded their expertise, first and foremost, in their own sensory experience: 'most tests for quality were direct, immediate, and sensory,' their success depended on 'the skilled senses of those involved.'[148] Not only looking and touching but also smelling and tasting, searchers would note, in surviving reports of their activities, coming across 'Mouldy, stinking & putryfyed' pills at an apothecary's shop; or they would put on record, for the benefit of future colleagues, that 'the best salt smelleth as sweet as any violet, and soe doth the salmon that hath beene salted theirwith, and rightlie handled, att the opening of the hogsheads; whereas otherwise it hath a very bad and rotten smell.'[149] Embodied experience would thus be introduced into sensory discourse, both in Foucault's regulatory-social and the conventional, more narrowly linguistic sense of the term.

Having moved from the everyday, 'everyman' situation of the marketplace to the more specialised one of the market searchers, the authoritative dimension of Foucauldian discourse comes into view. After all, regulatory institutions such as the guild searchers might be said to correspond to Foucault's 'authorities of delimitation,' meaning entities controlling the modes and confines of knowledge production or even reference across a given discourse.[150] That such discursive regulation extended to the sensory sphere in early modern England should be clear when considering various contentious issues of church government and religious worship, from the debates over the Eucharist and forms of service to the pervasive discourse of iconoclasm, in which Milton was

---

[146] See Welch, 'Senses in the Marketplace,' 67.
[147] Galileo presents this as a hypothetical case which could happen to anybody as 'any one of the senses is fallacious'; this is quoted and discussed by Welch, 'Senses in the Marketplace,' 66–7.
[148] See Patrick Wallis/Catherine Wright, 'Evidence, Artisan Experience and Authority in Early Modern England,' in: Pamela H. Smith et al. (eds), *Ways of Making and Knowing: The Material Culture of Empirical Knowledge* (New York: Bard Graduate Center, 2017), 138–63, quotations at 142, 146; the point about the relationship between the searchers' expertise and the sensory habits of consumers in general is made at 156.
[149] Quoted in Wallis/Wright, 'Evidence, Artisan Experience and Authority,' 142, 146.
[150] Foucault, *Archaeology of Knowledge*, 46.

himself directly implicated.[151] A well-documented and conveniently circumscribed instance, in which the institutionalised regulation of sensory discourse is rendered particularly clear, is the conflict, in 1630s London, between the long-established College of Physicians (chartered in 1518) and the up-and-coming Society of Apothecaries (chartered as recently as 1617).[152] This particular struggle related to the proper manufacturing, testing, and application of lac sulphuris ('milk of sulphur,' precipitated sulphur), at the time a new and cutting-edge drug in the treatment of skin diseases. Involving wider questions as to whether apothecaries were allowed to practice medicine at all (and, conversely, whether physicians were allowed to trade in drug products) such disputes were professionally and socio-economically essential. They centred on profits as well as on prestige. At the same time, however, they were representative of natural-philosophical divisions between Galenic traditionalists (represented by the majority of physicians) and a 'modern' chemical and Paracelsian countercurrent, represented by the apothecaries.[153] In the case at hand, both sides not only carried out trials by fire and through other analytical methods but also employed their senses to assert their professional and experiential superiority.[154] As the surviving examination protocols indicate, though, the traditionalist physicians relied almost exclusively on their eyes, and on the visual appearance of the samples investigated ('of a Yellow colour like brymston'), whereas the apothecaries involved resorted to a trial 'per Gustium [sic],' testing – and tasting – for sweetness and smell as well as for colour:

> Mr Lawrence his opinion is that this lac sulphuris made by Mr Harrison at the hall is agreable to his former lac sulphuris differinge only a litle in the smell.

---

[151] See in general Matthew Milner, *The Senses and the English Reformation* (Farnham: Ashgate, 2011). On the Eucharist, see also Moshenska, *Feeling Pleasures*, 33–45. On Milton and the discourse of iconoclasm, see Lana Cable, 'Milton's Iconoclastic Truth,' in: *Politics, Poetics, and Hermeneutics in Milton's Prose*, eds Loewenstein/Turner, 135–151, as well as her *Carnal Rhetoric*. For a concise outline of the relations between iconoclasm proper and a more general Protestant 'iconophobia' extending not least to the theatre, see Patrick Collinson, *The Birthpangs of Protestant England: Religious and Cultural Change in the Sixteenth and Seventeenth Centuries* (London: Macmillan, 1988), 115–21.

[152] For an account of this conflict see Wallis/Wright, 'Evidence, Artisan Experience and Authority,' 150–6. The authors point out that this investigation was an unusual, perhaps even unique, occurrence.

[153] As often, divisions were not all that clear-cut. Wallis and Wright point to the particular irony of the 'inversion of the tacit/propositional [sc. knowledge] contrast that is normally thought to hold for artisans (such as apothecaries) and learned, university-trained individuals (such as physicians). It is surprising to see the physicians advocating the intuitive sensory approach of guild regulation, while the apothecaries deploy an array of chemical procedures ...' ('Evidence, Artisan Experience and Authority,' 154). For the Paracelsian influence on early modern thought, working against traditional notions, see the concise account by Allen G. Debus, *Man and Nature in the Renaissance* (Cambridge: Cambridge University Press, 1978).

[154] For the general importance (yet controversial status) of the senses in early modern medical practice, see the essays in W. F. Bynum/Roy Porter (eds), *Medicine and the Five Senses* (Cambridge: Cambridge University Press, 1993).

> Mr Warden Stone his opinion is that the first lac sulphuris made by Mr Harrison is a litle sweeter then the last made at the hall.
> Mr Yeardly his opinion is that Mr Harrisons first lac sulphuris is sweter both in smell & taste then the laste made at the hall. ...[155]

In the end, the apothecaries managed to defend their charter, and their highly sensuous approach to the investigation of chemical materials became – for a while – the dominant paradigm.[156] By the power vested in them by their respective professional corporations, physicians and apothecaries not only defined the discursive object 'lac sulphuris' (which would remain subject to debate for a long time),[157] but they also negotiated, more generally, the role of the individual senses in medical-pharmaceutical discourse and vis-à-vis experimental as well as, from the perspective of embodied experience, externalised methods of analysis.

Returning to the concept of sensory discourse, and put in Foucauldian terms, both corporations, their joint investigation, individual members, and respective assaying practices as well as the resulting examination protocols all form part of the discursive formation that regulated – and hence gave rise to – such a 'discourse of the senses' in seventeenth-century England. At the same time, however, the rivalry between the two corporations as well as their discrepant approaches to how the senses should be employed *also* form part of sensory discourse, and these, too, find reflection in the sources. How, then, can this be reconciled with the notion of *a* sensory discourse? Referencing the 'possible *points of diffraction* of discourse,' Foucault addresses precisely this problem.[158] We would be in error, he argues, were we to seek complete homogeneity in the identification of discursive formations. Early on, he had emphasised the importance of discontinuity for his project.[159] Now it becomes apparent how this affects his theory on the level of discourse. Points of diffraction, he says, may emerge as

> *points of incompatibility*: two objects, or two types of enunciation, or two concepts may appear, in the same discursive formation, without being able to enter – under pain of manifest contradiction or inconsequence – the same series of statements. They are then characterised as *points of equivalence*: the two incompatible elements are formed in the same way and on the basis of the same rules; the conditions of their appearance are identical; they are situated at the same level; ... instead of constituting a mere defect of coherence, they form an alternative[160]

---

[155] Quoted in Wallis/Wright, 'Evidence, Artisan Experience and Authority,' 152–3, with three more opinions.
[156] See Lissa Roberts, 'The Death of the Sensuous Chemist: The 'New' Chemistry and the Transformation of Sensuous Technology,' in *Empire of the Senses*, ed. Howes, 106–127, on the process by which, finally, 'mathematical analysis ... replaced sensory analysis as the final step of chemical determination' (118).
[157] See H. Woods, 'What Is "Milk of Sulphur?",' *British Medical Journal* 1 (1891), 670–1.
[158] Foucault, *Archaeology of Knowledge*, 73.
[159] Foucault, *Archaeology of Knowledge*, 8–10, see also 15.
[160] Foucault, *Archaeology of Knowledge*, 73.

Following this understanding of 'discourse,' the discrepant approaches of London physicians and apothecaries to the sensory assessment of pharmaceuticals may be correlated not with contrasting or rivalling discourses, but with one complex sensory discourse and the discursive formation (relations of authority, etc.) underlying it. This arguably presents another instance in which the Foucauldian notion of discourse provides an angle which, by reference to other dimensions of the term, is not immediately graspable.

In further contrast to the usual approach to a definition of disciplines by objects, theories, and methods, then, each discursive formation in a Foucauldian sense is characterised by an even wider ensemble of governing rules, delimiting what can or cannot (or may/may not, or should/should not) be uttered within a given discourse. As my wording suggests (and the cases outlined have already illustrated), the respective scope of possible utterances in discourse – Foucault's *énoncés* – is not determined by 'factual' or contentual considerations alone (e.g., in the case at hand, by what is known or presumed about the senses at a given point in time); it is equally determined, according to Foucault, by the respective subject positions characterising individual *énonciations* ('utterance acts') and the power relations obtaining between them: by *social* rules, roles, and relations; these, too, are facts.[161] By separating the facts of discourse from the associations in which they are otherwise habitually regarded (e.g., the 'oeuvre' of a given author, already alluded to), we might be able to point out 'other forms of regularity, other types of relations' – 'relations between statements' and groups of statements.[162] With a view to sensory discourse, such statements would comprise any explicit or implicit references to the senses which, in connection to the discourse at large, should be seen as direct or indirect statements *about* the senses. Every such statement is characterised by certain 'subject positions,' the taking of which constitutes the subject in discourse.

By 'subject positions,' Foucault means the discursive loci at which the subject is constituted in discourse; put more simply, these are situations or attitudes or roles which a given discursive situation may occasion. Among the different facets of the subject in discourse he names, some indicate points of contact with the sensory sphere: the 'listening subject,' the 'seeing subject,' the 'observing subject' in general. In taking these positions, the subject may use 'instrumental intermediaries that modify the scale of information [and] shift the subject in relation to the average or immediate perceptual level,' just as Hooke or Galileo may shift their observational position 'from a superficial to a deep level' (Foucault) using a microscope or a telescope. Foucault refers to the totality of these subject positions related to the sensory sphere as 'perceptual situations'; they reveal sense perception to be an integral part of Foucauldian discourse.[163] Still, as a

---

[161] E.g., in the case of the medical practitioners cited, who examines or licences whom and by which standards – will the royal charter be revoked? On the questions of 'who ... is accorded the right to use this sort of language [*langage*]? Who is qualified to do so?' and the 'institutional *sites*' and respective subject positions related to those questions (pointedly discussed with reference to nineteenth-century *doctors*), see Foucault, *Archaeology of Knowledge*, 55–61.
[162] See Foucault, *Archaeology of Knowledge*, 30–2, quotation at 32.
[163] Foucault, *Archaeology of Knowledge*, 57–8. It could be argued that Milton himself posits a specific 'scale of information' in his references to Galileo, the telescope, and the superior vision of Raphael.

totality of 'disciplinary' rules (in both senses of the term), Foucauldian discourse is a social system as much as an epistemic one. Whether it was at work in the early Royal Society, in the markets and apothecaries' shops, or whether it regulated, for instance, the importance of an educated touch in literacy and handwriting:[164] *sensory* discourse, too, might serve exactly those functions. What is more, it might also do so with reference to political power in the most conventional sense.

Thus, when the 'Irish stroker,' the faith healer Valentine Greatrakes, appeared on the English scene in the 1660s, the obvious objection to his supposed powers was not so much that healing by mere touch was a medical impossibility – Boyle, Glanvill, More, and other virtuosi closely followed Greatrakes's activities and tried to account for his apparent successes in physical terms –; it was rather that someone 'who restoreth the Blind to sight, the Deaf to Hearing; the Lame to strength; … Cripples to walk without Crutches … [and] cureth all manner of Diseases, with a streak of His Hand and Prayer' arrogated to himself a tactile capability intimately associated with the monarch's power to cure 'the King's Evil' (i.e., scrofula, a tuberculous infection of the lymph nodes) by simple 'touching,' a practice which had seen a significant revival under the restored monarchy of Charles II.[165] The fact alone that tactile healing was the king's prerogative was precisely a reason to find a 'mere' physical explanation for Greatrakes's reported successes.[166] What might be thought or said about the specific powers and operation of touch in this particular context depended not only on the body of knowledge addressed in the discourses of medicine and physiology but also on the powers ascribed to the body of the king. Even apart from discourses concerned with the senses as part of their 'core business' (as physiology, the arts or certain others arguably were), the power relations obtaining in the wider Restoration polity were instrumental, therefore, in shaping

---

[164] On the last point, see Jonathan Goldberg, *Writing Matter: From the Hands of the English Renaissance* (Stanford, Calif.: Stanford University Press, 1990), esp. 13–107 on the close connections between literacy, proficiency in handwriting, and early modern social hierarchy in 'the formations of the Elizabethan hand' (49).

[165] The quotation is from the title page of *The Great Cures and Strange Miracles, Performed by Mr. Valentine Gertrux* [sic] … (London: Printed for John Thomas, 1666). On the ministry of Greatrakes and contemporary reactions, see Thomas, *Religion and the Decline of Magic*, 240–8; Constance Classen, *The Deepest Sense: A Cultural History of Touch* (Urbana, Ill.: University of Illinois Press, 2012), 159; Moshenska, *Feeling Pleasures*, 225–243, esp. 230–2 for the attack on Charles II's royal authority by Greatrakes and also earlier (Quaker) healers claiming to cure the King's Evil better than Charles I did. Stephen Brogan argues, to the contrary, that 'Greatrakes was only a mild threat to Charles II' and calls 'the fact that Greatrakes initially touched for scrofula … tactless' at most (*The Royal Touch in Early Modern England: Politics, Medicine, and Sin* [Woodbridge: Boydell, 2015], 113.) The fullest study of Greatrakes in his context is Peter Elmer's *The Miraculous Conformist: Valentine Greatrakes, the Body Politic, and the Politics of Healing in Restoration Britain* (Oxford: Oxford University Press, 2013); the classic account of the 'royal touch,' Marc Bloch's *Les Rois thaumaturges*, translated as *The Royal Touch: Sacred Monarchy and Scrofula in England and France*, tr. J. E. Anderson (London: Routledge & Kegan Paul, 1973 [1924]).

[166] This point is made by Uwe Pauschert, *Joseph Glanvill und die Neue Wissenschaft des 17. Jahrhunderts* (Frankfurt: Peter Lang, 1994), 223.

and delimiting a sensory discourse (or other discourses relevant to the Greatrakes affair) which, at first glance, may appear completely distinct from them.[167]

When, after his discussion of 'surfaces of emergence' and 'authorities of delimitation,' Foucault finally refers to the 'grids of specification' operative in manifesting a discursive formation as discourse, he points, as one example, to 'the soul, as a group of hierarchised, related, and more or less interpenetrable faculties' in nineteenth-century psychology.[168] The applicability of this, *mutatis mutandis*, to seventeenth-century debates in faculty psychology and the generally hierarchical nature of the early modern sensorium is obvious. As will become clear in later analyses, however, Foucault's category, with its heavy stress on *different kinds* of perception, and on *different ways* of employing individual senses in any one of those modes, may be even more relevant in the earlier period, as the early modern focus on morally and spiritually good sensory *practice* made for a highly particularised 'grid of sensory specification.'[169]

Finally, Foucault points to the importance of that which is outside of discourse. While discourses, in the last analysis, are always predicated upon (the potentialities of) language, they fulfil their various *functions* in '*a field of non-discursive practices.*'[170] In this regard, we might think of the silent topographies of (landed) power expressed through the axial vistas and long avenues cut or planted as landscaping measures on the country estates of the seventeenth century, where such sight lines 'radiating out from a single centre and stretching relentlessly over the countryside without regard to its natural features were a particularly obvious way of subjecting a whole district to the authority of the great house.'[171] Alternatively we might point, again, to the practice of royal 'touching' for the 'King's Evil.' Clearly, at its core, this was a gesture without words and was, in that sense, non-discursive. That did not mean, however, that it could not be addressed, and thus be made part of discourse, such as when John Browne, surgeon to Charles II, claimed emphatically that 'near half the Nation hath been Toucht and Healed by His Sacred Majesty since His Happy Restauration.'[172] By being addressed in the discourse of the senses (or of royal power), the non-discursive touch of the monarch could be rendered a 'statement' in favour of monarchical power.

How might these socio-political contexts be said to translate into an (inter-)texture of statements in the more narrowly linguistic meaning of the terms? A book, Foucault

---

[167] In the Foucauldian model, the relevance of a particular discourse is contingent upon the analytical perspective taken: whether we consider Greatrakes a medical professional or merely as challenging established healing practices from outside the medical field, his place would be in a medical discourse; if we focus on his background as a member of the Irish gentry or his implicit challenge to royal prerogative, we would be considering social and/or political discourses.

[168] Foucault, *Archaeology of Knowledge*, 46.

[169] This, again, conforms to Foucault's general notion of a 'high dispersion' of discursive objects; he names epistemological, moral, and aesthetic aspects (*Archaeology of Knowledge*, 49).

[170] Foucault, *Archaeology of Knowledge*, 75–6, quotation at 75.

[171] Thomas, *Man and the Natural World*, 207–8, quotation at 207, see also 256. The focus on vision is clear; at Badminton (Glos.), 'the lanthorn of the Duke of Beaufort's house formed the centre of a star cut through the woods' (207). Thomas does not follow up on the Benthamian-Foucauldian implications of this 'panoptic' school of landscape gardening.

[172] John Browne quoted in Moshenska, *Feeling Pleasures*, 231.

suggests, is 'a node within a network' of texts not intentionally related to it.[173] In this network, boundaries, whether of the individual work or a whole oeuvre, as referred to above, are quite difficult to draw, and every choice of inclusion or exclusion (among an author's works, prose works, great works, etc.) is already an interpretive operation. I have thus opted to refer, in the title of my study, to Milton's 'writings' rather than his 'works,' and to treat the Miltonic corpus, with its wide range of text types, as a 'corpus' in a heuristic rather than as an 'oeuvre' in an historical sense – not as monolithic, not as a given, and certainly not as 'majestically unfolding.'[174] This is not to play down the at times remarkable consistency of Milton's preoccupations, or the motifs and echoes connecting seemingly distant points of his writing. In my view, if we range the Miltonic corpus, for now, among what Foucault calls 'pre-existing forms of continuity,' i.e., 'syntheses that are accepted without question, [yet] must remain in suspense', it only serves to highlight those connections.[175] If we still isolate individual instances of sensory discourse in Milton and contextualise them, this is meant to balance the kind of psychologising synthesis which Foucault especially cautions against – but without which the study of statements made by a person in history, as opposed to the abstract statements of a discourse qua discourse, is hardly feasible; it was in this spirit that I referred above to the 'eigensense' of sensory discourse in Milton.

Accordingly, Foucault continues by arguing that any statements observed in a particular situation – although expressive of specific subject positions – must be seen as placed within an 'enunciative field', in which the statements ascribed to a given discourse coexist with other, associated statements from different discourses, regardless of their respective authors, purposes, etc.[176] In fact, it is this background (or cross-discursive context) against which the enunciative specificity of a given statement (i.e., the particular subject position taken in it) becomes traceable in the first place. Sentences may exist in isolation; statements depend on their discursive setting. Discourses, in other words, delimit one another, but this does not preclude borrowing or other forms of reference. These include 'forms of coexistence,' first in a 'field of presence' (i.e., 'statements formulated elsewhere and taken up in a discourse,' but also their critique, discussion, and possible exclusion) and also in a 'field of concomitance' (i.e., statements from quite unrelated discourses which may be referred to for 'analogical confirmation' or as an appeal to a higher authority).

If sensory discourse is not taken to be a strictly physiological, philosophical, or art-theoretical matter, as I have suggested, its 'field of presence' is all-important. Its 'field of concomitance would also be highly relevant, as analogical ascriptions (e.g., in the hierarchical structuring of the sensorium) play an important role. Foucault's own example – Linnaeus and his reference to theology as part of the field of concomitance for eighteenth-century natural history – readily suggests the adaptation of his model to early

---

[173] Foucault, *Archaeology of Knowledge*, 25–6.
[174] See Foucault, *Archaeology of Knowledge*, 26.
[175] Foucault, *Archaeology of Knowledge*, 28.
[176] For the following see Foucault, *Archaeology of Knowledge*, 64–5.

2.6 Foucauldian Discourse: Discourse as Context

modern sensory culture, which includes, for instance, the 'optical theology' of the Presbyterian minister Robert Dingley.[177]

As a last dimension of the enunciative field, Foucault points to the 'field of memory,' by which he means the discursive ambience of

> statements that are no longer accept or discussed, and which consequently no longer define a body of truth [sc. as the 'field of presence'] or a domain of validity [sc. as the 'field of concomitance'], but in relation to which relations of filiation, genesis, transformation, continuity, and historical discontinuity can be established ...[178]

As Foucault plausibly argues, the relationship between this latter field of discarded truths and the (ostensibly) more operative forms of coexistence is not fixed but historically variable; thus he points out that the field of memory in nineteenth-century biology 'seems much better defined and better articulated than the field of memory surrounding the history of plants and animals in the Renaissance: for at that time it could scarcely be distinguished from the field of presence; they had the same extension and the same form, and involved the same relations.'[179] The same, indeed, might be said of early modern discursive treatments of sense perception (and processes of cognition more generally). Whether we consider the conflict between the traditional Aristotelian physiology and new anatomical findings, related debates over the seat of cognition in the body – in the heart? or in the brain? –, or other scientific arguments of the day: it is often difficult to keep current and outmoded views apart, and conflicting ascriptions may arise in close discursive proximity.[180] Thus, incidentally, Foucault's account of the complex contextual setting of individual discourses may go towards resolving the much-debated question of Milton's enthusiasm (or lack thereof) for the new science.[181] One example is Milton's portrayal of Satan entering the serpent:

---

[177] For a discussion of Dingley's *Divine Opticks* (1654) in relation to Milton's treatment of vision in *Paradise Lost* see Gabel, 'Hierarchies of Vision.'

[178] Foucault, *Archaeology of Knowledge*, 64–5.

[179] Foucault, *Archaeology of Knowledge*, 65.

[180] See, for example, Suparna Roychoudhury, *Phantasmatic Shakespeare: Imagination in the Age of Early Modern Science* (Ithaca, N. Y.: Cornell University Press, 2018), 28–57, on the complex interplay of tradition and discovery regarding the placement of the various faculties of the soul in the body.

[181] According to the classic account given by Kester Svendsen, *Milton and Science* (Cambridge, Mass.: Harvard University Press, 1956), 'most of [Milton's] science is traditional and conventional, a literary as well as scientific commonplace' (3); this view has since been thoroughly modified, not least by Karen L. Edwards, *Milton and the Natural World: Science and Poetry in 'Paradise Lost'* (Cambridge: Cambridge University Press, 1999). Whereas Svendsen had restricted the sources of Milton's scientific knowledge largely to the encyclopaedic tradition (a discourse he dubs 'neo-Plinyism' [*Milton and Science*, 24, 238]), Edwards argues for his intimate familiarity with contemporary science, and in favour of 'a Milton who enjoys evoking and then gently debunking an old legend' (*Milton and the Natural World*, 113). Still, there remains a pronounced 'simultaneity of the non-simultaneous', for which Foucault's account arguably provides the best conceptualisation.

> ... in at his mouth
> The devil entered, and his brutal sense,
> In heart or head, possessing, soon inspired
> With act intelligential; (*PL* 9.187–90)

The serpent's 'brutal sense'[182] is embodied – but where to place it? Milton chooses to leave the matter in abeyance, a decision comparable to the more often discussed account of geo- and/or heliocentrism in Raphael's reply to Adam's request for instruction (*PL* 8.5–38, 66–178).[183] Whether the demonically induced 'act intelligential' unfolds in the heart (the traditional view) or in the head (current scientific teaching) is pointedly shown to be irrelevant to the situation at hand. That Milton was not, however, indifferent to the debate as a whole appears evident from other, related passages. On the whole, Foucault's conception of the enunciative field as conditioning discursive context serves to account for a number of ways in which contextual factors can be shown to have a bearing on how questions of sense perception and related aspects of cognition are put into language. I consider both, the contextual setting and its linguistic manifestation, to be aspects of 'sensory discourse.'

All told, Foucault's notion of 'discourse' diverges from the linguistic-conceptual one in two important respects. This side of language, as it were, is essentially predicated upon practice (he also notes that discourses are 'practices that systematically form the objects of which they speak').[184] I have already indicated a certain correlation here with sensory discourse in Milton, which also has a significant pragmatic element to it – albeit not in the sense intended by Foucault. On the other hand, Foucauldian discourse does make use of signs (linguistic and other); 'but what they do is more than use these signs to designate things. It is this *more* that renders them irreducible to the language [*langue*] and to speech. It is this "more" that we must reveal and describe.'[185]

If sensory discourse can also be said to indicate 'more' than what is referred to by its 'manifest, visible, coloured chain of words,' this, on a purely conceptual level, would be lived experience, the reconstruction of which is a persistent concern in sensory studies.[186] While I draw on such investigations for their contextualising and historicising

---

[182] I.e., his 'natural understanding or intelligence' (*OED*, 'sense, n.,' II.11) typical of a brute animal (even of the 'subtlest beast of all the field,' *PL* 9.86). A suggestion of 'the bodily senses considered as a single faculty in contrast to intellect, reason, will, etc.' (*OED*, 'sense, n.,' II.12b), and of the closely associated dangers of sensuality, most likely is intended.
[183] See Marjara, *Contemplation of Created Things*, 127–144, esp. his conclusion at 144: 'Milton evidently tries to have the best of both worlds. Even though he does not succumb to the temptation of giving the sun a central position in his universe, he ... gives it extraordinary dignity, power, and influence ...' For the contrasting view that, while 'Milton does not condemn [astronomy],' 'Raphael's reply is Ptolemaic,' see Lee A. Jacobus, *Sudden Apprehension: Aspects of Knowledge in 'Paradise Lost'* (The Hague: Mouton, 1976), quotations at 55, 58.
[184] Foucault, *Archaeology of Knowledge*, 54.
[185] Foucault, *Archaeology of Knowledge*, 54.
[186] As in Hoffer, *Sensory Worlds in Early America*; Rath, *How Early America Sounded*; Cockayne, *Hubbub*; and, from a literary studies perspective, Smith, *Acoustic World of Early Modern England*.

potential, my aim in the present study is not so much to reconstruct 'how Milton sensed,' but rather to examine how he employed the senses in language, as well as to give conclusive indications about why he conceivably did so and what meanings such language use can demonstrably have taken on or generated in its cultural context. The first of these objectives relates to sensory discourse in a linguistic sense, the second is reliant on it in a wider, more abstract and, if not an orthodox Foucauldian, then at least the 'Foucauldesque' sense outlined here.

It might be thought paradoxical to introduce Foucault's approach to discourse into what is essentially a single-author study. After all, Foucauldian discourse is not, as a whole, a matter of personal choice – 'not the majestically unfolding manifestation of a thinking, knowing, speaking subject, but, on the contrary, a totality, in which the dispersion of the subject and his discontinuity with himself may be determined.'[187] In this respect, particularly, my own notion of 'sensory discourse' consciously diverges from the Foucauldian model, as I do use the term to refer to concrete utterances, made by individual authors.[188] At the same time, however, Foucault's attention to the impersonal quality of discourse-as-context – the 'totality' of what, simply put, was 'in the air' at a given point in history – allows us to account for disparities and discontinuities, not only of individual statements, but also with a view to the very different kinds of text which form part of the Miltonic corpus. For this reason, the abstract, relational notion of the concept should not be disregarded, not even in connection with predominantly linguistic-conceptual analysis. In Foucault's delicate conception, discourse is defined by sets of relations that are 'not ... internal to discourse: they do not connect concepts or words with one another ... Yet they are not relations exterior to discourse, relations that might limit it, or impose certain forms upon it ... They are, in a sense, at the limit of discourse.'[189] In this view, discourse leads a precarious existence between context and texture, neither fully here nor there. As a sort of 'regulative idea' for further discussion, it will also be valuable to keep this precarious nature of (sensory) discourse in mind.

As has become clear, the Foucauldian concept of discourse connotes, in several ways at once, the idea of context. On the most basic level, (1) every text functions as 'a node within a network' of texts and should be considered as such. This is the classic notion of '(inter-)texture' referred to above. Then, there is (2) the mutual delineation of discourses, one against the other (e.g., of political theory, theology, literature); in the

---

[187] Foucault, *Archaeology of Knowledge,* 60.
[188] See Foucault, *Archaeology of Knowledge,* 84–5, quotation at 84. The extent of Foucault's supposed 'excision' of the individual from discourse has at times been overstated. In the concluding chapter of his book, he has a fictitious opponent accuse him as follows: 'Like a certain form of linguistics, you have tried to dispense with the speaking subject; you believed that one could cut off from discourse all its anthropological references, and treat it as if it had never been formulated by anyone, as if it had not come about in particular circumstances, as if it were not imbued with representations, as if it were addressed to no one.' Replying, the author concedes all charges but, at the same time, reiterates his earlier point that his concern is with those aspects of discourse his theory adds *above and beyond* the traditional, bringing into view the discursive potential for conflicting actualisations of those preconditioning aspects: 'I wanted not to exclude the problem of the subject, but to define the positions and functions that the subject could occupy in the diversity of discourse' (220).
[189] Foucault, *Archaeology of Knowledge,* 50–1.

early modern setting, this delineation might not always be clear on a material level, but it tends to be clearer in terms of intentionality.[190] And while a text like *Paradise Lost* may be said to align, in equal confidence and awareness, with poetic (and poetological), theological, and political discourses, the *discussion* of one or the other in analysis will also inevitably cast all other possible regards in the function of context. From a consideration of non-discursive reality (phrased by Foucault primarily in terms of power relations) and its implications for the experiential realm follows (3) the contextual relevance (for sensory discourse, too) of historical evidence in the wider sense of what we know about political or social practices; spatial or notional structures; or material culture. Again, however, these are analytical distinctions: a domain such as architecture, for example, might be said to satisfy each or all of those aspects just named, depending on the analytical perspective taken.[191] I adopt all of these contextual considerations, as well as some other aspects of discourse particular to Foucault's use of the term, including his regard for conflicting manifestations of one and the same discourse or his conception of subject positions as 'perceptual situations' (but excluding his strict assumption of the impersonality of discourse), into the notion of sensory discourse.

2.7 Conclusion: Sensory Discourse and Milton

In this chapter, I have started from Milton's notion of discourse, in one particular passage from *Paradise Lost*, as sensuous, potentially directed and epistemogenic language, later complemented with observations on passages from Milton's prose, to add an early modern contemporary notion of 'discourse' as both embodied and abstract, both concrete and metaphorical. I have then surveyed the respective implications of (1) language that is sensory yet not necessarily sensuous, including the question of a possible 'sensory idiom'; (2) linguistic and conceptual metaphors; and (3) a wider/contextual notion of discourse (including the potential of metaphor for contextual reference) for a comprehensive exposition of what 'sensory discourse' might mean. Having then considered, by reference to Foucault's theory of discourse, where the limits of applicability for our concept might lie, we are now in a position to give a full working definition of 'sensory discourse.'

In the first place, this cumulative definition can be seen as the systematic qualification and/or extension of commonplace assumptions about (1) poetic language, (2) metaphor, and (3) discourse, respectively. Thus, sensory language is not merely sensuous; it is 'botanical' as much as it is 'flowery.' By a similar token, metaphor, sensory or oth-

---

[190] See Kevin Sharpe/Steven N. Zwicker, 'Politics of Discourse: Introduction,' in: Sharpe/Zwicker (eds), *Politics of Discourse: The Literature and History of Seventeenth-Century England* (Berkeley, Calif.: University of California Press, 1987), 1–20. Of *Paradise Lost*, for example, Sharpe and Zwicker comment that it was 'written at the nexus of religion and politics; its spiritual language is freighted with political argument' (2).

[191] See Anna Barbara/Anthony Perliss, *Invisible Architecture: Experiencing Places through the Sense of Smell* (Milan: Skira, 2006), and Barry Blesser/Linda-Ruth Salter, *Spaces Speak, Are You Listening? Experiencing Aural Architecture* (Cambridge, Mass.: MIT Press, 2007) as examples of such sensory analyses (with Blesser/Salter more consistently interested in the socio-political implications of their subject than Barbara/Perliss).

2.7 Conclusion: Sensory Discourse and Milton

erwise, is neither just poetical – it is also epistemogenic – nor is it merely linguistic – it is also conceptual, and thus both more common and more fundamental than its poetic use might suggest. I conceive of sensory discourse, finally, as an oblique category, combining elements from the different conceptions outlined above and thus connecting early and later modern conceptions of 'discourse.' Sensory discourse, in particular, has sensory language as one important component, rather than its only one. It cannot, for my present purpose of analysing the sensorium presented in Milton's writings, be reduced to the impersonal and pre-expressive model outlined by Foucault but must, at its most fundamental linguistic level, account for the diverse 'sensory vocabularies' (from different languages and traditions) on which Milton could draw to address or evoke sense perception. The terms derived from these sources and brought into interplay in Milton's texts are the specific building blocks of his sensory discourse, expressing its more abstract, conceptual components. Conversely, sensory discourse cannot be complete without the various beliefs about the senses, the social and material underpinnings – all rather more abstract than that which could simply be collected in a glossary – which together constitute early modern sensory culture.

As the previous discussion has also indicated, the three source domains of sensory discourse (diverse notions of sensory language, metaphor, and discourse) are connected by (4) a shared concern with epistemic matters, as are all operating at the intersection of sense perception, language, and knowledge production. In none of the three cases, however, was this association taken for granted or considered wholly uncontroversial in the seventeenth-century context. The potential and reliability of the senses in knowledge production has always been subject to debate: which of the five senses was 'the sense of knowledge?' Vision? hearing? perhaps even touch? In the case of metaphor, we have seen how the traditional Aristotelian view – metaphor 'teaches and informs,' 'makes us learn something' by putting it before the senses – came under attack in the seventeenth century but was vindicated – on a different level – through conceptual metaphor theory and its suggestion that metaphor in the most fundamental sense operated by linking distinct bodies of knowledge (and drawing, quite frequently, on our knowledge of the human body). The early modern reaction against metaphor emerged, most noticeably, through calls for language reform. However, it has become equally clear that the real efficacy of this development was called into question by the frequent occurrence of (linguistic) metaphor in all kinds of texts, including ostensibly 'sober' ones.[192] In conjunction with the fact that, in seventeenth-century usage, the distinction of metaphorical

---

[192] In an answer worth considering to the question 'whether there has been a decline of metaphor, a reaction against metaphor, a gradual shift from a more concrete to a more abstract mode of thought' in the early modern era, Peter Burke has argued that such a process did indeed occur, and dates it (among Western European elites) to the middle of the seventeenth century; however, he suggests that this 'rise of literal-mindedness' corresponded not so much to an actual *abandonment of metaphor* per se but rather to a 'change in the conception of metaphor, from objective "correspondence" to mere subjective "analogy".' (*Varieties of Cultural History* [Cambridge: Polity, 1997], 180). It does not seem entirely clear, however, that the older, Aristotelian notion of 'teaching through the genus' was inapplicable to a 'merely' analogical approach.

and non-metaphorical uses is often difficult, this results in a situation in which we should assess the relevance of metaphor to (sensory) discourse higher rather than lower.[193]

The notion of discourse itself, finally, relates to knowledge in all three of the variants considered. The early modern understanding of 'discourse' as '(a) directed speech' often entails the aspect of instruction, of an impartation of knowledge. In part, this was due to the more fundamental association of the term with 'discourse of reason.'[194] In Milton specifically, discourse, the 'going to and fro' of inquisitive verbal exchange or discursive reason, is ideally a means to instruction; it may, however, be frustrated, perverted, or not heeded; it may be led astray or into mazes. In the way present-day (conceptual) metaphor theory treats discourse – namely, as the immediate verbal context in which linguistic metaphors are employed, and conceptual metaphors are invoked or developed –, there is also the implication of knowledge production, of discourse as the 'raw material' of metaphorical operation. Ultimately, in the Foucauldian model, discourse preserves, transmits, and generates knowledge – even without the deliberate contribution of individual discoursing subjects.

Possibilities for an analysis drawing on (3) context, variously conceived as linguistic, pre-linguistic, and non-discursive, have been opened up by conceptual metaphor theory and the Foucauldian notion of 'discourse.' This contextual approach allows us to conceive of sensory discourse as a (more or less deliberate, partly conventional) expression of meanings derived from or referring to the experience, evaluation, or functional principles of sense perception. In current understanding of the sensory domain, these last three aspects – the (aesthetic) experience, (moral) evaluation, and (physiological) functioning of the senses – would most likely be associated with more or less clearly demarcated discourses (e.g., the arts; theology or ethics; physiology or cognitive neuroscience). That they cannot be distinguished with any comparable clarity in Milton and his contemporaries is a circumstance particular to the discursive situation of the seventeenth century, and of early modern discourse more generally. With natural philosophers commenting on the aesthetic appeal of their specimens and theologians pointing to the latest anatomical discoveries, there was a distinctly 'shared responsibility' of contributors to sensory discourse.

In the light of these last reflections, it bears emphasising that sensory discourse 'has no home'; not even in physiology. It is a discourse which draws entirely on other dis-

---

[193] See Corns, *Development of Milton's Prose Style*, 43–4. Interestingly, the discourse on blindness (to which I return in Chapter 5 below) is also characterised by an ambiguous contiguity of literal-physiological and metaphoric references to blindness, see Barasch, *Blindness*, 9.

[194] *OED*, 'discourse, n.,' esp. senses 1, 2, and 3a. Just how much 'discourse' as a term really is characteristic of the seventeenth century is also suggested by a simple search using the Google Books Ngram Viewer <https://books.google.com/ngrams> (last accessed 18 June 2021). A search for 'discourse' indicates a 'boom phase' for the term between, roughly, 1580 (around the time of its first introduction) and 1680; the several 'peaks' in the popularity of the term observable during that period double as all-time highs, at about three times the relative incidence compared to the most recent peak in 1998. While this of course cuts across all semantic and pragmatic distinctions of actual usage, it indicates a certain long-term distribution pattern.

2.7 Conclusion: Sensory Discourse and Milton

courses, or, to adapt Foucauldian terminology, it is a purely 'interdiscursive configuration.'[195] As to the analytical potential of such 'configurations,' Foucault suggests that

> in confronting General Grammar, Natural History, and the Analysis of Wealth in the seventeenth and eighteenth centuries, one might wonder what ideas were shared at that time by linguists, naturalists, and economists; ... what implicit postulates they shared despite the diversity of their theories, what general, perhaps unstated principles they obeyed; ... what influence the analysis of language exercised on taxonomy, or what role the idea of an ordered nature played in the theory of wealth; ...[196]

A rather similar interplay of neighbouring (and indeed not-so-neighbouring) discourses may be observed, I have argued, with regard to the senses. As the contemporary discussion of sense perception indicates, sense perception was not consigned, in seventeenth-century England, to the particular attention of one specialist discourse. Rather, and mirroring the narrow/linguistic and the wide/contextual interpretations of 'discourse' outlined in this chapter, 'sensory discourse' is both the linguistic precipitate of such an interplay (in the form of concrete references to the senses in individual instances) and, at the same time, the aggregate totality of notions about the senses setting up the discursive space in which this interplay occurs. As a further element to be considered, the specifically Miltonic notion of 'discourse' as outlined in this chapter – situated, one might say, between the narrowly concrete and the widely contextual –, may be taken as expressive of Milton's own preconception of what discourse was and should be, and thus as a signpost along our way towards 'sensory discourse' in Milton.

The triple requirement I have put to the concept of 'sensory discourse' is that it (1) renders us able to account for sensory themes in both Milton's poetry and prose; that it (2) allows us to analyse relevant passages as part of a shared semantic field, whether they are direct or indirect statements about the senses, explicit ('technical') or implicit ('poetical') instances of sense-related language; and that it (3) permits the establishing of contextual connections to sensory culture in history, which includes extralinguistic aspects. Sensory discourse, then, covers the whole spectrum opened up by earlier approaches to the senses in language, including more recent endeavours in sensory studies, which reveal much of sensory language (as opposed to wider discourse) to be indicative of preconceptions or expressive of historically specific 'senseways', since forgotten. In some respects, this wide implication of sensory discourse is already inherent in the relationship between perception and language. In others, as demonstrated, it is a typical feature of the early modern discursive situation. Sensory discourse, ultimately, is sensory language considered in its wider conceptual and discursive context. This full conception of the term allows us to account for context (via its conceptual/general, abstract side) as well as for the particular (or peculiar) instances of sensory language formulated by Milton the individual author.

---

[195] See Foucault, *Archaeology of Knowledge*, 74–5, 174–82; quotations in the following lines at 74, 177.
[196] Foucault, *Archaeology of Knowledge*, 177.

Part Two: SENSORY DISCOURSE IN MILTON

3. Sensory Discourse in Milton's Latin Elegies (I, V, VII)

Among Milton's earliest poems, the elegy is the dominant form, both by number and by volume, and Latin is the dominant language.[1] Among the contents of the 1645 *Poems*, in fact, Milton's Latin elegies, seven in all, form a section of their own in the independently paginated second half of the volume, headed 'Elegiarum Liber primus.'[2] Several of these poems are marked out specifically as productions of the youthful poet, with his age at the time of their composition given as part of the heading (e.g., for Elegy V, discussed below: 'Elegia quinta, Anno ætatis 20'). As representative productions of Milton's early years, their sensory discourse exhibits a degree of continuity; at the same time, it already establishes certain preoccupations and sensory-discursive patterns which not only correlate the elegies amongst themselves but also re-emerge in Milton's later writings.

The elegies chosen for analysis in this chapter are examples of distinct subsets within the genre, representing the verse letter (Elegy I), love elegy (Elegy VII), and 'an erotic celebration of spring' (Elegy V), respectively.[3] Considering the high importance attributed to generic propriety in early modern literary discourse, however, it seems appropriate to begin with a brief reflection on what this genre of 'elegy' entails.[4] In fact, the elegiac genre has been singled out for its wide historical variety of forms and functions.[5] In classical Greek usage, the term *elegeia* covered almost any poem regardless of content, as long as it was composed in elegiac couplets (i.e., alternating lines of dactylic hexameter and pentameter, a stylistic convention to which Milton's Latin elegies conform). Common themes included love and warfare as well as, already, death and mourning. In classical Latin elegy, with its focus on erotic and satirical subjects, the topic of

---

[1] For a brief characterisation of the elegies in the context of Milton's early poetry see Lewalski, *Life of John Milton*, 16–17. See also Stella P. Revard, *Milton and the Tangles of Neaera's Hair: The Making of the 1645 Poems* (Columbia, Mo.: University of Missouri Press, 1997), 8–43.

[2] *Poems of Mr. John Milton, both English and Latin, Compos'd at several times* ... (London: Ruth Raworth for Humphrey Moseley, 1645), II, 11. Apart from the elegies proper, the 'Liber elegiarum' (11–43) comprises several poems inspired by the 1605 Gunpowder Plot (though not the long 'In Quintum Novembris,' which is in the following 'Sylvarum Liber') as well as by Milton's journey to Italy.

[3] The characterisation of Elegy V is Lewalski's, *Life of John Milton*, 17.

[4] See, with some qualifications, Alastair Fowler, *Kinds of Literature: An Introduction to the Theory of Genres and Modes* (Oxford: Clarendon, 1982), 25–6.

[5] For the following see Karen Weisman, 'Introduction,' in: Karen Weisman (ed.), *The Oxford Handbook of the Elegy* (Oxford: Oxford University Press, 2010), 1–12, and the various contributions on the history of elegiac discourse in the same volume, esp. Nagy, Miller, and Roberts on classical elegy, and Watterson, Braden, and Clymer on developments in early modern England; see also Fowler, *Kinds of Literature*, 136–7, on the the development of the 'historical kinds' of elegy.

death was treated indirectly at best (such as when Ovid, in an influential perspective referenced by Milton, described his experience of banishment as comparable to the experience of death). Whether it was concerned with actual mourning, social critique, frustrated love, or exile: one shared theme of the classical elegiac tradition can be described as 'the framing of loss.'[6] In later understandings of the term and the genre, elegy became restricted to a commemorative and mourning function, aspects still associated with the form today.

That Milton was very much aware of both the history and the presently prevailing version of these generic conventions is evident from his employment of the form. In several of his elegies not discussed here in detail, Milton conforms to the generic conception of elegy as threnody. His Second and Third Elegies, in particular, combine the traditional elegiac form with a more modern idea of what an elegy should be in terms of content.[7] Not very surprisingly, considering their thematic focus on death, the sensory world of these early threnodic elegies is rather restricted; what sensory discourse there is mostly refers to the plaintive quality of the commemorative poem itself, figured as living speech. Thus, in the final couplet of Elegy II, 'In Obitum Praeconis Academici Cantabrigiensis' ('On the Death of the University of Cambridge Beadle,' 1626), the speaker closes with a plea for vocal lamentation: 'Fundat et ipsa modos querebunda Elegëia tristes,/Personet et totis naenia moesta scholis' ('May plaintive Elegy herself pour sorrowful harmonies forth, and may all the schools resound with a song of lamentation,' 23–4).[8] And in Elegy III, 'In Obitum Praesulis Wintoniensis' ('On the Death of the Bishop of Winchester,' 1626), there is an embodying kind of nested or intrathrenody when the speaker announces that 'my voice [lit., 'mouth' or 'speech'], filled with grief, made this [i.e., the following] complaint' ('tristi sic ore querebar,' 15): 'Pitiless Death ... is it not enough ... that the lilies, the crocus and the rose sacred to lovely Cypris [i.e., Aphrodite/Venus] wither at the touch of your putrid breath?'[9] In this olfactory image, the conventional malodorousness of Death, experientially grounded in the stench of putrefaction, is juxtaposed for contrast to the lovely smell of Aphrodite's roses, representing another traditional subject of the elegy: love.[10] Even in the more conven-

---

[6] Weisman, 'Introduction,' 1.
[7] In a Venn diagram of Milton's poems representing '(classical) elegiac form' vs. '(modern) elegiac content,' Elegies II and III would be placed at the intersection of both categories. Other early poems, such as 'On the Death of a Fair Infant Dying of a Cough' (Winter 1625/6) or 'In Obitum Praesulis Eliensis' ('On the Death of the Bishop of Ely,' 1626) clearly have a comparable focus in terms of content but make different choices in terms of the metre and/or language used.
[8] In fact, there seems to be a certain insecurity here as to the speaker's belief in the efficacy of his own song – why else would there be a need to appeal to 'Elegy herself,' Elegy in the abstract? This too might be seen as typical of the genre: 'More than any other literary kind, elegy pushes against the limits of our expressive resources precisely at the very moment in which we confront our mortality, which is as much to say that it throws into relief the inefficacy of language precisely when we need it most. It follows naturally that the limits of poetic utterance have surfaced as recurrent motifs in elegy throughout its history ...' (Weisman, 'Introduction,' 11).
[9] '... afflata tuo marcescant tabo.' Compare/contrast this with the references to Venus and her Cypriot roses in Elegies I and V, discussed below.
[10] Via the Pauline correlation of sin and death (see Rom. 6:23), and in keeping with a general association of physical and moral matters, this metaphor could be applied to new targets: 'Words

tionally grieving of Milton's elegies, then, the 'classical other' of the elegiac genre may be said to show through.

As the following discussion of elegies I, V, and VII will indicate, the impact of that more flexible element of the elegiac tradition on Milton was considerable, and the various uses made of sensory discourse in the respective poems only attest to this.[11]

3.1 Elegy I ('Ad Carolum Diodatum,' April 1626?)
From the Sensuous Temptations of the City to a Sensory Conceptualisation of the Cityscape

In his 'Elegia prima' (April 1626?), written in the form of a verse epistle from the city to the country, and addressed to his friend Charles Diodati, Milton at first contrasts the attractions of London with dreary university life at Cambridge. This contrast is phrased as the contrast between bustling town and deserted country, between (sensorily) rich culture and barren nature. On the whole, then, the poem disappoints any generic expectations of pastoralism – or rather, it subverts them for its own purposes.

After some opening courtesies to Diodati, the elegiac speaker begins his counterintuitive account by contrasting London, 'the delightful place where I was born' ('patria dulcis,' 10), with Cambridgeshire, characterised by its 'bare fields which offer no gentle shades' as being a '[bad] place [for] the worshippers of Phoebus.'[12] The delight of the city, notably, is that it offers access to books, 'books, which are my life [mea vita libri]': 'here I can devote my leisure hours to the mild Muses' (25–6). With a view to the conflicted sensory discourse later in the poem, it is not particularly subtle to detect in this reference another allusion to the sensory sphere: even in their most abstract form on the printed page, each of the nine Muses is always the muse *of something*, and those 'areas of responsibility' are, for the most part, delineated in sensory terms (thus with music, the theatrical arts, astronomy – even Clio's customary attribute is a proclaiming trumpet).

After strenuous studies, then, even the restorative element of city life is not nature but (sensory) culture. In a movement materialising, in a sense, several of the 'mild Muses' at once, the speaker turns spectator and, in particular, auditor: 'When I am tired the pageantry of the rounded theatre [sinuosi pompa theatri] attracts me, and the play's babbling speeches [garrula scena] claim my applause' (27–8) – and this, apparently, is primarily an auditory experience, as the characters on stage are heard declaiming loudly ('auditur,' 29; 'Detonat … barbara verba,' 32) rather than being seen. The roundness of

---

to describe physical decay and putrefaction were commonly deployed when describing the moral degeneration of others. Immoral behaviour and dishonesty could be smelt, metaphorically at least, like physical corruption' (Cockayne, *Hubbub*, 236).

[11] It may be significant that *Lycidas*, written around ten years after the elegies and arguably the most prominent threnody in Milton's oeuvre, is explicitly designated in its headnote as a 'monody,' considered by its author, perhaps, the more narrowly mourning genre, and thus evading any unwanted associations of the elegiac form. See, however, Fowler, *Kinds of Literature*, 162–5, 259, on *Lycidas* and pastoral elegy.

[12] 'Nuda nec arva placent, umbrasque negantia molles,/Quam male Phoebicolis convenit ille locus!' (13–4). The conceit of these lines is sensory: bare fields are exposed to the sun (associated with Phoebus Apollo), but the scholar-poet speaker is more comfortable in the shade, although his pursuits, of course, are also associated with Apollo, only not so much with his capacity as a solar deity.

the early modern theatre, accentuated by Milton's use of *sinuosus* ('curved'), was the key factor in its architectural approach to sound amplification, and is thus directly connected to the highly auditory quality of the theatrical experience described.[13] That some contemporaries at least were aware of these connections is evident from a geometrically tinged remark in Sir Thomas Overbury's character of 'An excellent Actor' (1616): 'Sit in a full Theater, and you will thinke you see so many lines drawn from the circumference of so many eares, whiles the *Actor* is the *Center*.'[14]

A roll call of stock personages from ancient comedy ('a crafty old man', a pompous lawyer, 'some love-struck son' with his 'stern father') closes with 'a young girl who … falls in love without knowing what love is' (35–6). Milton then turns to Tragedy, personified 'with streaming hair and rolling eyes, brandish[ing] her bloody sceptre' (37–8),[15] and, accordingly, associated in reception with vision rather than hearing: 'It makes me sad to watch, yet watch I do, and find a pleasure in the sadness' ('Et dolet, et specto, iuvat et spectasse dolendo,' 39), concluding that 'sometimes there is a sweet bitterness even in weeping' (40).[16] It is, after all, the *'pageantry'* ('pompa,' 27, my emphasis) of the theatre which first attracts its *audience* – the combined appeal of the stage is clearly audio-visual.

The scene then changes and the speaker – somewhat surprisingly, considering his initial celebration of city life – admits to a certain attraction to the countryside, after all: 'Sed neque sub tecto semper nec in urbe latemus,/Irrita nec nobis tempora veris eunt' ('I do not always hide myself away indoors, or stay in the city: the spring does not pass by me unnoticed,' 47–8). It is in spring that nature works her sensory charms: a conventional theme prominently taken up in 'Elegia Quinta' and 'Song. On May Morning.' This apparent incursion of conventional nature-worship is partly undermined, however, by a return to the 'gentle shades' introduced early on in the poem: 'A dense elm grove nearby, and a magnificently shady spot just outside the city [suburbani … loci] are my haunts.'[17] It is at this point that the dominant theme of the remaining forty-two verses (almost half the poem) is introduced:

---

[13] See Andrew Gurr, 'Why Was the Globe Round?,' in: Idem, *Shakespeare's Workplace: Essays on Shakespearean Theatre* (Cambridge: Cambridge University Press, 2017), 167–180, and Smith, *Acoustic World of Early Modern England*, 206–245. That London theatres of the time actually strove to present a multi-sensory experience is suggested by the analyses in Hristomir A. Stanev, *Sensory Experience and the Metropolis on the Jacobean Stage (1603–1625)* (Farnham: Ashgate, 2014).
[14] Overbury quoted in Smith, *Acoustic World of Early Modern England*, 206. Consider also Milton's characterisation of the Edenic landscape (and sensescape) as 'a woody theatre/Of stateliest view' (*PL* 4.139–40). The circle or sphere, at the same time, is the 'natural' form of the sensescape, whether in Milton's epic or in the multi-sensory indoor setting of the earlier Elegy VI.
[15] Actually, Tragedy 'spins around her face' or 'mouth' ('ora rotat,' a poetic plural), but the focus still shifts away from sound at this point.
[16] 'Interdum et lacrymis dulcis amaror inest.' In the association of sweetness and bitterness (in relation to love), Carey detects a Catullian echo. Milton's following example ('as when some poor lad leaves joys untasted [indelibata] and dies', 41–2) makes the association with love explicit.
[17] 'Nos quoque lucus habet vicina consitus ulmo/Atque suburbani nobilis umbra loci' (49–50). Elms are a conventional element in pastoral poetry, noted for the deepness of their shade, and hence associated ambiguously with both idyllic nature and impending death. In the particular context of the lines immediately following, a reference to the traditional 'elm-and-vine' motif of

3.1 Elegy I ('Ad Carolum Diodatum,' April 1626?)

Saepius hic blandas spirantia sidera flammas
Virgineos videas praeteriisse choros.
Ah quoties dignae stupui miracula formae
Quae possit senium vel reparare Iovis;
Ah quoties vidi superantia lumina gemmas,
Atque faces quotquot volvit uterque polus; (51–56)

[Here you can often see parties of young girls walking by – stars which breathe forth seductive flames. Ah, how often have I been struck dumb by the miraculous shapeliness of a figure which might well make even old Jove young again! Ah, how often have I seen eyes brighter than jewels, brighter than all the stars which wheel round both the poles; …]

It is no coincidence that, after the various roles or actors described in the passage about the theatre, these girls are the second kind of human beings the speaker encounters: they, too, appear to exist (mainly?) to be looked at. More particularly, their beauty lies in the eye of the testifying beholder ('vidi') and the addressee ('videas') as much as in their own eyes ('lumina,' lit. 'lights'), which are singled out as the primary element of their attractiveness, and are compared to jewels and stars, both conventionally associated with light and vision.[18] Milton's further description also runs along established, Petrarchan lines: thus, he lists 'necks' whiter than the Milky Way, 'a forehead of exceptional loveliness, light-blown hair – a golden net spread by deceitful Cupid, and enticing cheeks beside which the flush of the hyacinth, and even the blushing red of your flower, Adonis, seem dull' (57–62).

Early in the poem, there had only been abstract, mythological figures: Phoebus and the Muses – as mediated, it seems reasonable to assume, through the books the speaker loves so much. Then, his attention had turned to actors – real humans, but portraying certain types, and only feigning to be, for example, a 'young girl' falling in love.[19] In the figure of the 'young girls walking by,' finally, the association of youth (contrasted with 'old Jove'), nature (and spring as nature's youth), romantic/erotic love[20] and sensory, above all visual appeal is epitomised and vitalised. Even if these girls, too, are described largely in stock phrases, for the purposes of the speaker, reducing them to objects of his appreciative regard, they *are* what they are perceived to be; and their prima-

---

(male/female) romantic love and marriage may also be intended (compare *PL* 5.215–9: '… or they [i. e., Adam and Eve] led the vine/To wed her elm; she, spoused about him twines/Her marriageable arms, and with him brings/Her dower, the adopted clusters, to adorn/His barren leaves.'

[18] Both of these images are repeatedly taken up in book 3 of *Paradise Lost*.

[19] It is worth pointing out that, in the late 1620s, the actors described in lines 29–36 would still have been exclusively male, even the one playing the last (and only female) role listed, the 'young girl' falling in love (Milton here uses *virgo*, the same term he later uses to refer to the British girls as 'virginibus … Britannis').

[20] Conceptually, I consider these alternatives as essentially equivalent, denoting different emphases, perhaps, within one conception of love opposed to another of love as charity – in the sense, that is, of *erōs* as opposed to *agapê*.

ry, concrete beauty in that sense is naturalised – and hence prioritised – vis-à-vis the abstract or secondary realms of the Muses and the theatre.

To such beauty, the speaker concludes, must yield not only all the heroines praised in antiquity; Persian princesses and other, more ordinary inhabitants of different cities and countries are also called upon to surrender:

> Cedite laudatae toties Heroides olim,
> Et quaecunque vagum cepit amica Iovem.
> Cedite Achaemeniae turrita fronte puellae,
> Et quot Susa colunt, Memnoniamque Ninon.
> Vos etiam Danaae fasces submittite Nymphae,
> Et vos Iliacae, Romuleaeque nurus.
> Nec Pompeianas Tarpeia Musa columnas
> Iactet, et Ausoniis plena theatra stolis. (63–70)

> [Admit defeat, you heroines so often praised: admit defeat, all you girls who have caught the eye of inconstant Jove. Admit defeat, you Achaemenian girls in your turreted hats, and you who live in Susa and Memnonian Niniveh. Surrender, you maidens of Greece and of Troy and of Rome. Let the Tarpeian Muse stop boasting about Pompey's colonnade, or about theatres crowded with the matrons of Italy.]

While Milton's choice of examples (cities of the ancient Near East) and detail (turreted hats) might at first seem curious, the passage as a whole refers back to themes already introduced – and links them to the further development of the poem's overarching theme. Most obviously, Milton's reference to the theatres of Italy and the Portico of Pompey – part of the great Theatre of Pompey, Rome's first permanent theatre – pick up on the poem's earlier preoccupation with spectatorship and the theatre; only it is now 'the matrons of Italy' crowding the theatres to watch.[21] Secondly, all of the individual cities named are united by the fact that they were famously conquered, looted, and/or razed, from the fall of Troy to the multiple sacks of Rome. This martial aspect of Milton's imaginary beauty contest is stressed not only by the repeated calls to 'admit defeat' ('cedite,' 65) and 'surrender' ('fasces submittite,' 67) but also by the distinctive headdress worn by the girls of the Achaemenids, named by Herodotus as the royal clan of the Persians: 'Admit defeat, you Achaemenian girls in your turreted hats' ('Achaemeniae turrita fronte puellae,' 65).[22] This detail is of more than merely antiquarian in-

---

[21] 'Ausoniis plena theatra stolis' (70), where the (married) women are identified metonymically by the garment they wear, the *stola*. Probably, the fact that they are married ('matrons,' in Carey's translation) should not, in itself, be taken to mean that they are less beautiful; see the repeated references to Eve as a 'matron' in *Paradise Lost*. As for women's attendance in the theatre, Carey points out that Ovid (the 'Tarpeian Muse' of line 69) in his *Ars Amatoria* specifically recommends the Portico and Theatre of Pompey as places to meet girls.

[22] Milton's 'turrita fronte,' literally, refers to the girls' 'turreted forehead.' In itself, this might also be taken to indicate a (natural or artificially augmented) high forehead, a common Renaissance ideal of beauty (see Victoria Sherrow, *Encyclopedia of Hair: A Cultural History* [Westport, Conn.: Greenwood Press, 2006], 329, on the common method of plucking or shaving eyebrows and

terest: in playfully suggesting that even their 'bastioned' headgear did not prevent them being 'conquered' by the more beautiful girls of Britain, Milton gives the conventional association of love and conquest (LOVE IS CONQUEST) a novel and concrete expression: the princesses with their tower-like hats appear as fortifications to be conquered. The third domain on which this union of the two concepts hinges is the visual sphere: the Persian girls with their conspicuous, turreted heads have to concede victory to the British girls with their lovely eyes.

That this visual subtext is indeed what motivates the whole passage, and connects it to the earlier treatment of both the spectacular theatre (with its feigned lovers) and the good-looking 'parties of young girls' (where, actually, Milton's 'virgineos ... *choros*' makes the theatrical connection explicit), is indicated by its conclusion and sequel:

> Gloria virginibus debetur prima Britannis,
> Extera sat tibi sit foemina posse sequi.
> Tuque urbs Dardaniis Londinum structa colonis
> Turrigerum late conspicienda caput,
> Tu nimium felix intra tua moenia claudis
> Quicquid formosi pendulus orbis habet. (71–75)

[The first prize goes to the British girls: be content, foreign woman, to take second place! And you, London, a city built by Trojan settlers, a city whose towery head can be seen for miles, you are more than fortunate for you enclose within your walls whatever beauty there is to be found in all this pendent world.]

After the dismissive enumeration of less-beautiful contenders that had come before, the concluding adjudication of 'gloria,' with its possible suggestion of a (visually) blazing glory,[23] provides the logical consummation of the earlier escalating comparison of girls' eyes first to jewels, then to stars. In addressing the personification of London with its 'towery head,' Milton reverses the earlier trope of 'turreted hats,' which had given the Persian princesses an architectural aspect and, seen collectively, the appearance of a miniature city. Again, there is an association here with visibility: London is an 'urbs ... late conspicienda,' a city that can be seen from afar on account of its high-rising battlements.[24] London as a city – traditionally figured as feminine – is a sight to behold;[25] its

---

'excess' scalp hair). As Carey's note ad loc. indicates, however, the main reference appears to be to a specific kind of ancient Persian royal headgear.

[23] Not necessarily according to its Latin sense of 'fame' (see *OLD*, 'gloria') but certainly in conjunction with the derivative 'glory' (see *OED*, 'glory, n.,' 5–7, 9).

[24] See also the discussion of this passage in Dobranski, *Milton's Visual Imagination*, 78 (in the context of Dobranski's discussion of fortification imagery in *Paradise Lost*). On the fortifications of London before and during the Civil War, and their relevance to early modern literature, see Adam N. McKeown, *Fortification and Its Discontents from Shakespeare to Milton: Trouble in the Walled City* (New York: Routledge, 2019).

[25] In the Latin context, this may be traced to the grammatical gender of *urbs* and *civitas*; in the Near Eastern context, to the common personification of cities as female in relation to their (male)

walls enclose the visible beauty of British girls; the reference to 'this pendent world' refers it all back to the cosmological scale and astronomical vision (echoing the earlier references to stars and the Milky Way).[26] Taken as a whole, Milton's association of girls, towers, and cities rests on the strong visual impact they all make. In its particular early modern setting, this association between the beauty of the conspicuous townscape and the beauty of the female human form is perhaps more obvious than it would seem from today's perspective. As Keith Thomas points out with regard to the 'visual pleasures of the townscape,' and the aesthetic status of urban fortifications in particular, 'for centuries town walls had symbolised security and human achievement; and to the traveller their sight was always reassuring.'[27] As a consequence, the high walls and towers of the fortified city are ornaments in their own right.[28]

Ultimately, then, both the image of the tower-like hats and that of the head-like towers, rest on the conceptual metaphor HEIGHT IS VISIBILITY, and both include an element of 'highness' as not just constitutive of beauty but also indicative of (social) rank:[29] the 'Achaemenian girls' are princesses, and London is the pre-eminent city of Britain. At the same time, (watch-)towers, in general, express the concept of VISION IS HEIGHT or VISION IS UP; this two-sided metaphor, which will recur frequently below, presupposes an ideal visual relation where seeing is, by the same token, being seen. While 'being seen,' in this concrete instance, refers to the aesthetic quality of the fortified townscape, the 'seeing' is connected to its primary, military purpose. In Milton's sensory imagery, however, the two aspects, and even the poem's more extensive preoccupation with female beauty, are fused: the superiority of London, 'a city built by Trojan settlers' (and

---

patron deity. See Christl Maier, *Daughter Zion, Mother Zion: Gender, Space, and the Sacred in Ancient Israel* (Minneapolis, Minn.: Fortress Press, 2008), esp. 61–73.

[26] Carey's translation 'this pendent world' – although of course quite literal – is echoing *PL* 2.1046–53, where Satan is 'at leisure to behold/Far off the empyreal heaven, extended wide/In circuit, undetermined square or round,/With opal towers and battlements adorned/Of living sapphire, once his native seat;/And, fast by, hanging in a golden chain,/*This pendent world*, in bigness as a star/Of smallest magnitude close by the moon' (emphasis added). The image of the golden chain is of Homeric origin, see Fowler ad loc. Fowler argues that Milton's 'undetermined square or round' means 'too wide to be obviously rectilinear or curved,' but a reference to the Heavenly Jerusalem/Zion may also be intended ('the city lieth foursquare, and the length is as large as the breadth,' according to Rev. 21:16; its heavy fortifications – built of jasper, sapphire, emerald, thus matching Milton's description of the walls of heaven – are described in 17–21).

[27] Thomas, *Man and the Natural World*, 243–4.

[28] The pervasive imagery of walls and towers may also have motivated Milton's reference to Ovid as 'the Tarpeian Muse' ('Tarpeia Musa,' 69), indicating the poet's place of residence within Rome, close to the Tarpeian Rock; see Carey ad loc.

[29] See the note by Carey ad loc.: 'The *tiara* or felt headdress of the Persians assumed different shapes according to the rank of the wearer: only royalty could wear it upright ..., in which case it became a high, sharp-pointed cap.' Citing *OED* 'tower, n.,' 6b, Carey further argues that Milton's '*turrita* suggests that he associated this with the high headdress worn by women in the seventeenth century.' However (and despite its earliest reference dating from c. 1612) the *OED* itself ascribes this vogue to 'the reigns of William III and Anne'; in a 1693 quotation also given, Dryden declares that it 'was an Ancient way amongst the Romans.' In my view, Milton appears more interested in the literalisation of the 'turreted' headgear as comparable to urban fortifications.

thus the enduring successor to another town famously destroyed), rests on the 'towery head' of its fortifications (including *the* Tower), just as the insuperable beauty of the *virgines Britannae* rest in their eyes. Both aspects, active military vision and passive aestheticising visibility, come under the rubric of early modern sensory discourse, and both may be referred to distinct preoccupations of the classical elegiac tradition: love and warfare, combined here into 'love as warfare' (or LOVE IS CONQUEST).

In the passage which immediately follows, the poem first 'zooms out' into the universe, then 'zooms in' on London:

> Non tibi tot caelo scintillant astra sereno
> Endymioneae turba ministra deae,
> Quot tibi conspicuae formaque auroque puellae
> Per medias radiant turba videnda vias (77–80)

> [The stars which spangle the calm sky above you – those hosts of handmaidens who wait on Endymion's goddess <i.e., Selene, the moon> – are fewer in number than the host which can be seen all a-glitter in your streets: girls whose good looks and golden trinkets catch the eye.]

As before, the poem draws a parallel between girls and the (technically) inanimate sphere: first, the point of reference was the city, now it is the cosmos; both are animated in order to render the association plausible: London was personified, and space, in the lines quoted, is populated with notionally female, mythological figures, themselves personifications of the stars and the moon. The latter, the speaker holds, cannot compare in number with the actual (not just notional) beauties crowding the streets of London; that they may even be more resplendent in a qualitative sense is at least suggested by the fact that they are 'conspicuae formaque auroque' – 'conspicuous through good looks and through gold,' a metal traditionally associated with the sun (as opposed to the moon's silver).[30] This is matched by their positively, actively 'beaming' with beauty ('radiant'), rather than, perhaps, just reflecting it.

In the final section of the poem, the speaker refers loveliness back to love, reporting that 'there is a story that kindly Venus came to this city, drawn by her twin doves and escorted by her quivered soldiery [pharetrigero milite cincta], ... destined to prefer it to Cnidos ... and to Paphos and rosy Cyprus' (81–4). Again, the approach of love is figured in military terms (since LOVE IS CONQUEST) and, again, there are sensory elements to consider. First, there is the reference to 'rosy Cyprus' (associated with Aphrodite/Venus on account of her important sanctuary at Paphos, Cyprus), evoking the sensuous, fragrant symbol of love, the rose. Then, however, in its concluding lines, the elegy takes an anti-sensuous turn – at least ostensibly –, and comes back to its academic point of departure by way of a renunciation, even rejection of all things sensuous, which are now figured as bewitching and hence dangerous:

---

[30] It is worth noting that, in the present passage, there is no trace of a 'Puritan' attack on jewellery, or on excessive attention to outer appearance more generally. Carey's (golden) 'trinkets' is an extrapolation of 'auroque' and should not be taken as deprecative.

> Ast ego, dum pueri sinit indulgentia caeci,
> Moenia quam subito linquere fausta paro;
> Et vitare procul malefidae infamia Circes
> Atria, divini Molyos usus ope.
> Stat quoque iuncosas Cami remeare paludes
> Atque iterum raucae murmur adire Scholae.
> Interea fidi parvum cape munus amici,
> Paucaque in alternos verba coacta modos. (85–92)

[But for my part I intend to quit this fortunate town as quickly as possible, while the blind boy's indulgence permits, and, with the help of divine moly, to leave far behind the infamous halls of faithless Circe. I am to return to the Cam's reedy marshes and face the uproar of the noisy University again. Meanwhile accept this little gift from a loyal friend – one or two words forced into elegiac metre.]

In this concluding passage, the earlier reference to the goddess of love and her escort – 'there is a story that kindly Venus came to this city ...' – is actualised as either an established or a directly imminent reality: 'the blind boy' (i.e., Cupid, her son, conventionally portrayed as a blindfolded archer) is imagined by the speaker to be present and about to strike.[31] While this image might appear playful rather than antisensuous, the next one, drawn from the *Odyssey*, clearly casts doubt over the earlier portrayal of female beauty: in his references to 'faithless Circe' and 'divine moly' (the potion used by Odysseus to ward off Circe's charms), Milton's elegiac alter ego figures himself as Odysseus narrowly escaping the dangers of sensuous bewitchment. Retrospectively, the 'seductive flames' ('blandas ... flammas,' 51) of the British girls appear in an altogether different light. So often they had 'struck [the speaker] dumb by the *miraculous* shapeliness of [their] figure' ('dignae stupui miracula formae,' 53, emphasis added), just as Circe had struck dumb Odysseus's companions by turning them into swine. Through Milton's retroactive introduction of the Circe motif, the girls' figures, indeed, are revealed as ambiguous, oscillating between innocent, aesthetic charm and nocent, seductive sorcery. The earlier association of vision, good looks, and military lookouts – grounded in the conceptual metaphor that LOVE IS CONQUEST – had already prepared this somewhat misogynistic presentation of erotic attraction as threatening and potentially dangerous.

The same final passage, however, is also riddled with significant contradiction, some of it traditional (as in the image of Cupid, the blind archer), some of it germane to the

---

[31] Milton would return to (and refashion) the image of Eros as an archer in Elegy V as well as in an extended passage of *The Doctrine and Discipline of Divorce* (1643/44); see CPW 2: 255–6. On the interpretation of Cupid's blindfold as indicating a tendentially contradictory 'combination or fusion of supernatural power and sinfulness,' see Barasch, *Blindness*, 129–30. The idea that the arrows of blind Cupid (and hence love) entered through the eyes was conventional, see for instance the account given by the French physician André du Laurens in his *Discourse of the Preservation of Sight ...* (tr. 1599), quoted in Jackie Watson, '"Dove-Like Looks" and "Serpents Eyes": Staging Visual Clues and Early Modern Aspiration,' in: *The Senses in Early Modern England*, eds Smith et al., 39–54, at 42.

speaking situation of Milton's elegiac persona. When the speaker declares his intention to retreat from the city after all in the face of advancing Venus, this is expressed in paradoxical terms: he suddenly is to leave London's 'moenia ... fausta' – walls happy because they enclose, as explained before, hosts of beautiful girls. The destination of his flight, Cambridge and its university, had earlier been characterised by reference to the country, the 'barren fields' surrounding the city and the student's abandoned rooms, from which he had been 'exiled' (13, 17, 20).[32] The 'uproar of the noisy University' now referred to belies expectations, attributing to a place of scholarly retirement the defining marks of the city soundscape.[33] Conversely, we may note the fuzzy quality of the intermediate realm in which the speaker actually encounters the London girls ('suburbani ... loci,' 'just outside the city,' 50) – neither here nor there, enticing with its pastoral haunts yet clearly associated with the big city. Taken together, this equivocal account raises the question of how (or whether) to reconcile the conflicting elements and, above all, the elegy's conflicting valuations of the British girls as, on the one hand, 'conquering' their imagined female competitors but, by the same token, threatening the speaker with their potentially harmful sensuality.[34]

Ultimately, and befitting the playfulness of Milton's tone, evident in his direct addresses to Charles Diodati, the conflict between these elements remains unresolved. Whether the passage about the speaker's flight from the approaching troops of Venus and his reliance on 'divine moly' as an antidote to female bewitchment is read as 'just' a humorous poetic conceit, included for the sake of ingenuity; or, in conjunction with his earlier professed love of books and study, as an ironic statement about the relative (de-)merits of sensuous enjoyment and ascetic studiousness;[35] or as both at once: at the end of the elegy it is clear that sensuous delights, represented by the theatrical attractions and visual beauty discussed for the greater, central part of the poem, are not without their ascetic (or dreary) alternatives – and, possibly, not without their dangers. The poem as a whole – though it may proceed playfully – serves to confront and thus, in the end, to mutually complicate, conflicting notions about the role of the senses – and of vision, in particular – in erotic relationships.[36]

---

[32] On this point, there has been some scholarly disagreement. Carey argues that 'Milton's "exile" is probably merely the university vacation' (*SP*, 19), whereas others have connected these references to Milton's alleged 'rustication' (i. e., temporary expulsion) from university in the spring of 1626. For this biographical aspect of the poem, not discussed here, see Lewalski, *Life of John Milton*, 20–22, and R. W. Condee, 'Ovid's Exile and Milton's Rustication,' *PQ* 37 (1958), 498–502.
[33] Contrast the sombre atmosphere of 'the studious cloister's pale' in *Il Penseroso* (154). On city noise generally, see Cockayne, *Hubbub*.
[34] This certainly would bear out Weisman's observation that qua its generic heritage, 'elegy inhabits a world of contradiction' ('Introduction,' 1).
[35] As Paul Allen Miller has remarked of Latin love elegy, its approach is 'ironic, darkly comic, ... self-conscious,' a tone which Milton appears to be imitating ('"What's Love Got to Do With It?": The Peculiar Story of Elegy in Rome,' in: *The Oxford Handbook of Elegy*, ed. Weisman, 46–66, at 46).
[36] Again, Milton's repeated references to Ovid, as well as wider elegiac-generic considerations, might offer clues regarding an inventive treatment of (erotic) love as the poem's intended theme.

3.2 Elegy V ('In Adventum Veris,' Spring 1629)
Multi-Sensory Perception and (Cyclical) Time – From Pleasing Shade to Looming Shadow

The theme of spring, Milton's editor John Carey notes à propos Elegy V, 'In Adventum Veris' ('On the Coming of Spring,' 1629), 'is a very common one among neo-Latin poets of the Renaissance.'[37] Accordingly, and on account of genre, one might expect from Milton's take on subject the kind of pastoral-sensory discourse that Elegy I so studiously subverts, or at least a sensuous celebration of springtime along the lines of the much shorter, ten-verse 'Song. On May Morning' (1629?). At the multi-sensory opening of this plausibly contemporaneous poem,

> ... the bright morning Star, Day's harbinger
> Comes dancing from the east, and leads with her
> The flowery May, who from her green lap throws
> The yellow cowslip, and the pale primrose. (1–4)

As a result, 'mirth and youth and warm desire' are kindled (6) and, ultimately, the poem is itself integrated into the vernal scene as an (audible) effect of the coming of spring, in an instance of the embodied kind of sensory discourse: 'Thus we salute thee with our early song/And welcome thee, and wish thee long' (9–10).

In Milton's elegy on the same theme, indeed, several aspects of the simpler, shorter lyric are also manifest: the association of spring and daybreak/sunrise (including the ambiguously 'early song': early in the day *and* the year); references to flowers as a kind of shorthand for the multi-sensory (visual and olfactory) aesthetic appeal of nature; even the conclusions of both poems exhibit certain similarities, as will become clear.[38] However, this brief inspection of the short lyric can only be a prelude to the elegy, in which those same and further sensory themes are developed at much greater length, and to a considerably higher degree of complexity.

Elegy V can be roughly divided into three parts: an opening section, in which the inspirational powers of spring are evoked (and invoked); a central section, in which this inspiration is 'acted out' through the depiction of succeeding mythological and pastoral scenes; and a short, tense conclusion, in which the speaker returns to the 'normal' lifeworld he shares with his audience. The diverse 'visionary' scenes of the poem's midsection are arranged, in turn, around *their* centrepiece, a detailed depiction of 'Tellus rediviva' (55), the reviving earth personified and longing for the embraces of returning Phoebus, the sun. This central passage, I argue, which alone accounts for roughly a third of the total line count, is the representational as well as the conceptual pivot of the whole poem.

---

[37] *SP*, 83, with several examples, most of them from Italy. *Variorum* I, 97–111 lists the elegy's numerous parallels with classical Latin poetry. A notable exception from the conventional association of nature in spring and multi-sensory perception may be found in Milton's Elegy VI with its multi-sensory indoor setting.

[38] In fact, Carey's tentative dating of the 'Song' to the spring of 1629 actually rests on (unspecified) 'similarities with *Elegia V*' (*SP*, 93).

3.2 Elegy V ('In Adventum Veris,' Spring 1629)

* * *

The elegy opens by establishing, quite literally, the time and place in which the following account is set. Both entities are personified, with the latter, Tellus (the Earth), doubling as the central female figure and, arguably, the general protagonist of the poem. Immediately afterwards, Milton's poet-speaker alter ego introduces himself by reference to the springtime inspiration which, he implies, made possible the composition of the elegy in the first place:

> In se perpetuo Tempus revolubile gyro
> Iam revocat zephyros vere tepente novos.
> Induiturque brevem Tellus reparata iuventam,
> Iamque soluta gelu dulce virescit humus.
> Fallor? an et nobis redeunt in carmina vires,
> Ingeniumque mihi munere veris adest?
> Munere veris adest, iterumque vigescit ab illo
> (Quis putet) atque aliquod iam sibi poscit opus.
>
> (1–8)

[Time, turning back upon his own tracks in a never-ending circuit, is now calling the fresh zephyrs once again as the spring grows warm. The Earth has recovered and is decking herself in her brief youth, and now that the frost has melted away the ground is growing pleasantly green. Am I imagining things, or are my powers of song coming back as well? Is inspiration here again as a gift from the spring? It *is* here again as a gift from the spring! From the spring it gains vigour again (who would have thought it?) and already it is clamouring for something to do.]

Between the allure of lush vegetation and the blowing of warm winds, the sensuous (visual and tactile) references of the passage, as well as their association with spring, are conventional.[39] The primary, gustatory meaning of 'dulce' ('sweetly'), however, as well as the *figura (pseud-)etymologica*[40] and multiple resonances in the quadruple relation of 'virescit ... vires .. veris ... vigescit,' lend the passage a thick sensory texture. The latter figure of speech, in particular, is noteworthy in that it immediately connects the sensory discourse of the poet-speaker (as vocal song: the 'vires' in question are 'in carmina vires') to the sensory discourse of the poem on a descriptive and, more particularly, on a depictive level (in its evocation of the visual impact of spring returning). It can also be

---

[39] On green as the colour not just of nature in general but of spring in particular, see Michel Pastoureau, *Green: The History of a Color*, tr. Jody Gladding (Princeton, N. J.: Princeton University Press, 2014 [2013]), 65–70.

[40] See *OLD*, 'uirescō' ('to begin to bear green growth'), not related to 'uīrescō' ('to regain strength'). If the latter is accepted as a (rarely attested) verb of its own, the scansion of Milton's line 4 makes it clear that the former meaning must be assumed (short first vowel in 'virescit'). Considered non-metrically, the wording of the passage implies an ambiguity: earth is turning green, but it is also regaining strength.

contrasted, in its consistent reliance on high-pitched and thus 'light, warm, dry' vowels, with the deep – and, conversely, 'dark, cold, damp' – sonority of 'soluta gelu dulce ... humus' (i.e., 'the soil, freed from ice, sweetly ...').[41] These lines, then, attempt the re-enactment of a particular kind of sense perception through language; they are 're-creative' in a literal sense.

From this 're-creation' of an experience familiar to most, the poem then turns to a more creative application of sensory discourse by ringing changes on the idea of poetic vision. In doing so, Milton draws on traditional images of inspiration, evoking another kind of 'spring': 'The Castalian fountain and the forked peak swim before my eyes, and at night my dreams bring Pirene to me' (9–10), where the references are to legendary fountains at Delphi and Corinth, as well as to Mount Parnassus, all three of them sacred to the Muses. Both waking and dreaming, the inspiring springs are before the speaker's eyes ('ante oculos'), and inspire him to compose the following lines.[42] His inspiration is not purely visual, however: 'Et furor, et sonitus me sacer intus agit' ('... I am driven on by poetic frenzy and the sacred sound which fills my brain,' 12). The poet-speaker's actual, vocal song, it seems, is first conceived as abstract, imaginary sound.

All of these sensory stimuli, however, constitute only a 'build-up' to the actual theophany, which occurs in lines 13–14, as none other than Phoebus Apollo himself approaches the speaker: 'Delius ipse venit, video Peneide lauro/Implicitos crines, Delius ipse venit' ('Apollo himself is coming – I can see his hair wreathed in Penean laurel – Apollo himself is coming'). The relevance to the elegy of Apollo, Greek god of (sun-)light, lyric poetry, and spring, is immediately clear. That he is also the classical deity associated with archery will become relevant in subsequent passages of the poem.[43] Structurally, the couplet is centred on the vision of laurel, an attribute of Apollo traced here, significantly, to his love of Daphne, daughter of Peneus, and, at the same time, a symbol of fame to the aspiring poet. This laurel, however, is not mentioned in the abstract but implies a (partial) vision of the deity himself *in the present*, announced in the grammatically fundamental 'video ... crines.' It is the laurel that is central structurally, but it is the god's laurelled hair which serves as the object of the speaker's vi-

---

[41] Research into the psychology of perception indicates that certain ideas or concepts are associated with vowel pitch in ways that are constant across cultures. One example of this is the 'bouba–kiki effect': asked which of two shapes presented (one pointed, one rounded) is 'bouba' and which is 'kiki,' the vast majority of subjects tested agreed that 'kiki' must be the the jagged, 'bouba,' the rounded figure; see V. S. Ramachandran/Edward M. Hubbard, 'The Emergence of the Human Mind: Some Clues from Synesthesia,' in: *Synesthesia*, eds Robertson/Sagiv, 147–190, at 171–2; see also Marks, *Unity of the Senses*, 75–83, esp. 76–8. On the triple quality of vowel sound as the result of a physical act, as sensory experience, and as an act of communication, as well as on early modern knowledge of the physiology of sound production, see Smith, *Acoustic World of Early Modern England*, 3–29, esp. 4–6 on vowel pitch.

[42] Compare a similar passage, referencing both Parnassus and the Castalian spring, in Elegy IV (1626), 29–32. As a mountain alone, Parnassus should be seen in conjunction with the mountain imagery occurring further on in Elegy V, as well as with the various 'mounts of vision' in *Paradise Lost* and *Paradise Regained* (as well as with their imitations or parodic uses by Satan).

[43] See M. C. Howatson (ed.), *The Oxford Companion to Classical Literature*, 2nd ed. [Oxford: Oxford University Press, 1989], 43–44. His epithet 'Phoebus,' related to *phōs*, 'light,' means 'the bright one' or 'the shining one.'

sion and his visionary exclamation. In a literalising reading of the couplet – in which Phoebus figures as the sun –, the couplet stages the sunrise, perhaps over a wooded ridge or seen through the fresh spring foliage: Milton's identification of sunbeams with Phoebus' hair is conventional (compare the subsequent occurrence of the same trope in line 86), and it may here be said to be laurelled in the sense that it touches or suffuses green leaves. In the early passages of the poem, then, the setting is a spring morning.

In its mythological sense, however, the ecstatic circularity of the couplet, in combination with the fragmented vision of the approaching deity, indicates the forceful, overwhelming quality of the visionary experience; this is established – or rather: approximated – as either not quite, or more than just, visual. Although the lines *are* emphatically visual, after all, their representational impulse reaches beyond the sphere of vision in a narrowly bodily sense. By this I do not mean that they depict a deity, and hence something categorically indepictable: Milton shows no such qualms in his later depiction of Tellus, and representations of Apollo as an athletic young archer were common and highly conventionalised. Rather, it appears to be a momentary insufficiency of physical vision itself that is the focus of these lines: *this* deity, in *this* situation, is only to be glimpsed. This, again, has its literal, naturalistic connotation, in that the (sudden appearance of the rising) sun may also dazzle the eyes into temporary blindness – an idea familiar from the tradition of visual discourse surrounding the Judaeo-Christian deity.[44] Phoebus, then, is both: Apollo and the sun, and a glimpse of the latter in spring may cause in the poet the onset of an inspiration traditionally associated with the former.

As the result of this outburst of poetic fervour, the main part of the poem opens with the speaker affirming, once more, his competence to visualise, verbalise, and vocalise the scenes he is about to portray:

> Intuiturque animus toto quid agatur Olympo,
> Nec fugiunt oculos Tartara caeca meos.
> Quid tam grande sonat distento spiritus ore?
> Quid parit haec rabies, quid sacer iste furor?
> Ver mihi, quod dedit ingenium, cantibitur illo;
> Profuerint isto reddita dona modo.   (19–22)

[I see in my mind's eye what is going on all over Olympus, and the unseen <lit., blind> depths of Tartarus do not escape my eyes.[45] What song is my spirit singing so loudly with wide-open mouth? What is being born of this madness, this sacred frenzy? The spring, which gave me inspiration, shall be the theme of the song it inspires: in this way her gifts will be repaid with interest.]

---

[44] See Avrahami, *Senses of Scripture*, 256. At *PL* 3.375–82, the Father is addressed as the 'fountain of light, thyself invisible/Amidst the glorious brightness where thou sitst/Throned inaccessible ... Dark with excessive bright thy skirts appear ...'; see Fowler's note ad loc. for possible influences from earlier poetry and theology.
[45] Compare the invocation to the Spirit at *PL* 1.27–8: 'Say first, for heaven hides nothing from thy view/Nor the deep tract of hell ...'

The poet-speaker's song is both reflective (open to outside experience, inspired by spring) and projective (springing from his own 'ingenium,' emanating from his own mouth); it is, as in a conflation of M. H. Abrams's classic, optical image, mirror and lamp at once.[46] The effect is deepened – or heightened to the point of paradox – by the fact that the subject or origin of incoming experience and the object or target of outgoing discourse are identical, a circumstance made explicit by the speaker: in the first instance, it had been from spring that he had obtained his inspiration ('munere veris,' 'by the gift of spring,' 6, 7); now, these repeated gifts are being repaid ('reddita dona,' 22) by giving birth, through inspiration, to spring itself. In these couplets, then, sensory discourse figures as a Moebius strip-like compound of (receptive and sensuous) perception fused to (expressive and sensuous) vocalisation, one generating the other without end.

This fusion continues throughout the following lines, in which the song of the nightingale is associated with the singing of the poet:

> Iam Philomela tuos foliis adoperta novellis
> Instituis modulos, dum silet omne nemus.
> Urbe ego, tu sylva simul incipiamus utrique,
> Et simul adventum veris uterque canat. (25–28)

> [You are already beginning your warbling song, Philomela, hidden among the unfolding leaves, while all the grove is silent. I in the city, you in the woods, let us both begin together and both together sing the coming of spring.]

The nightingale repeatedly occurs in Milton's poetry; its association with poetry and springtime is conventional and a long-lasting literary motif.[47] In the present instance, however, it appears to serve a particular purpose in that it further aligns the sensory discourse of the poet-speaker with the sensory discourse of his subject. More specifically, both nightingale and poet are moved to song by the coming of springtime, and both, through their singing, are contributing to spring itself: the poet because of the paradoxical relation just discussed (he is inspired by spring, yet produces spring through his song); the nightingale, because her song, to the speaker, is one of the perceptible signs of spring itself.

As in Elegy I, Milton invokes the contrast between the city and the country (here, woodland), and firmly identifies the poet-speaker with the former: 'Urbe ego, tu sylva ...' Now, however, his account conforms to the auditory characteristics ordinarily ascribed to (rural) nature in contrast to (urban) culture: the nightingale's 'warbling' is accentuated by the *active* silence of the surrounding woods (the euphonic '*silet* omne nemus').[48] This is an ideal as much as it is a natural scene: the sylvan soundscape is

---

[46] Abrams, *The Mirror and the Lamp*.
[47] See the survey by John Kerrigan, 'Milton and the Nightingale,' *EC* 42 (1992), 107–22.
[48] On early modern aesthetic appreciation of forests (by no means an invention of the Romantic age), see Thomas, *Man and the Natural World*, 202; in literary discourse, this was supplemented with 'the classical conception of woods as the haunt of sylvan deities' (215; Thomas cites Milton's *Il Penseroso*).

subjected wholly to the acoustic expression of the creative individual, represented by the nightingale.[49]

A rather similar setting is described in the opening lines of Milton's Sonnet 1, presumably written in the same year as Elegy V: 'O nightingale, that on yon bloomy spray/Warblest at eve, when all the woods are still ...' (1–2). Yet in the sonnet, the focus is on the effect of the nightingale's song on the listening speaker ('that amorous power [linked] to thy soft lay,' 8), whereas in the elegy, both are presented as singing together – each in their place but, emphatically, at the same time ('simul ... utrique, / ... simul ... uterque'). This is not to suggest that the speaker is not listening to, or cannot hear the nightingale's song ('Iam ... /Instituis modulos'). Clearly, however, his account of it must remain notional in the sense that we are not actually to imagine him as hearing Philomela sing with his bodily ears (he in the city, she in the woods ...); yet 'hear' it, in some way, he does, and is even able to place it in the surrounding silence of the woods. In the end, we must conclude, the reality of the duet between the speaker and the songbird is left in abeyance, and again, as in the case of seeing/not seeing Apollo approaching, there is an apparent concurrence of actual and notional perception.

By the same token, readers are to imagine the speaker as singing his own song – or rather, to imagine *his spirit* as singing it, with mouth wide open ('sonat distento spiritus ore'). Both instances of aural perception, then – the speaker hearing the song of the nightingale as well as our 'hearing,' in turn, the elegiac song of the poet-speaker – are suspended between emphatic assertions of their (phenomenal or embodied) reality and the simultaneous concession of their ultimate elusiveness. As one result of this equivalence, the speaker's perception and its expression merge: we, his audience, conceivably may hear *his* song as he hears the nightingale's; yet, at the same time, his song transports what he himself is 'hearing' – it is what makes Philomela's song 'perceptible' to us in the first place. On the auditory plane, too, Milton's elegy presents a mixture of concrete (embodied) and abstract ('spiritual') expression and perception.

After these, as it were, 'sensory-poetological' passages, the poem returns to the notion of spring as an 'advent of Phoebus,' understood both phenomenologically *and* in terms of underlying causes, as the return of the sun. This double perspective is the result of a superimposition taken up at the very end of the elegy: Milton presents, first, the *annual* return of the sun in springtime, which is then compared to the *diurnal* return of the sun at daybreak. In the first instance, 'the sun is running away from the Ethiopians and from Tithonus' fields, and is turning his golden reins towards the northern regions'; in the second, 'the course of night is short, short is the night's dark stay; wild night and his darkness are banished' – the result of Phoebus 'showing his hair,' as an earlier passage had already suggested. In combination, both returns of the sun contribute to the couplets just quoted, which fuse the two ideas of spring and of dawn:

---

[49] The fact that Milton refers to the nightingale by the traditional epithet, 'Philomela' (lit., 'song-lover'), apart from mythological conventions, is not immaterial: the name individualises it (the bird) and turns her (the bird) into a symbol in the Coleridgean sense involving the 'translucence' of a general idea in the particular. In the 'Elegiac Verses,' the nightingale had just been 'the Daulian bird,' singing alongside 'the gentle lark' (5–6, see Chapter 2.1 above); in Sonnet 1, she is addressed (i. e., personalised), but is addressed simply as 'O nightingale' (1).

Iam sol Aethiopas fugiens Tithoniaque arva,
Flectit ad Arctoas aurea lora plagas.
Est breve noctis iter, brevis est mora noctis opacae
Horrida cum tenebris exulat ille suis.   (31–34)

[Now the sun is running away from the Ethiopians and from Tithonus' fields, and is turning his golden reins towards the northern regions. The course of the night is short, short is the night's dark stay; wild night and his darkness are banished.]

The focus of the subsequent lines remains with the notion of daybreak and sunrise, which, after its introduction in mythological terms, is now presented as an actual, perceptible phenomenon. Incidentally, this suggests that the nightingale of the preceding passage had been singing while it was *still* dark, while that of Sonnet 1 is 'warbl[ing] at eve.' However, it also exemplifies, again, how Milton alternates abstract and 'naturalistic' representations of related sensory items – how, put paradoxically, he counterposes 'sensory noumena' and sensory phenomena. This was the case, most evidently, with the song of the nightingale, resounding in the silent woods and heard only by way of the poet's imagination, but contrasted even more harshly with the earlier reference to the abstract, imaginary 'sacred sound which fills my brain' (12, lit. 'which moves me inside'). This is also repeated in the instance of sunrise, first introduced in the traditional image of Phoebus' cart (31–36), which is not dropped but rather integrated and 'naturalised' in the still conventional, yet more concrete and, quite literally, more tangible image of a shepherd resting on the dewy ground at sunrise:

Forte aliquis scopuli recubans in vertice pastor,
Roscida cum primo sole rubescit humus,
Hac, ait, hac certe caruisti nocte puella
Phoebe tua, celeres quae retineret equos.
Laeta suas repetit sylvas, pharetramque resumit
Cynthia, Luciferas ut videt alta rotas,
Et tenues ponens radios gaudere videtur
Officium fieri tam breve fratris ope.
Desere, Phoebus ait, thalamos Aurora seniles (41–49)

[Perhaps some shepherd, stretched out on the top of a crag while the dewy earth grows red in the light of the dawn, exclaims: 'You certainly did not have your girl with you tonight, Phoebus, to delay your swift horses!' When from on high Cynthia [i.e., the Moon] sees the wheels of the sun's chariot [lit., 'the Luciferian,' i.e. 'light-bringing wheels'], she goes back joyfully to her woods and takes up her quiver again, and seems to be glad as she lays her weak moonbeams aside that her own job is made so short by her brother's help.]

The abstract generality of Milton's pastoral image ('aliquis ... pastor') combines with an equivocating suggestion of its actual fictionality ('Forte'): we are looking at 'some' shepherd, and even that is not entirely certain.[50] At the same time, however, the visual and tactile specification of the scene lends it a sensuous concreteness: the earth 'reddens' with the first light of the sun ('rubescit humus,' taking up in contrast the earlier 'virescit humus' of line 4); this may reasonably be associated with a contrast between the vegetative ('green') and the 'red' animal sphere of erotic love and sexual desire to which the focus of the elegy will shift over the next dozen lines.[51] Given Milton's frequent recourse to etymology, his use of the relatively uncommon 'scopulus' ('a projecting rock,' Carey's 'crag,' from Greek *skopelos*, 'a lookout place,' derived from *skopein*, 'to look, watch') seems significant, as it provides a complement to the visual focus established by the sunrise setting: the shepherd is not only positioned on rising ground (VISION IS UP), but on a kind of elevation that, already in its name, announces a wide prospect.[52] At the lower end of the sensory hierarchy, the image is 'grounded' by reference to the damp texture of the soil or turf, which is 'wet with dew': 'roscida … humus.'[53]

In the immediate continuation of the 'shepherd' passage, several voices are raised, again lending the poet-speaker's own expressive vocality to the characters of the poem, and shifting the focus of the elegy to erotic love. First, the shepherd himself 'exclaims [ait]: "You certainly did not have your girl with you tonight, Phoebus, to delay your swift horses!"' (43–44); then, Phoebus, in turn, 'shouts' ('ait') at Aurora (the Dawn) to 'come out of that old man's bedroom, what's the use of lying in bed with someone who's impotent' ('Quid iuvat effoeto procubuisse toro?', 49–50).[54] Luckily, there is an

---

[50] See the concluding chapter on Milton's use of 'perhaps' in Annabel Patterson's volume of essays, *Milton's Words*, 196–203. While Patterson does not discuss the present instance of 'forte' (lit., 'by chance,' ablative of 'fors'), her observation that, in Milton's usage of the English term, 'at times it seems to acquire a prophetic force of its own' (197) certainly applies to the general situation of the inspired speaker of Elegy V, too. *Variorum* I, 101, notes the pastoral associations of 'recubans,' 'from the line familiar to every schoolboy, Virgil, *E[clogue]* I. 1, "Tityre, tu patulae recubans sub tegmine fagi." …'

[51] On the conventional dimensions of this contrast, see Pastoureau, *Green,* esp. 54–70, and Michel Pastoureau, *Red: The History of a Color*, tr. Jody Gladding (Princeton, N. J.: Princeton University Press, 2017 [2016]), esp. 80–85. For reflections on how a history of colour(s) may be integrated into historical (sensory) scholarship see Pastoureau's *Couleurs, images, symboles: études d'histoire et d'anthropologie* (Paris: Léopard d'or, 1989), 9–84 ('Vers une histoire sociale des couleurs'), and his essay, 'Une histoire des couleurs est-elle possible?', *Ethnologie française* 20 (1990), 368–77, arguing that 'la couleur ne se définit pas tant par des considérations optiques, physiques ou chimiques mais, plus largement, parce que'en fait l'homme vivant en société' (368).

[52] *OLD*, 'scopulus^1.' There might even be an added pun here, as 'scopulus' also denotes an archer's mark; see *OLD*, '? scopulus^2' – a possible *hapax*, but attested in a work of Suetonius Milton appears to have used much, see Boswell, *Milton's Library*, 235. Compare the following references to the (chaste) hunter Diana's 'quiver' at 45 and the (passionate) hunter Cephalus ('Aeolides … venator') at 51; Phoebus, of course, is also an expert marksman; in the general (generic) context of love (elegy), we may also associate Cupid and his bow, especially after the repeated use of that trope in Elegy I, discussed above, and in the light of his later appearance in Elegy V (97–102).

[53] The element of 'wetness' is dominant, see *OLD*, 'roscidus.'

[54] The reference is to her aged husband, Tithonus, granted immortality but not eternal youth by the gods.

alternative, and he, too, has a soft bed to offer: 'Aeolides, the hunter, is waiting for you on the green grass [viridi ... in herba]. Get up! The man you love is on high Hymettus' ('Surge, tuos ignes altus Hymettus habet,' 49–52).[55] Again, there is the combination here of high placement and green grass,[56] as well as the reference to (erotic) love and redness: Carey's 'the man you love' rather disambiguates the original's 'tuos ignes,' i.e., 'your fires,' which reflects, at once, Aurora's rising (visible first on the high mountaintops), and the intensity of passion between her and her 'flame.'[57]

Finally, in the reference to Phoebus' early rising and the repeated to calls to 'get up' and 'leave that old man's bedroom,' there are distinct echoes of Milton's 'Theme on Early Rising' and 'Carmina Elegiaca,' composed about five years prior to Elegy V.[58] These may be traced right down to the lexical level, if we consider Milton's renewed use of the imperative 'Surge,' the repeated reference, in both earlier texts, to the soft and downy bed (*torus*; here in 50, cited above)[59] and the description of Flora in 'Elegiac Verses': 'vitreo rore madescit humus,' '[she moistens] the ground with dew as bright as glass' (12), where the use of the verb presents a tactile equivalent of Milton's later constructions of *humus* with the visual 'virescit' and 'rubescit.' The combined effect in all cases is comparable, however, as 'madescit' is supplemented with the visual 'vitreo rore,' while 'rubescit' and 'virescit' both are posited against tactile expressions of moisture and/or coldness ('roscida,' 'soluta gelu'). Overall, the parallels between Milton's earliest, mostly illustrative sensory writing and his (still early) Elegy V are pronounced. In the elegy, however, the elements concerned provide the basis for a more complex, deliberative usage of sensory discourse, as in the theophanic and poetological passages discussed. This duality of illustration and deliberation is also evident in the following passage, which opens the section pivotal to the entire poem.

After the address to Phoebus by the shepherd, the poet-speaker himself turns to the sun god, telling him that the reviving earth herself ('Tellus rediviva'), yearns for his embraces ('amplexus ... tuos'):[60]

---

[55] The lines refer to 'Aurora's love for Cephalus, son of Aeolus (called *Aeolides* by Ovid ...), whom she first saw spreading nets for deer on Mount Hymettus, as Ovid describes ...' (Carey ad loc.). Apart from its spectacular location, Hymettus might also indicate another sensory dimension, it being a 'mountain in Attica overlooking Athens on the coast, famous for its honey and its marble'; this honey was 'particularly famous for its flavour ... [,] credited with mystical qualities, and sometimes symbolized the natural blessings men enjoyed in the Golden Age' (*Oxford Companion to Classical Literature*, ed. Howatson, 286, 291).
[56] Late in his writing life, in *Paradise Regained*, Milton would again refer to Hymettus as one of the attractions of 'Athens the eye of Greece': 'there flowery hill Hymettus with the sound/Of bees' industrious murmur oft invites/To studious musing ...' (*PR* 4.240, 247–49), indicating his familiarity with the 'Hymettian honey' trope (see the preceding note).
[57] At 53, Milton also refers to her 'blushing face.'
[58] See Chapter 2.1 above.
[59] Metonymically, *torus* also refers to marriage or indeed any kind of sexual relationship (*OLD*, 'torus,' 5).
[60] Compare the suggestion of Aurora visibly reaching for the high mountaintops above, alluding, perhaps, to the tactile dimension of the Homeric, tri-sensory *rhododaktylos Êōs* ('rosy-fingered Dawn').

> Et cupit, et digna est, quid enim formosius illa,
> Pandit ut omniferos luxuriosa sinus,
> Atque Arabum spirat messes, et ab ore venusto
> Mitia cum Paphiis fundit amoma rosis.
> Ecce coronatur sacro frons ardua luco,
> Cingit ut Ideaeam pinea turris Opim;
> Et vario madidos intexit flore capillos,
> Floribus et visa est posse placere suis.
> Floribus effusos ut erat redimita capillos
> Tenario placuit diva Sicana Deo. (55–66)

[She yearns for them, and she deserves them too, for what is more beautiful than she as she voluptuously bares her breasts, mother of all things, and breathes out Arabian spice-harvests and pours Paphian roses and mild perfume from her lovely lips. Look! Her high forehead is crowned with a sacred grove, just as Idaean Ops is ringed with a turret of pine-trees; she has twined many-coloured flowers among her dewy hair, flowers which seem to give her the power to charm, as the Sicanian goddess once charmed the Taenarian god, when her flowing hair was plaited with flowers.]

Any possible distancing effect of their mythological content aside, the unabashed eroticism of these lines again casts strong doubt on any wholesale characterisation of Milton as hostile to the senses, or indeed to sensuality. Even their dismissal as a work of the poet's youth would not present a cogent objection, since they were still included in the 1673 *Poems*, published the year before Milton's death (and very likely with his close cooperation).[61]

The sensory discourse of the passage partly refers to individual senses, partly to specific connotations from the general sensory sphere. The reference to 'Arabian [spice-]harvests' combines olfactory and gustatory delights with the idea of faraway lands.[62] Another aromatic element of these lines – flowers, roses more particularly, the *Paphian* roses sacred to Venus, specifically – has already occurred in Elegy I.[63] There, as here, it actualises the conventional association of the sensuous mode, and of olfaction in particular, with romantic love. This aspect is further developed through Milton's depiction of the earth, 'mother of all things,' in the highly conventional – though pre-Petrarchan – classical vocabulary of a particularised, even itemised, beauty. At the same time, the sensuous imagery of the poem is again extended to include the tactile sphere by the clearly eroticising references to 'embraces,' 'dewy hair,' 'lovely mouth' ('ore venusto,' the latter related to 'Venus') and 'all-giving breasts' ('omniferos ... sinus').[64]

---

[61] See Carey's remarks about the production of the 1673 *Poems, &c. upon Several Occasions* ... in *SP*, 4.
[62] 'Spice-' is Carey's (I think justified) interpolation; compare *PL* 4.157–163.
[63] 'Paphos and rosy Cyprus' (84).
[64] Rendered by Carey more freely (and smoothly) as '... breasts, mother of all things.' Line 63, in its neat intertwining of the elements 'vario flore' and 'madidos capillos' with the verb 'intexit' – 'interweaves,' with all the usual connotations operative between '(in)texere' and 'textus' – mimics that which it describes, lending the verse further tactile force.

In the short excerpt cited, all the senses are already present. Indeed, several of the sensory items listed may be related to two or more of them: the spices of Arabia affect smell and taste at once; their odours are breathed by the 'lovely mouth' of a personified, female Earth,[65] which may reasonably also be associated with kisses (touch) and speech/song (sound); roses and other flowers, too, are valued for their smell as well as for their visual appeal. In their densely multi-sensory texture, these lines are closer to the impression of an encompassing sensuality evoked in the 'Elegiac Verses' or the 'Theme on Early Rising' than they are to the comparatively restricted – and sequentially compartmentalised – account of Elegy I: there, the speaker never evokes synaesthesia or even multi-sensoriality. In the theatre, presentation pertains first to vision, then to sound, then to vision again; in the subsequent comparison of London to its girls and of these to their foreign contenders, the focus undeniably shifts to vision. All the other senses, smell, taste, and touch, are practically absent in Elegy I.

In another respect, however, the two elegies do in fact share an important element in their approach to sensory discourse. After all, Tellus is represented not only as sensuous and enticing: she also embodies a kind of majesty – and literally so: 'coronatur' – whose representation reprises the imagery of towers and fortifications so conspicuous in the earlier poem:

> Ecce coronatur sacro frons ardua luco,
> Cingit ut Ideaeam pinea turris Opim; (59–60)

The personified Earth is 'crowned' with a circle or wreath of pine trees. The two alternative manifestations of this image presented in the couplet may, in both cases, be linked to the earlier Elegy I. In the first instance, there is the description of personified Earth as she appears to the speaker of Elegy V; in the second, this impression is extended by comparison to another entity not immediately 'present' to the poet-speaker (and spectator).

The first version (59) centres on the perceptual salience of the relevant detail: as the head conventionally is the highest part of the body, and the forehead, as the term implies, is its most anterior part, Milton's particularising reference to Earth's 'frons *ardua*' (her 'high' or 'steep forehead') suggests a triple elevation into visibility (as before, HEIGHT IS VISIBILITY). To this *potential visibility* corresponds an *actual* highlighting of the speaker's *vision*: 'Ecce!' Moreover, as a high forehead is part of the general Renaissance ideal of beauty, the description given indicates that the two aspects, majesty/strength and visual appeal, cannot actually be divided.[66] On a conceptual level, this conforms to the portrayals both of the British girls and of London given in Elegy I,

---

[65] Actually, she *is* breathing their 'harvests' ('messes'), which might offer an early expression of Milton's later views regarding the fundamental materiality of perception. In *Paradise Lost*, he returns several times to the idea of vapours rising from the ground (read here: Earth breathing) and solidifying into something material ('Arabian [spice-]harvests'), from Pandaemonium rising 'like an exhalation' (*PL* 1.711) to the invention of metallurgy at *PL* 11.563–73. For a discussion of this 'mists and vapours' motif, though without detailed reference to Milton's assumed materialism, see Marjara, *Contemplation of Created Things*, 178–88.

[66] See, again, Sherrow, *Encyclopedia of Hair*, 329.

where turreted heads and head-like towers had been approximated in an aestheticising display of military strength. Although in relation to the sun, the earth is DOWN, her sensory appeal and procreative powers justify her figuration as UP, as a 'towering,' formidable presence.

In Elegy V, also, the return to fortificatory imagery is inextricable from its figuration as embodied, inviting further lexical comparison to the earlier poem: whereas Earth's 'frons ardua' is crowned with a sacred grove, the 'Achaemenian girls' had been 'turrita fronte.' Furthermore, while the circular 'crown' on Tellus' head – its tines presumably represented by the tapering 'pine-trees' – bears only an associative relationship with the closed perimeter of a crenellated town wall, the second restatement of the relevant imagery from Elegy I makes the connection to fortification explicit: a 'pine-made tower' crowns Earth's head, 'just like Idaean Ops' (60).[67] In its conflicting descriptions (implying both the running length of a town wall – already suggested by *frons* alone – and the 'discrete' height of a tower), the couplet superimposes different kinds of military architecture, resulting in a 'realistic' yet composite image of ramparts and bastions. At that, the single enclosing tower ('cingit ... turris') in particular is reminiscent of the 'turreted' Persian headgear evoked in Elegy I.

Taking into account its mythological background, Milton's highly compressed comparison not only likens Tellus to Cybele, Phrygian goddess of plenty (equivalent to Roman Ops) by referring to Mount Ida, Cybele's place of abode close to Troy (also referenced in Elegy I); it also more closely associates her with 'the East,' in consonance both with the olfactory exoticism of the wider passage within Elegy V and the catalogue of Persian and other 'Eastern' women in Elegy I.[68] Although a typical mother-goddess just like Tellus, Cybele (in contrast to Tellus) was emphatically considered a *mountain* goddess, which might explain Milton's choice of the image in the context of the elegy's preoccupation with the importance of an elevated position to the actions and 'passions' of viewing and being viewed.[69] The transformation by comparison of Tellus into Cybele, then, reproduces in the mode of personification her earlier elevation into plain sight (HEIGHT IS VISIBILITY). Conversely, the elegy's insistent reference to towers and mountains as places of lookout ('scopuli'), which is also present in this passage, rests on the underlying sensory metaphor that VISION IS HEIGHT.

As in Elegy I, moreover, the 'visual-military complex' of Milton's imagery in Elegy V figures seeing and being seen as necessary antecedents of romantic love. The poem's emphatic association of Tellus/Cybele with the insignia of commanding (military) vision has just been established. Her lover Phoebus, as the sun, is essentially defined as

---

[67] *Pineus*, strictly speaking, is an adjective along the lines of 'oaken,' 'beechen,' or 'birchen' (but for which the *OED*, in distinction from those others, as yet records no English equivalent): 'pinen.'

[68] For the mythological background see Carey ad loc., who also points to possible literary sources of Milton's imagery; their relevance to my discussion will be obvious: 'Ida was crowned with pines (Virgil, *Aen.* x 230) and the pine was sacred to Cybele because, as Ovid relates, *Met.* x 103–5, her love, Attis, was turned into a pine. Ovid explains that Cybele wears a turreted crown because she first gave towers to cities (*Fast.* iv 219–21).'

[69] In Greek sources, she is referred to as *mētēr oreia*, 'the Mountain Mother'; see Lynn E. Roller, *In Search of God the Mother: The Cult of Anatolian Cybele* (Berkeley, Calif.: University of California Press, 1999), 198.

the epitome of vision; as an archer, he may use this vision as an archer does.[70] Despite this persistent characterisation of vision as associated with power and force, however, the connection established by sight in Elegy V is not presented as threatening or potentially harmful (as in Elegy I), but rather as linking two lovers. Its presentation ties into a sensory context not of deprivation, imitation, and doubt (the bare fields, theatrics, and potential Circean bewitchment of Elegy I) but rather of abundance, (pro-)creativity, and (self-)assurance, embodied in the speaker's vernal inspiration in his 'duet' with Philomela as much as in the figure of Tellus 'voluptuously bar[ing] her breasts.'

In the passages discussed thus far, the sensory discourse of Elegy V can be shown to comprise two distinct elements: (1) sensory (possibly sensuous) language as an *illustrative* or *descriptive* mode of expression centred on the appreciation (and potentially the enjoyment) of percepts (broadly speaking, the 'flowery language' of spring); and (2) the *deliberative* or *conceptual* use of those percepts to indicate more fundamental patterns of a structuring and/or argumentative nature. In both cases, individual elements may be interrelated among themselves in complex ways, either as *synaesthesia* or as *ideasthesia*, that is, the association of certain concepts with certain percepts (or with other concepts abstracted from related percepts). This latter phenomenon, I argue, is responsible for the repeated co-occurrence of mountain imagery and fortification imagery in relation to vision (and, ultimately, love, since 'love comes by sight' and LOVE IS CONQUEST).

Put in another, and perhaps more familiar, way, sensory discourse may (1) delight and (2) teach. Still, lest we ascribe to Milton, even to a twenty-year-old Milton, a straightforwardly positive, unconflicted view of the sensory sphere, we need to address the darker and altogether more serious undercurrent which is present even in the spring-like passage last discussed. The 'Taenarian god' of the last line, after all, is Hades/Pluto, 'so called because one of the mouths of hell was a cave in the promontory of Taenarus in Laconia,' as Carey notes. The 'Sicanian goddess,' accordingly, is Proserpina (or Proserpine), daughter of Demeter/Ceres, the Graeco-Roman goddess of agriculture and harvest (as in 'Arabian harvests'). The 'Rape' (i.e., abduction, but the modern-day sense of sexual violence is certainly implied) of Proserpina by Pluto, as recounted by Ovid and others, was a standard of Renaissance mythological imagery; when John Evelyn was travelling on the Continent in 1644, he noted seeing several versions of it in both painting and sculpture.[71] Its evocation in the present context gives us a first indication that all is not necessarily roses (or spices) in sensory language. Autumn, and with it the reckoning of harvest, is implicit in spring; violence and rape may be suggested in a

---

[70] Phoebus Apollo, however, is emphatically not a god of war or hunting, simply representing *good archery* (i. e., keen vision and a steady hand); see *Oxford Companion to Classical Literature*, ed. Howatson, 43.

[71] The 1621/2 marble by Gian Lorenzo Bernini, today in the Galleria Borghese, Rome, was then at the villa of Cardinal Ludovico Ludovisi, where Evelyn, on his grand tour, inspected it on 10 November 1644 (Evelyn, *Diary*, 126). Whether Milton had seen it when in Rome seven years earlier (i.e., between his reference to the subject in Elegy V and his subsequent use of it in *Paradise Lost*), we do not know.

3.2 Elegy V ('In Adventum Veris,' Spring 1629)

superficially amorous phrase.[72] The potentially overpowering, seductive appeal to the senses may bring forth appalling consequences.[73] If this darker, doubtful facet of sensory discourse is also teaching, it certainly does not present the senses as a source of delight.

At this point in the poem, however, such darker considerations form only an undercurrent of the dominant sensory discourse, which clearly focuses on the sensuous attractions of spring. In the two couplets immediately following the description of Tellus/Cybele, Elegy V continues its multi-sensory appeal to Phoebus:

> Aspice Phoebe tibi faciles hortantur amores,
> Mellitasque movent flamina verna preces.
> Cinnamea Zephyrus leve plaudit odorifer ala,
> Blanditiasque tibi ferre videntur aves. (67–70)

> [Look, Phoebus, easily won love is calling to you, and the spring breezes bear honied appeals. Fragrant Zephyrus lightly claps his cinnamon-scented wings, and the birds seem to carry blandishments to you.]

The passage commences, significantly, with an injunction to 'look!'; this again highlights the almost ekphrastic quality pervading much of the poem, and its central section, with the encounter between Tellus and Phoebus, in particular. At the same time, as in the initial description of Tellus, different sensory modes are cross-related, and are related to love. Taste, smell, touch, and hearing all are implied when a 'honied' and 'cinnamon-scented' breeze – personified as Zephyrus, conventional messenger of spring – 'lightly claps' its wings.[74] Simultaneously, the sense of hearing is addressed in each of the four lines: 'amores' (abstract 'love affairs,' but also personified Cupids) are 'calling out'; breezes transport (audible) prayers; 'plaudit' at once implies the clapping of applause; birds 'carry[ing] blandishments' suggest the pleasing aural ambience of birdsong.[75] Both the blowing of vernal breezes ('flamina verna') and the flapping/clapping of wings include in themselves a haptic element. Taken together, these concurrent sensations cover those parts of the sensorium not addressed by the earlier heavy emphasis

---

[72] The brutal fate of Philomela, introduced above as the sweetly 'warbl[ing]' nightingale's mythological persona, also illustrates this paradox; her mention also connects to the symbolism of the present passage.

[73] When, more than thirty years after composing his elegy, Milton reprises the Proserpina myth in *Paradise Lost*, the opposition of 'fair ... flowers' on the one side, gloom and pain on the other, all of them connected by the notion of 'gathering' or harvest, is made explicit and compressed into four and a half lines of blank verse: '... Not that fair field/Of Enna, where Proserpine gathering flowers,/Herself a fairer flower by gloomy Dis/Was gathered, which cost Ceres all that pain/To seek her through the world ...' (*PL* 4.266–70).

[74] Chaucer's prologue, exemplarily, is set in April, 'whan Zephyrus eek with his sweete breeth/Inspired hath in every holt and heeth/The tendre croppes ...' (*Canterbury Tales, General Prologue*, 5–7). At *PL* 5.15–17, Adam, waking Eve, 'with voice/Mild, as when Zephyrus on Flora breathes,/Her hand soft touching, whispered thus. Awake ...'

[75] With 'blanditiasque,' contrast, again, the ambiguously alluring 'blandas ... flammas' exuded by the British girls of Elegy I.

on vision; even so, birds 'are seen carrying blandishments' ('videntur').[76] On balance, and compared to the passage in which Tellus initially is presented, lines 67–70 again present an intensely multi-sensory account of reviving nature, and again fuse concretely sensuous and abstractly mythological considerations. In that they consistently equivocate on the ultimate allocation of referents to individual senses, however, they are more emphatically synaesthetic than the verses discussed before.

The elegy then further elaborates on the relationship between Phoebus, the Sun, and Tellus, the Earth, consummated in springtime. First, the focus is on the fruit of their union in the full bounty of nature, both above and below ground. Thus, the speaker continues to address Phoebus, commenting on Tellus' riches: 'She is bountiful and supplies you with health-giving herbs ... she lays before your eyes all the worth she keeps hidden away under the huge ocean and the heaped-up mountains' (73–74, 77–78).[77] The idea that minerals, precious stones and metals below ground are 'engendered' by the rays of the sun and the influence of the stars is a feature of early modern, more precisely Paracelsian natural philosophy.[78] In *Paradise Lost*, the doctrine is expressed most fully in the description of Satan's arrival on the sun, whose substance is described as an amalgam of different metals and gems, helping to account, perhaps, for the effects of the sun's rays down on earth:

> The place he found beyond expression bright,
> Compared with aught on earth, metal or stone;
> Not all parts like, but all alike informed
> With radiant light, as glowing iron with fire;
> If metal part seemed gold, part silver clear;
> If stone, carbuncle most or chrysolite,
> Ruby or topaz ...
> ...
> What wonder then if fields and regions here [i.e., in the sun]
> Breathe forth elixir pure, and rivers run
> Potable gold, when with one virtuous touch
> The arch-chemic sun so far from us remote
> Produces with celestial humour mixed

---

[76] Carey's translation of 'videntur' is of course viable but disambiguates Milton's original Latin: if the birds '*seem* to carry blandishments,' this arguably highlights their singing (as 'blandishments' typically are vocal), whereas a reading of 'videntur' in the non-deponential sense of 'are seen' focuses on the visual aspect. Later in the poem, there is an unambiguous instance of 'videri' in the sense of 'being seen' (129).

[77] 'Alma salutiferum medicos tibi gramen in usus/Praebet ... /Illa tibi ostentat quascunque sub aequore vasto,/Et superiniectis montibus abdit opes,' where 'superinectis montibus ... opes' arguably echoes the earlier comparison/identification of Tellus with 'Idaeam ... Opim' ('Idaean Ops,' i. e., Cybele, the Phrygian, mountain-goddess equivalent of Roman Ops, goddess of plenty, and *ops*, 'power, resources,' personified). The reference to healing herbs is also due to Phoebus Apollo's character as a god of medicine and healing.

[78] See Marjara, *Contemplation of Created Things*, 169–70, citing Paracelsus referring to the sun as an alchemist.

3.2 Elegy V ('In Adventum Veris,' Spring 1629)

Here in the dark [i.e., under the earth] so many precious things
Of colour glorious and effect so rare?' (3.591–7, 606–12)[79]

Kester Svendsen has commented on this passage that 'these are not casual associations [sc. of gems and metals] with brightness' – indeed, they go beyond a relationship of mere (sparkling) similarity to represent not only the almost trivial association of the sun with vision but also its proto-scientific association with the formation of certain precious materials (which materialise the powers of 'Phoebus' on earth).[80] In Elegy I, the comparison of the British girls' eyes to stars and jewels had touched upon the general domain of their shared relationship without making its natural philosophical foundation explicit. In Elegy V, the evocation of the idea primarily expresses the erotic union of Tellus and Phoebus while, to a lesser extent, continuing the poem's ongoing series of references to vision.

In the following lines, the elegy, without losing its multi-sensory quality, shifts its focus towards tactility. The lines in question open with the jealousy of Tellus over Phoebus' sinking into the ocean (figured as the sea goddess Tethys and hence a potential rival): 'Phoebus, why should the sky-blue mother take you into her western waves when you are exhausted by your daily journey? What have you got to do with Tethys ...?' Then, Tellus advertises to her lover the tactile delights of her own realm:

> Quid tibi cum Tethy? Quid cum Tartesside lympha,
> Dia quid immundo perluis ora salo?
> Frigora Phoebe mea melius captabis in umbra,
> Huc ades, ardentes imbue rore comas.
> Mollior egelida veniet tibi somnus in herba,
> Huc ades, et gremio lumina pone meo.
> Quaque iaces circum mulcebit lene susurrans
> Aura per humentes corpora fusa rosas.
> Nec me (crede mihi) terrent Semeleia fata,
> Nec Phaetonteo fumidus axis equo;
> Cum tu Phoebe tuo sapientius uteris igni,
> Huc ades et gremio lumina pone meo. (83–94)

['What have you got to do with Tethys or the waters of Tartessus? Why do you wash your heavenly face in dirty salt water? It will be more pleasant for you to seek coolness in my shades, Phoebus; come here, and bathe your gleaming hair in dew. You will find softer

---

[79] The notion is complicated however if we consider the epic speaker's comment at 1.690–2: 'Let none admire/That riches grown in hell; that soil may best/Deserve the precious bane' (ironically taken up by Mammon at 2.270–3). Marjara traces this qualification to a classical tradition, represented among others by Ovid, 'that deprecated the practice of mining precious metals' (*Contemplation of Created Things*, 174). See also Svendsen, *Milton and Science*, 117, as well as Roy Porter, *The Making of Geology: Earth Science in Britain, 1660–1815* (Cambridge: Cambridge University Press, 1977), 15, who points to 'prevalent [negative] attitudes, such as that to study the Earth was demeaning.'
[80] Svendsen, *Milton and Science*, 29.

sleep on the cool grass: come here, and lay your eyes against my breast. The breeze, murmuring gently around you where you lie, will soothe our bodies, stretched out on dewy roses. Semele's fate does not frighten me, I assure you, nor does the chariot which Phaëthon's horses caused to smoke. Come here, and lay your eyes against my breast, and you will put your fire to better use.']

Even without an exhaustive enumeration of individual elements and instances of sensory cross-referencing, the multi-sensory quality of the passage should be clear. What is new is the pervasive focus on the sense of touch or tactile sensations: Tellus calls Phoebus into the cool, and therefore pleasing, shade ('Frigora Phoebe mea melius captabis in umbra') and points out the coolness of the (dewy) grass ('egelida ... in herba');[81] even the roses, conventional symbols of Tellus' love for Phoebus (and, in a quite literal sense, their joint offspring), are not primarily of visual or olfactory interest, but provide the lovers with a soft and 'dewy' couch.[82]

However, the most significant aspect of this 'tactile turn' lies in *the way it relates* to the elegy's prior focus on vision and on the respective characterisations of the two mythological-allegorical figures. There is, after all, no simple displacement of the sensory focus from vision to touch or from general synaesthesia to touch-based synaesthesia. There is, rather, a *staging* of the shift from vision to touch as a process invested with meaning. To begin with, the sensory profile of Phoebus (earlier associated with vision) is made contrastable with that of Tellus by focusing on his secondary characteristic as a bringer of heat.[83] Accordingly, coolness (of dew, or Tellus) and warmth, even heat (of sunlight, or Phoebus' fire),[84] are present throughout the passage, and are directly confronted in the invitation to 'come here, and bathe your gleaming ['ardentes,' lit. 'burning'] hair in dew' (86). In the first instance, this visualises the idea of warming sunbeams (Phoebus' 'hair') touching, and perhaps glistening on, dewy grass.

At the same time, the image exemplifies certain early modern notions of cosmic order related to the distribution of elements, humours, and individual senses.[85] More precisely, Tellus, as a female figure, is associated with all the tactile qualities conventionally associated with the female temperament: she is soft, cold, and wet ('Frigora mea,' 'Mollior egelida ... in herba,' 'humentes ... rosas').[86] Phoebus, by contrast, figured as

[81] This constructs a parallel between Phoebus and the 'pastor' of lines 41–42; the corresponding 'Phyllis' appears at 114.
[82] Implicitly, Tellus' (sweet) dew is contrasted with the (salty) sea water of Tethys.
[83] To Milton, as to his contemporaries, the effects of the sun's light and heat were equivalent in their vitalising effect (see Marjara, *Contemplation of Created Things*, 170 and the passage from *PL* 4.655–71 quoted below); yet the primary symbolic association both of Phoebus Apollo and the sun is with light and vision (as in his first appearance in this poem, when his 'hair' is seen, not felt).
[84] The references to Semele and Phaeton allude to myths in which divine fire proves harmful; see Carey ad locc.
[85] For a concise account of early modern humoral theory see Harold J. Cook, 'Medicine,' in Katharine Park/Lorraine Daston (eds), *The Cambridge History of Science, Vol. 3: Early Modern Science* (Cambridge: Cambridge University Press, 2008), 407–434, at 410. A more comprehensive account of the Hippocratic–Galenic tradition is given by Jacques Jouanna, *Greek Medicine from Hippocrates to Galen: Selected Papers*, tr. Neil Allies (Leiden: Brill, 2012), 335–60.
[86] See Classen, *Worlds of Sense*, 122–126, at 123.

3.2 Elegy V ('In Adventum Veris,' Spring 1629)

male, contributes vigorous heat by means of his visible rays/burning strands of hair ('ardentes ... comas').[87] The resulting combination of moisture and heat is specifically associated in Galenic-Hippocratic humoralism with the season of spring, the age of youth, and blood as its predominant humour.[88] In this respect, Milton's presentation of the warm and humid fecundity of spring in Elegy V is not only conventional, but also conforms to Milton's later depictions of (pro-)creation as presented in *Paradise Lost*.[89] Phoebus and Tellus, sun and earth, male and female, hot and cold have to combine in order to make the 'coming of spring' possible.

Elegy V makes it clear, however, that the procreative union of Phoebus and Tellus should also be understood, altogether less conventionally, in terms of an approximation of vision and touch. This is first expressed, emphatically, through the nestling of Phoebus' eyes – *qua* sun, he is 'all eye' –[90] against the 'all-giving' breasts of Tellus – literally, in nature's bosom: 'Huc ades, et gremio pone lumina meo' (88, and repeated at 94). The call to 'come here' – 'Huc ades,' i.e., 'move your presence to this place,' repeated a total of three times in 86, 88, and 94 – is emphatic: even sunlight cannot really rely on an *actio in distans*. As in the passage from *Paradise Lost* quoted above ('... with one virtuous *touch*/the arch-chemic sun .../*Produces* ...'), Phoebus needs to *touch* to be *effective*, that is, procreative.[91] Whether or not one relates Milton's description to the notion of touch as the sense of procreation,[92] it enacts and embodies the abstract meteorological or botanical statement that 'in spring, sunlight touches the earth to produce vegetation,' as well as the circumstance that sunlight, once hitting the opaque earth, 'goes blind,' while its (tactile) warmth penetrates below the surface.

---

[87] Milton returns to this contrast and the associated sensory modes in *Paradise Lost*. When Adam and Eve are first presented, they are 'not equal, as their sex not equal seemed;/For contemplation [i. e., sight] he and valour formed,/For softness [i. e., touch] she and sweet attractive grace ...' (4.296–8). Adam, Eve later says, is 'less winning soft' than her own image (4.477).

[88] See Jouanna, *Greek Medicine*, 335, 339, 342. Both the notional blushing of Tellus (53) and the actual reddening of the dewy ground at daybreak ('rubescit,' 42) may be read as references to this association of spring with hot and wet blood. Accordingly, hot and dry summer corresponds to yellow bile; cold and dry autumn, to black bile; and cold and wet winter, to phlegm. Galen distinguishes the humours not only by colour but also by taste: blood is sweet; yellow bile, bitter; black bile, sour; phlegm, salty (339n20). Among the four elements, spring is associated with air. Arguably combining both, Milton's 'spring breezes bear honied appeals.'

[89] See the passages from Milton's account of the creation at *PL* 7.233–9, where 'on the *watery calm*/... the spirit of God ... /... vital virtue infused, and *vital warmth*/Throughout the *fluid* mass,' discarding 'downward' the '*cold* infernal dregs/*Adverse to life*' (emphases added), and 7.276–82: 'The earth was formed, but *in the womb* as yet/*Of waters*, embryon immature involved,/Appeared not: over all the face of earth/Main ocean flowed, not idle, but *with warm/Prolific humour softening* all her globe/Fermented *the great mother* to conceive,/Satiate with *genial moisture*, ...' (emphases added). In the second passage, in particular, Milton's account is remarkably close to conventional depictions of Tellus or comparable mother/earth goddesses.

[90] On Milton's later identification of sun and eye in *Paradise Lost*, see Chapter 5 below.

[91] His traditional characterisation as an archer represents the conceptual antithesis to this idea.

[92] This identification of touch and procreation ultimately went back to Aristotle; see Raphael's reference at *PL* 8.579–80 to 'the sense of touch, whereby mankind/Is propagated.'

Even beyond its account of vernal fertility, moreover, Milton's elegy can be shown to complicate the conventional sensory associations of its mythological characters. Thus, Tellus is associated with lying down – the most emphatic form of touching the earth – and sleeping, eyes closed ('Quaque iaces,' 'veniet tibi somnus'), whereas Phoebus is consistently associated with waking and rising, in the earlier parts of Elegy V as in 'Song: On May Morning' and, earlier, the 'Elegiac Verses' and the 'Theme on Early Rising.'[93] This characterisation corresponds not only to the phenomenal placement of the respective entities in everyday life (the sun is up above, the earth is down below) but also to the notional placement of the senses associated with them on the scale of sensory hierarchy: there, VISION IS UP, while TOUCH IS DOWN.

In fact, the poem's consistent sensory references to Phoebus and Tellus should be seen within the wider context of other paired attributes associated with the two figures. In some cases, the categories implied are binary (male/female, hot/cold, waking/sleeping); in others, they are elements of some more extensive category of order (vision and touch as two of the five senses; heat and cold as representative of the equally present fire and water, two of the four elements). All of these categories, whether binary or multiple in character, had their conventional early modern valuations: vision was nobler than touch; women were supposed to be subject to men. These valuations were expressed in terms of opposition, or hierarchical placement, or both (thus, in Elegy V, for vision and touch, where the confrontation of two extremes on the sensory-hierarchical scale constructs a quasi-binary). As in the case of humoral theory and its wide array of correspondences (humours associated with corresponding seasons, ages, elements, tastes, etc.), individual items placed at comparable ranks of their respective hierarchies might enter into multiple correlations: Phoebus, the sun, is hot, bright, and male; Tellus, the earth, is cool, shady/dark, and female. He is associated with vision; she, with touch. In terms of content, then, the relevant categories were subject to a high degree of interdetermination and cross-reference; structurally, they rested upon the hierarchical ordering implied by the most fundamental pair of orientational metaphors: GOOD IS UP and BAD IS DOWN.[94]

This brief excursus into the conceptual-metaphorical 'machinery' underlying the imagery of Elegy V was necessary in order to facilitate an understanding of how Milton, ultimately, breaks up the conventional, linked hierarchisation of categories, undercutting contemporary readers' expectations. In particular, this involves the traditional elevation of (male) vision over (female) touch. After all, the (presumable) closing of Phoebus' 'lumina' as he presses them against Tellus' breast signifies their reduction to an

---

[93] Of course, earth herself, too, is figured as 'sleeping' during winter, before being then woken up by the sun in spring (Milton's 'Tellus rediviva').

[94] See Lakoff/Johnson, *Metaphors We Live By*, 14–21. Among several examples (MORE IS UP, HAPPY IS UP, RATIONAL IS UP …), Lakoff and Johnson specifically name CONSCIOUS IS UP and UNCONSCIOUS IS DOWN, which correspond to the elegy's association of Phoebus and waking, Tellus and sleeping (15); their experiential basis is obvious. On the particular relevance of such orientational metaphors to the study of the early modern period, see Carlo Ginzburg, 'The High and the Low: The Theme of Forbidden Knowledge in the Sixteenth and Seventeenth Centuries,' in: Id., *Clues, Myths, and the Historical Method*, tr. John and Anne C. Tedeschi (Baltimore, Md.: Johns Hopkins University Press, 1986), 60–76, esp. 62–3.

organ of touch: while not denying the essentiality of both entities involved – it takes both, Tellus and Phoebus, to bring about spring –, Milton's image makes vision momentarily subservient to touch, and subordinates the sun to productive earth. The same tension-filled prioritisation of the tactile domain is at work in Milton's physical conceit of having Tellus call Phoebus (i.e., the sun himself) into the shade. This image combines two aspects. First, it takes two to cast a shadow – indeed, shade would not be pleasing without an excess of sun: in book 4 of *Paradise Lost*, Adam sits 'in the door …/Of his cool bower while now the mounted sun/Shot down direct his fervid rays to warm/Earth's inmost womb, more warmth than Adam needs' (4.299–302). At the same time, however, the emphasis with which Tellus extols the pleasantness of the cool spots she has to offer argues the comparative superiority of the tactile shade over the heat caused by Phoebus' sunbeams.[95] Ultimately, the elegy's tendency to prioritise touch in creation, while conforming to both Aristotelian and atomist natural philosophies, appears to express an early version, perhaps, of Milton's later, tactile-thermal cosmology, developed more fully in *Paradise Lost*.[96]

This relative ascendancy of Tellus and female, procreative tactility over vision corresponds to the overall emphasis of the elegy on the beauty and majesty of Tellus. She is the one who appears to control Phoebus, asking (or ordering) him to 'come here.' Phoebus, by contrast, may command Aurora to 'Come out of that old man's bedroom,' but he does not once even address Tellus. In terms of how the scene of the elegy relates its central figures to each other, Tellus, the earth, is presented as being the more authoritative of the two. At the same time, she is the main beneficiary of the return of Phoebus at the coming of spring – *not*, emphatically, the annual return of the earth to a certain position in relation to the sun: she is not the one who is moving. It would not be wrong to read this astronomical-mythological constellation of characters in the light of Milton's later concern with the place of the earth among the planets and, especially, vis-à-vis the sun.[97] Thus, Adam explains to curious Eve the utility of the stars ('But wherefore all night long shine these? for whom/This glorious sight, when sleep hath shut all eyes?,' *PL* 4.655–6):

---

[95] On the pastoral *otium in umbra* tradition of pleasing, *tactile* 'shade' as it relates to the more generally *visual* topos of 'shadow,' see John Hollander, *The Substance of Shadow: A Darkening Trope in Poetic History* (Chicago: University of Chicago Press, 2016), 33–36. Contrast/compare also the (similarly paradoxical) 'bare fields which offer no gentle shades' to the worshippers of Phoebus and the 'magnificently shady spot just outside the city' in Elegy I.

[96] Compare n89 above. On Lucretius' view of touch as fundamental, see Moshenska, *Feeling Pleasures*, 81–85.

[97] As far as I can see, Elegy V has not been considered in previous discussions of this theme in Milton, which have tended to focus on the astronomy of *Paradise Lost*. For a recent discussion of the epic's passages relating to the sun's and stars' 'ministering' to the earth see Dennis Danielson, *Paradise Lost and the Cosmological Revolution* (Cambridge: Cambridge University Press, 2014), 154–78. Marjara has argued convincingly that 'in the cosmology of *Paradise Lost*, heliocentrism is present in the spirit if not in the letter' (*Contemplation of Created Things*, 46, discussed more fully at 108–144). Elegy V, too, embodies traditional geocentrist values, yet it opens with a reference to the circular motion of Time that seems suggestive of the heliocentric model ('In se perpetuo Tempus revolubile gyro,' 1).

> These have their course to finish round the earth,
> By morrow evening, and from land to land
> In order, though to nations yet unborn,
> Ministering light prepared, they set and rise;
> Lest total darkness should by night regain
> Her old possession, and extinguish life
> In nature and all things, which these soft fires
> Not only enlighten, but with kindly heat
> Of various influence foment and warm,
> Temper or nourish, or in part shed down
> Their stellar virtue on all kinds that grow
> On earth, made hereby apter to receive
> Perfection from the sun's more potent ray. (*PL* 4.655–6, 659–71)

Although the *visual* aspect of the heavenly bodies, the stars and the sun, may be more conspicuous, their primary significance for the inhabitants of earth lies with their tactile 'influence' – they 'not only enlighten, but ... / ... foment and warm.'[98] Like the passage from *Paradise Lost*, composed almost forty years after Milton's first surviving poems, in its central passages Elegy V negotiates the respective visual and tactile implications of solar 'influence.'

With this rather complex, 'deliberative' use of sensory discourse evident in the confrontation of sun and earth, the conceptually central part of Elegy V closes. In the lines immediately following on from Tellus' impassioned address to Phoebus, the poem turns from its central figures to trace the amorous effects of spring in the world at large, stressing the close connection between the 'mother' and her 'creatures.' Here, Cupid is introduced as the mythological representative of these effects, and is characterised in a manner reminiscent of his representation in Elegy I:

> Sic Tellus lasciva suos suspirat amores;
> Matris in exemplum caetera turba ruunt.
> Nunc etenim toto currit vagus orbe Cupido,
> Languentesque fovet solis ab igne faces.
> Insonuere novis lethalia cornua nervis,
> Triste micant ferro tela corusca novo. (95–100)

[This is the way lascivious Earth breathes out her passion, and all the other creatures are quick to follow their mother's example. For now wandering Cupid speeds through the whole world and renews his dying torch in the flames of the sun. His deadly bow twangs with new strings and his bright arrows, freshly tipped, gleam balefully.]

---

[98] The passage continues with Adam's reference to 'millions of spiritual creatures ... behold[ing]' creation 'both day and night,' which reintegrates vision into the picture; still, from the human perspective, the life-giving (and tactile) powers of the sun and stars are more fundamental. The association of 'spiritual creatures' with vision and animal 'nourish[ment]' with touch is likewise not coincidental.

3.2 Elegy V ('In Adventum Veris,' Spring 1629)

In fact, not only the characterisation but also the placement of Cupid's arrival within the structure of the elegy as a whole parallels the appearance of the 'blind boy' toward the end of Elegy I: Milton's playful tone in the passage at hand, again pointing to the supposed dangers proceeding from Cupid's weaponry, appears to echo that of the earlier elegy. Although, in the absence of the pronounced military and Circean context of the earlier elegy, the present portrayal of Cupid might seem more innocuous by comparison, it is actually more decidedly martial ('deadly bow,' 'gleam balefully'). Its overall effect could be seen as subliminally threatening, particularly in connection with the following assertion that 'now he tries to subdue even the unconquerable Diana [invictam Dianam], and chaste Vesta.' Whilst unproblematic, perhaps, in the abstract sense of the personifications involved ('spring makes love conquer chastity'), on the figural level this indicates a rather more troubling degree of menace. As with the references to Philomela, Pluto, and Proserpina in earlier passages, conquering Cupid points to very real tension and indeed potential for sexualised violence implicit in the LOVE IS CONQUEST metaphor. Cupid, the paradoxically blind archer, pierces the objects of his desire with his arrows just as the primarily visual rays of Phoebus (Apollo, again, was also the god of archery) touch the earth.[99] As in the earlier instances, the sensuous discourse of love carries a significantly darker undercurrent.

At this point, the poem partly abandons the sphere of mythology for that of classicising and pastoral (yet, in both cases, humanising) typification. In the first instance, an abstractly urban scene is evoked (its abstractness implied by 'urbes' in the plural):

> Marmoreas iuvenes clamant Hymenaee per urbes,
> Litus io Hymen, et cava saxa sonant.
> Cultior ille venit tunicaque decentior apta,
> Puniceum redolet vestis odora crocum
> Egrediturque frequens ad amoeni gaudia veris
> Virgineos auro cincta puella sinus.
> Votum est cuique suum, votum est tamen omnibus unum,
> Ut sibi quem cupiat, det Cytherea virum. (105–112)

[Through marble cities the young men are shouting 'Hymenaeus!' – the sea-shore and the hollow rocks resound with 'Io Hymen!' Hymen arrives, all decked out and very spruce in his traditional costume: his fragrant gown has the scent of tawny saffron. The girls, with their virgin breasts bound about with gold, run out in crowds to the joys of the lovely springtime. Each one has her own prayer, but all their prayers are the same: that Cytherea will give her the man of her desire.][100]

---

[99] The association of archery, vision, and light had earlier been established in the reference to Diana's 'quiver' ('pharetramque,' 45), which is parallelised with her laying aside the 'weak rays' ('tenues ponens radios,' 47) of the (female) moon, and contrasted with the 'light-bringing wheels' ('Luciferas ... rotas,' 46) of Phoebus' chariot (the sun typically figures as male). As the appearance of Cupid is linked to the coming of spring and return of Phoebus, his own arrows, perhaps, are imagined to share in the more powerful rays of the sun.
[100] This early reference to Hymen, the Greek god of marriage, is non-judgemental and simply part of the elegy's mythological machinery. In *Paradise Lost*, by contrast, Milton creates a pointed

The fact that the notional cities described are 'made of marble' not only indicates a rather stark, classical setting but also suggests, in concert with the shouting young men and the resounding hollow rocks of the next line ('clamant,' 'cava saxa sonant'), a clearly discernible, resonant soundscape.[101] Lines 105–6, then, are primarily audio-visual in character. Hymen, when he appears, brings with him the added sensory dimension of odour, whose delicate quality matches the emphasis laid on Hymen's general urbanity ('cultior,' 'decentior') when contrasted with the boisterous urban youths. By tracing its origin to a species of crocus – associated with spring as an early flowering plant – and focusing on odour, in particular, Milton both expands the conventional reference to Hymen's saffron robe and reconnects it to the theme of his elegy: spring, repeatedly addressed in terms of its olfactory qualities in the central passages of the poem.[102] As Hymen is supposed to join male and female elements in matrimony, his appearance in the present passage comes in between that of the young men and that of the 'girls' (actually a representative singular: 'frequens ... puella'), who are silent (except, perhaps, for their prayers) but, as in Elegy I, are visually conspicuous on account of their golden ornaments ('auro cincta'). Both, emphatically *young* men and *young* women ('iuvenes,' 'puella,' 'virgineos ... sinus'), establish the conventional connection between their age in life (youth) and the corresponding season (spring).

---

contrast between the imagined pious nuptials of Adam and Eve (in their bower, 'espoused Eve decked first her nuptial bed,/And *heavenly choirs* the hymenean *sung*,' 4.710–1, emphases added) and the later pagan debauchery presented to Adam in his vision of the future: 'And now of love they treat till the evening star/Love's harbinger appeared; then, all in heat/They light the nuptial torch [Hymen's attribute], and bid invoke/*Hymen, then first to marriage rites invoked*;/With feast and *music* all the tents *resound*' (11.588–92, emphases added). As in Elegy V, the invocation of Hymen is characterised in strongly acoustic terms by its resounding quality (in the elegy: 'clamant,' 'sonant').

[101] While Milton himself had not yet travelled outside of England in 1629, the stony solidity of continental European cities was almost proverbial, and occurs with regularity in English travel accounts of the period. Thus, Evelyn, who frequently mentions individual buildings or whole towns as being 'of stone,' remarks à propos Paris that, while it appeared to him 'not so large as London ... there is no comparison between the buildings, palaces, and materials, this [i. e., Paris] being entirely of stone and more sumptuous ...' (*Diary*, 1 April 1644). Only after the great fire of September 1666, London, which had been primarily timber-framed, was rebuilt in brick, tile, and glass; see Cockayne, *Hubbub*, 118–21, 131 (arguing also that after reconstruction, 'sound would ... have travelled in a different way through the streets, lined with solid new buildings,' 118).

[102] Contrast the visual focus on Hymen's 'saffron robe' in 'L'Allegro' (1631?), 125–30: 'There let Hymen oft appear/In saffron robe, with *taper clear*,/And pomp, and feast, and revelry,/With *mask*, and antique *pageantry*,/Such *sights* as youthful poets dream/On summer eves by haunted stream' (emphases added). For another example of (possibly odorous-gustatory) saffron in an amorous context see Ceres' lines from the wedding masque in Shakespeare's *The Tempest*: 'Hail, many colour'd messenger [i. e., Iris], that ne'er/Dost disobey the wife of Jupiter [i. e., Juno, Roman goddess of love, marriage, childbirth];/Who with thy *saffron wings* upon my flowers,/Diffusest *honey-drops*, refreshing showers ...' (4.1.76–79, emphases added).

3.2 Elegy V ('In Adventum Veris,' Spring 1629) 147

After this last multi-sensory, partly olfactory passage reminiscent of a wedding masque, the poem, as in its opening sections prior to the appearance of reviving Tellus, focuses on the senses of hearing and sight, which are treated sequentially. In the first of these passages, human lovers are again presented, this time in the idealising mode of pastoral-piscatorial song:[103]

> Nunc quoque septena modulatur arundine pastor,
> Et sua quae iungat carmina Phyllis habet.
> Navita nocturno placat sua sidera cantu,
> Delphinasque leves ad vada summa vocat. (113–16)

> [And now the shepherd plays on his pipe of seven reeds, and Phyllis <a stock female name of classical pastoral> has songs of her own to add to this. At night the sailor sings to his stars to make them gentle, and calls up nimble dolphins to the surface of the sea.]

As in the earlier reference to cities and coastal cliffs (both made of stone, both characterised by their strongly vertical orientation or steepness), these couplets bring together dry land and sea, although this time the scene appears to be the open country and the open sea, respectively. In this sense, the shepherd and the sailor are parallel musical figures. The shepherd's 'pipe of seven reeds' is the syrinx or panpipe, named for its supposed inventor, the god Pan.[104] The shepherd, moreover, has his instrumental music joined by the singing of his female counterpart (who even 'adds songs of her own'), whereas the sailor – in a turn alluding, perhaps, to the proverbial solitariness/enforced celibacy of the seafarer – has to provide both, music and song (or music through song). The first possibility is established by the comparison of the sailor to the mythical Greek bard Arion, whose distressed singing charmed a school of dolphins – animals sacred to Apollo – into saving him from drowning; in pictorial representation, he is usually shown playing a lyre, a kithara, or some other stringed instrument.[105] The second possibility – of *a cappella* singing – is suggested by the strong vocal implications of the ablative-instrumental 'nocturno cantu' and of 'vocat.' Ultimately, both possibilities are equally present in the couplet, suggesting, as in the case of the elegiac speaker's 'distributed duet' with Philomela, an impression of notional music that oscillates between perception and abstraction. In his night-time solo performance, moreover, the sailor is both contrasted and paralleled with the shepherd: he does not have the shepherd's fe-

---

[103] On the piscatorial element in the pastoral tradition, see Peter V. Marinelli, *Pastoral* (London: Methuen, 1971), discussing Donne's 'The Bait'.
[104] See Alberto Ausoni, *Music in Art*, tr. Stephen Sartarelli (Los Angeles: J. Paul Getty Museum, 2009), 78.
[105] His lyre, too, connects him with his tutelary deity Apollo. See Ausoni, *Music in Art*, 116–7. Milton refers to Arion explicitly in 'Ad Patrem' (1631/2?), 60, wishing his musician father might 'deservedly inherit Arion's fame,' and, implicitly by reference to his dolphins, in *Lycidas* (1637), 163–4: 'Look homeward angel now, and melt with ruth./And, O ye dolphins, waft the hapless youth.' The young poet Edward King, who is commemorated in *Lycidas*, had drowned at sea (as Arion had not). In both cases, the reference to Arion is occasioned by the addressee-dedicatee of the poem.

male companion, but his song addresses and intends to move the stars ('*his* stars,' pointedly) and the creatures of the sea.[106] Likewise, his instrument (if he has one) is only suggested by the allusion to Arion and the (parallel? or contrasting?) mention of the shepherd's pipe. In taking up established themes of the poem, the shepherd and Phyllis appear to be mirroring the various romantic couples represented earlier, whereas the singing sailor is closer to the elegiac speaker's own poet persona. Together with the young men and women of the preceding lines, the shepherd, Phyllis, and the sailor form a human counter-element to the extended mythological-allegorical courtship represented in the central passages of the elegy.

In its concluding section, however, the poem returns to the mythological sphere. Taking up his initial visionary assertion, 'I see in my mind's eye what is going on all over Olympus' (19), the speaker now proclaims that 'Jupiter himself frolics on high Olympus with his wife, and summons his attendant gods to his feast' (117–8). As the following description establishes, this feast will take place at, or immediately after, sunset:

> Nunc etiam Satyri cum sera crepuscula surgunt,
> Pervolitant celeri florea rura choro,
> Sylvanusque sua cyparissi fronde revinctus,
> Semicaperque Deus, semideusque caper.
> Quaeque sub arboribus Dryades latuere vetustis
> Per iuga, per solos expatiantur agros. (119–124)

> [Now, as the evening twilight falls, the satyrs flit through the flowery meadows in a swift band, and with them Sylvanus, a god half-goat, a goat half-god, crowned with leaves from his favourite tree, the cypress. And the dryads who lay hidden beneath the ancient trees now wander about on hill-tops and through lonely fields.]

In a sense, the elegy, which had evoked the circularity of time in its very first line ('In se perpetuo Tempus revolubile gyro'), and which had early on staged the visual impressions of sunrise and red morning light, is about to come full circle: having followed the entirety of a spring day from early dawn to the falling of dusk, which now serves to put a stress on what light is left (conversely, the coming of dawn had earlier been established by the fact that 'wild night and his darkness are banished,' 33–34). The coming of evening at the poem's conclusion mirrors the banishment of night at its opening; the light-suffused appearance of Phoebus ('the shining one') in the central passages of the poem forms the bright zenith of vision between those two liminal visual experiences.

While the 'flowery meadows' of spring are still in evidence, Milton's reference to the cypress, associated in classical symbolism with death and mourning, signals, after the repeated hints at the 'dark side' of sensory discourse throughout the poem, a definite

---

[106] A similarly ambiguous presentation of a nocturnal poet-singer figure is later given to Milton's epic persona in the proem to *PL* 7, singing alone yet accompanied by his 'heavenly muse,' Urania: '… in darkness, and with dangers compassed round,/And *solitude*; yet *not alone*, while thou/Visitst my slumbers nightly, or when morn/Purples the east: …' (7.27–30, emphases added).

3.2 Elegy V ('In Adventum Veris,' Spring 1629)

shift in mood.[107] Likewise, the dryads' wandering through 'lonely fields' also continues the theme of solitariness introduced in the image of the singing sailor and contributes to the conventionally 'elegiac' tone, as per more recent understandings of the term, of these final lines. As Sylvanus, Pan, and 'lustful Faunus' ('cupidus Faunus') chase nymphs and goddesses ('mother Cybele and Ceres hardly find safety for themselves,' 126–7), the earlier theme of love as conquest is taken up as well. Now, this may be said to point to the savage nature of mere bodily lust: in fact, not just Sylvanus but all three gods named were figured as 'half-goat ... half-god,' and thus associated with an animal symbolising sensuality, fertility, and lust.[108] Two of them, the Greek Pan and the Roman Faunus, often identified with each other, are also associated with (pastoral) music. Their appearance here connects to the preceding pastoral scene featuring Phyllis and the piping shepherd.[109] In a further sensory detail, the present lines point out that not only love but lust, too, comes by sight: 'now she [i.e., a nymph] hides, but not very well, and even as she hides she hopes to be seen [cupit ... videri]; she runs away, but as she runs she is anxious to be overtaken' (129–30). Even in the 'otherland' of pagan pastoral, where gods may simply *be* what humans – according to Milton's views elsewhere – can only fall down to being, these scenes are cast in the fading light of dusk, and the declining year.

From the 'flowery meadows,' after all, the action has by now moved first to 'grainfields and thickets' (125), the former suggestive of harvest, and autumn rather than spring, and then further, into the woods. Much as they continue to celebrate the pleasures of the gods, the shades intensify over the course of these following lines, as 'the gods ... prefer these woods to their heavens [caelo], and each grove has its particular deities' (131–2). As they are pastoral deities, their pleasures are thoroughly *earthly*, enjoyed in the shades of woods and thickets, which are contrasted with the heavenly (and presumably bright) dwellings of the gods ('their heavens') above.[110] As in the earlier meeting of Phoebus and Tellus, distinct sensory spheres, characterised by their spatial differentiation in terms of UP and DOWN, are confronted. But whereas the earlier scene had centred on the affectionate, procreative meeting of sun and earth, however, the latter is concerned with mere enjoyment or even lust. That the line between the two is fine indeed is suggested by Milton's vacillating reference to 'god[s] half-goat[s] ...

---

[107] In the present instance, this symbolism is overdetermined by the mythical figure wearing the Cypress wreath: 'Sylvanus loved a boy called Cyparissus, who died of grief at the loss of a pet hind. The god turned the dead boy into a cypress, and wears leaves of this tree in remembrance' (Carey ad loc.).

[108] The goat is listed as one of the animals symbolising the quasi-Circean loss of human nature and submission to sensuality in *Comus*, 71.

[109] See Ausoni, *Music in Art*, 78–83 on 'A pastoral divinity, Pan is represented with animal features that underscore his connection with the feral aspects of nature' (78).

[110] There is a certain sense of doubtful, tendentially brutish embodiment in these lines, as if the classical gods' decision to enjoy earth(l)y pleasures, while basically blameless, had still somehow diminished their formerly exalted status. Milton's presentation of these scenes connects to a long tradition of classical and Renaissance debates over the materiality and tangibility of the gods/God; see Moshenska, *Feeling Pleasures*, 81–108. Moshenska's characterisation of Virgil's fluctuation 'between comforting presence and painful absence' (89) in his portrayal of divine tactility bears a family relation, perhaps, to Milton's more strongly moralised approach in Elegy V.

goat[s] half-god[s]'.[111] Beneath its superficial frivolity, the presentation of these classical scenes appears tinged by a doubt absent in the earlier depiction of Phoebus and Tellus, blameless and whole (not 'half-'anything) in their respective allegorical characters. Phoebus' touching is pure and still expressed in visual terms. The goatish half-gods' rustic groping in the final passages of the elegy is not condemned outright by the elegiac speaker, nor is it presented as unpleasant or undesirable from the nymphs' perspective; however, it is presented in a different mode compared to the procreative encounter 'at eye level' between Phoebus and Tellus: the fauns encounter their nymphs in terms of 'hide-and-seek,' in terms of playing tag. The difference between this and a 'rape' such as Proserpina's may, potentially, be hard to tell. As dusk falls on these scenes, Milton's presentation encourages the suspicion that pagan groves might be shady places in more senses than one.

In taking up, with slight grammatical variation, the pentameter of the couplet just quoted, thus turning it into the hexameter of the next elegiac couplet, Milton effectively links the last of the visionary scenes depicted in his elegy – the evening activities of fauns and nymphs – to the elegiac speaker's peroration, which now begins:

> Dii quoque non dubitant caelo praeponere sylvas,
> Et sua quisque diu sibi numina lucus habet.
> Et sua quisque diu sibi numina lucus habeto,
> Nec vos arborea dii precor ite domo. (131–4)

> [The gods, too, unhesitatingly prefer these woods to their heavens, and each grove has its own particular deities. Long may each grove have its own particular deities: do not leave your homes among the trees, gods, I beseech you.]

The speaker's appeal to the gods, 'precor,' constitutes the first explicit highlighting of the Milton's elegiac persona since the injunction, 'let us hymn [celebremus] the praises of spring' (29–30), uttered immediately after the speaker's 'duet' with Philomela. For the duration of the 'visionary scenes' at the poem's centre, the elegiac I had remained implicit; now it returns. In this sense, too, Elegy V is structured, concentrically, around the meeting of Tellus and Phoebus. The address to the gods at the poem's conclusion echoes, then, the passages at its beginning, in which the speaker had established the multilateral relation between himself, the season, and his own inspiration: spring brings inspiration to the poet, and the poet, helped by inspiration, evokes the coming of spring in the medium of the resulting poem.

At the end of the elegy, however, while the self-referential quality of the poetic discourse remains, its tone shifts appreciably: 'Te referant miseris te Iupiter aurea terris/Saecla, quid ad nimbos aspera tela redis?' ('May the golden age bring you back, Jove, to this wretched world!/Why go back to your cruel weapons in the clouds?', 135–6). Transporting an ambiguous feeling of recent or impending loss – have the gods left?

---

[111] See Carey ad loc. for possible sources of the formula, among them Ovid's reference to the Minotaur as 'semibovemque virum, semivirumque bovem' in *Ars Am.* 2.24. Considering the elegy's concern with divine and earthly senses and their conflicting valuations, Milton's substitutions (god for man and goat for bull) appear as significant as the context of the original.

3.2 Elegy V ('In Adventum Veris,' Spring 1629)

or may their departure yet be avoided? – lines 133–36, following on the extended poetic evocation of spring throughout most of the poem, express a painful longing for *eternal* spring. What Milton's elegiac speaker now wishes for, in effect, is the impossible continuation of a paradisiacal state of renewal and blossoming. This state, by definition, must be transitory, as it must be followed by the subsequent periods of maturation, harvest, and withering. Even poetry, Elegy V appears to demonstrate, can only truly eternalise spring at the cost of a corresponding fear of winter or, put differently: an adequate representation of sensory pleasure without the doubtful appreciation of its transience is simply not possible. The tension of this impossibility results, in the poem's final two elegiac couplets, in an imploration, directed at Phoebus himself, to please take his time, and thus prolong the pleasures of spring:

> Tu saltem lente rapidos age Phoebe iugales
> Qua potes, et sensim tempora veris eant.
> Brumaque productas tarde ferat hispida noctes,
> Ingruat et nostro serior umbra polo. (137–140)

> [At any rate, Phoebus, drive your swift team as slowly as you can, and let the passing of the springtime be gradual. May rough winter be tardy in bringing us his long nights, and may it be late in the day when shadows assail our sky.]

Significantly, the word on which the speaker's hope for the persistence of spring hinges at the same time offers a last salute to the sensory sphere that had dominated the poem's central scenes: the adverbial 'sensim' – 'let springtime pass *gradually*' – is derived from the participle 'sensus,' meaning 'felt or perceived through the senses.'[112] Its meaning in the context of the poem should be construed as twofold: 'let the passing of spring be so slow that it is *only just perceptible*' (the primary meaning) and 'let the passing of spring be such that it *affects the senses* [in all the ways laid out earlier in this poem].'

Significantly, too, Milton's only other use of 'sensim' also occurs in a markedly sensory context: in a short, ten-line poem, the first of three dedicated by Milton to the Roman singer Leonora Baroni and titled 'Ad Leonoram Romae canentem' ('To Leonora singing at Rome,' 1638/9), the speaker affirms that, in the addressee's heavenly singing, a divine 'third mind ... warbling ... creeps and graciously teaches mortal hearts how to grow accustomed, little by little [sensim], to immortal sound.' 'Little by little' – or 'audibly' – divine singing brings immortal sound to mortal hearts.[113] As the 'sensim' of Elegy V acknowledges both the sensuous appeal of an idealised spring and the very real constraints imposed upon that ideal, the elegiac speaker is begging Phoebus to, please, do the sensible thing – and make spring last. While the speaker's concluding wish is in tune with the final couplet of 'Song. On May Morning' ('Thus we salute thee with our early song/And welcome thee, and wish thee long,' 9–10), its tone is decidedly less assured.

---

[112] *OLD*, 'sentio,' 'sensim.'
[113] See Katherine R. Larson, *The Matter of Song in Early Modern England: Texts in and of the Air* (Oxford: Oxford University Press, 2019), 64–65, 89–94, on Milton's 'Leonora' sonnets.

The concluding couplets of Elegy V also expose the relativity of all sensuous pleasure in another way: on a lexical level, the 'umbra' of line 140 ('... when *shadows* assail our sky') corresponds precisely to 'umbram' in line 85 ('It will be more pleasant for you to seek coolness in my *shades*, Phoebus') although, on a pragmatic level, they are polar opposites (an opposition mediated, I have suggested, by the progressively darkening scene immediately preceding the poem's finale). The 'shades' of a warm spring are pleasing, the 'shadows' of approaching winter, on the other hand, are menacing. Both might share a similar visual quality, but their respective tactile force is clearly quite different. In this sense, the elegy's conclusion also presents a reverse image of the pleasing union of vision and touch – sunny, yet also shady – celebrated in the meeting of Phoebus and Tellus at the poem's centre.[114]

In again superimposing, finally, the two timescales of a day (from dawn to dusk) and the returning year (from spring to winter), and presenting them as substantially equivalent – spring comes with the redness of dawn, winter threatens as evening twilight falls –, the poem takes up another motif introduced at its outset. This also highlights the figurative dimension of the entities involved (i.e., the four seasons corresponding to morning, noon, evening, and night) and points to the conventional third equivalent: namely, the traditional four ages in a person's life (childhood, youth, maturity, and old age).[115] The poem does not seek a strict equivalence: the young women and men appearing in the Hymen scene are not children; however, their simultaneous association with spring and love seems clear. The third timescale of human aging arguably also bears some relevance to the poem's concluding lines. In the pagan universe of Milton's elegy, in any case, this last progression is unidirectional, in contrast to the others, which are cyclical (and are presented as such in the poem). The elegiac speaker's plea for a prolongation of spring, then, may also express a desire to prolong youth, and life in general, in the face of inescapable winter, or death.

***

Milton's elegy 'On the Coming of Spring' presents its subject as a time of multi-sensory, even synaesthetic pleasures; as a season of love, procreation, and growth. The first aspect is associated with his *illustrative* and *descriptive* use of sensory discourse (either referring to individual perceptions or illustrating 'what spring is like'). The second as-

---

[114] Regarding a similar thematic context, Hollander has pointed to the movement, in Virgil's 'First Eclogue,' from the '*umbrae* of pleasant shade [to] the encroaching *tenebrae* of night,' arguing that, in fact, '*umbra* in this poem starts out as what we may in English distinguish as the "shade" of foliage, and ends with the lengthening shadows that will lead to what we might call the *tenebrae* of fallen night' (*Substance of Shadow*, 35).

[115] Old age, traditionally, was associated not just with failing eyesight and hearing but with a general loss of sensory acuity and sensuous enjoyment (see, for instance, Avrahami, *Senses of Scripture*, 101, 202–205. When John Locke met a very old lady in 1680 (supposedly 108 years old at that time), he made a point of noting that 'her hearing is very good and her smelling so quick that as soon as she came near me she said I smelt very sweet, I having a new pair of gloves on that were not strong scented' – gloves were scented with ambergris to cover up the unpleasant smell of tanning residues. (Locke quoted in Laslett, *World We Have Lost*, 125.)

pect corresponds, primarily, to the *conceptual* use of sensory discourse, which is often based in metaphor, linking semantic domains related to each other by their shared association to the sensory sphere (as in the case of mountains and towers, or of love and warfare).

Many elements of the poem pertaining to those two uses are commonplace: mountains, for example, are an epitome of a high viewing position, as are towers. Their concrete combination with other sensory elements, however, and most of all the way they are presented in context, are not quite as fixed. Milton's specific treatment of his theme rests on the consistency with which he interfuses conventional depictions of sensuous vernal bliss with conceptually more complex, though not necessarily less sensory, components. His creative interweaving of references to abstract and concrete, notional and embodied forms of sense perception is a case in point, as is the repeated suggestion of 'darker' aspects through sensory discourse. At first, these are only implied in the context of conventionally pleasing uses, as with the references to Philomela and Proserpina; the latter's story would later be referenced in *Paradise Lost* in an image that neatly captures the 'bright' and 'dark' potentials of sensory discourse: '... Proserpine gathering flowers,/Herself a fairer flower by gloomy Dis/Was gathered ...' (4.267–9). At the conclusion of Elegy V, finally, the speaker's doubts and apprehensions are made explicit. This, also, is expressed in sensory terms as a fear of darkness and the end of sensuous spring (i.e., of love, of youth, of life in general).

Milton's presentation of spring in the structurally and conceptually central Tellus–Phoebus passage effects a complex superimposition of the two aspects of sensory discourse. On the one hand, the passage stages the multi-sensuousness of vernal abundance, phrased in the 'flowery language' of pleasantly descriptive sensory discourse (where 'cinnamon-scented' breezes follow on 'many-coloured flowers'); in its more complex form, this is figured as actual synaesthesia. On the other hand, the elegy considers the question of how the fertility of spring comes into being in the first place. Its answer, too, is put in sensory terms and points to the temporary 'lowering' (or, *sensu etymologico*, the 'humiliation') of Phoebus, the sun, thus implying a revaluation of customary sensory and other conceptual hierarchies.

These two distinct uses of sensory discourse in Elegy V may also be described in terms of the different perspectives on the sensorium they imply. In the first instance (of multi-sensuousness), the sensorium is fused into an equalised continuum, given added coherence by synaesthetic cross-referencing. In the second case (of its conceptual use), the two hierarchical extremes of the sensorium, (male) vision and (female) touch, are, as it were, short-circuited to account for the renewal of nature after winter. However, these two perspectives do not stand side by side, unconnected: Tellus advertises her potential, multi-sensuous springtime attractions in an attempt to hasten the coming of Phoebus, and thus spring.

In some respects, both Milton's conceptual preoccupations (e.g., with vision, towers, and fortifications) and his fusion of different aspects of sensory discourse (as in the theophany of Apollo and the duet with Philomela) are consistent across their repeated expressions, either within the elegy or even between poems (as became clear in numerous correspondences with Elegy I in particular). Other aspects, such as the poem's confrontation of vision and touch, its shifting sensory and conceptual valuation of *umbra* as 'cool shade' or 'cold shadow,' and the varying presentations of erotic tactility as either procreative or merely lecherous, indicate a principally fluid sensorium, in which individual senses or perceptions do not have a fixed meaning. The sensorium thus understood presents a 'conceptual toolbox' rather than a repertory of more or less pleasing sense perceptions. In allowing for considerable expressive variance, it appears geared towards deliberation and the production of *new* insights, not only about the senses but also about a variety of more abstract topics conventionally associated with them (again: love, youth, life in general). Insofar as they reflect creatively on the nature, capacities, and uncertain (i.e., potentially problematic) character of sense perception and further problems related to it, Milton's creative uses of sensory imagery and concepts thus fulfil what I have earlier called the *deliberative* function of sensory discourse. This is true of the poem's intricate reflections on vision and touch, procreativeness and lustfulness, and finally the (literal and metaphorical) precariousness of spring in the face of threatening winter.

Despite its vernal theme and overall optimism, then, Milton's poem is an elegy in an emphatic sense, with all the assumptions about the genre this implies: love and lament, pastoral ideality and pain all contribute to a generic pressure toward serious reflection.[116] Similar to Elegy I, which had combined (positive) elements of a traditional love elegy with a mock-Ovidian lament of the 'exile' from university, Elegy V displays a strain of (positive) love elegy that is displaced, towards the conclusion of the poem, by an 'elegiac' mood in the later understanding of the term. In fact, from its early celebration of inspired experience and meticulous description of vernal imagery through the focus of later passages on romantic love and to the gradual introduction of the themes of loss and mourning (begun with the reference to Persephone), Milton's Elegy V could be seen as tracing the thematic development of the elegy as a genre.

In addition, Elegy V reflects on time in two distinct senses at once, as abstract/cyclical *and* concrete/ephemeral – a superimposition resulting in a tension between the poem's initial assertion of the perpetual cyclicity of Time, on the one hand, and the elegy's actually directional (if concentric) structure, on the other. This concentricity of Elegy V is also reflected in the development of its sensory discourse, which reaches 'peak sensuality' in the description of Tellus and her subsequent address to Phoebus. In these lines (55–94), all the senses, including touch, are present. Immediately before and after, olfactory images occur, mixed with those of sight and sound. Even further away from the sensuous centre of the poem, vision and hearing are addressed separately: the early appearance of Phoebus at dawn and the 'warbling song' of Philomela are mirrored later by scenes of pastoral music-making and falling dusk, with the latter two already preparing the elegy's doubtful conclusion.

This doubt is connected to the fact that the poem itself is 'only' concentric, not itself cyclical, and is about what is *perceived*, not abstractly known, of spring. While the poem's mythological-allegorical figures ultimately belong to the abstract, cyclical sphere of nature (presupposing an eventual return of day, or spring), it is their presentation in terms of sensory experience, pleasure, and longing – Tellus 'yearns' for Phoebus' embraces – that individualises them. This individualising effect of the sensory sphere, in the end, facilitates the connection between *their experience* of spring and *the*

---

[116] See, again, *The Oxford Handbook of the Elegy*, ed. Weisman.

speaker's fear of losing spring. In the realm of allegory, individual seasons only stand for their cyclical recurrence; in the realm of experience, each season or year is a singularly precious piece of life.

The elegy does not conclude, however, with a Herrickian exhortation to 'gather rosebuds while ye may'; rather, readers are left with a conflicted and doubtful view of the subjects presented. At the end of the poem, the coming of spring has been made perceptible in its effects and intelligible in its implications – but the deliberative evaluation of these elements (ultimately left, perhaps, to the reader) has only been begun. At this point, the poem's emphasis on *potentiality* becomes significant. As the elegy's conclusion argues, the sensory moment of spring is precarious, subject to change and decay. At the same time, however, – and perhaps in a counter-movement to threatening loss – the elegy consistently presents spring as pure creative potentiality: as the *imagined* encounter of Tellus and Phoebus, never actually consummated, always expressed in terms of yearning, possibilities, and invitations. As such, Elegy V, despite its doubtful ending, also presents a confident assertion of the creative powers of the poet, wielding sensory discourse – with a certain didactic impulse – for his purposes of delighting, teaching, and admonishing or making the reader reflect on things beyond the immediate reach of the senses.[117]

3.3 Elegy VII (Summer? 1628)
'Paphian Fire,' Burning Passions, and the Individualising Experience of Love

Having considered the introduction of sensory discourse into Milton's sequence of elegies in Elegy I as well as its complex application in Elegy V – which has been called 'the peak of Milton's earlier Latin poetry' –, a review of the relevant themes in Elegy VII, composed between elegies IV and V by Carey's reckoning, will further qualify the observations made so far, and will serve as an epilogue to this chapter on Milton's Latin elegies.[118]

More similar in this respect to Elegy I than to V, Elegy VII focuses entirely on the topic of romantic love, and in particular on the effect of female visual attractiveness on the elegiac speaker. The vehicle for reflecting upon this attraction, its power and possible danger, is again classical mythology, represented in the main by Cupid ('Amor'), son of Venus. In fact, the speaker's involvement with Cupid – from taunting and being threatened by him, through Cupid's eventual 'attack,' to the speaker's ultimate vow of future worship – informs the elegy's entire structure. Consequently, the image of Cupid the archer is much more present than it is in elegies I and V, where his respective appearances near the end of the poems serve to illustrate certain points made earlier – namely, that romantic love is unpredictable and potentially dangerous –; but those

---

[117] Seen in this way, Milton's use of sensory discourse in Elegy V resembles the mechanisms explored in Clune, *Writing Against Time*.

[118] A. S. P. Woodhouse quoted in *Variorum* I, 95. While Elegy I actually appears to have been the first written of Milton's Latin elegies based on internal and external evidence, Elegy VII, though placed last upon publication, was not written last; most probably, Elegy VI was. On Milton's possible motivation for arranging the elegies non-chronologically in the 1645 *Poems*, see *SP*, 72, and *Variorum* I, 127–8.

points are made in the context of other, more prominent concerns. In Elegy VII, by contrast, the questions represented by Cupid afford the central points of deliberation, negotiated, as one might expect, in sensory terms.

In the opening lines of Elegy VII, the speaker looks back to a time when he was as yet oblivious to the powers of Venus: 'Nondum blanda tuas leges Amathusia noram,/Et Paphio vacuum pectus ab igne fuit' – 'I was still ignorant of your laws, seductive Amathusia [i.e., Venus], and my breast contained no Paphian fire' (1–2). The terminology ('blanda,' 'Paphio') is reminiscent of the other elegies, while the reference to fire introduces a motif most prominent in Elegy VII. In the speaker's following, dismissive references to Cupid, there appears none of the subliminal menace that had characterised corresponding passages in elegies I and V, quite the opposite:

> Saepe cupidineas, puerilia tela, sagittas,
> Atque tuum sprevi maxime, numen, Amor.
> Tu puer imbelles dixi transfige columbas,
> Conveniunt tenero mollia bella duci.
> Aut de passeribus tumidos age, parve, triumphos,
> Haec sunt militiae digna trophaea tuae:
> In genus humanum quid inania dirigis arma?
> Non valet in fortes ista pharetra viros.   (3–10)

> [I often made fun of Cupid's arrows, calling them childish weapons, and I scorned your godhead, O mighty Love. 'Go and shoot doves, lad; they can't hurt you,' I said, 'a tender campaigner like you is only fit for soft wars. Or go and boast about the triumphs you've won over sparrows, little boy: those are the sort of trophies which your warfare deserves. Why do you aim your idle darts at human beings? Your quiver's no good against grown-up men.']

By the double tactile reference to tenderness and softness ('tenero,' 'mollia bella'), associated with children and peaceable doves (and contrasted with 'strong men'), Cupid's paradoxical nature as an armed child is addressed. The paradox is not sustained, however, but is resolved by giving preference to one of the two sides. (This, as will become apparent, is the speaker's fundamental fallacy.) In comparison, it appears that the respective imagery of elegies I and V lays its emphasis rather on the opposite element of Cupid's warlikeness. The Cupid of the first lines of Elegy VII may be childlike – playing with arrows and sparrows –, but he is also irascible: he 'could not bear this [sc. disparagement] (not one of the gods is more easily irritated than he), and he grew twice as angry as before [duplici ... igne calet – lit., "he glows with twice the fire"]' (11–12), which takes up the fire imagery of line 2.

After the twelve-line prologue, Elegy VII, too, sets the scene, and does so in a way partially familiar from Elegy V, 'Song. On May Morning,' and the 'Elegiac Verses':

> Ver erat, et summae radians per culmina villae
> Attulerat primam lux tibi Maie diem:
> At mihi adhuc refugam quaerebant lumina noctem

Nec matutinum sustinuere iubar.
Astat Amor lecto, pictis Amor impiger alis,
Prodidit astantem mota pharetra deum:
Prodidit et facies, et dulce minantis ocelli,
Et quicquid puero, dignum et Amore fuit. (13–20)

[It was spring, and the dawn shining over the gables of the tall farmhouse had brought your first day, May. But my eyes still longed for the vanishing night, and could not bear the bright morning sunshine. Love stood by my bed, agile Love with his brightly coloured wings. His swinging quiver and his face and his sweetly threatening eyes gave him away, and whatever else was worthy of a boy, worthy even of Love.]

The poem's spring setting evidently honours the conventional association of the season with love, extensively reflected upon in Elegy V, where the dawn also played a significant structural role (opposite the subsequent dusk). Early morning settings feature prominently in 'Song. On May Morning' and, particularly, in the 'Elegiac Verses' and 'Theme on Early Rising,' where they accentuate the onset of perception after waking up. With reference to the visual sphere, more specifically, 'Elegiac Verses' had advocated early rising by special reference to the invigorating quality of morning light:

Get up, come on, get up! It's time! Shake off these worthless slumbers: it's getting light. ... Fiery Titan is rearing his head above the eastern waves, and flinging bright sunlight [nitidum ... iubar] over the gay fields. You sluggard, you're not likely to find such sights as these in that downy bed of yours, where feeble lethargy closes your eyes. (1–2, 5–6, 13–14)

Whereas the sun's 'radiance' or 'splendour' ('iubar') is 'nitidum' in the earlier verses – 'shining,' that is, or even 'beautiful,' in any case positive –, in Elegy VII it is just 'matutinum': neutrally 'matutinal' or (perhaps even too) 'early.'[119] Furthermore, while in 'Elegiac Verses' the sun and the speaker are parallelised through the personification of 'fiery Titan ... rearing his head above the eastern waves,' their confrontation in Elegy VII is characterised as unpleasant: 'my eyes still longed for the vanishing night, and could not bear the bright morning sunshine.' Elegy VII thus not only inverses the established trope of the pleasantness of early morning, but also presents the first genuinely unpleasant sensation in all the poems considered so far.[120] The speaker of

---

[119] '(Of a person, his features) Glowing with beauty, youth, or sim[ilar]' (*OLD*, 'nitidus,' 3); 'Of or belonging to the early morning' (*OLD*, 'matutinus'). For Elegy VII, it could be argued that the sun's rising above the roof of the 'highest' or 'very high' farmhouse ('summae ... villae') actually indicates that – the slowness of the speaker's 'biological clock' notwithstanding – morning has progressed quite far towards noon. In the concluding couplet of 'Song. On May Morning,' the earliness of the morning is also highlighted, but bears no negative or doubtful implications: 'Thus we salute thee with our early song/And welcome thee, and wish thee long' (9–10).
[120] Elegies I and V do refer to potentially unpleasant effects of sensation (possible bewitchment in the 'infamous halls of faithless Circe'), or the threat of unpleasantness in some other place ('bare fields which offer no gentle shades') or at some later date ('when shadows assail our sky').

Elegy VII clearly is a long way from the densely packed initial admonitions of 'Elegiac Verses,' 'Surge, age surge, leves ... excute somnos,/... tepidi fulcra relinque tori ...' (1–2). The positive association of early morning sunlight, waking up, and vision is not only denied but – more or less playfully – reversed.

When Cupid is now described as having 'sweetly threatening eyes,' staying within the general associative realm of vision suggested by the setting (dawn/sunrise, waking up), the elegy makes a first step towards a re-characterisation of the harmless figure evoked by the speaker's earlier remarks. In the reference to Cupid's 'brightly coloured wings,' as well, the focus is clearly on sight – a purely visual complement of sorts to the multi-sensory, 'cinnamon-scented wings' of Zephyrus in Elegy V. In its additive survey of visual features, jumping from Cupid's wings – most salient, probably, on account of their intense coloration – to his quiver to his face to his eyes, and concluding on the euphemistic 'whatever else was worthy of a boy,' this 'eye-witness description' of Cupid is in clear contrast to the speaker's earlier disparaging remarks, which had not been founded in (imaginary) perception: there, the only sensory references (to Cupid's tenderness and his 'soft wars') had been figurative and/or merely asserted by the speaker without actual (sensory) experience, possibly on the basis of the speaker's preconceived notion of the nature of Love. This is decidedly different in the lines at hand, in which Cupid's presence at the speaker's bedside is stressed ('Astat,' 'astantem'). He is there, and he is there to be *seen*.

The mini-catalogue of Cupid's visual appearance in lines 17–20 also anticipates a later and longer but similarly fragmented description of an attractive girl (69–76), which suggests the speaker's attraction to the beautiful boy Cupid.[121] On the one hand, this is necessary on an abstract, Platonising level: Cupid *is* 'Amor,' 'Love' – and Love must be lovely. On the other hand, the clear visual-perceptive focus on the surprise visitor's 'giving himself away' ('prodidit,' twice) through his attractive and/or conspicuous features stresses the 'thisness' of Cupid as seen and appreciated by the elegiac speaker. The figure by the bedside is no mere allegorical abstraction (if ever so perfect) but also a concrete object of the speaker's perception, and hence his attraction.[122] In comparing Amor by the bedside to Ganymede and Hylas, legendary for their handsomeness, the following lines also emphasise the bodily attractiveness of the figure: 'This is what the Trojan lad [i.e., Ganymede] looks like, while he mixes brimming goblets for infatuated Jove ...; and this is what Hylas ... looked like – Hylas, who lured the beautiful nymphs to his kisses and was stolen away by a Naiad.' Ganymede and Hylas – cupbearer to the gods and weapon-bearer/lover of Hercules, respectively – represent bodily love and sensuous enjoyment more generally. In the (intensely sensuous) banquet scene of *Paradise Regained*, one of the temptations offered by Satan to Christ, Milton would many

---

[121] This aspect of the elegy has recently been discussed by John S. Garrison, '"Overflowing Cups for Amorous Jove": Abundance and Attraction in Milton's Elegies,' in: David L. Orvis (ed.), *Queer Milton* (Cham: Palgrave Macmillan, 2018), 93–115.

[122] In this, the 'Coleridgean' sense of 'a translucence of the special [the species] in the individual, or of the general [genus] in the special ... above all, by the translucence of the eternal through and in the temporal,' the Cupid of these lines might be called a *symbol* of attractive beauty; Coleridge quoted in René Wellek/Austin Warren, *Theory of Literature*, 3rd ed. (Harmondsworth: Penguin, 1973 [1963]), 189.

years later refer to 'tall stripling youths rich-clad, of fairer hue/Than Ganymede or Hylas' (2.352–3). In the present context, no such ultimately negative evaluation seems intended, although the reference to Hylas' eventual abduction by the nymphs hints at the possible negative consequences of passion. Even without the later parallel passage, then, it is clear that the speaker is attracted to Cupid as an embodiment of Love.[123]

If he is lovely, Cupid is also still angry (earlier he had glowed with rage), and addresses the speaker accordingly:

> Et miser exemplo sapuisses tutius, inquit,
> Nunc mea quid possit dextera testis eris.
> Inter et expertos vires numerabere nostras,
> Et faciam vero per tua damna fidem.
> Ipse ego si nescis strato pythone superbum
> Edomui Phoebum, cessit et ille mihi;   (27–32)

['You miserable creature, you would have been wiser and safer is you had learned by the example of others. Now you will yourself witness what my right hand can do. You shall be numbered among those who have felt my strength: by your suffering I shall make people believe the truth about me. It was I, in case you don't know it, who tamed Phoebus while he gloried in the slaying of the Python. Even he yielded to me …']

In a context that is, perhaps, surprising, these lines introduce a theme which is closely connected to sense perception but has not been addressed explicitly in the elegies discussed so far: namely, the high significance of the senses in the realm of knowledge and wisdom, reached by direct experience ('expertos,' derived from *experior*) or the experience of others ('exemplo sapuisses,' with the etymological background of 'tasting'), and conceived in terms of witnessing ('testis eris') or suffering a particular experience ('Inter et expertos vires numerabere nostras', 'tua damna'). Conventionally, witnessing might be said to be connected more closely to vision, and suffering, to the sense of touch; their relationship in the present context, however, is less clearly assigned. Even so, they may be related to different subjects of knowledge, as the speaker's witnessing relates to the first-hand knowledge he himself gains, whereas his suffering, Cupid suggests, will be for the potential benefit of others. After all, Cupid intends to make the speaker an example to others, to make an example *of the speaker* and thus 'verily' to create faith in his own powers ('faciam vero per tua damna fidem').

The capstone of Cupid's achievement is that he himself 'tamed Phoebus' the god of archery, by making him fall in love: 'whenever he remembers Daphne he confesses that my arrows are more accurate and more painful than his own' (33–34). In elegies I and V, Phoebus Apollo figures (also) as the god of music and poetry, aspects of the deity that are all but absent in Elegy VII.[124] (In the present passage of Elegy VII, in fact, his only

---

[123] In the first half of the elegy, he is referred to exclusively as 'Amor' or by relating him to his mother, Venus ('Cyprius,' 11). At 65, he is called *Cupidus*.

[124] In Cupid's sneering remark that 'your muses will not be able to protect you, you fool' (45), there is a reference, rare in Elegy VII, to the sphere of poetry. Poetological deliberation plays a far

function is to be overcome by Cupid.) Three more figures with whom Cupid compares himself favourably – 'the Parthian horseman, who is trained to win a fight by shooting behind his back,' 'the Cydonian hunter,' and 'the giant Orion' (35–39) – are also presented as examples of skilful archery, but they, too, have succumbed to Cupid's arrows.[125] Love, Milton suggests, does indeed conquer all – not just *omnia* but *omnes*.

In a last, dramatic gesture, Cupid announces, then prepares his eventual assault on the speaker:

> Caetera quae dubitas melius mea tela docebunt
> Et tua non leviter corda petenda mihi.
> Nec te stulte tuae poterunt defendere musae,
> Nec tibi Phoebaeus porriget anguis opem.
> Dixit, et aurato quatiens mucrone sagittam,
> Evolat in tepidos Cypridos ille sinus.   (43–48)

['Whatever other doubts you may have will be resolved by my arrows better than by words, and also by your own heart, which must be my target – and I shall not shoot half-heartedly. Your muses will not be able to protect you, you fool, and Apollo's serpent will not provide you with any cure.' When he had finished speaking he shook a gold-tipped arrow at me and then flew away to nestle between the warm breasts of Cypris <i.e., Venus>]

Again, Cupid refers to the instructive quality of the (tactile) experience he is about to inflict ('docebunt'), before leaving, himself, for a markedly tactile destination. In the contrast between Cupid's shooting 'not ... half-heartedly' at the speaker's heart and his own nestling between Venus' 'warm breasts,' between piercing impact and soft caress, between inner 'corda' and outer 'sinus,' the figure's paradoxical nature is present. The speaker, however, still prefers to see only one side of Cupid, the harmless one: 'But I was inclined to smile at the threats which this furious little lad thundered at me: I had no fear of the boy' (49–50).

In the following passage, the scene shifts, and the focus of the poem, while not committed to either the urban or the pastoral sphere, is no longer on the mythological (if perceptibly present) but on the mundane (if quasi-divine):

> Et modo qua nostri spatiantur in urbe quirites
> Et modo villarum proxima rura placent.
> Turba frequens, facieque simillima turba dearum
> Splendida per medias itque reditque vias.
> Auctaque luce dies gemino fulgore coruscat,
> Fallor? an et radios hinc quoque Phoebus habet.
> Haec ego non fugi spectacula grata severus,
> Impetus et quo me fert iuvenilis, agor.
> Lumina luminibus male providus obvia misi

---

greater role in Elegy I (with references to both the muses and 'the worshippers of Phoebus') and Elegy V (with its several references to creative song).
[125] See Carey's notes ad locc.

3.3 Elegy VII (Summer? 1628)

Neve oculos potui continuisse meos.
Unam forte aliis supereminuisse notabam,
Principium nostri lux erat illa mali.
Sic Venus optaret mortalibus ipsa videri,
Sic regina deum conspicienda fuit. (51–64)

[Sometimes the city promenades provided me with entertainment, sometimes the countryside near the outlying houses. A whole host of girls, with faces just like goddesses, go to and fro along the walks, resplendently beautiful. And the day is twice as bright as usual because of the light they add to it. Am I mistaken, or is it from them that the sun borrows his beams? I was not puritanical: I did not run away from such delicious sights. I let myself be driven wherever the impulse of youth carried me. Heedlessly, I let my eyes meet theirs: I was unable to keep my eyes in check. Then, by chance, I caught sight of one girl who was far more beautiful than all the rest: that radiance was the beginning of my downfall. Venus herself, when she appeared to mortals, might have chosen to look like this girl: this is what the queen of the gods must have looked like ...]

The similarity of this passage to the encounter with the 'British girls' in Elegy I is readily apparent – so much so, in fact, that it has been suggested as a possible reason for the placement of Elegy VII at the end of Milton's elegy sequence.[126] Again, the girls' attractiveness is presented in emphatically visual terms through comparisons to celestial bodies. In Elegy I, there had been eyes 'brighter than all the stars'; now, it seems that 'the sun [Phoebus] borrows his beams [from them].' But whereas Elegy I had remained on an abstract level with its comparisons to walls and towers (implying the absolute aloofness of the girls as their comparison to the stars had implied their elusiveness), the speaker of Elegy VII shows no reservations in entering the fray: 'I was not puritanical [severus]: I did not run away from such delicious sights [spectacula grata].' These are the first preconditions for what follows: the speaker has to let himself in for an actual, eye-to-eye confrontation (not just a metaphorical contemplation of towers or stars). This he does in the following couplet, although the question of intention (of the beholder) vs temptation (by the beheld) or even a general 'ungovernability' of the senses (and the eyes, in particular) is not yet settled:

Lumina luminibus male providus obvia misi
Neve oculos potui continuisse meos.

[Heedlessly, I let my eyes meet theirs: I was unable to keep my eyes in check.]

---

[126] As Douglas Bush writes in *Variorum* I, 128–9, 'the experience described in [Elegy VII, 53–64] is a concrete illustration of the beauty of English girls and of the poet's susceptibility, which had been the subject of the second half of [Elegy I], so that these two poems make a sort of frame for the group, a frame in keeping with the traditionally erotic character of elegiac verse; ... [Elegy VII] is also a concrete example of the springtime activity of Cupid which had been a main theme of [Elegy V].'

In the dense phonetic texture of these lines, as well as the immediate confrontation of 'lumina luminibus,' the close contact established by an exchange of glances is replicated. When the speaker identifies himself as 'male providus' – 'hardly provident,' 'insufficiently circumspect' – there is a further, punning reference to the realm of vision: in letting his eyes wander, he precisely exhibits a lack of 'foresight' in a more abstract, restrictive sense. Significantly, this is also the moment in which the metaphorical *lumina* – Milton's preferred term for 'eyes' in his Latin poetry – gives way to the more precisely anatomical *oculi*: the fact that we are dealing with vision as an actual bodily process is thus underlined.[127]

Following the particularising impulse of the previous lines – from abstract Love to concrete girls, from mere looking on to eye contact, and from 'lumina' to 'oculos' –, it is only consistent that the attraction of the speaker focuses on one particular, namely the most beautiful girl among the group. She is so much more beautiful than the others, indeed, that her beauty raises her above the merely human sphere and occasions the comparison to Venus herself. The idea that such a degree of perfection in female beauty has something threatening to it – also present in the relevant passage of Elegy I – is expressed through the image of attractive light (suggesting, perhaps, the way that moths and other insects, seemingly reduced in that moment to their visual apparatus, are attracted to a flame): 'that light [lux illa] was the beginning of my/our misfortune [nostri ... mali].' In its tone of casual, conventional gynophobia (if not misogyny) the line also suggests – despite its reference to *the one* most beautiful girl – a more general application, underlined by the ambiguous use of 'nostri' (i.e., either referencing the speaker as an individual or men in general). The most conspicuous example of that generalising line of thought making female beauty and/or persuasiveness into the root of 'all our woe' would, of course, be treated by Milton in *Paradise Lost*.

As the speaker reflects on his reaction, it occurs to him that the divine beauty still capturing his attention can actually be little more than a pawn in Cupid's game: 'That wretch Cupid bore me a grudge and threw her in my way: it was he alone who had woven these nets for me in advance. The artful boy was hiding [latuit] close at hand with a good supply of arrows and the huge burden of his torch behind his back' (65–68). As Cupid is hiding, the speaker must infer his presence from the effect the sight of beauty has on him. When the focus returns to the most beautiful girl, both earlier images, hers and Cupid's, are fused, as her attractiveness is explained as a function of Cupid's presence:

> Nec mora, nunc ciliis haesit, nunc virginis ori,
> Insilit hinc labiis, insidet inde genis:
> Et quascunque agilis partes iaculator oberrat,
> Hei mihi, mille locis pectus inerme ferit.

---

[127] 'Lumina' for 'eyes' occurs in elegies I and V, as well as in 'Elegiac Verses,' and is generally more common in Milton's Latin poetry than forms of *oculus*. In Elegy V, after the speaker's claim to have the Castalian spring 'ante oculos' (9), he contrasts his *oculi* with the 'unseen [lit., "blind"] depths of Tartarus' in a line structurally reminiscent of the pentameter in the present couplet: 'Nec fugiunt oculos Tartara caeca meos' (20). In both instances, again, the active quality of actual bodily vision is highlighted.

3.3 Elegy VII (Summer? 1628)

Protinus insoliti subierunt corda furores,
Uror amans intus, flammaque totus eram.
Interea misero quae iam mihi sola placebat,
Ablata est oculis non reditura meis. (69–76)

[Losing no time he swung on the girl's eyelashes, then on her mouth, then jumped between her lips, then perched on her cheek – and wherever the nimble archer landed (alas for me!) he hit my defenceless breast in a thousand places. In an instant passions I had never felt before entered my heart – I burned inwardly with love: my whole being was aflame. Meanwhile the only girl who charmed me was taken away, never to be seen again.]

The particularising 'tracking shot' carried out over these lines imitates the jumping of visual attention from one salient aspect to the next; it thus breaks up the totality of perception into a multitude of constituent glances, suggesting that the whole is still greater than the sum of its parts. Structurally, the passage is similar to the earlier description of Cupid himself, but in its superimposition of male and female attractiveness, of abstract Love and concrete attraction, it constitutes the true culmination point of Elegy VII.

In its description of the passions ('furores') kindled by visual impressions of beauty, the passage combines a typically early modern conception of the passions as occasioned primarily by sense perception with the fire motif introduced earlier: the 'Paphian fire' (2) of Venus and the burning anger of Cupid now combine to set the speaker's 'whole being ... aflame.' And in the greatest possible contrast to the visual kindling of the speaker's passions, 'the only girl who charmed me was taken away, never to be seen again [oculis non reditura meis].'[128] Whereas love and the passions are kindled through the eyes, though, their continuation is rather intensified by absence: 'But I went on, madly in love, complaining to myself and irresolute ...' (77).

Interestingly, the passage in which the speaker expresses his longing after the beautiful girl's being 'taken away' (i.e., most likely, walking on) is the only one in which the marked visual focus of Elegy VII is supplemented, if ever so slightly, by references to the acoustic sphere. When the speaker '[goes] on ..., complaining to myself [tacite querebundus],' he does so quietly; when he confesses, 'I am torn apart: one half of me stays here, and the other follows my desire and takes pleasure in weeping for joys so suddenly snatched away' (80), the expression of his grief in terms of sound is more clearly noticeable. True, the reason for his grief is of a visual nature, as his comparing himself to the mythical seer Amphiaraus indicates: 'so Amphiaraus, carried down to Hades by his panic-stricken horses, looked back at the sun which was being snatched from his eyes' (83–84).[129] However, the speaker's goal, as presented in the next passage, is of a twofold nature, combining the earlier focus on visuality (and the visual triggers of falling in love) with his vocal expression of lovesickness:

---

[128] There is a similarity between the speaker's situation and the myth of Hylas, referred to earlier, who was taken from his *erastês* Hercules by water nymphs; Hercules continued to look for Hylas. See *Oxford Companion to Classical Literature*, ed. Howatson, 291.

[129] See *Oxford Companion to Classical Literature*, ed. Howatson, 32.

> O utinam spectare semel mihi detur amatos
> Vultus, et coram tristia verba loqui!
> Forsitan et duro non est adamante creata,
> Forte nec ad nostras surdeat illa preces.
> Crede mihi nullus sic infeliciter arsit,
> Ponar in exemplo primus et unus ego. (87–90)
>
> [O if only I may be allowed to see those beloved features once again, and to tell the story of my grief in her presence! Perhaps she is not made of unyielding adamant: it is possible that she may not be deaf to my prayers. Believe me, no one has ever fallen in love in such an unlucky way: I shall be chronicled as the first and only example!]

Notably, the wished-for contact between the speaker and the girl is imagined to consist in both, another glimpse of her beautiful face ('spectare ... amatos/Vultus') as well as her hearing – and, more importantly, listening to – the speaker's supplication ('coram ... loqui,' 'nec ... surdeat illa'). This, again, relates to contemporary theories of the passions: just as the speaker had not been blind to the girl's beauty (and was thus affected by it through vision), he hopes, in turn, to move his beloved to affection through the aural effect of his pleading voice. By imagining his addressee's receptivity in terms of an impenetrable 'stoniness,' the speaker draws on a conventional image.[130] In the specific context of 'making a stone cry' (or have mercy) through the medium of sound, however, Milton's lines conceivably allude to the myth of Orpheus, whose singing had moved even stones and trees.[131] In that case, the beautiful girl's previous sudden removal from the speaker's sight would associate her with Eurydice, Orpheus' own beloved. The last couplet quoted, finally, takes up both, the earlier references to fire and burning – 'nullus sic infeliciter arsit,' no one has ever caught fire in such an unhappy way – and the reflections on exemplarity and experience: the speaker, through his experience of lovesickness and loss, will be made an example. On account of their categorical quality ('nullus,' 'primus et unus'), these lines, addressed to an implied reading audience,[132] are both tongue-in-cheek – objectively speaking, the case described is neither unique nor a first – and descriptive of the speaker's (subjective) experience.

---

[130] Compare, for instance, the references to 'stony hearts' at *PL* 3.189 and 10.4.

[131] See *Oxford Companion to Classical Literature*, ed. Howatson, 399–400. Milton returned to the Orpheus myth throughout his writing life, stressing various aspects of the story, and identifying and/or distinguishing his own speaking position from that of the pagan prototype. Thus, in Elegy VI (1629) he refers to 'old Orpheus, when he tamed wild beasts among lonely caves' (69–70), who appears as a model of the 'sober' poet; in *Il Penseroso* (105–8), a reference to Orpheus' ability to make 'hell grant what love did seek' stresses his affective powers; in *Paradise Lost*, Milton's epic speaker points out that he is singing 'with other notes than to the Orphean lyre' (i. e., is not moved by poetic *furor*, 3.17) yet later feels threatened by 'that wild rout that tore the Thracian bard [i. e., Orpheus]/In Rhodope, where woods and rocks had ears/To rapture, till the savage clamour drowned/Both harp and voice; nor could the Muse defend/Her son' (7.34–38). Compare this last reference to Orpheus' mother Calliope with Cupid's threat in Elegy VII, 'Your muses will not be able to protect you, you fool' (45).

[132] The imperatives of the remaining lines all seem addressed to Cupid, but 'crede' (91) is ambiguous, at least.

3.3 Elegy VII (Summer? 1628)

With the speaker's playfully true *cri de coeur*, the elegy has reached its final state. In the remaining lines, the speaker concedes defeat and asks for mercy. Cupid has won; the speaker is convinced of his powers: 'Spare me, I beg you. ... Your altars shall smoke with my offerings, and you alone shall be supreme to me among the gods' (93, 97). At this point of the elegy, the speaker recognises what readers, aware of convention, may have been prepared to acknowledge from the poem's opening lines: namely, the primacy of Love. In its concluding couplets, the speaker highlights, in appropriately conventional terms, the paradoxical state of lovesickness, both pleasurable and painful:

> Deme meos tandem, verum nec deme furores,
> Nescio cur, miser est suaviter omnis amans:
> Tu modo da facilis, posthaec mea siqua futura est,
> Cuspis amaturos figat ut una duos. (99–102)

> [Take away my madness, then – but no, do not take it away! I don't know why, but every lover is miserable in a way which is somehow delightful. Only be gracious enough to grant that, if any girl is ever to be mine in the future, one arrow may pierce both of our hearts and make them love.]

Being 'sweetly miserable,' the speaker concludes, is the definition of love as experienced by him so far; the prospect of a possible future mutuality suggests that the bitter element of that bittersweet mixture might yet be removed.

The 'madness' the speaker of Elegy VII both wishes to lose and retain had earlier entered his heart at the sight of Cupid inhabiting the beautiful girl's eyelashes, lips, and cheeks ('subierunt corda furores,' 73). Those 'furores,' it should be noted, are the very 'passions' – Carey's earlier translation – that were excited by striking sensations according to early modern perceptual theory. In the poetological opening passages of Elegy V, the singular 'furor' had referred to the onset of the elegiac speaker's inspiration.[133] In both cases, an extreme event in the speaker's psyche (falling in love, feeling inspired) had been caused, ultimately, by a (quasi-)sensory stimulus (seeing the girl; 'seeing' the Castalian spring and other inspiring sights, perceiving the return of spring in general). Milton's conceptions of romantic passion and poetic inspiration may thus be said both to depend upon sensory imagery and on an underlying assumption of how the senses create *furores*.

In comparison with the two other elegies discussed in this chapter, Elegy VII clearly focuses the most on the sensory mechanisms underlying romantic attraction. While it resembles Elegy I in its description of the speaker's encounter with a group of attractive girls, Elegy VII then continues to present the effects of visual attraction in one individualised instance, and does not transpose its account onto the (conceptual-) metaphorical plane so conspicuous in both elegies I and V. In its depictions of Cupid standing by the speaker's bedside and, later, the speaker's encounter with the beautiful girls, the poem's focus is wholly on concrete visual perception, not its metaphorical

---

[133] 'Et furor, et sonitus me sacer intus agit'('... I am driven on by poetic frenzy and the sacred sound which fills my brain,' 12); 'Quid parit haec rabies, quid sacer iste furor?' ('What is being born of this madness, this sacred frenzy?,' 20).

abstraction. In contrast to Elegy V, finally, although the shared initial setting of both poems is a spring morning, the sensuous content of Elegy VII is concentrated on visual beauty: first, on the striking appearance of Cupid, then, in a parallel passage, on the girl in whose face Cupid – now shrunk to an ostensibly less threatening size – can be seen 'perch[ing]' and 'jump[ing].' In being *also* allegorical, this depiction loses none of its sensory immediacy; after all, Cupid had earlier been described in visual detail himself.

The tactile *heat* of love – figured in Elegy V as a natural feature of the sun's return in springtime – is presented in Elegy VII, less naturalistically, as a feature of love itself, from the 'Paphian fire' of its opening couplet to the burning altars of its conclusion. Whereas the image, in Elegy V, of Phoebus resting his eyes against Tellus' breast ('gremio lumina pone meo') is ultimately one of mutuality and fulfilment, Elegy VII presents a disjunction between incendiary sight and continued burning after the object of desire has been taken away. If, as Barbara Lewalski has argued, Elegy VII is one of the poems in which Milton 'had staged an awareness and imagination of erotic impulses not acted upon,' its presentation of the origins and the immediate effects of those impulses is emphatic – and emphatically sensuous.[134] Its unique contribution to our discussion so far lies in the added theme of experiencing and witnessing, which ultimately poses the question of the extent to which a poetical rendition of a highly individualised – and individualising –, experience may count as adequate 'testimony' to readers.

3.4 Songs of Experience
Places, Faces, and Sense-Based Deliberation in Milton's Elegies

In Milton's earliest poetry, sensory discourse starts from several sources established by his poetic precursors, especially from the elegiac tradition, and adapts them to the particular setting of his own poems. In Elegy I, the sensory ramifications of different locales are explored, and are partly ironised. The 'delightful' city is contrasted with the 'bare' country, leading to the conclusion that the speaker is 'gladly enjoy[ing]' his 'banishment,' a much happier exile than Ovid's had been. With the captivating atmosphere of the theatre, the elegy gives a glimpse of a particularly striking element of the contemporary urban sensescape; here, visual and audible stimuli combine to provoke in the spectator-auditor a feeling of 'pleasure in … sadness,' of a 'sweet bitterness even in weeping' (notions also expressed towards the end of Elegy VII).

In the shady, 'suburban' setting explored in the following passage, typically pastoral elements of the elegiac tradition come to bear, and the theme of love is both expanded upon and moved into the speaker's immediate sphere of experience: now, he is not watching acted love scenes on a stage, but sees himself confronted with real-life 'choirs' of girls, who do not, however, sing, or even speak, but are apprehended by the speaker in exclusively (and emphatically) visual terms. Part of this emphasis is provided by the metaphorical restatement of the striking visual impact the girls make on the speaker: when they are figured as towers and (inhabiting) walled cities (imagery prominently taken up in Elegy V), both the historical-contextual and the conceptual-metaphorical dimensions of sensory discourse come into play. The visual *and* martial

---

[134] Lewalski, *Life of Milton*, 45.

associations of these images lead, via the conceptual metaphor LOVE IS CONQUEST, to the concluding appearance of Venus accompanied by a guard of armed cupids (bearing close relation to comparable elements in elegies V and, especially, VII).

Elegy V presents the most complex and, in that sense, the fullest realisation of sensory discourse in Milton's sequence of elegies. This means that both the *illustrative* or *descriptive* and the *deliberative* or *conceptual* uses of sensory discourse are consistently present in the poem. Most fundamentally, the elegy harnesses the conventional, 'flowery' language of spring, frequently reminiscent of the 'Elegiac Verses.' In the central passages of Elegy V, this form of sensory discourse takes on a distinctly multi-sensory or even synaesthetic shape. This distinctly multi-sensory quality of the arrival of spring is then taken up or mirrored on the level of human experience.

On a conceptual level, the central encounter between Tellus and Phoebus has been shown to take up the visual imagery of towers and fortifications so conspicuous in Elegy I, while, at the same time, connecting to the later elegy's strong interest in elevated viewing positions more generally. Together, these images all contribute to a pervasive metaphorical pattern pitting UP against DOWN, whether this relates to the opposition of the (male) sun above and the (female) earth below, waking up as opposed to laying down, or the conventional valuations of vision and touch in a hierarchised sensorium. In that these elements are presented in the form of a *meeting* of opposites (e.g. Phoebus resting his eyes against Tellus' breasts), they help prepare the doubtful conclusion of the elegy.

In the passages preceding and following the central passages, Elegy V treats the visual and acoustic realms separately: first, at the arrival of Phoebus and in the speaker's duet with Philomela at dawn; later, in the scenes evoking the (nocturnal) song of shepherd and sailor and the wanton activities of pagan (half-)gods at dusk. At the arrival of Phoebus, the speaker's individual experience is highlighted, before progressively more abstract figures are described as coming into contact with him. These passages inaugurate a series of (quasi-)romantic couplings which answers to the genre's traditional function as love poetry. A brief appearance by Cupid, continuing in this vein, relates the poem to elegies I and VII but does not dwell on the theme as they do.

Elegy V also enlarges upon the embodying quality of sensory discourse that had been a feature of Milton's earlier, threnodic elegies. This time, however, the focus is not so much on the speaker's lamentation ('tristi sic ore querebar' in Elegy III) as on his exultation at the return of spring. In Elegy V, the speaker's spirit resounds (and rejoices) with wide-open mouth: 'sonat distento spiritus ore.' This time, the embodied quality of the speaker's song does not authenticate his grief but his inspiration, and his close connection to the (natural) phenomena by which he is inspired. When a more doubting perspective, which had earlier been adumbrated, is made explicit at the end of the poem, the speaker expresses his concern over the eventual cessation of spring and its sensuous comforts (which would also set an end to his inspiration, which had been brought back by spring).

In Elegy VII, several themes familiar from elegies I and V are taken up: the visual impact of female attractiveness; the menacing nature of Cupid; the possible effect of emotional song on an imagined addressee. In both its visual and aural varieties, the influence of sense perception on the self of the percipient is explained by reference to the passions ('furores') and thus should be seen in the context of contemporary theories of the perceptual-emotional nexus. Indeed, the historical specificity of Milton's references resides in the straightforward connection they assume between perception and emotional reaction, both aspects of experience being treated as part of a continuum.

In keeping with this experiential focus, the elegy also expands on the theme of personal experience as witnessing and learning, and the (im)possibility of learning certain things by example (i.e., *without* first-hand experience). This is first broached in Cupid's menacing declaration that 'you shall be numbered among those who have felt my strength [inter ... expertos vires ... nostras],' adding that 'by your suffering I shall make people believe the truth about me.' Later, the notion is taken up in the speaker's assertion that 'no one has ever fallen in love in such an unlucky way: I shall be chronicled the first and only example!' This is hyperbolic yet true: from an outside perspective, the speaker's situation appears generic in more senses than one – typical of the (love) elegy and of the human condition –; but as the expression of a state of mind, it is based in the ineluctable individuality of experience.

Through personal experience, the highly conventionalised category of 'love,' represented in the poem through mythological machinery and the established tropes of love poetry, is individualised for the speaker. In both cases, that of passionate response and the acquisition of knowledge, respectively, the senses of seeing and hearing play a crucial role, which conforms to the general dominance of those senses within the sensorium. It is through sense perception, ultimately, that (mythological, abstracting) tradition is converted into (lived, individualising) experience.

As becomes clear, the sensory discourse of Milton's elegies I, V, and VII satisfies several of the modes and functions of sensory discourse outlined in Chapter 2. Specifically, its concern with (1) language itself (in the guise of the poet-speaker's embodied 'song'), (2) knowledge-production/reasoning (reflections on love, mortality, and nature), and (3) (embodied) sense perception has been demonstrated. Individual expressions of these aspects can be categorised as descriptive/illustrative or conceptual/deliberative uses of sensory discourse, respectively. In the end, however, such distinctions remain analytical, as references to the song of Philomela, for example, evoke both the (illustrative) quality of birdsong and the (conceptual) dimension of the related mythology, as well as its relation to the speaker's own, embodied song. In their treatment of certain discernible themes with a 'sensory flair' (e.g., love, nature, or poetics), any two, or even all three, of the elegies have been shown to overlap. The concrete distribution of references to these themes is uneven, however, and each of the elegies features distinct emphases. With a view to their generic framework, Milton's poems exemplify the various concerns of the elegiac genre with love and loss, with (pastoralised) nature, observation, and description. Ultimately, the elegiac impulse toward a 'narration of ... experience' all but predestines Milton's elegies, too, as vehicles for reflecting on both the direct experiential impact and the wider implications of sense perception.[135]

---

[135] See Miller, "'What's Love Got to Do With It?'", quotation at 50.

4. Sensory Discourse in Milton's 'Prolusions' (I, II, VI)

The sensory discourse of Milton's elegies, composed during his time at Cambridge, appears to have developed, in form as well as in content, from the rudiments laid down only a few years before in his 'Elegiac Verses,' the earliest extant sample of his poetry.[1] Turning to Milton's non-poetic writings therefore, it seems appropriate also to trace the sensory discourse of his prose from the earliest surviving example. This is the 'Theme on Early Rising,' whose remarkable similarities to the 'Elegiac Verses,' in content as in wording, have already been pointed out. The 'Theme' had presumably been a school exercise, a short essay arguing the point of view suggested by a well-worn saying, 'Mane citus lectum fuge' ('Betimes in the morning leave thy bed').

In terms of function as well as genre, the logical 'successors' of the 'Theme' within the Miltonic corpus are Milton's 'prolusions': university exercises he was required to compose – and, more importantly, *perform* – while at Cambridge. As in the case of the 'Theme,' the respective themes and general thrust of the individual texts was most likely prescribed.[2] As I will argue in this chapter, Milton's prolusions may be fruitfully analysed for their sensory discourse on three counts: (1) as instances of embodied, explicitly rational and knowledge-oriented speech appealing to the senses; (2) with respect to the communicative situation connecting orator and audience; and (3) as regards their explicit references to the sensory sphere. While the first and second of these points apply to all of Milton's prolusions on generic grounds, the third relates to some more than to others, but is demonstrably relevant to all of them. In two of the examples discussed below – dealing with the comparative merits of day and night and the music of the spheres, respectively – sensory points of references are already given as part of the topic. As my discussion will indicate, however, the specific manifestation of sensory discourse within these texts may take on divergent and even contrasting forms.

Milton composed what later became known as his prolusions – seven of the pieces were preserved by their eventual publication, in 1674, close to the end of Milton's life – over a time span covering the better part of his time at Cambridge, from the third year of his studies to his eventual graduation as master of arts, and hence roughly coexten-

---

[1] Carey tentatively dates the 'Elegiac Verses' to 1624, and the elegies to the period between April 1626 (Elegy I) and December 1629 (Elegy VI).
[2] In the following, I will quote Phyllis B. Tillyard's English translation of the prolusions from CPW 1 and the Latin text from CW 12. CW offers an English translation of its own (by Bromley Smith), which tends to be more literal than that of CPW. For the sake of consistency (and with a view to the wider availability of the Yale edition), I refer to CPW first, and will point to CW where significant differences arise.

sive with the period of his life which also yielded his elegies.[3] As 'course requirements' for both his undergraduate and graduate degrees, Milton had to debate and speak a set number of times in the Public Schools of the university as well as at his own college.[4] These Latin *Prolusiones* (as Milton captioned them at their first publication) were intended for either of two purposes: as contributions to academic disputations, featuring two debaters (proponent and opponent) and often requiring novices to compete with more advanced students; or as stand-alone 'declamations,' rhetorical apprentice pieces delivered before an audience of students and faculty, often at formal occasions such as commencement or other celebrations. The general chronology and individual occasions of composition for Milton's prolusions are unclear; it cannot even be said with certainty which of them were part of his undergraduate and which were part of his graduate work.[5] That he did consider them at least respectable samples of his early work is suggested by their eventual publication.

Whereas, in disputation, students were to practice the art of logical argument, in declamation they honed their skills in rhetoric, and in the art of persuasion. The two are not unconnected, of course, especially as students would routinely be assigned to defend opinions that were contrary to their own, or were even considered contrary to common sense. They would then have to find good reasons in favour of 'their' position – or else were obliged to 'make the worse appear the better reason' in that sophistical sense of 'sweet discourse' already referred to.[6] Through the Prolusions' particular focus on rhetorical mastery and polemical effect, then, Milton honed the argumentative and persuasive strategies that would characterise some of his subsequent poetry (as in *L'Allegro* and *Il Penseroso*, but also the rhetorically conscious nature of many speeches in the epic poetry) and his prose (with *Areopagitica*, as a 'speech' to parliament, the pre-eminent example).[7]

In that they were ultimately all orations meant to be spoken – or more emphatically, to be declaimed – before an *audience*, each Prolusion individually constitutes an ur-scene, among Milton's prose writings, of sensory discourse as vocal speech appealing to the senses. In that specific understanding of the concept, then, these texts may be con-

---

[3] Milton went up to Cambridge in 1625, graduating BA at the end of March 1629 (around the time Elegy V was written) and proceeding MA in July 1632. For the general chronology of Milton's time at university, see Lewalski, *Life of Milton*, 15–52.

[4] On the practice of academic disputation at Cambridge in Milton's day and the Prolusions in general, see Gordon Campbell/Thomas N. Corns, *John Milton: Life, Work, and Thought* (Oxford: Oxford University Press, 2010), 35–37.

[5] The only prolusion that offers any substantive internal evidence regarding its date and occasion is Prolusion VI, on which see below. Including the tenuous circumstantial evidence that can be gleaned from the texts of the other prolusions, Campbell and Corns group IV, I, III, and V (in that chronological order) as belonging to Milton's undergraduate, and VII, VI, and II, to his graduate work (see *John Milton*, 37). Lewalski classifies prolusions I, II, III, and VII as declamations; IV and V, as disputations; and the much-discussed Prolusion VI, as a parody of those forms (*Life of Milton*, 28).

[6] See my remarks about Belial as an orator in Chapter 2 above.

[7] On the connections between Milton's rhetorical/disputational training and his later works, see Campbell/Corns, *John Milton*, 35, as well as Lewalski, *Life of John Milton*, 48–49.

sidered elements of sensory discourse *qua* genre.[8] The sense appealed to most of all through these declamations is, of course, that of hearing – though, in one case at least, Milton's casual allusion to his outer appearance (he was known among his contemporaries as the 'Lady of Christ's') suggests another, visual component of the communicative situation.[9] In several passages throughout the prolusions discussed below, Milton additionally *imagines* an ocular communication between the audience and himself as the speaker.

In any case, the generic format of the prolusions as texts written for public performance by their author brings with it an aspect of clear relevance to sensory discourse: they express a close convergence between the (conceptual) presence of the speaker in the text and the (historical) appearance of its author as a speaking subject, between the intratextual figuration and the extratextual concretisation of voice. This, to be sure, does not imply the unconditional and absolute identification of the two, quite the contrary: an orator's 'trying out' different personae was actually encouraged by the practice of academic disputation and, as Richard Steele would remark much later, in 1712, 'those who have been present at publick Disputes in the University, know that it is usual to maintain Heresies for Argument's sake. I have heard a Man a most impudent socinian for half an hour, who has been an Orthodox Divine all his Life after.'[10] Still, both the conceptualisation of the text as *written speech* and its association with an actually *speaking subject embodying it* (namely, its author), which, I have argued, form a consistent theme in Milton's elegies, appear even stronger in the case of his prolusions: both in what they were meant to be (a record of declaimed speech) and in how they came into public being (namely, in a declamatory performance by their author), the prolusions must be considered as sensory discourse of the embodied type.

At the beginning of several prolusions, Milton explicitly refers to the communicative position of the orator confronting his audience.[11] Thus, at the outset of Prolusion III ('An Attack on the Scholastic Philosophy'), he directly addresses his fellow students, admitting that 'I have been deeply occupied of late, gentlemen, in seeking, and indeed one of my chief anxieties has been to find, what device of rhetoric would best enable me to engage my hearers' attention ...' ('quo potissimum verborum apparatur vos Auditores meos exciperem').[12] On the face of it, this opening serves to highlight the peculiar communicative situation in which the speaker and his audience find themselves – and

---

[8] On this point see also Costello, *Scholastic Curriculum*, 146. The 1674 volume of Familiar Letters and Prolusions presents the latter as 'Prolusiones Quædam Oratoriæ' (see the title page reproduced in CPW 1: 215).
[9] Milton alludes to this nickname in Prolusion VI, see CPW 1: 283. Whether this was on account of his hairstyle and elegant clothing (as has been conjectured), his professed chastity, his general delicacy, or other factors, is not entirely clear. Aubrey reports that 'his complex[ion] [was] exceeding faire – he was so faire that they called him *the Lady of Christ's College*' (*Early Lives*, ed. Darbishire, 3, emphasis added). See also Lewalski, *Life of John Milton*, 31.
[10] Steele quoted in Campbell/Corns, *John Milton*, 36. Kathryn McEuen, in her short general introduction to the Prolusions, refers to their 'serious or pseudo-serious discussions' (CPW 1: 212).
[11] Prolusions I–III and VII, to be precise. These are exactly the texts identified by Lewalski as declamations, which may help to explain their rhetorical conventionality.
[12] CPW 1: 240.

find themselves united: one side voicing language in embodied discourse (i.e., speaking), the other perceiving this discourse as an acoustic impression (i.e., hearing and, as is to be hoped, listening). At the same time, the continuance of their communication requires a continuous effort on both sides, the orators presenting his thoughts engagingly and his hearers listening intently. As in the much later figurations of the epic speaker of *Paradise Lost* as a single voice opposing a tendentially hostile multitude, the speaker of the prolusion, apparently beset by a number of 'chief anxieties,' is singled out as a producer of meaningful *sound*. His discourse – written in manuscript, delivered, much later printed but, in any case, figured as vocal – is sensory not only on account of its genre (an exercise in declamation), and the communicative situation this implies (that of an academic oration), but also through its conscious reflection and express announcement of both these factors.

Indeed, the passage from Prolusion III does not intend to hide its function as a rhetorical journeyman's piece; that much is clear from the candid reference to the 'device[s] of rhetoric.' In that it is intended to capture the benevolence of his audience, moreover, Milton's (self-)portrayal of the rhetor as a timid young man should also be seen as a typical expression, and thus an implicit statement, of the classical rhetorical tradition itself.[13] Just as the mandatory public *delivery* of the Prolusions served to educate students in the traditional fifth 'canon' of rhetoric (following on invention, arrangement, diction, and memory), the direct addresses and self-reflection of Milton's *exordia* bespeak the lasting influence of classical rhetorical training.

Another significant aspect that is expressly present in the exordium to Prolusion III is what could be called the 'transitive purpose' of the rhetorical exercise.[14] As Milton declares (invoking Cicero), 'the fundamental duties of an orator are first to instruct, secondly to delight, and thirdly to persuade. And so I have made it my chief object to fulfil as nearly as possible this threefold function of a speaker.'[15] All three functions of rhetoric – *docere*, *delectare*, and *movere* – have been linked to the senses in our discussion so far: as sources of knowledge and of pleasure as well as, for better or for worse, as prompts to the passions.[16] In the Prolusions – being rhetorical exercises – they are obviously meant to co-occur, suggesting a particular affinity of the Prolusions to sensory discourse.

Of the three prolusions to be considered in detail in this chapter (I, II, and VI), the first two are of the declamatory type, intended to provide students an opportunity to hone their skills of rhetorical persuasion while arguing a given point. Prolusion VI takes a special role in more senses than one, but most of all because it may be seen as a self-conscious parody of the prolusion form and its claim to impart knowledge. Milton ex-

---

[13] In the exordium of Prolusion VII, Milton declares his reluctance to take the floor at all, seeing how 'he who would be an orator ... must first acquire a thorough knowledge of all the arts and sciences,' yet 'since ... this is impossible at my age, I would rather endeavour truly to deserve that reputation by long and concentrated study ...' (CPW 1: 288–89). Prolusions I and II, whose openings contain similar elements of self-deprecation, are considered in more detail below.
[14] As opposed to its 'intransitive purpose,' namely, the rhetorical education of the student delivering it.
[15] CPW 1: 240.
[16] Compare the pot simile from *Of Reformation*, discussed in Chapter 2 above.

plicitly reflects on this generic claim, and on questions of epistemology in the widest sense, in several of the prolusions not discussed in detail here, such as III ('An Attack on Scholastic Philosophy,' quoted above), V ('There Are No Partial Forms in an Animal in Addition to the Whole'), and VII ('Learning brings more Blessings to Men than Ignorance').

It seems worth pointing out that those texts, also, each in its distinct way, make reference to the sensory sphere, or to perception or cognition in a more abstract sense. Thus, in the strongly polemical Prolusion III, Milton repeatedly resorts to sensory metaphor, drawing on smell (scholastic disputations 'reek [olent] ... of the monkish cells in which they were written' whereas 'divine poetry' is characterised by 'the scent of nectar [quasi Nectareo halitu ǻfflans, totamque perfundens Ambrosia]'); touch and hearing (scholasticism is in a place 'tangled and matted with thorns and brambles [dumis & spinis asperum, atque horridum], overgrown with thistles and nettles ... where no laurels grow nor flowers bloom, and to which the sound of Apollo's lyre can never penetrate [nunquam pervenerit sonus]'); and vision (the scholastics in their aberration 'hide the light and shed deep darkness over the whole question [ipsam lucem adimant, rebusque profundum afferant caliginem],' it would be much better to 'let your eyes wander as it were [quasi oculis perambulare] over all the lands depicted on the map, and to behold the places trodden by the heroes of old [calcata vetustis Heroibus inspectare loca], to range over the regions made famous by wars ...' in order to gain knowledge of a new kind).[17]

In the rather more technical Prolusion V, by contrast, Milton – now himself taking a Scholastic position – might not argue through sensory metaphor, but he does cite Aristotle's *De anima* – thus establishing his familiarity with this most influential classical treatise on sense perception – and generally moves in an argumentative environment in which the constituent parts of the human soul, as well as its distinctive capacity for both 'sense knowledge' *and* 'reason' play a decisive role.[18]

In Prolusion VII, finally, Milton takes a Platonist position, and thus argues for the inadequacy of knowledge perceived through the senses, or, at the very least, through the senses alone: 'For who can worthily gaze upon and contemplate the Ideas of things human or divine [quis ... *ideas* intueri digne possit aut considerare], unless he possesses a mind trained and ennobled by Learning and study, without which he can know practically nothing of them ...'[19] Strikingly, however, even this downplaying of sense perception makes use of the traditional visual metaphor of Platonism, suggesting that the abstract contemplation of 'the Ideas of things' is itself a kind of transcendent 'gaze' and vision. Even in the case of astronomy, elsewhere the very symbol of actual, optical vision, the determinative force of the Platonic metaphor proves stronger – what is more, it also leads to a general scepticism regarding the validity of sense perception as a source of knowledge:

---

[17] CPW 1: 241, 243–44, 245–46.
[18] See CPW 1: 259, 261n8, 263n8. See also Costello, *Scholastic Curriculum*, 92–96, on the teaching of the Aristotelian theory of perception at Cambridge in Milton's day.
[19] CPW 1: 291.

> Can we indeed believe, my hearers, that the vast spaces of boundless air are illuminated and adorned with everlasting lights ... merely to serve as a lantern for base and slothful men, and to light the path of the idle and the sluggard here below? Do we perceive no purpose in the luxuriance of fruit and herb beyond the short-lived beauty of verdure? Of a truth, if we are so little able to appraise their value that we make no effort to go beyond the crass perceptions of the senses [ut nihil ultra crassum sensus intuitum persequamur], we shall show ourselves not merely servile and abject, but ungracious and wicked before the goodness of God; for by our unresponsiveness and grudging spirit He is deprived of much of the glory which is His due, and of the reverence which His mighty power exacts.[20]

The senses serve a purpose, then, and they present only the first stepping stone of a much longer and altogether different process; sense perception, represented first in its most distant and most immaterial form of astronomical vision, should lead 'upward' to higher things.[21] As he goes on to establish the importance and superiority of knowledge, Milton employs strikingly similar imagery, declaring that

> while the human Intellect shines forth as the lord and governor of all the other faculties, it guides and illuminates with its radiance the Will also, which would else be blind, and the Will shines with a borrowed light, even as the moon does,

but that only when Learning and Virtue are 'wedded in happy union ... then indeed Knowledge raises her head aloft and shows herself far superior, and shining forth takes her seat on high beside ... Intellect, and gazes upon the doings of the Will below ...'[22] More clearly than in the metaphors of Prolusion III, the sensory discourse of these passages is motivated by conceptual considerations.

This brief survey of three 'epistemological' prolusions already indicates another central aspect of sensory discourse in Milton: when the question of knowledge is being addressed in these early texts, the senses are never far away. As it also illustrates, however, this perceived affiliation of sense perception and knowledge-making could be expressed in markedly different terms. For instance, the sensory metaphors of Prolusion III may be read as polemical first – and thus, if in a negative way, illustrative or descriptive – and conceptual second (in the most conspicuous instance of this, fruitless learning is likened to thorny weeds because IDEAS ARE FOOD and UNDERSTANDING IS

---

[20] CPW 1: 292.

[21] This is an idea that will re-emerge in subsequent discussion, see Chapter 5.2 below. In the more immediate context of Prolusion VII, the notion of 'looking up,' in particular, relates to Milton's reference, in a later passage, to the relationship between humans' erect posture and their capacity for reasoning and abstract (or upward-directed) contemplation (303 and notes).

[22] CPW 1: 293. Milton takes the image up again later, exclaiming, 'What now of Ignorance? I perceive, gentlemen, that Ignorance is struck blind and senseless ...' (299). McEuen points out that 'in placing intellect (and knowledge) above will, Milton was following traditional beliefs' (293n6).

TOUCHING).²³ Conversely, the references to gazing at 'the Ideas of things' while shunning 'the crass perceptions of the senses' in Prolusion VII suggest a more abstract approach to the sensory sphere, and even if (linguistic) sensory metaphors are not wholly absent from the text, Milton's emphasis is on their conceptual, orientational application: VISION IS UP, KNOWLEDGE IS UP, KNOWLEDGE IS LIGHT, whereas THE WILL IS DOWN, etc. Apparent from this confrontation of 'crass perception,' on the one hand, and the 'vision of ideas,' on the other, is the irresolvable crux of sensory discourse in any Platonic/idealistic or sceptical context, where the sensory sphere is bound to provide the metaphors to conceptualise what the senses supposedly cannot apprehend. These emphases on an illustrative (Prolusion III) or conceptual use (Prolusion VII) of sensory discourse manifestly differ from the case of Prolusion V, in which the senses are scarcely referenced. Still, the psycho-philosophical deliberations of that text should be seen as part of the silent machinery of traditional concepts and presuppositions that underlies Milton's approach to sense perception.

Arguably the most consistent (and most varied) use of sensory discourse in Milton's prolusions, spanning both its illustrative and conceptual dimensions, occurs in numbers I, II, and VI, which I will now discuss in detail.

4.1 Prolusion I ('Whether Day or Night is More Excellent')
The Aesthetic, Social, and Moral Implications of Vision

In the case of Prolusion I, the sensory relevance of Milton's topic is hard to miss.²⁴ As Kathryn McEuen argues in her editorial introduction to the text, several remarks in the prolusion itself suggest that it was 'delivered in mid-winter,' and thus at a time when the relative excellence of night or day may have been particularly on peoples' minds.²⁵ Milton chooses (or was assigned) to uphold the side of day, defending a thesis with a long tradition in classical poetry and philosophy, as McEuen points out. Despite this aspect of conventionality, however, his treatment of the topic is generally playful and exhibits a marked subjective focus, closer in spirit to a 'Renaissance' mindset, perhaps, than to the mediaeval tradition of academic disputation.

Milton opens his speech with a self-conscious reference to rhetorical decorum. 'It is a frequent maxim of the most eminent masters of rhetoric,' he addresses his hearers, '... that in every style of oration, ... the speaker must begin by winning the good-will of his audience [ab aucupanda Auditorum gratia].'²⁶ The fundamental, auditory connection between a speaker and one or several listeners, which had constituted the *imaginary* baseline of sensory discourse in the elegies, is thus highlighted right at the outset of the

---

[23] The two conceptual metaphors are combined in a passage of Prolusion VII. There, Milton says of the teachers of logic (adding a quotation from Horace) that they 'are not like men at all, but like finches which live on thorns and thistles. "O iron stomachs of the harvesters!"' (CPW 1: 301).
[24] The text of Prolusion I is in CPW 1: 218–33. Some general remarks on the background and structure of Prolusion I may be found in the commentary at CPW 1: 216–18. I will refer to those (as to McEuen's notes on the text) only insofar as they are relevant to the discussion of Milton's sensory discourse in the prolusion.
[25] CPW 1: 216.
[26] CPW 1: 218.

prolusion which, in being originally delivered, created an *actual* perceptual event in the minds of the audience. With studied 'deviation' from the rhetorical norm, however, Milton immediately professes that he will have to say 'something contrary to all the rules of oratory,' and this, too, relates to the sensory connection between orator and audience: 'For how can I hope for your good-will, when in all this great assembly I encounter none but hostile glances [cum in hoc tanto concursu, quot oculis intueor tot ferme aspiciam infesta in me capita], so that my task seems to be to placate the implacable? [ut Orator venisse videar ad non exorabiles]'[27] Apparently, the speaker has come, in his role of orator (etymologically, one who uses his *os*, or mouth), to those fundamentally opposed to his attempts to win them over, and literally 'beyond the reach of speech' ('non exorabiles'); Milton's *figura etymologica* ('Orator,' 'exorabiles') drives home this point.[28] More significantly, however, the confrontation between the orator and his recalcitrant audience is figured as a confrontation of 'sensory channels,' with entreating, audible words pitted against hostile, silent glances.[29] The audience's favour, accordingly, is also imagined by the speaker in visual, ocular terms, and joined to an attack on talentless *oratorculi* ('speechifiers'):

> Yet to prevent complete despair, I see here and there [sparsim video], if I do not mistake, some who without a word show clearly by their looks how well they wish me [qui mihi ipso aspectu tacito, quam bene velint, haud obscure significant]. The approval of these, few though they be, is more precious to me than that of the countless hosts of the ignorant, who lack all intelligence, reasoning power, and sound judgment [in quibus nihil mentis, nihil rectæ rationis, nihil sani judicii inest], and who pride themselves on the ridiculous effervescing froth of their verbiage [verborum spuma]. Stripped of their covering of patches borrowed from new-fangled authors, they will prove to have no more in them than a serpent's slough, and once they have come to the end of their stock of phrases and platitudes you will find them unable to utter [*phthengesthai*] so much as a syllable, as dumb as the frogs of Seriphus [perinde mutos ac ranuncula Seriphia]. How difficult even Heraclitus would find it, were he still alive, to keep a straight face at the sight of these speechifiers (if I may call them so without offence) [si forte hosce cerneret, si Diis placet, Oratorculos], first grandly spouting their lines [quos paulo ante audiverit cothurnato] ... and then, their slender stock of phrases exhausted and their glory all gone, drawing in their horns and crawling off like snails.[30]

---

[27] CPW 1: 219.
[28] Tillyard's translation ('placate the implacable') reproduces the lexical echo of the original while highlighting the 'pleading' function of oratory suggested by it (as a more subdued kind of *movere*).
[29] Both the confrontational mise-en-scène of this opening, pitting the lone orator against a hostile multitude (a theme recurring throughout Milton's work) and the specifically ocular quality of their rejection are taken up and elaborated in Prolusion VI, discussed below.
[30] CPW 1: 220. The frogs of the island of Seriphus in the Aegean were said never to croak, except when moved elsewhere (then they were even noisier than the other frogs). Heraclitus was known as 'the mourner,' and a reclusive and serious man. (On both points see the notes ad loc.)

In this passage, Milton constructs a second opposition between those judicious few in the audience who wish him well (and show this by their 'silent looks') and the 'countless hosts of the ignorant,' *oratorculi*, as he calls them (literally, 'tiny orators'), who utter (borrowed) words and make (grandiose) sounds but are at a loss for either as soon as their supply of quotations and stock phrases runs out. Throughout, Milton's emphasis on the vocality of the uttered words is pronounced, and made clear through his choice of words ('*phthengesthai*,' 'audiverit'). That these are *mere sounds* – devoid of human 'intelligence, reasoning power, and sound judgment' – is underlined by the references to non-human nature, animate as well as inanimate ('ranuncula,' 'spuma'). The reference to frogs, in particular, serves to drive home Milton's point, as these are of course strongly associated with the incessant, tedious croaking noises they normally make.[31] In the particular case of the legendary frogs of Seriphus mentioned by him, their unnatural quietness argues that of the witless *oratorculi*: orators *should* be making sounds, but those should be their own, and carry meaning; these 'speechifiers,' however, *only* make sounds, and they are loudest when they croak on foreign territory.[32] Snails, finally, are not only as mute as the unnatural frogs of Seriphus but produce just as much 'spuma' as the *oratorculi* had done before falling silent. In early modern Europe, generally, 'reptiles, insects, and amphibians were especially detested, though the reasons for this loathing were seldom clearly articulated.'[33] Both to the classical rhetorical tradition and the early modern imagination, they are emblems of contempt. As creatures of the ground, moreover, both frogs and snails were inherently suspect.[34]

Having thus constructed, with merely ostensible modesty, a bond between himself – as an orator in the full meaning of the term, an orator with something to say – and the more intelligent (and thus favourably inclined) part of the audience, Milton turns to the actual topic of his speech. The question whether day or night is preferable, he declares, 'might seem [a subject] better suited to a poetical exercise than to a contest of rheto-

---

[31] Karen Edwards, 'Milton's Reformed Animals: An Early Modern Bestiary – D–F,' *MQ* 40 (2006), 99–187, at 168–73, names the present passage as the first occurrence of frogs in Milton's writings, cites Gervase Babington on the 'hatefull noise' frogs make (quotation at 168), and discusses Milton's later references to the repugnant croaking of frogs within their respective literary-historical contexts: thus, in Sonnet 12, Milton likens the 'barbarous noise' of his opponents to the croaking of frogs. Likewise, Alexander More's rhetoric is described, in the *Defensio Secunda*, as 'croaking like a frog from the hellish swamps in which he swims' (CPW 4: 594). In all instances, the focus is on the (hideous) auditory qualities of the frogs' croaking.

[32] Perhaps Milton intends this as a pun on the literal and rhetorical meanings of *loci* or *topoi*: the frogs of Seriphus croak loudest when they frequent the 'commonplaces' of rhetoric; they are mute when left to fend for themselves. Milton's Latin diminutives emphasise the parallel between the 'puny orators' (*oratorculi*) and the 'froglets' ('ranuncula').

[33] Thomas, *Man and the Natural World*, 57. Snails, however, were considered (shell)fish; see the illustration in Karen Edwards, 'Milton's Reformed Animals: An Early Modern Bestiary – S,' *MQ* 43 (2009), 89–141, at 118.

[34] See Edwards, 'Milton's Reformed Animals: An Early Modern Bestiary – S,' at 118–19. I owe to Edwards's analysis the point about the snails' 'spuma.' In sensory terms, their association would have been with touch; on the similar case of toads (and Milton's later association of Satan with a toad), see Moshenska, *Feeling Pleasures,* 269.

ric.'[35] Indeed, Milton treats a related theme – the coming of day at the end of night – in several of the poems discussed above and, in all cases, this topical focus is accompanied by a strong reliance on sensory discourse in descriptions of waking up, the coming of day, and (repeatedly) a change of season.[36]

In Prolusion I, the contrast between night and day is conceived in terms of a mythical struggle ('Did I say that Night had declared war on Day?'), as Milton references diverse episodes from the war between the gods and the titans of Greek mythology.[37] At the end of this digression, the appearance of Day is put in terms familiar from Milton's other treatments of the theme: 'And indeed I see Day herself, awakened by the crowing of the cock, hastening hither more swiftly than is her wont, to hear her own praise.'[38] The conceit is clear: Day herself – Latin *dies*, though grammatically masculine, was conventionally personified as feminine – is attracted by the voice of the orator, her champion, who thus constructs a parallel between himself and the crowing cock as the conventional herald of dawn. In that it usually is day awakening the speaker – as in Milton's diverse poems on the subject –, the prolusion inverts another conventional motif: now Day herself awakens and hastens to *listen*, her interest piqued by what she has *heard*.

Milton then announces the division of his speech along established rhetorical lines: to determine whether day or night is superior, he needs to 'enquire, first, which of the two is of nobler birth [Videndum primò utra genere sit clarior], secondly, which can trace back her descent the furthest, and thirdly, which is of the greater service to mankind?'[39] His phrasing, literally declaring that 'we have to *see* which one is more famous [or *brighter*] by descent,' is consistent with the common sensory-conceptual metaphor KNOWING IS SEEING (allied to the similar THINKING IS LOOKING). In the present context, however, a literalising pun seems likely: in suggesting to his audience the question as to whether day or night is (visibly) brighter, Milton might be said to anticipate the result of his discussion.

Milton then goes on to trace the respective lineages of night and day based on mythological accounts, citing Hesiod's *Theogony*: Day, Hesiod suggests, is the incestuous offspring of Night and Earth or of Night and Chaos (which would, in both cases, make day subordinate to night) – but can poets – and the poets of pagan antiquity at that – really be thought sufficiently reliable authorities 'in a question of such importance'?[40] The speaker will thus 'bring them to the test of reason [ad normam rationis revocare conor], and ... examine whether they can bear the scrutiny of strict truth [exploraturus ... num rigidæ possint veritatis examen pati].'[41] The purpose of the prolusion – as would be clear from its genre, but is stated here explicitly – is to establish the truth regarding a

---

[35] CPW 1: 221.
[36] In the 'Elegiac Verses,' 'Song. On May Morning,' and elegies V and VII, all discussed in Chapter 3 above.
[37] CPW 1: 221–22, quotation at 221.
[38] CPW 1: 222. [Video siquidem & ipsam diem Galli cantu expergefactam, cursu solito citiatori adproperâsse ad suas laudes exaudiendas.]
[39] CPW 1: 222.
[40] CPW 1: 223–24, quotation at 223.
[41] CPW 1: 224.

given question, and thus to lead to secure knowledge about it. This had been phrased in conceptual-metaphorical (visual) terms above; now it appears that the voice of the orator is equated with the proverbial 'voice of reason': by pronouncing on their validity, he will put the ancient traditions to the test. As will become apparent from the following discussion, however, the character of the prolusions as oratorical exercises was equally important, and Milton draws on all kinds of rhetorical flourishes as well as ample 'illustration' from (classical) literary sources.

As a first example of this approach, combining a claim to quasi-scientific/empiricist veracity with 'anecdotal evidence' from ancient Greek myth, he argues that 'first, then, the story that makes Night the Child of Earth [noctem Tellure ortam] is a learned and elegant allegory of antiquity; for what is it that makes night envelop the world [mundo noctem obducit] but the dense and solid earth [densa & impervia terra], coming between the sun's light and our horizon?' Similarly, the frustrated courtship of Night by the shepherd Phanes ('the bright/shining one'), mentioned by Milton in his paragraph of mythological exposition, has been explained by some in naturalistic terms: 'The ancients interpret Phanes as the sun or the day, and in relating that he at first sought Night in marriage and then pursued her to avenge his rejection, they mean only to signify the alternation of day and night.'[42] However, the speaker objects, it seems unreasonable to express the confrontation of night and day – 'their perpetual alternation and mutual repulsion' – in terms of love or passionate pursuit when, evidently, their relationship is one of 'implacable hatred from the very beginning of time.'[43] In order to save herself from Phanes' destructive brightness, the speaker suggests, Night simply had to seek refuge with her brother Erebus (i.e., Darkness).

Milton names their children, whose negative properties and associations of course do not speak in favour of Night: 'Misery, Envy, Fear, Deceit, Fraud, Obstinacy, Poverty, Want, Hunger, Fretfulness, Sickness, Old Age, Pallor, Darkness, Sleep, Death and Charon, her last child,' and roundly rejects the conflicting view, mentioned earlier, that Night was also the origin of day: '... who in his senses would not howl down and turn out the advocate of such a theory ...? Is it indeed probable on the face of it that black and gloomy Night [obscuram & fuscam noctem] should be the mother of a child so comely, so sweet, so universally beloved and desired [as Day]? [tam venustulum, tam amabilem, tam omnibus gratum acceptumque]'[44] Milton's description of the loveliness of Day, notably, is couched in terms resembling the language of his elegies, where indeed loveliness and attractive grace had not only been described in visual terms, but had been associated with related optical categories such as brightness, or with imagery relating to the same field of reference (such as stars or jewels). It is only fitting, then, that Day – representative of light as opposed to the black gloominess of night – should be described in a similar register, indicating that she is, literally, 'beautiful as day.'

Not only is such a parentage of Day unlikely, the speaker goes on to argue; due to their fundamental incompatibility of character (light and darkness being fundamentally opposed), the child 'would have caused her mother's death by her birth before due time [erumpens utero, i.e., as light breaking through darkness],' would have 'driven her fa-

---

[42] CPW 1: 224.
[43] CPW 1: 224–25.
[44] CPW 1: 225–26.

ther Erebus [Darkness] into headlong flight, and forced old Charon to hide his dazzled eyes [norcturnos abderet oculos] beneath the waters of the Styx ...'[45] It is clear that Milton makes the most of the allegorical qualities of his mythological personifications, focusing throughout on the visual implications of his images. Having rejected the ancient stories, the speaker suggests the opposite: 'Nay, I dare rather declare that Day is older than Night ...,' and in the following passages he presents Day as 'the oldest daughter of Heaven [i.e., Uranus/Coelus]' – implying, perhaps, but never explicitly naming the Judaeo-Christian tradition of light as either the first of created things or 'coeternal' with the Creator.[46]

When the speaker then turns to praise Day for its many positive qualities – and its benefits for humanity –, he draws on a kind of sensory discourse already quite familiar from Milton's early Latin poetry. In order to present its interlocking aspects in their full complexity, it seems advisable to quote the passage as a whole:

> In the first place, there is assuredly no need to describe to you how welcome and how desirable Day is to every living thing. Even the birds cannot hide their delight [gaudium], but leave their nests at peep of dawn [ubi primum diluculavit] and noise it abroad from the tree-tops in sweetest song [in verticibus Arborum concentu suavissimo deliniant omnia], or darting upwards [sursum librantes] as near as they may to the sun [Solem], take their flight to welcome the returning day [luci]. First of all these the wakeful cock acclaims the sun's coming [triumphat insomnis Gallus], and like a herald bids mankind shake of the bonds of sleep, and rise and run with joy to greet the new-born day [obviam effundant se novam salutatum auroram]. The kids skip in the meadows, and beasts of every kind leap and gambol in delight [totumque genus quadrupedum gestit & exultat lætitiâ]. The sad heliotrope [mœsta Clytie], who all night long has gazed toward the east [totam fere noctem, converso in Orientem vultu], awaiting her beloved Sun [Phœbum], now smiles and beams at her lover's approach. The marigold too and rose [Caltha quoque & Rosa], to add their share to the joy of all [communi gaudio], open their petals [aperientes sinum] and shed abroad their perfume [Odores suos ... profusè spirant], which they have kept for the Sun alone, and would not give to Night, shutting themselves up within their little leaves at fall of evening. And all the other flowers raise their heads, drooping and weighed down with dew [cæterique flores inclinata paulum, & rore languidula erigentes capita], and offer themselves to the Sun, mutely begging him to kiss away the tear-drops [tacite rogant ut suis osculis abstergat Lachrymulas] which his absence brought. The Earth too [Ipsa quoque Tellus] decks herself in lovelier robes to honour the Sun's coming [in adventum Solis cultiori se induit vestitu], and the clouds, arrayed in garb of every hue [variis Chamydatæ coloribus], attend [videntur][47] the

---

[45] CPW 1: 226.
[46] Compare *PL* 3.1–6: 'Hail, holy light, offspring of heaven first-born,/Or of the eternal co-eternal beam/May I express thee unblamed? since God is light,/And never but in unapproachèd light/Dwelt from eternity, dwelt then in thee,/Bright effluence of bright essence increate.'
[47] CW has 'seem to be maids ...' Compare the instances of *videri* in Elegy V (lines 70, 129), discussed in Chapter 3, n76.

4.1 Prolusion I ('Whether Day or Night is More Excellent')   181

rising god [surgenti Deo] in festive train and long procession. And last, that nothing may be lacking to proclaim his praise, the Persians and the Libyans give him divine honours; the Rhodians too have dedicated to his glory that far-famed Colossus of astounding size ...; to the Sun, too, we are told, the American Indians even to this day make sacrifice with incense and with every kind of ritual [thure cæteroque apparatu].[48]

In this richly multi-sensory description of daybreak, Milton blends a number of distinct elements, some of them familiar from the poetry already discussed. In particular, there are (1) an association of daybreak/sunrise and sense perception (including sense perception other than vision, which is conventionally associated with the sun); (2) an association of sunrise/sunlight and romantic/erotic love (figured on the two levels of animate nature and mythology); and (3) an associative extension of the notion of daybreak to signify, at the same time, spring as the beginning of the year (and sharing in the same sensory and romantic associations).

The first of these aspects, giving the passage a strongly multi-sensorial character reminiscent of Milton's other morning scenes, is expressed in terms of four general domains or 'contributors': birds (and other 'living things,' including humans); flowers; earth and sky; and finally, specifically named peoples. In the case of the birds, their singing is the defining element of their sensory contribution to the scene. It is caused by the return of light, which prompts them to raise a loud yet pleasant song, sung in polyphony ('concentu suavissimo') from the treetops, or to rise even further upward to welcome the sun in its own domain.[49] The crowing of the cock – called a 'herald' here, the 'guardsman cock' in the 'Elegiac Verses' – is chronologically prior but mentioned second, perhaps because his 'singing' lends itself less readily to the evocation of a strongly sensuous scene. His crowing, moreover, is functional (he 'acclaims' and 'bids'), whereas the singing of the birds is purely expressive of their 'delight' ('gaudium') about the return of day, conceived of in terms of its light ('luci'). In the depiction of the non-avian animals mentioned ('kids' and other 'beasts of every kind'), these are grouped with the birds – as participating in a shared rejoicing – and dissociated from them at the same time: their skipping, leaping, and gamboling is indeed expressive of happiness (*laetitia*) – but it is mute, a characteristic later shared by the flowers' 'mutely begging [the sun] to kiss away' the dew.[50] While the ambiguous notion of 'exultation' could be construed as auditory, and the animals' rejoicing thus as audible, the emphasis in all the verbs used is on their locomotory and gestural quality, and hence serves to heighten, by

---

[48] CPW 1: 227–28.
[49] Milton's remark that they fly upwards 'as near as they may to the sun [quam possunt prope Solem volitent]' appears to allude to the myth of Daedalus and Icarus.
[50] *OLD*, 'ex(s)ulto': '(1) To spring up, leap about ... (3) to show unrestrained pleasure, exult'; 'gestio': '(3) To act without restraint, be elated or triumphant, exult ... (4) To make expressive movements, gesture'; 'tripudio': 'to perform a *tripudium* (dance),' a ritual dance in triple time originally performed by priests.

contrast, the highly vocal quality of the birds' song.[51] Humans, in this first, 'avian' part of the passage, only appear as the 'audience' of the cock's crowing, roused by it to rise and greet the approaching, conspicuous, and delightful sun.[52]

The 'floral' second part of the morning scene is dominated by tactile and olfactory images but opens with a mythological reference to the story of Clytie, a daughter of Oceanus, whose unhappy love for and unceasing devotion to Phoebus Apollo (the Sun) at last turned her into a flower (the heliotrope, i.e., 'turning towards the sun').[53] As the birds had reacted to the return of light, Clytie's all-night gaze towards the east is finally rewarded, and she, too, reacts with (amorous) joy ('arridet & adblanditur ... Amatori'). The reference to Clytie/the heliotrope, therefore, introduces into the 'floral' passage the theme of romantic love. At the same time, the actual heliotrope flower was known and valued for its strong fragrance and had therefore been used as a scent from the beginnings of perfumery in Egypt and Mesopotamia.[54] In early modern England, it could be named alongside roses and lilies as one of the flowers representing the tantalising scents of a garden.[55]

The emphasis on scent is made explicit in the next image: just as the birds had contributed their song and the other animals their expressive gamboling, the marigold and the rose contribute their fragrance to the 'joy of all' by 'open[ing] their petals and shed[ding] abroad their perfume.' Roses, of course, are known for their smell, especially early in the morning and late in the day.[56] Their sweet odour thus contributes to the specific sensory profile – to the characteristic sensescape – of the prolusion's dawn

---

[51] According to the *OED*, 'exult,' the primary meaning of the English verb (now obsolete) accords with the Latin: 'to spring or leap up; to leap for joy.' This meaning was still current in the seventeenth and eighteenth centuries.

[52] Milton's 'obviam ... auroram' is ambiguous, covering all three aspects, see *OLD*, 'obvius': '(1) That is in the way or path (of a moving person, etc.), placed so as to meet. ... (4) Presenting itself (to the sight or other senses; also, to the mind). ... (7) (of persons ...) Ready, easy; affable, courteous.'

[53] See the note ad loc. in CPW 1: 228.

[54] See Frances Kennett, *History of Perfume* (London: Harrap, 1975), 38. In fact, both dimensions – the 'symbolic' and the 'olfactory' – could be connected: in ancient Mesopotamian perfumery, Kennett relates, the heliotrope was 'adopted in "sympathetic" magic because of its characteristic in turning its face to the sun. it was believed to act as a charm to induce a favourable glance towards the wearer' (58); it gave its name to a synthetic scent used in modern perfumery: heliotropin, first synthesised in 1885 (182).

[55] See Dugan, *Ephemeral History of Perfume*, 164, quoting from Henry Hawkins's *Partheneia Sacra* (1633).

[56] As early manuals for the distillation of rosewater taught, the rose petals required were to be picked early in the morning, as smells were then strongest (see Dugan, *Ephemeral History of Perfume*, 50). Bacon, too, noted in his influential essay 'Of Gardens' (1625) that the elusive perfume of the damask rose – 'farre Sweeter in the Aire, (where it comes and Goes, like the Warbling of Musick) then in the Hand' – was best apprehended (short of distillation) early in the day, if at all: 'Roses Damask and Red, are fast Flowers of their Smelles; So that; you may walke by a whole Row of them, and finde Nothing of their Sweetnesse; Yea, though it be, in a Mornings Dew' (Francis Bacon, *The Essayes or Counsels, Civill and Morall*, ed. Michael Kiernan [Oxford: Clarendon, 2000] 139–145, at 140.)

4.1 Prolusion I ('Whether Day or Night is More Excellent') 183

Fig. 4: John Parkinson, *Paradisi in Sole Paradisus Terrestris ...* (London, 1629), 297: Various flowers (including '3 *Calendula*. Marigolds.'). Source: UB Frankfurt.

scene. Milton's 'Caltha' today refers to a genus of flowering plants whose principal European representative is the (odorless) marsh marigold (*Caltha palustris*). In early modern usage, however, 'caltha' (a term referring to a strong-smelling yellow flower in Vergil, Ovid, and Pliny) was frequently taken to mean the common marigold (*Calendula officinalis*).[57] In his description of '*Calendula*. Marigolds,' the herbalist John Parkinson, apothecary to James I, notes that 'they are called *Caltha* of diuers, and taken to be that *Caltha*, wherof both Virgil and Columella haue written. Others doe call them *Calendula*, of the Kalendes, that is the first day of the monthes, wherein they are thought chiefly to flower; ... We cal them in English generally, eyther Golds, or Marigolds' (Fig. 4). They have, Parkinson reports, 'a pretty strong and resinous sweete sent.'[58] Today, by contrast, Marigolds are often considered to have an *un*pleasantly resinous odour (redeemed only by their visual appeal). Parkinson's reference to their 'resinous sweete sent,' however, appears to be positive rather than negative; Milton, too, puts them right next to roses for their perfume. This might, indeed, be an expression of the historical variability of olfactory preferences – of different conceptions of what it 'really means' to have a 'sweet scent.'

At the same time as emphasising olfactory perception, the description of 'Caltha' and 'Rosa' (female, as flowers, by convention but personified further through Milton's capitalisation) continues the threads of personification and amorousness begun in the allusion to Clytie: while, botanically, they may be opening their petals and exuding their fragrance, Milton literally has them open their bosom ('sinum') and 'exhale' or 'breathe forth' their scents 'in a lavish, excessive manner' ('profusè spirant').[59] As the mechanism of floral fragrance is described in corporeal terms, Milton's descriptions takes on a sensuousness bordering on (but never actually arriving at) reprehensible sensuality. This sensuous personification is continued with reference to the other flowers raising their 'heads' ('capita') and begging 'him [i.e., the Sun] to kiss away the tear-drops which his absence brought.' In parallelising the cold, moist quality of dew with tears, caused by the absence of the warm, drying sun – and figuring the process of that drying as 'kisses' – the tactile element of the scene is brought to the fore and the metaphorical notion of the 'romantic' attraction between the two parties is embodied.[60]

To an early modern audience, moreover, Milton's reference to dewdrops kissed away by sunbeams may also have served to underline the strong olfactory character of the passage. After all, both heat *and* moisture were thought to play crucial parts in the perception of scents. When Bacon discusses the importance of external parameters for olfaction in one of the 'experiments' of his *Sylva Sylvarum*, he particularly highlights

---

[57] For the classical references, see *OLD*, 'calt(h)a.'
[58] John Parkinson, *Paradisi in Sole Paradisus Terrestris. Or a Garden of All Sorts of Pleasant Flowers* ... (London, 1629), 296–98, quotations at 296, 298.
[59] *OLD*, 'profusê': '(2) With lavish or immoderate expenditure, extravagantly; (3) In an excessive degree, immoderately.' Smith's literal translation in CW captures the personificating, embodying quality of the description: 'The marigold and also the rose ... opening their bosoms, breathe forth profusely their odors ...'
[60] In several of the poems discussed in Chapter 3 above, references to dew have a similar function of highlighting the haptic quality of a scene; in Elegy V and 'Elegiac Verses,' references to (floral) scent are also prominent.

the connection between the scent of flowers and the humidity of the early morning setting in which it is to be experienced best:

> To *sweet Smells, heat* is requisite to concoct the *Matter,* and some *Moisture* to spread the *Breath* of them: For *heat,* we see that *Woods* and *Spices* are more *odorate* in the *Hot Countreys,* than in the *Cold.* For *Moisture,* we see that things too much dryed lose their *Sweetness,* and *Flowers* growing smell better in a *Morning* or *Evening,* than at *Noon.* ... (generally) those *Smells* are the most grateful, where the *degree* of *heat* is small, or where the *Strength* of the *Smell* is allayed; for these *things* do rather woo the *Sense,* than satiate it. And therefore the *smell* of *Violets* and *Roses* exceedeth in *Sweetness* that of *Spices*; and *Gums,* and the strongest sort of *Smells,* are best in a weft afar off.[61]

In that it represents the 'allay[ing]' of influences – neither too hot nor too cold, neither too wet nor too dry –, the perceptual framework established by a (spring) morning is supremely conducive to the perception of pleasing scents. In that he traces the pleasantness of their smell to this moderate yet indispensable influence of moisture and heat, Bacon offers a theoretical justification for the conventional notion of flowers – and, in particular, '*Violets* and *Roses*' – as possessing the most pleasing of odours.[62]

The relevance of such views for the parallel representation of different sensory modes is readily apparent. In the dawn scene of Prolusion I, as in the corresponding passages in Milton's poetry, smell and touch – two otherwise often contrasting senses – go hand in hand, linked by moisture. All in all, then, three sensory modalities are involved in this particular element of the scene, as the male sun and female flowers engage in an exchange of fragrance for light, mediated by touch.[63]

A similar confrontation of male and female elements can be detected in the following description of the Earth ('Tellus'), who appears as lovely as in Elegy V ('In Adventum Veris'). This time, however, her visual beauty is traced to the 'lovelier robes' ('cultiori ... vestitu') she dons 'in adventum Solis,' and which are reminiscent of those worn by Hymen, god of marriage, in the elegy.[64] The clouds, too, are described in terms of their visual appeal (they are 'arrayed in garb of every hue'), and 'are seen' attending the rising Sun as he makes his way across the sky – *surgens,* just like birds, humans, and formerly drooping flowers had been prompted to rise by him.

The association of daybreak and spring is established not only through the references to flowers and birds – which both 'return' in spring – but also, more specifically, through the references to procreation, to birds' nests, and suckling goats ('capellæ'), most often born, like lambs, in springtime. The romantic encounters between *Tellus* and

---

[61] Bacon, *Sylva Sylvarum,* 176 (no. 833 on 'Sweet Smells').
[62] See also Chapter 5.2 below, where I quote Bacon on the rainbow.
[63] Although the 'other flowers' ('cæterique flores') are masculine, the feminine quality of the flowers as a 'group' has arguably been established through the references to 'Caltha,' 'Rosa,' and – most of all – 'Clytie.' The notion of the Sun (= Phoebus) as a male lover is conventional, and is treated by Milton extensively in Elegy V (see Chapter 3.2 above).
[64] 'Cultior ille venit tunicaque decentior apta': 'Hymen arrives, all decked out and very spruce in his traditional costume,' 107–8.

Sol, familiar from Elegy V, between Phoebus and Caltha, as well as between the sun and the 'other flowers' are equally suggestive of spring.

The last section of the passage makes explicit the fact that the whole scene really is a miniature paean to Phoebus, who is referred to throughout by a variety of 'aliases' covering different aspects of his character: *Sol, lux, aurora, Phœbus, Deus*. As Persians, Libyans, and Rhodians worship the rising Sun, not only are representatives of all three 'classical' continents present (Asia, Africa, and Europe), but precedence is given to the Persians, arguably because the sun rises in the East, then the Libyans, because it is due south at noon and Africa, in the south, is associated with (mid-day) heat. The island of Rhodes, directly opposite the coast of Asia Minor, is the easternmost point of southern Europe, and its famed Colossus was a monumental statue of the sun god Helios, thus making an apt reference in the present context. The inhabitants of America, finally, are named last, not only because of their rather recent 'addition' to the received conception of the world, but also because the sun reaches them last and sets in the West: a fact echoed by Milton's original 'Occidentalis *Indiæ* Populi,' i.e., 'the peoples of the West/Sunset Indies.' Their use of incense brings this multi-sensory passage to a strongly olfactory conclusion – and possibly doubles as a quip directed against Roman Catholicism, as it associates the liturgical use of incense (native to the East) with the rituals of undeniable heathens in the extreme West (who had, more recently, been proselytised by the colonial powers of Catholic southern Europe).[65] Ultimately, it is the sun – representative of day, the ulterior object of Milton's encomium – which ties together the diverse sensory aspects of the scene: it is the sun that makes the beauty of the earth, clouds, and sky visible; that elicits harmonious sounds from the birds and sweet fragrances from the flowers; that touches all with warmth and, not least, creates the necessary preconditions for humans to be awake and perceive all these wonders in the first place.

Proceeding in his speech, Milton refers to certain aspects of the early modern environment which indicate how sensory discourse may be influenced by material and social contexts. First, he appeals to the experience of his audience: 'You yourselves, Members of the University, must bear witness how delightful, how welcome, how long-awaited is the light of morning, since it recalls you to the cultured Muses from whom cruel Night parted you still unsatisfied and athirst' – a tongue-in-cheek reference to the fact that, at daybreak, students were expected to continue their studies, but, at the same time, a comment on the difficulties imposed by early modern lighting practices: (good) candles were expensive and, even in the best of circumstances, the constant flickering of candlelight was, as Emily Cockayne observes, 'not conducive to the health of the eyes.'[66] Depending on students' financial means, moreover, it could just be too expen-

---

[65] At the conclusion of Milton's 1626 satire on the papacy, 'In Quintum Novembris' ('On the Fifth of November'), 'the Papists' cruel venture' (i.e., the Gunpowder Plot of 1605) is forestalled, '*pious incense* is burned and *grateful* honours paid to God' ('At *pia thura* Deo, et *grati* solvuntur honores,' 223, emphases added). The specification contrasts with an account, given earlier in the poem, of rites performed at St Peter's Basilica in Rome.

[66] See Cockayne, *Hubbub*, 146–47, quotation at 146.

sive to be 'burning the midnight oil.'[67] When Milton described the onset of the first symptoms of his later blindness in a letter to the physician Leonard Philaras, he specifically referred to the trouble he suddenly had reading, 'even in the morning,' when lighting conditions presumably were best: 'I noticed my sight becoming weak and growing dim [debilitari atque hebescere visum sensi], ... and even in the morning [mane], if I began as usual to read, I noticed that my eyes felt immediate pain deep within and turned from reading [oculi statim penitus dolere, lectionemque refugere] ...'[68] In this respect, too, the onset of blindness was a sort of premature nightfall.[69]

Milton substantiates his point with examples from Greek mythology and poetry. Saturn, hurled down from heaven into Hades, and even Pluto himself would prefer light over darkness, if they could. In particular, he quotes from the Orphic *Hymn to Dawn*, which, like his own prolusion, celebrates the pleasantness of daybreak to all men:

> Thus rejoiceth [*chairei*] she the race of clear-voiced
>   mortals [*thnêtōn meropōn genos*] –
> Nor doth a single one escape that watchful gaze, o'erhead
>   [*opsin kathuperteron*].
> When from their eyes [*apo blepharōn*], thou dost shake off
>   sweet sleep [*ton glukun hupnon*],
> Joy fills the soul of all [*Pâs de brotos gethei*], – of creeping beast,
>   the host
> Of quadrupeds, of birds, of the finny dwellers in the deep.[70]

The (multi-)sensory character of these lines is readily apparent. It resembles Milton's earlier portrayal of dawn as a time of mixed visual and auditory sense impressions, although the visual focus is more predominant than in his account with its elaborations on birdsong and the odour of flowers. Further sensory modes are indeed represented, however, in the *Hymn*'s gustatory-tactile metaphor of 'sweet sleep' being brushed or shaken off the eyes – literally, and more appropriately, the still drowsy 'eyelids,'

---

[67] In Prolusion VII, Milton proclaims to his audience that 'we allow ourselves to be outdone by labourers and husbandmen in working after dark and before dawn,' which appears to express a similar association of daylight and intellectual labour, now the subject of criticism.
[68] Letter 24, to [Leonard] Philaras, 28 September 1654, CPW 4: 867–70, at 869. By the count in CW, the letter in question is no. 15.
[69] In Milton's repeated references to his blindness after 1652, the image of an unnatural or endless night frequently recurs: thus at *PL* 3.24, where the speaker's blind eyes 'find no dawn.' See also Chapter 5.2 below. In Latin phraseology, moreover, *caecus* ('blind') may conventionally qualify *nox*, meaning 'a pitch-black night.' In a passage of Prolusion I addressed below, Milton refers to 'nox cæca & obnubila,' literally 'blind and clouded night.'
[70] *Hymn to Dawn*, 28.7–11, adapted from the more literal translation in *CW* 12: 141. Milton in his Latin text prints the original Greek; the five lines quoted by him amount to a little over a third of the fifteen-line *Hymn* and, apart from earlier references to 'light-bringing Day' as opposed to 'the black-coloured march of Night' and 'bright-beaming Eos, duly blushing/reddening (over) the earth [*Êōs lamprophaês, erythainomenê kata kosmon*],' form its 'sensory centre'; see *Orphei Hymni*, ed. Guilelmus Quandt (Berlin: Weidmann, 1962), 53.

blephara – of mortals.[71] The passage contains further parallels to Milton's own dawn scene discussed above in its references to various classes of animals, to birds and, in particular, to 'the host of quadrupeds' (*phula / Tetrapodōn*) which parallels Milton's '*totumque genus quadrupedum.*'[72] Similarly, Milton's 'every living thing' ('omnium animantium stirpi') is close to the Orphic hymn's *pâs ... brotos*, while the rejoicing described in the Greek verses (*chairei, gethei*) matches the *gaudium* and *laetitia* expressed by Milton's songbirds and other animals. It is impossible to determine, of course, whether Milton shaped his own prose depiction of dawn along the lines of these verses – which he obviously valued – or whether he chose the quotation because it echoes the notion expressed earlier in his speech. What is apparent is that the lines from the Orphic *Hymn to Dawn* blend seamlessly into the sensory discourse of Prolusion I.

In one particular point, however, the *Hymn* might be said to introduce a further layer of complexity into the sensory discourse of the prolusion thus far. Beyond their multi-sensorial quality, after all, the Greek lines transport an ultimately synaesthetic ambiguity in the interplay of their visual and auditory elements. This ambiguity rests on their use of the epitheton *merops* in a mixed visual/auditory context. *Merops* is a poetic word of disputed derivation. Conventionally, it just means 'mortal, human,' but this would create a tautology within the phrase *thnêtōn meropōn genos*, which already includes *thnêtos*, meaning 'mortal' more specifically (being derived from *thanatos*, 'death'); this meaning is matched by *brotos* towards the end of the passage. With a view to *merops*, two derivations, in particular, are being debated; these are derived from either of two possible meanings of *ops*, 'voice' or 'eye[s], face,' giving *merops* the meanings 'articulate, clear-voiced' (as in Smith's translation) or 'sharp-sighted, bright-eyed,' respectively.[73]

Since the latter *ops* is a poetic variant of *opsis*, present in the subsequent line of the *Hymn* (*opsin*, 'watchful gaze'), the 'optical' reading of *merops* – or rather, its reading with an optical connotation – may be thought adequate. This impression is reinforced by the verses' typical association of vision and height as per the orientational metaphor VISION IS UP. In fact, the phrase *opsin kathuperteron*, referring to Dawn's (i.e., by implication, the sun's) 'watchful gaze o'erhead,' presents an almost literal expression of the slightly more specific variant VISION IS HEIGHT. The full spatial extent of the positive influence of dawn/sunlight is also signified through the passage's comprehensive but spatially segmented listing of 'living things,' which includes (ground-dwelling) 'creeping beasts' and quadrupeds alongside birds and, perhaps somewhat hyperbolically, the 'finny dwellers in the deep.' The habitat of the latter constitutes the lower terminus of the UP–DOWN axis whose upper extreme had been established at the reference to dawn rising above the earth.[74] Humans are prominently excluded from this list of creatures in

---

[71] Derived from *blepein*, 'to look,' the term still retains a close relation to visual perception (see *LSJ*, 'blepō,' 'blepharon').

[72] Rendered by Tillyard as 'beasts of every kind' and by Smith as 'the whole race of quadrupeds.'

[73] See *LSJ*, 'merops' (acknowledging only the meaning 'articulate' as an 'epitheton of men'), 'ops¹,' and 'ops².' For the 'optical' interpretation of 'merops' (and the difficult derivation of the term in general), see *Frisk*, II, 'meropes' (211–12).

[74] To be fair, 'in the deep' is a translator's flourish; the *Hymn* calls the sea creatures *einaliōn* [sc. *ethnos*], '[the tribe] of those in the sea.'

4.1 Prolusion I ('Whether Day or Night is More Excellent') 189

sky, land, and sea; they are the *thnêtōn meropōn genos*, distinguished by the command of articulate speech and/or discerning vision.

However, through its repeated insistence that all living things 'rejoice' (*chairei*, *gethei*), the passage also creates a context in which *meropōn* may plausibly be taken to refer, more explicitly than either of those verbs, to the vocal, audible expression of rejoicing with a 'clear voice.' Ultimately, the ambiguous optical/auditory/'generic' meaning of the epitheton cannot be resolved, and either sensory reading fits the multi-sensory character of the passage, in which the 'watchful gaze' of Eos meets the eyes – literally, and more appropriately, the 'eyelids,' *blephara* – of mortals, still heavy with 'sweet sleep.' The looser, shorter translation given in the Yale edition of Milton's prose ('Then of a truth do mortal men rejoice'), though less cumbersome, conflates the conventional denotations of *thnêtos* and *merops* and excises the ambiguous sensory connotations of the latter from the passage, thus obscuring (or indeed muffling) the fullness of its sensory discourse.[75]

Apart from his general allusions to Greek and Roman mythology, then, Milton draws on classical literary sources to enrich the (sensory) discourse of his speech, even if never as extensively and complexly as in his quotation from the *Hymn to Dawn*.[76] As he continues his argument, however, his next appeal – much closer to home – is to the personal experience of his listeners. When he continues his argument, he combines both, the mixture of empiricism/pragmatism – now turned counterfactual in the form of a thought experiment – and the corresponding illustration from classical mythology: 'who would have the hardihood to sail the wide and boundless seas, without a hope that Day would dawn? He would cross the ocean even as the ghosts cross Lethe and Acheron, beset on every hand by fearsome darkness [horrendis ... tenebris].' While sea travel, quite probably, was for many of Milton's listeners beyond their immediate sphere of experience, his follow-up image seizes an everyday problem of early modern life and takes it to its logical extreme: in the hypothetical case of an endless night, he says, 'every man would ... pass his life in his own mean hovel [gurgustio], hardly daring even to creep outside [foras prorepere], so that the dissolution of human society must needs follow.'[77] Both the image of a dwelling hardly fit for human habitation and Milton's suggestion that its occupants might timidly 'creep out' only once in a while, if at all, portrays the benighted humanity of the image as a congregation of animals rather than humans.

While the notion of never-ending, 'fearsome darkness' has, after all, lost none of its potency, Milton's reference to nighttime as a time exclusively spent indoors is best

---

[75] CPW 1: 229: 'Then of a truth do mortal men rejoice, nor is there one who flees thy face which shines above, when thou dost shake sweet sleep from their eyes. Every man is glad, and every creeping thing, all the tribes of beast and bird, and all the many creatures of the deep.' Tillyard, moreover, renders the lines as prose whereas Smith aims to preserve their verse character. In Milton's original, *Epistolarum Familiarum Liber Unus* ... (London 1674), 78, they are typeset as poetry, including hanging indentation of long lines.
[76] Prolusion I contains several other verse quotations from Persius, Hesiod (twice), and Martial. The quotations from Hesiod have a bearing on the sensory discourse of the speech only inasmuch as they refer to the origins of Day and Night; this is why I have not discussed them individually.
[77] CPW 1: 229.

understood in its early modern context. This had two large and interrelated elements, a 'pragmatic' and an 'ideological' one. On the one hand, nighttime darkness in early modern Europe quite simply meant the sudden irruption of a particular sensescape – a 'nightscape' not recoverable under present-day conditions – which to humans was hard if not impossible to navigate, and which required individuals to carry lanterns or torches at all times and – prior to the eighteenth century – even in most urban areas.[78] On the basis of these pragmatic constrictions, social norms were formulated: the night was to be spent indoors, sleeping; any deviations from this norm were, tendentially, suspect. Hence, it was considered 'bestial to work at night, for the same reason that burglary was a worse crime than daylight robbery; the night, as Sir Edward Coke [d. 1634] explained, was "the time wherein man is to rest, and wherein beasts run about seeking their prey."'[79] Milton's animalising imagery, in which the perpetuation of nighttime leads to an inevitable collapse of human society, shares in precisely the same dichotomy: the day is for humans (and songbirds, and gambolling kids); nighttime is for wild beasts.

As he continues, Milton pursues these associations of day with culture, and, specifically, with painting as the epitome of *visual* culture. This opens a passage in which the visual appeal of different objects of vision is considered, first in culture, then in nature. In both aspects, Milton starts from the negative thought experiment of the preceding passage ('what if the sun would never rise again?'). Specifically, day, in that it implies the presence of the sun and of light, makes vision possible; painting is the art form representative of vision; hence, eternal night would make painting impossible – impossible to carry out but equally impossible to appreciate: 'To no purpose would Apelles have pictured Venus rising from the waves, in vain would Zeuxis have painted Helen, if dark, dense night [nox cæca & obnubila] hid from our eyes these wondrous sights [res tam visendas oculis nostris adimeret].' As in the elegies, female visual attractiveness is figured as the supreme kind of visual beauty in nature. Hence, Milton presents *paintings* of female beauty – of Venus herself, and of Helen of Troy, said to be the most beautiful woman in the world, and carried out by the legendary master painters of antiquity – as the supreme icons of visual culture in general. After discussing the every-*day* impact of vision (i.e., seeing) on human life, and day as the time of light and hence vision, Milton has turned to its rarefied version in art, and painting as the one art form uniquely addressed to the sense of sight. When he characterises the 'wondrous sights' of art, he refers to a heightened, yet thoroughly bodily, form of vision: to 'res tam visendas,' things calling for vision in its purest form.[80]

The passage continues by (re)turning to the visual appeal of nature, already alluded to earlier within Milton's miniature 'Hymn to Phoebus,' as Tellus 'deck[ed] herself in

---

[78] See Smith, *Sensory History*, 26. On developments in early modern lighting infrastructure in towns and cities, see Cockayne, *Hubbub*, 223–29.

[79] Thomas, *Man and the Natural World*, 39. For the cultural-historical (and material) context, see Sasha Handley, *Sleep in Early Modern England* (New Haven, Conn.: Yale University Press, 2016), and Janine Rivière, *Dreams in Early Modern England* (Abingdon: Routledge, 2017).

[80] These conventional declarations bear some contrast with the relative absence of painting from the literary and epistolary evidence surrounding Milton's subsequent tour of Italy (compared, for instance, with the countless descriptions of paintings in Evelyn's *Diary*); see, however, Frye, *Milton's Imagery and the Visual Arts*, and McColley, *Gust for Paradise*.

4.1 Prolusion I ('Whether Day or Night is More Excellent')

lovelier robes' and the clouds appeared 'arrayed in garbs of every hue.' This time, however, Milton not only expands on the theme by introducing some more elements familiar from the elegies but also connects the appreciation of visual beauty to the (necessary) use of vision, and thus to the more 'existential' perspective taken earlier in the passage:

> In vain too would the earth [tellus] bring forth in abundance vines twining in many a winding trail, in vain nobly towering trees [decentissimæ proceritatis arbores]; in vain would she deck herself anew with buds and blossoms [gemmis & floribus], as with stars [stellulis], striving to imitate the heaven above [cœlum exprimere conata]. Then indeed that noblest of the senses, sight, would lose its use to every creature [tum demum nobilissimus ille videndi sensus nullis animalibus usui foret]; yes, and the light of the world's eye being quenched [extincto mundi oculo], all things would fade [deflorescerent omnia] and perish utterly; nor would the men who dwelt upon the darkened earth [tenebricosam ... terram] long survive this tragedy, since nothing would be left to support their life, nor any means of staying the lapse of all things into the primeval Chaos [nihil denique obstaret, quo minus in antiquum Chaos ruerent omnia].[81]

As in elegies I and V, height (*proceritas*, 'loftiness') implies sight (VISION IS HEIGHT), and is referred to in the same breath with more obviously 'visual' imagery such as flowers, stars, and – possibly – precious stones.[82] Bringing together diverse aspects of vision alluded to earlier in the prolusion, Milton connects 'that noblest of the senses, sight' – following the conventional sensory hierarchy – to 'the light of the world's eye' – an equally conventional way of referring to the sun, and thus presents vision as uniting microcosm (the eye of man) and macrocosm (the eye of the world, the eye of heaven). Vis-à-vis the sun (the 'day-star'), all things, whether humans, animals, plants, stars, or even minerals, would wither away ('deflorescerent omnia'), underlining the symbolic centrality of plants and flowers – such as, paradigmatically, the heliotrope – in Milton's discussion of the interplay between day, the sun, and vision.

With the chain of being thus disrupted by the absence of light and day, finally, 'old Chaos' would reign. This theme, with its abstract association of Chaos and night, is alluded to frequently in *Paradise Lost* (e.g. at 1.543, 2.894–5, 970, and passim), where it contrasted even more strongly with its opposite, the order of God's creation. It also appears, fittingly, in *Comus* (*A Masque presented at Ludlow Castle*, 1634), Milton's masque set in a dark wood. At its original performance, the masque featured the children of the Earl of Bridgewater (for whom it was written), with the earl's two sons playing two brothers opposite their sister ('the Lady'), who has lost her way in the dark

---

[81] CPW 1: 229–30.
[82] *OLD* 'gemma': '(1) A bud or eye, esp. in the bark of vines, trees, etc.; (2) A precious stone, jewel, gem ...' The translation in CW, in fact, has '... to no purpose in fine would she bedeck herself with *gems and flowers* like little stars, trying to imitate heaven' (emphasis added). See also Milton's later reference to 'gemmarum nonnullæ,' quoted below, which unambiguously refers to precious stones. In the present instance, however, an ambiguity appears to be intended. Perhaps Milton is even thinking of how 'eye' may relate to the bud of a plant (*OED* 'eye,' II 10 b [a]).

wood ruled by the sorcerer Comus. In one particularly significant passage, Milton has the Elder Brother declare (as he enters):

> *Eld. Bro.* Unmuffle ye faint stars, and thou fair moon
> That wont'st to love the traveller's benison,
> Stoop thy pale visage through an amber cloud,
> And disinherit Chaos, that reigns here
> In double night of darkness, and of shades;
> Or if your influence be quite dammed up
> With black usurping mists, some gentle taper
> Though a rush-candle from a wicker hole
> Of some clay habitation visit us
> With thy long levelled rule of streaming light,
> And thou shalt be our star of Arcady,
> Or Tyrian Cynosure. (330–41)

In the gloomy wood's 'double night of darkness, and of shades,' Chaos and anarchy loom, and need to be brought under control by means of illumination, either by the moon and stars or else by artificial lighting. The connection between the two interlinked dichotomies of light/darkness and anarchy/(political) order is emphasised in the punning references to 'black usurping mists' and the 'long levelled rule of streaming light' which alone would be able to dispel them.[83] What is most striking when seen in juxtaposition to Milton's extolling of day and light over darkness and night in Prolusion I, however, is how the lines from *Comus*, too, supplement their references to the abstract notion of 'dark Chaos' with a more concrete awareness of how lighting might be provided and what this *means* in socio-cultural terms. In particular, Milton refers to different kinds of lighting available to more or less affluent social classes, respectively: the socio-economic connotation of 'some gentle [i.e., primarily: "kind, welcome"] taper' is turned denotative by the following, contrasting reference to 'a rush-candle from a wicker hole/Of some clay habitation.' Rushlights or rush candles – i.e., candles 'of little power made by dipping the pith of a rush in tallow or some other grease' (*OED*) – were the means of lighting available to poor people. Windows, conversely, often had a wickerwork covering where glass was too expensive. As in Prolusion I, the continuance of 'human society' is figured, in the lines from *Comus*, as contingent upon the availability of light. In contrast to the prolusion, however, the light in question, after the initial references to the moon and stars, is *artificial* lighting, and different kinds of lighting are evoked, each of them with its specific social connotation. Even a sputtering rush-candle gleaming from an almost opaque 'wicker hole,' Milton suggests, is able to institute 'gentle' (i.e., cultured) order and to repel the impending Chaos of darkness. In the prolusion as well as in the masque, the sensory discourse of the respective passages integrates views about light and vision that go beyond the immediate sphere of sense perception to address aesthetic, social, even political concerns. In their allusions to (social-

---

[83] On the biographical, political, and generic backgrounds of *Comus*, see Lewalski, *Life of Milton*, 63–64, 76–81.

4.1 Prolusion I ('Whether Day or Night is More Excellent')

ly connoted) lighting practices and devices – more pronounced in *Comus* than in Prolusion I, but present in both – the sensory discourse of Milton's texts offers a glimpse of the cultural context in which they were written: even a 'rush-candle from a wicker hole' would be as welcome as 'some gentle taper' to Milton's 'gentle'– aristocratic – actors.

In Prolusion I, Milton proceeds by dwelling further on the negative aspects of darkness, contending that 'with good reason ... have the poets declared that Night springs from Hell, since by no means whatever could so many grievous ills descend upon mankind from any other quarter.'[84] In picturing the horrors of the night, he initially refers to images familiar from the earlier praise of vision as the noblest sense, and specifically to the 'luxury problem' of nightfall precluding all possibilities of *aesthetic* vision:

> For when night falls [Obortâ enim nocte] all things grow foul and vile [sordescunt & obfuscantur omnia], no difference can be seen between a Helen and a Canidia, a precious jewel and a common stone (but that some gems [gemmarum nonnullæ] have power to outshine the darkness [noctis obscuritatem vincant]). Then too the loveliest spots strike horror to the heart, a horror gathering force from a silence deep and sad [alto & tristi quodam augetur silentio].[85]

At this point, hearing is referred to as a sense connected to nighttime vision: as darkness makes visual perception impossible, a deep, emotionally charged silence means the same kind of absence of stimuli with regard to the ears: the absence of sound and hearing, as the absence of light and vision, are disconcerting. In the immediate continuation of the passage from *Comus* already quoted, the younger of the two brothers, relating the darkness of the night to the simultaneous absence of any comforting sound, expresses a similar sentiment:

> *Sec. Bro.*   Or if our eyes
> Be barred that happiness, might we but hear
> The folded flocks penned in their wattled cotes,
> Or sound of pastoral reed with oaten stops,
> Or whistle from the lodge, or village cock
> Count the night-watches to his feathery dames,
> 'Twould be some solace yet some little cheering
> In this close dungeon of innumerous boughs. (341–48)

As before, Milton combines a comparatively abstract, conventional notion (the 'sound of pastoral reed') with the arguably more concrete evocation of sheep bleating and a cock – a 'guardsman cock' as in the 'Elegiac Verses' – making himself heard at night. Significantly, all of these images are connected to notions of shelter and safety (and their perversion): the 'folded' sheep are 'penned in their wattled cotes'; a 'lodge' and a

---

[84] CPW 1: 230.
[85] CPW 1: 230, noting that, as earlier, 'Helen represents the epitome of feminine beauty, [while] Canidia is a symbol of ugliness or venomousness in women,' referred to as such in several instances by Horace.

'village' are mentioned; the cock watches over his 'dames' – while the brothers are surrounded and enclosed (yet not sheltered) in a 'close dungeon of innumerable boughs.' The various sounds of (agri)culture and settlement – if they could only be heard – would make perceptible what cannot be seen. In a very similar way, the comforting sound of (village) bells is often mentioned as constitutive of what Bruce Smith has referred to as an 'acoustic community' situated within a shared 'acoustic horizon.'[86] And in *Il Penseroso*, Milton would construct the speaker's solitariness partly by reference to such a communally shared soundscape: 'Oft on a plat of rising ground,/I hear *the far-off curfew* sound,/Over some wide-watered shore,/Swinging slow with sullen roar.'[87] While the speaker of *Il Penseroso*, of course, does not miss the company of other people, the 'silence deep and sad' alluded to in Prolusion I seems very much akin to the frightful hush lamented by the younger brother of *Comus*.

As the passage in Prolusion I continues, Milton does not yet let go of individual fear (as 'man [and] beast ... shut their eyes against the dread aspect of Night') but also revisits the generally anti-social quality of night, again taking the acoustic as well as the visual dimension of the sensescape into account:

> All creatures lingering in the fields, be they man or beast, hasten to house or lair for refuge; then, hiding their heads beneath their coverings, they shut their eyes against the dread aspect of Night [ad aspectus noctis terribiles claudunt oculos]. None may be seen abroad [Nullum foris conspicies] save thieves and rogues who fear the light [Fures & Laverniones Lucifugos], who, breathing murder and rapine, lie in wait to rob honest folk of their goods, and wander forth by night alone, lest day betray them. For Day lays bare all crimes, nor ever suffers wrong-doing to pollute her light [haud passura lucem suam istiusmodi flagitiis inquinari]. None will you meet [nullum habebis obvium] save ghosts and spectres, and fearsome goblins who follows in Night's train from the realms below; it is their boast that all night long they rule the earth [totâ nocte terras in sua ditione esse] and share it with mankind. To this end, I think, night sharpens our hearing [noctem auditum nostrum reddidisse solertiorem], that our ears may catch the sooner and our hearts perceive with greater dread the groans of spectres, the screeching of owls and nightbirds, and the roaring of lions that prowl in search of prey [ut umbrarum gemitus, bubonum & strygum ululatus, ac rugitus Leonum, quos fames evocat; eò citius perstringerent aures, animosque graviori metu percellerunt].[88]

Whether it is for fear of darkness or of thieves and murderers (who, in turn, 'fear the light'): Milton keeps on reiterating the early modern commonplace that the night should

---

[86] See Smith, *Acoustic World of Early Modern England*, 31–33, 46–47 on bells in the countryside, 52–54 on bells within in the much different soundscape of London. See also Rath, *How Early America Sounded*, 3, 43–46; and Hoffer, *Sensory Worlds in Early America*, 43, 116. Corbin, *Village Bells*, analyses similar phenomena in nineteenth-century rural France.

[87] *Il Penseroso*, 73–76, emphasis added. From the perspective of the community at large, the speaker's seclusion would arguably be considered anti-social behaviour (on which see below).

[88] CPW 1: 230.

be spent indoors. Deviating from this norm would have to be considered either unnatural or anti-social behaviour, and would, if one were subjected to the experience against one's will – like the brothers of *Comus* –, be expected to cause fear.

Milton then takes up the equally conventional observation that 'night sharpens our hearing.'[89] This might seem paradoxical, since he had just referred to the 'deep and sad' silence of night – the apparent contradiction, however, captures precisely the nature of the experience: namely, that the silence of night somehow 'breeds' a heightened, more acute apprehension of sound – and the sounds to go with it. Thus, Francis Bacon had observed, regarding one of the experiments collected in his *Sylva Sylvarum*, that there appeared to exist an inverse relation between the acuity of hearing and the clarity of sight, and he had offered a physio-psychological explanation for this phenomenon:

> *Sounds* are *meliorated* by the *Intension* of the *Sense*; where the *Common Sense* is collected most, to the *particular Sense* of *Hearing*, and the *Sight* suspended: And therfore, *Sounds* are sweeter, (as well as greater,) in the *Night*, than in the *Day*.[90]

Since he has a thesis to argue, Milton does not consider the possibility that the darkness of night might make '*Sounds* ... sweeter,' or that it might 'meliorate' pleasant sounds as well as unpleasant ones. The examples he lists, however, do indicate that he intends to make the most out of the playful, 'ludic' potential of the prolusion form: even if the 'groans of spectres' were admitted as real sounds potentially disturbing the sleep of Milton's English contemporaries, the 'roaring of lions,' quite obviously, belongs to a different category. Moving away from the 'realism' of his earlier imagery, Milton capitalises on the potential of sensory discourse to stimulate his hearers' imagination. In the present instance, this creates an ostensible tension between Milton's rhetoric and his professed intention of establishing the truth about night and day, arrived at by argument and close scrutiny. Ultimately, however, and in keeping with the claim of rhetoric to offer both (imaginative) delight and (factual, argumentative) instruction, the prolusion genre is meant to accommodate conflicting demands of relatability and imaginativeness. As suggested at the outset of this chapter, sensory discourse affords both.

Whether imagined lions, the 'questionable shapes' of spectres, or harmless yet uncanny owls: the prolusion leaves no doubt regarding the potential of nighttime sounds to strike fear into the heart of whoever hears them (or imagines them in the profound silence of night). And while it is wrong to claim, therefore, that 'night brings respite from their fears to men and lulls every care to rest,' Milton argues, night is still the occasion of sleep, which revives and restores the body: 'but this is the merciful ordinance of God, for which we owe no gratitude to Night.'[91] As this first mention of (the Christian) God in the prolusion indicates, again, the delight of rhetorical argument for its own sake and

---

[89] For an example from classical antiquity, see Plutarch's *Quaestiones Convivales* (*Table Talk*), 8,3, on the question of why sounds appear to carry better at night; *Moralia, vol. IX: Table-talk, Books 7–9. Dialogue on Love*, trs E. L. Minar, F. H. Sandbach, W. C. Helmbold (Cambridge, Mass.: Harvard University Press, 1961).
[90] Bacon, *Sylva Sylvarum*, 55 (no. 235).
[91] CPW 1: 230–31.

references to more serious matters are not mutually exclusive in Milton's text. After all, 'what is sleep but the image of semblance of death?'[92]

As the main part of his argument draws to a close, the speaker points to the dependence of 'the moon and the other stars' on the original light of the sun, 'for they have no light to radiate but such as they borrow from the sun.'[93] On one level, this may be taken to refer to current discoveries in astronomy, where the realisation that the light apparently emitted by the planets was, in fact, reflected sunlight increasingly supplanted received (Aristotelian) notions about their inherent luminosity after Galileo's 1611 observation of the phases of Venus – resembling the more familiar ones of the moon – had established the reflection theory.[94] At the same time, Milton's remark mirrors certain views regarding the light of the sun, stars, and planets that were current in contemporary Platonism. According to the Platonists, not only the planets but also the (other) stars derived their visible light from the sun, while orthodox Aristotelians held that the stars were made of the fiery quintessence, which provided them with their light. Marjara has argued that Milton's alignment with the Platonist (and indeed Pythagorean) position is probably due more to a pervasive presence of Platonic/Pythagorean ideas in Renaissance thought than to any preoccupation with recent findings in astronomy.[95] However, we should not disregard the fact – indicated by Milton's later explicit references to Galileo, for example – that he demonstrably became aware, at some point, of these developments.[96] With particular reference to the passage from Prolusion I, Marjara further observes that, 'in *Paradise Lost*, Milton has moved distinctly away from this explicitly Platonic stance to the conservative Aristotelian opinion,' but that he 'does not totally abandon his Platonic belief; instead, he fuses it with the Aristotelian opinion ...'[97] At several points in the prolusions, however, Milton displays his familiarity with Aristotle's writings – they were set reading at university –, and defends broadly Aristotelian positions. It thus seems debatable whether any clear movement into a more or less Aristotelian or Platonic/Pythagorean direction should be assumed.[98] Moreover, Milton's references to Pythagoreanism, early or late, are not wholly without complications, either: in Prolusion II, discussed below, the power of Pythagoreanism to shape imagery and, in particular, sensory discourse, even in a context in which its claims to epistemic validity are being actively disputed, is evident. Both cases – that of (sun)light referred to in

---

[92] CPW 1: 231.
[93] CPW 1: 232.
[94] See Kuhn, *Copernican Revolution*, 222–24.
[95] See Marjara, *Contemplation of Created Things*, 63–68. As Milton's earlier reference to 'the dense and solid earth ... coming between the sun's light and our horizon' indicates, however, at least some aspects of empirical astronomy were on his mind during the composition of the speech.
[96] Apart from the passages in *Paradise Lost* quoted in Chapter 2 above, in *Areopagitica* (1644) Milton mentions his 1639 visit to Galileo (see CPW 2: 538). By contrast, *Of Education* (also 1644) only mentions geocentric works as parts of Milton's educational canon (see CPW 2: 390–92 and notes).
[97] Marjara, *Contemplation of Created Things*, 66.
[98] As Marjara himself acknowledges, Milton's cosmology in *Paradise Lost* depends to no small degree on the primacy of the sun (see *Contemplation of Created Things*, 118–23); this, again, could be seen to argue the greater relative importance of 'Pythagorean' or 'Platonic' ideas for the composition of the epic.

Prolusion I as well as the 'harmony of the spheres' discussed in Prolusion II – relate aspects of sense perception to more abstract, cosmological deliberation. It is on the side of their abstract implications that, as Marjara suggests, such sensory remarks of Milton's may be seen to conflict (either synchronically or diachronically); on the more immediately referential side of sensory discourse – that is, where it implies direct sensory experience of sunshine or of harmonious music –, such theoretically conflicting views may, in practice, contribute to a common sensory imagery.

After such spectral and cosmic considerations – of ghosts, 'fearsome goblins,' and remote planets – in his peroration Milton returns to matters closer at hand, and, in particular, to the negative social and, as he now reveals, downright immoral associations of night:

> Who then but a son of darkness [tenebrio], a robber, a gamester, or one whose wont it is to spend his nights in the company of harlots and snore away his days [inter Scortorum greges noctem pernoctare perpetem integrosque dies ronchos efflare solitus] – who, I ask, but such a fellow would have undertaken to defend a cause so odious and discreditable [sc. as a defence of night]? I wonder that he dare so much as look upon this sun [adspicere audeat Solem], or share with other men, without a qualm, that light which he is slandering so ungratefully [communi luce ... quam ingratus vituperat]. He deserves to share the fate of Python, slain by the stroke of the sun's hostile rays [dignus ... adversis radiorum ictibus ... interimat Sol]. He deserves to pass a long and loathsome life imprisoned in Cimmerian darkness. He deserves, above all, to see sleep overcoming his hearers even as he speaks [dignus denique cujus Oratio somnem moveat auditoribus], so that his best eloquence affects them no more than an idle dream [non majorem somnio quovis fidem faciat], till, drowsy himself, he is cheated into taking his hearers' nods and snores for nods of approval and murmurs of praise as he ends his speech [nutantes atque stertentes Auditores annuere sibi & plaudere peroranti deceptus putet].[99]

Considering his explicit reference to previous speakers in Prolusion II (discussed below), it seems not unlikely that, here too, Milton is (playfully) referring to a fellow student who had been assigned the ungrateful task of defending night and darkness in a preceding speech – something of an uphill battle considering the traditionally strong positive valuations of light, vision, day, and everything connected with it. As before, if in a morally reproachful and slightly comic register, the onset of night betokens 'the lapse of all things into the primeval Chaos.' Consequently, Milton's own association of darkness with 'robbers,' 'gamesters,' and 'harlots' is conventional; through his strong emphasis on the visual elements of his imagery (e.g., in the initial image, 'tenebrio,' 'noctem pernoctare perpetem'), however, he relates the passage more strongly still to the overall 'sensory program' of Prolusion I.

Ultimately, Milton's polemic speaks to a generally negative evaluation of night, based in socio-cultural preconceptions such as the ones outlined above: Milton's jesting

[99] CPW 1: 232.

marks itself off against this dark, negative foil. With his references to Phoebus Apollo's slaying of the Python and the 'Cimmerian darkness,' mentioned by Homer as surrounding the entrance to Hades, Milton again posits 'strong,' serious images of destructive negativity, only to resolve the tension through his reference to the supreme punishment, worse than being slain by Apollo or sent to Hades: falling prey to a comical subversion of the orator–audience relationship, in which the roles of speaker and hearers are inverted and unconscious snoring figures as a travesty of conscious, deliberate speech.

Still, the imagined snoring of the audience takes up the previous image of a dissolute 'shadeling ... wont to puff out snores for days on end' ('tenebrio ... integrosque dies ronchos efflare solitus'), and thus the reprehensible and the comically harmless both present in the passage cannot wholly be dissociated from each other. In both cases, the speaker draws on the perceptible, embodied expressions of sleep, making 'darkness' not so much 'visible' – as the oft-quoted tag from *Paradise Lost* goes – but rather audible.[100] Mindlessly snoring where they should be awake and attentive, they are shown up to be 'mere bodies.' In making jokes at the expense of a previous speaker as in castigating actual vices, in imagining a comical inversion of the speaker–audience relationship as in highlighting, thus, the actual relationship obtaining, in the present moment, between himself and his audience, Milton focuses on the *bodily expression* of *unnatural* sleep: if night is for sleeping, day and an academic function decidedly are not.

In drawing his audience's attention to the oratorical situation itself, Milton returns, close to the conclusion of his speech, to a farcical inversion of the setting he had evoked at its opening – only that now the tables have been turned: whereas at the self-referential outset of the prolusion, the speaker had seen himself at the mercy of *his* audience ('how can I hope for your good-will, when in all this great assembly I encounter none but hostile glances ...?'), he now imagines another speaker's audience in an absurd and ridiculous situation. Arguably, the two groups are identical – in that Milton and his imagined counterpart would both be addressing the same assembly of students –, but at the end of Prolusion I as at its beginning, Milton still needs to win *his* hearers' approval. And thus, the prolusion ends with a reference to its sensory subject-matter and links it to a renewed appeal to the audience's benevolence:

> But I see the black brows of Night [nigra video Noctis supercilia], and note the advance of darkness [sentio atras insurgere tenebras], I must withdraw, lest Night overtake me unawares.
> I beg you then, my hearers, since Night is but the passing and the Death of Day, not to give Death the preference over Life, but graciously to honour my cause with your votes; so may the Muses prosper your studies, and Dawn, the friend of the Muses, hear your prayers and may the Sun, who sees and hears all things, hearken to all in this assembly who honour and support his cause [exaudiatque Aurora Musis amica, exaudiat & *Phœbus* qui cuncta videt auditque quos habeat in hoc cœtu Laudis ejus Fautores]. I have done [Dixi].[101]

---

[100] See *PL* 1.61–64, in a description of Hell: 'A dungeon horrible, on all sides round/As one great furnace flamed, yet from those flames/No light, but rather darkness visible/Served only to discover sights of woe ...'
[101] CPW 1: 232–33.

4.1 Prolusion I ('Whether Day or Night is More Excellent') 199

In asking for the audience's favour, the speaker first appeals to his own imagined experience: in doing so, both his concrete reference to the 'black [eye]brows of Night' and his declaration of 'feeling' the shadows gather ('sentio') give his brief remark a marked sensory texture – not quite multi-sensory, but almost palpably visual.[102] Milton further amplifies this substantiation of his sensory discourse by again bringing into play the embodied dimension of perception presupposed by the speaker–hearer relationship: as he asks his audience for their support, applause, or other forms of audible approval, these are to be addressed to the ears of Aurora and Phoebus, personifications thus given the benefit of bodily hearing. Since both are primarily associated with vision, moreover, the image again approximates the visual and the auditory sphere, whose interplay had been related to the oratorical situation before, in the opposition of the orator's vocal speech and the audience's hostile glances as in the speaker's presentation of himself as the 'herald of dawn,' metaphorically crowing for bright Day to come. At the same time, Milton aptly takes up another theme he had introduced earlier, by reiterating the connection between the Muses, light, Phoebus, and Aurora as the bringers of that light. In giving to the speaker their audible support, Milton's listeners are ultimately doing themselves a favour, as their applause establishes a direct connection between themselves and Apollo as a representative of learning as well as to the Muses, representing all branches of culture.[103]

If the form of Prolusion I as an auditory event presupposes – and, as I have indicated, the speech itself repeatedly reflects on – the sensorily-based speaker–hearer relationship, Milton, at the conclusion of Prolusion I, as in the other prolusions discussed below, highlights this foundational aspect of his sensory discourse: namely, its being presented as vocal, embodied speech. In the elegies, this had been effected, consistently, by figuring the poet-speaker as a singer; in the prolusions, by presenting the orator, emphatically, as a speaker declaiming to be heard. Milton's closing formula accords with this emphasis of Prolusion I on embodied perception – even if it was conventional (he uses it to end four of his seven prolusions): 'Dixi' – 'I have spoken' and, by implication, 'you have listened.'

***

As its topic suggested right away, Prolusion I is characterised by frequent recourse to the sensory sphere. This involves all of the three categories outlined in Chapter 2: (1) illustrative sensory language (most notably in the multi-sensory description of dawn but also in Milton's frequent evocations of the nightscape); to a lesser extent, (2) sensory metaphor, as in the likening of less competent orators to noisy (or unnaturally quiet) frogs and, conceptually, in the pervasive association of darkness and light with negative

---

[102] In rendering 'supercilia,' CW actually has the more explicitly ocular 'But I see the black eyebrows of Night …'
[103] On the theme of *nightly* inspiration, prominently taken up/reworked in *Paradise Lost*, see Chapter 5 below.

and positive equivalents, respectively);[104] finally, and most of all, (3) sensory discourse as embodied speech: first directed by an orator at a crowd of 'non exorabiles,' then used to distinguish the speaker as the harbinger and champion of Day from his opponents, 'oratorculi' spearheaded by a 'son of darkness.'

This explicit focus on the speaker–hearer relationship as involving embodied speech on the one hand, and more or less intent listening on the other, is particularly pronounced at the outset and the conclusion of the speech, thus framing it and marking out Prolusion I in its entirety as 'a sensory discourse' in the oratorical meaning of the term. It co-occurs, in both cases, with a multi-sensory combination of vision and hearing as domains of reference: first in the confrontation of entreating vocal speech and silent hostile glances, later in the association of audible acclaim and its appeal – in more senses than one – to Dawn and Phoebus as representatives of all things visual, in nature as in culture.

This multi-sensory quality of Milton's discourse is extended – and indeed intensified through genuinely synaesthetic elements – in his own self-consciously 'poetical' depiction of dawn and in the quotation – the longest in Prolusion I – from the Orphic *Hymn to Dawn*. As I have suggested, Milton's own treatment of the theme displays marked parallels with the classical pre-text he subsequently quotes; not least among them is the fact that Milton's passage features a sort of 'Hymn to Phoebus' of its own, mimicking the general characteristics (and the cultic setting) of the ancient Greek form. With a view to the wider context of the sensory discourse in Milton's early writing, the passage can equally be related to the 'Elegiac Verses,' the elegies, and to Elegy V, in particular: this includes Milton's description of Day, in the prolusion, in terms of loveliness, (female) attractiveness, etc. – a perspective later taken up (twice) with regard to the respective visual appeal of art and nature. More generally, Milton, through his association of daybreak with perception, erotic love, and spring, introduces to the prosaic sensory discourse of Prolusion I a constellation of mutual significances which has also been shown to shape the sensory discourse of his early poetry.

This raises a question regarding the specificity of the sensory discourse in Prolusion I, and the applicability of the foregoing observations to the prolusions at large. What seems significant, first of all, is that Milton includes allusions to the scientific and socio-cultural contexts of his time. He refers twice to observational and/or theoretical astronomy: in his explanation of how the 'dense and solid earth com[es] between the sun's light and our horizon' at nighttime, and arguably again in his allusion to the planetary reflection of sunlight. In that they relate to the practice of astronomy as an observational and explanatory activity, both of these instances go well beyond the standard, mythologising allusions to 'Phoebus' or 'Diana' so prominent in the elegies. Although in most of Milton's allusions to space and the heavenly bodies, both 'astronomical' and 'mythologising,' concurrent references to light and vision place those passages within the sphere of sensory discourse, the strength of reference to the actual visual process is appreciably higher in the former case, as it relates to direct human experience and an

---

[104] The impact of conceptual metaphors involving the dichotomy of UP and DOWN is not as pronounced in Prolusion I as I will argue it is in Prolusion II; but it can certainly be observed in the various references to birds either flying high of being perched in lofty treetops, as well as in the clear vertical ordering present in the quotation from the *Hymn to Dawn*.

actual activity (namely, 'stargazing' in its various forms), rather than to an externalised abstraction (personification) or mythological tradition. Milton's references to celestial phenomena in Prolusion I comprise mythological as well as astronomical elements; in this, they differ from the elegies – which are wholly mythological – and are, at least in part, closer to Milton's mentions of Galileo as 'the Tuscan artist' in *Paradise Lost*.

In the discussion of Milton's references to the sensory realities of early modern (night)life, circumscribed and shaped by the disruptive force of darkness, the relevance of extratextual contexts to sensory discourse has become evident. Milton contrasts the spheres of order (personified by the light-loving Muses as representatives of the arts and sciences) and chaos (represented by wild animals, criminals, or mere lechers). As the passage from *Comus* suggested, artificial lighting played an important, if socially distinctive, role in this struggle between day and night. Another aspect of the same sensory complex, only hinted at in the prolusion's brief reflection on silence, is the acoustic profile of night, prompting characteristic responses on the part of (non-)auditors. Not everywhere was the confrontation between people and the nocturnal soundscape that surrounded them as pronounced as in the 'howling wilderness' experienced by colonists in North America; but the specific significance of (nighttime) sounds in the construction of community and belonging is evident from Milton's writings, too.[105] In the passages quoted from *Comus* and *Il Penseroso*, Milton makes explicit certain preconceptions about the interrelations between sound, darkness, and the social sphere which, in a more subdued manner, also contribute to the sensory discourse of Prolusion I.

Finally, Prolusion I represents yet another aspect of sensory discourse in its claims to truth and knowledge. At the outset of his speech, Milton announces that he will 'bring [the ancient traditions about Night and Day] to the test of reason' and expose them to 'the scrutiny of strict truth.' He does so in three distinct sections of the prolusion, arguing, in the first and second, the mythological superiority and seniority of Day and, in the third, its use to humankind. While the first and second points are treated in roughly the first half of the speech, the third is debated more extensively, taking up the second half of the prolusion. It is primarily in the passages concerned with the positive qualities of day and their benefits for humanity that the (multi-)sensory discourse of the prolusion comes to the fore. In its association of light and love; daybreak and spring; birdsong, the odour of flowers, and the lover's touch of the Sun, it resembles that of Milton's early Latin poetry. Milton's evocation of the nightscape, by contrast, is marked by (sensory) privation, which corresponds to a privation of knowledge in the forced absence of the Muses. Reinforcing a knowledge of social and moral norms, the respective passages also reflect on what is proper or appropriate for people to do during nighttime. As it turns out, not much is: night is for animals, and for the people who behave like them.

In stressing the importance of truth and reasoning for the prolusion genre, Milton acknowledges its formally epistemogenic character: these are orations held at university before an audience of scholars; they had better relate to their hearers' knowledge of

---

[105] On the terrifying quality of the American forest soundscape (especially since it implied sound without sight, even during the day), see Hoffer, *Sensory Worlds in Early America*, 43–44; see also Rath, *How Early America Sounded*, 145–71, on Native American soundscapes and early settlers' reactions to them.

some sort. After only a brief consideration of cosmological matters, however, Milton's discussion quickly turns to the aesthetic, social, and moral implications of his topic. This does not detract from his claims to accuracy and validity – after all, his aim is to establish the superiority of day, which already implies a value judgment rather than a detailed exposition of celestial mechanics. The knowledge about day and night transported in Prolusion I is of a 'holistic' kind, in which scientific, aesthetic, social, and moral considerations go hand in hand.

4.2 Prolusion II ('On the Harmony of the Spheres')
Laughable Pythagoras and the Resounding Consequences of Man's 'Brutish Desires'

In Prolusion II, a 'powerfully eloquent piece' despite its comparative brevity, Milton considers the age-old notion of a 'harmony of the spheres,' which originated from the Pythagorean tradition.[106] In its most straightforward interpretation, this meant that the heavenly bodies, orbiting around the earth in their concentric spheres, each sounded a particular note as they moved along, together creating a perfect harmony.[107] The idea appears repeatedly throughout Milton's writing life but is never treated more consistently than in this academic exercise.[108]

Probably a product of Milton's graduate studies, Prolusion II was delivered in the 'public schools' of Cambridge (i.e., before an audience drawn from the university as a whole); in this respect, it differs from Prolusion I, which appears to have been presented by Milton as an undergraduate to his peers at Christ's College.[109] As Milton himself states in his opening remarks, 'many eminent speakers' have spoken before him on the

---

[106] Prolusion II is in CPW 1: 234–39. The assessment of its eloquence is that of Campbell/Corns, *John Milton*, 36. Campbell and Corns also comment on the 'soaring quality of Milton's Latin prose' in Prolusion II, and argue that it is expressive of 'a consummate skill that is never glimpsed in Milton's earlier Latin prose, and not be realized again until Milton wrote the visionary passages of the *Defensio Prima*' (63).

[107] A concise survey of the 'harmony of the spheres' tradition before Kepler (arguably its last great exponent) is given by Bruce Stephenson, *The Music of the Heavens: Kepler's Harmonic Astronomy* (Princeton, N. J.: Princeton University Press, 1994), 16–46; an account of its wider implications, by Leo Spitzer, *Classical and Christian Ideas of World Harmony: Prolegomena to an Interpretation of the Word 'Stimmung'* (Baltimore, Md.: Johns Hopkins University Press, 1963); for the impact of the tradition in early modern England, more specifically, see Penelope Gouk, *Music, Science, and Natural Magic in Seventeenth-Century England* (New Haven, Conn.: Yale University Press, 1999), 145–56. The often ignored place of *dis*harmony within this tradition has more recently been analysed by Daniel Heller-Roazen, *The Fifth Hammer: Pythagoras and the Disharmony of the World* (Cambridge, Mass.: MIT Press, 2011).

[108] A survey of Milton's references to the idea is undertaken by M. N. K. Mander, 'Milton and the Music of the Spheres,' *MQ* 24 (1990), 63–71.

[109] In their published versions, prolusions I and II are headed 'In Collegio, &c.' and 'In Scholis Publicis,' respectively. On the problem of dating the individual prolusions (whose conventional numbering is derived from their first publication in print), see, again, the most recent assessment by Campbell/Corns, *John Milton*, 35–36. Lewalski, *Life of John Milton*, 28–29, by contrast, cautiously assigns prolusions I, II, and VI to 'Milton's third year, the usual time for sophisters (second- and third-year students) to begin public disputations.'

4.2 Prolusion II ('On the Harmony of the Spheres')

occasion of 'this day's appointed celebrations.'[110] This ceremonial setting of its original delivery allies it to Prolusion VI, discussed below; in contrast to the much longer 'salting' prolusion delivered as a 'vacation exercise.' However, the specific occasion of Prolusion II remains unknown. In that it is a 'declamation,' i.e., an exercise in rhetorical persuasion, Prolusion II is closer to Prolusion I, discussed above. This is in spite of its slightly different format, contemplating an idea rather than arguing a fixed thesis. On the level of content, finally, Prolusion II is remarkable for taking a topic with an obvious sensory implication – the 'harmony' or 'music of the spheres' – and turning that very implication into the subject of the orator's reflection: to what extent can the idea of an actual 'music' of the spheres (still) be taken seriously?[111] As I will argue with reference to the three prolusions discussed in this chapter, the subtle differences distinguishing them in terms of their setting, rhetorical approach, and content are mirrored in the distinct features of Milton's sensory discourse in the respective texts. In certain of these respects – such as the chosen approach to its stated topic, the speaker's self-presentation, and the awareness of his audience he displays – Prolusion II can be shown to occupy a middle ground between prolusions I and VI.

Milton begins his oration 'De Sphærarum Concentu' by downplaying, right away, the logical rigour of what he is about to say.[112] The impressive performances of the previous speakers, as well as the solemnity of the occasion, he says, both put eminent pressure on him to find a novel and captivating theme for his own speech: 'So I conceived the idea of making a few preliminary remarks with open hand [dilatatâ ... manu], as we say, and rhetorical exuberance, on the subject of that heavenly harmony [illo

---

[110] CPW 1: 234.

[111] The process which arguably led to the more skeptical view of the tradition at the time of Milton's writing is discussed by John Hollander, *The Untuning of the Sky: Ideas of Music in English Poetry, 1500–1700* (Princeton, N. J.: Princeton University Press, 1961). See also the more cautious introductory account in Diane Kelsey McColley, *Poetry and Music in Seventeenth-Century England* (Cambridge: Cambridge University Press, 1997), 7–52, on the various 'concinnities' ascribed at the time to abstract sphere music, the music of the soul, and practical/audible music, respectively. It should be noted, however, that the literal truth of the 'sphere music' paradigm had been called into question from at least the time of Basil the Great in the fourth century CE. This skepticism was founded in part on certain interpretations of Ps. 19:1–4: 'The heavens declare the glory of God;/and the firmament sheweth his handywork./Day unto day uttereth speech, and night unto night sheweth knowledge./*There is no speech nor language; their voice is not heard* ...' (emphasis added; adapted from KJV, which reads, with a significant difference: 'There is no speech nor language where their voice is not heard.') On this Christian critique of the 'harmony of the spheres' tradition, see Albert L. Blackwell, *The Sacred in Music* (Louisville, Ky.: Westminster John Knox Press, 1999), 176–84.

[112] Latin *concentus*, by contrast to the more definitely auditory *musica*, suggests both audible and inaudible – though not necessarily imperceptible – harmonies: '(1) a singing together (esp. of birds); a playing together, sounding (of musical instruments) ..., (2) an agreeable combination of sounds, concord' and '(3) an agreement of things other than sounds, concord, harmony; a blending (of scents or colours)' (*OLD*). In Prolusion I, Milton uses the term to refer to the 'sweetest song' of birds at sunrise and the 'sweet harmony' of instrumental music as performed by Orpheus and Amphion.

cœlesti concentu] which is presently [mox] to be discussed as it were with closed fist [contracto pugno] ...'[113]

Since his short essay, in its totality, is closer to a rhetorical exploration of its topic than to a strictly logical analysis, it appears that, when Milton announces a later treatment of the 'harmony of the spheres' with a 'closed fist,' he is referring to a speech following his own. Perhaps surprisingly, the first sensory image of the prolusion is tactile, as Milton contrasts the 'soft' and 'hard' approaches to his theme through 'suave' rhetoric and 'hard-hitting' logic, respectively. The image itself is conventional.[114] While the general implication of its two opposed elements was clear, however, its specific thrust would be subject to context and intention. Thus, in *The Censure of the Rota upon Mr Miltons book, entituled, The ready and easie way to establish a free commonwealth* ..., an anonymous Restoration satire directed against Milton and published in March 1660, it is imputed to him 'that you fight always with the flat of your hand like a Rhetorician, and never Contract the Logical fist ...'[115] In this case, rhetorical 'softness' is equated with censurable weakness, and the argumentative substance of Milton's book is denied. While the similar (self-)denial of Prolusion II – the speech's actual focus on rhetoric over logic aside – is meant to win the audience's benevolence, Milton's later detractors use the image to challenge his self-presentation as a serious orator and a stern, prophet-like figure, and move him close to the sophism Milton himself loved to castigate.[116]

An equal command of both modes, the proving and the persuasive, was the rhetorical ideal, as is evident from a characterisation of the English Ramist George Downham: 'It is seldome seen, that the *Clunchfist of Logick* (good to *Knock* a man down at a blow) can so open itself as to smooth and *stroak* one with the *Palme* thereof. Our Dounham could doe both.'[117] As this example illustrates once more, the sensory images contributing to early modern sensory discourse cannot simply be dismissed as 'dead metaphors,' quite the contrary: even where they were highly conventional, they were apt to be taken up and 're-sensualised' through concretisation or amplification, in this case by reference to the sense of touch. The '*Clunchfist of Logick*' was not merely a figure of speech: it could hit, and hit hard. Words had effects, and sensory discourse, with its high capacity for 'putting things before the senses,' was particularly suitable for maximising those effects.[118]

---

[113] CPW 1: 234.

[114] Cicero (in *De Finibus*) and Quintilian (in *Institutio Oratoria*) attribute the comparison of dialectic to a closed fist to the pre-Socratic Greek philosopher Zeno of Elea; see CPW 2: 402n167.

[115] Quoted in CPW 7: 200.

[116] On Milton's rhetorical self-presentation in the two editions of *The Readie and Easie Way*, see Fallon, *Milton's Peculiar Grace*, 177–81. Whereas the present image reduces Milton's rhetoric to 'mere (because soft) touch,' harmless because it is lacking both 'punch' and 'grip,' Milton's own description of Belial, whose 'tongue/Dropped manna,' suggests 'mere (because nutrient-poor) taste,' worthless because of its sweet appeal to appeal itself (see also Chapter 2 above).

[117] Quoted in CPW 3: 131.

[118] Positing a similar metaphorical correlation between the Trinity and the human hand, William Langland in the fourteenth century had compared the (powerful) Father to a clenched fist, the (effective) Son to the fingers, and the (gentle) Spirit to the palm; see Moshenska, *Feeling Pleasures*, 6.

When Milton himself returns to the image in *Of Education* (1644), it is in the context of his outline for a balanced and effective instruction of young scholars. After an extensive course of study in various preparatory fields, he at last arrives at rhetorical training:

> And now lastly will be the time to read with them those organic arts which inable men to discourse and write perspicuously, elegantly, and according to the fitted stile of lofty, mean, or lowly. Logic therefore so much as is usefull, is to be referr'd to this due place withall her well couch heads and Topics, untill it be time to open her contracted palm into a gracefull and ornate Rhetorick taught out of the rule of *Plato, Aristotle, Phalereus, Cicero, Hermogenes, Longinus*. To which Poetry would be made subsequent, or indeed rather precedent, as being lesse suttle and fine, but more simple, sensuous and passionate.[119]

Here, the double association of the fist/palm image is instructive: on the one hand, it refers to the ornateness of rhetoric (conceived of, again, as positive), on the other, to its artfulness and subtlety, which distinguishes it from the more strongly 'sensuous and passionate' nature of actual poetry, the capstone of Milton's educational plan.[120]

In Prolusion II, likewise, the tactile image of the soft, smooth, palm of rhetoric serves to highlight the author's present agenda: Milton's stated purpose is to entertain rather than to argue. This first impression is borne out when he turns to his subject proper. If the target of his introductory remarks had been, as suggested above, the (lacking) logical rigour of his speech, he now aims at its epistemic substance by calling into question the soundness of the Pythagorean 'harmony of the spheres' tradition as a whole:

> Now I beg you, my hearers [auditores], not to take this theory as seriously intended [Hæc ... accipiatis ... quasi per lusum dicta]. For who in his senses would suppose that Pythagoras, a very god among philosophers, whose name all men of that time hailed with the most profound reverence – who, I ask, would suppose that he had ever put forward a theory based on such very poor foundations [tam lubrice fundatam opinionem]? Surely, if he held [docuit][121] any doctrine of the harmony of the spheres [Sphærarum ... harmoniam], or taught that the heavens revolve in unison with some sweet melody [circumactos ad modulaminis dulcedinem cœlos], it was only as a means of suggesting allegorically [sapienter]

---

[119] CPW 2: 401–403.

[120] On the relevance of this idea of the pre-eminent 'sensuousness' of poetry for the sensory discourse of *Of Education*, see CPW 2: 402–403, as well as Balachandra Rajan, 'Simple, Sensuous and Passionate,' *RES* 21 (1945), 289–301.

[121] Milton is not suggesting that Pythagoras had not held or might not have held such a doctrine, *pace* McColley, *Poetry and Music*, 256n2. As McEuen points out in her commentary, Pythagoras did indeed perceive (mathematical) 'regularity, correspondence, beauty, proportion, and harmony' in the universe, but he also explicitly 'made musical principles prominent in his system, because, presumably, the heavenly bodies were divided by intervals in accordance with the laws of musical harmony.' However, she does also refer to Milton's explanation of the Pythagorean notion as 'merely a poetic representation of a scientific theory' as 'both ingenious and apt' (CPW 1: 235n2).

the close interrelation of the orbs and their uniform revolution in accordance with the laws of destiny for ever.[122]

In making the ludic element of his prolusion explicit – his words are 'quasi per lusum dicta' –, Milton both characterises his own speech and takes the ground from under the following speaker's: a theory not to be taken seriously may provide the topic for a rhetorical exercise, but it cannot be made the subject of fruitful logical disquisition. Accordingly, Milton describes the – supposed – doctrine of Pythagoras as his *opinio*, founded on slippery ground, and thus distinguishes it from the traditional conception of actual knowledge as *true and rational* belief.[123] The Pythagorean concept is put forward with ingenuity ('sapienter') to express an ulterior truth, and 'in this [Pythagoras] followed the example of the poets, or (what is almost the same thing) of the divine oracles.'[124]

Having grouped the philosopher – indeed, Milton calls him 'a very god among philosophers' – with poets and oracles on account of their shared recourse to figurative language, Milton proceeds to trace the insertion of the 'harmony of the spheres' metaphor into the philosophical tradition. Thus, Pythagoras was followed by Plato, who relates, in Milton's paraphrase, that 'upon each one of the celestial orbs is seated a being called a Siren, at whose mellifluous song [quæ mellitissimo cantu] both gods and men are rapt in wonder.'[125] Building on this clearly more specific, literalising statement of a similar notion – in Plato's version, the rather abstract Pythagorean 'harmony' figures as a vocal 'song' performed by distinct, if mythical, individuals –, Milton argues, was the later misreading of Pythagoras' original intent. Specifically, it was Aristotle, Milton says, 'the rival and constant detractor of Pythagoras and Plato,' who 'foisted on Pythagoras the literal doctrine of the unheard symphony of heaven and of the melody of the spheres [inauditam hanc Cœlorum symphoniam, Sphærarumque modulos affinxit *Pythagoræ*].'[126] In the remaining half of Prolusion II, Milton sets out – in a combination of rhetorical play and actual demonstration – to clear Pythagoras from the imputations of his literalist misinterpreters.

At this point, Milton draws the audience's attention to himself as speaker, employing a conceit which alludes to another famous doctrine of Pythagoreanism, namely, that of the transmigration of souls: 'if only fate or chance had allowed your soul, O Father Pythagoras, to transmigrate into my body, you would not have lacked a champion to deliver you without difficulty, under however heavy a burden of obloquy you might be labouring!'[127] While this remark is clearly meant to amuse – rather than, for instance, move the audience to compassion –, it emphasises the fact that the speaker, indeed, is

---

[122] CPW 1: 234–35.
[123] In a less dichotomous manner, Milton would later argue (in *Areopagitica*, 1644) that 'opinion in good men is but knowledge in the making' (CPW 2: 554).
[124] CPW 1: 235.
[125] CPW 1: 236. Earlier, Milton points out, Homer had used the metaphor of a golden chain to indicate 'universal concord and sweet union of all things [conspirationem rerum universam, & consensum amabilem].'
[126] CPW 1: 236. 'The literal doctrine of' is Tillyard's interpolation.
[127] CPW 1: 236–37.

4.2 Prolusion II ('On the Harmony of the Spheres')

'embodying' the teachings he has presented and is now vowing to defend. Caught between oratorical pathos and plain banter, but more obviously leaning towards the latter than in similar self-referential passages in the other prolusions, Milton's allusion ties in with his stated intention of offering some 'open-handed' rhetorical exuberance. In that it nonetheless contains an element of truth, however slight, it resembles the half-joking 'acceptance' of the harmony of the spheres offered by Milton at the conclusion of his speech.

For the time being, however, Milton has his fun imagining possible consequences of an actually *audible* harmony of the spheres and relates these, comically, to the teachings of Aristotle, still the dominant figure in academic philosophy at the time:

> After all, we may well ask, why should not the heavenly bodies give forth musical tones [Musicos efficiant sonos] in their annual revolutions? Does it not seem reasonable to you, Aristotle? Why, I can hardly believe that those Intelligences of yours could have endured through so many centuries the sedentary toil of making the heavens rotate, if the ineffable music of the stars [ineffabile illud Astrorum melos] had not prevented them from leaving their posts, and the melody, by its enchantment, persuaded them to stay [& modulationes delinimento suasisset moram]. If you rob the heavens of this music [illas pulchellas], you devote those wonderful minds and subordinate gods of yours to a life of drudgery, and condemn them to the treadmill.[128]

What makes this notion so absurd – and thus, in the rhetorical context of Milton's prolusion, comical – is that Aristotle had, in fact, *refuted* the Pythagorean doctrine of the harmony of the spheres, which he had taken to posit an actually audible celestial music; it had been in this sense that Aristotle had 'foisted on Pythagoras the literal doctrine of the unheard symphony of heaven and of the melody of the spheres,' as Milton had claimed earlier.[129] Milton may reasonably assume his audience to detect this discrepancy – otherwise, the main point of his auditory image would be lost. Milton twists the tradition to his purpose to yield a comical digression about the Aristotelian intelligences being entertained by the music of the spheres; he thus makes good on his earlier announcement to put rhetoric over logic. While this kind of behaviour would normally not be acccaptable in an orator, the playful quality of the prolusion sanctions it. As one would expect, the more explicitly *auditory* vocabulary Milton uses in this passage underlines the shift in his understanding of *sphaerarum concentus* from an ambiguous harmony – which might be audible but could equally mean an abstract, pleasing proportion – to a definitely audible phenomenon: his reference to 'musical tones' ('musicos sonos') and repeated mention of melody (as opposed to harmony) make this clear.

Milton thus introduces the image of 'heavenly beings' delighted and even sustained by the music of the spheres by reference to Aristotle's 'intelligences,' abstract noetic substances that certainly would not be expected to 'have an ear' for music (this is another aspect of Milton's comical digression). When, in the interpretations of mediaeval

---

[128] CPW 1: 237.

[129] Aristotle refuted the Pythagorean theory of the harmony of the spheres in his *De Caelo*; see McEuen's note ad loc.

theologians, these 'intelligences' were identified with the more or less anthropomorphic angels of Christian tradition, this 'clash' of abstract intelligence and concrete perception was attenuated, since the association of the – ethereal, yet somehow concretely *present* – angels with music remained and, indeed, may have facilitated their identification with the Aristotelian concept. As Raphael explains to Adam in book 6 of *Paradise Lost*, referring to the angels,

> All heart they live, all head, all eye, all ear,
> All intellect, all sense, and as they please,
> They limb themselves, and colour, shape or size
> Assume, as likes them best, condense or rare. (*PL* 6.350–53)[130]

Posited in this way halfway between abstract harmony ('all intellect') and actual music ('all ear,' 'all sense'), Milton's angels, too, often 'limb themselves' in order to strike their harps, play 'the solemn pipe,' the 'dulcimer [and] organs of sweet stop,' or simply singing.[131] In Milton's poetry, generally, references to the music of the heavenly hosts abound, with the most prominent example in his earlier writing the 'Nativity Ode' ('On the Morning of Christ's Nativity'), written in 1629 and thus roughly contemporary with the elegies and prolusions. In stanzas IX and XIII, Milton describes the annunciation to the shepherds as an eminently auditory event and relates it firmly to the 'harmony of the spheres' tradition:

> When such music sweet
> Their hearts and ears did greet,
> As never was by mortal finger strook,
> Divinely-warbled voice
> Answering the stringed noise,
>   As all their souls in blissful rapture took:
> The air such pleasure loth to lose,
> With thousand echoes still prolongs each heavenly close.
>
> [...]
>
> Ring out, ye crystal spheres,
> Once bless our human ears,
> (If ye have power to touch our senses so)
> And let your silver chime
> Move in melodious time;
> And let the base of heaven's deep organ blow,
> And with your ninefold harmony
> Make up full consort to the angelic symphony. (93–100, 125–32)

---

[130] On the angelological context of this and other passages in *Paradise Lost* referring to angelic (non-)corporeality and perception, see Raymond, *Milton's Angels*.

[131] *PL* 7.594–96. The passage describes the joyful rest on the seventh day, after Creation is completed.

4.2 Prolusion II ('On the Harmony of the Spheres')

In stanza IX, the music described is unearthly, too sweet to have been performed by 'mortal finger[s],' and accompanied by 'divinely-warbled' voices; the air itself contributes to the overall impression by adding her echoes to the 'heavenly' sound. This last detail, in particular, highlights the structural similarity between the celestial music of the angels and the older 'harmony of the spheres' tradition. In stanza XIII, this similarity is made explicit, as the traditional music of the spheres is assimilated into – or rather, made into an accompaniment for – the angelic 'symphony.' Milton does appear to register a hint of doubt in the parenthetical qualification, '(If ye have power to touch our senses so),' but he undeniably presents the music of the spheres as fundamentally similar to, and hence compatible with, the music of the heavenly hosts.

In Prolusion II, however, Milton does not immediately follow up on the theological implications of his topic; this would arguably not have fitted the generally comical approach of the prolusion. Instead, he expands on the idea of having 'celestial' beings listen to the music of the spheres by reference to several figures from classical mythology:

> ... even Atlas himself would long since have cast down the burden of the skies from his shoulders to its ruin, had not that sweet harmony soothed him with an ecstasy of delight [nisi dulcis ille concentus ... lætissimâ voluptate permulsisset] as he panted and sweated beneath his heavy load. Again, the Dolphin [Astra Delphinus] would long since have wearied of the stars and preferred his proper element of the sea to the skies, had he not well known that the singing spheres of heaven far surpassed Arion's lyre in sweetness [vocales Cœli Orbes Lyram *Arioniam* suavitate longe superare]. And we may well believe that it is in order to tune their own notes in accord with that harmony of heaven to which they listen so intently, that the lark takes her flight up into the clouds at daybreak and the nightingale passes the lonely hours of night in song [quod credibile est ipsam alaudam prima luce rectà in nubes evolare, & Lusciniam totam noctis solitudinem cantu transigere, ut ad Harmonicam cœli rationem, quam attente auscultant, suos corrigant modulos].[132]

Listing three further examples of how the music of the spheres may be taken to charm its hearers, Milton moves from a merely cosmological association with the firmament (in the case of Atlas) through a mixed or double reference to the sky and to music (the Dolphin and Arion), to a wholly musical and (almost) 'down-to-earth' image (the lark and the nightingale as the two conventional representatives of birdsong). Within the overall structure of Milton's conceit, therefore, and with a view to his strategy of 'literalising' and 'concretising' the Pythagorean notion for comic effect, his reference to the constellation of the Dolphin is particularly apt. More precisely, it serves as a kind of conceptual pivot, since it affords a double reference to heaven and earth as well as a double reference to music: namely, as a literally audible expression both of the harmony of the spheres *and* of the legendary talent of Arion, whose feat of calling dolphins to the surface by his musical skill Milton also alludes to in Elegy VI. In 'moving down' from

---

[132] CPW 1: 237.

the abstract sphere of Aristotelian intelligences through mythology to the more or less terrestrial level of birdsong, Milton links the cosmic and the mundane spheres through their shared participation in the phenomenon of musical sound, and playfully 'defends' the Platonic and (literalised) Pythagorean concepts against the sceptics.

From these concrete effects of the music of the spheres, Milton claims, were derived other myths: that of the Muses continuously dancing at the altar of Jove, for instance, or 'the attribution to Phoebus, in the remote past, of musical skill [hinc *Phœbo* lyræ peritia ... attributa est],' as well as the ancient belief that 'Harmonia was the daughter of Jove and Electra, and that at her marriage to Cadmus all the choirs of heaven sang in concert [totus Cœli chorus concinuisse dicitur].'[133] Again, the harmony of the spheres is translated into the concrete expression of heavenly music-making.

Introducing a theme taken up again in the concluding passages of his speech, Milton then turns to the relevance that all these ancient traditions might have for himself and his contemporaries, to their anthropological and – quite possibly – their moral implications:

> What if no one on earth has ever heard this symphony of the stars [audiverit ... hanc astrorum Symphoniam]? It does not therefore follow that everything beyond the sphere of the moon is mute and utterly benumbed in silence [muta ... torpidoque silentio consopita]. The fault is in our own deaf ears [aures nostras incusemus debiles], which are either unable or unworthy to hear these sweet strains [quæ cantus & tam dulces sonos excipere aut non possunt, aut non dignæ sunt].[134]

Taken for themselves, these lines might be read as commenting on a possible critical potential of the 'harmony of the spheres' tradition. However, they are immediately followed by a return to the earlier comical mode, and to Aristotle specifically, presented by Milton as its paradoxical 'father.' Alluding to a passage in Aristotle's *Meteorologica*, Milton suggests that 'this melody of the heavens is not all unheard' – after all, certain celestial phenomena (popularly known to the Greeks as 'goats') skip and jump in the sky 'for [no] other reason than that when they plainly hear the orchestra of heaven [præcinentes cœlos ... clare cum audiant], being so near at hand, they cannot choose but dance.'[135] As before, Milton achieves a comic effect by identifying Aristotle's natural philosophy with the Pythagoreanism Aristotle rejected.

In concluding, Milton returns to Pythagoras himself, and thus to the starting point of his reflections. More particularly, he refers to the belief that, on account of his righteousness and overall integrity of character, 'Pythagoras alone among men is said to have heard this music [concentum hunc audisse]' of the spheres.[136] As it turns out, the preceding joke about Aristotelian 'goats' skipping and jumping to the music of the spheres offered only a short return to the all-out comicality of Milton's earlier references to Aristotle. Indeed, Milton's allusion to Pythagoras' singular goodness –

---

[133] CPW 1: 237–38.
[134] CPW 1: 238.
[135] Ibid.
[136] Ibid.

4.2 Prolusion II ('On the Harmony of the Spheres')

represented through his ability to hear the music of the spheres – constructs a positive foil to sinful, depraved – and hence deaf – humanity:

> The fact that we are unable to hear this harmony [Quod autem nos hanc minime audiamus Harmoniam] seems certainly to be due to the presumption of that thief Prometheus, which brought so many evils upon men, and robbed us of that happiness which we may never again enjoy so long as we remain buried in sin and degraded by brutish desires [dum sceleribus cooperti belluinis cupiditatibus obbrutescimus]; for how can we become sensitive to this heavenly sound [qui enim possumus cœlestis illius soni capaces fieri] while our souls are, as Persius says, bowed to the ground and lacking in every heavenly element [in terras curvæ ... & cœlestium prorsus inanes]? But if our souls were pure, chaste, and white as snow, as was Pythagoras' of old, then indeed our ears would ring and be filled with that exquisite music of the stars in their orbits [tum quidem suavissimâ illâ stellarum circumeuntium musicâ personarent aures nostræ, & opplerentur]; then would all things turn back to the Age of God [in aureum illud sæculum redirent], and we ourselves, free from every grief, would pass our lives in a blessed peace which even the gods might envy.[137]

Being able to hear, and hear well, in this scenario is tantamount to moral rectitude. By positing as the originator of its negative counterpart 'that thief Prometheus,' Milton stays true to his former use of classical (and pagan) references, although the general thrust of the passage – lamenting how humanity's degradation to the level of 'brutish desires' makes a return to an earlier happiness impossible – certainly allows for its association with the biblical account of the Fall. In that it gives a markedly positive valuation to the sense of hearing (which is, in fact, contrasted with the said degradation and brutishness), the passage illustrates how auditory perception, representing, along with vision, one of the 'distance senses,' would often be considered purer than and morally superior to the 'brutish' contact senses of – above all – touch but also taste and smell.

In the image of 'souls ... bowed to the ground,' Milton reinforces this negative association of earthiness, 'touching down,' and that kind of embodiment which is understood in terms of a degradation of the soul's original purity. This (de)valuation mirrors the conventional hierarchical ranking of the senses, where, at the lower of two extremes, TOUCH IS DOWN, while VISION IS UP. It is this polar opposition of the two extremes which informs Milton's depiction of the fallen angel Mammon, in book 1 of *Paradise Lost*, as

> the least erected spirit that fell
> From heaven, for even in heaven his looks and thoughts
> Were always downward bent, admiring more
> The riches of heaven's pavement, trodden gold,
> Than aught divine or holy else enjoyed
> In vision beatific: (*PL* 1.679–84)

---

[137] CPW 1: 238–39.

Mammon's 'looks and thoughts' (the former expressive of the latter) are 'downward bent' in his greedy (and thus proto-tactile) admiration of 'trodden gold,' a material that, among the spiritual splendours of heaven, is only fit to be stepped on. The moral valuation implied by the passage, expressed through the sensory reference to an (unnatural) downward gaze, is clear, as is its structural similarity to Milton's reference, in Prolusion II, to 'souls ... bowed to the ground and lacking in every heavenly element.' In the Prolusion, however, the positive counterpart to negative tactility/earthiness is not played by (ideally elevated) vision, which – in contrast to Prolusion I, discussed above, and Prolusion VI, discussed below – is not at all conspicuous in the sensory discourse of the speech. Instead, hearing – or rather, (sphere) music as the most sublime object of hearing – is consistently associated with elevated positions (of the spheres themselves, of the stars and constellations, or of meteorological phenomena) or upward movement (as the lark 'takes her flight up into the clouds at daybreak').

In the absence of sight-based sensory discourse, hearing, as the other 'noble' distance sense, thus figures as a positive foil to 'evils,' 'sin,' and 'brutish desires' – *even though* Milton expressly disclaims the actual audibility of the music of the spheres at the outset of his prolusion. This illustrates the capacity of sensory discourse to transport, on a conceptual level, ideas or valuations by using references to sense perception even if the phenomenal reality of that sense perception is denied. In the concluding paragraph of Prolusion II, Milton fuses references to actual sound ('cœlestis illius soni,' 'suavissimâ ... musicâ') and references to a more abstract 'purity' or 'harmony' of the soul ('pure, chaste, and white as snow') to convey an ultimately moral judgment. Even within his mostly comical prolusion – and despite the possible pun on 'aures' and 'aureum [saeculum]' even in this last passage –, he introduces a slight serious element, expressed in a deliberative application of sensory discourse.[138]

At this – halfway – serious point in his speech, however, Milton acknowledges that his speaking time is running out and, true to the prevailing temperament of his speech, ends on a lighter note:

> time cuts me short ... and luckily too, for I am afraid that by my confused and unmelodious style [ne incondito miniméque numeroso stylo] I have been all this while offending against that very harmony of which I speak [huic quam prædico harmoniæ], and have myself been an obstacle to your hearing it [fuerímque ipse impedimento, quo minus illam audiveritis]. And so I have done.[139]

Milton had started out by claiming that the harmony of the spheres was a mere trope expressing the close, harmonic, and eternal interrelation of the heavenly orbs; he had then employed the notion of an actually audible music of the spheres for comic effect; at the end of Prolusion II, he draws his audience's attention both to the overlooked – or perhaps rather overheard – 'critical potential' of the harmony of the spheres tradition as

---

[138] Compare the reference to the golden age at the conclusion of Elegy V, 185–86, discussed in Chapter 3.2.
[139] CPW 1: 239.

well as to the audible quality of his own, the speaker's, voice. As announced at the outset of the prolusion, Milton makes the 'contracted fist' of logic secondary to rhetorical embellishment, but the claim to knowledge inherent in the prolusion form is not, after all, wholly denied: Milton still has something to teach his audience about the moral implications of the 'harmony of the spheres' tradition. Throughout Prolusion II, there is only a very slight, intermittent focus on the speaker *as speaker*, represented, at the beginning of the speech, in the tactile metaphor of rhetoric as a soft, open palm, and expressed at its conclusion by reference to his audible voice. For reasons to be explored, this focus on the person of the orator is much more pronounced in Prolusion VI, to which I now turn.

4.3 Prolusion VI ('Sportive Exercises ...')
'Nugae' Served with Salt – Milton's 'Morosophical' Banquet and the Reductio ad Corpus

In Prolusion II, the minimal focus on the speaker's persona corresponds to a relatively weak 'presence' of his listeners in the text – they are referred to only in passing, and the relationship between them and the speaker is never addressed at length. In combination, the relative weakness of the speaker and that of his listeners result in a straightforward oratorical situation, in which the speaker delivers his text to a passive and fairly nondescript audience. In other prolusions, however, the communicative situation imagined by the rhetorical subject is not necessarily a one-way affair. In Prolusion III, for example, this becomes clear from the speaker's reaction to the mere *presence* of his audience (e.g., his admissions of insecurity or inadequacy to capture their goodwill). At other times, the ultimately sensory relation between orator and auditors is presented as more explicitly bilateral, including the active participation of the latter.

The highly self-referential, eminently humorous Prolusion VI, which argues that 'Sportive Exercises [such as itself] on occasion are not inconsistent with philosophical Studies,' presents several intriguing examples of this latter kind of bilateral communication between the orator and his audience. Divided into two parts, the 'oration' and the 'prolusion' proper, it was delivered by Milton acting as 'Father' (i.e., master of ceremonies) at a 'Vacation Exercise,' a traditional, raucous kind of student entertainment. Milton's eponymous poem, 'At a Vacation Exercise,' originally formed part of the same cluster of texts. In the heading of the published version, the prolusion is described as 'Delivered in the college summer vacation, but in the presence of almost the whole body of students, as is customary.'[140] Traditionally, Prolusion VI was dated to the summer of 1628, and thus to Milton's undergraduate days, though more recently, it has on plausible grounds been reassigned to 1631, the year before Milton's final departure from Cambridge.[141] Its genre could be described as either a parody of conventional academic orations (which, after all, *were* 'exercises,' i.e., examinations of a kind, and an integral part of serious studies), or, with more specific reference to university traditions, as the performance text of a 'salting' – an initiation ceremony through which first-year students at Cambridge were admitted into the social body of their college, but which, at

---

[140] CPW 1: 266.
[141] For the traditional view, see Lewalski, *Life of John Milton*, 28–29; on the reasons for re-dating Prolusion VI, see Campbell/Corns, *John Milton*, 36, 58–60.

the same time, presented a welcome opportunity for lampooning authority figures and fellow students in equal measure.[142]

From this background, it seems clear that Prolusion VI would allow for an even greater latitude in staging and self-presentation than would regular academic orations.[143] As I will argue in the following, Milton indeed does all he can to subvert the usual focus of academic orations on decorum and the impartation of knowledge. At the same time, however, he places a strong focus on the relationship between the orator and his auditors, stressing the bodily presence of both and their sharing in a space of common experience. On one level, this may be construed as expressing the comparatively stronger engagement between the two parties demanded quite suggestively by the very terminology of the occasion: as the 'Father' of the assembled congregation, Milton the speaker (quasi-)naturally bears a closer relation to his listeners than a 'normal' orator would at a regular academic exercise.

The particular significance of Prolusion VI for the present analysis lies in the way Milton accomplishes both these objectives, oratorical self-assertion and academic (self-)deprecation, at once – and he does so by drawing on the same, sensory imaginary. In its original performative context, both functions of the prolusion can be traced, then, to a shared source in Milton's deployment of sensory discourse. On the most fundamental level, this refers to the constant highlighting of the speaker–hearer connection and thus, again, to the property of sensory discourse as vocal, embodied speech. This is implied, to a degree, in the very notion of a live oration, but also made 'palpable' by Milton through an array of distinctly 'sensory' rhetorical strategies lampooning both the (usually serious) setting and different individuals and groups from among the audience. The whole comical *and* rhetorical impetus of Prolusion VI, then, rests on its frequent recourse to sensory discourse, and the ways in which that discourse serves to link the comical to the self-consciously rhetorical elements of the speech.

Milton opens his oration with a topos familiar from his elegies and, as an introductory topos, from Elegy I, in particular. This is the juxtaposition of the city, full of 'good things,' on the one hand, and the quiet country life, ideal for study, on the other:

---

[142] The relevance of the 'salting' tradition to Milton's Prolusion VI was first pointed out by Roslyn Richek, 'Thomas Randolph's *Salting* (1627), Its Text, and John Milton's Sixth Prolusion as Another Salting,' *ELR* 12 (1982), 103–112, and 'Appendix: Milton's Salting,' *ELR* 12 (1982), 127–31. The fact that salting speeches apparently were most often given by advanced students is one of the arguments for assigning Prolusion VI to Milton's later years at Cambridge. However, Thomas Randolph (whose 'Salting' I address below) is known to have acted as 'Father' in 1627, his third year as an undergraduate (and thus the year before the date traditionally assigned to Prolusion VI). The exact date of Prolusion VI is not decisive to my reading; in any case, it seems clear that Milton's text was written after Randolph's.

[143] This is argued, with a particular focus on the tension between Milton's role as 'Father' and his public image as 'the Lady,' by Jessica Tvordi, 'The Comic Personas of Milton's *Prolusion VI*: Negotiating Masculine Identity Through Self-Directed Humor,' in: Albrecht Classen (ed.), *Laughter in the Middle Ages and Early Modern Times: Epistemology of a Fundamental Human Behavior, Its Meaning, and Consequences* (Berlin: De Gruyter, 2010), 715–34.

4.3 Prolusion VI ('Sportive Exercises ...')

> On my return from that city which is the chief of all cities,[144] Members of the University, filled (I had almost said 'to repletion') [usque ad saginam, prope dixerim, satur] with all the good things which are to be found there in such abundance [deliciarum omnium ... affluit], I looked forward to enjoying once more a spell of cultured leisure, a mode of life in which, it is my belief, even the souls of the blessed find delight [gaudere]. I fully intended at last to bury myself in learning and to devote myself day and night to the charms of philosophy [jucundissimæ Philosophiæ]; for the alternation of toil and pleasure [Laboris & Voluptatis vicissitudo] usually has the effect of annihilating the boredom brought about by satiety [satietatis tædium] and of making us the more eager to resume our interrupted tasks.[145]

With its references to *voluptas* and being 'filled ... "to repletion [usque ad saginam ... satur],"'[146] this opening paragraph already introduces a theme of pleasure – most likely the kind of urban(e) sensuous pleasure also presented in Elegy I – and (over-)indulgence that will resonate throughout the text. At the very outset of the speech, this theme is associated, conventionally enough, with London, the 'city of all cities,' which had played a similar role in Elegy I. This pleasurable city life is contrasted with a restless dedication, 'day and night' ('perdius & pernox') to the 'charms of philosophy' – a philosophy whose study, however charming, generally still requires 'toil' (*labor*) as opposed to bringing 'pleasure' (*voluptas*). In this particular instance, however, and vis-à-vis 'the boredom brought about by satiety,' a contrary, even adverse stimulus may be perceived as pleasant solely on account of its being *different*. This notion of *variatio delectat* – originating, incidentally, in rhetorical theory, where it referred to a pleasing modulation of volume and speaking styles – was a commonplace of seventeenth-century aesthetics.[147] It was also applied, early on, to sense-experience in a more fundamental, physiological sense. Thus, Thomas Hobbes highlights the importance of a variation in sensory input if the resulting perceptions are to remain acute and thus useful, and if attention is to be maintained: 'it being almost all one for a man to be always sensible of the same thing and not to be sensible of anything.'[148]

---

[144] 'Caput urbium': the phrase resonates with the imagery of Elegy I.
[145] CPW 1: 266. The conceit of Elegy I had of course been that the speaker had devoted himself to the Muses in the city, whereas the barren country had had nothing to offer to 'the worshippers of Phoebus.' The hint of irony at the expense of academic overachievers present in the exordium can only be conventional or perhaps self-deprecating, considering Milton's actually ambitious programme of private study.
[146] Literally, *sagina* refers to (1) 'the cramming, fattening of animals, poultry, etc.'; (2) 'food used for fattening, the diet of gladiators and athletes'; (3) 'fatness, corpulence' (*OLD*, 'sagina'). The reference thus is not just to the *feeling* of 'being full,' but to the *action/mode*, *material*, and the *corporeal effects* of cramming.
[147] See, with reference to Milton's later positive valuations of variety in *Paradise Lost*, the 'Companion Poems,' Nativity Ode, and *Lycidas*, as well as several passages in his prose (though not Prolusion VI), H. V. S. Ogden, 'The Principles of Variety and Contrast in Seventeenth-Century Aesthetics, and Milton's Poetry,' *JHI* 10 (1949) 159–82.
[148] Hobbes, *Elements of Philosophy*, ch. 4, 5 (*English Works of Thomas Hobbes of Malmesbury*, I, 394).

By introducing 'philosophy' – that is, academic study – on the same level of enjoyment (and not, for instance, by reference to its utility or higher inherent worth), Milton presents the joys of the mind and of the body as fundamentally commutable: philosophy, too, can be *jucundissima*, 'most pleasant, most delightful.'[149] On balance, then, there is a slight emphasis on joy of the latter kind, on visceral rather than purely intellectual enjoyment: it is as an inherently *pleasing* countermeasure to sensory fatigue that the 'charms' of philosophy take full effect.[150] Regardless of what it is meant to achieve (what its ulterior motivation might be), *labor* is presented as just another kind of *voluptas*. If toil and pleasure alternate, everything can be pleasure; nothing must be toil.

Just as he had settled down to continue his studies, however, the speaker was summoned to preside over the festivities of the vacation exercise ('the yearly celebration of our ancient custom'), and hence 'commanded to transfer that zeal, which I had intended to devote to the acquisition of knowledge [acquirendæ sapientiæ], to foolery and the invention of new jests [ad nugas ... & novas ineptias] – as if the world were not already full of fools [stultorum plena], as if that famous Ship of Fools, as renowned in song as the Argo herself, had been wrecked, or finally as if there were not matter enough already to make even Democritus laugh.'[151] The fundamental opposition, then, seems to be between the alternation of 'real' pleasures on the one hand, and 'mere' foolery. As Milton hastens to clarify, however – asking 'your pardon, my hearers [Auditores]' – 'the custom which we celebrate to-day is assuredly no foolish one [non est ineptus], but on the contrary most commendable,' and he himself will 'play the wise fool for a while' ('aliquantisper *morosophōs* nugari'), fusing two of the traditional functions of rhetoric, *docere* and *delectare*.[152] According to the speaker's paradoxical announcement, Prolu-

---

[149] See OLD, 'iucundus,' including overtones of being 'agreeable to the senses, delicious, etc.' (sense 3 of 3). Both translations, 'the charms of philosophy' (CPW) and 'most gracious Philosophy' (CW) miss one important aspect of the phrase: Milton characterises philosophy by reference to the *pleasing effect* it has *on the speaker*.

[150] 'Sensory fatigue' or 'sensory adaptation' is what the phenomenon described by Hobbes (and alluded to by Milton) would be called in current psychological terminology; see Myers/DeWall, *Psychology*, 218–19.

[151] CPW 1: 266. Whereas CPW ('acquisition of knowledge') stresses the academic and perhaps natural-philosophical facets of *sapientia*, CW ('acquisition of wisdom') points to its loftier connotations of knowledge leading to virtuous behaviour (the classical meaning, see *OLD*). The ambiguity of the passage arguably illustrates the Renaissance idea that there was 'wisdom in knowledge' (see Rice, *Renaissance Idea of Wisdom*, quotation at 149) or, conversely, pokes fun at the idea (derided since Heraclitus) that the teaching of knowledge will automatically impart wisdom. The etymological dimension of *sapientia* as derived from *sapere*, 'to taste,' (heavily capitalised on by Milton elsewhere, e.g. at *PL* 9.1017–18) is not exploited here – surprisingly, perhaps, considering the Prolusion's later focus on the culinary domain. Milton's 'navis stultifera' alludes to the title of Sebastian Brant's *Ship of Fools* (*Das Narrenschiff*) in its Latin translation; Democritus was known as 'the laughing philosopher' on account of his habitual derision of human folly.

[152] CPW 1: 266–67. Milton appears to be inverting the two components of the Greek-derived 'sophomore' (meaning a second-year student, originally a Cambridge term,
see *OED*, 'sophomore'), playing on its original meaning ('wisely foolish') now fitted to his own purpose: he will be 'foolishly wise.' For this etymology of 'sophomore,' which Milton's allusion

4.3 Prolusion VI ('Sportive Exercises ...')

sion VI will be all at once: the silly inversion of an academic exercise but not devoid of wisdom, and a celebration that has been 'commanded' to supplant serious study.

Turning to his assigned task, the speaker remembers – and imagines – the last occasion on which he had delivered an 'academic oration' (a serious academic exercise, presumably) before the same assembly. Then, he had 'felt sure that any effort of mine would have but a cold reception from you' – when suddenly, and 'quite contrary to my expectation, quite contrary indeed to any spark of hope I may have entertained, I heard, or rather I myself felt [accepi, imo ipse sensi], that my speech was received with quite unusual applause on every hand ...'[153] In a curious equivocation, Milton figures his hearers' reaction in sensory, yet not quite explicitly auditory, terms.[154] Perhaps we are to imagine this as some slight commotion among the audience, indeed more properly felt than heard. Be that as it may, the speaker's felt or heard, in any case 'sensed' impression of his listeners' immediate 'feedback' is the image that most readily suggests itself to him when he returns to the rostrum for another attempt to win them over. Their shared communicative situation is characterised, to an extent, by reciprocity.

For now, however, he has not won over his listeners just yet, and thus the speaker resorts to the two-pronged strategy of flattery and humility to capture their benevolence:

> I am quite overcome with pride and joy [mirum in modum voluptate perfundor] at finding myself surrounded on all sides [circumfusum me, & undique stipatum] by such an assembly of learned men; and yet, when I take stock of myself and turning my eyes inward contemplate in my own heart the meagre powers I possess [cum in me descendo, & quasi flexis introrsum oculis meam tenuitatem secretus intueor], I blush to myself and a sudden uprush of sadness overwhelms and chokes my rising joy [subsilientem deprimit & jugulat lætitiam].
>
> But, gentlemen, do not, I beg of you, desert me as I lie here fallen [jacentem & consternatum], and stricken by your eyes as by lightning [acie oculorum vestrorum tanquam de cœlo tactum]. Let the soft breeze of your goodwill [vestri favoris aura] refresh my fainting spirit, as well as it can, and warm it into life again [erigat ... quod potest, & refocillet]; so shall my sickness, thanks to you, be less acute, and the remedy, since it is you who apply it, the more willingly and gladly accepted; so that it would be a true pleasure [perquam gratum] to me often to faint thus, if I might as often be revived and restored by you.[155]

In an image familiar from much later works, Milton figures himself, the speaker, as a lone individual surrounded by a potentially hostile, in any case expectant and observing

---

arguably supports (while the *OED* does not), see Eric Partridge, *Origins: An Etymological Dictionary of Modern English* (London: Routledge, 2009 [1977]), 416.

[153] CPW 1: 266–67. An editorial note ad loc. suggests that 'this is another of the autobiographical passages.' Perhaps, then, the passage should be read as informed by the recollection of 'real' (i.e., audible) applause.

[154] CW has the less specifically auditory 'as I noted, nay rather, I myself felt.' *Accipere* allows for both interpretations, 'to take in one's grasp ... to receive in or on the body' (*OLD* 1) and 'to receive (sense impressions), (spec.) to hear (sounds)' (9).

[155] CPW 1: 268.

multitude.[156] More specifically, the qualitative distinction of the two sides (pitting erudition against tenuous powers) is inextricably connected to the quantitative opposition of the speaker vis-à-vis (!) his many hearers. Most likely, the description of the scene is meant to be taken with a grain of salt – after all Milton, an advanced student ranking high among his contemporaries, is addressing a crowd composed to a considerable extent of new students and 'sophisters.' This does not fundamentally affect, however, the functioning of the evidently sensory discourse of the passage.

I have above referred to the shared communicative situation of speaker and audience, which is constituted (or, in the case of the printed text, imagined) through the audible presence of the authorial voice as embodied sensory discourse. In Milton's imaginary confrontation of audience and speaker as an overpowering and a defeated force, respectively, this conception of communicative reciprocity is taken to its cold extreme: not as a relation of true mutuality – this is what Milton's speaker rhetorically begs for as the 'soft breeze of [the audience's] goodwill' – but rather as a conduit of influence that is bilateral only potentially, not in actual operation.

The individual steps of the imagined confrontation are phrased in terms of sensory perception and affect. It all begins with the speaker's delight *at the sight of* the illustrious crowd surrounding him; Milton's 'joy' is *voluptas*, the pleasing, para-sensuous feeling alluded to in the introductory paragraph of his speech (where it had been rendered by his translators as 'pleasure'). This feeling of joy, at the outset, cannot be divided from the encompassing presence of the audience; in fact, the two appear to merge, literally flowing one into another, as Milton's wording suggests: derived from *perfundere* and *circumfundere*, respectively, both 'perfundor' (of the speaker's joy) and 'circumfusum' (of the relation between speaker and audience) refer to relations of (bodily) immersion and the 'soaking' of an individual or object in an amorphous substance. What curbs this pervasive, quasi-bodily pleasure (later also referred to, perhaps with a slight accentuation of emotion over indulgence, as *laetitia*) is again *a view*, namely the speaker's metaphorical look into the depths ('in me descendo, & quasi ... intueor') of his 'own heart,' that is, his psyche. What he sees there, his own intellectual poverty ('meam tenuitatem') is what distinguishes him from his hearers; in effect, he imagines looking at himself, as it were, from *their* superior point of view.

As the speaker begins his appeal to the audience, the focus again is on his 'low' (notionally prostrate) and afflicted position, 'fallen' and 'stricken by [lit., the sharpness or blade of] your eyes as by lightning [lit., "as if touched from heaven"].' The strongly synaesthetic, visual-tactile metaphor is clear: 'if looks could kill' – with the sharpness of a blade, no less – they would have to be thought of as tactile; indeed, they have an effect comparable to being 'touched from heaven,' by lightning, thunder, or divine in-

---

[156] See, again, *PL* 7.27–30, discussed in Chapter 5.3 below, and similar passages in *Paradise Lost* (e.g., in Milton's presentation of Abdiel). Regarding the particular speaking position in the academic exercises, Stephen Fallon has pointed out that, on the whole, 'Milton's self-representation [in the Prolusions] is shaped also by the agonistic ethos of the academic disputation. He paints a picture of an embattled self, joined by the pure and right-thinking few and opposed by the promiscuous many' (*Milton's Peculiar Grace*, 50). On the conceptual metonymy SURROUNDING SOMEBODY FOR PAYING ATTENTION TO THAT PERSON, see Kövecses, *Where Metaphors Come From*, 145.

tervention.[157] The antidote to the speaker's despair, conversely, is figured as a fundamentally *agreeable* tactile sensation, as the 'soft breeze' ('aura') of the audience's favour.[158] This is underlined by the way in which the positive effects of that 'breeze' are characterised as 'refresh[ing]' (lit., 'raising up') and 'warm[ing].'[159] The speaker's spirit had been 'fainting' ('semianimum,' lit. 'only half animate,' i.e., 'half-dead'), lying down, but by the favour of his hearers may be revived, may be 'raised up.' In addition to the more conspicuously sensory elements of the passage, the spatial attributions present in these phrases (as in the references to 'descending [down] into oneself' and 'being touched from heaven' above) rehearse conceptual metaphors familiar from earlier discussion, based in the dichotomy of UP vs DOWN and connected, here as there, to notions of power, control, and consciousness (i.e., control over perception and power over the self).

In one brief yet dense episode, then, Prolusion VI manages to flesh out the even briefer remarks about 'none but hostile glances' in Prolusion I, turning a conventional, only tenuously sensory reference to the exposed position of the lone orator in plain view into a miniature drama phrased in synaesthetic terms. Combining visual and tactile images, Milton imagines an unequal confrontation between potentially deadly looks – the speaker is left 'half-dead' on account of their 'sharpness' – on the one side, and timid introspection on the other. Again, Milton's presentation corresponds to the hierarchical valuation of sight over touch: whereas the looks darted at the speaker by his hearers are powerful (and directed outward), the speaker himself can only take a look into the depths of his 'own heart'; he does not command the same kind of ocular authority. The speaker is at the receiving end of the (metaphorically tactile) effects of the audience's glances; in entreating them for the remedy, he is at their mercy. The question of whether or not the passage, melodramatic as it appears, has an ironic edge – to my mind it does – has no immediate bearing on the metaphorical and conceptual-metaphorical structure of its sensory discourse. In fact, an ironic tinge to the speaker's plea for his audience's favour could well be seen as connecting the present passage to Milton's later, rather less timid allusions to the audience's noxious breath.

---

[157] To the early modern imagination, generally, it was not lightning but thunder (conceived of as directly effective sound) that did the damage during a thunderstorm (hence, a 'thunderbolt'); see Rath, *How Early America Sounded*, 10–21. The association of eyes and light(ning), however, suggests either flashes of lightning (as in Tillyard's interpolation) or a more abstract 'act of God,' also strongly associated with vision.

[158] *OLD* 'aura' points to various relevant facets of the term: 'air in gentle motion' (1); 'the [proverbial] breath (of favour, etc. … also the favour of fortune' (3); 'air issuing from the lungs, breath' (5); by metonymy (the vehicle of the smell for the smell): 'an odour, fragrance, aroma; an effluvium, stench' (6); by transfer to the visual realm, 'radiation, gleam' (7b). While it is clear that the 'breath' (= voices) of the audience may stand for (expressions of) their approval, possible references to meanings 5 and, in particular, 6 might be thought ambiguous and/or prefiguring later passages teasing the audience regarding their supposed bad breath (discussed below).

[159] 'Warm it into life' (CPW) captures the derivation of *focillare*, 'to revive,' from *focus*, 'hearth'; CW has the more neutral 'revive me.'

At this point of the Prolusion, however, the speaker still needs to win the goodwill of his hearers (not just their hearty laughter), and thus he continues with lavish praise of their qualities ('what matchless power, what marvellous virtue is yours ...') – as well as with a bit of thinly veiled self-praise:

> ... let no one wonder that I triumph, as though exalted to heaven, at finding so many men eminent for their learning, the very flower as it were of the University, gathered together here; for I can scarce believe that a greater number flocked of old to Athens to hear those two supreme orators [ad audiendum duos Oratores summos], Demosthenes and Aeschines, contending for the crown of eloquence [de principatu eloquentiæ certantes] ...[160]

What Milton disguises as a continued astonishment at the sheer size of the congregation in fact flatters both himself and his hearers, whom he figures as successors to the ancient Athenians. The consistent emphasis on the act of speaking, on Milton's oration as oratory, is clear; it may be emphasised still through his highlighting of the agonistic, almost visceral element present in the confrontation of two famous orators of antiquity. Turning from the Greeks to the Romans, Milton continues his thought by naming Hortensius and Cicero, their most eminent orators, and again flatters both himself *and* his audience:

> ... or that such felicity ever fell to the lot of Hortensius at any declamation of his [peroranti *Hortensio*], or that so great a company of cultured men ever graced a speech of Cicero's [orantem *Ciceronem*]. So that with however poor success I perform my task, it will yet be no mean honour to me merely to have opened my lips [verba fecisse] before so large and crowded an assembly of our most eminent men.[161]

Through Milton's use of participles in these lines, Hortensius and Cicero are *presented* (in a very literal sense) in the act of speaking, and speaking with verve.[162] Milton's speaker himself would feel honoured only to have 'made words,' produced vocal speech before such an illustrious assembly – but even then, his performance would resemble those of his classical models in that it is emphatically presented as corporeally performed, embodied discourse.[163] Milton's phrasing serves to emphasise his own perceived closeness to the great orators of antiquity: they had bodies, too; they spoke be-

---

[160] CPW 1: 268, with an editor's note on 'the fulsomeness of the praise to which Milton resorts in this passage.'

[161] CPW 1: 268.

[162] This is expressed by the intensifying 'per-' in Milton's evocation of Hortensius, see *OLD*, 'peroro': '(1) To argue a case to the end, plead, harangue, etc.,' which includes the technical rhetorical meaning of '(2) To deliver the final part of a speech, wind up a case, conclude ...'

[163] The Latin idiom used by Milton, *verba facere*, expresses precisely this aspect of speech as vocal, embodied discourse, see '*OLD*, 'uerbum': '(5) (pl.) Spoken words, talking, utterance, discourse, etc. ... (c) *verba facere*, to talk, speak; ...' CPW's 'opened my lips' arguably captures this emphasis on the body; CW has 'to have uttered words.'

fore an assembled audience, just as he does; in the case of the Romans, they even spoke the same language. But it also constructs a particular kind of closeness between the present orator – Milton himself – and his audience of contemporaries.

The theme of vocal speech as embodied discourse is continued, and a new facet is added to it, in the next passage, where the respective powers of the orator and the lyre player are contrasted. Specifically, Milton's extended comparison is between the most accomplished musicians and singers of ancient myth (he names Orpheus and Amphion) and himself, whose 'instrument' is his command of speech:[164]

> And by heaven, I cannot help flattering myself a little that I am, as I think, far more fortunate than Orpheus or Amphion; for they did but supply the trained and skilful touch to make the strings give forth their sweet harmony [hi enim chordulis suavi concentu adsonantibus digitos tantum docte & perite admovebant], and the exquisite music was due as much to the instrument itself as to their apt and dexterous handling of it [eratque in ipsis fidibus, & in apto dextroque manuum motu æqualis utrinque pars dulcedinis]. But if I win any praise here to-day, it will be entirely and truly my own, and the more glorious in proportion as the creations of the intellect are superior to manual skill [quanto ingenii opus vincit ac præstat manuum artificium].[165]

After the focus on the vocal 'madeness' of embodied speech in the previous passage, Milton's conventionally synaesthetic references to the 'sweet harmony' ('suavi concentu') and overall 'sweetness' ('dulcedinis') of instrumental music carry the notion to its logical extreme: the orator's voice, too, is first and foremost an acoustic phenomenon; it is his 'instrument'; and it is actually superior to the most skilled instrumental music, usually considered the epitome of pleasant sound.

Milton emphasises the confrontational quality of his comparison in several ways. First, he completely passes over the fact that the two musicians he names are *singers* as well; in making them lyre-players only, he not only reduces the extent of their artistry by half but minimises, at the same time, the potential overlap between their sphere of activity and his own as an orator. In connection with this, the speaker displaces half of the musicians' remaining artistry onto their (inanimate) instruments. In a third stroke of devaluation, the remainder of musical prowess left to them is dismissed as a purely manual skill, in keeping with the conventional valuation of touch as the lowest of the five senses. Their touch may be 'trained and skillful' ('docte & perite'), but it is, ultimately, external to the actual generation of their music by the vibrating strings, and alien to its true, ethereal quality: they 'moved their fingers close to the strings resounding in sweet harmony' ('chordulis suavi concentu adsonantibus digitos ... admovebant'). The passage does not go so far as to *deny* that Amphion's and Orpheus' strings were moved by their fingers; but Milton's phrasing, in its entanglement of direct and indirect objects ('digitos' and 'chordulis ... adsonantibus,' respectively), creates a subtle rift

---

[164] Amphion, like Orpheus, could move stones with his playing but applied his skill to a more constructive purpose when he used his harp to raise the walls of Thebes (see *Oxford Companion to Classical Literature*, ed. Howatson, 41).
[165] CPW 1: 268–69.

between the direct 'manipulation' of the strings and its indirect, yet all-important, audible effect.[166] What reaches the ears of the audience, quite obviously, is not the sound of fingers moving and touching but rather that of strings resounding; and even if half of the lyre players' music resides 'in apto dextroque manuum motu,' they are still inferior to the speaker on two counts: one step removed from the production of sound, they *have* instruments, whereas the speaker's body *is* an instrument of oratory. At the same time, since Milton has them play songs without words, their performance lacks the *ingenium* that distinguishes the orator's speech, a creation not of coarse handiwork but of the intellect.[167]

All things considered, then, Milton's account offers faint praise indeed for the actual (manual) skill of the two musicians. It is worth remembering at this point, however, that Milton – himself a skilled organist and player on the bass viol, according to the testimony of contemporaries – is speaking *in persona oratoris*: the strategic devaluation of musicians (and, ultimately, of music) to the advantage of the virtuoso orator is directly connected to the character of the prolusion as an oratorical exercise; as far as its embodied vocal (and hence auditory) quality is concerned, its sensory discourse can suffer no rivals.

In elaborating on the comparison, Milton reiterates its two most important, if at first sight conflicting, points:

> Besides, Orpheus and Amphion used to attract an audience consisting only of rocks and wild beasts and trees, and if any human beings came, they were at best but rude and rustic folk; but *I* find the most learned men altogether engrossed in listening to my words and hanging on my lips [at ego doctissimas mihi deditas aures, & ab ore meo pendentes video]. Lastly, those rustics and wild beasts used to follow the stringed music which they already knew well and had often heard before [jam satis notam & complureis exauditam sequebantur nervorum harmoniam]; *you* have been drawn hither and held fast here [huc rapuit, & jam detinet] by expectation alone.[168]

As Milton argues throughout, the relationship between himself (as speaker) and his audience (as hearers/listeners) is marked by a strong emphasis on sound (comparable in this respect to the relationship between Orpheus, Amphion, and their listeners); yet the orator (and, by extension, his audience) are cleared from any suspicions of a 'rude and rustic' sensuality through Milton's references to the ultimately intellectual and at least semi-deliberate nature of their association. Ultimately, a tension remains, as the audience are charmed into listening, as if against their will; yet their expectation – a quality

---

[166] CPW's 'for they *did but supply the touch* to *make the strings* give forth their ... harmony' strives to capture this nuance, as does CW's 'they *merely applied their fingers ... to little strings*, attuned with pleasing harmony' (emphases added).

[167] Milton's remarks should be seen in the context of the traditionally close but fraught relationship between (instrumental or vocal) music and rhetoric, which ultimately came down to the question of the (intellectual) *use* vs the (sensual) *abuse* of music; see Winn, *Unsuspected Eloquence*, esp. 30–55.

[168] CPW 1: 269.

which sets them apart from wild beasts and rustics – is predicated upon their intellect and learning.

Through its quality of being 'ingenii opus' and composed for a learned audience, we may expect the orator's speech to be instructive; on account of its *dulcedo*, we know it to be 'sweet' and pleasing; in that the audience was literally 'drawn hither and held fast here,' 'hanging on [the speaker's] lips' to hear it, its affective potential has become manifest. All told, then, the passage reflects on the three Ciceronian functions of rhetoric, and it does so in the medium of sensory discourse, pitting sound against touch and sensuous hearing against perceptive listening. Milton's playful 'dis-identification' with the most renowned bards of classical antiquity thus also reproduces, in a nutshell, the fundamental tension between pleasure and utility that is the driving force of Prolusion VI as a whole.

Despite such distinguished points of reference as Demosthenes or Orpheus, however, the speaker wants his audience to know that 'I have not spoken thus in a spirit of boastfulness.' Rather, his comparisons are simply meant to express a desire for 'such a stream of honeyed, or rather nectared, eloquence [melleum illud, seu verius Nectareum Eloquentiæ flumen] ... as of old ever steeped and as it were celestially bedewed [quasi cœlitus irrorabat] the great minds of Athens and of Rome.'[169] If the general thrust of the image – a sweet 'mellifluence' of discourse – is conventional enough, its contextual embedding and deliberate restatement – not honey but nectar – deserve some comment. The meaning of the image is not necessarily positive; we have already encountered Milton's later subversion of it in book 2 of *Paradise Lost*, where Belial's sophistical 'tongue/Dropped manna.' Appearing as it does in close contextual proximity to two related gustatory references (to honey and nectar), the present allusion to heavenly dew may also reasonably be associated with the sweet manna of Exodus. In effect, the significance of the allusion rests wholly in the sweet taste of the manna; Milton's reference to 'the great minds of Athens and of Rome' precludes a more specifically theological reading. In decidedly wishing for 'nectared' rather than 'honeyed' eloquence, moreover, the speaker emphasises that his concern is with the *sourcing* of rhetorical ingenuity, a theme elaborated upon in the continuation of the sentence: 'would that I could suck out all the innermost marrow of persuasion, pilfer the notebooks of Mercury himself, and empty all the coffers of wit ...' Now, in wishing for a stream of 'nectared' rather than 'honeyed' eloquence, Milton draws on the conventional image of sweet discourse but remakes it into an ambiguous assertion of the orator's own creativity: the speaker thrives on the nectar of inspiration or tradition (ingested just as the 'marrow of persuasion' is 'suck[ed],' etc.). This he passes on to his audience as the honey of his own mellifluous rhetoric – yet, if all is gathered from elsewhere, just how much of that honey may be said to be his own?[170] Taken as a whole, the passage highlights the potential of sensory discourse not just for auditory, visual, and tactile but also for gustatory conceptualisation. This, it appears in the present, oratorical context, is facilitated by the association of the tongue with both, embodied speech and taste.

---

[169] CPW 1: 269.

[170] CPW notes ad loc. that 'Mercury not only presided over orators and merchants but also was the god of thieves and pickpockets': if even Mercury steals, this is the common *modus operandi* of all orators.

A concern with the three senses of touching, seeing, and (above all) hearing had dominated Prolusion VI so far; images of eating and taste will become more central as the oration continues. At present, however, the two notions of tasting and hearing are closely connected, fused even, in the speaker's ambition to integrate 'nectared eloquence,' persuasion, and wit, in order to finally 'produce something worthy of such great expectations [tanta expectatione], so notable a concourse, and so polished and refined an audience [tam denique tersis & delicatis auribus dignum].'[171] Through its attributes ('tersis & delicatis'), the conventional metonymy of Milton's original Latin ('ears' for 'hearers') is particularised and embodied: in the most fundamental senses of both terms, these ears are clean ('tersis') and delightfully tender to the touch ('delicatis'). Both descriptions may well be read as ironic or teasing references to undergraduate hygiene and immaturity. Any further positive or negative connotations attached to them ('neat, refined' for *tersus*, 'discerning' or 'self-indulgent' for *delicatus*) are based in these perceptible or perceptual, in any case bodily qualities.[172] Throughout the passage, then, the embodied quality of the oratorical moment is again brought to the fore, oscillating between metaphorical taste and touch ('nectared eloquence' is witty, 'tender ears' are receptive and discerning) on the one side and literal hearing (as well as *listening* on the part of an expectant audience) on the other.

As Milton continues, the sensory focus extends to again include hearing *and* vision and, explicitly, the pleasure derived from both: 'So behold, my hearers ... [Ecce, Auditores], whither my consuming desire and longing to please you [ardor & prolubium placendi vobis] drives me and carries me away ...' It would be no use to visit the shrines and sanctuaries of the Muses, the speaker concludes, 'for I find myself surrounded by men in whom the Muses and the Graces are incarnate' – that is, who 'breathe them' with every breath they take: 'qui Musas omnes spirant & Gratias.' Here, the breath of the audience, re-appearing throughout the prolusion in different, positive or negative, valuations, figures as a cipher of their cultivated and noble character. Consequently, Milton continues,

> barbarity, Error, Ignorance, and all that tribe which the Muses loathe must needs take flight with all speed at sight of you [ad aspectum vestrum], and hide themselves in a far distant clime. And then, why should not every barbarous, vulgar, or outworn word or phrase be forthwith banished from my speech, and I myself become straightway eloquent and accomplished, through the working of your influence [afflatu vestro] and secret inspiration [arcano instinctu]?[173]

In this explicit return to his earlier imagery, suggesting a relationship of influence between the audience and the orator, Milton first conceives of this influence, as before, in visual terms. Then, however, it is figured as an *afflatus*, or breath, which takes up the respiratory image ('Musas ... spirant') of the previous passage. On the whole, the speaker–audience relationship now appears more benign than it had done before; the speaker

---

[171] CPW 1: 269–70.
[172] CW renders the relevant phrase as 'ears so pure and fastidious,' which arguably covers both its literal and its figurative dimension.
[173] CPW 1: 271.

is not struck down by sharp, hostile looks, but rather inspired and supported in his endeavour to please. It is at this point in the oration that Milton shifts the focus of its sensory discourse from the auditory and visual to the gustatory realm:

> ... I entreat you, my hearers, not to grudge a little of your time to my frivolities [nugis], for even the gods themselves are said often to have laid aside for the moment the cares of the commonwealth of heaven and to have been present as spectators of the wars of puny man [depugnantium homunculorum spectaculo]. Sometimes, indeed, the stories tell, they did not disdain humble homes, but accepted the hospitality of the poor and gladly made a meal of beans and herbs [fabas & olera narrantur esitasse]. So too I beg and beseech you, my kind hearers [Auditores optimi], to accept what I can offer as in some sort a humble banquet [quale conviviolum] for your delicate and discerning taste [ad subtile vestrum & sagax palatum].[174]

In its double reference to (literal) perception and (metaphorical) discernment, Milton's description of the collective palate of his audience as 'subtile' and 'sagax' parallels the earlier, similar reference to their ears ('tersis & delicatis auribus'). Its hyperbolical elevation of his hearers to the level of gods, looking down on his rhetorical efforts, then deigning to partake of the 'humble banquet' of his speech, continues another strand from the earlier confrontation between speaker and audience, in which the latter figured as overpowering vis-à-vis the helplessness and insignificance of the former. That the image of the speaker's 'conviviolum' (literally, a 'small feast') indeed focuses on eating – and, in particular, the tasting of food or drink – is made clear by the subsequent reference to his listeners' palate.

On a conceptual level, this notion of a 'humble banquet' being offered by the speaker to his hearers actualises the metaphor IDEAS ARE FOOD, already referred to above: in delivering his speech, the orator gives them 'something to digest' as well as, what may be thought more important in this parody of an academic oration (valuing style over content), something to *taste*. However, the speaker's supposedly lowly 'frivolities' (the foolishly wise *nugae* promised earlier) may turn out to be more substantial than initially thought, just like 'beans and herbs' might – after all, even the gods did not refuse those. Or perhaps they might provoke bloating and indigestion – this ambiguity is taken up in a subsequent passage.

When the speaker then warns his audience of the detrimental effects of excessively strict living – '... if we made it our daily custom to go to sleep and so to speak die in philosophy and grow old among the thorns and brambles of logic ...' –, this again is referred to a classical example as well as to the question of diet: living a life that was oriented wholly towards (scholastic) learning would mean 'following the over-rigid rule of Cato,' whose prescripts had included a strict temperance of diet. 'Why, the very rustics would say that we live on mustard [sinapi nos victitare].'[175] In this case, a meagre

---

[174] Ibid.
[175] CPW 1: 271–72. Milton's reference to mustard suggests the practices of contemporary English religious ascetics. During Milton's time at Cambridge, one well-known example was 'the future mining projector Thomas Bushell, who in the 1620s lived for three years in a hut on a diet of

diet is what the orator's humorous offerings are meant to overcome, arguing in favour of the 'sportive exercises' his own sportive exercise has set out to defend. This is in manifest contrast to the preceding reference to 'beans and herbs,' which had stood for the negligibility or else underestimation of the speaker's *nugae*. Both references serve their function arguing in favour of the prolusion's thesis, and both relate to the IDEAS ARE FOOD metaphor; their respective actualisations of that metaphor, however, are inconsistent with each other.

Indeed, the speaker now turns in earnest to a deliberation of his thesis (that 'Sportive Exercises on occasion are not inconsistent with philosophical Studies'). In accordance with explicitly stated rhetorical custom – 'Would you now, gentlemen, have me build up a structure of proof from instances upon this foundation of reason?' –, he adduces examples for the appropriateness of jesting: Homer, Socrates, and Cicero all used jokes and wit to bring their points across. 'The conversation of the ancient philosophers,' in particular, 'was always sprinkled with witty sayings and enlivened by a pleasant sparkle [sale sparsa, & lepore venusto passim ... referta].'[176] The idea that witty invention is the metaphorical 'salt' of discourse is conventional, but it chimes particularly well with the prolusion's pervasive theme that IDEAS ARE FOOD.[177] In fact, Milton highlights the literal meaning of *sal* when he suggests that the 'conversation' of the ancient philosophers was 'sprinkled' ('sparsa') with wit, just as a dish would be sprinkled with salt to improve its taste.

Milton then goes on to reference Erasmus's *In Praise of Folly* (1509), as well as several 'great generals, kings, and heroes' who 'overflowed with humorous and witty sayings [salsè dictorum],' and those classical authors 'pre-eminent among their contemporaries for wit'; he points out that the classical gods themselves are represented as merry jesters, notably 'at their feasts and carouses [inter epulas & pocula]'; and, finally, he names his own audience: 'yourselves, which I consider worth all the rest. For that jests and jollity [sales & joculi] are far from displeasing to you is proved clearly enough by your coming here in crowds to-day, and to this every one of you seems to nod assent.'[178] If the younger generation of students – in the same passage, Milton specifically refers to 'the newly-created Bachelors' – is united in its appreciation of witty 'jests and jollity,' there is the distinct danger of 'some bearded Masters of crabbed and surly nature ... shak[ing] their obstinate heads,' complaining that 'to-day's exercises, which our forbears undoubtedly instituted with the proper and honest purpose of winning some solid gain [insignem aliquem fructum inde percipiendum], either of rhetoric or of philosophy, have of late been perverted into a show of feeble witticism [insipidos sales].'[179] Again, the qualification of the witticisms presented ('sales') as 'insipidos' ('tasteless')

---

herbs, oil, mustard and honey' (Thomas, *Man and the Natural World*, 289). Milton's tactile reference to the 'thorns and brambles of logic [inter dumos & spinas Logicæ]' resembles his other uses of similar imagery, see the passage about 'thorns and brambles' [dumis & spinis] in Prolusion III, quoted above.

[176] CPW 1: 272–73.

[177] See *OLD*, 'sal,' 6: 'a quality which gives "life" or "character" to a person or thing; b) (of speech) wit; (pl.) examples of wit, jokes, witticisms.'

[178] CPW 1: 274.

[179] CPW 1: 275–76.

4.3 Prolusion VI ('Sportive Exercises ...')

serves to actualise the literal, gustatory meaning of *sal*: according to those opposed to the 'sportive exercises' defended in Prolusion VI, they only yield tasteless wit, conceived of as 'stale salt'.[180] As Milton has already begun to point out, however, his objective is to supply his audience with a banquet of well-seasoned and 'fruitful' dishes not devoid of wit and wisdom.

In presenting the particular utility of university exercises as their metaphorical 'fruit,' Milton deploys another variation of the IDEAS ARE FOOD metaphor. In this, the verb *percipere* proves ambiguous, with several facets of meaning relevant to the present passage: its fundamental meaning is one of harvesting fruit (the literal 'plucking' of the *fructus* mentioned); its reference to sensory or mental 'perception' – the way in which, we are constantly reminded, the oration is transmitted from speaker to audience – is an abstracting extension of this; its result, the acquisition of abstract things (in particular, knowledge) is what regular academic exercises are for – and what the current, parodic one discusses.[181] Whether or not Milton had in mind conventional ideas about the loss of the sense of taste in old age: the particular savour (i.e., the wit) of his speech is appreciated only by his contemporaries; the senior faculty (the 'bearded Masters') just lack the palate for it.[182]

In the following passage, Milton argues, in essence, that times have changed and will always be changing, and that both curricula and rules have to be adapted to find 'the right mean.' Still, he concludes, wit and learning both have their place, and are dependent, ultimately, on the right, serious kind of mindset: 'no one can be master of a fine and clever wit who has not first learnt how to behave seriously.'[183] With this, the 'oration' arguing for the admissibility of occasional foolishness comes to an end, and the 'prolusion' proper is about to begin: 'In a moment, we shall shake off the fetters of rhetoric and throw ourselves into comic licence.'[184] In closing his first speech (and opening his second), Milton again refers to the two-sided, acoustically determined relationship between speaker and audience: 'And so I entreat at the beginning of my enter-

---

[180] The more literal 'tasteless witticisms' of the Columbia edition is closer to the gustatory image of Milton's original Latin (*insipidus* is derived from *sapere*, 'to taste'). The same applies to 'gathering some remarkable fruit' (CW) as against 'winning some solid gain' (CPW).

[181] See *OLD*, 'percipio': 'to take (natural produce) from the place of growth, source of production, etc., harvest ...' (1); 'to acquire possession of (esp. as the proceeds or reward of one's efforts), earn, reap, ... reap (abst. things)' (2, 3); 'to perceive, apprehend, notice ... to take in or grasp with the mind' (6, 7).

[182] See Locke's visit to a very old lady, referred to in Chapter 2 above, and compare *PL* 11.538–46, where Michael explains to Adam, commenting on his vision of the future: 'This is old age; but then thou must outlive/Thy youth, thy strength, thy beauty, which will change/To withered weak and grey; *thy senses then/Obtuse, all taste of pleasure must forgo,*/To what thou hast, and for the air of youth/Hopeful and cheerful, in thy blood will reign/A melancholy damp of cold and dry/To weigh thy spirits down, and last consume/The balm of life' (emphases added).

[183] CPW 1: 276.

[184] Ibid. This does not mean, of course, that the second speech abandons rhetorical strategies; Milton's announcement of a fundamental shift from rhetoric to non-rhetoric is itself a rhetorical gesture. A change in *tone*, however, is quite apparent.

tainment the favour which actors beg at the end of theirs: give me your laughter and applause [Plaudite, & ridete].'[185]

Prolusion VI is unique among Milton's surviving academic exercises in that it consists of several parts: an initial 'oration' (which I have just discussed), the 'prolusion' proper, and a section in English verse.[186] As Milton embarks on the second prose section, he continues, after a short introductory anecdote of recent student exploits, on the theme of speaker–audience communication. This had also been alluded to at the beginning of the first part and, now as then, Milton conjures up an audible reaction on the part of his hearers. This time, however, the acoustic component is joined by other imagined sensations, and the sensory compound as a whole is deployed to quite different effect. The reference, now, is not so much to a scene remembered – Milton had earlier alluded to the last occasion on which he had addressed his fellow students – but to one wished-for or expected. The result, a densely multi-sensory passage that both acknowledges and teases his hearers, is worth quoting at some length:

> I ask you now to imagine, gentlemen, [fingite, Auditores] although it is not the first of April, that we are celebrating the Hilaria in honour of the Mother of the Gods, or a festival sacred to the god Laughter [deo Risui]. Laugh [Ridete], then, and raise a roar from your saucy lungs [petulanti splene sustollite cachinnum], smooth out the wrinkles of your brows [exporrigite frontem], make a long nose if you like, but don't turn it up at anything [uncis indulgete naribus, sed naso adunco ne suspendite]; let the whole place resound with shouts of mirth [profusissimo risu circumsonent omnia], let unbridled hilarity make the tears of merriment flow freely [solutior cachinnus hilares excutiat lachrymas], so that laughter may drain them dry [iis risu exhaustis], leaving not a drop to grace the triumph of grief [ne guttulam quidem habeat Dolor quà triumphum exornet suum]. For my part, if I see anyone not opening his mouth as wide as he should to laugh [nimis parce diducto rictu ridentem], I shall say that he is trying to hide teeth which are foul and decayed, and yellow from neglect [scabros & cariosos dentes rubigine obductos], or misplaced and projecting, or else that at to-day's feast he has so crammed his belly that he dares not put any extra strain upon it by laughing [aut inter prandendum hodie sic opplevisse abdomen, ut non audeat ilia ulterius distendere ad risum], for fear that not the Sphinx but his sphincter anus [non *Sphinx* sed *Sphincter* anus] should sing a second part to his mouth's first and accidentally let out some enigmas [ne praecinenti ori succinat, & ænigmata quædam nolens effutiat], which I leave to the doctors instead of Oedipus to explain. For I should not like the cheerful sound of laughter [nolim enim hilari vocis sono obstrepat] to be drowned by groans from the posterior of the assembly [in hoc cœtu posticus gemitus]. I leave it to the doctors [Medici], who can loosen the bowels, to loosen up all this. If anyone does not raise his voice loud and clear enough [Si quis strenuum & clarum non ediderit murmur], I shall swear that his breath is so foul and poisonous [tam gravem & mortiferum faucibus exhalare spiritum] that the

---

[185] CPW 1: 277.

[186] These are the lines 'At a Vacation Exercise in the College,' which, in their published form, are headed 'The Latin Speeches ended, the English thus began' (*SP*, 79).

fumes of Etna or Avernus could not be more noisome [nihil spiret tetrius], or at any rate that he has just been eating onions or leeks [allium aut porrum comedisse dudum] so that he dare not open his mouth for fear of making his neighbours choke with his evil-smelling breath [adeo ut non audeat aperire os, ne vicinos quosque fœtido halitu enecet].[187]

The passage is as ribald as its sensory discourse is complex. In the first instance, Milton invites, or rather *commands* his hearers to raise their voices in laughter, and to make themselves heard. His emphasis on intensity and volume, on the audible and arguably even tactile dimension of the phenomenon is insistent, as *cachinnus* and *circumsonare* indicate.[188] This roaring laughter is figured as an all-engrossing, and eminently physical, bodily event: at the same time as encouraging them to 'raise a roar of laughter,' Milton prompts his fellow students to grimace and gesticulate (and appends an ominous first admonition not to turn up their noses at anything). The immediate outer and inner effects of this combined bodily effort are clear: 'the whole place [will] resound with shouts of mirth' (a multiplied, amplified acoustic effect of the orator's own speech) and 'tears of merriment [will] flow,' indicating that the orator has indeed, as the Ciceronian triad of rhetorical functions demands, moved his audience to passion. This is also suggested by the involvement of the hearers' spleen, an organ associated in early modern psychology and humoral theory, most of all, with the black bile of melancholy but also with the passions more generally.[189] This wider association of the organ with emotive movements of the soul helps to explain how, in diametrical opposition to its being the source of melancholy, the spleen could also be 'regarded as the seat of laughter or mirth.'[190] From the context, as from Milton's references to laughter, it should be clear what general kind of 'spleen' he has in mind here (mirth, not melancholy); but it is his contrasting of *risus* and 'Dolor' – Grief personified – that makes matters explicit. As long as laughter reigns, 'Dolor' will be denied her triumph. In this, the passage is close to the confrontation of melancholy and mirth in the companion poems of 1631/32, and to the banishment of 'loathed Melancholy' in the opening lines of *L'Allegro*, in particular.[191] Still, Milton's qualification in the present passage – 'petulanti splene' – indicates his notion more precisely: the mirth of the audience is to be directed outward in the active, borderline aggressive manner which – *petulans* suggests – is right next to immo-

---

[187] CPW 1: 277–78.
[188] *OLD*, 'cachinnus': 'a laugh, esp. of a loud or boisterous kind, guffaw.'
[189] See Jouanna, *Greek Medicine*, 231n4 on how the spleen became associated with black bile. The physio-psychological subtext of the passage (i.e., its connection to beliefs about the passions) is not captured by CPW's 'from your saucy lungs,' which obviously aims to render the image intelligible for a present-day audience associating laughter, quite understandably, with the *lungs*; CW has 'from your saucy spleen.'
[190] *OED*, 'spleen,' 1c, dated 'frequently c1600.' Sense 1b is given as, 'regarded as the seat of melancholy or morose feelings' (similarly 8c). Senses 2a, 3, and 8a also relate to the cheerful effects of the spleen, various others to its potential to raise the passions more generally.
[191] See lines 1–10. The raucous mirth of the prolusion is in fact a long way from the 'heart-easing Mirth' (13) of *L'Allegro*, which is characterised by its 'unreprovèd pleasures' (40).

rality.[192] Such are the effects of the orator's craft in action, and their bodily and (in the technical sense) passionate operation is palpable from Milton's wording.

Notably, the sensory imagery of the passage then moves beyond the acoustic sphere, and thus beyond the immediate sensory-discursive groundwork of the speaker–hearer relationship. In evoking the noxious smells of flatulence and bad breath, Milton extends the sensory reference of his discourse to the intensely affective (but inherently 'silent') realm of olfaction. At the same time, Milton's conceit suggests that the two imagined perceptions – smell and sound – are closely connected: the wide-open mouths laughing and shouting are, simultaneously, the source of reeking exhalations, while the 'sphincter anus' not only 'let[s] out some enigmas' but also 'sing[s],' and the 'posterior of the assembly' emits audible 'groans.'[193] When contrasted with the corresponding imagery used at the outset of the 'oration,' the audience's imagined foul breath and flatulence appear like a travesty of the earlier 'soft breeze' ('aura') of the audience's favour.

Both foul breath and (in)digestion are associated with the ingestion of food, an area of reference consistently alluded to in earlier passages actualising the conceptual metaphor that IDEAS ARE FOOD. The present passage instead makes explicit reference to the food ingested by the audience: on the festive occasion on which Prolusion VI was delivered, the speeches had been preceded by a 'feast' whose opulence, Milton implies, had tempted his hearers to cram their bellies until they were close to bursting.[194] Apart from its gustatory aspect (which is only implied here, and is explored more fully in a later passage of the speech), Milton's image evokes an internal perception of 'being full' which, in today's technical parlance, would be described as an instance of 'interoception.'[195] While the perceptual quality of this particular image might be less obvious than that of the others relating to hearing and smell, it is particularly effective at highlighting the *embodied* quality of the discursive experience, since it draws auditors' attention to the physical feeling of their bodies as such.

When Milton refers to 'onions or leeks' as causing 'evil-smelling breath,' this implies a devaluation of those foods. Leeks, in particular, had been a firmly entrenched staple of the English diet for a long time and, up to the beginning of the early modern period, were acceptable to all social strata. Due to changes in culinary fashions and general attitudes toward certain foods, however, by the early seventeenth century, 'leeks had fallen from grace, and only the poorest people and the vulgar gentry of Wales re-

---

[192] *OLD*, 'petulans': 'impudently or boisterously aggressive, self-assertive, forward, insolent, unruly; (with reference to sexual behaviour) wanton, immodest.'

[193] Milton's pun on 'Sphinx' and 'sphincter' is etymologically well-founded: both are derived from Greek *sphingein*, 'to grip tightly.'

[194] This theme is already introduced in the opening sentences of the prolusion, quoted above: 'On my return from that city which is the chief of all cities, … filled (I had almost said "to repletion" [usque ad saginam]) with all the good things which are found there in such abundance ….' (CPW 1: 266).

[195] See Drew Leder, 'Visceral Perception,' in: *The Book of Touch*, ed. Classen, 335–41, at 335: '*Interoception* refers to all sensations of the viscera, that is, the internal organs of the body. It is usually distinguished from *exteroception*, our five senses open to the external world, and *proprioception*, our sense of balance, position, and muscular tension, provided by receptors in muscles, joints, tendons, and the inner ear.'

mained loyal to this vegetable.'[196] As if this was not enough, medical authorities frequently cautioned against fruits and vegetables that provoked indigestion, flatulence, or bad breath, as they were thought to cause serious health problems.[197] In fact, the social valuation of vegetables in general was low in Milton's day. They were associated with typically 'Puritan' (i.e., religiously strict and lower middle class) arguments for moderation, just as, conversely, Puritan attacks against drunkenness and gluttony – the very 'cramming of the belly' to which Milton alludes – were frequent.[198] At bottom, then, Milton's reference to leeks and onions in the context of crude manners (and their sensory repercussions) appears to rest on a socio-cultural ascription: crude foods imply crude manners, which in turn imply low status.[199] This circumstance might help to explain why food, in this particular passage, appears more or less only as a nuisance, causing unwanted smells, sounds, and bloating.

The same close connection between the social, religious, and culinary realms is operative in the following passage from a 1642 pamphlet mocking Puritan lay preaching, in which the standing orders of a 'parliament of roundheads' are imagined to include provisions for an annual 'Feast ... of *Turnips*':

> That every Yeare there shall be the *Round-heads* Feast Celebrated, a well-lung'd-long-breathed Cobler shall preach a Sermon six houres, and his Prayers two houres long, and at every Messe in this Feast shall be presented a goodly Dish of *Turnips*, because it is very agreeable to our Natures; for a *Turnip* hath a round head, and the Anagram of *Puritan* is ATURNIP.[200]

No doubt, many of the young gentlemen in Milton's audience would have appreciated the joke.[201] Apart from the fact that a diet of turnips is also apt to cause flatulence, the presentation, comical from a more high Anglican point of view, of a mere artisan in the

---

[196] Joan Thirsk, *Food in Early Modern England: Phases, Fads, Fashions, 1500–1760* (London: Hambledon Continuum, 2006), 73. Referring to observations made in the botanist William Coles's *The Art of Simpling* (1656) and *Adam in Eden* (1657), Thirsk also notes that, by the middle of the century, 'leeks [were] now unacceptable to the snobs' (119).
[197] See Cockayne, *Hubbub*, 86, 93–94.
[198] See, for example, Thirsk, *Food in Early Modern England*, 78–81, on the views of the staunchly Calvinist physician James Hart (d. 1639). Even Hart, however, held meat to be the most nourishing and appropriate food humans could consume.
[199] In a passage of the earlier 'oration,' Milton had referred to the classical gods' occasional eating of beans and herbs, with an editorial gloss pointing out that '"to dine off vegetables" was proverbial for a simple meal' (CPW 1: 271).
[200] *New orders new, agreed upon by a parliament of Roundheads; avowed by Ananias Dulman, alias Prick-eares* (London 1642), quoted in CPW 1: 187. The supposed author's name is a telling one ('inane,' 'dull'), and his alias appears an (obscene) allusion to the fate of the Puritan hero, William Prynne, whose ears had been cut off in punishment in 1637 (an event Milton alludes to in one of his sonnets and, possibly, in *Lycidas*; see *SP*, 53, 72).
[201] When Milton, later in his speech, explains his own effeminate image as 'the Lady' of his College by pointing out that 'my hand has never grown horny with driving the plough, ... I was never a farm hand at seven or laid myself down full length in the midday sun,' some of the comedy is, most likely, derived from the fact that neither had most of his fellow students (CPW 1: 284).

incongruously 'high' role of preacher should be noted (a 'well-lung'd-long-breathed Cobler,' no less, i.e., roaring, long-winded, possibly stinking, and a shoddy workman). His confrontation with an equally 'low' (indeed subterranean) vegetable may also be perceived as comical.[202] As in Prolusion VI, the form and occasion of the discourse held are in comical opposition to their actual setting and its (bodily) implications. Turnips, just as leeks and onions, form part of a multi-faceted social–culinary–sensory hierarchy; they are classified – and themselves serve to 'classify' individuals – accordingly. As Milton's learned 'doctors, who can loosen the bowels,' might have pointed out, both leeks and onions were considered 'hot' foods in humoral terms, and would thus have matched the kind of 'sanguine' conviviality suggested by the context of the passage.[203] Ultimately, however, their effects are presented as symptoms, not as benefits; in the para-academic context of Prolusion VI, the scatological outweighs the medicinal.

The crudity of Milton's remarks – markedly different in tone from the first part of Prolusion VI – amplifies their comic potential, playing on the conventional opposition of food entering at the top/front of the body, and waste being excreted at the bottom/back – what Milton addresses as 'the posterior of the assembly.' In the parody of an academic oration presented in Prolusion VI, this obvious breach of rhetorical decorum (i.e., the use of a style appropriate to the occasion, surroundings, audience, speaker etc.) subverts the expectations addressed to a 'normal' academic oration.[204] Since all of the audience's perceptible 'contributions' to the imagined scene – the twin sounds of laughter and flatulence as well as the noxious smells accompanying both – are ultimately derived from their laughing and good cheer, they are presented as direct effects of the speaker's rousing oratory. This mechanism is both synaesthetic (audible/olfactory) and potentially self-reinforcing: the harder the laughs, the louder the farts, and vice versa. It is the sensory-discursive function of these images to draw attention to the embodied quality of the oratorical experience shared by the speaker and his audience. Milton's willingness to dwell on them with some relish cannot obscure the fact that they owe their humoristic effectiveness precisely to their fundamental (if culturally relative) 'distastefulness.'[205] The sensory discourse of the passage at hand is clearly not geared towards an appreciation of pleasant perceptions; nor is it, necessarily, deliberative or conceptual (although it does appear to draw, as indicated, on certain physiological and

---

[202] About the culinary and social valuations of animal or vegetable foods based on their placement on a vertical axis from underground to the sky, Niall Atkinson has remarked that, 'in general, the higher the animal lived, the more refined its taste. The same was true for the vertical difference that separated root vegetables from food that grew on trees' ('The Social Life of the Senses: Architecture, Food, and Manners,' in: *Cultural History of the Senses in the Renaissance*, ed. Roodenburg, 19–42, at 31).

[203] See Shapin, *Changing Tastes*, 9.

[204] The university context is arguably highlighted through the repeated references to 'the doctors,' i.e., academically trained physicians. Early in his speech, Milton had pointed to the incongruity between the content and the style of his oration: 'I am to-day to praise mirth in a serious style, which seems an arduous task indeed and far from easy' (CPW 1: 271).

[205] Erasmus had already advised schoolboys to drown out any farting sounds at table with intentional coughing; see Herman Roodenburg, 'Introduction: The Sensory Worlds of the Renaissance,' in: *Cultural History of the Senses in the Renaissance*, ed. Roodenburg, 2–17, at 15–16.

4.3 Prolusion VI ('Sportive Exercises ...')

socio-cultural preconceptions). It serves, rather, to disrupt expectations and seize the audience's attention through its evocation of the unpleasant, the inappropriate, and the ordinarily repressed. In this, above all, it is entertaining.[206]

In the subsequent passages of the speech, references to 'fiery Cerberus barking forth smoke' [fumido latratu ... favillas pleno ore egerit], 'that burning and all-consuming Furnace of ours belch[ing] forth [eructat] lurid flames and pour[ing] out [evolvit] coiling wreaths of smoke,' as well as to 'the fire-vomiting Chimaera [ignivomam *Chimæram*]' continue the string of coarse allusions to oral ejection/emissions begun in the passage on laughter and bad breath.[207]

Considering the possible failure of his attempts to win the audience's goodwill (and to offer them the pleasure promised at the outset of the 'oration'), the orator is already anticipating an equally perceptible effect, namely, the conventional sound of the audience's *dis*pleasure:

> Next, there must be no trace of that dreadful and infernal sound, a hiss [horrendus & tartareus ille sibili sonus], anywhere near this assembly; for if it is heard here to-day [si hic audiatur hodie], I shall believe that the Furies and Eumenides are skulking somewhere among you, that their snakes and serpents have found their way into your bosoms, and that the madness [Furores] of Athamas has come upon you [vobis inspiravisse].[208]

In evoking the sounds of disfavour, Milton again figures his audience as inwardly moved – albeit not, this time, by the influence of the speaker (who thus remains blameless), but rather by factors beyond his control, and wholly dissociated from his ability to teach (as in the 'oration'), move (as when he stirs up laughter and merriment), and delight (as is the declared purpose of both speeches). The 'Furores' 'breathed into' ('inspiravisse') the audience as they themselves hiss the orator must be attributed to some malicious higher power. In Elegy VII, we had encountered them as the passions caused by the sight of the beloved; here, they figure as the notional counterforce opposing the orator's efforts to win the audience's goodwill.

Following more punning remarks on furnaces, sparks, and fires, Milton returns to the culinary realm when he – having promised his audience a 'humble banquet' in the earlier part of his speech – elaborately imagines a banquet much more grandiose:

---

[206] Milton's concern with table manners in book 9 of *Paradise Lost* arguably bears greater conceptual import: on his description of (post)lapsarian eating as portraying a 'fall into [merely superficial] civility,' see Arvind Thomas, 'Milton and Table Manners,' *MQ* 40 (2006), 37–47.

[207] CPW 1: 279. According to an editorial note ad loc., the various references to Cerberus, the Furnace, and many more references to fire in the immediate context probably constitute puns on the names of two college servants (one of whom apparently was named Sparks). This would suggest a greater degree of embodiment than a reference to a mere mythological figure.

[208] At the instigation of Juno, Athamas, king of Thebes in Boeotia, suffered an episode of madness during which he mistook his wife and children for a lioness and her cubs, and killed one of his sons. He was later restored to his senses (see CPW, note ad loc.)

234 Chapter 4 – Milton's Prolusions

> To return to yourselves, gentlemen. That you may not regret having taken so difficult and dangerous a journey, here is a banquet ready prepared for you! Here are tables decked with all the luxury of Persia and loaded with rarest dainties, fit to delight and captivate the palate of a very Apicius [*Apicianiam* gulam oblectent & deliniant]. For it is said that eight whole boars were set before Antony and Cleopatra at a banquet, but behold, before *you* are set, as a first course, fifty fatted boars which have been pickled in beer for three years [quinquaginta saginatos apros cervisià conditaneà per triennium maceratos], and yet are still so tough [adhuc adeo callosos] that they may well tire out even our dog-teeth. Next, the same number of excellent oxen with magnificent tails [boves insigniter caudatos], just roasted before the door by our fiery servant; only I am afraid all the juice has gone into the dripping-pan. After them come as many calves' heads, fat and fleshy enough, but with so little brains [adeo pertenui cerebro] as not to be enough for seasoning. Then again a hundred kids, more or less, but too lean, I think, from over-indulgence in the pleasures of love [*Veneris* usu nimium macros]. We expected a few rams with fine spreading horns, but our cooks have not yet brought them from the town ... [209]

The list continues, with the focus shifting to birds ('long fattened on dough and flour and grated cheese') of an uncertain kind but 'as green in character as in plumage' and 'apt to produce a rash in those who eat them [scabiem ... comedentibus protrudunt] if our epicure [Comestor] is right.'[210] Next are 'an enormous turkey, so fat and stout after three years' fattening that one vast dish is scarcely big enough for it'; then 'some Irish birds' ('... I would ... warn you not to taste them [his itaque abstineatis moneo], for they are very apt ... to produce lice'); and, finally, 'several geese.' The latter 'have good loud voices noisier than the frogs of Aristophanes [ranis Aristophanicis vocaliores]. You will easily recognise them – in fact it is a wonder that they have not already betrayed themselves by hissing, and perhaps you will hear them in a moment [mirum enim est ni se jam prodiderint sibilando, statim fortasse audietis].'[211]

From the nature of Milton's descriptions, which now combine culinary/gustatory and auditory aspects, it appears highly likely that the speaker has individual groups from among his audience in mind, and is singling them out for lampooning, perhaps indicating their places in the auditorium as he proceeds. The 'animals' served have themselves been fattened or have even been 'pickled in beer for three years,' thus mirroring the gourmandising behaviour imputed to the audience earlier.[212] They make

---

[209] CPW 1: 280–81. In full, his description of it runs to two full pages (280–82), from which I quote in excerpt.
[210] As with the reference to pubic lice (discussed below), that to scabies has distinct sexual *and* tactile overtones. Cockayne lists the disease (caused by parasitic mites) among those emblematic of an altogether 'itchier' era (see *Hubbub*, 54–56 on the connections between itching, parasites, and venereal disease). Tillyard's less specific 'a rash' arguably transports similar connotations; CW has 'the mange,' i.e., scabies. A *comestor* is 'a glutton, gourmand' (*OLD*, 'comesor, comestor').
[211] CPW 1: 281.
[212] At the very outset of his 'oration,' Milton had already referred to his being filled by the pleasures of London 'usque ad saginam,' a phrase suggestive of animal fattening (see n.149 above).

themselves heard, and the audience 'will easily recognise' their voices once they start hissing (as geese are wont to do) – 'perhaps you will hear them in a moment.' Again, the bodily presence of the audience is emphasised by reference to their own audible contribution to the oratorical moment, at the same time as they are 'transformed,' by the speaker's rhetoric, into a series of animals to be eaten. Ultimately, it is the audience themselves who are being 'served' at this rhetorical banquet and who are being 'given a taste' of their own ridiculousness.

Apart from being gluttons, drunkards, and fools ('quite weak-brained'), the animal stand-ins for Milton's audience are also prone to sexual overindulgence. All of this is in keeping with the mediaeval and early modern association of (certain) animals – such as boars, bulls, rams, or apes – with sensuous and, in particular, with sexual indulgence and excess.[213] As Robert Burton sums up contemporary views on the matter,

> [lovers depraved by lust] become at last void of sense; degenerate into dogs, hogs, asses, brutes; as Jupiter into a Bull, Apuleius an Ass, Lycaon a Wolf ... For what else may we think those ingenious Poets to have shadowed in their witty fictions and Poems, but that a man once given over to his lust ... is no better than a beast.[214]

Beasts – and certain species, in particular – are defined by their sexuality, and humans who let their sexuality define them are no better than beasts. While Milton's teasing, of course, is 'all in good fun,' the transgressive and downright de-humanising potential of animal imagery such as his should not be underestimated. The mainstream of early modern views regarding the ascendancy of humans over animals was unequivocal: animals were inferior, and likening people to animals was, in general, no slight matter. In particular, Keith Thomas has argued, 'it was ... a serious matter when controversialists tried to dehumanise their opponents, as when ... Milton compared his enemies to "owls and cuckoos, asses, apes and dogs" ... In early modern England [such language] was a regular weapon of religious and political polemic. Animal analogies were equally conspicuous in popular satire and abuse.'[215] Seen within the wider cultural context of the oration, then, it is clear that Milton's jokes are meant to sting, if only a little.

In the passage from Prolusion VI, however, the beasts are dead, and are being served as food – will the association of certain kinds of animal with sexual licence still prove valid? The sexually sensuous dimension of Milton's passage is made explicit through reference to the (active) 'pleasures of love' ('*Veneris* usu'), but it is also present in the

---

[213] Milton draws on this tradition with regularity. See Wentersdorf, 'The "Rout of Monsters" in *Comus*'; Karl P. Wentersdorf, 'Images of "Licence" in Milton's *Sonnet XII*,' *MQ* 13 (1979), 36–42; and the various instalments of Karen Edwards's 'Milton's Reformed Animals: An Early Modern Bestiary,' *MQ* 39–43 (2005–2009), passim.
[214] Robert Burton, *The Anatomy of Melancholy*, ed. Holbrook Jackson (London: Dent, 1977), 737.
[215] See Thomas, *Man and the Natural World*, 30–50, quotation at 47. Thomas quotes from Milton's Sonnet 12 ('On the Detraction which followed upon my Writing Certain Treatises'), 4.

characterisation of the 'boves' as 'insigniter caudatos,'[216] in the full description of the turkey ('with such a long and horny beak [rostro eousque prælongo & eduro][217] that it could attack an elephant or a rhinoceros with impunity; but we have had it killed for today, just at the right moment, since it was beginning to be a danger to young girls and to attack women, like the large apes'), and that of the 'Irish birds,' whose 'lice' are actually 'pediculos inguinales' (literally, 'lice of the groin'), that is, pubic lice.[218] Even prior to overtly sexual associations, Karen Edwards has pointed out, lice in the early modern period were 'regarded as inseparable from the fallen human condition,' and their wide prevalence in the general population was, accordingly, taken for granted.[219] In a quite literal sense, moreover, an infestation with lice was considered the concretisation of human depravity. Thus, Sir Thomas Browne could comment in a discussion of spontaneous generation that it was 'the corrupt and excrementous humours in man' that were 'animated into Lice.'[220] The association of lice with the genital region was, however, a recurrent theme, and is present, for instance, in Hooke's generally marvelling description 'Of a Louse' in his *Micrographia*:

> ... it is troubled at nothing so much as at a man that scratches his head, as knowing that man is plotting and contriving some mischief against it, and that makes it oftentime sculk into some meaner and lower place, and run behind a mans back, though it go very much against the hair ...[221]

In the various animal images Milton employs in the passage quoted, then, sexually charged elements abound. They are represented, moreover, with a marked emphasis on tactility and (haptic) texture – observable in the reference to tough boar meat and the turkey's 'long and horny beak,' but arguably also in the reference to lice, whose feeding on their host would have caused intense itching. Ultimately, the passage fuses culinary, sexual, and tactile imagery, associating sexuality, in particular, with exhaustion, violence, and parasitic infestation – jokingly, no doubt, but with a distinct moral overtone (and in keeping, also, with Milton's subsequent self-presentation: as the chaste antithesis to his lecherous fellow students).

---

[216] *OLD* 'cauda': (1) 'the tail (of an animal ...)'; (2) 'the penis.' The translation 'oxen' in both CPW and CW matches culinary practice but arguably obscures the sexual connotation of Milton's wording, which 'bulls' might have brought out more clearly (Latin *bos* covers all, bulls, oxen, and cows).
[217] CW has '... and its beak is so very long and very hard that it can without fear of punishment enter into a contest with an elephant or a rhinoceros.'
[218] CPW 1: 281. See *OLD*, 'inguen': 'the part of the body around the sexual organs, groin. b) (used to denote the sexual organs themselves)' (2). It is unclear why Tillyard sanitises the passage; CW has the rather technical but at least complete 'they are very effective ... in the generation of inguinal lice.'
[219] Karen Edwards, 'Milton's Reformed Animals: An Early Modern Bestiary – L,' *MQ* 41 (2007), 223–251, surveys Milton's mentions of Lice at 245–46; quotation at 245.
[220] Thomas Browne, *Pseudodoxia Epidemica*, ed. Geoffrey Keynes (London: Faber & Faber, 1964), 143.
[221] Hooke, *Micrographia*, n. p. ('Observ. LIV: *Of a Louse.*').

The order of courses continues with eggs ('but they are "bad eggs"')[222] and fruit: 'we have only apples and medlars [mala & mespila], and they are gallows-fruit [infelicis arboris] and are not quite ripe [nec satis matura], so that it would be better to hang them up again to ripen in the sun.'[223] Again, a sexual connotation seems intended: both considering the traditional, para-biblical associations of apples from an 'unfortunate tree' – many years later, *Paradise Lost* will open with a reference to 'the fruit/Of that forbidden tree, whose mortal taste/Brought death into the world' (1.1–3) – and of medlars, popularly called 'open-arses,' and symbols of sexual depravity and promiscuity.[224] As earlier in the description of his 'banquet,' Milton connects eating and sex, and presents both in at least a doubtful light.

In closing this long culinary passage, Milton again addresses his hearers directly, calling them to action, and effectively bringing together several thematic strands in the sensory discourse of his speech: 'You see what we have provided, so I beg you to help yourselves to what you fancy [quibus palato sunt]. But I expect you will say that this banquet, like the nocturnal feasts offered by the devil to witches, is cooked without salt [nullo condiri sale], and I am afraid that you will go away hungrier than you came.'[225] In the sexual and gluttonous associations of the witches' sabbath, the theme of the immediately preceding passages is continued; in the speaker's mock-apologetic concession that his own 'feast' (i.e., speech) may have been 'cooked without salt' (i.e., wit), the earlier punning on *sal* as both 'wit' and 'salt' is taken up again, and is at last made explicit. As pointed out above, in fact, Prolusion VI has been identified as belonging to the seventeenth-century genre of mock-academic exercises or speeches in verse that were delivered at Cambridge and known as a 'salting.'[226] Prior to Roslyn Richek's analysis of Prolusion VI as a salting script, the first and only extant example known was the poet and playwright Thomas Randolph's 316-line poem titled 'Thom' Randolfs Salting,' preserved in a manuscript miscellany and first described by Fredson Bowers.[227] Randolph had entered Trinity College, Cambridge, in 1624, graduating BA in 1628, and was promoted to MA in 1632, whereupon he became a fellow of his college; he acted as 'Father' of the salting ceremony in 1627, during his third year at Cambridge, delivering

---

[222] Milton here alludes to an ancient Greek proverb ('From a bad crow a bad egg') by saying that the eggs served are *kakou korakos*, 'of a bad crow.' The same proverb is quoted in Prolusion I, see CPW 1: 225.

[223] CPW 1: 281–82.

[224] Compare, for instance, the reference in Shakespeare's *Romeo and Juliet* (2.136–41) to 'that kind of fruit/As maids call medlars, when they laugh alone' but more commonly called, as Mercutio instantly acknowledges, 'an open-arse' (because of their appearance). Medlars (not as common today as they were in pre-industrial times) ordinarily require a prolonged period of after-ripening during autumn and winter, a process referred to as 'bletting.' Apples were also commonly seen as causing indigestion and flatulence; see Cockayne, *Hubbub*, 94.

[225] CPW 1: 282.

[226] See Richek, 'Thomas Randolph's *Salting* (1627).' References to salting ceremonies have variously been found, but Randolph's and Milton's remain the two only known salting scripts. According to Anthony à Wood (who gives an account of his own Oxford salting as a freshman in 1647/8), the custom stopped at some point before the Restoration; see Anthony à Wood, *Athenæ Oxonienses* …, 4 vols (New York: Johnson Reprint Corporation, 1967 [1691–92]), I, 140.

[227] See Fredson Bowers, 'Thomas Randolph's *Salting*,' *MP* 39 (1942), 275–280.

the speech in rhymed iambic pentameter couplets now known as his 'Salting.' [228] From the opening of Randolph's speech, it is clear that actual salt, not just 'salty wit,' was associated with the ceremony:

> No salting here these many yeares was seene
> Salt hath w[th] vs long out of season bene.
> Whence then this plenty now? How have we more
> This yeare than other? hence p[r]ceeds o[r] store;
> o[r] Fleet hath late either frō France or Spaine
> (as y[e] nevves goes) y[e] salt Islands tane. (1–6)[229]

Randolph's reference is to a disastrous (for the English) naval expedition of 1627, whose target had been the Île de Ré and two neighbouring islands, off the western coast of France; Randolph calls them 'ye salt Islands.' In fact, as Bowers points out, one of the reasons for the English attack on the Île de Ré had been its valuable salt marshes and salt pits which, in the event of a successful conquest, would have provided not only salt for English consumption but also a considerable source of income to the English crown.[230]

In the concluding paragraphs of his speech, Milton humorously contrasts his role of 'Father' (of the ceremony) with his nickname, already mentioned: 'Some of late called me "the Lady."'[231] In particular, 'Lady' Milton asks, 'how does it happen that I have so quickly become a Father? ... that I should be thus suddenly changed from woman into man?'[232] In fact, he says, his supposed sex change is merely illusory: they have wrongly attributed the female gender to him not because of anything he had done but rather on account of the things he had *not* done, and of how this had influenced his appearance:

> It is, I suppose, because I have never brought myself to toss off great bumpers like a prize-fighter [quia Scyphos capacissimos nunquam valui pancratice haurire], or because my hand has never grown horny with driving the plough [quia manus tenendâ stivâ non occaluit], or because I was never a farm hand at seven or laid myself down full length in the midday sun [ad meridianum Solem supinus jacui]; or last perhaps because I never showed my virility in the way these brothellers do [nunquam me virum præstiti, eo modo quo illi Ganeones]. But I wish they could leave playing the ass [exuere asinos] as readily as I the woman.[233]

---

[228] See *ODNB*, 'Randolph, Thomas (bap. 1605, d. 1635).
[229] The full text of Randolph's poem is given by Roslyn Richek, 'Thom Randolfs Salting,' *ELR* 12 (1982), 113–126.
[230] See Bowers, 'Thomas Randolph's *Salting*,' 277–78.
[231] CPW 1: 283. On the critical potential of this particular aspect of Prolusion VI, see Tvordi, 'The Comic Personas of Milton's *Prolusion VI.*' The designation of the orator as 'Father' of the salting ceremony seems to have been traditional, as it also appears in Randolph's 'Salting.'
[232] CPW 1: 283.
[233] CPW 1: 284. In Milton's enumeration, Stephen Dobranski detects a 'bawdy list of possible explanations' for his nickname, translating more freely, '... because my hand has never hardened with gripping the shaft of a plough-handle, or because I have never lain down with someone,

4.3 Prolusion VI ('Sportive Exercises ...')

Never one to drink heavily, not used to working with his hands,[234] pale, and frugal to chaste: Milton's persona is defined, first and last, in opposition to the excessive behaviour he has been describing throughout the prolusion. In the reference to 'Ganeones,' in particular, the consistent conflation of sexual and culinary/gustatory excess familiar from earlier passages of the speech is taken up again: these may be culinary 'gluttons' or 'debauchees' in a wider sense of sensual, including sexual, excess.[235] By also figuring them as 'asses,' Milton makes a further – half-admonishing, half-joking? – statement about the sensuous licence (and the brutish ignorance) of his fellow students. Apart from associations of stupidity or stubbornness, persisting today, in the early modern imaginary, asses were among those animals associated with sexual excess.[236] Thus, according to various versions of the Circe legend, the sorceress was accompanied by an ass, a goat, a swine, and a dog, as four emblems of excessive, brute sensuality.[237] In the present context, both symbolic dimensions of the ass appear relevant: presumably neglecting their studies on account of their excessive revelling, the students referred to remain 'asinine'; but it is only in subordinating everything to the gratification of their senses that they may be called 'Ganeones' and 'asinos' at once.

Milton proceeds to point out the irrelevance of what others say about him – especially when they taunt him as 'the Lady': Demosthenes and Hortensius (another famous orator) were both mocked, respectively, as 'too little of a man' or as 'Dionysia the lyre-player.'[238] They had been above such taunts, Milton says, and so is he. Also, he has no desire to be called either 'Lord' or 'Lady,' and declares – in an early expression of republican sentiment? – that 'it is only in your courts and on your platforms that I have any ambition to lord it.' Consequently, Milton as speaker resigns himself to his role of the 'Father.' If he is the 'Father' of the festivities, then, according to the 'salting' traditions, the first-year students in the audience will be his sons: 'and I see that the jolly rascals acknowledge me as their father by a furtive nod.'[239] Tradition then demands that he introduce his sons to the congregated members of the college. Randolph had, after some theatrical deliberation, decided to introduce them as dishes to be served at the night's banquet – a clear parallel to Milton's Prolusion VI, whether the latter was delivered in 1628 or 1631.[240] Milton, for his part, had used the conceit of turning people into

---

supine in the midday sun.' (*The Cambridge Introduction to Milton* [Cambridge: Cambridge University Press, 2012], 9).

[234] Compare the depreciation of 'manual labour' in the allusions to Orpheus and Amphion above.

[235] See *OLD*, 'ganeo': 'a glutton, debauchee.' CW has 'these gluttons' instead of CPW's 'these brothellers'; the point seems to be that they are both.

[236] See Wentersdorf, 'Images of "Licence,"' esp. 38, on the ass of Milton's Sonnet 12 as a symbol of lechery (pointing to classical and biblical sources, as well as to Shakespeare's *A Midsummer Night's Dream*).

[237] See Wentersdorf, 'The "Rout of Monsters" in *Comus*,' 119.

[238] CPW 1: 284. An added barb in the case of Hortensius would have been that 'lyre-player' can be construed as a euphemism for 'prostitute' (frequently trained to play musical instruments in antiquity).

[239] CPW 1: 284. This suggesting, of course, that Milton had *not* been sexually continent – but had, to the contrary, been to bed with several of his fellow students' mothers.

[240] See the discussions of Bowers, 'Thomas Randolph's *Salting*,' 276; and, for the parallels between Randolph's text and Milton's, Richek, 'Thomas Randolph's *Salting* (1627).'

food not in his introduction of the freshmen but had employed it to lampoon other, more advanced students; this seems clear, for instance from his reference to 'fifty fatted boars which have been pickled in beer for three years.' When it is his turn to introduce the first-year students, however, he does appear to allude to Randolph's earlier 'Salting' (and conceivably to other salting scripts that have not survived):

> Do you ask their names? I should not like my sons to be given the names of various dishes [fericulorum], and to furnish forth a banquet for you [epulandos vobis], for that would be too like the savagery of Tantalus and Lycaon; and I will not give them the names of the parts of the body, lest you should think me the father of so many bits of men instead of whole ones; nor do I fancy calling them after the various kinds of meat [nec ad vinorum genera], lest in my remarks I should not keep to my muttons [sit *aprosdionyson*, & nihil ad *Bacchum*], as the proverb says.[241]

Instead, Milton announces, he will 'have them called after the Predicaments of Aristotle,' suggesting an identification of himself, the 'Father' as *Ens*, or Being.[242] This very scholarly joke is in marked contrast to the earlier passages of his speech (as well as, it appears, to the salting speeches of preceding years; perhaps he is poking fun at his own image as a hard-working, rather austere student (and a bit of a killjoy).

Milton's introduction of his new fellow students along Aristotelian lines – as well as their prose replies, which are lost – are included in the English verse of 'At a Vacation Exercise.' The English poem thus elaborates on Milton's own salting conceit. When, in the final part of his Latin prose oration, Milton resumes his defence of himself *as an orator*, however, the similarity to Randolph's 'Salting' is again conspicuous. In particular, Milton alludes to the failed invasion of the Île de Ré, and thus to the same military episode that had furnished the opening conceit for Randolph's speech. Milton, too, avails himself of the island's association with salt and links the reference to his earlier uses of *sal* and related terms to indicate (pungent or stale) wit:[243]

> As for my jokes [Quod ad Sales meos], I don't want them to have no bite in them, or you may well say they are hackneyed and stale [tritos, & veteres] ... Certainly

---

[241] CPW 1: 284. Both Tantalus and Lycaon were known as having offered human flesh to the gods (Tantalus had even slaughtered his own son, Pelops). In Milton's original Latin, the pun at the end of the passage ('kinds of meat ... keep to my muttons') actually refers to different kinds of wine ('vinorum genera') and the Greek and Latin idioms '*aprosdionyson*' and 'nihil ad *Bacchum*,' 'nothing to do with Bacchus,' that is, 'not on the point, irrelevant' (see translator's note ad loc.).
[242] This would make his 'Sons' the ten Aristotelian categories or predicaments (substance, quantity, quality, relation, place, time, action, passion, posture, and habit); see the note in CPW ad loc. and also the 'stage directions' and commentary for 'At a Vacation Exercise,' *SP* 78–83. Perhaps not wholly coincidentally, considering the critical thrust of the preceding parts of the speech, Milton's 'Father' as Aristotelian 'Ens' is wholly detached from this world of sense perception, while his 'sons,' related as they are to the 'accidents' of Aristotelian perceptual theory, are the ones immersed in it.
[243] See Richek, 'Thomas Randolph's *Salting* (1627).'

4.3 Prolusion VI ('Sportive Exercises ...') 241

on this occasion I could wish that my lot were the same as Horace's, and that I were a fishmonger's son [salsamentarii filius], for then I should have just the right amount of salt [tunc enim sales mihi essent ad unguem], and I should send you all off so nicely pickled [sale ita pulchre defricatos] that you would be as sick of salt water [non magis pœniteret salis petiti] as were those soldiers of ours who lately managed to escape from the island of Ré.[244]

In their respective translations of Milton's 'salis petiti,' neither Tillyard ('salt water') nor Smith ('the sought-for briny deep') take into account the ultimately commercial background of the Île de Ré expedition, as is suggested by their references to salt *water*. Given that context, however, the meaning of the phrase should probably be construed along the lines of 'I will rub you all in salt [i.e., I will lampoon you] so thoroughly that our soldiers who recently escaped from the Île de Ré would not have felt sorrier [than you will] *about the much-coveted salt* [they ultimately failed to capture from the French].'

Milton's multiple references to *sal* in this passage constitute the 'grand finale' to his consistent punning on its senses of 'wit' and 'salt' throughout Prolusion VI. Jokingly suggesting that he would be better furnished with 'sales' as the son of a lowly fishmonger (instead of an upwardly mobile scrivener), he again capitalises on the socio-cultural associations of a certain food. As with 'onions or leeks' before, the snide insinuation is partly based in smell: the stench of rotten fish was proverbial, and fishmongers were often on the receiving end of complaints about the bad odours exuded, if not by the wares on sale, then by fish scraps and cuttings.[245] At the same time, fish itself did not enjoy its former standing as a mandatory fasting dish; this was true, in particular, of salted fish, once a universal staple, but relegated by the seventeenth-century to the lower rungs of the socio-alimentary ladder: 'readily available common crude foods such as ... salted fish were at the bottom of the food hierarchy.'[246] In his fanciful designation of Horace's father as a fishmonger, Milton draws on these preconceptions, and fuses the diverse associations of salt into a single satirical barb: by subjecting them to the 'salting' remarks of his wit, the speaker will turn certain among his hearers into salted fish – ready for consumption but revolting to all but coarse palates.[247] On the level of early modern culture at large, such imagery might not have seemed ridiculous, *per se*; thus, the nonconformist theologian John Owen held that 'there is a salt in spiritual things,

---

[244] CPW 1: 285.
[245] See Cockayne, *Hubbub*, 98–99.
[246] Cockayne, *Hubbub*, 84; dried salt fish was falling out of favour from the seventeenth-century (98), a development comparable to the concurrent devaluation of leeks and onions. See also Thirsk, *Food in Early Modern England*, 265–70 on fish, esp. 269 on the low status of salt herring.
[247] CPW notes ad loc. that 'though Horace's father was a freedman and in poor circumstances, there is no evidence that he was a fishmonger.' It seems likely that Horace appears here as a fellow satirist (well stocked with 'sales') and that Milton's reference to a *salsamentarius* (lit., 'one who salts,' 'one who sells *salsamentum* [salted fish],' i.e., a fishmonger, *OLD*) is for the sake both of the pun and the distinctly low-class associations of both the salesman and his wares.

whereby they are conditioned and made savoury unto a renewed mind ...'[248] As English sources of the period suggest, there even existed the converse notion that, 'spiritually, preaching was "salt" that made hearers tasty to God.'[249] However, in conjunction with the sum total of his remaining imagery in Prolusion VI – and perhaps even drawing on such other, more serious applications of the 'salting and eating' image in public discourse (a characteristic his prolusion shares with preaching) –, Milton's final variation on the theme of wit is salt unites the critical and the coarse impulses struggling for dominance throughout the text.

In concluding, Milton alludes to the dual nature of his speech, which has been both a ribald student entertainment and, at the same time, the 'edifying' address of a 'Father' to his 'sons.'[250] The latter is a function of his speech which Milton does not, I suggest, disavow completely; still, he fuses punning references to intemperance with half-serious, half-joking admonition towards the end of his speech. Thus, he urges, by alluding both to his own role of 'Father' and to Liber (often called 'Liber pater,' i.e., 'free, licentious Father'), the Roman god of wine: 'let not my sons [liberique mei] worship Father Liber [liberum], if they wish me to be their 'Father.'[251] Having arrived at the end of his Latin oration, Milton announces what is to come (the English verses 'At a Vacation Exercise') and once more asks for the undivided attention of his hearers – or rather, his listeners: 'Now I will overleap the University Statutes as if they were the wall of Romulus and run off from Latin into English. Lend me attentive ears and minds, you whom such things amuse [Vos quibus istæc arrident aures atque animos nunc mihi attentos date].'[252]

***

The second part of Prolusion VI ends as it had begun: by highlighting the vocal–aural connection between orator and audience. As my discussion has indicated, however, this aspect of the prolusion – its conceptualisation of discourse as embodied, vocal speech – forms just one strand of its rich sensory discourse. The same references to speech and hearing – and various others to other senses – pattern the interaction between the speaker and his audience, which is upheld by the orator's voice on the one side, and the audience's mixed contribution of applause, laughter, almost deadly glances and hissing, not to mention bad breath and potential flatulence, on the other. Apart from the voice of the orator as heard by his audience, the other main constituent of sensory discourse in both the 'oration' and the 'prolusion' is a variety of sensory references; to different extents, Milton refers to all five senses. While the sensory-discursive categories of embodied speech and (above all) taste are present throughout the text, there is a clear shift in emphasis from an initial concern with the oratorical towards a later focus on the culinary sphere. If Milton's use of sensory imagery is persistent, however, it is not necessarily

---

[248] Owen quoted in William J. Wainwright, 'Jonathan Edwards and His Puritan Predecessors,' in *Spiritual Senses*, eds Gavrilyuk/Coakley, 224–40, at 229.
[249] Milner, *Senses and the English Reformation*, 113–14.
[250] 'I want to avoid being heavily sententious in my advice to you, my sons, so as not to seem to have taken more pains in educating than in begetting you' (CPW 1:286).
[251] Translation adapted from CW 13: 245.
[252] CPW 1: 286, perhaps suggesting that English was to Latin as salted fish was to finer food.

consistent across the component parts of the prolusion. A synopsis of distinct elements in the sensory discourse of Prolusion VI will indicate some of the functions they serve in the different parts of the text.

Among the sensory-discursive elements of the prolusion not immediately relating to the speaker–hearer relationship of orator and audience, Milton's diverse references to food offered for the audience's consumption are the most conspicuous. As I have indicated, these serve a parodic and/or transgressive function in both parts of the speech, albeit in demonstrably different ways. In the 'oration,' with its strong focus on the speaker–audience relationship (expressed through laughter as well as through diverse other kinds of positive or negative influence), even Milton's mention of a 'small banquet' ('conviviolum') is made in the context of the speaker's offering it to 'so polished and refined an audience [tam denique tersis & delicatis auribus],' with an obvious focus on their ears rather than their palates. The contents of this 'banquet,' the speaker calls his 'frivolities [nugis].' At this point of the speech, they are firmly presented within the general framework of the ideas are food metaphor: even such (notionally edible) frivolities may, at times, be worthy of consideration, as the thesis of the prolusion states; they may play their role even within the serious discourse of philosophers and statesmen. In this first part of his speech, Milton nonetheless subverts the conventions surrounding a serious academic oration with its claim to epistemic authority. What he himself communicates, after all, is that a suspension of high seriousness every once in a while – the alternation of *labor* and *voluptas* described at the outset of his speech – ultimately benefits both, study and pleasure. Thus, the pleasure of foolishness is justified by reference to the (renewed) pleasure of learning – this is the 'foolish wisdom' of the 'oration,' and at the same time a vindication of pleasure within bounds.

In the later 'prolusion,' by contrast, most of Milton's references to the culinary and gustatory domains provide not so much a conceptual-metaphorical justification of the orator's role – IDEAS ARE FOOD, and he is the purveyor of both – but rather a comical leitmotif taken through variations: first as the shared bodily basis for coarse references to bad breath and flatulence (both construed as 'vocal' and olfactory at once); then as the structuring element in a long catalogue of 'courses' in an imagined banquet, in which some of those present figure as 'meats' to be served. Both versions invert the partially fraught relationship between speaker and hearers as Milton had presented it in the 'oration': there, the speaker had been at the mercy of an either hostile or gracious audience, either half-killed by their sharp looks or revived and inspired by their favour. Now, it is the speaker who first exposes the grotesqueness of the assembled student body through his various remarks relating to 'the posterior of the assembly,' then rhetorically dresses and serves individuals and groups from the audience for the remaining hearers' notional consumption (i.e., amusement).

Where the first part of the prolusion had taken regular, serious academic exercises as the basis of its oratorical burlesque, the second part is patterned on the actual banquet that was part of the salting celebrations (and which had apparently already taken place by the time Prolusion VI was delivered). There, the students had feasted; in Milton's hyperbolical transmutation of the scene, they figure as animals both fattened and feasted upon. At the most fundamental level, the sensory discourse of Prolusion VI, in drawing hearers' attention to the acts of speaking/listening and non-verbal communication as in its repeated references to matters of digestion, serves to emphasise the corporeal materiality of both orator and audience. In the case of the audience, this *reductio ad corpus* is emphatically exceeded twice, first by de-humanisation (members of the audience are presented as mere animals, governed by sensuality), then by suggestions of disembodiment and dismemberment (these animals have been killed and cooked). In several steps, the young scholars in the audience – not just Aristotle's 'rational animals' but budding intellectuals, we may assume – are demoted first to the degree of brute beasts and then placed on the level of inanimate nutrients. This not only implies, in two ways at once, the audience's being made subject to the low-ranking senses of touch and taste; it also argues their downgrading on the scale of nature. To conceive of the 'chain of being' in terms of consumption and nourishment was no novel idea. As Bacon had put it, 'nourishment should be of an inferior nature and a simpler substance than the body nourished. *Plants* are nourished with the Earth and Water, *Living Creatures* with Plants, *Man* with living Creatures.'[253] In *Paradise Lost*, Milton himself would have Raphael point out to Adam during a discussion of angelic eating habits how, in a manner rather similar to the ingestion of food by angels and men,

> whatever was created, needs
> To be sustained and fed; of elements
> The grosser feeds the purer, earth the sea,
> Earth and the sea feed air, the air those fires
> Ethereal, and as lowest first the moon ... (5.414–18)[254]

Long before *Paradise Lost*, the satirical banquet of Prolusion VI also draws on the idea that the hierarchical relationships conventionally observed within nature correspond to the ordering of the food chain. By connecting this to the equally conventional hierarchy of the senses – animals are in thrall to their sensuality, and especially to the lower senses of touch and taste – Milton effects a thoroughgoing hierarchisation of the relationship between the speaker and his audience (those spoken to *and* those spoken about): in the imagined environment of the prolusion, which sets out to demonstrate that 'the creations of the intellect are superior to manual skill,' the well-spoken and witty eat the mute and dull.

From Milton's repeated references to the palate (*palatum, gula*) and to Apicius, the legendary gourmet of Roman antiquity, and from his punning remark about the old 'bearded Masters[']' rejection of his 'insipidos sales,' it is clear that his culinary imagery always includes gustatory associations. Because of their predominance over purely alimentary significations, moreover, it can clearly be said that, in deploying sensory discourse to stimulate his hearers' imagination, Milton addresses their sense of taste first, their already glutted stomachs second.[255] This impression is strengthened if we

---

[253] From the translation of Bacon's *Historia Vitae et Mortis* as *History of Life and Death*, contained as an appendix in *Sylva Sylvarum*, 271–340, quotation at 289. Marjara quotes a later translation of this passage in *Contemplation of Created Things*, 54.

[254] Marjara considers the notion that 'the grosser feeds the purer' one of a few 'keystone ideas' structuring *Paradise Lost* (see *Contemplation of Created Things*, 36).

[255] The two Latin terms convey different emphases: whereas *palatum* implies a discerning, naturally able or well-trained taste, its tasting deliberate and situated in the mouth (*OLD*, 'palatum':

4.3 Prolusion VI ('Sportive Exercises ...') 245

consider the kind of meal imagined by the speaker, which is a banquet or feast arranged for pleasure, not primarily, perhaps, for sustenance. In this, the two banquets of the night – one actual, one imaginary – resemble the prolusion delivered at the 'vacation exercise' in its character as the pleasure-oriented version of a genre and an event (the academic oration and exercise, respectively) otherwise geared towards utility – namely towards that impartation of knowledge which, in the wider frame of the IDEAS ARE FOOD metaphor, corresponds to eating for sustenance.[256]

Since the culinary imagery of Prolusion VI – despite its gustatory focus – ultimately implies both, eating *and* tasting, it proves an ideal repertory of metaphors for negotiating the fundamental duality of *labor* and *voluptas* introduced at the outset of the speech. In this, 'pleasure,' specifically, plays more than one role: on the one hand, it corresponds to the prolusion's valuation of 'taste' (i.e., wit or style) over 'nutritional value' (i.e., knowledge imparted); on the other hand, its negative twin – excessive sensuality, i.e., an excess of pleasure – is subjected to critical examination and lampooning at the hands of a speaking subject who describes himself as 'never [having] showed [his] virility in the way these brothellers do.'

Part of the critical potential of Milton's culinary imagery is derived from the conventional socio-cultural associations of certain foods (onions and leeks, apples and medlars, salted fish), ascribing to them a 'low' status on account of their effects on the body, their symbolical significance, their spatial associations, or quite simply their ubiquity and availability to the population at large. As a result, the two hierarchies previously referred to (that of the senses and that of the human–animal segment of the food chain) are joined by a third, expressing the ordering potential of social distinctions, and the hierarchy of comestibles, in particular, is supplemented, as fish and vegetable foods take their rightful place below prestigious meat and different kinds of fowl. Such pre-gustatory considerations would, arguably, have been of high significance for a culture in which, prior to much later advances in transport and refrigeration, 'freshness was not always of prime consideration when judging food quality.' This does not mean, of course, that early modern noses were stopped, taste buds or fingers were numbed by conventional significations; quite the opposite, as 'reactions [to food] were based on lifelong experience and relied on all the senses.'[257] Over the course of his two-part ora-

---

'(1) the roof of the mouth, palate esp. (b) with reference to the process of eating and drinking ... (2) capacity for appreciating food and drink, sense of taste, palate'), *gula* suggests an epicurean indulgence halfway between connoisseurship and gluttony: its tasting *is* swallowing: *OLD*, 'gula': (1) the throat with its passages; ... the oesophagus, gullet; (2a) (regarded as the seat of the appetite), (b) (regarded as the seat of taste).' On Apicius and the recipes attributed to him, which make use of both luxury and common foods, see Andrew Wallace-Hadrill, 'The Senses in the Marketplace: The Luxury Market and Eastern Trade in Imperial Rome,' in: Jerry Toner (ed.), *A Cultural History of the Senses in Antiquity* (London: Bloomsbury, 2014), 69–89, at 75–78.

[256] Regarding one of the dishes of 'poultry' he announces, the speaker even jokes that these birds are 'lacking in solid nutriment [nihil in se habeant solidi nutrimenti]' (CPW 1: 281).

[257] Cockayne, *Hubbub*, 86, also sensibly suggesting that, as today, 'individual experiences led to personal preferences within culturally proscribed limits,' while 'foods with unpleasant side-effects such as flatulence, indigestion or bad breath were ... avoided.'

tion, Milton, too, draws on references to all the senses – including the sounds of the body and even interoception – to make his rhetorical banquet palpable to the audience.

The third and final series of culinary images and wordplay spans both the 'oration' and the 'prolusion.' It comprises Milton's references to the speaker's wit, or 'salt,' a fundamental requirement of the 'salting' ceremony for which the speeches were composed. Various parallels between Milton's Prolusion VI and Randolph's 'Salting' have been pointed out by Richek, among them their focus on heavy drinking (characteristic of the occasion on which both were delivered) and, most strikingly, their shared description of individuals or groups from among their fellow students as different foods or dishes.[258] On the whole, Milton appears to be drawing heavily on Randolph's earlier text as well as, possibly, on a tradition of other salting scripts. What is striking in the context of this book, however, is how Milton's almost conventional references to 'salty wit' and notionally 'anthropophagic' satire – conventional within the framework of the 'salting' tradition– tie in with the wider sensory discourse of the speech, and thus contribute to a dense web of references to sensory exchanges between orator and audience.

In any case, in Prolusion VI Milton manages to combine both, an association of his own text with the salting tradition revived and shaped by Randolph *and* a dissociation from that tradition: the first aspect is clear from his own extensive revival of Randolph's anthropophagic trope in parts of his speech and from his persistent use of bawdy allusion; the second, from his ostensible rejection both of the trope and the tradition (of gluttony, heavy drinking, etc.) towards its conclusion. Milton thus approaches the salting tradition from two sides at once: one affirmative, one critical. As both the affirmation of sensuous pleasure (the *voluptas* of his opening) and the critique of sensual indulgence relate to the sphere of the senses, Milton may employ sensory discourse in both 'modes' of his speech. In the end, Milton appears to come down on the side of – intermittent, reflected – pleasure, and thus to uphold the thesis of the prolusion that 'Sportive Exercises *on occasion* are not inconsistent with philosophical Studies.' Indeed, as his stated intention of wanting to 'play the wise fool for a while' ('aliquantisper *morosophōs* nugari') suggests, a 'sportive exercise' such as Prolusion VI may very well *include* philosophical reflection.

The most versatile element of Milton's sensory discourse throughout the text is the one conceptual metaphor prominent in the generally more frivolous second part of Prolusion VI: in taking up the conventional notion that WIT IS SALT, Milton activates a variety of connotations: both elements of the metaphor indicate a high value/scarcity, actual or intellectual 'savouriness' (and sharpness), and both 'give "life" or "character" to a person or thing,' as the *OLD* has it. Ultimately, then, the notion of *sal* as both ingenuity and an ability to present circumstances and people in novel and surprising ways (e.g., through punning, double entendre, or metaphor) points to the power of wit to '[set] things before the eyes' (or ears, tongue, or nose), much in the way Aristotle had claimed was characteristic of metaphor as a means to knowledge. As becomes clear, WIT IS SALT belongs in the same conceptual-metaphorical milieu as IDEAS ARE FOOD. And while wit, on its own, is not tantamount to knowledge, its absence leaves the best ideas hard to

---

[258] See Richek, 'Thomas Randolph's *Salting* (1627),' for a detailed discussion. Consider also the conceptual parallels to the twentieth- and twenty-first-century phenomenon of the 'comedy roast' (I am grateful to Francis Ipgrave for pointing this out to me).

4.3 Prolusion VI ('Sportive Exercises ...')

digest – its contributions to Milton's oratorical performance include both mirth and argumentative force. In that they allow him to showcase his wit, even Milton's cruder culinary tropes feed into the same conceptual-metaphorical paradigm of IDEAS ARE FOOD. The same conceptual metaphor, we recall, is operative in a key passage, already quoted, from book 7 of *Paradise Lost*.[259]

There, the archangel Raphael admonishes Adam, in an image deeply resonant with the adolescent humour of Prolusion VI, that

> knowledge is as food, and needs no less
> Her temperance over appetite, to know
> In measure what the mind may well contain;
> Oppresses else with surfeit, and soon turns
> Wisdom to folly, as nourishment to wind (7.126–30)

In following his argument for the occasional permissibility of 'sportive exercises' with the description of a banquet of folly seasoned by wit, the young Milton of Prolusion VI reverses the process outlined by Raphael, turns gluttons themselves into food for thought and – making good on his promise of '*morosophōs* nugari' – folly into wisdom. In polemicising, at the same time, against excessive sensuality and sexual licence, he not only defends himself against the teasing of his peers but, ultimately, salvages his own rhetorical performance from the imputation of 'mere' folly.

From the outset of Prolusion VI, when it is posited explicitly by the speaker, the central opposition of the speech – that between *labor* and *voluptas* – is put to work, in individual images – such as the allusions to Orpheus and Amphion – but also in the general structure of its two parts: first, and fundamentally, as the 'sportive exercise' of the prolusion subverts an established academic form (i.e., preference is given to 'pleasure'); then, and more subtly, as that subversion itself – the 'salting' tradition – is employed to criticise students' excessive sensuality and – somewhat anachronistically put – aggressive machismo (i.e., preference is given to intellectual 'toil'). With this double subversion of academic and para-academic conventions, Prolusion VI performs two of the traditional functions of rhetoric, *delectare* and *docere*. As I have indicated in my discussion, both relate to the sensory discourse of the speech, and both are accomplished through the prolusion's efforts to make the audience laugh. The remaining, third rhetorical function (*movere*) rests on an appeal to the passions, a connection which is also made explicit in Prolusion VI. In Milton's anticipatory description of his hearers' side-splitting, spleen-rousing laughter, the speaker's twin concerns of his audience's embodied perception and impassioned reaction are equally present. In being, first and foremost, geared towards making listeners laugh, the sensory discourse of Prolusion VI contributes in equal measure to the three rhetorical functions fulfilled by the text. While the sense of taste, represented in the prolusion's various culinary images, governs its

---

[259] *Paradise Lost*, of course, was nowhere near written at the time Prolusion VI was composed (even considering that the earliest conceptual traces of the later epic among Milton's surviving notes reach as far back as 1640). I am not suggesting any direct connection between the two texts but rather a shared relation of both texts to that sub-strand of sensory discourse covered by the conceptual metaphor IDEAS ARE FOOD.

overall structure and satirical-critical purpose, all the other senses are drawn upon in Milton's imaginative exploration of the speaker–hearer relationship. Ultimately, it is the specific occasion for which Prolusion VI was composed, and which allowed for both sensory and anti-sensual rhetoric, that accounts for the prominence and variety of its sensory discourse.

4.4 Pre-Ludes to Knowledge
Milton's Prolusions as Sensory-Rhetorical Showpieces

Although Milton's prolusions are, by generic default, deliberative texts, their sensory discourse has emerged as not exclusively — perhaps not even predominantly – deliberative. In fact, the preceding discussion of prolusions I, II, and VI has indicated that, going beyond conceptualising references to the 'intellectual' senses of sight and hearing, these texts not only contain references to *all* the senses, but also run the full gamut of sensory discourse as outlined in Chapter 2, combining illustrative/descriptive and deliberative/conceptual uses.

On the whole, Prolusion I has been shown to represent the strongest focus on knowledge and, despite some banter – all the prolusions contain *some* elements making light of the high seriousness of the academic speaking situation – spares no effort to argue its point. In particular, Milton presents arguments ranging from the classical tradition to contemporary everyday experience. The latter elements not only make his speech relatable to its original audience but also – seen from today's perspective – ensure that Prolusion I as a text transports at least some of the sensory-cultural context of its composition.

The sensory discourse of Prolusion II is of a much more sceptical bent, disclaiming from the outset the phenomenal truth of the harmony of the spheres, and even only allowing its conceptual application after ostentatious comic hedging. (By contrast, the earlier Prolusion I had not questioned the fundamental significance of the micro-/macrocosmic 'eye of day' metaphor at all.) It is striking, moreover, that Prolusion II – despite its auditory topic – is the least concerned of the three texts discussed with sound as an actual perceptual phenomenon implied by (the) speech. This is true in comparison with Prolusion VI, in particular, but even Prolusion I bespeaks a greater interest in the sounds produced by the orator (and the *oratorculi*) or in the stillness of night. Apart from the atypical Prolusion VI – delivered not as a regular academic exercise but as the parody of one –, Prolusion II is the speech most plainly geared towards entertaining its audience with conceits and surprising twists. In that Prolusion I has most recently been dated to the beginning of Milton's time at university, whereas II and VI are considered products of his graduate studies, this contrast between Prolusion I on the one hand, and prolusions II and VI on the other, may also be indicative of a greater self-assurance of Milton as a mature student.[260] In a number of respects, then, both as regards its topic and the speaker's chosen approach to that topic, Prolusion II takes a middle ground between prolusions I and VI.

---

[260] For these dating considerations see, again, Campbell/Corns, *John Milton*, 37. Lewalski, *Life of John Milton*, 28–29, dates all three prolusions to Milton's third year at university.

If Prolusion VI is atypical in both form and occasion and unabashedly farcical to boot, is has been shown to reflect on the delicate interplay of (bodily) pleasure and (intellectual) labour, and thus to transmit, in its extended consideration of sensual licence, a kind of knowledge, occasioned by the senses (and what are perceived as their defects) but not immediately derived from them. This is also true, by extension, of the moral deliberations of prolusions I and II, where the truth of what is said is argued by reference to, but not necessarily on the experiential basis of, sensory experience.

If we relate these differences between the three texts to the three Ciceronian functions of rhetoric, it becomes clear that, while all three prolusions quite expressly function as rhetorical exercises, they each aspire to fulfil the respective 'offices of the orator' to varying degrees: while *docere* – the academic or moral instruction of the audience – is most explicitly pursued in Prolusion I, disclaimed yet still carried out in Prolusion II, and re-introduced through the back door – the 'posterior of the assembly' – in Prolusion VI, the purpose of *delectare* is foregrounded through meta-rhetorical remarks in prolusions II and VI (about the 'open hand' of rhetoric and the cheerful occasion of the speech, respectively), yet it is not absent from Prolusion I with its mythological and quasi-poetical digressions. The function of *movere*, finally, is emphasised with gusto in the references to the passions in Prolusion VI, but it is equally present in the appeals to the more worrying aspects of night in Prolusion I and, conceivably, even in the semi-pathos of Milton's lament for the human condition at the conclusion of Prolusion II – serious and moving in content yet situated in close textual proximity to jokes about Arion's Dolphin and sky goats skipping to the music of the spheres. In all three functions of rhetoric, I have argued in this chapter, sensory discourse, with its power to evoke and 'set before the eyes' experiences relating to the orator's theme, played a central role.

As has also become clear, the rhetorical orientation of the prolusions – toward teaching, delighting, and moving an audience – forms just one of two tightly interlocking facets of those texts. The other is a constant reflection on their oratorical setting (i.e., on their being written for actual delivery before that audience). Here, too, the prolusions make a distinctive contribution to Milton's sensory discourse: in that they repeatedly focus on the direct, embodied interaction between the speaker and his audience, they express a distinct appreciation of the senses as a means to communication. This aspect figures much more strongly in these prose orations than it does in the elegies, where it is only implicit in the elegiac speaker's 'song.' Again, this communicative aspect relates not only to its most obvious sensory channel – the orator's vocal speech and his listeners' audition – but also includes 'hostile,' 'sharp' glances passing between the two parties, not to mention, in the case of Prolusion VI, diverse smells, a variety of body sounds, metaphorical touch (both healing and harmful), even an imagined ritual feasting on parts of the audience. That many, if not most of these sense-impressions are imaginary, evoked by the speaker in the form of (ostensible) apprehensions or downright 'make-perceive' – imagining some of those present as animals about to be eaten – does not detract from their status and importance as functioning elements of sensory discourse, employing appeals to the sensory sphere as a means to evoke sensations and communicate perceptions.[261]

A considerable proportion of the perceptions communicated thus relate to the sphere of morals, evaluating and, at times, condemning certain kinds of behaviour. In all three prolusions (most obviously, again, in Prolusion VI), such reproaches serve a double purpose of exhortation *and* (teasing) entertainment. However, whereas prolusions I and II simply posit their more or less specific, more or less hard-hitting sensory-moral grievances – 'night is the time of criminals and lechers' and 'humanity as a whole is depraved and thus deaf to the music of the spheres,' respectively –, Prolusion VI presents its moral critique as an integral part of its sensory discourse: the depravity and lacking academic commitment of at least some students (those opposed to the 'Lady'/'Father' speaker) are not only asserted but, as it were, *staged*, and represented at length in the second half of the speech. This does not make the prolusion any less enjoyable, even for those so addressed, but the speaker's moral critique should not be dismissed as mere banter; its fundamental validity is established not least by its sense-based animal imagery, which is in keeping with prevailing socio-moral norms.

In the texts discussed in this chapter, sensory discourse performs a variety of functions, some of which are familiar from the discussion so far: in the tradition of the 'Theme on Early Rising,' it serves to embellish and put certain scenes 'before the eyes,' but by the same token also to surprise, entertain and possibly disgust the respective audiences, all in the guise – and with the oblique goal – of teaching them a lesson. All things considered, Milton's recourse to the sensory sphere makes a major contribution to his earliest prose and, in particular, to the characteristic oscillation between truth and play implicit in the prolusion genre: here, *jucundissima philosophia* is placed right next to caustic or poignant words that are 'quasi per lusum dicta,' letting epistemogenic and ludic elements intermingle. What McEuen calls the 'serious or pseudo-serious discussions' of the prolusions should thus be read both ways: as making light of a conventionally serious form, but also as doing so by telling serious jokes. With a view to Milton's subsequent writing, specifically, these texts have been 'pre-ludes' to more momentous rhetorical and polemic engagements, but they also form one source of his continuing interest in the relationship between sensory knowledge and sensual temptation. The trace of their sensory discourse will carry on into his later poetry and prose.

---

[261] I borrow the phrase 'make-perceive' from Robert Briscoe, who, however, uses it in a more strictly technical sense to refer to a psycho-phenomenological model of cognitive 'top-down imagining,' in which existing mental imagery is superimposed on sensory (specifically, visual) impressions. See his 'Vision, Action, and Make-Perceive,' *M&L* 23 (2008), 457–97, as well as the more recent 'Superimposed Mental Imagery: On the Uses of Make-Perceive,' in: Fiona Macpherson/Fabian Dorsch (eds), *Perceptual Memory and Perceptual Imagination* (Oxford: Oxford University Press, 2018), 161–85.

5. Sensory Discourse in the Proems of *Paradise Lost*

Paradise Lost forms, in many senses, the culmination of Milton's writing life up to that point. This was certainly how he himself presented it, referring to the diffidence with which he had been 'long choosing, and beginning late' (*PL* 9.26) on his epic, whose subject – designated over the years for a variety of genres – had been on his mind since the early 1640s. In the ten-, then twelve-book versions of 1667 and 1674, Milton merged poetic and political, historical, (natural-)philosophical and theological considerations, and thus topics which had preoccupied him, with varying intensity over time, his whole life. *Paradise Lost* also presents a culmination of sorts in the development of Milton's sensory discourse, bringing together elements originally associated with all those different tributaries to the epic, the original 'omnivorous genre.'

A full and exhaustive sensory reading of *Paradise Lost* would merit a book-length study of its own, but my concern here is to outline the various roles played by sensory discourse in different kinds of texts from different stages of Milton's career, as well as to indicate how sensory discourse could function as a conceptual conduit between those different texts (and kinds of texts), written at diverse times and for divergent purposes. In this chapter, therefore, I will confine myself to a discussion of the four proems interspersed throughout *Paradise Lost*. These not only constitute a link between Milton's earlier, non-epic poetry and *Paradise Lost*, but also contain the sensory leitmotifs of Milton's epic, and thus offer a glimpse of the poem's sensory discourse at large. Not least, the blind speaker of the poems has been plausibly read as a persona closely related to the blind author of the poem. The proems thus allow for a degree of comparison between the epic speaker of *Paradise Lost* and the oratorical persona of Milton's early prolusions.

The four proems of *Paradise Lost* – prefixed to books 1, 3, 7, and 9 – contain as in a nutshell Milton's narrative and conceptual agenda for the respective books, as well as providing both a 'general roadmap' to his poem and a sort of running commentary on the progress of its epic design as a whole. When Roger H. Sundell identifies three main subjects present in all of the proems – 'the poet, his muse, and the poem' –, this already points to three possible foci for sensory analysis.[1] Indeed, the relationship between the poet-speaker and the Muse, as it is presented in these 'invocations' (as they have also been called), provides a first point of reference. In particular, it is the voice of the speaker, addressing and 'invoking' the Muse, which forms a vital part of the sensory discourse of *Paradise Lost*, both highlighting and deliberating on the vocal quality of

---

[1] See Roger H. Sundell, 'The Singer and his Song in the Prologues of *Paradise Lost*,' in: John Max Patrick/Roger H. Sundell (eds), *Milton and the Art of Sacred Song* (Madison, Wisc.: University of Wisconsin Press, 1979), 65–80, quotation at 67. See also the discussion of Milton's self-representation in the proems in Fallon, *Milton's Peculiar Grace*, 210–32.

the epic's notional 'song.' Sundell further argues for a separation between the 'voices' of Milton's epic persona in the proems (the 'singer') and the rest of the poem (where this persona figures as the 'narrator').[2] Following up on this thought, I will consider the explicitly singing voice of Milton's proems a more or less distant descendant of the explicit 'singer' of Elegy V, and of the explicit oratorical personae put forward in the prolusions, where they are likened to bards or singers on more than one occasion. John Hale, in his discussion of different 'voices' in the epic – the poet's, Satan's, the voices of heaven, Adam's and Eve's in their innocent and experienced varieties, etc. –, has underlined one important aspect of these voices that has also formed the basis of my discussion of Milton's sensory discourse so far:

> Whatever else 'voice' may mean, the discussion of it should keep contact with how voices speak. It should stay aware that voices are to be heard; that, indeed, Milton composed out loud; and that, for their greater pleasure, readers read him aloud. Milton keeps faith, by conviction and habit and the misfortune of blindness alike, with epic's original orality.[3]

Whatever is spoken (or sung) in *Paradise Lost*, in other words, should be conceived of as expressed by actual, embodied vocality. This is all the more true as, I argue, the generally dense sensory discourse of *Paradise Lost* as a whole – i.e., across and beyond the proems – continuously reinforces readers' construal of the voices presented in the poem as actually grounded in (and subject to) embodied experience.

Within the proems, specifically, the express vocality of the speaker contrasts, as Hale pointed out, with his blindness, yet also with a special kind of inner or 'alternative' vision. Whether or not we feel comfortable with the observation that 'the blind bard of the epic may recall Homer, but he undoubtedly is Milton' himself, the speaker's experience of blindness, similar to that reflected earlier in some of Milton's most searching sonnets, clearly forms the negative perceptual backdrop to the sensory discourse of the proems at large, whereas the focus on embodied vocality forms its positive foundation.[4] In the following sections, I will discuss the four proems in turn, focusing on the (self-)presentation of the epic speaker and the relationship between the positive and negative potentials of voice and blindness, as well as on possible connections between the sensory discourse of the proems, that of the wider epic, and their shared roots going back to Milton's earliest writing.

---

[2] See Sundell, 'Singer and his Song,' 68.
[3] See the chapter on 'Milton's Languages and the Voices of *Paradise Lost*' in his *Milton's Languages*, 131–45, quotation at 132.
[4] Stephen Orgel/Jonathan Goldberg, 'Introduction', vii. Accordingly, Orgel and Goldberg also note that 'there is ... one genuinely mediating voice in *Paradise Lost*, and it is Milton's own, entering at critical moments,' most of all in the proems; 'in passages [like the proems], Milton becomes the central figure in the poem' (xxv).

5.1 Proem I (*PL* 1.1–26)
Milton's View of the Poet's Song in Proem I and the Note on 'The Verse'

> Of man's first disobedience, and the fruit
> Of that forbidden tree, whose mortal taste
> Brought death into the world, and all our woe,
> With loss of Eden, till one greater man
> Restore us, and regain the blissful seat,   5
> Sing, heavenly Muse, that on the secret top
> Of Oreb, or of Sinai, didst inspire
> That shepherd, who first taught the chosen seed,
> In the beginning how the heavens and earth
> Rose out of chaos: Or if Sion hill   10
> Delight thee more, and Siloa's brook that flowed
> Fast by the oracle of God[,] I thence
> Invoke thy aid to my advent'rous song,
> That with no middle flight intends to soar
> Above the Aonian mount, while it pursues   15
> Things unattempted yet in prose or rhyme.
> And chiefly thou O Spirit, that dost prefer
> Before all temples the upright heart and pure,
> Instruct me, for thou knowst; thou from the first
> Wast present, and with mighty wings outspread   20
> Dovelike satst brooding on the vast abyss
> And mad'st it pregnant: what in me is dark
> Illumine, what is low raise and support;
> That to the height of this great argument
> I may assert eternal providence,   25
> And justify the ways of God to men. (*PL* 1.1–26)

In the opening lines of *Paradise Lost*, multiple sensory modalities are referenced. However, even though they are put side by side in the text, these various sensory references function on different levels of abstraction, and thus cannot be considered as contributing to a common *multi-sensory scene*.[5] In contrast to the later proems, in which the speaker refers to concrete (if imagined) settings of sense perception outside of himself, however, most of the concrete elements of sensory discourse in Proem I concern the speaker's own persona, his embodied voice (shared or confused with that of his Muse) and inner illumination (a theme taken up in later proems).

The first and most obvious instance of sensory discourse in the proem, however, is made even more conspicuous by the line-end position of its two parts, connecting the first two verses: this is the double reference to 'taste' and its object, the 'fruit' employed

---

[5] Eden, and more particularly Paradise, presented as *the* archetypical multi-sensory sensescape in later parts of the poem, is named but not described in any way.

by Satan to corrupt Eve and, through her, Adam. While 'taste and temptation' is obviously a defining sensory theme for *Paradise Lost* as a whole, its discursive centre is in book 9, where the thematic complex of eating, food, and taste is developed at length, and is present throughout, from the opening lines to that book's conclusion. Owing to the conceptual metaphor underlying both (IDEAS ARE FOOD or, as Raphael later puts it, 'knowledge is as food'), the theme of 'mortal taste' is also connected to the archangel's visit to Paradise in book 5, where he has dinner with Adam and Eve and, in an after-dinner conversation, informs Adam about the limits of human knowledge – explained in terms of ingestion and digestion – and the human couple's duty to obey God's commands (and, in particular, his prohibition of eating from the tree of knowledge). In the present context, too, taste and (dis)obedience are associated: they are the twin subjects of the epic 'song' that is *Paradise Lost*. In later passages of the poem, Milton highlights the auditory subtext of '(dis)obedience': derived from Latin *oboedire*, and thus, ultimately, from *audire*, 'to hear,' the term transports, in Milton's etymologically conscious usage, an acute awareness of the fact that, as Hale observes, '"listening to" a voice means, not simply hearing it but heeding it, all the way up to obeying it, or disobeying it.'[6] For now, however, this auditory dimension is not explored further, but is only implied in the light of later references.

Similarly, the speaker's blindness is not yet explicitly discussed, but is alluded to in Milton's mention of 'Siloa's brook,' meaning the stream – actually an artificial, man-made canal – that fed the biblical Pool of Siloam, a water reservoir outside Jerusalem which figures prominently in one of Jesus's miracles as related by John and frequently represented in Christian art:

> And as Jesus passed by, he saw a man which was blind from his birth. And his disciples asked him, saying, Master, who did sin, this man, or his parents, that he was born blind? Jesus answered, Neither hath this man sinned, nor his parents: but that the works of God should be made manifest in him. I must work the works of him that sent me, while it is day: the night cometh, when no man can work. As long as I am in the world, I am the light of the world. When he had thus spoken, he spat on the ground, and made clay of the spittle, and he anointed the eyes of the blind man with the clay. And said unto him, Go, wash in the pool of Siloam, (which is by interpretation, Sent.)[7] He went his way therefore, and washed, and came seeing.[8]

---

[6] Hale, *Milton's Languages*, 133. Hale notes the equivalent etymologies of Latin *oboedire*, Greek *hupakouein*, and German *gehorchen*, and points out that, even so, 'etymology defamiliarizes what the Bible also emphasizes: "If thou wilt *diligently hearken to the voice* of the Lord thy God ..."' – quoting Ex. 15:26, where the Authorised Version's 'diligently hearken' renders an intensifying repetition of the Hebrew root *shama*, 'to hear,' literally amounting to something like, 'if you will *hear a hearing* ...,' that is, 'if you will *indeed hear* ...'

[7] Milton's nephew Edward Phillips glosses the actual Hebrew term, '*Shiloh*,' as 'a Saviour, it is a word used in the Scripture for our Saviour Christ' (*New World of Words*, sig. [Mm4r]).

[8] John 9:1–7; on the central place of this and Jesus's other miracles of healing the blind in the (Western) cultural history of blindness, see Barasch, *Blindness*, 47–55, esp. 47 on early Christian art and 49–50 on the theological significance of the motif.

5.1 Proem I (PL 1.1–26)

With respect to Milton's own situation and his self-representation as the poet-speaker of Proem I, two aspects of John's account appear pertinent. On the one hand, there is Jesus's innovative rejection of the common and long-lived idea that blindness (even congenital blindness) was indicative of some heinous transgression or sin committed by the blind person (or their ancestors).[9] On the other hand, there is the strong sense of mission – quite literally – that brings together both participants in the healing miracle: the blind man is blind so 'that the works of God should be made manifest in him,' and is sent by Jesus to be cured; Jesus himself is sent to 'work the works of him that sent me while it is day.'[10] Being the 'light of the world,' it is part of his mission to heal the blind.[11]

Milton had earlier addressed both of these thematic complexes – that of blindness as punishment and that of blindness in connection to work or duty – by reference to the very same biblical text, in *Defensio Secunda* (1654). There, part of his reply to the imputation of being 'a monster, dreadful, ugly, huge, deprived of sight,' had been to point out that 'it is perfectly certain from the divine testimony of Christ our Saviour that the man who was healed by him had been blind from the very womb, through no sin of his own or of his parents.'[12] Milton himself, we are to understand, is not suffering his blindness as a punishment for his mediate transgression against God in the person of the king, as royalist writers suggested he was well into the Restoration period.[13] In fact, he says – and here the second aspect, that of fulfilling one's mission, comes into play –, he has lost his vision due to a conscious decision, after the first symptoms of his condition had already become manifest, to pursue the task assigned to him:

> Hence, when the business of replying to the royal defense had been officially assigned to me, and at that same time I was afflicted at once by ill health and the virtual loss of my remaining eye, and the doctors were making learned predictions that if I should undertake this task, I would shortly lose both eyes, I was not in the least deterred by the warning. I seemed to hear, not the voice of the doctor (even that of Aesculapius, issuing from the shrine at Epidaurus), but the sound of a certain more divine monitor within. And I thought that two lots had now been set before me by a certain command of fate: the one, blindness, the other, duty. ….[14]

---

[9] On the widespread notion – common to the Graeco-Roman and Judaeo-Christian traditions – of blindness as the (inherited) effect of transgression, and as a punishment for transgressing against God or the gods, in particular, see Barasch, *Blindness*, 11, 21–27, and passim. This aspect all but disappears, Barasch argues, in Renaissance interpretations of blindness (136). Avrahami, *Senses of Scripture*, 198, disagrees with respect to the Hebrew Bible.

[10] In both the literal sense of nocturnal darkness and the figurative sense of night as blindness, Milton, according to his self-representation in Proem VII, would belie the conventional (and biblical) notion that 'no man can work' at night, referred to in his own work as early as Prolusion I; see also my discussion of Milton's repeated use of the term 'nightly' in the proems below.

[11] For the healing of the blind as emblematic of God's (creative) power in the Hebrew Bible, see Avrahami, *Senses of Scripture*, 194–95.

[12] CPW 4: 587.

[13] See my discussion of attacks on Milton on account of his blindness below.

[14] CPW 4: 587–88.

Spurred into action by the 'audible' intervention of conscience, God's representative within the individual, the Milton of *Defensio Secunda* had, as the speaker of his roughly contemporary Sonnet 22, lost his eyesight 'overplied/in liberty's defence, my noble task.'[15] The epic speaker of *Paradise Lost*, though thus far only implied to be blind, shares in the blamelessness of their affliction (as witnessed by his 'upright heart and pure') as well as in their being destined for momentous, godly work. Ultimately, then, the reference to 'Siloa's brook' links Proem I not only to the rich Christian tradition surrounding Jesus's healing of the blind but also to Milton's earlier treatments of the same motif. It casts a light on both the speaker's image of himself as blind yet personally blameless – worth pointing out in a context centred on original sin – and on his conception of the poetic task at hand: he too is 'sent,' both to be 'illumine[d]' and to perform his task and 'justify the ways of God to men.'

Indeed, the speaker's call for inner, spiritual illumination is next in the proem's sequence of references to vision. This is to be granted by the 'Spirit;' in proems III and VII, it will be presented as compensating for a lack of outside, physical vision. In contrast to this inner vision, Milton's 'heavenly Muse,' the other higher power invoked (and, indeed, invoked first), is a figure of the outside world; later, in Proem VII, she is introduced as Urania (literally, 'the heavenly one'), the Greek Muse of astronomy, an identification which is then immediately qualified.[16] In Proem I, she is consistently correlated with mountaintops, a visual trope familiar from Elegy V with its references to Mount Ida, Parnassus, 'high Hymettus,' and other *scopuli* or elevated viewing positions. In the passage at hand, three biblical mountains or peaks are named: Oreb, Sinai, and Sion are associated with visionary power, priestly duty, and newly purified or purifying vision, respectively.[17] Their association with arcane (and thus HIGH) knowledge – 'secret top' – and inspiration or prophecy is equally clear:[18] 'that shepherd' inspired by the Muse is Moses, a biblical mirror figure to Milton's epic speaker.[19] Moses, incidentally, was known for his perfect vision, even in old age; when he died at the age of 120, his sight had not diminished.[20] The 'Aonian mount,' finally, is Helicon, sacred to the Muses (and thus comparable in function to the similar references in Elegy V).

---

[15] Compare the Father's audio-visual characterisation of conscience in *PL* 3.194–97: 'And I will place within them [i.e., humankind] as a guide,/My umpire conscience, whom *if they will hear,/Light after light* well used they shall attain,/And to the end persisting, safe arrive' (emphasis added). On Protestant views of conscience as 'a remnant of that intimacy once found between Adam and God *talking together* in the garden,' see Julia Ipgrave, *Adam in Seventeenth-Century Political Writing in England and New England* (London: Routledge, 2017), 59–62, quotation at 62, emphasis added.

[16] See Chapter 5.3 below. Milton had used the designation as early as 1629, in his 'Nativity Ode': 'Say heavenly Muse, shall not thy sacred vein/Afford a present to the infant God?/Hast thou no verse, no hymn or solemn strain,/To welcome him to this his new abode …?'

[17] These associations are given by Sundell, 'Singer and his Song,' 73.

[18] On the close metaphorical association of 'high' (arcane) knowledge, power, and divine wisdom, see Ginzburg, 'The High and the Low,' 63.

[19] 'Implying Moses' superiority to Hesiod, who as a *shepherd* had a vision of the Muses' (Fowler ad loc.).

[20] See Avrahami, *Senses of Scripture*, 62n, 202, 256.

If the Muse is associated with mountaintops and thus (prophetic) vision, her closest connection in terms of sensory discourse is with singing and song. In terms of both, the act (of singing) and the artefact (song), she is supposed to lend the speaker her support. In asking *the Muse* to sing 'of man's first disobedience …' and everything else that defines the scope of the epic, of course, the speaker has already embarked on his own 'advent'rous song.' The resulting situation resembles that of the poet-speaker of Elegy V, whose duet with Philomela was similarly characterised by a diffuse superimposition of both voices, while the subject of his song – the coming of spring – was, at the same time, that which inspired it in the first place. In a comparable movement of thought, Milton in Proem I places the origin of poetic inspiration in a paradoxical entanglement of spontaneous expression and external stimuli, conceived of as vocal and auditory, respectively. In the context of the early modern physiology of perception, in which sound and hearing were the sensory-perceptual categories most closely associated with the spirits, it would only have seemed natural to express matters of inspiration in this manner.[21]

When the poet-speaker invokes, first, the Muse and then the Spirit, both of these supporting agents are meant to help the speaker redeem his double claim to poetic worth and epistemic probity; the necessary moral component (an 'upright heart and pure') appears to lie within his own responsibility.[22] By virtue of her being a goddess of the arts, his Muse is qualified to inspire the poet to create an aesthetically pleasing – 'lyrical,' hence musical – *form*; her knowledge of arcane *content* – of the kind which enabled Moses to teach the children of Israel – is supplemented by the knowledge of the (Holy) Spirit, which is that of the experiential witness: 'instruct me, for thou knowst; thou from the first/Wast present.' Just as the speaker himself hopes to be 'instruct[ed]' by the Spirit and as Moses had 'taught' the Israelites, the purpose of the following poem will be to 'justify' – and that means, first and foremost, 'explain,' 'render comprehensible' – 'the ways of God to men.'[23] From its very beginning, then, and in several distinct ways, *Paradise Lost* is a poem of knowledge, and the ways in which this knowledge is made accessible to the poet-speaker, transformed by him, and passed on to his audience, are all informed by sensory discourse: as illumination, voices joined in a duet, and soaring epic song.

While each of the two supporting entities invoked is mainly associated with one of the two defining aspects of the poem – the Muse, with poetic inspiration, and the Spirit, with factual and spiritual corroboration –, they are both ultimately connected to both dimensions: the Muse, in that she is invoked, also, as having inspired Moses to '[teach] the chosen seed;' and the Spirit, in that its 'brooding' and, literally, impregnating operation ('mad'st it pregnant') is intimately associated with the creative process. As the speaker makes clear, in fact, through his repeated references to song, delight, and un-

---

[21] See Gouk, *Music, Science, and Natural Magic*, 164–66.

[22] Contrast, however, *PL* 11.1–8, quoted again below, where it is God's 'prevenient grace' which 'remove[s]/The stony from their hearts.' In this point, Proem I clearly does not aim at the same level of theological rigour; its focus is on poetic inspiration and the transfer of knowledge.

[23] As Edward Phillips explains in his dictionary of hard or unusual words, '*Justification* … is a shewing a good reason why a man did such a thing as he is called to answer' (*New World of English Words*, sig. X4v). Note the focus on showing and thus 'putting before the eyes.'

precedented artistry, his work – knowledge-based though it is – will *not* be a dry, systematic disquisition; and it is sensory discourse, to a great extent, which will serve to maintain that distinction throughout the epic: the speaker's song, as presented in Proem I, is both, knowledgeable *and* aesthetically daring (pursuing 'things unattempted yet in prose or rhyme'). *Paradise Lost* will also be morally sound, as it is conceived in an 'upright heart and pure,' and will thus aim to clear the high bar Milton sets up in his poetological preface on 'The Verse,' written after the fact.

The orientational metaphors at work in the proem – Milton's 'upright heart' is the one I referred to last – run through the lines from its initial references to mountaintops in general and the soaring of the poet's (Christian) song above the peaks of (pagan) classical culture in particular. Song, instruction, and spiritual edification; artistic creation and the '[rising] out of chaos' of heaven and earth at God's Creation (as the Sprit-Dove is sitting perched 'on the vast abyss'); as well as inner illumination and the 'rais[ing] and support[ing]' of 'what is low' and 'what … is dark' in the speaker, all are associated with upward movement and/or elevated positions. It is hard to reduce this complex of images to its lowest common denominator, its fundamental orientational metaphor. It may be GOOD IS UP – Milton, if pressed, might have given this as GOD IS UP –; but in terms of sensory discourse, it certainly implies, as its closest approximations, VISION IS UP, LIGHT IS UP, and HARMONY IS UP – namely, above blindness, darkness, and chaos/discord, respectively. These valuations, conventional as they may be, will reappear and will be put to various uses throughout the epic. In the form in which they appear in Milton's proems, they form the sensory discursive nexus between the hierarchy of the senses and the conceptual substructure of *Paradise Lost* as a whole.

The Blank-Verse Poetics for 'Paradise Lost' and Milton's Sensory Discourse

True to the traditional role of the epic as a literary vehicle of knowledge, Milton characterises *Paradise Lost*, from the beginning, by reference not just to his own artistic aspirations but also to the poem's value as an instrument of instruction. The first of these two aspects is expressed, in the proem, through the ultimately orientational-metaphorical image of the speaker's song 'soar[ing]/Above the Aonian mount … pursu[ing]/Things unattempted yet in prose or rhyme.'[24] It is explicated more fully and technically – and more consistently phrased in sensory terms – in Milton's 'Note on the Verse,' prefixed to *Paradise Lost* from the fourth printing of its first edition in 1668.[25]

---

[24] 'Unattempted' arguably suggests a tactile element of 'reaching out to touch, reaching out and touching;' see *OLD*, 'tempto,' 'tendo.' In any case, the semantic resonances of '-tempt-' in the present context should be clear: 'the tempter' (as Milton repeatedly refers to Satan throughout *Paradise Lost*) is the one who reaches out, touches, and, by touching, defiles ('overweening/To overreach,' as Adam puts it at 10.878–79), just as the poet's song 'intends to soar' as it 'pursues' – and, hopefully, reaches – 'things unattempted yet.' Both readings, whether focused on tactility or temptation, speak to Milton's often disconcerting association of his own poetic undertaking with Satanic presumption; see the lucid examination of this point by Steven Blakemore, '"With no middle flight": Poetic Pride and Satanic Hubris in *Paradise Lost*,' *KR* 5 (1985), 23–31.

[25] Milton wrote this at the prompting of his printer-publisher, Samuel Simmons. As Simmons himself explains in an announcement headed 'The Printer to the Reader,' 'Courteous reader, there

In this note, significantly, Milton not only deliberates on the formal make-up of his verse but also makes explicit reference to the auditory qualities of the kind of poem he considers ideal, dissociating himself from the prevailing use of the rhyming couplet:

> The measure [of *Paradise Lost*] is English heroic verse without rhyme, as that of Homer in Greek, and of Virgil in Latin; rhyme being no necessary adjunct or true ornament of poem or good verse, in longer works especially, but the invention of a barbarous age, to set off wretched matter and lame metre; graced indeed since by the use of some famous modern poets, carried away by custom, but much to their own vexation, hindrance and constraint to express many things otherwise, and for the most part worse than else they would have expressed them. Not without cause therefore some both Italian and Spanish poets of prime note have rejected rhyme both in longer and shorter works, as have also long since our best English tragedies, as a thing of it self, to all judicious ears, trivial and of no true musical delight; which consists only in apt numbers, fit quantity of syllables, and the sense variously drawn out from one verse into another, not in the jingling sound of like endings, a fault avoided by the ancients both in poetry and all good oratory. This neglect then of rhyme so little is to be taken for a defect, though it may seem so perhaps to vulgar readers, that it rather is to be esteemed an example set, the first in English, of ancient liberty recovered to heroic poem from the troublesome and modern bondage of rhyming.[26]

In his reflections on the precise metrical texture of the 'song' of *Paradise Lost*, Milton fuses poetological and political considerations, mediated through sensory discourse. Specifically, he contrasts general barbarism and 'bondage' (i.e., literary and political cruelty and compulsion) with the 'ancient liberty' of the quintessential epic poets of antiquity, Homer and Virgil; the latter must be 'recovered' through 'the first [example of it] in English.' Milton's argument here resembles a figure of thought influential in early modern English political thinking, according to which current (i.e., 'modern') abuses are just deviations from a traditional ('ancient') norm; any form of resistance against these abuses can thus be conceptualised as reactionary (restoring the traditional norm) rather than revolutionary (breaking with the past, creating a new and better norm).[27] When Milton calls rhyme 'the invention of a barbarous age,' it should be acknowledged that the phrase contains a double blow: 'invention,' in Milton, is a dirty word, associated in *Paradise Lost* with the fallen angels' hubris in their construction of

---

was no argument [i.e., introduction] at first intended to the book, but for the satisfaction of many that have desired it, I have procured it, and withal a reason of that which stumbled many others, why the poem rhymes not.' (Fowler, 51).

[26] The note on 'The Verse' is printed in Fowler's edition of *Paradise Lost*, 54–55, with a concise assessment of the poem's metrical structure and characteristics at 23–25. It is also printed, with commentary by Robert J. Wickenheiser, in CPW 8: 12–14. On the generic and political implications of Milton's formal choice see my *Paradise Reframed: Milton, Dryden, and the Politics of Literary Adaptation, 1658–1679* (Heidelberg: Universitätsverlag Winter, 2016), 91–98.

[27] See J. G. A. Pocock, *The Ancient Constitution and the Feudal Law: A Study of English Historical Thought in the Seventeenth Century* (Cambridge: Cambridge University Press, 1987 [1957]).

artillery; Satan's scheming and the dangers of Adam overstepping the prescribed bounds of knowledge; with death and postlapsarian impiety.[28] The way forward, again, is not to find a new solution but to 'recover' and make amends – to return, in effect, to a previous ideal state.

The ancient ideal to be recovered, of course, is that of classical Graeco-Roman culture, not of some more genuinely British past, and the casualness with which Milton equates the two spheres is indicative of his own identification with both. Even though it was lacking rhyme, he argues, and thus the superficially salient auditory element of 'modern' verse, classical poetry was not lacking 'true musical delight' (delight being, notably, also a factor in the invocation of the Muse in Proem I).[29] This *true* delight implies a triple awareness – of 'apt numbers,' 'fit quantity of syllables,' and 'the sense variously drawn out …' –, and thus a kind of 'multiple' or even 'consonant' understanding.[30] The key terms featured in the triad ('numbers,' 'fit,' 'the sense') suggest as much, as does Milton's use of them elsewhere. 'Numbers,' in a musical or poetological context, apart from its marked Pythagorean connotation, highlights the orderliness or deliberation of the creative process. In Proem III, discussed more fully below, the speaker refers to his 'thoughts, that voluntary move/Harmonious numbers' (3.37–38) and, later in the same book, Milton's description of the sun includes the remark that the heavenly bodies revolving around it 'move/Their starry dance in numbers that compute/Days, months, and years … [and]/Turn swift their various motions' (3.579–82).[31] In both instances, orderly ('numbered') movement – i.e., a 'dance' – implies harmony (of words and thoughts; of the spheres or planets), even though the 'voluntary' movement in the mind

---

[28] See *PL* 2.60–70, 6.464–71, and 6.498–99; 4.520–24 and 7.121; 9.766–67 and 11.610, respectively.

[29] In addition to 'Oreb, or … Sinai,' the speaker offers a third alternative: 'Or if Sion hill/*Delight* thee more …' (emphasis added). As Milton would doubtless have known (but of course cannot readily acknowledge in the present context), rhyme was not *wholly* unknown in classical Latin verse; in fact, Milton himself not only used rhyme in much of his own earlier English poetry, but even deploys occasional internal and even end rhymes throughout the blank verse of *Paradise Lost* for special effect.

[30] On the at times problematic differentiation and the political implications of these terms, see G. Stanley Koehler, 'Milton on "Numbers," "Quantity," and Rime,' *SIP* 55 (1958), 201–217, and Thomas N. Corns, 'Cultural and Genre Markers in Milton's *Paradise Lost*,' *RBPH* 69 (1991), 555-562, at 559–60; on the reception history of Milton's use of them in his note on 'The Verse,' see Leonard, *Faithful Labourers*, I, 110–13.

[31] In *Paradise Regained*, Satan, presenting to Jesus the wonders of Greece, and Athens in particular, invites him to pay a visit to 'painted Stoa next:/There thou shalt hear and learn the secret power/Of harmony in tones and numbers hit/By voice or hand, and various-measured verse,/Aeolian charms and Dorian lyric odes,/And his who gave them breath, but higher sung,/Blind Melesignes thence Homer called,/Whose poem Phoebus challenged for his own' (*PR* 4.253–60). Again, there is a striking entanglement of Milton's own poetic aspiration and poetological endorsement (in *Paradise Lost*) and Satanic ambition and temptation (in *Paradise Regained*).

of the poet-speaker indicates a greater degree of freedom even within the orderliness of harmony.[32]

When Milton refers to the 'fit quantity of syllables' characteristic of good verse, this is one aspect of a more encompassing notion of fitness and appropriateness which links metrical stylistics in a narrower sense to concepts of rhetorical decorum – as an epic poem, *Paradise Lost* would require recourse to the *genus grande*, or high style – and, ultimately, to that constant preoccupation of Milton's, the notion of a 'fit audience,' addressed more fully in Proem VII.[33] Within the action of the poem itself, it is Adam and Eve who embody Milton's ideal of poetical-rhetorical stylistic 'fitness,' as characterised in his account of their morning prayer:

> Lowly they bowed adoring, and began
> Their orisons, each morning duly paid
> In various style, for neither various style
> Nor holy rapture wanted they to praise
> Their maker, in fit strains pronounced or sung
> Unmeditated, such prompt eloquence
> Flowed from their lips, in prose or numerous verse,
> More tuneable than needed lute or harp
> To add more sweetness, and they thus began … (*PL* 5.144–152)

In the primordial expressiveness of Adam and Eve, poetry, oratory, and song are combined: their 'fit strains' are 'pronounced or sung … in prose or numerous verse,' where 'numerous' includes the meaning of frequency ('each morning duly paid') as well as the notion of 'apt numbers' already mentioned. Their 'various style' – a notion Milton emphasises through repetition – suggests a diversity of creative expression reminiscent of the multiplicity of genres contained within *Paradise Lost* itself.[34] In fact, there are a number of significant parallels between Milton's presentation of his speaker persona in the proems of his epic, his conception of embodied speech more generally, and his presentation of Adam and Eve's morning prayer. Specifically, they begin their worship 'lowly,' just as the speaker in Proem I asks for 'what is low' in him to be raised. In contrast to Milton's speaker however, they never have to ask for inspiration – they are never lacking in 'holy rapture' –, whereas the main point of three or even all four of the proems in *Paradise Lost* is to secure the inspiration and instruction necessary to fulfil the epic task.[35] Still, Milton aspires to the prelapsarian ideal of an 'unmediated' (i.e.,

---

[32] For the notion of a 'cosmic dance,' see E. M. W. Tillyard, *The Elizabethan World Picture: A Study of the Idea of Order in the Age of Shakespeare, Donne and Milton* (New York: Vintage Books, 1959 [1942]), 101–106.

[33] See Chapter 5.3 below.

[34] See Barbara Kiefer Lewalski, 'The Genres of *Paradise Lost*,' in: Dennis Danielson (ed.), *The Cambridge Companion to Milton*, 2nd ed. (Cambridge: Cambridge University Press, 1999 [1989]), 113–128, as well as her *'Paradise Lost' and the Rhetoric of Literary Forms* (Princeton, N. J.: Princeton University Press, 1985).

[35] Fallon notes that there are 'three or four invocations in *Paradise Lost*, depending on how one counts' (*Milton's Peculiar Grace*, 212).

spontaneous) and unconstrained poetic outpour, and sometimes manages to get close to it. In Proem IX, discussed below, the speaker refers to his Muse as

> my celestial patroness, who deigns
> Her nightly visitation unimplored,
> And dictates to me slumbering; or inspires
> Easy my unpremeditated verse:
> (*PL* 9.21–24)

The poet-speaker's verse is 'unpremeditated,' Adam and Eve's morning prayer, wholly 'unmeditated' – a subtle difference, and yet expressive, perhaps, of the asymptotic – close yet ultimately frustrated – convergence of even the optimum of poetic inspiration to the fullness of prelapsarian rhetorical perfection. All three, however, are blessed – Adam and Eve, always; the speaker, at the Muse's mercy – in that their inspiration and/or 'holy rapture' comes over them 'unimplored.' In some other respects, however, Milton's portrayal of Adam and Eve praying is firmly rooted in his (quite material and terrestrial, as opposed to 'celestial') conception of sensory discourse as embodied vocal speech. On the one hand, there is the *flow* of 'sweetness' from the lips of Adam and Eve – a partial elucidation of the ELOQUENCE IS SWEETNESS metaphor through its literalising association with mellifluousness and thus the sweetness of honey but, at the same time, insisting on the 'various style' of their prayer, which changes with the quickness of a flowing stream (DISCOURSE IS A FLOWING LIQUID, a metaphor perhaps also present in the reference to 'Siloa's brook' in Proem I).[36] On the other hand, Milton's emphasises the sufficiency of the human voice as an instrument for both speech and song, and indeed its superiority over other (musical) instruments: Adam and Eve do not need 'lute or harp.' This, too, is wholly in keeping with Milton's earlier references to the power of embodied speech, as exemplified by his (self-)assertive claim in Prolusion VI that an orator such as himself was 'far more fortunate than Orpheus or Amphion' on account of his self-sufficiency in producing resounding 'creations of the intellect,' rather than displaying mere 'manual skill' in playing the harp.[37]

Milton's use of 'orisons' in this particular passage to describe the devotions of Adam and Eve is also significant. He would most likely have been aware of the shared etymology of 'orison' on the one hand, and 'orator,' 'oration,' and 'oratory,' on the other.[38] Its occurrence in the account of the morning prayer in book 5 of *Paradise Lost* is the first of only two occurrences within the poem; 'prayer(s)' is by far the more frequent term used. The second instance of 'orisons' refers to Adam and Eve's contrite

---

[36] More precisely, 'various style' implies change (as do 'apt numbers,' 'fit quantity of syllables,' and 'the sense variously drawn out from one verse into another'), CHANGE IS MOVEMENT, and MOVEMENT IS A FLOW.

[37] See Milton's references to Orpheus in Prolusion VI, discussed in Chapter 4.3 above. The same notion is present, if with an ironic tinge, in Milton's parenthetical remark about the debating devils at *PL* 2.556, '(For eloquence the soul, song charms the sense),' discussed in Chapter 2.

[38] See *OLD*, 'oro': '(1) To pray to, beseech, supplicate (a person, god, etc. for a favour) ...; (2) To speak before a court or assembly, plead ...'

prayers of repentance after the Fall (see *PL* 11.137), which only just before, at the opening of book 11, had been characterised as follows:

> Thus they in lowliest plight repentant stood
> Praying, for from the mercy-seat above
> Prevenient grace descending had removed
> The stony from their hearts, and made new flesh
> Regenerate grow instead, that sighs now breathed
> Unutterable, which the spirit of prayer
> Inspired, and winged for heaven with speedier flight
> Than loudest oratory; (*PL* 11.1–8)

Again, there is the act of inspiration; again, the raising from 'lowliest plight' and up 'for heaven with speedier flight;' again, the comparison involving oratory. After the Fall, however, the orisons of Adam and Eve are no longer compared *to* oratory; they are compared *with* it. In the process, they are found lacking, as they are mere, inarticulate 'sighs ... unutterable' (representing the 'creations of the intellect' had been oratory's claim to glory in Milton's earlier account); and yet, by the 'prevenient grace' of God, they transcend the effect of 'loudest oratory' in that they still reach the divine ear. Unlike before the Fall, when prayer – a prayer of praise, however, not of repentance – had shared *all* the characteristics of the sensory discourse of poetry, song, and rhetorical performance, these latter 'orisons' may retain a resemblance of the old paradigm; yet, they really are emblematic of the new, postlapsarian one. They are *more piercing and sincere* than oratory, yet *less articulate*: we have witnessed the fundamental dissociation of rhetoric and godliness as an effect of the Fall.[39] Before, oratory in the full-bodied sense of the term had been 'fit' for divine worship; after, the proof of devotion is in the heart, which, instead of the bodily voice, has become the relevant organ for any effective communication to and with the deity.[40] In terms of wider cultural context, this matches the Protestant distrust of 'liturgical speech' as opposed to actual prayer and preaching. For the latter, audition – and indeed audibility: a clear and sonorous voice on the part of the minister – was a key requirement; but the former – associated with the sung liturgies and half-sung chants of pre-Reformation piety – was highly suspicious.[41] What had been 'fit' for Adam and Eve – prayer that was both oratory and song – was not necessarily appropriate for their most recent descendants. Milton's clear focus on the extempore quality of Adam and Eve's praying both before and after the Fall, on the

---

[39] This matches Milton's frequent portrayal of the fallen angels as (sophistical, insincere) orators, and of their enticingly 'sweet' discourse as the epitome of 'fallen' rhetoric. See the references to Belial as an infernal rhetorician in Chapter 2 above.

[40] *Paradise Lost* as a whole plays out as a drama of God being (not) visible (yet, anymore, still ...), an aspect which forms a central element in the poem's reflections on human–divine communication.

[41] See Milner, *Senses and the English Reformation*, 112–14. Milner specifically notes preachers' conviction that 'contrition, thanksgiving, and supplication were beneficial to their hearers because they gave God his due, and moved others towards godly virtue,' a position that clearly is present in the passages at hand.

other hand – their orisons are first 'unmeditated,' then simply 'breathed' –, is entirely in keeping with prevailing Protestant ideas of a more 'godly' bent.[42] All in all, his reflections on the nature, (bodily) mechanics, and purpose of prayer thus appear as closely connected to contemporary debates about the proprieties and improprieties of praying and preaching – which formed a sizeable segment of early modern English sensory culture – as they undeniably are to the preoccupations of Milton's highly programmatic first proem to *Paradise Lost*, and to the aspirations and anxieties surrounding his own sensory discourse as a notionally speaking, singing poet.

The third and last hallmark of 'true musical delight' Milton names in his note on 'The Verse' – going beyond the foundational elements of 'apt numbers' and a 'fit quantity of syllables' – is that, in the verses in question, 'the sense [is] variously drawn out from one verse into another.' This may, of course, be taken to refer to Milton's known fondness of run-on lines, whether exemplified by his sweeping verse paragraphs, his strategy of letting a line break change the reader's construal of a given grammatical structure, or simply by what has been called, in John Broadbent's memorable phrase, 'the typically Miltonic half-line of derision.'[43] In this reading of the phrase, it is the *meaning* conveyed through Milton's lines which is 'variously drawn out' and flowing effortlessly, as it were, from verse to verse.

Since Milton often exploits the ambiguity of 'sense' (as perceptual faculty, meaning, or understanding), a sensory reading of the phrase readily suggests itself, as in keeping with the general focus of the passage on auditory perception. There are parallels for such a use of 'sense' in *Paradise Lost*. Thus, in the passage on the fallen angels' diversions from book 2, discussed in Chapter 2 above, it is in the context of singing and spoken discourse or oratory – and thus clearly in relation to hearing – that 'eloquence the soul, song charms *the sense*' (*PL* 2.556, emphasis added). A slightly more ambiguous version occurs in book V, when Raphael ponders the difficulty of accommodating the war in heaven to both Adam's *hearing* and his *understanding*: 'Sad task and hard, for how shall I relate/*To human sense* the invisible exploits/Of warring spirits …' (*PL* 5.564–6, emphasis added).

---

[42] On the conflicts surrounding extempore prayer vs set prayer, see, for instance, Hunt, *Art of Hearing*, 41, and the editor's introduction in CPW 1: 26, 35, 136. Preaching, however, was a different matter entirely, and the traditional postulate of High Anglican 'metaphysical' vs Puritan 'plain' styles of preaching has now been exploded; see, again, Hunt, *Art of Hearing*, esp. 81–94, and Debora K. Shuger, *The Christian Grand Style in the English Renaissance* (Princeton, N. J.: Princeton University Press, 1988), for an earlier challenge to the dichotomy.

[43] John B. Broadbent, *Some Graver Subject: An Essay on 'Paradise Lost'* (London: Chatto & Windus, 1960), 69. Broadbent's own example is at *PL* 1.41–44: '… and with ambitious aim/Against the throne and monarchy of God/Raised impious war in heaven and battle proud/*With vain attempt*' (emphasis added). Examples of the first two varieties also abound; see, for instance, the passage in Proem III, 3.26–40, forming the immediate context of the phrase 'thoughts, that voluntary move/Harmonious numbers,' already quoted above. Fowler ad loc. quotes Donald Davie on the reader's uncertainty regarding the (in)transitivity of 'move,' occasioned by the line break: 'The flicker of hesitation about whether the thoughts move only themselves, or something else, makes us see that the numbers … are the very thoughts themselves, seen under a new aspect.' This would make the passage a striking instance of sensory discourse as a vehicle of thought or knowledge. See also Chapter 5.2 below.

Milton's use of 'variously' – 'the sense *variously* drawn out' – also appears to signal an involvement of the sensory sphere. As in the parallel occurrences already referred to – the 'various style' of Adam and Eve's morning prayer, and the 'various motions' of the constellations around the sun –, the term implies the notion of *variatio delectat*, an idea inherently connected to that of sensuous enjoyment.[44] Further parallels in *Paradise Lost* include the description of Paradise as 'a happy rural seat of various view' (*PL* 4.245), offering to its inhabitants 'various fruits' (*PL* 5.390), and the appearance of flowers and herbs at Creation, 'opening their various colours' and making 'gay/[Earth's] bosom smelling sweet' (*PL* 7.318–19).

That the tempting richness of such variety may prove problematic is suggested, ironically, by Adam's characterisation of God's prohibition as 'this easy charge, of all the trees/In Paradise that bear delicious fruit/So various, not to taste that only tree/Of knowledge, planted by the tree of life ...' (*PL* 4.419–22), as well as by Satan's temptation of Eve in a dream, displacing – and supposedly improving on – the 'various view' of Paradise in an even wider vision of the earth:

> ... he drew nigh, and to me held,
> Even to my mouth of that same fruit held part
> Which he had plucked; the pleasant savoury smell
> So quickened appetite, that I, methought,
> Could not but taste. Forthwith up to the clouds
> With him I flew, and underneath beheld
> The earth outstretched immense, a prospect wide
> And various ...   (*PL* 5.82–89)[45]

And when Adam, conversing with an alarmed Raphael in book 8, admits to the full power of his attraction to Eve, not only are his simultaneous protestations of marital harmony undermined – to those familiar with Milton's auditory poetics – by the 'jingling sound of like endings' ('Harmony to behold in wedded pair/More grateful than harmonious sound to the ear'); Adam's assertion of self-control is also predicated upon his (supposed) ability to deal with the dangers of pleasing sensory variety:

> Yet these [i.e., Eve's beauty and 'decencies'] subject not; I to thee disclose
> What inward thence I feel, not therefore foiled,
> Who meet with various objects from the sense
> Variously representing; yet still free
> Approve the best, and follow what I approve.[46]
>   (*PL* 8.605–611)

---

[44] See the discussion of *variatio delectat* in Chapter 4.3 above.

[45] Compare and contrast *PL* 11.377–411 (the kingdoms of the earth as they appear to Michael and Adam on the mount of vision) and the corresponding passages in *PR* 3.251–346 and 4.25–108 (Satan tempting Jesus with a mountaintop view, offering him, first, the throne of David and, then, all the kingdoms of the world).

[46] Milton has Adam allude, ominously, to a famous sensory-discursive pre-text: Medea's line in Ovid, 'Video meliora proboque, deteriora sequor': 'The best I see and like: the worst I follow

In this passage, the repetition of 'various' is striking: in Adam's account of the situation, it is as if the variety of sense objects, multiplied by the variety of sensory representation through the organs of perception, results in an almost exponential barrage of sense impressions. Adam is completely guileless, as he has never been confronted with any actually harmful sensual temptation meant to 'subject' him; Milton makes a point of presenting him as ignorant of any danger.

Eve, conversely, *is* confronted with a real threat of temptation when Satan approaches her in the guise of the serpent. After she has reacted to Satan's fulsome praise with studied bashfulness ('Serpent, thy overpraising leaves in doubt/The virtue of that fruit, in thee first proved'), she cannot hold back her curiosity:

> But say, where grows the tree, from hence how far?
> For many are the trees of God that grow
> In Paradise, and various, yet unknown
> To us, in such abundance lies our choice,
> As leaves a greater store of fruit untouched,
> Still hanging incorruptible, till men
> Grow up to their provision, and more hands
> Help to disburden nature of her birth.   (*PL* 9.615–24)

Again, the variety of fruit in the garden is highlighted – albeit not, as before, in a neutral manner, or as a justification of God's prohibition ('the variety of fruit-bearing trees in the garden is so great that we can easily spare the one prohibited,' as Adam's statement at *PL* 4.419–22 could be paraphrased). Rather, in Eve's mind, it is the very idea of *an unknown variety* ('many are the trees ... / and various, yet unknown') that lays the foundation for her subsequent lapse. When Milton has her declare that 'in such abundance lies our choice' to leave a great quantity of fruit 'untouched' and 'incorruptible' for future generations, these words carry a cruel irony. Whereas Adam seems aware (without really understanding it) of the nexus between 'variousness' and sensual temptation, Eve from the outset reveals a fascination with unknown variety (and an ironic misjudgment of where exactly she will have to make a necessary 'choice') that between them will eventually cause her downfall.

In all of the passages cited, variety – the 'variousness' of the objects of perception – is related to sensuous enjoyment or, in the more problematic cases, sensual temptation. Through their slight differences in presentation – combining different valuations of variety with different perspectives on God's prohibition –, Milton makes this element of his sensory discourse into an effective dramaturgical tool, suitable to transport subtle (often ironic) judgments and contrasting characterisations on the part of the epic narrator. After the Fall, he will refer to Adam and Eve's 'sad discourse, and various plaint' (*PL* 10.343), just as Adam will have to confront 'the inclement seasons, rain, ice, hail

---

headlong still,' *Metamorphoses*, 7.20; English translation by Arthur Golding [1560], (Baltimore, Md.: Johns Hopkins University Press, 2002), 201.

and snow,/Which now the sky with various face begins/To show us in this mountain' (*PL* 10.1063–65).[47]

In comparison with the complex interplay of significations enabled by the three prerequisites of 'true musical delight' – 'apt number,' 'fit quantity of syllables,' and 'the sense variously drawn out' – the 'jingling sound of like endings' is, as I have suggested, merely superficial; it only simulates – thus Milton's claim – the semantic and auditory concord that the more complexly interacting elements of the classical model actually produce.

Again, there is a convergence of auditory and political or moral considerations, encapsulated in the concept of – albeit not, in the present passage, the term – 'concord.' When Milton in *Paradise Lost* refers to 'concord,' the term often takes on a similar – and a similarly mixed and complex – signification. Thus, when the fallen angels begin 'rejoicing in their matchless chief,' Satan, after the great consultation in Pandaemonium, the narrator illustrates this outburst of emotion by means of a highly significant epic simile:

> As when from mountain tops the dusky clouds
> Ascending, while the north wind sleeps, o'erspread
> Heaven's cheerful face, the louring element
> Scowls o'er the darkened landscape snow, or shower;
> If chance the radiant sun with farewell sweet
> Extend his evening beam, the fields revive,
> The birds their notes renew, and bleating herds
> Attest their joy, that hill and valley rings. (*PL* 2.488–95)

The image amounts to an ironic inversion of Milton's earlier sensory discursive descriptions of spring and/or dawn scenes, and of animals' audible reactions to them, in particular.[48] More precisely, it is ironic in that it grants the fallen angels a brief moment of glory and transposes the metaphorical scene of that glory from the conventional spring morning to an autumn or winter evening; less ironically, it presents Satan's sun as setting, and the return of spring (i.e., the eventual redemption of humankind through Satan's final downfall) as only a matter of time. Having set this scene before the eyes of the reader (or hearer), Milton's epic narrator then comments: 'Oh shame to men! Devil with devil damned/Firm concord holds, men only disagree/Of creatures rational ...' (*PL* 2.496–98). In a later, more straightforward instance, Milton describes the musico-communal cohesion in the polity of heaven, saying of the angels that

---

[47] Further instances of problematic sensory variety after the Fall are at *PL* 11.557 ('tents of various hue,' inhabited by reprehensible sensualists) and 12.52–61 (angered at the pretensions of Babel, God 'sets/Upon their tongues a various spirit ... /To sow a jangling noise of words unknown:/Forthwith a hideous gabble rises loud' which causes 'great laughter' in heaven 'to see the hubbub strange/And hear the din').

[48] Compare the bleating of sheep evoked in *Comus*, discussed as an element of Milton's sensory discourse in Chapter 4.1 above.

> their golden harps they took,
> Harps ever tuned, that glittering by their side
> Like quivers hung, and with preamble sweet
> Of charming symphony they introduce
> Their sacred song, and waken raptures high;
> No voice exempt, no voice but well could join
> Melodious part, such concord is in heaven. (*PL* 3.365–71)

Significantly, this is the angelic hosts' reaction to the Father's exaltation of the Son; the scene from book 3 forms a mirror-image (or rather, a mirror-inversion) of the fallen angels' reaction to Satan's act of self-empowerment in book 2. In heaven, there is no discord: even the angels' harps are 'ever tuned.'[49] This corresponds to Adam and Eve before the Fall, who perform 'orisons' without fail, or failure of 'holy rapture,' themselves the supremely 'fit' and sufficient instruments. In both cases, too, the production of harmony and concord is a joint, or communal activity.[50] In heaven, as Milton particularly stresses, no one is left out, all are allowed – and are able – to join in.[51] Musical and political harmony go hand in hand with a deep and vocal piety. The only ones who do not participate, ultimately, will be those who choose to disobey.

In different ways, the three poetological demands posited by Milton as prerequisites to 'true musical delight' – namely, 'apt numbers,' 'fit quantity of syllables' and 'the sense [being] variously drawn out from one verse into another' – can be shown to connect to the sensory discourse of the epic at large: through a persistent association, in *Paradise Lost*, of both verse and oratorical speech (as both oratory and orison) with music and song; through deliberation on the notions of fitness and appropriateness in performing such instances of embodied speech; and through a sophisticated narrative exploration of how an enticing variety of sense impressions – the notion of *variatio delectat* familiar to early modern perceptual theory and aesthetics alike – may, in fact, present the risk of sensual corruption. In several instances, Milton draws on sensory discursive elements familiar from his earlier writings (notably, the spring scenes from

---

[49] Having reportedly mastered the bass viol as a young man, Milton would have had an acute understanding of what this meant. The practice of historically informed performance has made his point easier to grasp for modern audiences.

[50] As becomes clear from the further course of their morning prayer, not even Adam and Eve are performing a duet. They are accompanied, rather, by the surrounding nature and natural forces, and by the angels themselves (see *PL* 5.153–208).

[51] Milton's depiction reflects the value given to communal music-making in the genteel social context of his own upbringing, as is suggested by an anecdote related in Thomas Morley's *A Plaine and Easie Introduction to Practicall Musicke* (1597). The scene is a dinner party, and Philomathes, the unhappy protagonist of Morley's introduction, is left out of the conversation due to his complete and utter ignorance of musical matters; things then get worse: 'Supper being ended and music books (according to the custom) being brought to the table, the mistress of the house presented me with a part, earnestly requesting me to sing; but when, after many excuses, I protested unfeignedly that I could not, every one began to wonder; yea, some whispered to others demanding how I was brought up, so that upon shame of my ignorance I go now to seek out my old friend Master Gnorimus, to make myself his scholar' (Morley quoted in Le Huray, 'The fair musick that all creatures made,' 243). In Milton's heaven, of course, no such tutoring is needed.

Prolusion I and Elegy V but also the notion of embodied oratorical speech most fully explored in Prolusion VI). Matching the often-ironic perspective of the epic narrator of *Paradise Lost*, however, these borrowings are at times inverted, or their validity called into question.

The judgment of poetry, Milton's note on 'The Verse' suggests, is a task for 'judicious ears,' but its characteristic effect on the hearer is 'true musical delight.' Critical awareness and sensuous enjoyment are thus shown to interact. This makes it easy to see how, in Milton's account, aesthetic judgment ultimately becomes political judgment and hence, on account of its taking place in the mind of the individual, a sort of moral trial. The medium of political and moral discourse, in Milton's classically trained and shaped understanding of the term, is oratory. As my discussion of the prolusions in Chapter 4 has indicated, Milton's earliest notion of rhetoric and the oratorical situation rested on a sensory discursive foundation, expressed through the embodied vocal speech of the orator – a notion that he later reiterated in *Areopagitica* and other more narrowly political writings. Forty years on from the prolusions – and some twenty-five after writing *Areopagitica* –, Milton's association of oratory with 'true musical delight' renews this sensory discursive foundation and sets it side by side with poetry, the discursive form of the epic on which he is about to embark. In associating poetry with 'all good oratory,' Milton emphasises the shared auditory dimension of both.

***

In Proem I, as I have argued, the auditory and embodied dimension of poetry, its immediate sensuous force, again plays a decisive role, whether this be in the poet's actual *song*, in his association with (spiritual) vision, or insinuations of (physical) blindness. With respect to the *function* of poetry, the poem highlights its capacity to act as a literary vehicle of knowledge, moral and otherwise. The moral dimension, in fact, cannot be meaningfully distinguished, in Milton's model, from epistemic or sensory-aesthetic considerations: on the level of its sensory discourse, both the proem and Milton's poetological note on 'The Verse' present *Paradise Lost* as a work that will certainly demand the judgment of 'judicious ears' in the ultimately moral senses outlined above. On the level of teaching, instruction, and knowledge (all lexemes occur in the proem), Milton's ulterior purpose, again, is to enable his audience to assess correctly the questions posed by the epic's 'great argument' – to judge, as it were, and judge correctly – in the matter of God's ways to men.

5.2 Proem III (*PL* 3.1–55)
Two Kinds of Vision and Blindness; Proem III as a Companion Piece to Samson's Lament

> Hail[,] holy light, offspring of heaven first-born,
> Or of the eternal co-eternal beam
> May I express thee unblamed? since God is light,
> And never but in unapproachèd light
> Dwelt from eternity, dwelt then in thee,   5
> Bright effluence of bright essence increate.
> Or hearst thou rather pure ethereal stream,
> Whose fountain who shall tell? Before the sun,
> Before the heavens thou wert, and at the voice
> Of God, as with a mantle didst invest   10
> The rising world of waters dark and deep,
> Won from the void and formless infinite.
> Thee I revisit now with bolder wing,
> Escaped the Stygian pool, though long detained
> In that obscure sojourn, while in my flight   15
> Through utter and through middle darkness borne,
> With other notes than to the Orphèan lyre
> I sung of Chaos and eternal Night,
> Taught by the heavenly Muse to venture down
> The dark descent, and up to reascend,   20
> Though hard and rare: thee I revisit safe,
> And feel thy sovereign vital lamp; but thou
> Revisitst not these eyes, that roll in vain
> To find thy piercing ray, and find no dawn;
> So thick a drop serene hath quenched their orbs,   25
> Or dim suffusion veiled. Yet not the more
> Cease I to wander, where the Muses haunt
> Clear spring, or shady grove, or sunny hill,
> Smit with the love of sacred song; but chief
> Thee Sion and the flowery brooks beneath,   30
> That wash thy hallowed feet, and warbling flow,
> Nightly I visit: nor sometimes forget
> Those other two equalled with me in fate,
> So were I equalled with them in renown,
> Blind Thamyris and blind Maeonides,   35
> And Tiresias and Phineus prophets old.
> Then feed on thoughts, that voluntary move
> Harmonious numbers; as the wakeful bird
> Sings darkling, and in shadiest covert hid
> Tunes her nocturnal note. Thus with the year   40
> Seasons return, but not to me returns

5.2 Proem III (PL 3.1–55)

>   Day, or the sweet approach of even or morn,
>   Or sight of vernal bloom, or summer's rose,
>   Or flocks, or herds, or human face divine;
>   But cloud instead, and ever-during dark   45
>   Surrounds me, from the cheerful ways of men
>   Cut off, and for the book of knowledge fair
>   Presented with a universal blank
>   Of nature's works to me expunged and rased,
>   And wisdom at one entrance quite shut out.   50
>   So much the rather thou celestial Light,
>   Shine inward, and the mind through all her powers
>   Irradiate, there plant eyes, all mist from thence
>   Purge and disperse, that I may see and tell
>   Of things invisible to mortal sight.
>   (PL 3.1–55)

Proem III signals a change of scenery: from the dark and oppressive sensescape of hell (where books 1 and 2 of the epic had predominantly been set, prior to Satan's excursion into the realm of 'Chaos and eternal Night' referenced in line 18 above) to the 'bright confines' of heaven.[52] It thus acts as a point of contact between the proems, which generally focus on the persona of the poet-speaker, and the contrastive presentation of different sensescapes in the narrative parts of the poem. The most prominent sensory theme of this specific proem is light and vision, and this is a theme that will define book 3 as a whole, from the opening scene in heaven, with its dialogue between the Father and the Son ('the radiant image of his glory'), to Satan's visit to the sun and conversation with the archangel Uriel (lit., 'God is my light').[53] In the question of which *kind* of light the 'bright essence' addressed in the proem ultimately is, several options have been suggested in scholarship: the Son of God as the 'living light' of the world? physical light? or both, possibly as a divine emanation in the Platonist sense (Milton's 'effluence')?[54] As my discussion will indicate, both Milton's presentation of light in Proem III and the connections that can be traced between the proem and the wider sensory discourse of *Paradise Lost* suggest a complex notion of light as a physical as well as a metaphysical force, with these two elements interacting yet not interchangeable.

Alastair Fowler has commented that Proem III is 'more personal' than Proem I, 'yet richer in theological and aesthetic implications, with autobiography kept in proportion.'[55] Indeed, the persona of the poet-speaker is given considerably more room in

---

[52] *PL* 2.395. Regarding the allusion to Satan's journey (which is presented as a parallel to the poet-speaker's) in the proem, compare *PL* 1.543 ('the reign of Chaos and old Night') as well as 2.959–63 (Satan arriving before 'the throne/Of Chaos ... With him enthroned/Sat sable-vested Night, eldest of things,/The consort of his reign').
[53] *PL* 3.63. See Isabel McCaffrey, 'The Theme of *Paradise Lost* Book III,' in: Thomas Kranidas (ed.), *New Essays on 'Paradise Lost'* (Berkeley, Calif.: University of California Press, 1971 [1969]), 58–85.
[54] See Fowler ad *PL* 3.1–8.
[55] See Fowler, 165.

Proem III (which, in any case, is more than twice as long as Proem I). This greater focus on the speaker is reflected in the internal structure of the proem, which can be subdivided into three partitions or stages, the longest and central of which is dedicated wholly to the speaker persona. This is in contrast to Proem I, in which the speaker addresses first the Muse and then the Spirit, resulting in a bipartite structure as well as in a proportionally slighter emphasis on the speaker himself. The first section of Proem III comprises lines 1–26a and contains the speaker's address to light proper, including a detailed characterisation of the addressee and a reflection on the progress of the epic so far; this latter part, which begins in line 13, already introduces the persona of the poet. It may therefore be considered a connecting piece leading into section 2 (lines 26b–50, and thus of similar length), in which the speaker gives an account of himself. In the brief concluding section 3 (lines 51–55), which opens with a renewed address to light, the two previous foci are combined, as the speaker now not only greets and praises light (as in the first section) or reflects on his own blindness (as in the second) but asks to be given inner vision as a necessary prerequisite for his continued poetic labour: 'that I may see and tell/Of things invisible to mortal sight.' It is in this last section, consequently, that Proem III most resembles Proem I, with its double request for poetic inspiration and spiritual illumination.

The imagery of sections 1 and 3 is largely sight- and light-based, with the significant exception of two distinct references to sounds and voices: first, there is the speaker addressing light, a speech act whose auditory quality is highlighted by the subsequent question, 'Or hearst thou rather pure ethereal stream …?,' glossed by Fowler as 'do you prefer to be called?'[56] That light possesses hearing is something of a conceit,[57] but it is a consistent one; immediately after the speaker's wavering question about naming conventions, he refers to light heeding the voice of God at its creation: 'at the voice/Of God … [thou] didst invest/The rising world of waters dark and deep …'[58] In that the two individuals shown in the poem as addressing light are God and the poet-speaker – *poeta alter deus* –, Milton draws a parallel, despite all the obvious differences, between the act of Creation and the poetic act of creation, as in Proem I with reference to the Spirit of God brooding over and impregnating 'the vast abyss.' Apart from these spoken addresses to light explicitly conceived of as auditory elements, Proem III mentions the poet having sung 'with other notes than to the Orphèan lyre' in the preceding two books of the epic; a statement matching the speaker's declared intention in Proem I of soaring 'above the Aonian mount' (i.e., above pagan poetry) with the help of his heavenly muse. Its precise formulation is particularly apt since Orpheus, too, had famously visited the

---

[56] Fowler ad loc. Fowler calls this a 'Latin idiom, not earlier instanced in *OED*,' but Hale points out that it is, in fact, also a Graecism: 'But does it arrive from Greek *akoueis* direct, or through Latin's imitative *audis*? My vote is for both …' (*Milton's Languages*, 121).

[57] Consider the speaker's insecurity on this point: 'May I express [i.e., represent symbolically or image] thee unblamed?' (see Fowler ad loc.).

[58] Compare *PL* 7.243–55, beginning, 'Let there be light, said God, and forthwith light/Ethereal, first of things, quintessence pure/Sprung from the deep …'

underworld.[59] Generally, Milton's interweaving of a dominant visual and a supporting auditory discourse in these proems matches the sensory characteristics of biblical prophetical discourse as outlined by Yael Avrahami.[60] In that they relate to both sacred and secular poetry, to human and to divine creativity, the auditory references in sections 1 and 3 of Proem III hearken back to central themes of Proem I. In its central section 2, by contrast, the sensory discourse of Proem III becomes more diversified and introduces more fully themes only hinted at in the earlier poem. In order to trace these echoes and new entries in the sensory discourse of Proem III, I will now consider each of the three sections in more detail.

The 'Holy Light' Revisited: Milton's Visual-Tactile Imagery in Proem III, section 1

In the opening lines of Proem III, Milton deliberates on the precise nature of the entity he is invoking. In this, Fowler notes, 'each form of address (*offspring, beam, stream*), associates divine light or wisdom with a distinct aspect of deity.'[61] The identification of God with light, his first creation, and the characterisation of light as the hallmark of God's inaccessibility will be taken up again later in book 3, where, after the Father's exaltation of the Son, the paradoxical image of a blazing invisibility (complementary, perhaps, to the 'darkness visible' of hell) is made more explicit:

> Thee Father first they sung omnipotent,
> Immutable, immortal, infinite,
> Eternal king; thee author of all being,
> Fountain of light, thyself invisible
> Amidst the glorious brightness where thou sitst
> Throned inaccessible, but when thou shad'st
> The full blaze of thy beams, and through a cloud
> Drawn round about thee like a radiant shrine,
> Dark with excessive bright thy skirts appear,
> Yet dazzle heaven, that brightest seraphim
> Approach not, but with both wings veil their eyes.
>
> (*PL* 3.372–82)

In these lines, as in Proem III, God figures as the twin source of light and life – the two are connected in the sensory imaginary underlying Milton's presentation, just as are, conversely, blindness, old age, and death.[62] In fact, in both passages, God is presented as the *source* of light ('fountain of light') in a more than trivial sense, just as the proem,

---

[59] Milton's ambiguous identification with/dissociation from the problematic figure of Orpheus appears in his writing as early as in Prolusion VI (see Chapter 4.3 above) but reaches its full complexity in *Paradise Lost*; see Chapter 5.3 below as well as Gabel, *Paradise Reframed*, 150–52.
[60] See Avrahami, *Senses of Scripture*, 266, 274.
[61] Fowler ad *PL* 3.1–8. See Fowler's commentary for the theological niceties of the proem, esp. Milton's equivocating between different pairs of alternatives (e.g., the Arianism often ascribed to his *De Doctrina Christiana* and Athanasian Trinitarianism).
[62] See Avrahami, *Senses of Scripture*, 256–57. On LIFE IS LIGHT, see Kövecses, *Metaphor*, 50, 55.

too, inaugurates a series of images associating the divine light with flowing water.[63] This includes rather direct references ('effluence,' 'stream,' 'fountain') as well as the more oblique 'offspring.'[64] The latter term, in particular, has a double resonance, reinforcing the connection between light and the Son, i.e. Christ, who is also dispensing the 'water of life,' associated with the Spirit.[65] In their general thrust, these images indicate – and make more palpable, *almost* graspable, like a running stream – the directedness of light in general, and the directedness of divine illumination towards the speaker, in particular. They also chime with Milton's reference, in his account of Creation, to 'the sun's orb, made porous to receive/And drink the liquid light' (*PL* 7.361–62).[66] At the same time, they renew the association, familiar from Proem I, between inspiration, on the one hand, and the cheerful rapidity of running water, on the other.[67] Milton's 'rising world of [sc. standing] waters dark and deep' – the 'vast abyss' of Proem I – functions as a twofold conceptual antithesis to the agile liquidity of light, as does his reference to another body of standing water – or rather, fire: that 'Stygian pool' (i.e., lake of fire) into which the fallen angels had been plunged at the opening of book 1.[68]

---

[63] Compare Kövecses, *Metaphor*, 55, on LIGHT IS A SUBSTANCE, citing Shakespeare's Sonnet 73. In Milton's materialist cosmology, this metaphor is particularly apposite, since he views 'light and ether [i.e., the quintessential matter of which the sun's body is formed] as two forms of a single essence' (Thomas N. Corns quoted by Fowler ad *PL* 3.356).

[64] At the creation of light in *Paradise Lost*, it '*sprung* from the deep' (*PL* 7.245, emphasis added).

[65] See, for instance, John 4:14: 'But whosoever drinketh of the water that I shall give him shall never thirst; but the water that I shall give him shall be in him a well of water springing up into everlasting life,' and Rev. 21:6, interpreted to refer to Christ as well: 'And he said unto me, It is done: I am Alpha and Omega, the beginning and the end. I will give unto him that is athirst of the fountain of the water of life freely.'

[66] Continuing, 'hither as to their fountain other stars/Repairing, in their golden urns draw light' (*PL* 7.364–65). Proem III had announced as much: 'Before the sun, before the heavens thou wert, …' Consider also the etymological implication of Milton's frequent references to the 'influence' of the heavenly bodies. The notion that the planets and stars receive their light from the sun is basically Platonic; see Marjara, *Contemplation of Created Things*, 65–66. At the same time, this ur-scene of the Christian metaphysics of light – the distinction between 'light' itself, created on the first day, and 'the lights' of sun and moon, created on the fourth – is what makes the present invocation to abstract 'holy light' possible in the first place; see Hans Blumenberg, 'Light as a Metaphor for Truth: At the Preliminary Stage of Philosophical Concept Formation' [1957,] in: David Michael Levin (ed.), *Modernity and the Hegemony of Vision* (Berkeley, Calif.: University of California Press, 1993), 30–62, at 41.

[67] 'Siloa's brook that flowed/Fast by the oracle of God' (*PL* 1.11–12), associated with the Muse, was *flowing right next to* ('fast by') the oracle, but the phrase is ambiguous, and the additional sense of its flowing *fast* (i.e., rapidly) may well be intended.

[68] See *PL* 1.221–22: 'Forthwith upright he [i.e., Satan] rears from off the pool/His mighty stature,' and 265–66: 'The associates and copartners of our loss/Lie thus astonished on the oblivious pool …' 'Stygian' carries a distinct connotation of darkness, see *OED*, 'Stygian,' 3: 'black as the river Styx; dark or gloomy as the region of the Styx,' citing Milton's reference to 'Stygian darkness' in *Comus*, 132. Another reference, to the 'unfathomed `pool of Styx´ Stygian pool' in the ultimately cancelled Trinity MS insertions to *Comus* (see *SP*, 180n), appears a more direct precursor to the phrase from *Paradise Lost*. An even earlier one to 'tenebras Stygis' occurs in line 8 of the funeral poem 'In Obitum Procancellarii Medici' (1626). The darkness of hell, more

5.2 Proem III (PL 3.1–55)

In an extension of the orientational metaphors of Proem I (LIGHT IS UP and VISION IS UP, specifically), the speaker of Proem III literally rises to the poetic occasion: 'Thee I revisit now with bolder wing,/Escaped the Stygian pool ... / ..., while in my flight/ .... /I sung of Chaos and eternal Night ...' The speaker has moved up from the darkness, singing of dark matters; as he changes his subject, he also changes, appropriately, his visual surroundings, 'taught by the heavenly Muse to venture *down*/The dark *descent* and *up* to *reascend* ...' Accordingly, this movement on the part of the speaker is a movement towards light: hence, light is not the only entity characterised by its directedness and motion in these lines. The speaker's movement is presented, with striking insistence, in the personalising and familiarising terms of a habitual social call, of a mutual (if partly frustrated) relationship between the speaker-as-seer and light as his counterpart: 'Thee I revisit now ... /... thee I revisit safe,/ ... but thou/Revisitst not these eyes ...' This intimacy is heightened further when the speaker alludes to the *tactile* quality of (sun)light[69] – its warmth: 'thee I revisit safe,/And *feel* thy sovereign vital lamp.'[70] It is characteristic of Milton's fundamentally tactile cosmology that he does not consider the life-giving ('vital') properties of light in the abstract but rather explains them by reference to its concurrent administering of warmth, a tactile quality further emphasised by his subsequent reference to light's 'piercing ray.'[71] In a passage from later in book 3, the heavenly bodies are presented in strikingly similar terms in their relationship to the sun, 'the great luminary':

> ... they as they move
> Their starry dance in numbers that compute
> Days, months, and years, towards *his all-cheering lamp*
> Turn swift their various motions, or are turned
> By *his magnetic beam, that gently warms*
> *The universe, and to each inward part*
> *With gentle penetration, though unseen,*
> *Shoots invisible virtue even to the deep:*
> So wondrously was set his station *bright*.
> (*PL* 3.576, 579–87, emphases added)

---

generally, is a persistent theme of the first two books of *Paradise Lost*; Milton specifically emphasises that from its 'flames [emerges]/No light, but rather darkness visible.' In its remoteness from God, the 'Stygian pool' of hell is antithetical both to the divine stream of light and the deep and dark waters involved in Creation.

[69] Compare the references to the sun as an 'all-cheering lamp' at *PL* 3.581, also in the next quotation below, and those to the 'glorious lamp' of the sun as 'regent of day' in *PL* 7.370–71 ('regent' as in '*sovereign* vital lamp').

[70] See the various tactile senses, often with particular reference to warmth and cold, particularly, in *OED*, 'feel, v.,' I.1, 2, and see n.190 below.

[71] On the significance of 'piercing' in Milton's theory of vision see Erin Webster, '"Presented with a Universal blanc:" The Physics of Vision in Milton's Invocation to Light,' *MS* 56 (2015), 233–71, esp. 234–35, 250–51, 256, as well as her *The Curious Eye*, 116–125, esp. 120.

In the account of Creation in book 7, furthermore, even before the creation of the sun itself, the relevant imagery and vocabulary appears with reference to the Spirit of God 'brooding[,] wings ... outspread,' as familiar from Proem I:

> Thus God the heaven created, thus the earth,
> Matter unformed and void: *darkness* profound
> Covered the abyss: but *on* the watery calm
> His brooding wings the spirit of God outspread,
> And *vital virtue infused*, and *vital warmth*
> Throughout the fluid mass, but *downward* purged
> The *black* tartareous *cold* infernal dregs
> *Adverse to life*: (*PL* 7.232–39, emphases added)

In Proem III, it is the poet-speaker who benefits from the same vitalising and illuminating 'infusion,' administered before, apparently, in a familiar, mutual 'visit' of one partner to the other. Even this term, however, is not, in Milton's usage, sensorily neutral. Through its root meaning of 'seeing' (from Latin *videre*), 'visit' carries the notion of 'in-spection.'[72] Hence the conspicuous wording in Milton's multi-sensory account of Eve leaving the dinner table during Raphael's own 'visit' to Paradise:

> So spake our sire, and by his countenance seemed
> Entering on studious thoughts abstruse, which Eve
> *Perceiving* where she sat retired in *sight*,
> With lowliness majestic from her seat,
> And *grace that won who saw* to wish her stay,
> Rose, and went forth among her fruits and flowers,
> To *visit how they prospered*, bud and bloom,
> Her nursery; they at her coming sprung
> And *touched* by her fair *tendance* gladlier grew.
> (*PL* 8.39–47, emphases added)

Despite the conventional suggestion that thinking (conceptualised, as contemplation, most often in visual terms) is a characteristically male activity, while women's work properly relates to the sense of touch,[73] what is striking in the passage at hand is that Eve, too, is presented as an agent of vision, seeing as well as being seen: sitting (if 'retired') 'in sight;' 'perceiving' the situation and 'visit[ing],' finally, not simply her plants but rather '*how they prospered.*' Her touch, her 'fair tendance' (from Latin *tendere*, 'to reach for, touch') are clearly administered with a discerning eye – after, and on the basis of, sound visual judgment, and hence with all the sensory hallmarks, at least, of reason. In Eve's prelapsarian gardening, as in the illuminating, warming visitation of 'holy

---

[72] See *OED*, 'visit, v.,' 2 (citing *PL* 12.48–50) and 9: 'to go to look at; to inspect or examine; to look into or see to ...'; the sense of a social visit is *OED* meaning 8.
[73] On touch-based conceptions of what constitutes 'women's work,' see Constance Classen, 'Feminine Tactics: Creating an Alternative Aesthetics in the Nineteenth and Twentieth Centuries,' in: *The Book of Touch*, ed. Classen, 228–39, with glances at early modernity (229–30).

light' on the speaker of Proem III, the twin aspects of vision and touch are inseparable. Correspondingly, Eve phrases her lament when, after the Fall, the impending 'loss of Eden' appears inevitable:

> Must I thus leave thee Paradise? ...
> ...
> O flowers,
> That never will in other climate grow,
> *My early visitation and my last*
> *At even*, which I bred up *with tender hand*
> From the first opening bud, and gave ye names,
> Who now shall rear ye to the sun, or rank
> Your tribes, and water from the ambrosial fount?
> (*PL* 11.269–79)

Eve's flowers, whose reaction to her tending had already been emotional, almost human, in the earlier passage (they 'gladlier grew'),[74] are now further humanised by reference to their 'names' and 'tribes.'[75] Occasioned by the sense of losing everything she had valued about her life in Paradise, perhaps, Eve highlights the quasi-social implications of her 'visitation' to her flowers (the 'fruits' also named in the prelapsarian passage are conspicuously absent from the postlapsarian one). In both cases, her multi-sensory involvement with the Edenic environment argues the 'at-one-ness' of the human inhabitants of Paradise with their surroundings, just as the visual and tactile involvement of the speaker in Proem III argues the close (if precarious) connection between himself and the 'vital lamp' of divine light.

In a final, suggestive passage in book 12, Michael relates to Adam the events preceding the confusion of tongues at Babel:

> ... God who oft descends to *visit* men
> *Unseen*, and through their habitations walks
> To *mark* their doings, them *beholding* soon,
> Comes down to *see* their city, ere the tower
> Obstruct heaven towers ...   (*PL* 12.48–52)

Significantly, it is the construction of the Tower of Babel – a symbol of human presumption but also, as all towers, representative of vision itself – which occasions God's 'unseen' visitation on humankind: in this case, his 'beholding' is an act whose clear

---

[74] I.e., they both 'became more glad' and 'grew more willingly;' for the first reading, see *OED*, 'gladly, adj.,' a now obsolete form of the adjective. On the orientational metaphor HAPPY IS UP, see Kövecses, *Metaphor*, passim (references given in his index of metaphors).

[75] See, however, *OED*, 'tribe, n.,' 5: 'a group in the classification of plants, animals, etc. ...,' citing Milton's line as the second attestation. Whether or not Milton was aware of the similarity – he apparently had a working command of Dutch –, English 'tribe' (from Latin *tribus*) and German *Trieb* ('the shoot of a plant,' derived from the Germanic root that also yields English 'drive') are not related.

perceptual asymmetry expresses the twofold visual omnipotence of God, all-seeing yet invisible.

The Anti-Enthusiastic Attack on Milton in 'The Transproser Rehears'd' and Platonising Elements in Milton's Sensory Discourse

When the speaker of Proem III complains that 'thou/Revisitst not these eyes,' all of the distinct connotations of 'visit' outlined above are in play: visual attentiveness; (quasi-)social engagement; and effective agency (whether in Eve's tending her flowers or in God's visiting punishment on the people of Babel).[76] That, out of the over 10,000 verses of *Paradise Lost*, it was these lines from Proem III, specifically, and the image of easy familiarity with the divine light which they evoke, that struck a nerve with Milton's contemporary audience, is suggested by the circumstance that they were alluded to – parodied, in fact – in the 1673 pamphlet *The Transproser Rehears'd*,[77] whose title alludes to Andrew Marvell's two-part defence of toleration for religious dissenters, *The Rehearsal Transpros'd*, published in 1672/3.[78] Thus, the author pokes fun at nonconformist claims to personal divine inspiration and – importantly, given its sensory discursive significance – to inner illumination. Among the dissenting individuals who had fallen foul of the restored monarchy, Milton came in for particular ridicule, and Proem III served as a welcome peg.

From a sensory discourse perspective, the immediate context of the attack on Milton – its precise occasion in this pamphlet directed primarily against Marvell – is remarkable. This attack follows, after all, on the image of 'our Author' (i.e., Marvell) ranging his satirical troops for battle. This military image, however, is related to the faculties of the soul, posited in the brain:

> ... And though I will not deny, that these hostile *Shapes* and Military *Figures*, which our Romancer had quarter'd in the three Ventricles of his Capacious Brain (his *Memory, Fancy,* and Judgement being transform'd into Fortification and Garrison) might raise such tumults in his Sconce,[79] & so far invade his civil

---

[76] These senses are those of *OED*, 'visit, v.,' II.9, II, and I, respectively.

[77] *The Transproser Rehears'd: of the Fifth Act of Mr. Bayes's Play* (Oxford, 1673), the relevant passages are at 41–43. They are partially printed by John T. Shawcross (ed.), *Milton: The Critical Heritage* (London: Routledge & Kegan Paul, 1970), 77–78 (no. 24), and excerpted more extensively in Elizabeth Story Donno (ed.), *Andrew Marvell: The Critical Heritage* (London: Routledge, 1995 [1978]), 28–36 (no. 1).

[78] Both titles are themselves indebted to Buckingham's anonymously published play, *The Rehearsal* (1671), an attack on Dryden and the high seriousness of his heroic drama. See Sharon Achinstein, 'Milton's Spectre in the Restoration: Marvell, Dryden, and Literary Enthusiasm,' *HLQ* 59 (1996), 1–29. See also Lewalski, *Life of John Milton*, 499–501, and Gabel, *Paradise Reframed*, 128–31. *The Transproser Rehears'd* has been variously attributed, traditionally to Richard Leigh (an ascription followed by Achinstein), but also to Samuel Parker and others; for an attribution to Parker (followed by Lewalski, *Life of Milton*), see Nicholas von Maltzahn, 'Samuel Butler's Milton,' *SIP* 92 (1995), 482–95.

[79] This remarkable usage amalgamates three distinct homophones recorded by the *OED* as 'sconce, n.¹' ('A lantern or candlestick with a screen to protect the light from the wind,' from

Peace, as to make the Gentleman startle at his own dreams: yet to those who consider that these are but the fumes of Melancholy, such *Visionary Battalia's* are no more frightful than those fighting *Apparitions*; which Exhalations raise in the Clouds. But to indulge our Author in the love of his *Chimerical* conceits, struck blind with his own daz'ling *Idea* of the *Sun*, and admiring those *imaginary* Heights which his fancy has rais'd. Since even timerous Minds are Couragious and bold enough to shape prodigious Forms and Images of Battels; & dark Souls may be illuminated with *bright* and shining thoughts.[80]

Marvell is presented as a crazed poet (a 'Romancer'), a melancholic, and a (religious) enthusiast.[81] These three categories had large areas of overlap in the early modern English imaginary, as is evidenced, not least, in Robert Burton's discussion of enthusiasm as a kind of 'religious melancholy' and its connections to the 'phrenzy' of the inspired poet.[82] In describing Marvell's imaginings and mental faculties in terms of armies and fortifications, the author of *The Transproser Rehears'd* is drawing on established tropes of of sense perception and cognition more generally; his association of 'the fumes of Melancholy' and the passions they cause with civil unrest belongs in the same general area of metaphorical conceptualisation.[83] Notably, especially in view of the subsequent close association of Marvell and Milton as the twin targets of the author's invective, Marvell is also figured as blind: 'struck blind,' in fact, by his own excessive imagina-

---

Latin *absconsus*, 'hidden'), 'sconce, n.[2]' ('A jocular term for: The head; esp. the crown or top of the head ...;' of obscure origin), and 'sconce, n.[3]' ('*Fortification*, A small fort or earthwork ...;' from the Dutch; a cognate of modern German *Schanze*).

[80] *Transproser Rehears'd*, 40–41; Marvell, ed. Donno, 34.

[81] See *OED*, 'romancer, n.': '(1) The author of a romance; a writer of romances; (2) A person prone to wild exaggeration or falsehood; a teller of false stories ... Also: a person given to romantic speculation, a fantasist.' Both senses are attested by mid-seventeenth-century citations.

[82] See, for instance, Burton on religious melancholy (*Anatomy of Melancholy*, pt. 3, sect. IV; 311–432); see also Michael Heyd, 'Robert Burton's Sources on Enthusiasm and Melancholy: From a Medical Tradition to Religious Controversy,' *HEI* 5 (1984), 17–44.

[83] On the associations of the human body, and especially its mental and perceptual faculties (including the five senses), with fortifications – brilliantly captured by the anonymous author's use of 'sconce,' see McKeown, *Fortification and Its Discontents*, as well as Martha Pollak, *Cities at War in Early Modern Europe* (Cambridge: Cambridge University Press, 2010), who comments on 'the extraordinary fashion of the pentagonal citadel between 1534 and 1680,' pointing out that 'Italian architectural writings [of that era] still imagined the city as a human body with the citadel as its head, or inscribed a "Vitruvian man" onto the pentagonal citadel, with hands and feet corresponding to four bastions and a crowned head at the fifth, oriented towards the enemy' (12). See also some of the contemporary illustrations discussed by Pollak (13, 20–21). Although Pollak suggests that 'there is scant evidence that the pentagon was chosen for occult, Neoplatonic, or Pythagorean reasons' (25), its associations with the body, the head, and the five senses – even in the concrete context of fortification building – are well documented; see Paolo Marconi, "Una chiave per l'interpretazione dell'urbanistica rinascimentale: la cittadella come microcosmo,' *Quaderni dell'Istituto di storia dell'architettura* 15 (1968), 53–94, esp. 64, 69, citing the Renaissance architect Lorini on bastions: '... essendo questi gli occhi del baluardo, che è capo del corpo della Fortezza ... onde potrassi assimigliare essa Fortezza al corpo humano.'

tion.[84] The language in which this imaginary blinding is described, in turn, is phrased in another contemporary idiom, allied to those of anti-enthusiasm and faculty psychology (or, considering Burton's claim to medical efficacy, 'faculty psychiatry'): that of anti-Platonism, which likewise had a strong investment in sensory discourse owing to the marked visual component of much Platonic imagery (I will return to this point below in my discussion of Milton's own use of the visual-Platonic idiom).

The passage quoted from *The Transproser Rehears'd* is pervaded by the twin themes of cognition and perception – or rather, by their malfunctions: passionate 'tumults,' blindness, and melancholy madness. Right down to the level of terminology, the 'shapes' and 'figures' referred to by Marvell's and Milton's detractor form part of what Suparna Roychoudhury has called the 'lexicon of imagination,' i.e., they are *termini technici* from faculty psychological discussions of the 'fancy.'[85] However, the '*Shapes*' and '*Figures*,' the *Visionary* [!] *Battalia's*' and '*Apparitions*' mentioned also relate to symptoms of madness as phenomena of visual perception.[86] Melancholy itself, by virtue alone of its etymological and conceptual link to 'black' bile, is associated with the notion of darkness as opposed to light. Connected to this, however, is the strong – and more explicitly sensory – association of melancholy and dreaming, in Burton as in other early modern authorities on the condition.[87] Thus, in his 1659 character of 'A Melancholy Man', Samuel Butler comments that 'his sleeps and his wakings are so much the same, that he knows not how to distinguish them, and many times when he dreams, he believes he is broad awake and *sees visions.*'[88] Marvell's supposedly pathological imagination is thus consistently linked to the sphere of (visual) perception, most explicitly through the references to his being 'struck blind with his own daz'ling *Idea* of the *Sun*,' to 'dark Souls' and '*bright* and shining thoughts.' What is introduced as a figurative way of speaking about how 'Souls may be illuminated' (another ironic dig at the enthusiasts) is swiftly literalised, however, as the pamphleteer's attention turns to Milton:

> As, to seek no farther for an instance; the *blind* Author of *Paradise lost* (the odds betwixt a *Transproser* and a *Blank Verse Poet*, is not great) begins his third Book thus, groping for a beam of *Light*. ...[89]

---

[84] Marvell and Milton were connected by their work and personal relations. It is assumed that Marvell was appointed to his first post at Milton's recommendation; he became the blind Milton's personal assistant in 1657, and would later, as a member of parliament, use his influence to make sure that Milton was released from his temporary incarceration in the autumn and winter of 1660; see Lewalski, *Life of John Milton*, 293, 344, 400.

[85] See her *Phantasmatic Shakespeare*, 22 (on Theseus' terminologically precise references to 'toys,' 'shapes,' 'forms,' and 'fantasies' in *A Midsummer Night's Dream*.)

[86] On this complex of issues central to early modern sensory history, see the seminal study by Clark, *Vanities of the Eye*.

[87] See Clark, *Vanities of the Eye*, 56–57; Rivière, *Dreams in Early Modern England*, 107–109.

[88] Samuel Butler, 'A Melancholy Man,' in: Id., *Characters*, ed. Charles W. Daves (Cleveland, Ohio: P of Case Western U, 1970 [1659]), 96–98, at 97, emphasis added.

[89] *Transproser Rehears'd*, 41; *Marvell*, ed. Donno, 34.

The image of blind Milton groping because he cannot see conforms to traditional mocking representations of blind people as 'fumbling and stumbling,' groping with their hands to find their way around. 'The outstretched hand,' Moshe Barasch comments, 'is the most characteristic gesture, and it became a shorthand emblem for blindness.'[90] Along with other negative attributes associated with blindness – such as stupidity, licentiousness, and indeed the madness also attributed to Marvell –, this tactile 'shorthand' for blindness can be found in classical as well as biblical sources, as Barasch notes. Thus, one of the curses of Deuteronomy 28 reads, 'The Lord shall smite thee with madness, and blindness, and astonishment of heart: And thou shalt grope at noonday, as the blind gropeth in darkness.'[91] Even more specifically, the author of *The Transproser Rehears'd* appears to invert and thus negate Milton's material conception of 'holy light,' which is the – literally – palpable aspect of its approachability, as outlined above: whoever claims direct, personal familiarity with the divine, the image implies, is as ridiculous as a blind man groping at (immaterial) light.[92]

This first attack is followed by quotations of *PL* 3.1–2 ('Hail, holy Light, …') and 21–26 (ending in 'Or dim suffusion veil'd. ——'), which provide the points of reference for the author's subsequent taunts. Then the main part of the attack on Milton begins, picking up on specific formulations from Proem III:

> No doubt but the thoughts of this *Vital Lamp* lighted a *Christmas* Candle in his brain. What dark meaning he may have in calling this *thick drop Serene*, I am not able to say; but for his *Eternal Coeternal*, besides the absurdity of his inventive Divinity, in making *Light* contemporary with it's [sic] Creator, that jingling in the middle of his Verse, is more notoriously ridiculous, because the *blind Bard* (as he tell[s] us himself in his Apology for writing in blank Verse) studiously declin'd Rhyme as a *jingling sound of like endings* …[93]

These remarks, in particular, are noteworthy for a number of reasons. For one thing, they deflate Milton's quasi-prophetical claim to theological authority by reducing his 'holy light' to the – still reasonably Christian yet much less awe-inspiring and thus less threatening, not to mention less politically subversive – Christmas candle of popular folklore.[94] The literalising, materialising image – a lone candle lighted in this poor maniac's brain, as opposed to Milton's original plea in Proem III to 'irradiate' his mind 'through all her powers' – of course is meant to strike the reader as absurd and ridiculous. Its form and thrust are directly parallel to the earlier jeering remarks about Marvell's 'sconce' (i.e., his head as a lantern or candlestick). The obscurity of nonconformist writing, moreover, – Milton's 'dark meaning' – was a standard trope of anti-

---

[90] See Barasch, *Blindness*, 102–103, quotation at 102.
[91] Dtn. 28:28–29.
[92] Compare also the many other slanders of Milton aimed at his blindness, some of which are quoted below.
[93] *Transproser Rehears'd*, 42; *Marvell*, ed. Donno, 34–35.
[94] See Ronald Hutton, *The Stations of the Sun: A History of the Ritual Year in Britain* (Oxford: Oxford University Press, 1996), 9, 37, on mediaeval and early modern Christmas traditions involving candle-lighting.

enthusiasm rhetoric.[95] Here it is directly related to Milton's – *prima facie* paradoxical – reference to the condition of blindness as a 'drop *serene*' (i.e., clear or bright), actually an opthalmological term of art.[96]

To the author of *The Transproser Rehears'd* (as to Milton himself, I have suggested), the term and concept of 'invention' – in spiritual matters, most of all – are anathema; and one of the more ludicrous aspects of blind Milton's 'inventive Divinity' must be his 'making *Light* contemporary with it's Creator,' otherwise Proem III would not have been singled out for special comment. This disambiguating reading is part of the pamphleteer's agenda, of course; Milton's actual phrasing ('... offspring of heaven firstborn/*Or* of the eternal co-eternal beam/*May I express thee unblamed?*') suggests greater wariness in both its deliberative and cautiously questioning quality and in the sequence in which two distinct possibilities are named – *first* comes the reference to light as heaven's 'offspring ... first-born,' a epithet often associated with the Son.[97] And 'Christ,' as Donne puts it in a Christmas sermon on John 1:8 ('[John] was not that Light, but was sent to bear witness of that Light') – 'Christ is not so called light, as he is called a rock, or a corner-stone; not by a metaphor, but truly, and properly.'[98] Milton combines these three orthodox notions into an unorthodox fourth: Christ as the firstborn Son is a conventional idea, so is Christ as light, and so is light as the first creature.[99] However Christ (*qua* light), as the Father's firstborn *creature*, would make the Son not a fully co-equal member of the Trinity, but a secondary or less powerful one. Only after this Christological assessment of light, based in his unorthodox conception of the Trinity, does Milton consider its possible 'co-eternality' and identity with the Father. Ultimately, it appears that both possibilities named by the speaker of Proem III are expressive of Milton's 'inventive Divinity' – but their (im)precise signification is more dynamically complex than the author of *The Transproser Rehears'd* allows. All things considered, Milton's lines combine the theological self-assurance perhaps to be expected from the author of a treatise named *De Doctrina Christiana* (just like Augustine's) with a tentativeness and even an insecurity ('May I express thee unblamed?') that is characteristic of the proems in general, and of their oscillation between soaring confidence and a preoccupation with the dark, both metaphorically and literally.

---

[95] See Gabel, *Paradise Reframed*, 60n46, 129.
[96] See n.142 below. Arguably, Milton diverts some of that paradoxical force for his own ends: the blindness occasioned by the 'drop serene' is itself 'serene' in the sense that it enables a kind of beatific vision.
[97] See, for instance, Col. 1:15: '[The Son] is the image of the invisible God, the firstborn of every creature.' Compare also Fowler ad loc. As *logos*, the Son was in fact 'co-eternal' with the Father according to the prologue to John ('In the beginning was the Word ...') – and thus, in mainstream theology; this view clashes, however, with Milton's unorthodox understanding of the Trinity, often labelled as 'Arian.' See the section on Milton's antitrinitarianism in Maurice Kelley's introduction to the *Christian Doctrine* (*De Doctrina Christiana*), CPW 6: 47–73. For a critical assessment of that designation of 'Arianism' (by Kelley and others), see C. A. Patrides, 'Milton and Arianism,' *JHI* 25 (1964), 423–29.
[98] Sermon CXVII, Preached at St. Paul's upon Christmas-Day, 1621; quoted by Fowler ad *PL* 3.2.
[99] See, again, *PL* 7.243: 'Let there be light, said God, and forthwith light/Ethereal, *first of things*, quintessence pure/Sprung from the deep ...' (emphasis added).

Perhaps most significantly, however, the author of *The Transproser Rehears'd* perceives a connection between Milton's 'inventive Divinity' and his more properly inventive activity as a poet. In this, he recognises but refutes – and, immediately afterwards, explicitly cites – Milton's own amalgamation of poetics and politics (which in turn are closely connected to his religious views) in the note on 'The Verse':

> You see Sir, that I am improved too with reading the Poets, and though you may be better read in *Bishop Dav'nants Gondibert;* yet I think this *Schismatick in Poetry* [i.e., Milton], though nonconformable in point of Rhyme, as authentick ev'ry jot, as any *Bishop Laureat* of them all.[100]

The philosophical epic *Gondibert*, dedicated by its author, the royalist theatre impresario and poet laureate Sir William Davenant (no 'Bishop' he), to Thomas Hobbes, is put side by side with *Paradise Lost* to mock both the theological and poetological pretensions of Milton's epic (and, at the same time, the pomposity of Davenant himself). In accusing Milton of being 'nonconformable in point of Rhyme' and simultaneously pointing out 'that jingling in the middle of his Verse' – i.e., the internal rhyme of 'eternal co-eternal' –, his detractor aims to expose him as a hypocrite: a poetic fraud and a spiritual pretender at once. What else to expect from a blind man claiming to be so intimately familiar with light?

Throughout the passages of *The Transproser Rehears'd* that are directed against Milton, he and Marvell – the main target of the pamphlet – are closely associated by means of cross-relating references to their darkly confused minds, beset with dangerous enthusiasm yet maniacally sure of their own private illumination. When the pamphleteer had denounced Marvell's 'chimerical conceits,' being 'struck blind with his own … *Idea* of the *Sun*, and admiring those *imaginary* heights which his fancy had rais'd,' this not only draws on the 'lexicon of imagination,' as discussed above, but is also intended – as is evident from the reference to 'his own … *Idea* of the *Sun*' – to evoke another perceptual-cognitive discourse of the seventeenth-century debate: namely, that of contemporary Platonism. Within the confines of that discourse, i.e., among early modern Platonists and their opponents, the term 'idea' – derived, incidentally, from the same visual root that gave us Latin *videre* – could have distinct meanings still recognisable today. On the one hand, the term suggests, now as it did then, diverse ways in which something may be said to be 'just an idea,' whether as a mere suggestion or an insubstantial flight of fancy.[101] On the other, there is the neutral or positive, more or less technical, more or less explicitly Platonic use of the term to signify, generally, 'a standard or principle to be realised or aimed at; a conception of what is desirable or ought to be' – an *ideal*.[102] In mid-seventeenth-century Britain, however, the two notions

---

[100] *Transproser Rehears'd*, 43; *Marvell*, ed. Donno, 35.

[101] See most expressly on the negative side *OED*, 'idea, n.,' 11b: '*depreciative*. A conception to which no reality corresponds; something merely imagined or fancied. Usually with modifying word, as *mere*.' Among Milton's writings, see also *Il Penseroso*, 1–10 and the discussion of those lines in the context of early modern faculty psychology by Roychoudhury, *Phantasmatic Shakespeare*, 59–60, 93–94.

[102] *OED*, 'idea, n.,' 2.

– 'Platonic ideas' and 'mere ideas' – were not necessarily distinct, as is suggested by a quotation from the puritan witch-hunter John Gaule's *Pys-mantia: The Mag-Astro-Mancer, or the Magicall-Astrologicall Diviner Posed and Puzzled* (1652), given by the *OED* to illustrate the Platonic sense of 'idea': 'chymericall figments, Platonicall Ideaes, Cabbalisticall fancies.' All six of those words, clearly, are meant to sting; three of them ('*Idea*,' 'chimerical,' 'fancy') are also levelled against Marvell by the author of *The Transproser Rehears'd*. At this point, it becomes clear how personal considerations and emphases could shape individual authors' investments in the discourses surrounding and imbuing perception and the senses: the anonymous pamphleteer's (negative) assessment of the imagination or 'fancy' is quite in tune with Milton's own personifying references to that faculty in *Paradise Lost*. Both authors are suspicious of the supposed unruliness of the imagination, apt to lead the conscious, ruling intellect astray at the instigation of the senses, whether sleeping and dreaming or waking and, perhaps, day-dreaming. On the contrary, by his own usage of the term 'idea', the author of *The Transproser Rehears'd* shows that he would not have accepted Milton's generally positive valuation of the term in *Paradise Lost* and elsewhere (to which I will return below).[103]

In the passage from *The Transproser Rehears'd*, '*Idea*' is certainly intended to evoke its technical, Platonic/Platonist meaning, considering the simultaneous allusion to the extended metaphor involving the sun in Plato's *Republic*, which already points ahead to the subsequent focus on (personal) light and (merely imaginary) truth in the subsequent attacks on Milton.[104] As in these attacks, characterised by the puncturing of Milton's high theological pathos at its most vulnerable point – his metaphysics and poetics of light –, the pamphleteer aims to deflate the lofty term, '*Idea*,' and he does so with remarkable efficiency: if something is someone's 'own … *Idea*,' it cannot be an idea in the absolute, Platonic sense at all, even if it is accompanied by a dazzling, Platonic sun. The 'daz'ling' itself, of course, makes the image complete: Marvell – and by association, Milton – thinks he has glimpsed the truth, but in fact he has been struck blind.

Although Milton is not attacked directly in this image, he and Marvell are consistently tarred with the same brush throughout the relevant passages of *The Transproser Rehears'd*. In addition, Milton's own frequent recourse to a remarkably similar visual-Platonic idiom is striking and relates, not least, to his unorthodox conception of the Deity, the precise occasion for the attacks on him in *The Transproser Rehears'd*. As the

---

[103] *PL* 7.557, quoted above, is Milton's only use of the term 'idea' in *Paradise Lost* and – as far as I can see – in his English poetry generally. See, however, the semi-serious 'De Idea Platonica quemadmodum Aristoteles intellexit' ('Of the Platonic Ideal Form as understood by Aristotle,' June 1628?), which not only references 'the visionary Tiresias, whose blindness gave him piercing sight' ('cui profundum caecitas lumen dedit/Dircaeus augur,' 25–26) but also, in its concluding lines, names Plato as 'the greatest fictional writer of them all' ('fabulator maximus,' 38) for positing the existence of the ideal form of man (Milton is channelling an arch-Aristotelian persona throughout). Milton's reference to 'sotto nova idea/Pellegrina bellezza' (6–7) in the Italian Sonnet 4, probably written at the end of 1629, – 'a foreign beauty, modelled on a new idea of loveliness' – appears to indicate a generally Platonic understanding of the term, as well.
[104] *Republic* 507b–509c. Plato has Socrates offer the sun as an accessible analogy for the idea of the Good (*to agathon*).

use of Platonising sensory discourse in the respective passages ties in with the visual/optical theology of Proem III, it reflects back on the sensory discursive situatedness of the proem in the wider context of Milton's epic. In one pertinent passage from book 7 of *Paradise Lost*, the Father, having accomplished his six-days' work of Creation,

> up returned
> Up to the heaven of heavens his high abode,
> Thence to behold this new created world
> The addition of his empire, how it showed
> In prospect from his throne, how good, how fair,
> Answering his great idea. (*PL* 7.552–57)

As the proliferation of visual language ('behold,' 'showed,' 'prospect') and the corresponding conceptual metaphorics ('up,' 'high') already suggest, 'idea,' in Milton's clearly less negative conception of the term, belongs in the same sensory-metaphorical domain. This is caused, most likely, by the Platonic notion of a 'vision (or contemplation) of the ideas' – ideas of which, incidentally, (the) 'good,' (the) 'fair,' and (the) 'great,' apart from being attributes of the Godhead, would make almost textbook examples. Even apart from the passage just quoted, there are a number of passages throughout *Paradise Lost* in which Milton – an Aristotelian, generally, if not a very enthusiastic one – appears comfortable with Platonic notions, and appears to be flirting with the idea of 'ideas.'

This Platonic idiom and conceptual framework can be shown to have deep roots in Milton's earlier writing.[105] In several of his prolusions, specifically, the young Milton had harshly critiqued (and yet shown a firm grasp of) Aristotelian-based scholasticism, and had made some positive references to Platonic metaphysics and epistemology. Most notably, this had been the case in Prolusion VII, where the concept of knowledge required aspirants, in the same visual-Platonic idiom discussed above, to 'gaze upon and contemplate the Ideas [*ideas* intueri] of things human or divine.'[106] This, one could

---

[105] See Marjara, *Contemplation of Created Things*, 45–46. Marjara argues that Milton's scientific Aristotelianism is based not wholly on personal admiration but also on the needs of his epic poem for consistency and coherence. Still: 'The non-Aristotelian opinions that [Milton] adopted amounted to no more than minor adjustments to his basic Aristotelian position.' The opposition, however, may not even be all that rigid; see Lloyd P. Gerson, *Aristotle and Other Platonists* (Ithaca, N. Y.: Cornell University Press, 2005).

[106] CPW 1: 291. In the *Art of Logic* (which, however, is largely a translation), the following passage is significant, because it demonstrates the very fine calibration – Platonic, but *not too* Platonic, or rather: not too Platonist – of which the concept is capable: 'For the notion of what is essential and common to all species is called *genus*, and by the Greeks often *idea*, not indeed one separated from things, as they would hold the Platonic ideas to be – which are nonsense according to Aristotle [in his *Metaphysics*] – but something which in thought and reason is one and the same thing common to many species in which in fact and by nature it occurs individually, as Plato says in the *Meno*. The Stoics, too, as Plutarch reports ..., said that the ideas were our own notions' (CPW 8: 299). Of the very few terminologically significant references to 'ideas' in Milton's other prose, the remaining are either to a (rather Platonic) 'idea of beauty' (as in Sonnet IV) or – in the two passages of *De Doctrina Christiana* – to ideas in the mind of God (as in *PL* 7.557).

argue, is exactly what the God of *Paradise Lost* is doing when he 'behold[s]' the newly created world with his 'great idea' in mind. In his theological treatise *De Doctrina Christiana* (*Of Christian Doctrine*), Milton would indicate that this was, in fact, the conceptual place of the passage from book 7 of *Paradise Lost*, right at the intersection of divine vision (God beholding) and a vision of the divine (contemplating God's works and precedent 'idea'): 'For God's foreknowledge is simply his wisdom under another name, or that idea of all things which, to speak in human terms, he had in mind before he decreed anything.'[107] This much is common dogma, and the act of God's beholding, in a way and in an idiom that usually indicates the generation of *knowledge*, the product of his own 'great idea' (i.e., his own fore*knowledge*) could thus be construed as yet another portrayal of perfect divine (self-)knowledge, as in the Father's and the Son's earlier visual communication and, indeed, communion in the light-and-sight-based book 3 of *Paradise Lost*:

> Beyond compare the Son of God was seen
> Most glorious, in him all his Father shone
> Substantially expressed, an in his face
> Divine compassion visibly appeared,
> Love without end, and without measure grace ...   (*PL* 3.138–42)

However, Milton's divine epistemology is rather more unorthodox than this, as becomes apparent when, discussing the problem of free will in *De Doctrina*, he declares that

> it is neither absurd nor impious to say that the idea of certain things or events might come to God from some other source [sc. than his foreknowledge]. Since God has decreed from eternity that man should have free will to enable him either to fall or not to fall, the idea of that evil event, the fall, was clearly present in God from some other source: everyone admits this. It cannot be deduced from this that something temporal may cause or limit something eternal; for nothing temporal, but rather eternal wisdom supplied a cause for the divine plan.[108]

This account of the divine management of (fore-)knowledge, just like Adam's contention that 'evil into the mind of God ... May come ...' in book 5, is an unorthodox take on the functioning on God's mind – and perhaps it is forced to be so, as Milton intends seriously to tackle a looming contradiction. Ultimately, even a brief consideration of these theological underpinnings of Milton's use of Platonic terminology indicates that, considering Milton's conception of what divine perception could mean, the precise mode of his portrayal of God beholding his Creation in book 7 – clearly presented as a visual event geared towards the acquisition of knowledge – is far from gratuitous.

In further instances of 'Platonising' sensory discourse in *Paradise Lost*, the axis of sight is upended, as various characters contemplate the sun, and the question of the

---

[107] CPW 6: 154. The translation is John Carey's. The fair copy of *De Doctrina* – by the hands of diverse of Milton's amanuenses – dates from around 1660; it was rediscovered in a Whitehall cupboard in 1823 and first printed in 1825.
[108] CPW 6: 162–63.

relationship between perceptible appearances and underlying realities is raised – whether these are understood to be, e.g., 'the Good,' 'Truth,' or 'God' is not entirely immaterial but does not affect the structure of presentation, partly because the solar image Milton uses can be related both to Plato's own 'sun analogy' from the *Republic* and to conventional associations of the Christian God with the sun.[109] Thus, in Adam's and Eve's prayer-address, 'Thou sun, of this great world both eye and soul,/Acknowledge [God] thy greater' (*PL* 5.171–72), the intricacies of the Christian identification of God and sun are subtly reproduced: their invocation is to the sun, but its ultimate honoree is God. Contrast Satan's both aggressive and self-pitying apostrophe to the sun after his earlier alighting on the summit of Mount Niphates:

> O thou that with surpassing glory crowned,
> Lookst from thy sole dominion like the God
> Of this new world; at whose sight all the stars
> Hide their diminished heads; to thee I call,
> But with no friendly voice, and add thy name
> O sun, to tell thee how I hate thy beams
> That bring to my remembrance from what state
> I fell, how glorious once above thy sphere;
> Till pride and worse ambition threw me down
> Warring in heaven against heaven's matchless king:
>
> (*PL* 4.32–41)[110]

In his contemptuous punning ('sole dominion') and misapprehension, Satan's address differs markedly from that of Adam and Eve. Even if he appears to recognise that the sun only 'looks ... *like* the God/Of this new world,' he does not make the crucial further step of 'acknowledg[ing God irs] greater;' he does mention God as 'heaven's matchless king,' but is not able – or does not want – to fully grasp the multiple connections – representational, representative, and genetic – between the two entities: in Satan's account the sun is just a light in the sky (albeit a splendid one), not a stand-in for its creator; and God is just a despot (albeit a powerful one), and not *the* Creator.[111] Still, Satan employs the same visual idiom familiar from both, references to God beholding his Creation and Adam and Eve's address to the sun.[112] Ironically, how-

---

[109] See Marjara, *Contemplation of Created Things*, 46, 118–144, on the presence of a typically Renaissance exaltation of the sun in Milton (and in *Paradise Lost*, specifically).

[110] For this and the previous quotation, see also Fowler ad locc. and Marjara, *Contemplation of Created Things*, 218, 292 on the diverse non-Aristotelian resonances of Milton's images in both passages.

[111] This perspective ties in with the fallen angels' consistent (and wilful?) misrepresentation of God in terms of 'normal,' secular kingship and rule in books 1 and 2 of *Paradise Lost*, as well as with Satan's frequent questioning of God's creative powers.

[112] It might be worth asking, however, whether the respective addresses of the sun as 'thou' do not represent distinct usages of the familiar pronoun: either, by Adam and Eve, to express 'solidarity' with the sun (as in St Francis's 'Brother Sun'); or, in Satan's case, to express 'contempt' for it; see Terry Walker, *'Thou' and 'You' in Early Modern English Dialogues: Trials, Depositions, and Drama Comedy* (Amsterdam: John Benjamins, 2007), 39–64.

ever, Satan's use of the appropriate vocabulary does not result in knowledge – and thus acknowledgment – of God but in error and misrepresentation, leading further on towards his subsequent actions.

When, to address one last instance of the visual-Platonic idiom in *Paradise Lost*, Adam replies to Raphael's explanations regarding the scale of nature, nurture, perception, and cognition ('So from the root/Springs lighter the green stalk …'), he does so in a way that highlights the Platonic roots of this notion of a 'great chain,' and gives a first intimation as to the connections between visual perception and the acquisition of secure – because divinely warranted – knowledge:[113]

> O favourable spirit, propitious guest,
> Well hast thou taught the way that might direct
> Our knowledge, and the scale of nature set
> From centre to circumference, whereon
> In contemplation of created things
> By steps we may ascend to God.
>
> (*PL* 5.507–512)

In her sweeping study of the reception and various restatements of the classical *beatus ille* tradition in the early modern period, Maren-Sofie Røstvig has argued that, partly as a reaction to the experience of the Civil War, the ideal-typical and active 'Happy Husbandman [modelled on Adam in Paradise] was being metamorphosed into a [rather passive] Serene Contemplator ' in the 1640s and 1650s.[114] In the case of Milton's Adam – who, after all, is meant to represent the original 'Happy Husbandman' –, the turn towards contemplation, though innocent in itself, brings with it a premonition of his ultimate downfall. Significantly, Milton has Adam refer to 'created things' in general (which includes, for instance, Eve and the forbidden fruit). In other authors' statements of the same theme, contemplation is almost invariably contemplation of the heavens, and the importance of God or Wisdom as the ultimate goals of that contemplation outshines any possible obstacles along the way. Thus, in Joseph Hall's characterisation of 'The Happy Man' (from his *Characters of Virtues and Vices*, 1608), 'His eyes stick so fast in heaven, that no earthly object can remove them; yea, his whole selfe is there

---

[113] On the 'great chain' metaphor, see, still, Tillyard, *Elizabethan World Picture*, 25–82; and Arthur O. Lovejoy, *The Great Chain of Being: A Study in the History of an Idea* (Cambridge, Mass.: Harvard University Press, 1978 [1936]). Lovejoy refers to *PL* 5.507–512 at 89–90. For an account of the 'great chain of being' from the perspective of conceptual metaphor theory, see Kövecses, *Metaphor*, 151–56.

[114] Maren-Sofie Røstvig, *The Happy Man: Studies on the Metamorphoses of a Classical Ideal*, 2 vols (Oslo: Akademisk Forlag, 1954–58), I, 143. 'Beatus ille' refers to the opening lines of Horace's Second Epode (*Beatus ille qui procul negotiis/ut prisca gens mortalium/paterna rura bobus exercet suis/solutus omni faenore …*), rendered by Dryden as 'How happy in his low degree/How rich in humble Poverty, is he,/Who leads a quiet country life!/Discharg'd of business, void of strife …'

before his time.'[115] Raphael, in the lines following on Adam's quoted above, emphatically denies that such a contemplative transport to a higher plane of vision or knowledge can *on its own* bring true happiness:

> Son of heaven and earth,
> Attend: that thou art happy, owe to God;
> That thou continu'st such, owe to thyself,
> That is, to thy obedience; therein stand.
> This was the caution giv'n thee; be advised.
> …
> Myself and all the angelic host that stand
> In sight of God enthroned, our happy state
> Hold, as you yours, while our obedience holds …
> (*PL* 5.519–23, 535–37)

As Raphael's juxtaposition of (insufficient) human contemplation and the (superabundant) *visio beatifica* that is predicated upon a firm obedience to the will of God insinuates, the scale of contemplation – leading, 'by steps,' upward but focused, ultimately, on 'created things' – may ultimately prove a slippery slope downward into ruin: 'And some are fallen, to disobedience fallen,/And so from heaven to deepest hell; oh fall/From what high state of bliss into what woe!' (*PL* 5.541–43).[116]

Both accounts of contemplation, Hall's and Milton's, may be said to meet, then, in that Hall's reference to the 'Happy Man' being 'there [sc. in heaven] before his time' also calls up the notion of *visio beatifica*, a concept strongly associated throughout *Paradise Lost*, as in the passage just quoted, with closeness – and obedience – to God. On the other hand, Adam's appreciation of the materiality – 'of created things' – and gradualness implicit in the enterprise of acquiring knowledge – 'by steps we may ascend' – , both combining as if to postulate a quasi-Baconian assemblage of tangible micro-insights, contrasts with the pronounced other-worldliness of Hall's description: 'no earthly object can remove [his eyes from heaven].'[117] In this respect, at least, Hall's portrait of an (albeit 'Happy') skygazer is much closer in conceptual structure to Milton's descriptions of Melancholy in *Il Penseroso* – another heavily Platonising early text – as having 'looks commercing with the skies,/Thy rapt soul sitting in thine eyes,' and of that poem's speaker as

---

[115] Hall quoted in Røstvig, *Happy Man*, I, 123; compare Hall's character of the 'wise man,' who is 'an apt scholler … for … *everything he sees* informes him' (quoted in Røstvig, *Happy Man*, I, 159, emphasis added).

[116] In all of the accounts of contemplation cited in this section, of course, VISION IS UP, KNOWLEDGE IS UP, HAPPINESS IS UP; in the passages from *Paradise Lost*, in addition, OBEDIENCE IS UP (expressed in the opposition of 'standing' vs 'falling'). Note also the semi-explicit association of hearing and obedience in Raphael's admonition: 'Attend [i.e., listen]: … thy obedience; therein stand.'

[117] It also contrasts with the later view of Jonathan Edwards that, in the ascent to divine knowledge, there was no 'long chain of arguments; the argument is but one … the mind ascends to the truth of the gospel but by one step, and that is its divine glory' (Edwards quoted in Wainwright, 'Jonathan Edwards,' 233).

>   seen in some high lonely tower,
> Where I may oft outwatch the Bear,
> With thrice great Hermes, or unsphere
> The spirit of Plato to unfold
> What worlds, or what vast regions hold
> The immortal mind that hath forsook
> Her mansion in this fleshly nook: (*IP* 39–40, 86–92)

Here, the speaker's watching, actually a somewhat unnatural (because nocturnal) 'outwatch[ing]', is allied to the 'immortal mind' soaring above, and contrasted with the world of the senses.[118] The first correlation makes use of the spiritualised kind of vision implied by the Platonic notion of contemplation – as evoked by Milton's reference to 'the spirit of Plato' – and, as often, it is represented by an engagement in, at bottom, *practical* astronomy: the metaphorical 'unspher[ing]' of Plato's spirit is subsequent to the stargazer's placement in 'some high lonely tower.'[119] The second is represented by the 'mansion' of the body, a 'fleshly nook' for the mind (figured as female on account of Latin *mens*) to dwell in – or rather, to 'fors[ake]' at the first possibility. There is a striking similarity – in the sense of an inversion, a conceptual complementarity – between those lines from *Il Penseroso* (1632?) and the following, the second stanza of Milton's 'Nativity Ode' ('On the Morning of Christ's Nativity,' 1629):

> That glorious form, that light unsufferable,
> And that far-beaming blaze of majesty,
> Wherewith he wont at heaven's high council-table,
> To sit the midst of trinal unity,
> He laid aside; and here with us to be,
>   Forsook the courts of everlasting day,
> And chose with us a darksome house of mortal clay.   (8–14)

At the Incarnation – as I have mentioned, the only kind of dynamic embodiment Milton feels comfortable with –, it is *Christ* who 'fors[akes]' the high regions of light, choosing instead 'a darksome house of mortal clay,' i.e., both the lowly stable of Bethlehem (lit., 'house of bread') and the 'mansion' of the body 'in this fleshly nook.' His descent, as Milton presents it, is as humbling as the 'outwatch[ing]' of the speaker in *Il Penseroso*

---

[118] The term 'outwatch' is multiply ambiguous, see *OED* 'watch, v.': '(1) To be or remain awake …; (2) to remain awake for purposes of devotion; to keep vigil …; (3) to be on the alert, to be vigilant; to be one's guard against danger or surprise …; (4) to be on the look out; to keep a person or thing in sight, so as to be aware of any movement or change …' as well as, more specifically, 'outwatch, v.': '(1) To watch (an object) until it disappears; to watch through and beyond (a period of time); (2) to surpass in watching; to watch longer or be more vigilant than.' Milton's line is cited in support of sense 1 of 'outwatch.'

[119] See *OED*, 'unsphere, v.': 'to remove (a star, etc.) from its sphere. Also in figurative context.' The *OED*'s first attestation of the literal sense is from Shakespeare's *The Winter's Tale* (1.2.49); Milton's line is the first figurative use attested.

is ambitious. Both images associate light with the sphere of the incorporeal and with supreme, i.e., either Platonically 'ideal' or divine wisdom (promulgated, we may assume, at 'heaven's high-council-table'). The negative foil to this blazing wisdom of absolute minds is constituted by the human, all-too-human body and the darkness associated with it, either the darkness of night (in *Il Penseroso*) or the a 'darksome house of mortal clay.'

And what of Adam, 'this man of clay,' as Satan sneeringly calls him?[120] His own idea – in a non-Platonic sense – of the patient ascent to the divine (and to knowledge) is as far from the hermetic and magical suddenness suggested by the lines from *Il Penseroso* as it is from that other sudden epistemic transformation: the one promised to Eve by the Serpent. But does his assumption that 'in contemplation of created things ... / ... we may ascend to God,' even as it is set to follow 'the way that might direct/Our knowledge,' actually imply the acquisition of *divine* knowledge of the kind solicited as well as professed in Milton's proems? A subsequent passage clarifies the point. When, after Raphael's comprehensive account of the war in heaven, which takes up the second half of book 5 and all of book 6, it is Adam's turn to contribute to the conversation, he relates to the angel his own earliest memories, and these, too, relate to the connection between vision, contemplation (of 'created things' *and* of the divine), and, ultimately, to the acquisition of knowledge:

---

[120] At *PL* 9.176. Satan knows his Hebrew: *adamah* is 'the red tilled soil,' (red) clay or arable ground; the verbal stem *adam* itself means 'to be red' or ruddy, often used, suggestively, of skins or leather (*HALOT*, s. vv.). Compare Adam's (postlapsarian) cry, also associating 'clay' with 'darkness': 'Did I request thee, Maker, from my clay/To mould me man, did I solicit thee/From darkness to promote me, or here place/In this delicious garden?' (*PL* 10.743–46), which is based on Isa. 45:9: 'Woe unto him that striveth with *his* Maker [*yotzro*]! Let the potsherd strive with the potsherds of the earth. Shall the clay say *to him that fashioneth it* [*le'yotzro*], What makest thou? or thy work, He hath no hands?' In both instances, the Hebrew uses the term *yotzer*, 'a potter, a worker in clay'; as with many Hebrew nouns of occupation or function, this is actually a present participle (i.e., 'the forming one'), in the present case of *yatzar*, 'to form, fashion; (of God) to create' (*HALOT*, s. vv.). This is also the verb used at Gen. 2:7 ('And the Lord God *formed* [*wayyitzer*] *man of the dust of the ground* [*eth-ha'adam afar min-ha'adamah*] ...'). Generally, the association of clay with touch is clear – clay being *the* emblematic raw material to be worked with the hands; its association with darkness, in Milton as in Isaiah, rests on the interconnected conceptual metaphors LIGHT IS UP, TOUCH IS DOWN, and DARKNESS IS DOWN (realised as, e.g., 'darkness falls,' 'descent into darkness,' etc.), as well as on the impenetrability of clay (and the earth, more generally, as in Elegy V) to light. With particular reference to the act of creation, consider also the orientational metaphors CONSCIOUS IS UP and UNCONSCIOUS IS DOWN, special cases being LIFE IS UP and DEATH IS DOWN. For a detailed discussion of how the visual language of book 3 of *Paradise Lost* (concerned with seeing and images) relates to Milton's reflections on God's creation and works in the same book (concerned with how these might instill faith) see David Quint, '"Things Invisible to Mortal Sight:" Light, Vision and the Unity of Book 3 of *Paradise Lost*,' *MLQ* 71 (2010), 229–69.

For man to tell how human life began
Is hard; for who himself beginning knew?[121]
...
... As new waked from soundest sleep
Soft on the flowery herb I found me laid
In balmy sweat, which with his beams the sun
Soon dried, and on the reeking moisture fed.
Straight toward heaven my wondering eyes I turned,
And gazed a while the ample sky, till raised
By quick instinctive motion up I sprung,
As thitherward endeavouring, and upright
Stood on my feet; about me round I saw
Hill, dale, and shady woods, and sunny plains,
And liquid lapse of murmuring streams; by these
Creatures that lived, and moved, and walked, or flew,
Birds on the branches warbling; all things smiled,
With fragrance and with joy my heart o'erflowed.
Myself I then perused, and limb by limb
Surveyed, and sometimes went, and sometimes ran
With supple joints, as lively vigour led:
But who I was, or where, or from what cause,
Knew not; to speak I tried, and forthwith spake,
My tongue obeyed and readily could name
Whate'er I saw. Thou sun, said I, fair light,
And thou enlightened earth, so fresh and gay,
Ye hills and dales, ye rivers, woods, and plains,
And ye that live and move, fair creatures, tell,
Tell, if ye saw, how came I thus, how here?

---

[121] This remark of Adam's relates both to the problem of accommodation and serves as an ironic counterpart to Satan's sneering reply to Abdiel, 'That we were formed then sayst thou? And the work/Of secondary hands, by task transferred/From Father to his Son? Strange point and new!/Doctrine which we would know whence learned: who saw/When this creation was? Rememberst thou/Thy making, while the maker gave thee being?/We know no time when we were not as know;/Know none before us, self-begot, self-raised/By our own quickening power, when fatal course/Had circled his full orb, the birth mature/Of this our native heaven, ethereal sons' (*PL* 5.853–63). While Satan's ridicule is directed at the traditional image of the Creator as a divine artisan (and, disparagingly, at the Son as a 'demi-demiurge': 'secondary hands'), his last phrase contains a bitterly ironic pun (not by Satan but by his creator, Milton) on the 'ethereal mould' of the sun (see *PL* 7.354–56), and thus, again, contrasts the touch-based agency of the Creator with a supposedly higher sphere associated with vision.

5.2 Proem III (PL 3.1–55)

> Not of my self; by some great maker then,
> In goodness and in power pre-eminent;
> Tell me, how may I know him, how adore,
> From whom I have that thus I move and live,
> And feel that I am happier than I know.
>
> (*PL* 8.250–82)

Throughout, Adam's report draws on several relevant orientational metaphors: CONSCIOUSNESS IS UP (while UNCONSCIOUSNESS IS DOWN: 'from soundest sleep') just as VISION IS UP (while TOUCH IS DOWN: 'soft ... laid'). His first movement is an upward movement of the eyes, a gaze towards heaven; from this, he draws the 'instinctive' impulse to spring up and stand 'upright' on his feet; he then looks around and surveys his surroundings, sees 'creatures' (i.e., 'created things'), hears brooks 'murmuring' and birds 'warbling,' absorbs 'fragrance' and 'joy' at once. On the 'soft ... flowery herb,' touch had provided the first of his sensations, then vision had taken the lead, triggered an instinctive upward movement and outward exploration; the other senses (minus, for now, taste) then joined in. A visual (possibly also tactile) 'perus[al]' of himself closes this first section, in which no knowledge other than instinctive awareness has been gained.

When Adam gains language (this, too, comes to him by instinct), he addresses his surroundings (in parallel to the prior reaching outward of his senses), begins asking questions, and thus has taken a swift first step toward (literally) discursive reason: 'Tell, if ye saw, *how* came I thus, *how* here?/*Not* of my self; by some great maker *then*.'[122] (The almost too neat and rapid logical conclusion with which Adam arrives at his proof of the existence of 'some great maker' was later parodied by John Dryden in his operatic reworking of *Paradise Lost* as *The State of Innocence*, in which a 'rising' Adam declaims, in mock-Cartesian language: 'What am I? or from whence? For what I am/I know, because I think ...')[123] Significantly, it is the sun whom Adam addresses first, using the same words – 'thou sun' – used later in the epic plot (though earlier in the narrative) by himself and Eve to worship God (as well as resembling, ironically, Satan's address to the sun, though 'with no friendly voice'). Adam's (sensory, visual) perception of this most conspicuous presence in the sensescape – prefigured, perhaps, in the reference to 'balmy sweat' at the very beginning of the passage[124] – leads immediately to the acknowledgment of 'some great maker.' And even though this 'maker' is as yet unknown, he is comprehensively described by Adam as 'in goodness and in power pre-eminent,' and thus – unbeknownst to Adam – known by these attributes, after all.

---

[122] See John Leonard, *Naming in Paradise: Milton and the Language of Adam and Eve* (Oxford: Clarendon, 1990), esp. 23–39 on the passage at hand.

[123] *The State of Innocence* (pr. 1677), 2.1.1–2. See Gabel, *Paradise Reframed*, 9–10, Dryden quoted at 10.

[124] Sweat which 'with his beams the sun/Soon dried, and on the reeking moisture feed,' immediately establishing a give-and-take relationship. On the importance of such processes of sublimation in the cosmology of *Paradise Lost*, see Marjara, *Contemplation of Created Things*, 178–88. See also Geoffrey Hartman, 'Adam on the Grass with Balsamum,' *ELH* 36 (1969), 168–92, esp. 168–73 on this particular passage and its connection to Adam's (and Satan's) attitude to the sun as representative of God.

At the same time as he is forced to confess that he still is 'happier than I know,' Adam has, unconsciously, gained considerable knowledge: knowledge of God and also – having 'surveyed' himself and concluding that he had come into being 'not of my self' – an awareness of what Milton presents, in contrast to the self-aggrandisement of the fallen angels, as the bedrock of self-knowledge.

Throughout the passage, which presents, as in a nutshell, a model of all experiential knowledge of both the macrocosm and the microcosm, Adam's sense perception is a necessary, not a sufficient, factor. It is necessary because it triggers Adam's instinctive movement towards knowledge of God and of himself – an upwards movement, mostly, since KNOWLEDGE, too, IS UP) –, and sustains it through facilitating Adam's sensory – and sensuous, joyful – engagement with his created surroundings. It is insufficient, however, because the transcendent trigger of those insights – God himself – is presented to the senses through his representative, the sun, yet remains, ultimately, unperceived. Adam is happy – his heart 'o'erflow[ing]' with joy –, but he is 'happier than I know.' Apart from ironically foreshadowing – to the reader – the danger already approaching at the time of Adam's conversation with Raphael, the ambiguous phrase, 'happier than I know,' indicates the insufficiency of (sense-based) knowing alone for a full analysis or understanding of that happiness. At the same time, Adam's proposition, '… that I am happier than I know,' is, significantly, something he 'feel[s],' i.e. perceives as part or as a symptom of his sensuous enjoyment.[125] At this point of his as yet short life, Adam is wholly wrapped up in this 'feeling of certain knowledge', evoked in him from the outside. At a later point – though, again, earlier in the narrative, and in a passage already quoted –, Raphael will remind him of the contingency of that condition – and of the responsibility it places on him: 'that thou art happy, owe to God;/That thou continu'st such, owe to thyself,/That is, to thy obedience …' (*PL* 5.520–22). The senses are one factor contributing to Adam's happiness; in the further development of Milton's plot, they will become its most consequential threat. In the first moments of his conscious being, Adam's knowledge is occasioned by the senses, but it is not created by them, nor is it, ultimately, dependent on them: in a subsequent passage, relating his first encounter with and spontaneous naming of the various animals, Adam explains that he 'named them, as they passed, and understood/Their nature, with such knowledge God endued/My sudden apprehension …' (*PL* 8.352–54).[126]

This, then, is the wider conceptual setting of Adam's hope, expressed in book 5, that 'in contemplation of created things/By steps we may ascend to God.' If it is (haplessly) optimistic regarding the acquisition of ever more (or superior) divine knowledge – Adam has actually acquired the key elements of his knowledge of God immediately after his creation –, the view that this knowledge of God is firmly grounded in a knowledge of Adam's immediate, earthly surroundings is borne out, also, in the passage relating the first moments of his conscious being, even though Adam himself might overestimate the role the senses had actually played then. Half 'Happy Husbandman,' half 'Serene Contemplator,' Milton's Adam still treads the middle ground between the two extremes of absolute unthinkingness and excessive intellectualism. A comparable bal-

---

[125] On the ambiguity of 'feeling,' see n.190 below.
[126] On the place of this passage in relation to Milton's wider conception of knowledge in *Paradise Lost*, see Jacobus, *Sudden Apprehension*, 46–47.

ance, in fact, appears to be struck in another seventeenth-century character of a studious 'contemplator,' John Earle's character of 'A Contemplatiue Man':

> [He] is a schooler in this great Vniuersity the World, and the same his book and studie. He cloysters not his meditations in the narrow darkness of a roome, but sends them abroad with his eyes, and his brayne trauells with his feet. He lookes vpon man from a high tower, and sees him truelier at this distance in his infirmityes, and pooreness. ... He lookes not vpon a a thing as a yawning stranger at Nouelties: but his search is more mysterious and inward, and he spells Heauen out of Earth. He knitts his obseruations together, and makes a Ladder of them all to climbe to God. ... He has learn'd all can here be taught him, and comes now to Heauen to see more.[127]

Earle appears to combine both, the high-flying contemplation at a remove favoured by the speaker of Milton's *Il Penseroso*, and the comparatively more 'hands-on' approach favoured, all 'created things' considered, by Adam in *Paradise Lost*: in fact, Earle's 'schooler' of the world combines attributes of the two Miltonic figures as he 'lookes vpon man from a high tower.' In his focus on vision, not to be satisfied 'in the narrow darkness of a roome,' he resembles both. And where Adam seeks, 'in contemplation of created things,' to 'ascend to God,' Earle's 'Contemplatiue Man,' in an image remarkably similar to Milton's, 'knitts his obseruations together ... to climbe to God.' In a seeming parallel to the promise given to Adam, towards the conclusion of *Paradise Lost*, of 'a paradise within thee, happier far' (*PL* 12.587), Earle conceives of contemplation as a 'search [that] is more mysterious and inward' as it 'spells Heauen out of Earth.' In contrast to Milton's conception, finally, Earle presents the divine knowledge gained by contemplation as, in a sense, transcending the accretions of worldly knowledge ('all can here be taught him') and ultimately entering a new sphere of knowledge – still conceived of in visual terms – as he 'comes ... to Heauen to see more.'

In the portraits of the respective 'contemplators' drafted by Hall and Earle, as well as in Milton's diverse statements of the same theme, vision and light are given a key role. However it is Adam in *Paradise Lost* who, in his first conscious steps, going (and, sometimes, running) 'with supple joints as lively vigour led,' perhaps embodies best Røstvig's observation that, in its later iterations, 'the figure of the Serene Contemplator was joyous rather than severe or ascetic,' a circumstance she traces, aptly, to 'the introduction of the new theme of the Golden Age or the Earthly Paradise, which is basically a soft' – like Adam's 'flowery bed' – 'and rather sensuous motif.'[128] Not every setting of contemplation is as sensuous as Adam's in Paradise; but in all of the instances of contemplation from his writings considered above, Milton makes intensive use of sensory discourse and, especially, of the same visual-Platonic idiom that the author of *The Transproser Rehears'd* ridicules. This connects, on the one hand, to the corresponding theme in the history of ideas about Ideas (as traced by Røstvig); on the other, it relates to Milton's very own, and quite distinctive, metaphysics and theology of light as ex-

---

[127] John Earle, *Micro-cosmographie: Or, A Peece of the World Discovered (1628)*, ed. and tr. Alexander Eilers (Würzburg: Königshausen & Neumann, 2018), 91–92.
[128] Røstvig, *Happy Man*, I, 175–76.

pressed in Proem III of *Paradise Lost*. Whereas the visual-Platonic idiom of contemplation, more generally, prioritises vision, in accordance with one influential version of the conventional sensory hierarchy, as the sense of knowledge, Proem III, in a somewhat unexpected extension of the theme, also considers the effect of light on the contact sense of touch (as the light of the sun had touched, and dried, newly created Adam; as the hands of the Creator had formed his creature).

In his address to light in Proem III, Milton fuses the imageries of Christian and Platonic (visual) contemplation, and supplements them with his own conception of light as a tactile and creative/generative force in the cosmos, signified most commonly by the sun as God's representative in the world. Ultimately, this triple presentation of light serves to establish the epic speaker's claim to inspired authority, and this is the reason why Milton's pamphleteer detractor, who aims to deny any nonconformist claim to personal inspiration and illumination, not only ridicules Milton's address to 'holy light' as pathos-laden but, immediately before, had smeared Marvell as a solipsistic, perhaps even self-deifying Platonist – someone who is 'struck blind with his own ... *Idea* of the *Sun*.' Since the author of *The Transproser Rehears'd* considers Milton and Marvell as, basically, birds of a feather, his claim that the latter was merely 'admiring those *imaginary* heights which his fancy had rais'd' would also brand the former, for all his claims to soaring sublimity, as a self-deceiving, day-dreaming enthusiast.

In its conceptual associations, its sensory domains of reference, and even its terminology, Milton's invocation to light comes dangerously close, then, to the 'Magicall-Astrologicall Diviner' attacked by John Gaule. Gaule's attack, significantly, is directed against the self-declared purveyors of secret knowledge, whether these consult magic, astrology (not yet wholly divorced from astronomy), or other means, such as the contemplation of 'Platonicall Ideaes.' For the author of *The Transproser Rehears'd*, as for Gaule, 'Platonicall' would have been a term of abuse; not so for Milton, even if his *explicit* acknowledgement of Platonising thought patterns ceased at some point after the composition of his earlier poetry.[129] As Erin Webster has argued, however, Milton's Platonising visual idiom in Proem III – speaking of 'holy light' and inner irradiation – should not be considered as completely abstracted from corporeal vision but should be seen rather as one aspect of a visual complex transcending later disciplinary or estimative distinctions.[130] This same close connection between physical and spiritual vision, between insight in spite of blindness and the crushing reality of sensory embodiment, is also apparent in the continuation of Proem III.

---

[129] The one reference to Plato in *Paradise Lost* also comes in book 3, and in the context of Satan reaching the limbo of vanity, which prompts Milton to a mention of '[him] who to enjoy/Plato's Elysium, leaped into the sea,/Cleombrotus' (*PL* 3.471–73).

[130] See Webster, "'Presented with a Universal blanc,'" Webster traces the terminological and conceptual parallels (as well as distinctions) between Milton's account of vision in Proem III and the models of Kepler and Descartes, and explores Milton's theological and epistemological development of those foundations. See also her *The Curious Eye*, 125–131.

The Defiance of a 'Blind Beetle': Milton and the Blind Speaker's Confidence in Proem III

Lewalski points out that the 'Transproser' reacts with force to a perceived 'political–religious–aesthetic linkage;' Milton's sensory discourse in Poem III as well as his use of blank verse in the poem at large – an aesthetic choice also justified in sensory discursive terms – provide important links between those three spheres.[131] In a similar blending of domains, the pamphleteer's attack against Milton draws on contentual as well as deeply personal aspects of vision: when he refers to Milton as a '*blind* Author ... groping for a beam of *Light*,' this reverses the visual-tactile thrust of the invocation itself, but it also chimes with other attacks of Milton on account of his blindness. As early as 1653, only a year after Milton's blindness had become total, a Dutch diplomat recognised in it the just reward of a malicious slanderer: 'Now there is no need for [Salmasius] to reply anything to that trifler Milton; since you tell me that he has been injured in both eyes, I recognise the punishment of divine justice ...'[132] In 1660, as Charles II returned to England, the royalist John Heydon recorded a rumour about the precise circumstances under which this punishment had supposedly occurred: 'If *Milton* beginning to write an Answer to the late Kings Book against Monarchy, was at the second word, by the power of God strucken blind: What shall fall upon them that endeavour to destroy his Son[?] verily they that fight against him, fight against Providence.'[133] Likewise, three years later, the firebrand preacher Robert South, in a court sermon about the martyrdom of Charles I, could trust his congregation to remember that '*Latin* advocate, Mr. *Milton*, who like a blind Adder has spit so much Poison on the King's Person and Cause.'[134] South's correlation of Milton's blindness to the blindness of a poisonous snake[135] indicates that, after the Restoration, in particular, Milton was at the receiving end of the sense-based animal imagery he himself had deployed in his early university prose and the polemical writings of the 1640s but also in his sonnets. A similar piece of invective can be found in the 1660 reference, by the biographer David Lloyd, to 'that mercenary *Milton*' as a 'blind Beetle.'[136] And Salmasius, who had been Milton's opponent in his first *Defensio* of 1651, would later term his former adversary a 'filthy beast, who has retained nothing manlike, except his bleary eyes. But with them, nearly blind as they are, he sees more keenly than with that vicious mind, blinded to everything by madness and stupidity,'[137] and calls him 'ipse cœculus' – 'this little blind fellow': 'This little blind

---

[131] Lewalski, *Life of John Milton*, 500.
[132] French, *Life Records*, 3: 252.
[133] French, *Life Records*, 4: 320.
[134] French, *Life Records*, 4: 379.
[135] The proverbial – ultimately, biblical – association of the adder with another kind of sensory impairment may play a role in South's image: 'deaf as an adder' (see *OED*, 'deaf, adj.,' 1d.). The relevant verse is Ps. 58:5.
[136] French, *Life Records*, 4: 327. For the proverbial phrase, 'blind as a beetle,' see *OED*, 'blind, adj. (and adv.),' 1.
[137] *Claudii Salmasii ad Johannem Miltonum Responsio, Opus Posthumum* (London 1660); quoted in French, *Life Records*, 4: 344–48, at 346–47.

fellow sees, if he sees anything, that those royal expenditures [a point on which Milton had rested his attack] count for nothing, or next to nothing, against Salmasius ...'[138]

These various associations of blindness with divine punishment, and also implying 'madness and stupidity,' are in keeping with long-established sensory discursive traditions (already Deuteronomy 28, quoted above, had associated 'madness ... blindness, and astonishment of heart').[139] Consequently, the various attacks by Salmasius and others – and more specifically Salmasius's quotation from Virgil alluding to the blinded Cyclops, had occasioned Milton's reminder, in the *Defensio Secunda*, that the blind man healed by Jesus in the Gospel of John had been blind 'through no sin of his own or of his parents.'[140]

Proem III, for all the ethereal metaphysics of its first section addressed to 'holy light,' does not eschew the topic of physical blindness, quite the opposite. Section 2 of the proem opens with the speaker's plaintive acknowledgment, quoted above, that the visual-tactile connection which had linked himself to 'holy light' in its physical manifestation as the light of the sun has broken down forever: 'thou/Revisitst not these eyes ...' His blank eyeballs 'roll in vain,' emphasising the gross corporeality of his affliction (which, by the conclusion of the proem, is attenuated to a 'mere corporeality'). In its conventional association with multi-sensory morning scenes, Milton's remark that the speaker's blind eyes 'find no dawn' implies both a visual and a wider sensory reference: here, as elsewhere in Milton, 'dawn' or 'Morn' (often personified) appears primarily as a representative of *vision*, although, in contrast to the frequent occurence of the image not just in the early writings but throughout *Paradise Lost* as well, the reference now, for the first and only time, is to an absence – to '*no* dawn.'[141] This curious inversion extends to the fact that usually it is dawn who is figured as approaching (as at the opening of book 5: 'Now Morn *her rosy steps in the eastern clime/Advancing*, sowed the earth with orient pearl ...,' emphasis added). In Proem III, by contrast, it is the speaker's eyes who move ('roll') 'in vain/To find thy piercing ray, and find no dawn.' However, the *wider* signification of dawn, even in its absence, arguably remains the same as in the various dawn scenes of Milton's early writing: namely, as that time of day associated, before all others, with the pleasant experience of multi-sensory yet blameless perception, often personified in the sensuous and multi-sensory Homeric figure of *rhododaktylos Êōs*, 'rosy-fingered Dawn.'

---

[138] 'Videt ipse cœculus, si quid videt ...,' *Claudii Salmasii* ...; quoted in French, *Life Records*, 4: 347. In the same passage, Salmasius sneers that, 'as you yourself are blind with rage [furore cœcus], not less in mind [mente] than in body, it was hardly fitting for you to impose that same blindness of mind [animi cœcitatem] on everybody ...'

[139] See also Barasch, *Blindness*, 35–36 and 55 on ancient Greek and early Christian associations between blindness and *atê* ('delusion') and ignorance, respectively.

[140] See Chapter 5.1 above.

[141] At *PL* 2.1034–37, in particular, describing the final stage of Satan's journey towards Eden and, significantly, immediately preceding the opening of book 3, dawn is associated with 'the sacred influence/Of light,' creating a link between other, more conventional accounts of dawn (e.g., at *PL* 5.1–2; 6.2–4; 9.192–97, also referring to 'sacred light;' as well as 11.173–75) and the reference in Proem III.

5.2 Proem III (PL 3.1–55)

The terms used to describe the speaker's condition in the following lines ('drop serene' and 'dim suffusion') have been traced to early modern ophthalmological terminology, indicating 'the *gutta serena* [lit., 'serene drop'], in which the eye appears normal, and the cataract, which covers it with an opaque film.'[142] Not surprisingly, this whole passage has traditionally been regarded not so much as an imaginative exploration of blindness through the persona of a fictitious or vaguely mythic speaker along the lines of those mentioned – Homer and others – but rather as Milton's thinly fictionalised or mythologised and, at the same time, heavily, even brutally, autobiographical account of his own experience of blindness.[143] In my following discussion of these lines, I aim to trace the specificity of Milton's representation of blindness in Proem III, including by reference to another blindness-centered late work, *Samson Agonistes* (1671).

When the speaker of Proem III opens the central passage of section 2 proper (at *PL* 3.26), one might be justified in detecting a hint of defiance in the face of affliction: 'Yet not the more/Cease I to wander …'[144] – a remarkable declaration considering the traditionally strong association of blindness and immobility, or at least dependence on outside help. In his study of blindness in Western cultural history, Moshe Barasch not only gives examples throughout of representations of blindness as 'fumbling and stumbling' but specifically discusses the subject, in both artistic and literary works, of 'the blind man and his guide.'[145] The speaker of Proem III, by contrast, shows no inhibition

---

[142] Fowler ad loc. Contrast the (wilful?) incomprehension of 'drop serene' on the part of the author of *The Transproser Rehears'd*, quoted above. As Eleanor Brown cautions, however, 'medical terms were not fixed in the seventeenth century. "Drop serene" is the translation of *gutta serena*, a term applied to all blindness in which the eye retains a normal appearance … [and, quoting a medical specialist,] "It is the condition in which the patient sees nothing and the doctor also sees nothing."' Another specialist cited by Brown, however, argues that 'Drop serene and dim suffusion are not so much different diagnoses as two names for very much the same thing' (Brown, *Milton's Blindness*, 22–23).

[143] See, generally, Brown, *Milton's Blindness*. Brown, who was born blind, discusses Proem III (as 'by far the more important' of two blindness-centered passages in *Paradise Lost*) on pp. 59–64 of her study: 'Taken as a whole the passage seems to me to be a hallelujah rather than a lament' (59). For a more recent discussion from a disability studies perspective, see Angelica Duran, 'The Blind Bard, According to John Milton and His Contemporaries,' *Mosaic* 46 (2013), 141–157.

[144] Consider also the inverse parallel in phrasing to the apocalyptic (and, hence, 'visionary') allusion in the abrupt opening of *Lycidas*: 'Yet once more, O ye laurels …', on which see Michael Lieb, '"Yet Once More:" The Formulaic Opening of *Lycidas*,' *MQ* 12 (1978), 23–28, esp. 23–24, with reference to the Father's declaration in *PL* 3.175–76, 'Once more will I renew/[Man's] lapsèd powers …' The allusion in *Lycidas* is to Heb. 12:26: '… Yet once more I shake not the earth only, but also heaven.'

[145] See Barasch, *Blindness*, esp. 103–114. A special instance of this, also discussed by Barasch, is the case of 'the blind leading the blind' – from Matt. 15:14: 'Let them alone: they be blind leaders of the blind. And if the blind lead the blind, both shall fall into the ditch' –, an image turned against Milton in the title of the royalist Sir Roger L'Estrange's 1660 pamphlet, *No blinde guides, in answer to a seditious pamphlet of J. Milton's intituled Brief notes upon a late sermon …*, with the verse from Matthew for its epigraph. See Lewalski, *Life of John Milton*, 379–80 on this and another attack of L'Estrange on Milton, whom he wrongly thought to have written a pamphlet titled *Eye-Salve for the English Army*, called by L'Estrange 'a medicine of the same Composition, which (by general report) strook *Milton* Blind.' L'Estrange's response was titled *Physician Cure Thy Self*.

whatsoever in striking out on his own – and whether or not this is intentional on Milton's part, his route includes some rather difficult to navigate terrain: '…where the Muses haunt/Clear spring, or shady grove, or sunny hill.' In contrast to Proem I, the Muses – and 'chief[ly]' the heavenly Muse of Sion, competent to inspire 'sacred song' – are not 'invoke[d]' for their 'aid' to the speaker's 'adven'trous song' but inhabit (or 'haunt') various destinations which the speaker, though blind, is confident to reach by his own efforts.

All of those destinations bear poetological and/or sensory connotations. The 'clear spring' of the Muses, here as in the references to the Castalian fountain and to Pirene in Elegy V, is a conventional symbol of poetic inspiration but in the present instance it also connects to the strong presentation of (divine) light as a liquid in the opening lines of the proem.[146] This latter point is then reinforced by the subsequent specification that it is chiefly 'Sion and the flowery brooks beneath' that attract the speaker. Milton thus relates the speaker's situation in Proem III back to Proem I with its mentions of, among other mountaintops, 'Sion hill' and 'Siloa's brook' (in Proem III, the height of Zion is emphasised through the reference to its 'hallowed feet' 'beneath'). While the alternation of 'shady … or sunny' surroundings is not visible to the speaker, it is differentiated by temperature and thus open to his tactile perception; as the primary reference of those terms is visual, however, the speaker's visual impairment is highlighted. That the brooks of Proem III are 'flowery' enhances their sensory profile: this, too, is a perception open to the blind speaker (the sensory associations of flowers being divided between their visual beauty and pleasing scent).[147] The same goes for the 'warbling' motion of the water, an audible 'flow' which again connects the present passage of the proem with the repeated references to the fluidity of light in section 1. When the speaker refers to his 'nightly' visits to these places of inspiration ('Nightly I visit'), the meaning of the phrase oscillates between distinct adverbial as well as adjectival uses:[148] it certainly expresses a habitual action (and, perhaps, implies a habituation to his condition); it presents that action as taking place *at night* (temporally) as well as in a *darkened* (because blind) and perhaps even *benighted* condition (as in need of inspiration and illumination); finally, it allows a biographical reading, as Milton is known to have

---

[146] Bearing in mind Milton's reference to the return of the seasons later in the proem (*PL* 3.40–44), consider also, again, the ambiguity of 'spring.'

[147] In Parkinson's *Paradisi in Sole Paradisus Terrestris* of 1629, for instance, the visual appearance and the sweet smell of flowers are routinely considered in conjunction, although one or the other may take precedence, or they may reach a perfect equilibrium; thus with '*Out-landish flowers* … whereof although many haue little sweete sent to commend them, yet their earlinesse and exceeding great beautie and varietie doth so far counteruaile that defect (and yet I must tell you with all, that there is among the many sorts of them some, and that not a few, that doe excell in sweetnesse, being so strong and heady, that they rather offend by too much than by too little sent, and some againe are of so milde and moderate temper, that they scarce come short of your most delicate and dantiest flowers) that they are almost in all places with all persons … desired and accepted …' (8).

[148] See *OED*, 'nightly, adv.': (1) 'every night, whenever it is night;' (2) 'at or by night; during the night' (citing *PL* 2.642); and 'nightly, adj.': (1) 'that comes, happens, or occurs during the night; accomplished or done at night; that occurs every night' (citing Milton's *Arcades*); (2) 'belonging to, peculiar to, or characteristic of night … operating by night … dark as, or with, night (literal and figurative); that resembles night.' It is the last sense, in particular, that relates the phrase to the speaker's blindness.

composed *Paradise Lost*, for the most part, at night or very early in the morning.[149] In addition, the distinct visual force of 'visit,' already discussed above, comes into play: the speaker's 'nightly' visits to the haunts of the Muses are, in a sense, spiritual return visits ('thee I revisit safe') to make up for the discontinued visitations of physical light ('but thou/Revisitst not these eyes'). In proems VII and IX, discussed below, this complex of images is taken up once more.

From Bank to Prison: Samson as a Contrast Figure to the Blind Speaker of Proem III

After a sorrowful opening to section 2, then, the proem's blind speaker evidently presents himself in a state of sensory self-assurance: as an unceasing wanderer, independently navigating groves and hills, springs and brooks. In the opening lines of *Samson Agonistes*, by contrast, set 'before the Prison in Gaza,' the blinded Samson is presented as in need of help to master even the shortest distances and to reach even the most trivial – yet, to him, welcome and relieving, sensuously pleasing – goal:

> *Sam.* A little onward lend thy guiding hand
> To these dark steps, a little further on;
> For yonder bank hath choice of sun or shade,
> There I am wont to sit, when any chance
> Relieves me from my task of servile toil,
> Daily in the common prison else enjoined me,
> Where I a prisoner chained, scarce freely draw
> The air imprisoned also, close and damp,
> Unwholesome draught: but here I feel amends,
> The breath of heaven fresh blowing, pure and sweet,
> With day-spring born; here leave me to respire.
> (*SA* 1–11)

Milton's connection of the 'guiding hand' to Samson's 'dark steps' encapsulates the latter's dependence on the sense of touch.[150] Again, as in the epic speaker's visiting of 'shady grove, or sunny hill' in Proem III, the alternation of 'sun and shade' offers a pleasing variation (in the sense of 'variousness' discussed above) even to blind Samson, who cannot see but feel the difference between both. In addition, and owing to Samson's particular situation, this variation is presented here as the only 'choice' amid the otherwise completely unchosen predicament of the blinded prisoner, 'eyeless in Gaza at the mill with slaves' (*SA* 41). (There is a particularly cruel irony in Milton's phrase,

---

[149] See Fowler ad *PL* 3.32 and Lewalski, *Life of John Milton*, 448–49 for the relevant biographical sources (and 305–6 for the connection to Sonnet 19, 'When I consider how my light is spent'). See also Chapter 5.3 below. Of the nine instances of 'nightly' in *Paradise Lost* (all of them more or less ambiguous in the way suggested here), four occur in the poetological proems (which only account for about 1.5 per cent of the epic as a whole).

[150] Compare the lines from Euripides' *Phoenician Women* in which blind Teiresias asks to be led by the hand: 'Now lead me on, my daughter. You're the eye/for my blind steps, as star is to the sailor' (834–35; quoted by Barasch, *Blindness*, 164n67).

'eyeless in Gaza,' suggesting both a 'gaze' that has been lost and Samson's being exposed to the gaze of others: only a few lines earlier in the opening scene, Samson – 'both my eyes put out' – deplores being 'made of my enemies the scorn and gaze' [*SA* 33–34]; later, and with yet another pun on the visual connotation of 'visit,' he feels himself 'to visitants a gaze/Or pitied object' [*SA* 567–68].)[151]

At the very opening of the play, however, Samson can 'feel amends' and enjoy a brief period of respite. This happens, significantly, at 'day-spring,' i.e., in the freshness of the morning.[152] Considered more fully, Milton's 'the breath of heaven fresh blowing, pure and sweet,/With day-spring born,' proves multiply ambiguous, as it suggests not only an association of 'day' and 'spring' (morning as the 'spring' of day, in the senses both of the season and the fountainhead) but also the natural association of '(being) born' at birth (and hence also of freshness and youth) and the notion of freshness being 'borne' on the morning air.[153] The 'breath of heaven,' finally, is 'blowing' in the sense of a (notionally deliberate) movement of the air; however, the wider associations of the passage and its setting (on which more presently) argue for a further ambiguity: the morning air itself is 'fresh blowing, pure and sweet' in the sense that fragrant flowers may be said to be 'blowing,' i.e., 'blossoming.' All of these same associations have played into the multi-sensory morning and/or spring scenes I have considered in earlier chapters.

In Samson's lines, there appears also to be a distant, bitter echo of the contrast between *labor* and *voluptas* mentioned in Prolusion VI – between (forced) 'toil' and (modest) 'pleasure,' the latter made more pleasurable by variation. In any case, Samson establishes a parallel between breathing 'freely' and being free – not 'enjoined' to labour, 'chained.' His drawing the 'pure and sweet' air blowing around the 'bank' is clearly an act of sensuous enjoyment. At the same time, his relishing the 'pure and sweet' air figures as an act of sensory emancipation: here is an instance of pleasing sense perception that has not been taken from him, and it contrasts, markedly, with the 'unwholesome draught' of his prison.[154] It thus marks an act of liberation from his dou-

---

[151] See on this thematic complex of seeing and being seen Brendan Prawdzik, *Theatrical Milton: Politics and Poetics of the Staged Body* (Edinburgh: Edinburgh University Press, 2017), 186–87.
[152] Carey ad loc. notes the parallel with the 'dayspring' of Luke 1:78 KJV (newer translations have 'sunrise' or 'dawn'). The immediate context of the verse in the Canticle of Zacharias (the 'Benedictus') also seems significant: 'And thou, child [i.e., John the Baptist], shalt be called the prophet of the Highest: for thou shalt go before the face of the Lord to prepare his ways; …
Through the tender mercy of our God; whereby the dayspring from on high hath visited us, to give light to them that sit in darkness and in the shadow of death, to guide our feet into the way of peace' (Luke 1:76–79). Note the orientational and visual contrast between walking/guiding and a light 'from on high,' on the one hand, and sitting in darkness, on the other.
[153] Consider also *OED* 'bourn/bourne, n.': 'a small stream, a brook …,' citing Milton's *Comus* (312): 'And every bosky bourn from side to side …,' glossed by Carey as 'bushy stream.'
[154] Consider the possible parallel with Samson's destructive act of self-empowerment at the climax of the drama: '… Now of my own accord such other trial/I mean to show you of my strength, yet greater;/As with amaze shall strike all who behold,/This uttered, straining all his nerves he bowed,/*As with the force of winds and waters pent,*/When mountains tremble, those two massy pillars/With horrible convulsion to and fro/He tugged …' (*SA* 1643–50, emphasis added): Samson moves from the pleasingly gentle, harmlessly empowering and invigorating 'breath of

ble slavery of imprisonment and blindness. After the strong emphasis on his imprisonment in the opening lines already – note the sequence of 'prison,' 'prisoner,' and 'imprisoned' in three consecutive lines –, this parallel is subsequently made explicit by the Chorus as they approach Samson sitting on the bank:

> Which shall I first bewail,
> Thy bondage or lost sight,
> Prison within prison
> Inseparably dark?
> Thou art become (O worst imprisonment!)
> The dungeon of thyself; thy soul
> (Which men enjoying sight oft without cause complain)
> Imprisoned now indeed,
> In real darkness of the body dwells,
> Shut up from outward light
> To incorporate with gloomy night;
> For inward light alas puts forth no visual beam.
> (*SA* 151–63)

According to the extended metaphor introduced by the Chorus, blindness is like imprisonment in that it severs the soul's communication with the outside world (evoking the notion of the senses as 'windows of the soul').[155] More specifically, Samsons soul is now forced 'to incorporate with gloomy night,' which presents an inverse variant of the dynamic kind of embodiment Milton consistently rejects. In *Comus*, the risk that 'the soul .../Embodies, and imbrutes' (466–7) is created by the senses, and an excessive indulgence in them; in Samson's case, the 'incorporat[ion]' – i.e., the embodiment – of the soul is caused by his degeneration from the natural and good state of embodiment in which the senses – well used – form an integral part of the whole human being.[156] This is in keeping, too, with the Hebraic conception of the soul as fundamentally embodied (the primary reference of the Hebrew term, *nephesh*, is to the throat and the breath).[157] As Milton has the Chorus clarify in their parenthetical remark, the common devaluation of the embodied state *per se* is to be rejected: when 'men enjoying sight' complain

---

Heaven' and (river?) 'bank' of the opening scene to the tempestuous, torrential 'force of winds and waters pent' of the catastrophe.

[155] See Jütte, *History of the Senses*, 77.

[156] On the Hebraic conception of the soul and its reception in early modern England, see Moshenska, *Feeling Pleasures*, 63–65 (on Lancelot Andrewes) and 253 (on Milton). A different account of Milton's conception of the 'living soul' (e.g., *PL* 7.528) in terms of traditional Western faculty psychology is given by Svendsen, *Milton and Science*, 180. On Milton's view of the fundamental 'inseparability of the body and spirit,' see Stephen M. Fallon, 'The Metaphysics of Milton's Divorce Tracts,' in: David Loewenstein/James Grantham Turner (eds), *Politics, Poetics, and Hermeneutics in Milton's Prose* (Cambridge: Cambridge University Press, 1990), 69–83, esp. 73–76, as well as his *Milton among the Philosophers*, esp. 50–78 (on the 'Cambridge reaction' to seventeenth-century accounts of the incorporeal soul) and 83–110 (on Milton's 'animist materialism').

[157] *HALOT*, s. v.

about the situatedness of the soul within the body, this is 'without cause.' The very fact of perception, finally, is a cause of enjoyment ('men *enjoying* sight'). In the outside judgment of the Chorus, moreover, the insufficiency of Samson's 'inward light' when compared to the powers of physical vision is striking (the Chorus's reference to the extramission theory of vision – 'no visual beam' – might imply a subtle devaluation of their opinion on the part of Milton, who in *Paradise Lost* clearly advocates a variety of the intromission theory).[158] The speaker of Proem III, despite further parallels with Samson, and after some lament and hesitation of his own, will arrive at a different conclusion.

In the opening lines of Milton's drama, Samson's frequenting of 'yonder bank' is habitual ('there I am wont to sit,' as a welcome break from his 'daily' toil), as is the parallel 'nightly' visiting of the speaker in Proem III. In contrast to the speaker's unceasing 'wander[ing],' however, Samson, once he has been led to his customary spot, remains stationary: 'there I am wont *to sit*.' This notion of 'sitting' (down), in fact, is connected throughout the drama to the humiliation caused by Samson's blindness; in the immediate context of a passage quoted earlier, this paralysing aspect of blindness is conceptualised in terms of inefficiency and uselessness:

> Now blind, disheartened, shamed, dishonour'd, quelled,
> To what can I be useful, wherein serve
> My nation, and the work from heaven imposed,
> But to sit idle on the household hearth,
> A burdenous drone; to visitants a gaze,
> Or pitied object, these redundant locks
> Robustious to no purpose clustering down,
> Vain monument of strength; till length of years
> And sedentary numbness craze my limbs
> To a contemptible old age obscure.
>
> (*SA* 563–72)

In language reminiscent of that employed by Milton in *Defensio Secunda* ('… two lots had now been set before me …: the one, blindness, the other, duty …') and Sonnet 22 ('… in liberty's defence, my noble task …') to come to terms with the tension between his own blindness and services to *his* 'nation,' Samson reiterates the link between blindness, immobility, and helplessness. Imagining his sitting 'idle on the household hearth,' enduring a 'sedentary numbness' for many years to come, Milton has him associate – and, ultimately, conflate – the premature loss of his sight with the eventual loss of vigour and perceptual acuity conventionally associated with 'obscure' (i.e., dark) old age. In the opening lines of *Samson Agonistes*, by contrast, his sitting on the 'bank' at least allows him the invigorating perceptions of 'day-spring.'

Given the generally sensuous nature of the opening passage, the fact that Samson is led to a 'bank' also seems significant, as it can be related to a number of similar passages in Milton's earlier poetry. As a result, the term and notion of a 'bank' alone should be

---

[158] See Webster, "'Presented with a Universal blanc.'"

considered a meaningful element of Milton's sensory discourse in the opening lines of *Samson Agonistes*. The word 'bank,' in early modern as in current usage, can refer either to any kind of rising ground or, more specifically, to the side of a lake, river, or brook.[159] Considering the sensuous focus of the following lines (as well as the punning 'day-spring born'), a reference to running water appears not unlikely, contrasted with Samson's imprisonment and immobility as 'the breath of heaven fresh blowing' is contrasted with the 'imprisoned' air. (This could be read not only in parallel to 'Siloa's brook … flow[ing]' in Proem I of *Paradise Lost* but also to the 'flowery brooks' of Sion that 'warbling flow' in Proem III.) In any case, the reference in *Samson Agonistes* ties in with Milton's references to riverbanks (or 'banks' more generally) in numerous passages of his earlier poetry, where they most frequently set the scene for multi-sensory perception and, often, sensuous enjoyment. A brief glance at *Comus* will illustrate the point: in the masque, there are various references to 'banks,' and most of them are in the context of sensuous, multi-sensory riverside settings. Thus in the Attendant Spirit's address to the river nymph, Sabrina: 'May thy lofty head be crowned/With many a tower and terrace round,/And here and there thy banks upon/With groves of myrrh, and cinnamon' (933–36). The visual imagery of towers and battlements is present but is trumped, as it were, by the reference to odorous spices. And after a change of scenery and a song, the Spirit declares, with greater emphasis on the perceptual act itself,

> To the ocean now I fly,
> And those happy climes that lie
> Where day never shuts his eye,
> Up in the broad fields of the sky:
> There I suck the liquid air
> All amidst the gardens fair
> Of Hesperus …
> …
> There eternal summer dwells,
> And west winds, with musky wing
> About the cedarn alleys fling
> Nard, and cassia's balmy smells.
> Iris there with humid bow,
> *Waters the odorous banks that blow*
> *Flowers of more mingled hue*
> Than *her purfled scarf* can shew,
> And drenches with Elysian dew
> (List mortals if your ears be true)

---

[159] Among the possible relevant senses in *OED* 'bank, n.,' are (1) 'a raised shelf or ridge of ground;' (3) 'the slope of a hill, a hillside; an area of high ground, a hill' (ironically, considering the implication of a wide view); (9) 'the sloping … edge of a river or other watercourse; (also more broadly) the land running immediately alongside a river or other watercourse …' or of (11) '… a lake shore' (citing *PL* 4.262). Compare also the close association (and habitual 'sensory utilisation') of both in *Il Penseroso* (73–75): 'Oft on a plat of rising ground,/I hear the far-off curfew sound,/Over some wide-watered shore …'

> Beds of hyacinth, and roses,
> Where young Adonis oft reposes ...
>
> (975–81, 987–98, emphasis added)[160]

The scene has all the makings of a multi-sensory pastoral scene, resembling the one that represents the coming of spring in Elegy V: sunshine, pleasant odours, dewy 'beds' of flowers upon flowers perfect for 'repos[ing].' The dominant visual elements of the scene – the sun, the rainbow, and the multi-coloured flowers – all may be said to contribute, at the same time, to the passage's main focus, which is on olfaction ('musky wing,' 'cedarn alleys,' 'nard, and cassia's balmy smells,' 'odorous banks'). In Chapter 4 above, I have referred to seventeenth-century notions about the generation of odours through an interplay of warmth and moisture, animated by the rays of the sun. In the present passage, Milton's reference to 'Iris' and her 'humid bow' argues an even more specific amplification to the odorousness of his scene, due to an inherent association of the rainbow not only with vision but also with smell. In the paragraph of *Sylva Sylvarum* immediately preceding the passage cited in Chapter 4, Bacon discusses several theories regarding the apparent olfactory effect of rainbows; again, sunlight, moisture, and dew interact:

> It hath been observed by the *Ancients*, that where a *Rainbow* seemeth to hang over, or to touch, there breatheth forth a *sweet smell*. The *cause* is, for that this happeneth but in certain matters which have in themselves some *Sweetness*, which the *gentle Dew* of the *Rainbow* doth draw forth; and the like do *soft Showers*, for they also make the *Ground* sweet: But none are so delicate as the *Dew* of the *Rainbow* where it falleth. ...[161]

In the lines from *Comus*, too, the 'humid' rainbow is not, primarily, *seen* (as in *PL* 11.875–79) but 'waters the odorous banks' – and, in fact, the flowers growing there are more colourful ('of more mingled hue') than the rainbow itself.[162] In referring to Iris' '*purfled* [i.e., seamed or fringed] scarf,' Milton further identifies the rainbow and

---

[160] Compare also these ultimately deleted lines from the Trinity MS version of *Comus*: 'amidst the `gardens´` Hesperian gardens, ON WHOSE BANKS `where the banks´/` Bedewed with nectar and celestial songs / Eternal roses grow, `yield´` `blow´` `bloss´m´` `grow´` and hyacinth / And fruits of golden rind ...' (*SP* 179n.)

[161] Bacon, *Sylva Sylvarum*, 176 (no. 832 on 'Sweetness of Odor from the Rainbow').

[162] At the conclusion of Michael's account of the Flood in book 11, Noah 'with uplifted hands, and eyes devout,/Grateful to heaven, over his head beholds/A dewy cloud, and in the cloud a bow/Conspicuous with three listed colours gay,/Betok'ning peace from God and covenant new.' Earlier in the same book, Michael is described as follows: 'over his *lucid* arms/A military vest of *purple* flowed/Livelier than Melibœan, or the *grain*/Of Sarra, worn by kings and heroes old/In time of truce; *Iris had dipped the woof*' (*PL* 11.240–44, emphases added). Here, the reference to the rainbow is primarily visual. There is an added ambiguity, however, as 'Iris' refers both to the goddess of the rainbow and the iris flower (*Lilium purpureum*); see Fowler ad loc. (In book 5, Raphael's three pairs of wings are similarly described in the tactile terms of textile dyeing: 'colours dipped in heaven ... sky-tinctured grain,' *PL* 5.283–85.) Compare also the reference in *Comus* to 'sky-robes spun out of Iris' woof' (83).

the river(banks), connected through their shared attributes of colourfulness, odorousness, and moisture. The Spirit's eager absorption of the 'liquid air' of these gardens – he is almost drinking it in – also corresponds to the image and highlights the corporeality implied in Milton's detailed description of his sensuous scene.

Even in the comparatively sober *Paradise Regained* (printed, with *Samson Agonistes*, in 1671), a 'green bank' provides the setting to a heavily multi-sensory scene. Jesus, having been tempted by Satan on the pinnacle of the Temple towards the end of book 4, is 'received … soft/From his uneasy station' by a 'fiery globe/Of angels' who carry him through the air 'as on a floating couch,'

> Then in a flowery valley set him down
> On a green bank, and set before him spread
> A table of celestial food, divine,
> Ambrosial, fruits fetched from the tree of life,
> And from the fount of life ambrosial drink,
> That soon refreshed him wearied, and repaired
> What hunger, if aught hunger had impaired
> Or thirst, and as he fed, angelic choirs
> Sung heavenly anthems of his victory
> Over temptation, and the tempter proud.
> (*PR* 4.581–95)

In this counterpart to the strongly sensuous earlier scene in which Satan had tempted Jesus with a refined banquet served up by 'tall stripling youths rich-clad, of fairer hue/Than Ganymede or Hylas' (*PR* 2.337–67), the 'green bank' on which 'celestial food' is laid out by the angels appears to represent a simpler yet superior, positively Edenic kind of sensory enjoyment. In fact, the angels fetch everything necessary from 'the fount of life' and 'the tree of life,' and thus straight out of Paradise.[163] (During the earlier banquet temptation, the narrator had commented, ironically, that 'Alas how simple, to these cates compared,/Was that crude apple that diverted Eve!,' *PR* 2.348–49.)

As a final example of how Milton has different types of 'banks' serve as a setting for deliberations surrounding sensory enjoyment, consider the following, strongly multi-sensory, even synaesthetic passage from *Lycidas*. This – also the most sensuous passage in the poem – opens with an invocation to the Arcadian river(god) Alpheus:[164]

> Return Alpheus, the dread voice is past,
> That shrunk thy streams; return Sicilian muse,
> And call the vales, and bid them hither cast
> Their bells, and flowrets of a thousand hues.
> Ye valleys low where the mild whispers use,
> Of shades and wanton winds, and gushing brooks,

---

[163] The 'fount of life' is mentioned in *PL* 3.357. The image is from Rev. 21:6; see n.65 above.
[164] In *Arcades* (1629/30? or 1634?), Milton refers to it (him), in a quite similar setting, as 'Divine Alpheus, who by secret sluice,/Stole under seas to meet his Arethuse;/And ye *the breathing roses of the wood,*/Fair silver-buskined nymphs as great and good …' (30–33, emphasis added).

> On whose fresh lap the swart star sparely looks,
> Throw hither all your quaint enammelled eyes,
> That on the green turf suck the honied showers,
> And purple all the ground with vernal flowers
> Bring the rathe primrose that forsaken dies,
> The tufted crow-toe, and pale jessamine,
> The white pink, and the pansy freaked with jet,
> The glowing violet,
> The musk-rose, and the well-attired woodbine,
> With cowslips wan that hang the pensive head,
> And every flower that sad embroidery wears:
> Bid amaranthus all his beauty shed,
> And daffadillies fill their cups with tears,
> To strew the laureate hearse where Lycid lies.
> (132–51)

What characterises the micro-sensescape of the riverbank in *Lycidas* – whether it is that of Alpheus or of other 'gushing brooks' –, is a profusion of flowers (implying, again, both sight and smell) and a luscious 'green turf' (softness), overlaid with suggestions of acoustic ('their bells,' 'mild whispers') and gustatory ('suck the honied showers') sensations. As in the poems discussed in Chapter 3, this is the quintessential sensescape of spring, as is made explicit by Milton's reference to 'vernal flowers.' These flowers are fading, however, because they have been gathered; metaphorically, they are in mourning ('pale,' 'wan,' 'hang[ing] the[ir] pensive head[s]') because they have been gathered in their prime. This provides the connection, taken up again explicitly only at the very end of the passage, between them and Lycidas, 'dead ere his prime' (8), whose death is made more poignant by comparison to that of the 'vernal flowers.'[165]

Despite their manifest differences in tone and thrust, what these diverse multi-sensory evocations of 'banks' in Milton's poetry all share is that they are, in short, quite Edenic. In fact, they all resemble, to varying extents, another 'Miltonic bank,' namely the 'green shady bank, profuse of flowers' on which Adam can be found sitting just after his first conscious steps and thoughts (*PL* 8.286). Seen through the lens of *Paradise Lost* and its various sensescapes (to which I return below), such flowery banks are like fragments or – in the sense of self-similarity – like fractals, of Paradise itself.[166] In different ways, all of the riverbank scenes considered are concerned with different kinds of 'prime': with spring (as the prime of the year), morning (as the prime of day), the

---

[165] In the opening lines of the elegy, also, the seasons are evoked, albeit with all the rough tactility proper to a *winter* setting: 'Yet once more, O ye laurels ... /... /I come to *pluck your berries harsh and crude,*/And with *forced fingers rude*/Shatter your leaves *before the mellowing year.*/Bitter constraint, and sad occasion dear,/Compels me to *disturb your season due*:/For Lycidas is dead, dead ere his prime ...' (1–8).

[166] For glimpses of the sensescape of Milton's Paradise, see *PL* 4.244–61; 4.323–38, as well as Eve's first experiences in contrast to Adam's. (esp. *PL* 4.447–63). At *PL* 9.437–41, 'flowers [are]/Imbordered on each bank' by Eve. At *PL* 9.1034–41, Adam and Eve rest on a 'shady bank' after the Fall for their first postlapsarian sexual intercourse.

loss of youth (as the prime of life) – and, in an abstracting idealisation of all these, allude to primeval scenes of sensuous enjoyment, whether in Arcady, the isles of the Hesperides, or, again, Paradise. By virtue of their multiform sensory content – the 'variousness' also suggested by their running brooks, these scenes at the same time stand for the 'prime' of perception, undulled by repetition, unbored by monotony, keen and astute on account of the crispness of the medium and the superiority of the perceptual apparatus involved.[167] They thus represent the culmination of an associative pattern present in the sensory discourse of Milton's writings both early and late. In their tendency to focus on smell and touch – the scent of flowers wafting over a soft, grassy 'couch' – they make a fitting sensescape both for Samson and for the blind speaker of Proem III, to be enjoyed by the one and to be explored by the other.

In fact, the 'nightly' wandering of the speaker in Proem III is directed not, primarily, towards a sensuous enjoyment of 'shady grove, or sunny hill' but of poetry, understood as both song and prophecy. The speaker is, in an ultimately tactile image, 'smit with the love of sacred song,'[168] but he also pays his dues to the most famous blind poets of pagan antiquity, 'blind Thamyris, and blind Maeonides [i.e., Homer]/And Tiresias and Phineus prophets old.' All four references imply a contrastive, paradoxical association between (physical) blindness and (poetical, spiritual, or cognitive) insight and inspiration, partly figured in tactile terms.[169] As the comparison to Moses in Proem I (promising 'things unattempted yet in prose or rhyme'), the speaker's consideration of these blind role models prompts a reflection – now doubtful – on his own ambition ('were I equalled with them in renown'). Pondering their works, the speaker 'feed[s] on thoughts' – IDEAS ARE FOOD – and is moved to compose poetry of his own. This is compared, in another conventional image already familiar from Milton's earlier poetry, to 'the wakeful bird,' i.e., the nightingale, that 'sings darkling' – just as the speaker operates 'nightly' – 'and in shadiest covert hid/Tunes her nocturnal note,' just as the speaker wanders through, among other places, 'shady grove[s].' As in Elegy V, then, the nightingale, itself (or herself) conventionally representative of 'voluntary' (i.e., unconstrained and spontaneous) song as the most natural form of embodied sensory discourse, acts as a figure of identification for the speaker. By singing 'darkling,' the nightingale signifies a temporary movement, within the imagery of the proem, from the visual to the auditory sphere (i.e., towards a substitute for light and vision). With respect to the poet-

---

[167] Regardless of the particulars of their functioning, in other words, these passages *make a claim for* that which Michael W. Clune has argued poetry (or literature more generally) should aim to *perform* (see Clune, *Writing Against Time*).
[168] Fowler ad loc. points a passage in Virgil's *Georgics* in which the speaker declares himself 'ingenti percussus amore' – 'smitten with a great love' for the Muses. Compare also Jesus's references in *Paradise Regained* to 'our Hebrew songs and harps in Babylon' as well as to 'Sion's songs, to all true tastes excelling' (*PR* 4.336, 347).
[169] For details on the four figures named, see Fowler ad loc. as well as Barasch, *Blindness*, 26 (on Phineus), 28–32 (on the figure of 'the blind seer,' including Thamyris and Teiresias), 38–43 (on visual representations of Teiresias and Homer), 130–36 (on 'the revival of the blind seer' in the Renaissance and Renaissance representations of Homer). In particular, Barasch suggests that 'Raphael's blind Homer [in his *Parnassus* in the Vatican] is a spiritual hero,' cleared of all traditional associations of blindness with guilt and transgression (136). A similar focus on the formative power of the inspired artist creating by introspection is also present in Proem III.

speaker, this signifies a movement from inactivity (the uselessness of Samson) and a fear of failure (faced with his more 'renown[ed]' precursors) to inspired productivity in spite of blindness.

This on the whole positive movement towards a sound-based notion of inspiration and poetic production is immediately undercut, however, by the speaker's returning memory of what he has lost. Occasioned, perhaps, by the very appearance of the nightingale as an emblem not only of love and lyric poetry but also of spring and summer,[170] the following passage (lines 40–44) abounds with references to the cycle of the year and to the seasonal-pastoral imagery which, in several of the earlier texts already discussed, formed such an important part of Milton's sensory discourse. Specifically, it is the *non-return* of the seasons (as earlier in Proem III it had been the non-return of dawn) that – beyond even the absence of vision – marks the condition of blindness as sensorily defective in a more encompassing sense. In fact, as in Samson's ambiguous reference to the 'day-spring,' the respective significances of the seasons or of the times of day, both representative of changes in sense perception, are practically interchangeable: 'Thus with the year/Seasons return, but not to me returns/Day, or the sweet approach of even or morn,/Or sight of vernal bloom, or summer's rose …' Spring and summer, the seasons of roses and nightingales along with other staples of pastoral such as 'flocks, or herds,' conventionally indicate multi-sensory perception and the corresponding sensuous enjoyment. In the case of Samson on the bank at 'day-spring,' we have seen how Milton could stage the enjoyment of such a multi-sensory setting even in the case of blindness. In the grief-stricken account of Milton's blind speaker, by contrast, it appears that his loss of sight has brought with it the annihilation of those multi-sensory complexes in their totality, as if – in his subjective experience – his blindness had encroached on other sensory modes still available to him. According to the letter, it is the 'sight' of all those things which has been taken from him; but the spirit of Milton's lines is that of complete sensory deprivation. This becomes particularly clear in Milton's reference to the loss of 'human face divine,' which is more than just its seen image but implies communication, affection, love, and 'the cheerful ways of men' more generally.[171] In presenting his speaker as 'surround[ed]' by 'ever-during dark,' Milton emphasises the complete isolation of the speaker, thrown back on himself and his cruelly diminished capacities, and thus introduces a theme that will be taken up in Proem VII. In Milton's earlier Prolusion VI, the orator had figured himself as 'surrounded on all sides' by a threatening audience – which, however, had been presented as a kind of ocular

---

[170] As in Shakespeare's Sonnet 102: 'Our love was new, and then but in the spring/When I was wont to greet it with my lays;/As Philomel in summer's front doth sing,/And stops his pipe in growth of riper days' (5–8). In his own Sonnet 1, Milton associates the nightingale with 'propitious May' (4).

[171] Compare Eve's first words to Adam after Satan has disturbed her dreams: 'O sole in whom my thoughts find all repose,/My glory, my perfection, glad I see/Thy face, and morn returned …' (*PL* 5.28–30). Milton's phrase 'human face *divine*' resonates with both the numerous references, throughout *Paradise Lost*, to humans' being made in God's image (see, for instance, *PL* 4.289–93), and with the equally prominent references to the face of God himself, Father or Son (see, for instance, *PL* 3.138–42). As these examples indicate, there is considerable overlap between the two categories (which, again, makes the phrase, 'human face divine,' so appropriate).

5.2 Proem III (PL 3.1–55)

communication between him and his hearers: the epic speaker of Proem III does not even have that left to him.

Only as a third thought – following on the loss of sensuous enjoyment and the loss of human communication and companionship –, does the speaker address another aspect of sense perception, and this is its potential to generate knowledge: with 'nature's works to [him] expunged and rased,' any chance at the successful 'contemplation of created things,' to borrow Adam's phrase, appears to have been destroyed. At that, the distinction between 'wisdom' (more closely associated, perhaps, with an 'ascen[t] to God') and 'knowledge' appears to be one of perspective, not of substance, considering the equivocal manner in which Milton uses both terms.[172] In particular, his reference to the 'book of knowledge' evokes both the conventional trope of nature as a book to be read *and* the man-made codification of knowledge about nature, represented in its physical form.[173] As would be conventional, the passage presents vision as *the* sense of knowledge – or does it?[174] Milton's precise wording appears to combine conflicting notions: wisdom is 'quite shut out,' i.e., it is completely shut out, but it is shut out 'at *one* entrance' (only?).[175] While the 'entrance' of vision is 'shut,' the others may still be open – a possibility held in suspense by Milton's phrasing. Still, the epic speaker's quest for knowledge, initiated by his appeal to the Spirit in Proem I to 'instruct me, for thou knowst,' appears to have reached an impasse. Even if other sensory 'entrance[s]' of wisdom remain available, the specific sensory discursive configuration of Proem III as an invocation to light demands an appropriate consideration of the common conceptual metaphor TRUTH IS LIGHT.[176] The latter image relates to a commonplace allegorical representation of the five senses as gates, leading into the city or citadel of the human soul.[177] In John Bunyan's allegorical *The Holy War ... or, The Losing and Taking Again of the Town of Mansoul* (1682), this frequent metaphor is made explicit, as the endangered town in question ('man's soul') boasts five gates, each associated with one of the senses, and ranked in order of precedence as follows:

> This famous town of *Mansoul* had five gates, in at which to come, out at which to go, and these were made likewise answerable to the Walls: to wit *Impregnable*, and such as could never be opened nor forced, but by the will and leave of those

---

[172] This relates to the question of the proper *application* of the senses.
[173] On the idea of a book of nature (*liber naturae*) and its history, see Hans Blumenberg, *Die Lesbarkeit der Welt* (Frankfurt am Main: Suhrkamp, 1981). See also John K. Hale, 'Books and Book-Form in Milton,' *R&R* 23 (1999), 63–77, esp. 73–74, where Hale argues that, in *Paradise Lost*, Milton 'appropriates ... and renews' the 'traditional book-topoi' such as the book of nature, for instance by terming both book and knowledge 'fair' and thus aestheticising both. This clearly relates to Milton's focus on sense perception in the passage at hand.
[174] For opposed claims of hearing as an 'Aristotelian commonplace' see Hunt, *Art of Hearing*, 23.
[175] This is Milton's usage of 'quite,' generally; compare, for instance, *PL* 2.92–93, 95–97.
[176] See Blumenberg, 'Light as a Metaphor for Truth.' This is the translation of a paper originally published, in 1957, as 'Licht als Metapher der Wahrheit: Im Vorfeld der philosophischen Begriffsbildung.'
[177] See Vinge, *Five Senses*, 11–12, 63–68; Jütte, *History of the Senses*, 77.

within. The names of the Gates were these, *Ear-gate, Eye-gate, Mouth-gate, Nose-gate,* and *Feel-gate.*[178]

A marginal note against this passage drives the point home – these gates are 'The five Sences' –, as does Bunyan's frontispiece, which prominently displays 'Heart Castle' alongside the two most important gates to the town of Mansoul, 'Eye gate' and 'Eare gate' (Fig. 5). Usually, as in the case of Bunyan's *Holy War*, the idea in comparing the human senses to the gates of a fortified city is that of a threat – a threat to the 'besieged' citadel of the human soul. In the present case, however, Milton is rather thinking of the access previously given to knowledge and wisdom through the 'entrance' of the eyes.[179]

In moving from (personal) sensuous enjoyment to (interpersonal) communication to (ideally 'transpersonal,' i.e. objective) knowledge, in this passage of the proem Milton may be said to touch on three distinct domains in which the speaker's blindness has had an impact. In the end, of course, it is the speaker's very own experience that matters: his being 'from the cheerful ways of men/Cut off' – an instance of Milton's characteristically suggestive use of line breaks and half-lines – and having 'wisdom at one entrance quite shut out.' In his reference to 'the book of knowledge fair,' Milton fuses aesthetic and epistemic regards on the sense of sight. In section 3 of the proem, he will return to the spiritual dimension with a renewed address to 'celestial light,' figured as both a restorative to his blindness and a corrective to mere 'mortal sight.'

In *Samson Agonistes*, by contrast, the protagonist's initial moment of rest on the pleasant bank remains the only element of relief amidst his blindness. Milton's further portrayal of Samson's affliction focuses not on possibilities of compensation but on the irreversible loss of his sight. In fact, parts of Samson's first soliloquy read like a variation of the epic speaker's lament in the central section of Proem III:

> but chief of all,
> O loss of sight, of thee I most complain!
> Blind among enemies, O worse than chains,
> Dungeon, or beggary, or decrepit age!
> Light the prime work of God to me is extinct,
> And all her various objects of delight
> Annulled, which might in part my grief have eased,
> Inferior to the vilest now become
> Of man or worm; the vilest here excel me,
> They creep, yet see, I dark in light exposed

---

[178] John Bunyan, *The Holy War, made by Shaddai upon Diabolus, for the Regaining of the Metropolis of the World, or, the Losing and Taking Again of the Town of Mansoul* (London: Printed for Dorman Newman, 1682), 4.

[179] Milton's wording in the phrase 'of nature's works to me expunged and *rased*' answers to both, the image of the 'book of knowledge' but also that of the senses as gates into the city of the soul. See *OED*, 'raze, v.: (2) 'To erase or obliterate (writing, a record, etc.), originally by scraping …' and (6) 'to tear down, demolish, or level (a building, town, etc. …'

5.2 Proem III (PL 3.1–55)

Fig. 5: John Bunyan, *The Holy War* … (1682), frontispiece: 'The Towne of Mansoul' with 'Eare gate,' 'Eye gate,' and 'Heart Castle.'   Source: EEBO

> To daily fraud, contempt, abuse and wrong
> Within doors, or without, still as a fool,
> In power of others, never in my own;
>
> (*SA* 64–78)

As in the opening lines of the drama, blindness is figured as helplessness, the blind man 'dark in light exposed' to attacks, and powerless. Crucially, even worms, conventionally associated with the sense of touch ('they creep ...' on the ground) and introduced into the present passage as the creatures furthest both from humanity and from the top of the sensory hierarchy, are superior to the blind man on account of their possessing vision at all ('... yet see').[180] The orientational inversion is clear: Samson should be 'on top' of both the sensory hierarchy and the hierarchy of creation;[181] instead, he is 'inferior,' i.e., literally, 'lower' (which, in turn, is related to the focus on his 'sitting down' throughout). Comparable to Proem III, however, Samson now particularly deplores the loss of the 'various objects of delight/ ... which might in part my grief have eased' (as had, indeed, other pleasant perceptions in the opening lines of the drama). As Samson's reference to 'all her various objects of delight' – 'her' as Latin *lux* is feminine – makes clear, he now restricts his conception of sensuous enjoyment to one sensory mode only, that of vision. Concurrent with this (self-)restriction of the perceptual range, however, and somewhat paradoxically, his phrase evokes the notion of a pleasing 'variousness' of sense perception (across both sense-objects and sensory modes) discussed earlier.

What ultimately separates Samson's attitude from that of the speaker in Proem III is the different way in which he relates light to its creator. Whereas, in Proem III, it is first introduced as 'holy light,' 'offspring ... first-born' and representative of God, Samson presents it as merely one – if the 'prime' one – of God's works. When he, too, addresses light directly in the continuation of the soliloquy ('O first-created' – not 'first-born'! – 'beam ...'), he immediately turns this address into a reproach:

> Scarce half I seem to live, dead more than half.
> O dark, dark, dark, amid the blaze of noon,
> Irrecoverably dark, total eclipse
> Without all hope of day!
> O first-created beam, and thou great word,
> Let there be light, and light was over all;
> Why am I thus bereaved thy prime decree?
> The sun to me is dark
> And silent as the moon,
> When she deserts the night
> Hid in her vacant interlunar cave. (*SA* 79–89)

---

[180] For the association of worms and touch, see Classen, *Deepest Sense*, 104. On Milton's numerous references to and 'predominantly negative portrayal of worms,' see Karen Edwards, 'Milton's Reformed Animals: An Early Modern Bestiary – T–Z,' *MQ* 43 (2009), 241–308, at 289–94 (with commentary on the present passage at 294).

[181] Compare Milton's close association of Adam's vision with human superiority and rule.

5.2 Proem III (PL 3.1–55)

To Samson, quite simply, and in addition to being a prison, blindness is death. This is in marked contrast to the (equally blind) epic speaker's persistent connection to, and enjoyment of, holy light as a 'vital lamp.' More radical still than the Chorus in this respect, Samson does not even consider the possibility of inner illumination raised by them ('For inward light alas puts forth no visual beam …'), and he thus presents his darkness, in several ways, as all-encompassing: it is 'dark, dark, dark' (epizeuxis to indicate vehemence) 'amid the blaze of noon' (pathetic paradox); it is 'irrecoverabl[e],' 'total,' 'without all hope;' it extends to the sun itself (the source of light and vision) and, similar to the central passage of Proem III, it appears to encroach on another sensory mode as well, rendering the sun and moon as 'silent' as they have become invisible. In fact, Milton's wording is ambiguous, creating a complex association between Samson's sight and his hearing. This extends to the term 'silent'[182] as well as to the phrase 'vacant interlunar cave.'[183] Even when considering the testimony of sensory modes other than vision, then, Samson is invariably thrown back on his blindness.

As the blind speaker of *Paradise Lost* makes clear in the final section 3 of Proem III, for him, in contrast to blind Samson, whose fate will be quite different, there is a way forward. Similar to the speaker's earlier declaration at the opening of section 2, 'Yet not the more/Cease I to wander …,' section 3 opens with an affirmation of resistance to blindness – or rather, with an insistent plea, addressed, again, directly to light, to help the speaker battle the adverse effects of blindness. In contrast to the contention of the Chorus in *Samson Agonistes* that 'inward light … puts forth no visual beam,' the epic speaker's concluding appeal specifies two ways in which 'celestial light' would counteract his blindness: through a *restoration* of sight as internal sight ('Shine inward, … /Irradiate, there plant eyes') which, in the end, would amount to an *improvement* on regular, external sight ('that I may see and tell/Of *things invisible to mortal sight*'). When he asks for celestial light to enlighten him 'through all [the] powers' of his mind' and 'there plant eyes,' this, too, may mean more than the usual pair.[184] What in Proem I had been the joint responsibility of the 'heavenly Muse' ('Of man's first disobedience …. Sing') and the 'Spirit' ('what in me is dark/Illumine'), namely the

---

[182] 'The time when the moon is in conjunction with the sun is called, says Pliny xvi 74, either the day of the silent moon (*silentis lunae*) or the interlunar day (*interlunii*). *OED* first records the word "silent" meaning "not shining", as applied to the moon, in 1646. Samson translates a visual fact, the moon's absence, into the terms of the sense he still retains, hearing' (Carey ad loc.). Without contesting the validity of this reading, I would argue that, in the context of this passage focused on the *totality* of blindness, Milton's technical use of 'silent,' at the same time, suggests a sensory deprivation going even beyond blindness proper. Not least, the sun and moon *are* silent, and are only perceptible to vision (if we disregard the possibility of sphere music, which may provide a further point of association).

[183] Compare *PL* 6.4–8: 'There is a cave/within the mount of God, fast by his throne,/Where light and darkness in perpetual round/Lodge and dislodge by turns, which makes through heaven/Graceful vicissitude, like day and night …' (compare also *PL* 5.642–46). As for sound, the association of 'caves' and 'concaves' with resonance and resounding pervades *Paradise Lost*, especially with reference to hell; see, for instance, *PL* 1.541–43, 2.787–89. Consider also Bacon's repeated reference, in *Sylva Sylvarum*, to the 'Caue of the Eare' and the ear as 'a sinuous Caue' (§§ 272, 282).

[184] As, perhaps, in Milton's description of the cherubim at *PL* 11.129–131: 'all their shape/Spangled with eyes more numerous than those/Of Argus …'

expressive and perceptual reinforcement of the epic speaker, is now left to holy light alone.

In his call on this light to 'irradiate' 'the mind through all her *powers*,' the speaker draws on the traditional language of faculty psychology, in which the capacity of the soul to function is derived from the interplay of different 'faculties' or 'powers.'[185] In its most basic versions, these powers may be designated as *imaginatio* (usually referred to by Milton as 'fancy'), *cogitatio* ('reason'), and *memoria* ('memory'), but more complex classifications abound.[186] The significance of this comprehensive support to the blind speaker would lie in a strengthening of his imagination (to make up for lost sight), which, however, would have to be balanced and kept in check by reason; the relevance of memory, finally, lies in its (correct, precise) retention of earlier experience. The 'mists' to be 'purge[d] and disperse[d]' in the process corresponds to the 'cloud' of 'ever-during dark' to which the speaker had referred earlier. At the same time, both images connect to Milton's solar imagery throughout *Paradise Lost*; in operating on the 'mists' of physical blindness and metaphysical (i.e., in Milton's world, spiritual) ignorance, God's inward light, too, functions like the sun.[187]

The speaker's image of a full and pervasive internal illumination expands on his more restrained request to the Spirit, in Proem I, to illumine 'what ... is dark.' In fact, (holy) light *itself*, addressed throughout the proem with reference to both its theological signification and the superior role played by it in the physical universe (represented by the sun), as well as to the connections between both (God made it, and he made the sun), gives reason to expect an appropriately greater degree of illumination: total illumination. In the continuation of the passage from *Samson Agonistes* quoted last, Samson, too, reflects on the implications of the totality of light, both as a life-giving force and as an inner power:

> Since light so necessary is to life,
> And almost life itself, if it be true
> That light is in the soul,
> She all in every part; why was the sight
> To such a tender ball as the eye confined?
> So obvious and so easy to be quenched,
> And not as feeling through all parts diffused,
> That she might look at will through every pore?
>
> (*SA* 90–97)

---

[185] 'The mind,' again, is feminine, on account of Latin *mens*. Compare Samson's similar references to light/*lux* (quoted above) and the soul/*anima* (quoted below).

[186] See Park, 'Organic Soul;' see also the surveys in C. S. Lewis, *The Discarded Image: An Introduction to Medieval and Renaissance Literature* (Cambridge: Cambridge University Press, 1964), 152–68, and E. Ruth Harvey, *The Inward Wits: Psychological Theory in the Middle Ages and the Renaissance* (London: Warburg Institute, 1975).

[187] Compare also 'Beelzebub's hope that the devils may "purge off this gloom" at heaven's "orient beam"' in *PL* 2.399–400 (Fowler ad loc.).

By labelling the eye 'a tender ball,' Samson paradoxically (yet fittingly) assigns it to the tactile sphere: both a 'mere thing' and a toy, a trifle, the blind eye has forfeited its place at the top of the sensory hierarchy. As in the reference in Proem III to 'these eyes, that roll in vain' because 'so thick a drop serene hath quenched their orbs,' Samson's disparaging remarks – disparaging the useless because incapacitated sense-*organ*, i.e. 'tool' – emphasises the embodied quality of vision: the noble eye, too, is a part of the merely tactile body, and this simple fact becomes shockingly obvious in the event of blindness.[188] In a different sense (that of touching rather than eating/tasting) and with a different impetus (aiming at pathetic heightening rather than bathetic putdowns), these portrayals of the blind eye as a material *thing* are fundamentally akin to what I have called, in my discussion of Prolusion VI, the *reductio ad corpus*.[189]

However, while the image from *Samson Agonistes* indicates the same precariousness of vision lamented by the speaker of Proem III, there is an important difference. Paradoxically, Samson, at the same time as *deploring* the demotion of the blind eye to the realm of the merely tactile, wishes for vision to be *more like* touch ('feeling'). The paradox, as the earlier pathos, rests on the diametrically opposed placement of vision and touch in the hierarchised sensorium. At the same time, Samson's reference to 'feeling' is ambiguous, and arguably also relates to his current emotional state of abject despair: this is what he *feels* 'through all parts diffused.'[190] The speaker of Proem III also *feels* – namely, 'thy sovereign vital lamp' –, and he concludes his reflections on light with the image of a complete and interiorised repletion: his loss of *outer* vision will correspond, hopefully, to a commensurate gain in *inner* vision, a visionary totality pervading his 'mind through all her powers.' This, while it resembles Samson's description of 'feeling through all parts diffused' and 'look[ing] at will through every pore,' is in contrast to the confrontation of vision and touch – in terms of the sensory hierarchy, the ultimate in non-vision – that Samson's images imply. Whereas the speaker of Proem III hopes to be given vision for vision – new eyes in exchange for his old, blind ones –, Samson's totality remains that of the 'total eclipse/Without all hope of day.'

---

[188] Significantly, both the speaker of Proem III and Samson refer to their eyes as having been 'quenched;' the notion of 'quench[ing]' (a fire, a candle, etc.) also encapsulates the idea of tactility overcoming light or vision. Samson's complaint about the 'obvious[ness]' of the eye works in a similar way: the eye is both 'clearly visible' and 'situated in the way' of harm, hence 'exposed or open to (an action or influence; liable' (*OED*, 'obvious, adj. and n.,' 1, 3 and 4). Strikingly, several of the *OED*'s citations for the now obsolete sense 3 refer to light and sight, and one, to touch: 'They [sc. the horns of the bee] serue to giue warning in the darke ... of any obuious thing quicke or dead that might offend her' (from Charles Butler's *The Feminine Monarchie*, 1623).
[189] See Chapter 4.3. Eating and ingesting, of course, could be considered an applied combination of the two lowest senses, touch and taste.
[190] For the intricate relationship in early modern discourse between the two aspects – 'feeling' as tactility and as experience of emotion – see Moshenska, *Feeling Pleasures*, 6–7. In early modern usage, 'touching' and 'feeling' are often synonymous and, indeed, the underlying primary meaning of 'to feel' is 'to touch' (see *OED*, 'feeling, n.,' I). Moshenska argues that it is precisely this 'fluctuation between meanings ... that distinguishes accounts of touch in sixteenth- and seventeenth-century England,' and that today, still, 'feeling' aptly encapsulates the ambiguity between literal and figurative language which is characteristic of many references to touch.

'Taste and See': Proem III and the Spiritual Senses Tradition

To at least some of Milton's contemporaries, the image of spiritual vision presented in Proem III constituted an instance of reprehensible Platonising, as the attack to this effect by the author of *The Transproser Rehears'd* indicates. Such readings did have a point, as the presence of Platonising sensory discourse in Milton, in earlier texts as well as in *Paradise Lost* itself, can hardly be disputed: it appears plausible to read the symbolism of Proem III, too, as expressive of a (neo-)Platonic metaphysics of light, contiguous to Milton's emphatically visual idea of 'contemplation.' There is, however, another tradition of conceptualising non-physical (i.e., 'metaphysical' or 'spiritual') vision that also has a bearing on Milton's account in Proem III, and in the concluding section particularly. This is the tradition of the 'spiritual senses' in Western Christianity.[191] In several ways, Milton's poetic conception of inner sight also evokes the concepts and terminology of that tradition; in his seventeenth-century English context, however, there was a convergence of the spiritual senses tradition and wider Platonic influences, exemplified in the theological writings of the Cambridge Platonists.[192]

The spiritual senses tradition, as it has been delineated by scholars, starts from Origen's rendering of Proverbs 2:5 (in the Authorised Version, 'Then shalt thou understand the fear of the Lord, and find the knowledge of God') as, in effect, '... thou shalt acquire a divine sense [*aisthêsis theia*].'[193] As a consequence, sensory language in Scripture was taken literally: if the Psalms invited readers and hearers to 'taste and see [!] that the Lord is good' (Ps. 34:8), this was taken indeed to indicate something that could be perceived in mystical experience; when Paul, conversely, referred to believers as 'a sweet savour of Christ [unto God],' their godliness was equally conceived in sensory terms, as a taste pleasant to the divine palate.

In the exegetical tradition, this notion of a specialised perception of the divine sometimes developed into elaborate, more or less consistent doctrines of the spiritual senses as an additional 'set' of perceptual faculties, resulting in 'two different sets of powers or faculties [that were understood] as *two states of the same fivefold sensorium*.'[194] One way of conceptualising Milton's intricate intermingling of physical and spiritual vision, then, might be as switching between or blending those 'two states' of what, essentially, was a unified conceptual model. What unites all the different approaches to the spiritual senses complex is their use of 'expressions in which "sense" in general or a particular sensory modality ... is ... qualified by reference to spirit ..., heart ..., soul ..., mind or intellect ..., the inner [man] ... or faith' – that is, by reference to 'the ear of the heart,' the 'touch of one's soul,' or – as in the case of Proem III, 'inward' eyes.[195] In some authors, the language of the spiritual senses is closely linked

---

[191] See the contributions in *The Spiritual Senses*, eds Gavrilyuk/Coakley. My remarks in the following are based on the editors' 'Introduction,' 1–19.

[192] See Wainwright, 'Jonathan Edwards,' 225, 229–30.

[193] The Septuagint has *epignōsin theou* ('knowledge of God'), which corresponds to the KJV. On Origen's account of the spiritual senses, see Vinge, *Five* Senses, 26–29, and the chapter by Mark J. McInroy, 'Origen of Alexandria,' in *Spiritual Senses*, eds Gavrilyuk/Coakley, 20–35.

[194] Gavrilyuk/Coakley, 'Introduction,' 5, emphasis added.

[195] Gavrilyuk/Coakley, 'Introduction,' 2.

to their conception of the Trinity, and to their pneumatology, in particular; this, too, is true of Milton's proems, both with regard to the invocation of the Spirit in Proem I (called on to 'illumine' the speaker) and the strong association in Proem III between light and the Son – he, too, the 'offspring of heaven first-born' – as the dispenser of the 'water of life.'[196]

As Sarah Coakley and Paul Gavrilyuk have argued regarding the fuzzy fringes of the spiritual senses discourse, there are 'dead metaphors describing various forms of thinking. For example, we speak of "seeing a point," "having a point of view" … "grasping a concept," "touching upon a subject," … "smelling trouble" and so on' and that 'there appears to be no need to invoke a special mode of perception to account for these ordinary forms of reflection, imagination and judgement.'[197] In terms of sensory discourse, however, there should be no such thing as a 'dead metaphor,' and the examples given by Coakley and Gavrilyuk certainly have firm conceptual-metaphorical roots in actual, bodily sense perception. They also acknowledge that not even every correlation of the senses to the intellect can be reduced to a metaphor for ordinary mental activity. Their example to illustrate this point, significantly, also figures prominently in Milton: it is the Platonic contemplation of the forms, conceived of in terms of 'a direct, perception-like apprehension of the intelligibles.'[198] With regard to the proems to *Paradise Lost*, more specifically, this point might not even have to be raised: there, inner vision is explicitly introduced not as a manner of speaking but in its relation to physical blindness. This blindness, in turn, is an emphatically corporeal affliction, in the proems as in *Samson Agonistes* (the decisive difference being that Samson is *denied* spiritual vision). All aspects or 'states' of vision – physical vision, the speaker's physical blindness and hope for spiritual vision, Samson's physical blindness without hope for spiritual vision – are treated by Milton as part of a conceptual continuum; the consistency of his sensory discourse in addressing them reflects this.

In early modern England, the spiritual senses tradition was still prominent,[199] and in keeping with the Protestant emphasis on personal piety, the 'bestowal of a new spiritual sense [upon conversion] was a Puritan commonplace.'[200] Against this close cultural context, Milton's plea for inspiration, 'there plant eyes,' appears like the restaging of a conversion experience. As William J. Wainwright points out, the Puritan conception of what was also called the 'sense of the heart' could just refer to a 'feeling' of being fully convicted of the truth of the Gospel; but it could also refer to a cognitive engagement with the divine. This, Wainwright argues, could conform to either of two models: one

---

[196] See Gavrilyuk/Coakley, 'Introduction,' 4. According to some early proponents of the spiritual senses doctrine, the spiritual senses were activated, as it were, at baptism (see Gavrilyuk/Coakley, 'Introduction,' 13).

[197] Gavrilyuk/Coakley, 'Introduction,' 6. The authors explain that, in this 'metaphorical' use of the spiritual senses idiom, 'no close similarity with the functioning of a physical sensorium is intended.' Milton, clearly, consistently parallelises the two; see Webster, '"Presented with a Universal blanc."'

[198] Gavrilyuk/Coakley, 'Introduction,' 6–7, quotation at 7.

[199] See Wainwright, 'Jonathan Edwards,' for an overview covering the seventeenth and early eighteenth centuries.

[200] Wainwright, 'Jonathan Edwards,' 225.

he terms 'Platonic' (meaning an immediate intuition of the divine); the other conceived of the way in which divine knowledge was acquired as structurally similar to sense perception. Again, then, there is a close affinity between the Platonic notion of contemplation and the spiritual senses tradition, raising the question of their relation in Milton.

In the case of *Paradise Lost*, in fact, the relationship between contemplative insight and spiritual vision may be indicated by reference to two passages already referred to. Exemplary of the first is Adam's conviction that, through persistent attention to the scale of nature, 'in contemplation of created things,/By steps we may ascend to God' (*PL* 5.511–12). Apart from the Platonic tradition of contemplation, this notion has its roots in the 'argument from Creation' presented throughout the Christian tradition.[201] Its canonical statement is in Romans 1:20: 'For the invisible things of him from the creation of the world are clearly seen, being understood by the things that are made, even his eternal power and Godhead ...'[202] Through contemplation of 'the things that are made,' then, – they are instrumental both in a linguistic and a general sense – the 'invisible' qualities of God, 'even his eternal power and Godhead,' may be 'understood,' may be made *nooumena*. As the latter term implies, the 'things that are made' appear to us as *phainomena*; they are the 'visible things' to which God's 'invisible things' are opposed. The notion thus wholly corresponds to Adam's idea of gaining knowledge *of God himself* through attentive scrutiny of his Creation. This is one way, then, of gaining insight into 'things invisible to mortal [i.e., physical as opposed to spiritual] sight.' The speaker of Proem III is *not* suggesting, after all, that he is anything other than human. It is just that, to him, 'wisdom [has been] quite shut out' at the 'one entrance' associated, by Plato as by Paul, with the contemplative ascent. Thus his request for another kind of vision, for a second chance of reaching the same goal by a different route. Platonic contemplation and the spiritual senses tradition both contribute to Milton's sensory discourse in *Paradise Lost*, but they are not mutually exclusive; rather, spiritual vision refers to the potential already inherent, by divine grace, in physical vision to apply the senses in pursuit of divine knowledge. In much the same way that, at the roots of the spiritual senses tradition, 'epistemology and spirituality ... were intrinsically united,' Milton presents both as aspects of the same sensory continuum.[203]

In keeping with the valuation of the individual (spiritual) senses in Christian mysticism, the acquisition of divine knowledge was often figured in terms of the contact senses of touch and taste.[204] Again, the literalness with which these spiritual-sensory experiences could be related to actual bodily perception is striking. Thus, the puritan clergyman Robert Dingley could write, in his treatise *The Spirituall Taste Described;*

---

[201] See also Gabel, 'Hierarchies of Vision,' 122–26.
[202] In the original Greek, 'the invisible things,' meaning God's transcendent attributes, are *ta ... aorata*; the KJV's 'clearly seen' renders *kathoratai*, i.e., '[they] are fully seen, seen through and through' (as the neuter plural *aorata* takes a singular predicate). Both terms are derived from the same verb root, *horân*, 'to see;' the close connection between the (formerly invisible) objects of vision and the act of seeing is thus more evident in the Greek than it is in the KJV's rendering into English. 'Understood' is *nooumena*, qualifying *ta ... aorata*.
[203] Gavrilyuk/Coakley, 'Introduction,' 13.
[204] On the development of this aspect of the spiritual senses tradition see Gordon Rudy, *The Mystical Language of Sensation in the Later Middle Ages* (New York: Routledge, 2002).

and a Glimpse of Christ Discovered (1649) that 'there is a corporall taste, and hereby occasionally we may taste God,' namely when 'even in bodily food, a Beleever tastes how good the Lord is; ... and he tastes Divine goodnesse in every morsell of bread he eates.'[205] Dingley promptly explains that the main focus of his treatise is on what he pointedly calls 'a Mysticall and Spirituall taste, which is to examine, try, consider, and relish divine goodnesse, and partake of its sweetnesse and joy,' and he goes on to indicate the diverse ways in which that concept might be understood.[206] Still, it is clear from his statements how the bodily and the spiritual taste were understood as two versions of, essentially, the same mechanism. And even in such emphatically non-visual accounts of contemplation, the Platonic tradition could be named as a point of reference. Witness the description of a gustatory perception of 'divine truth' given by the Cambridge (Platonist) philosopher, John Smith: 'There is an inward sweetness and deliciousness in divine truth, which no sensual mind can taste or relish. ... Divinity is not so well perceived by a subtle wit ... as by a purified sense, as Plotinus phraseth it.'[207] In fact, the concepts of (more direct?) divine taste and (more intellectual?) spiritual vision, in Smith's view, do not seem to be ranked, but appear as equal contributors in a unified spiritual sensorium, one giving rise to the other:

> We must shut the eyes of sense, and open that brighter eye of the understanding, that other eye of the soul, as the philosopher calls our intellectual faculty ... the light of the divine world will then begin to fall upon us ... and in God's own light shall we behold him. The fruit of this knowledge will be sweet to our taste, and pleasant to our palates. ...[208]

Shutting the 'eyes of sense' in order to let 'the light of the divine world' reach 'that other eye of the soul' – Smith's Platonising language seems of a piece with that of Milton's Proem III, right down to the question of (in)voluntariness: if a detachment from bodily perception is the duty of every Christian intent on spiritual self-improvement ('*We must* shut the eyes of sense ...'), this might offer at least some comfort to those struck blind without being given a choice.

To be sure, Smith's immediate return to the gustatory domain distances him from Milton, who, on his part, does not go as far as addressing a 'taste or relish' of the divine; the closest Milton's sensory discourse gets to a similar spiritualisation of taste is in his description of food and dining in the prelapsarian 'Garden of Eating.'[209] Still, Milton's

---

[205] Robert Dingley, *The Spirituall Taste Described; and a Glimpse of Christ Discovered. In two Parts; grounded on Psal. 34.8. and Malac. 4.2.* (London: Matthew Simmons, 1649), B3ᵛ, F3ʳ–F3ᵛ. Dingley's treatise was also distributed under the alternative title *Gods Sweetnesse Made out in Christ; or Divine Relishes of Mathlesse Goodnesse*. Dingley's printer Matthew Simmons also printed several of Milton's early tracts; his son Samuel would later be the printer of *Paradise Lost*.
[206] Dingley, *Spirituall Taste Described*, F3ᵛ.
[207] Smith quoted in Wainwright, 'Jonathan Edwards,' 230.
[208] Ibid.
[209] I borrow this phrase from Michael C. Schoenfeldt, *Bodies and Selves in Early Modern England: Physiology and Inwardness in Spenser, Shakespeare, Herbert, and Milton* (Cambridge: Cambridge University Press, 1999), 139.

reflections on light and (in)sight in Proem III do not disregard the contact senses altogether: the speaker, after all, 'feel[s]' the sun-like radiation of 'holy light' as a life-giving, 'vital lamp.'[210] Significantly, it was this image – the element of Milton's sensory discourse in the proem most suggestive of spiritual perception as a mystical and immediate experience of the divine – that bore the brunt of the anti-enthusiastic attack on Milton in *The Transproser Rehears'd*.

Through their declarations of a 'joyful' and 'pleasant' perception of God – and the conventionally 'lower,' more physical ones, in particular –, the proponents of the spiritual senses tradition among Milton's contemporaries meant to supplement the conventional discourse of theology with some much-needed *experiential* knowledge. As Owen put it, 'speculative notions about spiritual things, when they are alone, are dry, sapless and barren. In this gust [i.e., spiritual taste] we taste by experience that God is gracious, and that the love of Christ is better than wine, or whatever else hath the most grateful relish unto a sensual appetite.'[211] At the same time, however, both he and John Smith stressed that this experience led to genuinely 'intellectual' insight or intuition, courtesy of 'that reason that is within us' (Smith).[212] However, if divine knowledge, in the final analysis, is an 'intellectual intuition, why employ the language of the physical senses' in the first place?[213] Wainwright's answer is twofold: first, because it was the convention of a still very influential tradition; and, secondly, because the senses provide apt metaphors for the immediacy and affective overtones of the religious experience. Milton's sensory discourse in Proem III, in as far as it can be traced to the spiritual senses tradition, also aims at precisely this application.

***

Since, in the third and final section of Proem III, the speaker takes up his earlier invocation to light (from section 1) and aims to (re-)connect it to his personal fate (laid out in section 2), it might seem obvious to consider the proem in its entirety as a kind of extended syllogism. In fact, Milton's language in the first two sections would support this approach: they are composed largely of statements of fact, repeatedly implying reasons, conclusions, qualifications, and conscious oppositions ('*since* God is light ... dwelt *then* in thee ...,' '... *though* long detained ... *though* hard and rare ...,' '*but* thou/Revisitst not ...,' '*Yet not the more* ... *then* feed on thoughts ... *Thus* with the year/Seasons return, *but not to me* returns/Day ...'). Section 3 takes up this train of thought and continues it ('*So much the rather* ...'); crucially, however, it does not proceed by statements of fact but wholly in the imperative or rather, in the given context, in the 'implorative' mood: '*Shine* inward ... there *plant* eyes ... *purge* and *disperse*.' This, again, results in a conclusion, which now indicates the hoped-for effect of the invocation: '*that* I may see and tell ...' At this point, finally, the dialectic of hope and

---

[210] In addition, Erin Webster has pointed out 'Milton's figuration of the mind's vision of divine things as a luminous *piercing of the dark body* – the "ir-" prefix on "irradiate" stressing the inward movement – by celestial light' ('"Presented with a Universal blanc," 234–35, emphasis added).
[211] Owen quoted in Wainwright, 'Jonathan Edwards,' 229.
[212] Smith quoted in Wainwright, 'Jonathan Edwards,' 230.
[213] Wainwright, 'Jonathan Edwards,' 230.

despair which had informed the first two sections of Proem III – figured, as in the sensory discourse of Milton's proems more generally, as vision and blindness –, while not *resolved*, is presented as fundamentally *resolvable* through divine inspiration.

In its repeated confrontation of vision and blindness, Proem III indicates that the orientational certainties of the hierarchised sensorium are not to be taken for granted. If VISION, conventionally, IS UP in the sense that it outranks the other senses, that it is placed highest in the sensorium and is associated with all the epistemic, social, and cultural prestige an elevated viewing position implies, the experience of the poet-speaker in Proem III brings to light the precariousness of this privileged ranking (its hovering, in the case of the already blind speaker, between hope and despair). This, ultimately, is the sensory discursive significance of the proem's focus on movement, and the speaker's movement UP towards the light, in particular. Whereas, in several of Milton's earlier writings, VISION IS UP had indeed corresponded to an elevated viewing *station*, the proems, more dynamically, express the orientational metaphor in terms of up- or downward *movement*: Proem I in its hope to 'soar above the Aonian mount,' Proem III in looking back on a 'dark descent,' hoping to 'reascend' to light.[214] Precariousness implies the threat of an imminent change for the worse, and since CHANGE IS MOVEMENT, the use of orientational-directional metaphors to express precariousness seems only natural. Since the faculty and organs threatened – and, in one sense, already lost – are the speaker's vision and eyes, it is equally obvious to express both the positive and negative faces of that precariousness in optical/ocular terms: either as a movement towards light (or a movement of light towards the speaker) or as a movement away from light (or, correspondingly, an unwillingness of personified light to 'revisit' the speaker's eyes).

Through its inclusion of the speaker's individual fate (much more extensive than the corresponding parts of Proem I), Proem III derives its force, ultimately, from a pathos similar to that expressed in Samson's embittered lament. But whereas blind Samson's predicament is sealed by the circumstance that he simply cannot conceive – as the speaker of Proem III can – of a source from which his vision could be renewed, the speaker is torn between the assurance of spiritual vision and the conflicting – and, fundamentally, proto-empiricist – awareness that for him, 'wisdom' has been 'quite shut out' on account of his blindness.[215] Milton does not, ultimately, confuse physical and spiritual light and vision; that much becomes clear from the dialectic of hope and des-

---

[214] Strictly speaking, this difference could be indicated by distinguishing, for instance, VISION IS UP (movement) from VISION IS HIGH (placement), but since ' … IS UP' (covering both movement *and* placement) is the conventional formulation in conceptual metaphor literature, I will adhere to that formula and indicate any differences in signification.

[215] In his *Essay Concerning Human Understanding* (1689), Locke would put forward the notion that 'all ideas come from sensation or reflection,' specifying this by reference to the established philosophical metaphor of the 'tabula rasa': 'Let us then suppose the mind to be, as we say, white paper, void of all characters, without any ideas …' (Book II, ch. 1., 'Of Ideas in general, and their original; *Essay*, ed. Nidditch, 104). Milton uses a similar image (though with a more negative thrust) in his reference to a 'universal blank' (construed as referring to an empty white page in contrast to the 'book of knowledge fair' by Hale, 'Books and Book-Form in Milton,' 74).

pair that pervades the proem, and whose synthesis can only be prayer.[216] However, in order for that dialectic to be set in motion, he must present physical and spiritual vision as correlated and structurally comparable faculties – an approach in tune with the spiritual senses tradition. If, after all, the speaker had been entirely certain of his spiritual illumination – if his invocation to 'holy light' had not been tinged, that is, by the anxiety physical blindness causes him – Proem III would not have risen to the level of pleading insistence reached in its concluding section ('*So much the rather* thou …'). And yet, in contrast to Samson – 'O dark, dark, dark, amid the blaze of noon,/*Irrecoverably* dark, total eclipse/*Without all hope* of day!' – the speaker of Proem III, like Samson, may be past (physical) recovery, but he is not past praying for. The synthesis of section 3 – more an uneasy settling on hope than an actual conclusion from his earlier premises – is his peroration: as a prayer, to an audience of One; and to the reading public, as the provisional capstone to his sensory self-fashioning.

5.3 Proem VII (*PL* 7.1–39)
The Insecurity of Vision and the Speaker's Access to 'Eternal Wisdom'

> Descend from Heaven, Urania, by that name
> If rightly thou art called, whose voice divine
> Following, above the Olympian hill I soar,
> Above the flight of Pegasean wing.
> The meaning, not the name, I call: for thou   5
> Nor of the Muses nine, nor on the top
> Of old Olympus dwellest; but, heavenly-born,
> Before the hills appeared, or fountain flowed,
> Thou with eternal Wisdom didst converse,
> Wisdom thy sister, and with her didst play   10
> In presence of the Almighty Father, pleased
> With thy celestial song. Up led by thee
> Into the Heaven of Heavens I have presumed,
> An earthly guest, and drawn empyreal air,
> Thy tempering: with like safety guided down   15
> Return me to my native element:
> Lest from this flying steed unreined, (as once
> Bellerophon, though from a lower clime,)
> Dismounted, on the Aleian field I fall,
> Erroneous there to wander, and forlorn.   20
> Half yet remains unsung, but narrower bound
> Within the visible diurnal sphere;
> Standing on earth, not rapt above the pole,
> More safe I sing with mortal voice, unchanged
> To hoarse or mute, though fallen on evil days,   25

---

[216] On this point see also Judith H. Anderson, *Light and Death: Figuration in Spenser, Kepler, Donne, Milton* (New York: Fordham University Press, 2017), 199.

On evil days though fallen, and evil tongues;
In darkness, and with dangers compassed round,
And solitude; yet not alone, while thou
Visitest my slumbers nightly, or when morn
Purples the east: still govern thou my song, 30
Urania, and fit audience find, though few.
But drive far off the barbarous dissonance
Of Bacchus and his revelers, the race
Of that wild rout that tore the Thracian bard
In Rhodope, where woods and rocks had ears 35
To rapture, till the savage clamor drowned
Both harp and voice; nor could the Muse defend
Her son. So fail not thou, who thee implores:
For thou art heavenly, she an empty dream.

(*PL* 7.1–39)

Coming after Raphael's extended report of the war in heaven in books 5 and 6 of *Paradise Lost*, Proem VII opens the second half of the epic in its twelve-book form, a structural peculiarity both addressed and mirrored in the proem itself, which divides into two roughly equal halves: in the first, lines 1–20, Milton renews his invocation to the 'heavenly Muse' addressed in Proem I ('sing, heavenly Muse,' *PL* 1.6) and referred to in the third person in Proem III ('taught by the heavenly Muse to venture down …,' *PL* 3.19); in the second half of Proem VII (lines 21–39), the focus again is on the personal fate of the speaker, as it had been in Proem III, as well as on the Muse's support of him. In Proem VII, as in the first two proems, the orientational axis of UP versus DOWN plays a crucial role, and again is connected to the sensory hierarchy. However, both this movement and the sensory imagery derived from it emerge as paradoxical; as at the end of Proem III, the speaker, ultimately, can only resort to supplication. The uncertainty of the speaker's position, I argue, relates to the respective valuation of the senses of sight and hearing.

Who Is Urania?

After the strong focus on light and vision, on physical and spiritual sight and blindness, that characterised Proem III, Proem VII takes up the fundamentally balanced, audio-visual disposition of Proem I. This is apparent from the very first lines, as the speaker's hesitant address to the Muse's hearing – 'if rightly thou art called,' rehearsing the doubtful 'or hear'st thou rather …' of *PL* 3.7, one of the few auditory elements in Proem III – is contraposed to the Muse's own 'voice divine.' Since the speaker is still 'following' the Muse's voice upward – and as we have been able to witness by this point in the poem – his earlier request for the Muse to 'sing' (*PL* 1.6) appears to have been successful. This movement of 'soar[ing]' (at *PL* 7.3 as at 1.14), pointedly, is 'above' the tops of mountains, presented in Proem I as privileged sites of vision. Whereas the speaker of Proem I had hoped to 'soar/Above the Aonian mount,' i.e., above Mount Helicon, sacred to the Muses, Proem VII repeats the movement but turns it factual: the speaker now is indeed soaring 'above the Olympian hill,' seat of the pagan Greek pantheon and, also, the Muses. From the hopeful 'my advent'rous song ... intends to soar,' the speaker has arrived at the factual 'I soar.'

The enormity of the movement is expressed as a shift in perspective: seen from the great height attained with the help of the 'heavenly,' 'divine,' ultimately Christian Muse, Mount Olympus is reduced to a mere 'hill.'[217] This indicates the transcending of a boundary which, seen from below, does indeed seem high, but pales in comparison to the vast vertical extension of the Christian cosmos: in the catalogue of pagan deities in Book 1, Milton had already commented that 'the snowy top/Of cold Olympus,' where the Greek deities 'ruled the middle air,' was 'their highest heaven' (*PL* 1.515–17) – the authorial sneer in the last, typical 'half-line of derision' is unmistakable.[218] In what appears an echo of that earlier reference, Milton's Muse of Proem VII does *not* originate from 'the top/Of old Olympus' but is 'heav'nly born' in the theological sense.[219] As the first lines of the speaker's invocation emphasise, then, the Muse is both associated with heaven and – in a deeper sense – dissociated from the mere, visible sky: as the ancient Greek Muse of astronomy, Urania is narrowly identified as a representative of the latter but Milton's Muse emphatically is *not* one 'of the Muses nine.'

Hence the speaker's preoccupation with how to 'rightly' address the Muse, a quandary resolved into the distinction between the 'name' Urania (standing for the ancient Greek Muse it designates) and its 'meaning' (i.e., 'the heavenly one,' Milton's 'heavenly Muse'), derived from Greek *ouranos*, 'sky, heaven.'[220] Despite her capacity to convey the speaker up into the heavenly sphere ('Up led by thee/Into the heav'n of heav'ns I have presumed ...'), Milton's Muse is *not* the identically named Muse of astronomy; she is not the Muse of 'blind Maeonides' (from Proem III) but rather of Moses (from Proem I). Her contribution to the song of the poet, if forthcoming, will exceed the worth of mere speculation, astronomical or otherwise, conceived, in any case, as based in visual perception.

Vision, in the first half of Proem VII, is again primarily the sense of insufficiency and endangerment, either at risk or already lost. In contrast to Proem III, however, where the precariousness of (bodily) vision had been the dominant theme, the relevant elements in the sensory discourse of Proem VII relate to the poet-speaker's seer-like

---

[217] Fowler ad loc. points out that by the time of Milton's writing 'Mountain and *hill* were already distinguished.' In fairness it should be said, however, that throughout *Paradise Lost* the opposition is not a rigid one (consider the reference, certainly not disparaging, to 'Sion hill' in Proem I).

[218] The reference to 'high Olympus' at *PL* 10.583, significantly perhaps, is postlapsarian. In the sense that these instances of Milton's sensory discourse finally relate, also, to embodied perception, I am not convinced that, as Marjorie Hope Nicolson has argued by reference to a line from Byron ('to me ... high mountains are a feeling'), 'high mountains were not "a feeling" to ... Milton' (*Mountain Gloom and Mountain Glory: The Development of the Aesthetics of the Infinite* [Seattle, Wash.: University of Washington Press, 1997 (1959)], 1).

[219] She *is descended from* heaven and thus the speaker's plea 'Descend from heav'n Urania,' apart from its spatial reference, has about it something of a performative positing, as in the opening of a mathematical proof: 'let Urania descend from heaven ...'

[220] In New Testament Greek usage, too, it refers both to the sky and – more commonly – to heaven, frequently in the plural, a usage alien to classical Greek (compare Milton's 'the heav'n of heav'ns' at *PL* 7.13, at the same time, fittingly, an instance of *genitivus hebraicus*, emulating the way a superlative is expressed in Hebrew; see Fowler ad loc.).

inspiration first, and to mundane eye-sight only second. In Proem VII, as will become clear, the two aspects – natural vs inspired vision – are not completely detached from each other (neither had they been in Proem III) but are, again, considered in conjunction.

In Proem VII, the theme is taken up, first of all, in the speaker's deliberations on the appropriate meaning of 'Urania.' Is amplified, purified vision – and, above all, such a vision of 'celestial' things –[221] best represented by traditional approaches to or the cutting-edge technology of astronomical observation, with all that this implies in terms of human effort and the perfectibility of the senses by human means? After only a short hesitation ('if rightly thou art called …'), Milton's decision is unequivocal: 'the meaning, not the name, I call.' The reason is straightforward: the speaker's Muse quite simply *is not* the identically named pagan Greek Muse. Still, why *use* her 'name' to express the 'meaning' ('the heavenly one') when 'heavenly Muse' had been entirely adequate in Proem I? Apart from a possible influence of Renaissance literary pratice,[222] the conceptual uncertainty introduced along with the name, 'Urania,' appears to be precisely Milton's point. Earlier in *Paradise Lost*, Milton had contrasted the astronomical optics of Galileo (already alluded to as 'the Tuscan artist' at *PL* 1.287–91) with the perfect vision of the steadfast angel Raphael, who is about to depart heaven for Paradise to admonish Adam, and is looking down towards the earth:

> From hence, no cloud, or, to obstruct his sight,
> Star interposed, however small he sees,
> Not unconform to other shining globes,
> Earth and the garden of God, with cedars crowned
> Above all hills. As when by night the glass
> Of Galileo, less assured, observes
> Imagined lands and regions in the moon:
> Or pilot from amidst the Cyclades
> Delos or Samos first appearing kens
> A cloudy spot.
>
> (*PL* 5.257–66)

The specific contrast in this passage is between angelic vision on the one hand, unobstructed by either 'cloud' or 'star', and human vision on the other. Human vision appears in two forms: as technologically enhanced/amplified (Galileo) and as natural/unaided (the Greek pilot). Angelic vision, clearly, is supreme; in the visual hierarchy of *Paradise Lost*, it is second only to the all-seeing eye of God himself.[223] In Milton's phrase, 'no cloud, or, to obstruct his sight,/Star interposed,' there is a suggestive echo of Proem III: Raphael is at the furthest distance from blindness possible among created

---

[221] In the first half of Proem VII, terms relating to the sky or heaven abound: 'heaven,' 'heavenly,' 'celestial,' 'Heaven of Heavens,' 'empyreal.'
[222] The 'Christianisation' of Urania was a well-worn trope of the 'divine poetry' movement of the Renaissance; see the examples given by Fowler ad loc.
[223] See Gabel, 'Hierarchies of Vision.'

beings.[224] If a progressive gradation downward is intended by the two human points of comparison, Galileo, equipped with his 'glass' (i.e., telescope), is superior to the pilot, who has to trust his unaided eyes to discern 'a cloudy spot' (rounding off the passage opened with Raphael's vision inhibited by 'no cloud'). Nevertheless, Galileo's vision is 'less assured,' that is, more uncertain both in the physical/physiological sense (even with the telescope, his eyesight is inferior to Raphael's) and in what could be called a sense of bearing or inner certainty: his vision is less *self*-assured; he has reason to doubt whether the 'imagined lands and regions' he sees in the moon are really there. Milton presents practical, instrumental astronomy as riddled with a double uncertainty: it may aspire to superior vision, but it can only go so far, and is running the risk of overestimating its own potential.[225] The pilot, by contrast, at least appears to be sure of *what* it is he is seeing: the cloud he 'kens' is not shaped 'very like a whale' (as Hamlet would have Polonius believe, and as would correspond to Galileo's 'imagined lands and regions') but is quite simply 'a cloudy spot': the outer limit of his vision itself. Being a pilot, moreover, this minimum of (unaided) self-assuredness is essential. To Raphael, who in the continuation of the passage 'through the vast ethereal sky/Sails between worlds and worlds,' an angelic counterpart to the humble human sailor, perfect vision is part of his nature, not the result of technological or other enhancement: he descends further

>   ... till within soar
> Of towering eagles, to all the fowls he seems
> A phoenix, gazed by all, as that sole bird
> When to enshrine his relics in the sun's
> Bright temple, to Ægyptian Thebes he flies.
> At once on the eastern cliff of Paradise
> He lights, and to his proper shape returns
> A seraph winged ...   (*PL* 270–77)

In the densely packed sensory discourse of this passage, Raphael is presented as the embodiment of physical vision. More specifically, Milton is combining conceptual-metaphorical language ('towering') with references to mythology and natural history (Raphael is a phoenix among eagles, both bearing distinct visual/optical assocations), and his habitual solar imagery ('the sun's bright temple,' 'the eastern cliff of Paradise'), with puns ('that *sole* bird,' 'he *lights*') and etymology ('seraph,' from Hebrew *saraph*,

---

[224] Compare the reference to 'cloud ... and ever-during dark' at *PL* 3.45 (and 5.266!), as well as *OED* 'star-blind, adj.¹': 'totally or partially blind; (sometimes) spec. having vision obscured by a cataract or cataracts.' 'Star-blind,' related to German *grüner/grauer Star* ('glaucoma' and 'cataract,' respectively, the two kinds of blindness mentioned in Proem III) is attested from Old English times. Any physiological connotation of 'no ... star interposed' would relate both to the poet-speaker and to Galileo, who went blind around the time Milton possibly met him in the late 1630s; see Neil Harris, 'The Vallombrosa Simile and the Image of the Poet in *Paradise Lost*,' in: Mario A. Di Cesare (ed.), *Milton in Italy: Contexts, Images, Contradictions* (Binghamton, N. Y.: Medieval & Renaissance Texts & Studies, 1991), 71–96, at 76.

[225] See the various senses of *OED* 'assure, v.'

5.3 Proem VII (PL 7.1–39)

'to burn').[226] All of this forms an important part of what Raphael *is*; it is the polar opposite of the technologically enhanced (yet still 'less assured') telescopic vision of astronomy.

In Proem VII, the speaker's pointed rejection of 'Urania' as the Muse of astronomy implies a simultaneous rejection of over-confident yet 'less assured' human vision. Moving up to meet the descending Muse ('Descend ... I soar'), the speaker makes his way through a milieu more or less equivalent to that traversed by Raphael (he, too, descending) in book 5. Although this upward movement is his own ('*I* soar'), Milton's reference to Pegasus ('above the flight of Pegasean wing') conjures up a conventional image of the poet's need (and hope) for assistance but also of the dangers inherent in overestimating one's visionary reach: a symbol of poetic 'inspiration, contemplation, imagination, and sometimes ordinary inspiration excelled,' the winged horse Pegasus was said to have struck the Muses' spring ('Hippocrene,' i.e., 'the horse's spring') from Mount Helicon.[227] At the conclusion of the proem's first half, Milton rehearses the image of the empowering yet dangerous winged horse in his explicit comparison of the proem's speaker with Bellerophon, the mythical rider of Pegasus: having 'presumed' on his upward journey above Olympus,[228] above even the level reached by Pegasus and into 'the Heaven of Heavens,' and mindful of the harrowing conclusion to Bellerophon's story, the speaker entreats the Muse to be 'guided down' back to earth 'with like safety [sc. as in his ascent],'

> Lest from this flying steed unreined (as once
> Bellerophon, though from a lower clime),
> Dismounted, on the Aleian field I fall
> Erroneous, there to wander and forlorn.

In its integration of both upward and downward movement into the speaker's appeal for divine transport, the passage resembles the speaker's retrospective comment in Proem III that he had been 'taught by the heavenly Muse to venture down/The dark descent, and up to reascend,/Though hard and rare ...,' followed by a momentary sigh of relief: 'thee I revisit *safe*' (*PL* 3.19–21). In Proem VII, by contrast, the speaker's assurance of 'like safety' appears to be hanging by a thread, courtesy of the looming precedent set 'once' by Bellerophon – his story is cited not as timeless myth (perhaps in contrast to 'eternal Wisdom') but by way of historical example. Having compared himself *with* Bellerophon – and having found a disturbing degree of agreement –, the speaker is anxious not to be compared, ultimately, *to* Bellerophon, who had 'presumed' to fly Pegasus

---

[226] On the superior sight of the eagle (and Milton's references to it) see Edwards, 'Milton's Reformed Animals ... D–F,' 134–38; on the phoenix, accordingly, Karen Edwards, 'Milton's Reformed Animals: An Early Modern Bestiary – P–R,' *MQ* 42 (2008), 253–308, at 263–67.
[227] Fowler ad *PL* 7.4. Hesiod refers to it as 'the horse's spring' (*hippou krênês*) in his invocation to the Muses that forms the proem to the *Theogony*. In this sense, Milton's references to Pegasus in Proem VII also connect to the various other 'fountains' and 'brooks' mentioned in proems I and III.
[228] See *OED*, 'presume, v.': (1) '... to undertake without adequate authority or permission' and several related senses, among them (5) 'to aspire or press forward presumptuously; to make one's way overconfidently into an unwarranted position,' citing Milton's verse *PL* 7.13.

up to the top of Mount Olympus in order to set himself among the gods. He was thrown off and fell down 'on the Aleian field,' losing both Pegasus and Olympus (Milton's punning 'dismounted' captures this notion of a double downfall). A circumstance not explicitly mentioned by Milton, but highly relevant with a view to the sensory discourse of the proems, is that Bellerophon's 'forlorn' wandering was made worse by disability: as a result of his fall, he had lost his eyesight.[229] This familiar source of anxiety for the speaker is taken up again in the second half of the proem. At present, however, he is preoccupied with the danger of falling itself, made all the more menacing by the circumstance that Bellerophon had fallen 'from a lower clime.'[230] Bellerophon's 'erroneous ... wander[ing],' moreover, implies a misapplication or loss of knowledge contrary to the speaker's own, generally knowledge- or wisdom-centred approach.[231]

The theme of presumption and downfall in the story of Bellerophon obviously resonates with several elements central to the narrative of *Paradise Lost* as a whole: Satan's 'pride', which had 'cast him out from heaven ... hurled headlong flaming from the ethereal sky' (*PL* 1.36–37, 45); Eve's, then Adam's transgression and Fall. Similarly, the speaker of Proem VII is worried that his 'soar[ing]' ascent, though fostered by the Muse, might end in a crashing fall, and that the double visionary exaltation (above Olympus, above the flight of Pegasus flying over Olympus) might not be without its dangers, and might leave him, in the end, not just bereft of physical vision (the theme of Proem III) but also without the (in)sight of divine inspiration (hoped for at the end of Proem III). But whereas the speaker of Proem III had been torn between hope and despair regarding his lost physical vision, Proem VII discusses the precarious nature of inner vision, now conceptualised – with a slight shift of emphasis compared to Proem III, where 'see[ing] and tell[ing]' appeared rather as secondary effects of the speaker's personal illumination – as poetic inspiration, intended to sustain the 'song' of *Paradise Lost* (a conception of the epic poem as fundamentally sensory discourse to which Milton returns throughout).

Urania's Song and Eternal Wisdom

There is, then, a distinct visual theme to the first half of Proem VII, a theme that connects to Milton's preoccupation, familiar from the first two proems, with the speaker's illumination and insight – his 'vision' in that sense of the term – but also with his physical vision. In contrast to the latter half of Proem I, however, as well as to Proem III in its entirety – yet entirely in keeping with the invocation to the 'heavenly Muse' in the very first lines of *Paradise Lost* –, Proem VII figures Urania's contribution to the speaker's undertaking not in visual terms – not as an 'illumin[ing]' or 'irradiat[ing];' that is the domain of the 'Spirit' and of 'holy light.' *Her* contribution, rather, is her song, performed with 'voice divine.' This introduces, already in the second line of the proem, the theme of auditory (as opposed to visual) perception. The performance of Urania's

---

[229] See Fowler ad loc. ('he wandered blind and lonely till death'); Goldberg/Orgel ad loc. (he 'lived out his last years ... in blindness and alone').
[230] Fowler ad loc. points out a relevant homophony: 'from a lower *clime*,' i.e., region/'from a lower *climb*.'
[231] Compare also the description of the fallen angels 'in wandering mazes lost' in book 2, discussed in Chapter 2 above.

5.3 Proem VII (PL 7.1–39)

song is the subject, more specifically, of the passage *PL* 3.7–12a, inset into the invocation like a miniature flashback to a time before the speaker's present – or, indeed, before *any* present in a humanly conceivable sense:

> Before the hills appeared, or fountain flowed
> Thou with eternal wisdom didst converse,
> Wisdom thy sister, and with her didst play
> In presence of the almighty Father, pleased
> With thy celestial song.

Urania's song, 'convers[ing]' with eternal wisdom, should be capable of satisfying the speaker's quest for knowledge. More explicitly than in Proem I, and in keeping with the often quoted Pauline declaration that 'faith cometh by hearing, and hearing by the word of God,' auditory perception is thus posited as an alternative to sight in a situation in which 'wisdom' – the speaker's – is 'at one entrance quite shut out.'[232] At the same time, the passage continues a distinct preoccupation with questions of testimony, presence, and precedence – points which had been either raised or addressed at various times in proems I and III: the Spirit of Proem I is able to 'instruct' the speaker, by illumination, 'for thou knowst,' and he knows precisely because he had been present at the earliest stages of sacred history ('… thou from the first/Wast present …'). In a similar entanglement of temporal precedence, superior knowledge, and the authority to teach, Moses had figured as 'that shepherd, who *first taught* the chosen seed,/*In the beginning* how the heavens and earth/Rose out of chaos,' later taken up in similar attributions of precedence in relation to Creation: to light in Proem III ('before the heavens thou wert') and Urania in Proem VII ('before the hills appeared, or fountain flowed …').[233] And in the opening passage of Proem III, the speaker's first question is whether to address the

---

[232] Rom. 10:17. See Hunt, *Art of Hearing*, 30–42, on the repercussions of this verse in contemporary debates over preaching; see also Fried, '*Comus* and the Truth of the Ear,' esp. 128–29, on the 'primacy of the spoken word in communicating saving truth' and the development of this principle both in *Comus* and in the final books of *Paradise Lost*. In his last prose treatise, *Of True Religion* (1673), however, Milton advances a skeptical position regarding the value of hearing (the word of God) in and of itself. Catholics, he points out, are forbidden to read Scripture, and 'hence comes implicit faith, ever learning and never taught, much hearing and small proficience, till want of Fundamental knowledg easily turns to superstition or Popery …' (CPW 8: 434–35).

[233] *PL* 1.8–10. Milton's 'in the beginning' alludes to the opening of Genesis ('In the beginning [*be'reshit*] God created the heaven and the earth,' Gen. 1:1), from which that book takes its *incipit* title in the Hebrew Bible, as well as to that of John's gospel ('In the beginning was the Word …,' John 1:1). Genesis, of course, is a major source of *Paradise Lost*. John the Evangelist was traditionally thought to be identical with John of Patmos, the self-named author of the Book of Revelation, also a major source of Milton's epic (see, for instance, the micro-proem at the opening of *PL* 4: 'Oh for that warning voice, which he who saw/The Apocalypse, heard cry in heaven aloud …,' and compare Rev. 8:10–13). Fowler argues that by 'mimetic inversion' (i.e., by placing 'in the beginning,' conspicuously, at the beginning of a line, Milton emphasises his reference to the biblical pre-text (ad loc.).

recipient of his invocation as the '*offspring* of heaven *first-born*'[234] or rather, as '*of the eternal co-eternal* beam.'

In Proem VII, these questions of filiation and – approximate? – coevality recur: Urania is accompanied by 'wisdom [her] sister;' the audience of her song consists of 'the almighty Father.' Milton leaves open the precise relationship between wisdom and the Father, but since wisdom is '[sc. God's] eternal wisdom,' there is again the insinuation of coevality. In this different kind of trinity, Urania and wisdom are (roughly) coeval; so are wisdom and the Father; the Father, being the Father of all, is the fixed point in the triad. Whether Urania's 'convers[ation]' with wisdom is identical with or precedent to their 'play[ing]' together, moreover, it is clear that the 'song' that pleases the Father is Urania's alone ('thy celestial song').[235]

Urania's authority, ultimately, is derived from the idea of her almost absolute temporal precedence and spatial closeness to God himself – a closeness bordering on that ascribed to the persons in the Trinity. What may 'please' the ear of God can, through 'convers[ation]' with 'eternal wisdom,' acquire an instructive value for the benefit of the proem's speaker – he has been 'following' Urania's 'voice divine' – and, by extension, for that of *his* audience and readers. God, of course, cannot be taught by his own wisdom. His 'plea[sure]' may derive, perhaps, from a continual awareness of it, with Urania's song its accommodating representation: Urania's song unrolling, in temporal sequence, the static totality of 'eternal wisdom.' When the speaker declares that the Muse had 'converse[d]' with eternal (and hence transtemporal) wisdom, moreover, this is presented as happening *at some point in time* – namely, 'before the hills appeared or fountain flowed,' and thus prior in existence even to 'old Olympus.' This is the *temporal* equivalent to the *spatial* gesture of transcending classical, pagan culture that is implicit in the speaker's 'soar[ing]' 'above the Olympian hill …/Above the flight of Pegasean wing.' Urania existed, 'play[ing],' before even 'old Olympus' (and all other 'hills'). Milton's phrase, reminiscent of or echoing the idiom 'as old as the hills,'[236] most likely derives from the same passage in the Book of Job, in which Job's friend,

---

[234] I have suggested above a possible pun, – considering the context of 'effluence,' 'stream,' 'fountain' in the continuation of Proem III – on 'off*spring* … first-*born*' (i.e., 'bourne'). Consider, from Proem VII, '… nor on the top/Of old Olympus *dwellst* [i.e., wellst?], but heav'nly *born*,/Before the hills appeared, or *fountain flowed* …' The relevant passage from Proem III also has '*Dwelt* from eternity, *dwelt* then in thee …' See *OED*, 'well, v.': (5) 'of water: to rise up to the surface of the earth … and flow in a steady or copious stream. Also with a well or spring of water as subject …'

[235] The whole passage seems based on several verses from Proverbs 8 (24–25, 27, 30). Where the KJV has 'rejoicing,' Milton's 'play' appears to follow the Vulgate ('ludens'), with the possible suggestion of 'musical play' (see Fowler ad loc.), a derivation made more likely, perhaps, by Milton's use of the Vulgate forms 'Sion' and 'Siloa' (see Fowler ad *PL* 1.11).

[236] *OED*, 'old, adj.': (P3) '(as) old as the hills [perhaps in allusion to Job 15:7 …] exceedingly or immeasurably old,' gives a first attestation dating from 1819; but consider the lines from Coleridge's 1797 semi-pastiche of *Paradise Lost*, *Kubla Khan*: 'And here were gardens bright with sinuous rills,/Where blossomed many an incense-bearing tree;/And here were forests *ancient as the hills*,/Enfolding sunny spots of greenery …' (8–11, emphasis added, quoted from *Romanticism*, ed. Wu, 639–43, at 641. It seems likely that the idiom and association themselves are, in fact, even older.

5.3 Proem VII (PL 7.1–39)

Eliphaz, rebukes Job for his accusations against God (a theme resonant with the situation of the blind speaker of *Paradise Lost*):

> Should a wise man utter vain knowledge, and fill his belly with the east wind? [IDEAS ARE FOOD] ... Thine own mouth condemneth thee, and not I: yea, thine own lips testify against thee. Art thou the first man [*adam* and Adam] that was born? *or wast thou made before the hills?* Hast thou heard [*tishma*] the secret of God? and dost thou restrain wisdom to thyself? What knowest thou, that we know not? what understandest thou, which is not in us?[237]

As in Proem VII, temporal precedence – being made or just being present 'before the hills' – implies precedence in terms of knowledge and wisdom. As in Proem VII, too, the communication or expression of that wisdom is conceived of, above all, in auditory terms. Job, Eliphaz's questions imply, has *not* 'heard the secret of God,' and thus is lacking in wisdom, knowledge, and understanding. In a movement descending from the height of abstraction to the level of particularised observation, the Hebrew terms used suggest supreme wisdom (*chokhmah*), knowledge possessed (*yada*), and understanding (*binah*), gained through 'insight' or 'discernment': by perception through the senses.[238] Job has not succeeded on any of these successive levels. Excusably, perhaps, he has not heard God's secret counsel; but neither has he attained the lower levels of sense-based knowledge, as might have been expected of him. When the delineation of wisdom is taken up again in the 'Poem to Wisdom' of Job 28, the speaker's repeated questions – 'But where shall wisdom be found? and where is the place of understanding?' 'Whence then cometh wisdom? and where is the place of understanding?' – are made relatable in their urgency by a long list of disappointments ('... the depth saith, It is not in me: and the sea saith, It is not with me ...') before being given the following answer:[239]

---

[237] Job 15:2, 15:6–9, emphasis added.
[238] See Avrahami, *Senses of Scripture*, 129–30, on the central role of the verb *bin* ('to discern, perceive with the senses') in the epistemology of the Hebrew Bible. In individual instances, *bin* may refer to seeing, hearing, touching, tasting, or to understanding in the abstract. *Yada*, also, carries a connotation of 'perceiving' (with the senses), but it is not associated as particularly with any one sensory modality. See *HALOT* s. vv. Ultimately, there is a further parallel here to Milton's use of the argument from Creation ('in contemplation of created things ...'); as Avrahami points out, the relevant passages in Job are 'in complete harmony with the notion that understanding and acknowledgment of creation come from watching the created universe (*Senses of Scripture*, 70). In the first passage from Job quoted above, it is the gradation of types of knowledge that seems most to resemble the Miltonic notion of ascent to God 'by steps.' In the whole Book of Job, however, this approach is presented as problematic, as 'Job uses his body as a critical tool for testing wisdom and God-talk. He uses the faculties of his body to discern what is Right about God: the eye ..., the ear ..., and the palate,' and is criticised for it by his so-called comforters. See Scott C. Jones, 'Corporeal Discourse in the Book of Job,' *JBL* 132 (2013), 845–863, quotation at 846–47.
[239] The parallelism of these questions is a device typical of Hebrew poetry; however, again, *chokhmah* ('wisdom') and *binah* ('understanding') carry a slightly different force, the first acting almost as a 'regulative idea' – ultimately unattainable – to the pursuit of the second. On the opposition of the two terms in the in the passage at hand, see Scott C. Jones, *Rumors of Wisdom:*

> Seeing it is hid from the eyes of all living, and kept close from the fowls of the air. Destruction and death say, we have heard the fame thereof with our ears. God understandeth the way thereof, and he knoweth the place thereof. For he looketh to the ends of the earth, and seeth under the whole heaven ...[240]

Ultimately, divine wisdom is 'hid from the eyes of all living,' but even those furthest from God – the personified, rather Miltonic abstractions of destruction and death – have heard rumours about it.[241] God, by contrast, understands understanding, and he knows wisdom, both their way and their place: their totality. Both facts are expressed in sensory terms opposed to the earlier negation – wisdom is 'hid from the eyes of all living,' and even from the high-flying birds, emblematic of superior sight – by reference to God's encompassing vision: 'by pairing the horizontal and vertical dimensions, the parallel phrases ["ends of the earth" and "under the whole heaven"] create a spatial merism which is equivalent to "everywhere and everything."'[242] God's 'eternal Wisdom' and his total vision are more or less interchangeable aspects of his being.

Milton's 'heavenly Muse,' then, is privy to the kind of divine wisdom whose possibility of attainment by the human senses is so persistently questioned in the Book of Job. In its full perspicuity, this wisdom is available to God alone; but its diluted versions are said to make the rounds as 'rumors' (lit., 'things that are heard'). In the conceptual source domain from which important elements of Milton's sensory discourse in Proem VII derive, auditory perception may not be the key to divine wisdom in its superhuman totality (associated with the sense of sight); but it is presented as the only way of attaining an approximation of that wisdom in the first place. The activity of Milton's 'heavenly Muse,' Urania, in inspiring the speaker of Proem VII through her 'voice divine' and 'celestial song' should be read within this conceptual framework. Her song is pleasing, but it is also marked by its association with wisdom and its corresponding potential to impart wisdom to the speaker and *his* audience. When Milton describes the association of Urania and Wisdom, two points stand out: first, it is presented as 'convers[ation],' a term oscillating between static and dynamic meanings, between mere presence and

---

Job 28 as Poetry (Berlin: De Gruyter, 2009), 173–76. Jones argues that *binah*, 'a *Leitwort* of the poem,' is 'related to specific objects in a way that [*chokhmah*] is not' (176). In a dialectic relationship similar in structure to the notion of the 'hermeneutic circle,' *binah* is a process (of perception and understanding), *chokhmah* both a precondition and the ideal result of that process.

[240] Job 28:12–24.

[241] The Hebrew is insistent as to the embodied and auditory quality of their coming to know *about* wisdom; more literally, the relevant phrase reads 'we have heard a hearing [i.e., a rumour] in our ears' (*be'oznenu shamanu shimah*). This, too, could be read as part of the 'corporeal discourse' pervading Job; see Jones, 'Corporeal Discourse.' The KJV's 'fame' expresses *OED* sense 1a (now rare): 'that which people say or tell; public report, common talk; a particular instance of this, a report, rumour.' See also Jones, *Rumors of Wisdom*, 184–85: 'The nature of this phrasing [sc. *be'oznenu shamanu shimah*] suggests a contrast between aural recollection and firsthand visual perception. The statement that God "gazes to the end of the earth" [Job 28:24a] underscores this contrast between seeing and hearing ... In Job 28:22, wisdom remains hidden from view. Its fame is known, but all news is only hearsay' (quotation at 185).

[242] Scott, *Rumors of Wisdom*, 190.

5.3 Proem VII (PL 7.1–39)

discursive exchange; and second, it is characterised in terms of an aestheticised or, in any case, autotelic activity ('and with her didst *play*'), again suggesting some kind of dynamic interaction.[243] To early modern speakers of English, 'conversation,' as Bruce R. Smith points out, meant not just 'what one might say with one's voice,' but rather implied a whole bundle of habits and behavioural norms; anything one might do frequently or with any regularity.[244] Wisdom itself, as Milton makes clear, is 'eternal' (and thus static, unchanging). Only in its regular, cohabiting interaction with the Muse does it 'come into play.' In its first half, Proem VII itself 'plays' with the contrast between eternity and temporal sequence (including questions of precedence among pagan and Christian sources of inspiration), between a spatial 'surmounting' of Pegasus and the 'Muses nine,' on the one hand, and, on the other, the sphere of a God who is, in one of Milton's earlier authorial comments, 'high throned above all height,' looking down (*PL* 3.58).

Urania's activity in inspiring the speaker implies the transfer (i.e., the 'discursification') of divine knowledge already countoured in the ambiguous image of her 'play[ing]' with 'eternal Wisdom.' In contrast to the static totality of the divine mind 'knowing knowledge' perfectly, the inspiration of the speaker, by occuring *at a point in time* or *over the length of their shared song*, either inaugurates or marks the process through which divine wisdom is not only made into discourse, but is made into 'celestial song,' the kind of sensory discourse that pleases even the ear of God. This may also be conceptualised in terms of a paradigmatic/syntagmatic relationship between the speaker and the Muse. In that it is static, complete, and unchanging, divine wisdom is 'pure paradigm.' The language of the speaker (before inspiration), is mere syntagma. Its overdeterminacy (being 'song') is a function of its being inspired by the Muse, i.e., of its conveying an inkling, at least, of divine wisdom. Milton's conception of inspired 'song' shares this interaction or superimposition of paradigmatic and syntagmatic regards with secular poetry. In less theological and more musical terms, the two dimensions may be said to relate to each other like harmony and melody.

Sight – or rather, the aspiration to a superior, elevated kind of vision – is present in the first half of Proem VII only by implication, and only in terms of its precariousness and danger of being lost. Still, if attained, it is the sense of perfect, simultaneous perception and of God's 'eternal wisdom' in its purest sense, as the passages from Milton's pre-text, the Book of Job, suggest. Hearing, by contrast, appears as a sequential way to wisdom (via knowledge, if the two are indeed distinguished), both in Proem VII and Job; in Job, it also is, at least by tendency, the less trustworthy or comprehensive sense of knowledge, relaying 'rumours of wisdom.' The 'secret [counsel] of God' is something Job has not heard; Milton's Muse, by contrast, has played 'in presence of the Almighty

---

[243] Consider the various relevant senses given by *OED*, 'converse, v.,' some of them obsolete now but in early modern use: (1) 'to move about, have one's being, live, dwell in ... a place, among (with) people, etc.;' (2) 'to associate familiarly, consort, keep company; to hold intercourse, be familiar with' (citing *PL* 2.184); (4) 'to communicate or interchange ideas (with any one) by speech or writing or otherwise; to hold inward communion, commune with;' (5) '"to convey the thoughts reciprocally in talk" (Johnson); to engage in conversation, to talk with (a person) ... the ordinary current use;' (6) 'to keep company with ...'
[244] See Smith, *Acoustic World of Early Modern England*, 252–53.

Father' and has 'converse[d]' with (his) 'eternal Wisdom.' She is in a position, then, to pass at least a rumour of that wisdom on to the speaker.

When Milton pays tribute to the *temporal* precedence of his Muse by associating her with a time 'before the hills appeared and fountain flowed,' moreover, this also relates back to the imagery of inspiration deployed in the two earlier proems, and specifically to the main sites of inspiration, mountain/hills and fountains/brooks. It also suggests that the speaker's address to Urania in Proem VII, by virtue of her close association with 'eternal Wisdom,' ultimately surpasses the two earlier invocations in terms of incisiveness or pertinence. In Proem I, the speaker had associated his 'heavenly Muse' with 'the secret top/Of Oreb, or of Sinai,' and with 'Sion hill;' now we learn that her authority actually reaches much further back in time. A similar connection can be established to the address to 'holy light' in Proem III:

> Or hearst thou rather pure ethereal stream
> Whose fountain who shall tell? Before the sun,
> Before the heavens thou wert, and at the voice
> Of God, as with a mantle didst invest
> The rising world of waters dark and deep
> Won from the void and formless infinite.
>
> (*PL* 3.7–12)

Whereas light existed 'before the sun' and 'before the heavens,' its metaphorical 'fountain' came into being through God's command, motivated by his 'eternal Wisdom.' In that she was present 'before ... fountain flowed,' and able to 'converse' with that wisdom directly, Urania is closer to the source still. Every aspect of divine knowledge that is discursified and presented to the audience's senses by the speaker must, ultimately, derive from her mediation.

The Speaker's 'Mortal Voice, Unchanged'

The first half of Proem VII ends with the speaker's reflections on the fate of Bellerophon and the precariousness of his own position as a frail (and possibly presumptuous) human in need of divine assistance. As the second half opens, the speaker's plea for safe conduct down from the height of visionary inspiration appears to have been answered: the speaker is now 'standing on earth, not rapt above the pole.' At the same time, both the visual and auditory discourses of lines 1–20 are continued, while the repositioning of the speaker 'on earth' amounts to a return to 'the visible diurnal sphere.'[245] As the speaker's later remarks suggest, this visibility is strictly a feature of the cosmos in its objective existence; just as, in Proem III, 'with the year/Seasons return; but not to me ...,' the subjective experience of the speaker does not correspond to the objective facts (as is expressed, perhaps, in the tendentially tactile image of his 'standing on earth'). Generally, the passage brings with it a profusion of astronomical termi-

---

[245] 'The starry heaven, which seems to revolve with a *diurnal* motion. In the first half [of *Paradise Lost*], Milton has sung "things invisible" [*PL* 3.55] ...' (Fowler ad loc.)

nology that appears to belie, on the face of it, the speaker's earlier protestations that *his* Urania is not, in fact, who his classically informed readers might think she is. Apart from Milton's reference to 'the visible diurnal sphere,' this includes the references to 'earth' and 'the pole,' glossed by Fowler as 'the celestial pole; synecdoche for the cosmos,' but certainly also suggestive of the earth's two poles ('*standing on* earth, not *rapt above the pole* ...').[246] Taken together, these terms evoke a context of (practical as well as theoretical) astronomy which the speaker's actual sense experience cannot substantiate, as becomes clear in the further course of the proem.

Turning from the 'visible diurnal' to the auditory and audible sphere, the quality of the speaker's song as embodied sensory discourse is highlighted through his declaration, 'More safe I sing with mortal voice, unchanged/To hoarse or mute ...' Milton's notion of 'epic song' in *Paradise Lost* is not abstract; it includes reflections on the actual bodily, 'mortal voice' of his speaker – in fact, it might be more appropriate to call him a 'singer.' This conception of the epic poem as, fundamentally, audible connects to Milton's insistence on the primacy of 'true musical delight,' voiced in his note on 'The Verse.' It also echoes numerous earlier instances in which Milton had commented on the power of the (beautiful) human voice to 'charm,' in the ambivalent sense of an enchanting song.[247]

The speaker's voice, if 'mortal' (i.e., not duetting with the Muse as in Proem I or the opening lines of Proem VII) is 'unchanged/To hoarse or mute': capable but chastened. This fundamental change in tone announced at the beginning of the proem's second half relates both to the *apprehension* of a possible catastrophe (rehearsing the fate of Bellerophon just recounted) but also, as the speaker now explains, to an *actual* downfall that he has already suffered. He may not have fallen off Pegasus and been blinded for his presumption, like Bellerophon, but he is '*fallen* on evil days,/On evil days ... *fallen*, and evil tongues [i.e., exposed to other, malicious voices];/*In darkness*, and with dangers *compassed round,*/And *solitude* ...' If not for the same justifying reasons,[248] the speaker *has*, in a sense, suffered the fate of Bellerophon: he has fallen (emphasised through Milton's chiastic repetition); he is alone (in 'solitude'); he is surrounded ('compassed round') by darkness. As in the speaker's earlier reference to 'the visible diurnal sphere' (invisible to him, it is now revealed), the circle or sphere (in the present case, of 'darkness') constitutes the most fundamental structural feature of the sensescape, and of the *threatening* sensescape in particular. Milton had employed similar imagery in those passages of his prolusions in which the lone orator is facing a hostile crowd; however,

---

[246] Fowler ad loc. For parallel appearances of both terms in clearly astronomical or cosmological contexts, see, for instance, *PL* 2.924–27 (earth); 4.721–22 (Adam and Eve 'beh[olding] ... the starry pole;' and 10.668–71 ('the poles of earth').

[247] See, for instance, Milton's three poems dedicated to the Italian singer and theorbo-player, Leonora Baroni, whom he had heard performing at Rome ('Ad Leonoram Romae canentem,' nos 55–57 in *SP*, 257–60). For historical context, see Susan McClary, *Desire and Pleasure in Seventeenth-Century Music* (Berkeley, Calif.: University of California Press, 2012), 79–103, on professional female singers in early modern Italy. See also Larson, *The Matter of Song in Early Modern England*, esp. 64–65, 89–94 for a discussion of Milton's 'Leonora' sonnets in the context of contemporary theories of acoustics and the human voice.

[248] This point, ultimately, is left open: has he 'presumed' (*PL* 7.13) too far?

the most recent parallel to the present image of darkness encroaching on the epic speaker is his lament, in Proem III, that 'ever-during *dark/Surrounds me.*' The speaker of Proem VII, Milton's imagery reiterates, shares the defining quality of the speaker in Proem III – and both may be more like Bellerophon than they would hope: not just blind but (justly?) punished, isolated, and maligned.

This portrayal of the speaker as beset with doubts and anxieties in the face of precariousness and (quote possibly mortal) danger can certainly be linked to Milton's own experience in the Restoration era.[249] In the context of the overarching sensory discourse of the proems, however, it is more important to acknowledge, again, the constant oscillation between positive and negative valuations in the sensory discourse of the proems that has set in with the speaker's uneasy deliberation of the dialectic between insight and blindness in Proem III. (The much shorter Proem I had been focused entirely on the two entities addressed, the Muse and the Spirit, and had disregarded the exact circumstances of the speaker's predicament.) The same precariousness is present, however, in both halves of Proem VII, and it spans both the visual and auditory strands of Milton's sensory discourse. In the first half, vocal expression and the sense of hearing (represented by Urania's 'voice divine' and 'celestial song') had been reassuring, whereas vision (more precisely, the hope for inspired insight, represented by what could be termed the speaker's 'Bellerophon complex') was a source of anxiety; this latter aspect is restated and connected more explicitly to the speaker's blindness in the first lines of the proem's second half.

His voice, by contrast, is 'unchanged,' even if his qualification, 'mortal,' as well as the mere introduction of the notions of 'hoarse' and 'mute,' argue a certain degree of precariousness even here. Corresponding to this (relative) self-assurance of his vocal abilities on the part of the speaker, his 'solitude,' surrounded by darkness and dangers, is mitigated through the reassuring presence of Urania, whose re-appearance helps to connect both halves of the proem – the 'celestial' and the 'terrestrial' – into a conceptual whole. Through her agency, the speaker is 'not alone,' and her company is described in terms rather similar to those used in Proem III to describe the complicated relationship between the blind speaker, Mount Sion, and 'holy light.' Specifically, Urania *visits* the speaker's 'slumbers nightly, or when morn/Purples the east.'[250] The first alternative echoes the speaker's nocturnal/benighted excursions in search of inspiration ('Thee Sion ... /Nightly I visit ...').[251] The second alternative, through the association of daybreak with vision, underlines the speaker's visual – albeit, with Urania's help, not visionary – deprivation (in any case, he is still 'slumber[ing]'). In both senses, Milton's use of 'visit,' again, carries a distinctly visual connotation. In his image of Urania visiting the speaker's 'slumbers,' moreover, Milton draws on the traditional topos of (pre-

---

[249] See Gabel, *Paradise Reframed*, 125–27, 148–50 on the interplay of metaphorical and actual imprisonment (through the imagery of blindness, affliction, persecution) in the imagery of blindness that informs the proems of *Paradise Lost* as well as *Samson Agonistes*.
[250] At *PL* 4.596, 'purple' is the colour of the sun*set*.
[251] Fowler (ad loc.) also points to Ps. 17:3: 'Thou hast proved mine heart; thou hast visited me in the night.'

5.3 Proem VII (PL 7.1–39)

monitory or inspirational) dream visions, very much alive in early modern culture.[252] In a biographical reading of the similar situation described in Proem IX, Milton's early biographer Richardson appears to argue against inspired dreaming, reporting that 'he frequently Compos'd lying in Bed in a Morning ... I have been Well inform'd, that when he could not Sleep, but lay Awake whole Nights, he Try'd; not One Verse could he make; at Other times flow'd *Easy his Unpremeditated Verse* [*PL* 9.24], with a certain *Impetus* and *Æstro*, as Himself seem'd to Believe.'[253] Milton's final address to Urania in the last line of Proem VII, 'For thou [sc. Urania] art heavenly, she [Calliope] an empty dream,' leaves the question unresolved, as the speaker does not quite say whether or not Urania herself is (or appears to him in) a dream that is not 'empty.' Still, and whether or not we are to conceive of the poet-speaker as dreaming or waking during his inspired '*Impetus*,' the contrast between the physical blindness of Milton's speaker – certainly the most strongly autobiographical element of *Paradise Lost* – and the 'visit' of the Muse, presented in visual terms, is clear.

In the 'terrestrial' second half of Proem VII, then, Milton conceives of the speaker's inspiration in mostly visual terms. This is in clear contrast to the 'celestial' first half of the proem, in which the speaker had been 'following' Urania's 'voice divine.' Now, it is the speaker himself who is 'sing[ing],' and singing 'with mortal voice.' The speaker's precarious singing needs the Muse's support in order to be kept up, and it requires a sympathetic audience in order to be successful. It is in this sense that the speaker addresses his Muse with the double request, 'Still govern thou my song,/Urania, and fit audience find, though few.' Following on the speaker's reference to his 'mortal voice,' i.e., a weak or fallible voice, the literal meaning of 'audience' as 'those who hear' comes to the fore. The two notions establish the producing and the receiving end, respectively, of the speaker's song as *embodied* sensory discourse.

In his prolusions, Milton had repeatedly highlighted the physical character of the auditory connection between a speaker and his audience that is implicit in the oratorical situation. This often coincided with a distinct sense of danger, of being at the mercy of the audience. In the following lines, Milton's characterisation of the audience he does *not* want, and his extended reference to the myth of Orpheus, take this notion to its extreme: not only is Orpheus' singing countered, at the acoustic level, by a 'barbarous dissonance' and 'savage clamor' that ultimately 'drowned/Both harp and voice,' but his

---

[252] See Rivière, *Dreams in Early Modern England*; Clark, *Vanities of the Eye*, 300–328; Thomas, *Religion and the Decline of Magic*, 151–53. Milton's 'slumbers' (in the plural) may indicate a particularly close association with dreaming, as may his specification, 'or when morn purples the east' (most dreaming occurs during the latter parts of a night's sleep). According to the *OLD*, the plural of *somnus* is 'not usually distinguishable from [the singular],' but the phrase *in somnis* ('in one's sleep') occurs '[usually] in references to dreams.' In any case, there is a close lexical and conceptual association between *somnus* and the more readily countable, more specifically oneiric *somnium* ('a dream, a vision;' see *OLD* s. vv.). The *OED*, 'slumber, n.,' does not comment on the plural specifically, but all the relevant instances cited are post-1660 (first attested in Dryden's 'To His Sacred Majesty, A Panegyric on His Coronation'). Milton's plural in particular, whether or not referring to dreams, appears to be a Latinism, inspired by Latin usages such as the one in his own early 'Elegiac Verses': 'Surge, age, surge ... excute *somnos*' ('shake off these ... *slumbers*').
[253] *Early Lives*, ed. Darbishire, 291.

body – the instrument of the speaker or singer according to Milton's own reference to the Orpheus myth in Prolusion VI – is torn to pieces, and the physiological basis of vocal sensory discourse thus destroyed.[254] Apart from his blindness and the precariousness of his spiritual/inspired vision, this is the second great sense-related anxiety troubling Milton's epic speaker. In the form of the Orpheus myth, it dominates the second half of Proem VII, as the fate of Bellerophon had dominated the first half of the proem. In the speaker's concluding plea for Urania's support, Milton again takes up the question of her fundamentally doubtful identity. Orpheus' mother Calliope, the Muse of epic poetry, had not been able to 'defend/Her son.' Since Milton's Muse Urania is 'heavenly' – in the sense of 'the meaning, not the name' –, she will be able and, hopefully, willing both to support the speaker and to protect him against his detractors. As at the end of Proem III, the speaker's various anxieties and insecurities – related to a loss of his vision as well as to violence directed against his voice – can only be resolved into supplication.

***

More so even than Proem III, Proem VII is a statement of the speaker's insecurity. This cautious-to-anxious tone in Milton's authorial self-presentation stems from a suspicion of having 'presumed' too far above 'the reach/Of human sense' (*PL* 5.571–72), that is, of human perception and understanding. Whereas the sensory point of reference for this insecurity is at first figured in visual terms – as the danger of falling and being blinded, just like Bellerophon – and thus questions the poet's visionary powers, Milton's subsequent reference to Orpheus serves to cast doubt on the permissibility and sufficiency of his vocal song as well. If there is a slight advantage to the poet's song (as opposed to his vision), it lies in its capacity to address the poet's heavenly Muse, which will then continue to 'govern' (i.e., limit and direct) it.

Another aspect of audition in Proem VII (and another slight point in its favour) pertains to its relation to wisdom. In Proem III, Milton had more or less equated access to the 'book of knowledge fair' – a common metaphorical reference to natural knowledge gained through the senses – with access to 'wisdom.' In Proem VII, however, wisdom is 'eternal Wisdom,' and as such it is both an epistemic ideal and an attribute of God. Here Milton appears to follow the traditional distinction between knowledge (only implied here through his references to sense perception) and wisdom, more specifically, as the 'knowledge of divine things.'[255] 'Eternal Wisdom' accompanies Urania's 'celestial song,' and Milton's sensory discourse in this passage arguably transposes a fundamental distinction from the Book of Job into his own epic poem: the acquisition (or rather expression) of wisdom by vision is a prerogative of God; wisdom (like faith) coming by hearing, on the other hand, is an established trope of spiritual teaching (and being

---

[254] On the Orpheus myth and its representations in visual art, see Ausoni, *Music in Art*, 108–15. Orpheus' head and his lyre were thrown into a river and carried out to sea; Milton's phrase, 'till the savage clamor *drowned both harp and voice*,' appears to refer to this aspect of the story.

[255] Rice, *Renaissance Idea of Wisdom*, 59. This distinction, taken up in Renaissance Neoplatonism, corresponds to the prior, Aristotelian distinction between conditional and absolute wisdom (of things which are subject to change and things which are immutable, i.e., 'eternal,' respectively).

taught). Urania may thus discursify 'eternal Wisdom' for the benefit of the speaker – and hence, ultimately, for the benefit of *his* audience.

5.4 Proem IX (*PL* 9.1–47)
'Tempering' Sense Perception and the Passions through Food and Music

> No more of talk where God or angel guest
> With man, as with his friend, familiar used,
> To sit indulgent, and with him partake
> Rural repast, permitting him the while
> Venial discourse unblamed: I now must change 5
> Those notes to tragic; foul distrust, and breach
> Disloyal on the part of man, revolt,
> And disobedience: on the part of heaven
> Now alienated, distance and distaste,
> Anger and just rebuke, and judgment given, 10
> That brought into this world a world of woe,
> Sin and her shadow Death, and Misery
> Death's harbinger: sad task, yet argument
> Not less but more heroic than the wrath
> Of stern Achilles on his foe pursued 15
> Thrice fugitive about Troy wall; or rage
> Of Turnus for Lavinia disespoused;
> Or Neptune's ire, or Juno's, that so long
> Perplexed the Greek, and Cytherea's son:
> If answerable style I can obtain 20
> Of my celestial patroness, who deigns
> Her nightly visitation unimplored,
> And dictates to me slumbering, or inspires
> Easy my unpremeditated verse:
> Since first this subject for heroic song 25
> Pleased me long choosing, and beginning late;
> Not sedulous by nature to indite
> Wars, hitherto the only argument
> Heroic deemed, chief mastery to dissect
> With long and tedious havoc fabled knights 30
> In battles feigned; the better fortitude
> Of patience and heroic martyrdom
> Unsung; or to describe races and games,
> Or tilting furniture, emblazoned shields,
> Impreses quaint, caparisons and steeds, 35
> Bases and tinsel trappings, gorgeous knights
> At joust and tournament; then marshalled feast
> Served up in hall with sewers and seneschals;
> The skill of artifice or office mean,
> Not that which justly gives heroic name 40

>   To person, or to poem. Me of these
>   Nor skilled nor studious, higher argument
>   Remains, sufficient of itself to raise
>   That name, unless an age too late, or cold
>   Climate, or years damp my intended wing   45
>   Depressed, and much they may, if all be mine,
>   Not hers who brings it nightly to my ear.
>   (*PL* 9.1–47)

Unlike proems I and VII, Proem IX does not break down into two halves (one addressed to the Muse, the other, to the Spirit; one concerned with the fate of Bellerophon, the other with that of Orpheus). Unlike Proem III, it cannot easily be divided into a sequence of thematically distinct sections reflecting on the situation of the blind speaker, then leading to a (precarious) synthesis. Rather, Proem IX revolves around a twofold shift in the discursive fabric of the poem: a shift from the pastoral or georgic setting of Paradise (where Adam, Eve, and Raphael had shared their 'rural repast' in books 5 to 8) to the 'tragic' events leading up – or rather, leading down – to the Fall; and a shift in narrative responsibility, as the relation of the main story, Raphael's responsibility since his arrival in book 5, is left wholly to the 'mortal voice' of the epic speaker. This shift, with its two correlated aspects, is addressed from a succession of angles: as a 'discursive fact' at the level of the poem's mediation; as a matter of generic conventions; and finally, by reference to the speaker's situation and background.

In terms of its sensory discourse, Proem IX dismisses the visual or visual-auditory focus of proems I, III, and VII, and instead focuses on the auditory quality of the epic poem as song. This is complemented, however, by a striking series of food- and taste-based imagery. These changes in sensory discourse relate, also, to the major shifts announced in the proem. While the topical focus on food and eating signals the shift by which the narrative will be gathering pace towards the Fall, the discursive focus on audition concerns the relationship between the speaker and his Muse. This relationship is now conceived of more narrowly – 'narrower bound,' as Proem VII had had it – as a physical event in the speaker's life-world; it is no longer related to the ultimately metaphorical sphere of illumination and insight. Crucially, and marking the most notable formal difference between the prior three proems and Proem IX, the latter does not contain *any* invocation to the 'heavenly Muse' (nor to the Spirit or 'holy light'). In the following, I will consider first the sensory discourse of taste in Proem IX, and then that of hearing, before offering some suggestions as to their relevance in the wider context of *Paradise Lost*.

Taste and Talk in Eden and Beyond

In the opening lines of Proem IX (*PL* 9.1–5), Milton looks back on books 5 to 8 of *Paradise Lost*, in which Raphael had related to Adam the events of the war in heaven, and Adam had, in turn, recounted how God had walked with him in the garden prior to the creation of Eve (*PL* 8.311–452). This had been dinner 'talk' – as opposed, perhaps, to its framing through the poet-speaker's 'song' – and 'venial discourse unblamed,' since

5.4 Proem IX (PL 9.1–47)

Adam had been rather inquisitive about cosmology and the origins of Creation – somewhat worryingly but not excessively so.[256] A similarly complex valuation, hovering between the two poles of the culpable and the (only just?) permissible, is implied in the description of the 'rural repast' shared by the angel with Adam and Eve. In fact, the two elements of food and speech (as expressive of thought) are described, in strikingly similar ways, as things to be both relished and restricted. These two aspects of the conceptual metaphor IDEAS ARE FOOD (which connects the two poles of 'rural repast' and 'discourse,' i.e., dinner talk) had been made explicit at different points over the preceding books. In a positive sense, the metaphor is actualised through Adam's confession to Raphael, containing several verbal parallels to Proem IX, that

> while I sit with thee, I seem in heaven,
> And sweeter thy discourse is to my ear
> Than fruits of palm-tree pleasantest to thirst
> And hunger both, from labour, at the hour
> Of sweet repast; they satiate, and soon fill,
> Though pleasant, but thy words with grace divine
> Imbued, bring to their sweetness no satiety.
> (*PL* 8.210–16)[257]

And earlier in the poem, the metaphor had been represented in its negative, problematic aspect in Raphael's stern admonition, already referred to, that

> knowledge is as food, and needs no less
> Her temperance over appetite, to know
> In measure what the mind may well contain,
> Oppresses else with surfeit, and soon turns
> Wisdom to folly, as nourishment to wind.
> (*PL* 7.126–30)[258]

This is the wider context in which the speaker of Proem IX, enjoying the benefits both of hindsight and of prophetic foresight, looks back on the dinner conversation in Eden and looks forward to its inevitable sequel. In Proem IX itself, the problematic dual nature of both food and (inquisitive) discourse – blamelessly pleasing yet forever slipping toward blameful excess – is encapsulated in a few significant phrases. When the speaker notes, for instance, that Raphael had sat with Adam and Eve 'indulgent,' he makes use of an ambiguity: the term relates just as much to their shared sensory enjoyment of food

---

[256] See Fowler ad loc.
[257] Compare the passage *PL* 5.544–48, in which Adam calls Raphael his 'divine instructor,' and his words more delightful than the 'aërial music' of the angels.
[258] 'Knowledge' is figured as feminine ('*her* temperance') on account of Latin *sapientia* – from *sapere*, 'to taste' –, which may be rendered as either 'knowledge' or 'wisdom.' Fowler ad loc. points to a parallel in Davenant's *Gondibert* (1651), equally based on the conceptual metaphor that IDEAS ARE FOOD: 'For though books serve as diet of the mind;/if knowledge, early got, self-value breeds,/By false digestion it is turned to wind;/And what should nourish, on the eater feeds.'

as it does to Raphael's forbearing response to Adam's curiosity.[259] Raphael *indulges in the food* offered to him, as he clearly states in the earlier account of their dinner in book 5: when Adam expresses doubts regarding the appropriateness of their human food for angelic ingestion, he replies that 'God hath here [sc. in Paradise]/Varied his bounty so with new delights,/As may compare with heaven; and to taste/Think not I shall be nice.'[260] However, he also *indulges Adam's questions*, 'permitting him the while/Venial discourse unblamed.' In both instances, judgment and moderation are key. And in both the bodily/sensory sphere (represented by the taste of food) and the abstract/intellectual sphere (of 'discourse'), restraint and gusto must also enter into a synthesis. Both are connected by the twin promises of acquisition or ingestion (of nourishment, of knowledge) and of enjoyment (the physical satisfaction of taste or the intellectual satisfaction of understanding) but also by the threat of a dangerous *over*indulgence. All these aspects combine in the underlying conceptual metaphor that IDEAS ARE FOOD. In the relevant passages of book 5, and now in Proem IX, that metaphor finds expression in Milton's sensory discourse.

In Proem IX, the meal shared by Adam, Eve, and their 'angel guest' is described as 'rural,' which indicates a degree of simplicity easily judged as a lack of refinement.[261] In his depiction of the event in book 5, however, Milton is careful to point out that, in prelapsarian Paradise, simplicity and refinement do not contradict each other. Witness the consonance, rather than the contrast, between the 'frugal[ity]' of a 'small store' and 'choice' (i.e., qualitative excellence) or 'bounties' (quantitative excellence) in Eve's account of her plans for dinner:

> small store will serve, where store,
> All seasons, ripe for use hangs on the stalk;
> Save what by frugal storing firmness gains
> To nourish, and superfluous moist consumes:
> But I will haste and from each bough and brake,
> Each plant and juiciest gourd will pluck such choice
> To entertain our angel guest, as he
> Beholding shall confess that here on Earth
> God hath dispensed his bounties as in Heaven.
> (*PL* 5.322–30)

When Eve puts these plans into action, Milton expands on the two notions of exquisiteness and abundance:

> … on hospitable thoughts intent
> What choice to choose for delicacy best,

---

[259] See *OED*, 'indulgent, adj.': (1a) 'that indulges or tends to indulge; disposed to *gratify by compliance with desire* or humour, or to *overlook faults or failings* …' (emphases added). See also the relevant senses of *OED*, 'indulge, v.': (7) 'to indulge in: … to gratify one's desire or appetite for …;' (8) 'to gratify a desire, appetite, etc.'
[260] See the whole passage, *PL* 5.388–443.
[261] See the relevant senses in *OED*, 'rural, adj.'

> What order, so contrived as not to mix
> Tastes, not well joined, inelegant, but bring
> Taste after taste upheld with kindliest change,
> Bestirs her then, and from each tender stalk
> Whatever earth all-bearing mother yields
> In India east or west, or middle shore
> In Pontus or the Punic coast, or where
> Alcinous reigned, fruit of all kinds, in coat,
> Rough, or smooth rined, or bearded husk, or shell
> She gathers, tribute large, and on the board
> Heaps with unsparing hand; for drink the grape
> She crushes, inoffensive must, and meaths
> From many a berry, and from sweet kernels pressed
> She tempers dulcet creams; nor these to hold
> Wants her fit vessels pure; then strews the ground
> With rose and odours from the shrub unfumed.
>
> (*PL* 5.332–49)

Eve's preparations are generous – a 'tribute large,' which she 'heaps with unsparing hand' – but they also are well thought out: 'so contrived as not to mix/Tastes, not well joined, inelegant, but bring/Taste after taste upheld with kindliest change.' This is the principle of a pleasing 'variousness' of sensations, introduced above by reference to sound in particular, now applied to the sense of *taste*. In basically singing the praises of this rather suspicious and, given the context, ominous sense, Milton emphasises the prelapsarian harmlessness of the scene: the drink is not wine but 'inoffensive must;' the odorous decorations are taken 'from the shrub unfumed' (i.e., are not burned; as yet, there is no fire, neither for cooking, heating, nor for other purposes). In the reference to 'earth all-bearing mother,' which is related to Eve's earlier observation that 'store,/All seasons, ripe for use hangs on the stalk,' Milton's imagery resembles that of Elegy V, in which Tellus (the Earth) 'voluptuously bares her breasts [*omniferos ... sinus*], mother of all things.' In Paradise, however, even such tempting abundance is, for now, harmless.

This is the general sensory context in which Raphael could 'sit indulgent,' both savouring the delicious food of Paradise and tolerating Adam's curious questions. Elsewhere in Milton, the combination of food, drink, and discourse is also presented as typical of the humble yet pleasing pastoral meal. Thus, in a relevant passage of *L'Allegro* (1631), a pair of stock pastoral characters, Corydon and Thyrsis, 'are at their savoury dinner set/Of herbs, and other country messes,' followed by a serving of 'spicy nut-brown ale/With stories told of many a feat …' (84–85, 100–101).[262] And in Sonnet 17 (Winter 1655?), addressed by Milton to his young friend Henry Lawrence, the speaker asks, after evoking a dreary winter scene,

---

[262] 'Messes' here has the general sense of *OED*, 'mess, n.,' I: 'a portion of food, and related senses.' It is not related, etymologically, to the Latin *messes* ('harvests'), which occurs several times in Milton's earlier Latin poetry. In the present context, however, an interlingual pun might be intended.

> Where shall we sometimes meet, and by the fire
> Help waste a sullen day ...
> ...
> What neat repast shall feast us, light and choice,
> Of Attic taste, with wine, whence we may rise
> To hear the lute well touched, or artful voice
> Warble immortal notes and Tuscan air?
> He who of those delights can judge, and spare
> To interpose them oft, is not unwise.
>
> (3–4, 9–14)

Although the setting of the sonnet is different both from that of *L'Allegro* and that of the dinner scene in *Paradise Lost*, a coincidence of several elements suggests that all three relate to an underlying ideal. The imagined 'meet[ing]' between the speaker and his addressee 'by the fire' implies 'talk' in the form of the proverbial fireside chat. And when the sonnet's 'neat repast,' at the same time, serves to 'feast' its partakers (note the sumptuous word-music in Milton's use of assonance and consonance), this also conforms quite closely to the 'rural repast' of *Paradise Lost*, which nevertheless is compared to the manna of heaven.[263] Similarly, the reference to an 'Attic taste' – according to the *OED*, a taste 'marked by simple and refined elegance' – that is 'light and choice' resonates with Eve's description of her own 'frugal store.'[264] In fact, the presence of wine, rather than 'inoffensive must,' marks the single biggest difference between the culinary ideal of the sonnet and that of the epic. Even the multi-sensory addition of music resonates with the sensescape of Milton's Paradise.

However, the sonnet is written from a postlapsarian point of view. Not only are the ideal scenes of culinary and musical delights merely imagined; they are placed at a further remove – in some remote winter's utopia – by the speaker's interrogative phrasing: 'Where shall we ... meet ...? ... What neat repast shall feast us ...?' Even so, it is not entirely clear that such a thing as a truly 'neat' (i.e., simple) meal could ever qualify as a 'feast' in the postlapsarian world *in the same way* the food of Adam and Eve had. As soon as 'wine' comes into play, in fact, the suspicion of fallen overindulgence is hard to ward off. How is one to assess, therefore, the relative permissibility of a given instance of sensuous pleasure without falling into complete sensual indulgence?

The sonnet states this problem in its highly ambiguous conclusion without resolving it. Milton's ideally judicious partaker – 'he who of those delights can judge' – is also the ideal aficionado: he has tried 'those delights' and is experienced in them; he is acquainted with pleasure. At the same time, 'spare' could mean either, 'refrain from' or 'spare time to,' and 'interpose' could mean either 'indulge in' or 'abstain from.'[265] When confronted with the lure of pleasure, Milton appears to be saying with a wink, one can either take it or leave it. In the immediate context of the sonnet, with its dreary

---

[263] See *OED*, 'feast, v.': (1) 'to make or partake of a feast, fare sumptuously, regale oneself.'
[264] *OED*, 'Attic, adj. and n.^{1}.'
[265] See *OED*, 'spare, v.' and 'interpose, v.,' as well as Carey ad loc. Carey concludes, rightly I think, that 'the idea that the sonnet would be improved if the ambiguity were resolved seems questionable.'

winter imagery, the first option is clearly put forward as the more desirable one. On the more general level of how the senses *should* be 'governed,' however, Milton appears to be rather more cautious, suggesting that the necessary balance between indulgence and restraint can only be achieved through a judgment of particular cases, and that doing so falls within the responsibility of the individual – both points clearly resonating with the role played by judgment and taste in *Paradise Lost*. Whoever has grasped as much is perhaps not much wiser than before, but at least he is 'not unwise' – Milton's litotic conclusion, too, indicates the precarious quality of the point under discussion.

In Paradise, before the Fall, the questions raised in the first twelve lines of Milton's Sonnet 17 were meaningless; but the problem contained in its couplet-like conclusion[266] – the question of when to say yes and when to say no to sensuous pleasure, traditionally exemplified by an indulgence in the sense of taste (and allied, via IDEAS ARE FOOD to the problem of curiosity and forbidden knowledge) – is precisely the question at the centre of *Paradise Lost*, and of book 9, in particular. The presence of taste-based sensory discourse in Proem IX suggests as much right at the outset of the book. After the speaker's reminiscence on the 'rural repast' in Paradise, the next significant reference belonging to this theme is to the 'distance and *distaste*' of heaven, meaning God's reaction to Adam and Eve's transgression. Christopher Ricks has commented on how the phrase, 'distance and distaste,' really forms the culmination to Milton's prior crescendo of 'discourse ... distrust ... disloyal ... disobedience,' leading from words exchanged over a meal (Adam's questions to Raphael and Raphael's admonition to Adam) to the fatal 'taste' of the Fall:

> There does not at first seem to be much in the immediate context which will invigorate the metaphor in "distaste." But the pressure is not exerted only locally. It is exerted also by the countless times that the Fall is described as the *tasting* of the apple.[267] The real structure of the phrase is of a brilliantly unspoken pun. On the part of man, *taste*; on the part of Heaven, *distaste*.[268]

Through the early reference to '(dis)taste', then, Proem IX is connected to the wider sensory discourse of book 9. At the same time, the conjunction of '(dis)taste' and 'disobedience' in the passage – soon complemented by the phrase, 'that brought into this world a world of woe,/Sin and her shadow Death ...' – hearkens back to the opening of Proem I: 'Of man's first *disobedience*, and the fruit/Of that forbidden tree, whose mortal *taste*/*Brought death into the world*, and all our *woe* ...' Simultaneously, the notion of God's 'distaste' in Proem IX connects to the further development of Milton's plot after the Fall, including the operation of divine grace in the 'hearts contrite' of repentant Adam and Eve (*PL* 10.1072). When the Son – in his role of intercessor –

---

[266] Sonnet 17 combines a 'Petrarchan'-style rhyme scheme (abba abba cdc eed) with a roughly 'Shakespearean' (i.e., 4+4+4+2) structure.

[267] While most of the references throughout the poem are just to a 'fruit,' Satan refers to the fruit of the forbidden tree as 'those fair apples' at *PL* 9.585 (in tempting Eve) and 'an apple' at *PL* 10.487 (reporting his 'success' in hell).

[268] Ricks, *Milton's Grand Style*, 70–71. Ricks then goes on to cite several instances of 'taste' from book 9 in context, arguing that 'the whole story of the Fall is told in them.'

draws the Father's attention to the human couple's 'sorrow unfeigned, and humiliation meek' (*PL* 10.1073, 1085) early in book 11, he does so in imagery that not only *reverses* the taste-based stigma of the Fall but, through its incorporation of olfactory discourse, aligns it with conventional images of sacrifices pleasing to God:

> See Father, what first fruits on earth are sprung
> From thy implanted grace in man, these sighs
> And prayers, which in this golden censer, mixed
> With incense, I thy priest before thee bring;
> Fruits of more pleasing savor from thy seed
> Sown with contrition in his heart, than those
> Which his own hand manuring all the trees
> Of Paradise could have produced, ere fallen
> From innocence. Now therefore, bend thine ear
> To supplication, hear his sighs, though mute;
> Unskillful with what words to pray, let me
> Interpret for him, me his advocate
> And propitiation, all his works on me,
> Good or not good engraft, my merit those
> Shall pèrfect, and for these my death shall pay.
> Accept me, and in me from these receive
> The smell of peace toward mankind ...
>
> (*PL* 11.22–38)

While the close connection between taste and smell is evident across cultures, that between smell and God's wrath in sacrifice, which aims to convey to heaven 'the smell of peace,' becomes clearer if we consider the importance of Milton's biblical frame of reference for the sensory discourse in the passage – a frame of reference in which Hebrew *aph* means both 'nose, nostrils' and 'anger, wrath,' and is used accordingly in passages combining references to both, God's anger and his sense of smell.[269]

For now, however, book 9 will be concerned with God's 'distaste' and, accordingly, not 'the smell of peace toward mankind' but rather God's wrath and judgment ('anger and just rebuke, and judgment given'). This theme of *God's wrath*, the speaker points out, is an integral part of the 'great argument' already announced in Proem I; it is 'not less but more heroic than the wrath/Of stern Achilles' (in the *Iliad*) or 'Neptune's ire [in the *Odyssey*], or Juno's' (in the *Aeneid*). Being an expression of '[distaste] on the part of heaven,' it bears a mediate relation to Milton's imagery of taste in Proem IX.

After a first reference to his Muse (to which I will return presently), the speaker continues his reflection on the proper 'subject of heroic song' in the passage beginning in line 25. War, he notes, had 'hitherto [been] the only argument/Heroic deemed.' The ways in which Milton characterises these earlier treatments of war in epic ('heroic') poetry are, again, significant with respect to the *sensory* side of Milton's own epic dis-

---

[269] Compare the account of Abel's sacrifice in *PL* 11.436–42; it is Cain, on the other hand, who sacrifices 'first fruits' (*PL* 11.435). See also Avrahami, *Senses of Scripture*, 19, 124–25 on smell in Biblical sacrifice and God's nose as an organ of wrath or affection.

course (I comment on the lines 29b–37a below). The passage beginning in line 37b, however, returns to the general theme of food and feasting, now understood not, as in Sonnet 17, as the enjoyment of a 'neat repast ... light and choice' but, in its more common sense, as a lavish and perhaps even overindulgent kind of meal, substituting gustatory excess for the balance of relish, nutritional value, and the 'Attic' sense of proportion Milton had advocated in his sonnet.

After their accounts of 'fabled knights/In battles feigned' – knights both legendary and fictitious in battles both fictional and pretended, as the following reference to 'joust and tournament' suggests –, previous epics had depicted, according to Milton, 'marshalled feast/Served up in hall with sewers and seneschals;/The skill of ... office mean,/Not that which justly gives heroic name/To person, or to poem.' Such 'marshalled feast[s],' apart from evoking the kind of gourmandising excess just outlined, abandon the ideal of an unconstrained conviviality, irrespective of rank, as it is advocated both earlier in Proem IX ('where God or angel guest/With man, as with his friend, familiar used ...') and in Sonnet 17 (Henry Lawrence was Milton's junior by some twenty-five years).[270] In *Paradise Lost*, the hope that metaphorical as well as physical nourishment is to be gained by the 'discourse' of such occasions is made explicit when Raphael leaves at the end of book 6, admonishing Adam one last time to 'let it profit thee to have heard,/By terrible example [i.e., Raphael's account of Satan's rebellion], the reward/Of disobedience ...' (*PL* 6.909–912). And as if in contrast to the now famous conclusion of Milton's Sonnet 16 ('they also serve who only stand and wait'), Milton's disparaging reference to 'sewers and seneschals' makes clear that not all who serve are serving a worthy cause.[271] Taken together, both the outer extravagance of and the inherent misplacement of focus implied by the conventional notion of a 'feast' contradict Milton's ideal of what communal eating – and tasting, and gustatory enjoyment – should be.

Coming in the wake of an attack on ekphrasis, moreover, the lines not only present feasting as an undue indulgence in the sense of taste but, what may be worse, as merely ornamental, offering appropriate nourishment neither to its fictitious partakers nor, since IDEAS ARE FOOD, to readers: Milton's concern that 'nourishment' be not 'turn[ed] to wind' applies here as well. In fact, for Milton, both aspects – the 'governing' of taste and a regard for nutritional value (whether literal or metaphorical) – are closely connected, as the dietary advice given to Adam by Michael in book 11 suggests:

> There is, said Michael, if thou well observe
> The rule of not too much, by temperance taught
> In what thou eatst and drinkst, seeking from thence

---

[270] When Edward Phillips reports how, in the 1650s, Milton used to be visited, among others, by 'young *Laurence* (the Son of him that was President of Oliver's Council), to whom there is a Sonnet among the rest in his Printed Poems,' (*Early Lives*, ed. Darbishire, 74), his emphasis on this difference in age is clear.

[271] *OED*, 'sewer, n.2': (a) 'an attendant at a meal who superintended the arrangement of the table, the seating of the guests, and the tasting and serving of the dishes.' *OED*, 'seneschal, n.': (1) 'an official in the household of a sovereign or great noble, to whom the ... entire control of domestic arrangements [was] entrusted.'

> Due nourishment, not gluttonous delight,
> Till many years over thy head return:
> So mayst thou live, till like ripe fruit thou drop
> Into thy mother's lap, or be with ease
> Gathered, not harshly plucked, for death mature,
> This is old age ...   (*PL* 11.530–38)

The first part of the admonition is conventional enough, citing the classical maxim of *mêden agan*, 'nothing too much' or 'all in moderation.' What appears characteristic of Milton's approach to the theme, however, is Michael's precise wording, 'by temperance taught,' which echoes several earlier instances of structurally and functionally similar phrases in the poem. Thus, the steadfast angel Abdiel reproaches Satan in book 5 by pointing out that '*by experience taught*, we know how good,/And of our good and of our dignity/How provident [God] is' (*PL* 5.826–28, emphasis added). More pertinently still, Adam warns Eve in book 8 that

> apt the mind or fancy is to rove
> Unchecked, and of her roving is no end;[272]
> Till warned, or *by experience taught*, she learn,
> That not to know at large of things remote
> From use, obscure and subtle, but to know
> That which before us lies in daily life,
> Is the prime wisdom, what is more, is fume,
> Or emptiness, or fond impertinence ...
>   (*PL* 8.188–95, emphasis added)[273]

There are strong similarities, both in wording and in thought, between the last passage on 'fancy' and that other one, from book 7, in which 'folly' figures as 'wind' (i.e., flatulence) when compared to the 'nourishment' of wisdom. There, too, 'temperance' had been the crucial, mediating factor ('But knowledge is as food, and needs no less/Her *temperance* over appetite,' *PL* 7.126–27). What emerges even more strikingly from the structural and conceptual parallel between these statements on experience, however, is the *mechanics*, as it were, of temperance. Temperance is not something one *has* but something one *does*; it is not an inbred virtue but 'the action or fact of tempering; mingling or combining in due proportion, adjusting, moderating, modification, toning down, bringing into a temperate or moderate state.'[274] Temperance, then, is structurally equivalent to (sense) experience, in that it can only be acquired (or aspired to) through the

---

[272] Compare the endless discursive 'roving' of the fallen angels in the passage discussed in Chapter 2 ('... in wandering mazes lost,' *PL* 2.561) as well as the epigraph from Wordsworth taken up in the Epilogue below.

[273] Compare also the ironic authorial comment, at *PL* 2.9, that Satan is 'by success *un*taught' (emphasis added).

[274] *OED*, 'temperance, n.,' 3a, marked as 'obsolete' and last attested in 1596. I would argue that Milton's usage at *PL* 11.531 carries this (manifestly humoralistic) definition as its primary meaning.

experience of things which are best enjoyed in moderation. The crucial skill is discernment – 'if thou well observe ...,' Michael says – and appropriate judgment, based in reason.[275] In this sense, Michael's advice to Adam is a restatement of the ambiguous concluding lines of Sonnet 17: 'He who of those delights can judge, and spare/To interpose them oft, is not unwise.'

It might seem ironic that Adam is given precisely this kind of advice at precisely this point in the poem: after the Fall. In fact, the imagery of the second half of Michael's instruction from book 11 evokes the forbidden tree of knowledge, Eve's plucking of the Fruit, and 'mother' Earth's reaction in book 9 ('So saying, her rash hand in evil hour/Forth reaching to the fruit, she plucked, she ate:/Earth felt the wound ...,' *PL* 9.780–82). The similarity is treacherous, though, as the prohibition of the tree of knowledge had been a test of obedience (i.e., hearing plus reason), not of taste or even temperance, which becomes necessary only after the Fall. The contrast between the original transgression – 'foul distrust, and breach/Disloyal' leading to 'revolt,/And disobedience,' and only finally to taste and 'distaste' – and Michael's admonition to temperance-as-practice only serves to underline that, for Milton, sense perception is not, per se, evil – not even taste, and not even the enjoyment of taste. If coupled with reason and *the proper kind* of discernment and restraint – 'if thou *well* observe (the rule of not to much)' – taste, even postlapsarian taste, can lead to valuable experiential knowledge, namely, to the practical knowledge of how to live the best possible postlapsarian life ('So mayst thou live ...').[276] Temperance, as a *modus operandi*, not a fixed mindset, is the central concept of Milton's – by all means sense-based – eudaimonism. Taste, paradoxically, being the sense that had been so intimately connected to the Fall, will play a key role in that process in times to come.

In fact, the problematic and challenging nature of taste after the Fall, when the relation between sensory enjoyment and the attainment or even the retention of knowledge is no longer self-evident, rests on – or results in? –[277] a confusion involving those con-

---

[275] Milton at this point plays on the unstable meaning of 'observe' as 'look' – Michael is actually presenting a series of visions to Adam – and 'consider' or 'discern,' as well as 'follow, practise, or keep to,' its primary meaning (see *OED*, 'observe, v.'), revealed to be the fundamental meaning of the present passage by the line break ('if thou well observe/The rule of not too much'). Ultimately, temperance can only arise from the experiential dialectic of observation and observance. On CONSIDERING IS LOOKING and THINKING IS LOOKING, see Kövecses, *Metaphor*, 271. This is the visual equivalent of the gustatory/dietary CONSIDERING IS CHEWING (as opposed to the gobbling of 'gluttonous delight'); see Kövecses, *Metaphor*, 84.

[276] Contrast Raphael's earlier admonition to Adam regarding the prelapsarian connection between (sensory) enjoyment and the proper conduct of life: '... *joy thou/In what [God] gives to thee*, this Paradise/And thy fair Eve; heaven is for thee too high/To know what passes there; be lowly wise:/*Think only what concerns thee and thy being*' (*PL* 8.170–74).

[277] The equivocation is by no means trivial: Adam's earliest use of language in *PL* 8.250–82, quoted above, is informed by innate knowledge: 'My tongue obeyed and readily could name/Whate'er I saw.' Things are *named* by Adam (he calls them by their name, because he knows what they are), but they are also named *by him* (given their specific name, because his is the first use of it); compare the respective senses in *OED*, 'name, v.' The case of 'taste,' I argue, is roughly comparable in that whatever Adam and Eve *refer to as* 'taste' after the Fall has a

cepts. After he, too, has tasted the forbidden fruit, Adam indulges in the illusion of judgment and 'sapience' (i.e., wisdom) attained through the act of tasting for pleasure alone:

> Eve, now I see thou art exact of taste,
> And elegant, of sapience no small part,
> Since to each meaning savour we apply,
> And palate call judicious; I the praise
> yield thee, so well this day thou hast purveyed.
> Much pleasure we have lost, while we abstained
> From this delightful fruit, nor known till now
> True relish, tasting; if such pleasure be
> In things to us forbidden, it might be wished,
> For this one tree had been forbidden ten.
> (*PL* 9.1017–26)

As in the case of Satan's 'scoffing in ambiguous words' during the war in heaven, Milton uses wordplay to expose the potential dangers of wordplay.[278] William Empson called this characteristically Miltonic, self-reflexive use of punning 'a bitter and controlled mood of irony ... so much above mere ingenuity that the puns seem almost like a generalisation.'[279] In Adam's case, this is lamentably true: his near-equation of elegance with 'sapience,' understood as wisdom, as well as his misattribution of 'judicious[ness]' to the palate, the conventional (and merely) bodily seat of taste, both express a false conception of taste that, Milton suggests, would become general after the Fall if left unchecked. This is the notion that Raphael's explanation, 'knowledge is as food' – essentially a conceptual metaphor – could be taken literally, like a bad pun taken at face value, or even inverted, meaning that food – that is, taste: that is, sensual indulgence alone – might lead to knowledge. This 'sensual shortcut' to knowledge amounts to an echo of Satan's promise to Eve that 'this fruit divine,/Fair to the eye, inviting to the taste' was 'of virtue to make wise: what hinders then/To reach, *and feed at once both body and mind*?' (*PL* 9.776–79, emphasis added). Michael's call to temperance, by contrast, is intended to correct the confusion and one-sided exaltation of sensuality. In the immediate continuation of the passage, Milton makes clear that the Fall, quite contrary to Adam's claims, has brought both a 'downward spiral' of sensual indulgence – moving from gustatory to sexual licence – and a corresponding lack of discernment, collapsing the various modalities of the sensorium into one overbearing 'sense,' the imperative of indulgence:

> But come, so well refreshed, now let us play,
> As meet is, after such delicious fare;
> For never did thy beauty since the day

---

specific meaning; but this semantic (re)determination rests on a prior lapse of judgment (a misapprehension of what constitutes 'taste' in any particular sense).
[278] See *PL* 6.558–68, and passim.
[279] William Empson, *Seven Types of Ambiguity* (London: Hogarth Press, 1991 [1930]), 103.

> I saw thee first and wedded thee, adorned
> With all perfections, so inflame my sense
> With ardour to enjoy thee, fairer now
> Than ever, bounty of this virtuous tree.
>
> (*PL* 9.1027–33)

These are the culmination and the wider repercussions of the theme of tasting, food, and eating, treated by Milton both in its literal and metaphorical senses (of IDEAS ARE FOOD and related metaphors), connected to his conception of temperance as an ongoing process, and introduced into book 9 – the 'book of taste' in *Paradise Lost*, as book 3 had been 'the book of light and vision' – right from its proem. In the concluding lines of book 9, as Adam and Eve's fit of passion is deteriorating fast into the first marital dispute in history, Milton revives this strand of his sensory discourse for one final, bitter pun: 'Thus they in mutual accusation spent/The *fruitless* hours, but nether self-condemning,/And of their vain contèst appeared no end' (*PL* 9.1187–88, emphasis added).[280] From the 'venial discourse unblamed' referred to in the proem, the discursive reality of Adam and Eve – as that of the fallen angels earlier – has been transformed, over the course of book 9, into a 'vain' maze of never-ending blame.[281]

Milton's Tragic Mode and the Speaker's Epic Voice

It is through a *deliberative* use of sensory discourse that Milton reflects on the ambiguous meanings of food and taste, a theme introduced early in book 9, taken up throughout, and consistently related to the ultimately epistemological metaphor that IDEAS ARE FOOD. As Proem XI unmistakably states in its programmatic opening line, however, there will now be 'no more … talk' of such things; instead of the angel Raphael reporting, the merely human speaker now assumes the key role of narrator. While his references to his 'heavenly Muse,' addressed extensively in the previous Proem VII, do not cease, Proem IX does not include a formal invocation, underlining the speaker's precarious and ultimately fallible status even more strongly than the conflicted sensory discourse of the earlier proems had. This strong emphasis on the speaker's (mere) humanity goes along with connected emphases on the corporeality of his epic 'song' and the autobiographical dimension of the author's self-(re)presentation in the text.[282]

In the speaker's first reference to himself, beginning in line 5b, the vocal quality of his song is highlighted: 'I now must change/*Those notes* to tragic …' As becomes clear in the continuation of the passage, this 'tragic' quality pertains to his epic song as a whole, both its texture or style (its 'notes') and its content or 'argument,' and this helps explain why questions of generic propriety take up such a large portion of Proem IX. Even though the speaker's enterprise, from its beginning, had been presented as something *to be undertaken* ('my *advent'rous* song;' *PL* 1.13), moreover, and had involved much descending and ascending, wandering and soaring in all of the proems, not to

---

[280] Compare the similarly punning use of *fructus* in Prolusion VI, discussed in Chapter 3.3.
[281] Compare the passage *PL* 2.557–65, discussed in Chapter 1.
[282] Apart from the relevant chapter in Fallon, *Milton's Peculiar Grace*, see J. Martin Evans, 'The Birth of the Author: Milton's Poetic Self-Construction,' *MS* 38 (2000), 47–65.

mention the threat of a violent death, it is only now that his song becomes a 'sad task,' as if the quality of the subject matter and the corresponding tone of its mediation through 'tragic [notes]' had carried over to the speaker himself. The phrase 'sad task' resonates with Raphael's cautious response to Adam's initial request for a 'full relation' of events in heaven in book 5:

> High matter thou enjoinst me, O prime of men,
> Sad task and hard, for how shall I relate
> To human sense the invisible exploits
> Of warring spirits; how without remorse
> The ruin of so many glorious once
> And perfect while they stood; how last unfold
> The secrets of another world, perhaps
> Not lawful to reveal? Yet for thy good
> This is dispensed, and what surmounts the reach
> Of human sense, I shall delineate so,
> By likening spiritual to corporal forms,
> As may express them best, though what if earth
> Be but the shadow of heav'n, and things therein
> Each to other like, more than on earth is thought?
>   (*PL* 5.563–76)

Raphael distinguishes three areas of concern: first, it is 'hard' to 'relate/To human sense the ... exploits/Of ... spirits' (the problem of *accommodation*);[283] second, it is 'sad,' even upon reflection, to reconsider what had been the cause for such great 'remorse[,]/The ruin of so many glorious once/And perfect while they stood' (the problem of *compassion*);[284] and, finally, the problem of *epistemic propriety*, i.e., the question of whether what he is about to relate should be made available to a wider audience at all.[285] Spread out across the proems, Milton's speaker, likewise, refers to those same points, thus establishing further parallels between himself and Raphael: while the problem of accommodation is addressed in the speaker's request, 'that I may *see and tell*/Of things invisible to mortal sight' in Proem III, the problem of epistemic propriety is less pressing to him, since, in the upcoming crucial passages of book 9 in particular, he mostly recounts what had already been 'taught [to] the chosen seed' (*PL* 1.8) by his predecessor, Moses, and stays close to his (biblical) sources in other respects as well (what has been revealed in the Law and the Scriptures in general must be 'lawful to reveal').

---

[283] See C. A. Patrides, '*Paradise Lost* and the Theory of Accommodation,' in: W. B. Hunter/C. A. Patrides/J. H. Adamson (eds), *Bright Essence: Studies in Milton's Theology* (Salt Lake City, Utah: University of Utah Press, 1973 [1971]), 159–63.

[284] Even Satan is moved to an inkling of pity (and, significantly, remorse) when he reviews his troops in book 1: '... cruel his eye, but cast/Signs of remorse and passion to behold/The fellows of his crime, the followers rather/(Far other once beheld in bliss) condemned/For ever now to have their lot in pain,/ ... / Their glory withered' (*PL* 1.604–12).

[285] See Ginzburg, 'The High and the Low,' on the early modern notion of arcane, forbidden knowledge.

5.4 Proem IX (PL 9.1–47)

It is the second aspect, that of compassion, which relates most directly to the speaker's announcement, in Proem IX, that he 'now must change/Those notes to tragic.' This statement connects not only to Milton's reflections on the passions in general (*compassion* also falls in this domain), but more specifically to those passages in *Paradise Lost* informed by traditional notions about the power of music to move the passions and, most specifically, to those which appear informed by ancient Greek musical theory. One fundamental assumption in the musical theory of the Greeks, pioneered by the philosopher-performers of the Pythagorean school, was that the different scales or *modes* – in Greek, *harmoniai* – of music had a clearly specified psychological effect on hearers, and were able to put them in certain *moods* (*ethê*, plural of *ethos*).[286]

This notion of 'moods' covered a variety of what would today perhaps be referred to as emotions or virtues – anything the soul could be 'moved' to through the either inciting or placating influence of music. Reflecting a strong convergence of musical and rhetorical theory on this point, however, it has been suggested that 'the whole notion of *musical effect* [was] intimately involved with the notion of the *sense of a text*, and, ultimately, of the meaning of words.'[287] Thus, in his *Republic*, Plato would point out that the Dorian and Phrygian modes were not manly or noble 'in themselves,' but were, rather, habitually associated with serious and patriotic texts and had therefore acquired a certain stable connotation along those lines.[288] Such niceties were often ignored in later tradition, and the ancient doctrine was generally understood to indicate a clearly defined effect of specific *ethê* on the mind of anyone who listened to or even heard them. Milton refers to the doctrine at several points in both his poetry and his prose, and appears to presuppose a general understanding of the modes on the part of his audience. Thus, in the final verse paragraph of *Lycidas*, the 'uncouth swain' is presented as a *serious* singer, 'with eager thought warbling his Doric lay.'[289]

The Greek musical modes appear to have been much on Milton's mind in 1644, since both *Of Education* and *Areopagitica*, respectively published in June and November of that year, contain references to them. Both examples throw further light on Milton's use of the concept in Proem IX. The passage in *Areopagitica* ironically demands a regulation of musical modes similar to the pre-press censorship against which Milton's 'Speech ... to the Parliament of *England*' argues. As in *Lycidas*, Milton's reference to the 'Doric' mode implies high seriousness, although, in the present context of polemicising against a forced and unwanted 'rectifi[cation of] manners,' it rather serves to expose the plans of the licensers as inspired by the strong-handed regime of Plato's ideal republic:

> If we think to regulat Printing, thereby to rectifie manners, we must regulat all recreations and pastimes, all that is delightfull to man. No musick must be heard, no song be set or sung, but what is grave and *Dorick*. There must be licencing dancers, that no gesture, motion, or deportment be taught our youth but what by their allowance shall be thought honest; for such *Plato* was provided of; It will

---

[286] See Winn, *Unsuspected Eloquence*, 22–24.
[287] Hollander, *Untuning of the Sky*, 35–36.
[288] See Winn, *Unsuspected Eloquence*, 22.
[289] Carey ad loc. points to the pastoral associations of Doric Greek, the dialect of Theocritus, Moschus, and Bion.

> ask more then the work of twenty licencers to examin all the lutes, the violins, and the ghittars in every house; they must not be suffer'd to prattle as they doe, but must be licenc'd what they may say. And who shall silence all the airs and madrigalls, that whisper softness in chambers?[290]

In *Of Education*, the imagined function of musical modes – namely, to 'rectifie manners' – is similar to that presumed in *Areopagitica*; however, since it is now Milton who intends to propose the rectification guidelines, the thrust of the passage in question is quite different. Athletic and martial exercise, Milton writes of his ideal school, 'will inspire [pupils] with a gallant and fearlesse courage, which being temper'd with seasonable lectures and precepts to them of true fortitude, and patience, will turn into a native and heroick valour, and make them hate the cowardise of doing wrong.' After such combat training – which includes fencing and sword-fighting ('to guard and to strike safely with edge, or point') as well as 'all the locks and gripes of wrastling, wherein English men were wont to excell' – they may use

> the interim of unsweating themselves ... and convenient rest before meat ... with profit and delight ... in recreating and composing their travail'd spirits with the solemn and divine harmonies of musick heard, or learnt; ... some times the Lute, or soft organ stop waiting on elegant voices either to Religious, martiall, or civill ditties; which if wise men & prophets be not extreamly out, have a great power over dispositions and manners, to smooth and make them gentle from rustick harshnesse and distemper'd passions. The like also would not be unexpedient after meat to assist and cherish nature in her first concoction, and send their mindes backe to study in good tune and satisfaction.[291]

More sustainedly and more seriously than *Areopagitica*, the open 'Letter' *Of Education* (addressed by Milton to Samuel Hartlib, the educator and academic reformer) presents the classic statement of the doctrine of musical modes as put forward by Plato: physical and mental strength are to be pursued in parallel, although Milton does allow for some 'temper[ing]' of raw courage by means of 'seasonable lectures ... of true fortitude, and patience,' that is, for Christian sermonising to domesticate pagan belligerence. Through this tempering, the resulting 'native and heroick valour,' though designated with the emotive term emphatically controverted in Proem IX – 'heroic' occurs five times in the course of its roughly fifty lines, and Milton is consistently employed in draining the word of its conventional associations –, seems none too far removed from the 'better fortitude/Of patience and heroic martyrdom' of the proem, with some allowance made for swordplay.

In his subsequent comments on musical education, Milton strikes a conceptual triad that resonates even more clearly with the sensory discourse of Proem IX. Not only is there a close temporal relation between the ingestion of food ('before meat ... after meat,' i.e., before and after meals) and the tempering of 'distemper'd passions' by

---

[290] CPW 2: 523–24.
[291] CPW 2: 409–411.

5.4 Proem IX (PL 9.1–47)

means of music; but the two aspects are correlated on the level of the body as well as that of the soul: music – more precisely, the 'Religious, martiall, or civill ditties' assigned by 'wise men & prophets' to those respective uses – will serve to 'cherish nature in her first concoction'[292] (i.e., assist the *body* in digestion), but it will also work on the pupils' *minds* and 'send [them] backe to study *in good tune and satisfaction*;' in this last phrase, Milton combines musical and culinary metaphors.[293] Finally, this whole alimentary-musical process of strengthening and tempering occurs in the overall context of the strengthening of the pupils' courage and the subsequent tempering of that into 'heroick valour,' marked by 'fortitude' and 'patience' – a dialectical process between nurture and *another kind* of nurture. In Milton's perspective, music – and the views on its effect handed down by 'wise men & prophets' – makes a key contribution to the successful outcome of that process.

In *Paradise Lost* prior to Proem IX, there are two passages in which Milton refers to the ancient Greek musical modes and to their use or effect. As on other occasions, these passages present hell and heaven as inverted mirror images of one another. In book 1, Milton describes the parading of the fallen angels:

> anon they move
> In perfect phalanx to *the Dorian mood*
> Of flutes and soft recorders; such as raised
> To *height of noblest temper heroes* old
> Arming to battle, and *instead of rage*
> *Deliberate valour* breathed, firm and unmoved
> With dread of death to flight or foul retreat,
> Not wanting power to *mitigate and swage*,

---

[292] This appears to be digestion as the 'first concoction,' as opposed the conversion of chyme into blood (the second) and secretion (the third 'concoction'); see CPW: 411n24. See also Charles Webster, *The Great Instauration: Science, Medicine and Reform, 1626–1660*, 2nd ed. (Oxford: Peter Lang, 2002 [1975], 139–40, on the mid-century debate over 'concoction' (i.e., digestion): was it driven by heat or caused by an acid ferment? Milton's phrasing – '*cherish* nature in her first concoction' – suggests that he accepted the first variant, since 'cherish' could mean 'to keep warm; to give warmth to' (see *OED*, 'cherish, v.,' 6, citing *PL* 10.1068). This also matches Milton's description of how the stars 'with kindly heat/Of various influence *foment and warm,/Temper or nourish*' all creatures on earth (*PL* 4.666–68), as well as the other 'concoctive' imagery of his generally heat-based cosmology; see Marjara, *Contemplation of Created Things*, 229–38. On Milton's use of similar language to express the IDEAS ARE FOOD metaphor in his prose (*The Doctrine and Discipline of Divorce* as well as *Areopagitica*), see Svendsen, *Milton and Science*, 186, 221.

[293] See the various musical senses at *OED*, 'tune, n.,' but also 3b: '*figurative* in "in tune, out of tune," in or out of order or proper condition; in or out of harmony with some person or thing …,' as well as *OED*, 'satisfaction, n.': 5a: 'the action of gratifying (an appetite or desire) to the full …; the fact of having been gratified to the full or of having one's desire fulfilled' – the pupils are 'in … satisfaction' because their appetite or even hunger for music has been sated, just as, immediately before, their bodies had been fed. (As in *Twelfth Night*, 1.1, MUSIC IS FOOD.) Now they go back to study to feed their minds (IDEAS ARE FOOD). For other close associations of the two parallel metaphors, see Proem III: 'Then *feed on thoughts*, that voluntary move/*Harmonious numbers* …,' as well as the parallel references to food and music in Sonnet 17, discussed above.

> With solemn touches, troubled thoughts, and chase
> Anguish and doubt and fear and sorrow and pain
> From mortal or immortal minds. Thus they
> Breathing united force with fixèd thought
> Moved on in silence to soft pipes that charmed
> Their painful steps o'er the burnt soil; ...
>
> (*PL* 1.549–62, emphases added)

As Fowler notes, 'the devils use the best mode (*mood*) for calm firmness – the Doric, as against the soft and indolent Ionian and Lydian modes.'[294] In other respects, as well, Milton's description resonates with his earlier references to the topic. The 'height of noblest temper' to which he refers is indeed the result of a tempering process, by which 'rage' (a term more negative than the 'gallant and fearlesse courage' of *Of Education*, but conceptually equivalent) is 'mitigate[d] and swage[d]' (i.e., assuaged) into 'deliberate valour' – the 'heroick valour' of the earlier treatise. Ultimately, though, the fallen angels moving 'in perfect phalanx' are only compared to the 'heroes old' of pagan antiquity; Milton makes no reference to any further tempering towards Christian virtue.

During the mobilisation for the war in heaven, by contrast, and thus later in the sequence of the poem but earlier in terms of its plot, Milton describes the heavenly host in similar terms. After God's 'wrath' has been 'awaked,' 'the loud/Ethereal trumpet from on high gan blow':

> At which command the powers militant,
> That stood for heaven, in mighty quadrate joined
> Of union irresistible, moved on
> In silence their bright legions, to the sound
> Of instrumental harmony that breathed
> Heroic ardour to advent'rous deeds
> Under their godlike leaders, in the cause
> Of God and his Messiah.   (*PL* 6.59–68)

In both passages, the celestial and the infernal, the troops are marching 'in silence,' which highlights the importance of the music that is playing. Significantly, Milton does not refer to a specific Greek mode but just to the 'instrumental harmony' with which the angels are associated throughout *Paradise Lost* (both in the musical sense and in the sense of 'firm concord' already referred to earlier). From the overall similarity in structure and several verbal parallels to the passage in book 1, it is nevertheless clear that Milton has in mind the same conceptual complex of a musical tempering to 'heroic ardour.' The loyal angels, however, have internalised Christian virtue and 'the better fortitude' extolled in Proem IX; they are marching 'under their godlike leaders, in the cause/Of God and his Messiah' and are thus superior to the merely pagan dependence of the fallen angels on 'the Dorian mood.'

---

[294] Fowler ad loc.

The last passage, with its reference to 'heroic ardour' and 'advent'rous deeds,' takes us back to Proem IX, in which the speaker contemplates how his own 'advent'rous song' (*PL* 1.13), though technically an instance of 'heroic song' (*PL* 9.25), i.e., an epic poem, could be justified as such, even if its 'great argument' (*PL* 1.24) rejects most elements of the 'only argument/Heroic deemed' (*PL* 9.28) by earlier epic poets. The key to how this aspect of Proem IX connects to the sensory discourse of the proems at large (which, most fundamentally, relates to the embodied voice of the speaker as expressed through his epic 'song') lies in the notion of appropriateness. This is first referred to when the speaker announces that he 'now must change/Those notes to tragic,' which indicates a change of mode and mood in the sense just outlined. Instead of merely following the pagan model of epic poetry, however (as the fallen angels do), the content to be related by the speaker in that tragic mode constitutes an 'argument/Not less but more heroic,' and hence the heroism instilled by this change of mode and mood will be different from the heroism instilled by the 'Dorian mood' into 'heroes old' and the 'perfect phalanx' of Satan's troops.[295] Milton's epic speaker – if self-questioning or even self-demonising in other respects – is to the bards of ancient pagan epic as the marching devils are to the marching angels: he, too, is active 'in the cause/Of God and his Messiah.'

The second respect in which the speaker of Proem IX addresses the appropriateness of his song concerns the quality and nature of his inspiration, a consistent theme of the previous three proems. In stark contrast to his earlier invocations, however, Proem IX does not address the Muse directly (in the second person) but only refers to her (in the third person) in two passages bracketing the second half of the proem. In the first of these, Milton's conditional phrasing again betrays insecurity, and a sense of the precariousness of the speaker's position (it is similar in this respect to the questions and requests of the earlier proems): 'If answerable style I can obtain/Of my celestial patroness ...,' that is, Urania, the 'heavenly Muse' to whose 'celestial song' the speaker had referred in Proem VII. Milton's phrase, 'answerable style,' is highly ambiguous, and has been interpreted in a variety of ways.[296] Fundamentally, however, Milton appears to be thinking of a style 'answerable,' that is, 'appropriate' or 'matching' his own 'great argument' (just as God, in a passage from book 7 quoted above, had examine whether Creation 'answer[ed] his great idea'). In other words, the speaker wishes for a style (of song) that matches the tragic content of his argument, the very 'tragic [notes]' referred

---

[295] This understanding of the tragic mode connects to *Samson Agonistes*, Milton's tragedy, in which the proto-Christian patience and fortitude of the protagonist are repeatedly addressed (see, for instance, *SA* 1287–96. See also *PR* 1.424–26 and 3.88–95, naming 'patient Job' as worthy to be mentioned. Barbara Kiefer Lewalski has demonstrated how the Book of Job was a model for *Paradise Regained* in her *Milton's Brief Epic: The Genre, Meaning, and Art of 'Paradise Regained'* (Providence, R. I.: Brown University Press, 1966).

[296] The fundamental ambiguity is between 'answerable' meaning 'equivalent' or 'corresponding' and 'answerable' meaning 'accountable' or 'responsible.' See Fowler ad loc., who points to Milton's 'theme of Christian responsibility.' Arnold Stein, in his *Answerable Style: Essays on 'Paradise Lost'* (Minneapolis, Minn.: University of Minnesota Press, 1953), 119–62, explored the ways in which Milton's style in *Paradise Lost* may be said to be 'answerable' to contemporary concepts of the Christian epic but also to Milton's own idea of an appropriate style. See also Leonard, *Faithful Labourers*, I, 238–40.

to earlier. In the controversial question of whether the Platonic notion of the various *harmoniai* – the *form* of song – could be contemplated independently from any textual *content*, it appears, Milton would most likely have argued in favour of a synthetic approach, conforming to Plato's original position.

What is the outdated heroic *content* Milton rejects, just as he rejects the outmoded *form* of (pagan) heroic song? Apart from tedious accounts of martial exploits, he turns against *descriptive* passages containing the ekphrastic, i.e., in a sense, *visual* representation of striking appearances or worldly splendour. Accordingly, earlier heroic poets used to

> describe races and games,
> Or tilting furniture, emblazoned shields,
> Impreses quaint, caparisons and steeds,
> Bases and tinsel trappings, gorgeous knights
> At joust and tournament …

This passage is focused heavily on the outer appearance of the elements represented, and thus on the *visual* sphere. Milton's terminology indicates as much: '*emblazoned* shields,' 'impreses *quaint*' (i.e., heraldic devices designed to have an attractive appearance), '*gorgeous* knights.'[297] This focus on the visual sphere, the speaker suggests, must be rejected; a surprising turn after the speaker's explicit plea in Proem III to be given the power to 'see and tell [even] of things invisible to mortal sight.'

Indeed, while numerous examples from both classical and romantic/modern epic poetry can be found to indicate Milton's targets (for instance, the description of Achilles' 'emblazoned' shield in the *Illiad*, book 18, is the *locus classicus* for ekphrasis),[298] this does not mean that *Paradise Lost* is free from the elements Milton criticises, whether these be martial exploits (the war in heaven in books 5 and 6), 'races and games' (the devils in book 2, the loyal angels in book 4), or ekphrasis (throughout, but see particularly the heavily ekphrastic description of Michael in *PL* 11.239–48). As in the other cases of such 'contradictive mirroring' in *Paradise Lost* (e.g., between conditions or events in hell and in heaven, or between the speaker and Satan, or the speaker and Eve), these re-emergences of – according to Milton – outmoded epic practice should not be seen as gratuitous; nor should they be considered as lying beyond the poet's deliberation ('… even Milton nods …'). Rather, Milton's point appears to be stated, as in those other cases, by way of a fine yet significant contradistinction: all the ekphrastic and crudely heroic elements Milton criticises are fixated on perceptual surfaces and untempered by Christian virtue – they had 'hitherto [been] the *only* argument/Heroic deemed …' –, but Milton's 'great argument' is different, as the speaker had first announced at the conclusion of Proem I. The point is taken up again in Proem IX – it had not played any signifi-

---

[297] See *OED*, 'emblazon, v.': 'to … portray conspicuously, as on a heraldic shield; to adorn … with heraldic devices …'; *OED*, 'quaint, adj.,' 3b; *OED*, 'gorgeous, adj.,' 1: 'adorned with rich or brilliant colours …'. 'Caparisons,' too, cloth coverings for horses or saddles, are 'often gaily ornamented' (*OED* s. v.).

[298] Fowler ad loc. names Boiardo, Ariosto, Tasso, and Spenser as (near-)contemporary epic poets to whose works Milton's characterisation applies.

cant role in proems III and VII – and is restated in terms of a shift to the tragic mode. Whenever Milton deploys the machinery and imagery of traditional epic in *Paradise Lost*, it is *in the service of* his own, novel 'argument' – conceived of as 'heroic' in a new way, as 'the better fortitude/Of patience and heroic martyrdom,' which had previously had been left 'unsung' but now is sung by Milton's epic speaker, just as Milton's angels are allowed to approximate epic clichés as long as they do so 'in the cause/Of God and his Messiah.' In this respect, too, Milton distinguishes sharply between 'the meaning' and 'the name;' between the intention and the (speech) act itself. Milton's 'answerable style' would serve to indicate the one by means of the other.

Milton's 'higher argument,' as he calls it in Proem IX, is sufficiently lofty not to need the poet's exaltation: it is 'sufficient of itself to raise/That name,' namely, that of 'heroic song,' characterised *de facto* by those things 'which justly [give] heroic name/To person, or to poem.'[299] Still, the speaker has been 'soar[ing],' as indicated at several points throughout the proems, in order to meet his descending Muse and be able to produce the song that is *Paradise Lost*. In the speaker's reflection on this process of inspiration, Proem IX connects Milton's deliberations on the properties and meaning of the tragic mode (which, among the proems, are exclusive to Proem IX) with the consistent presentation of *Paradise Lost* as a song attributed to the bodily voice of its poet-speaker. This song is sometimes joined by the 'celestial song' of the Muse; sometimes the speaker's 'mortal voice' is heard solo but 'unchanged/To hoarse or mute.' In Proem IX, as mentioned, there is no invocation to the Muse, as Milton indirectly acknowledges in his account of past inspiration: 'If answerable style I can obtain/Of my celestial patroness, who deigns/Her nightly visitation *unimplored*.' Still, the Muse does come, unbidden, as, accordingly, does the speaker's song, which is 'easy' and 'unpremeditated.' Milton's reference to the 'nightly visitation' of the Muse rehearses both the speaker's own 'nightly' visits to Sion in Proem III and Urania's 'nightly' visits to the speaker's 'slumbers' in Proem VII; in Proem IX, again, the Muse 'dictates to me slumbering.' This latter image also concludes Proem IX, with Milton's periphrastic naming (antonomasia) of his Muse as '[she] who brings it *nightly* to my ear.'

***

As far as the proems are concerned, this is Milton's last word in the sensory discourse of *Paradise Lost*: both inspiration and expression of the poet's 'higher argument' belong, ultimately, in the auditory sphere, where they may employ the appropriate tragic mode. In the remaining sensory discourse of book 9 (and much of book 10), however, the rest is *taste*, taking up the other pronounced theme of the proem. (Overall, there appears to exist, over the course of the four proems, a movement from sight/vision through voice/hearing to a preoccupation with taste. In the 'visionary' books 11 and 12, which follow on the part of *Paradise Lost* segmented by the proems, there is a corresponding movement from sight to hearing to taste, a shift from the visual mode of book

---

[299] Compare Sonnet 16: '… God doth not need/Either man's work or his own gifts … / … his state/Is kingly.'

11 to the auditory mode of book 12 and on to the indispensable 'formation of taste' in a postlapsarian world.)[300]

In Proem IX, Milton reiterates the theme of the speaker's ultimate helplessness and fallibility, being wholly at the mercy of '[her] who brings it nightly to my ear.' When the threat of such failure – a kind of deafness to inspiration, shutting out wisdom at its only remaining 'entrance' – is conceptualised in spatial terms ('*higher* argument ... sufficient of itself to *raise*/That name, unless an age too late ... / ... *damp my intended wing/Depressed*'), Milton takes up the theme of soaring song introduced as early as Proem I. In its celebration of a moderate, 'rural repast,' its attention to what is permissible and 'venial' in discourse, as well as in its concern for what is the appropriately 'tragic' tone for the following account of the Fall, Proem IX also connects to the sensory discursive traditions – present in numerous of Milton's other writings – of moderation and 'tempering.'

In a way, the sensory discourse of the proems has come full circle although, in the meantime, the speaker's reasons for his reliance on the Muse's auditory inspiration have been presented at length: by reference to his blindness, but also through a privileged association of hearing with 'eternal Wisdom' and a corresponding devaluation of the visual sphere as providing merely the 'tinsel trappings' of epic (and thus, ideally, knowledge-bearing) song. On both sides, however, insecurities remain: the cruel fate of Orpheus evokes the potential endangerment of even an inspired singer; and the blind speaker's quite substantial deprivation (aesthetic, epistemic, social) and desolation, addressed in proems III and VII, have not, ultimately, been redeemed.

5.5 From Blindness through Song to Insight
Bodily and Spiritual Perception, Knowledge and Wisdom in the Proems of 'Paradise Lost'

As has become clear, the sensory discourse of Milton's proems revolves around the problematic figure of the poet-speaker. Caught between the hope for (visionary or vocal) inspiration and an apprehension of failure (as well as the painful awareness of his existing blindness), the speaker negotiates the inherent potentials and dangers of sense perception.

While all the senses make an appearance in the proems, there is a distinct emphasis on visual and auditory perception. The shifting focus within this audio-visual field of reference can be described in terms of a quasi-circular motion: after Proem I had set in with sound, and the speaker's preoccupation with vision had occupied Proem III and the first half of Proem VII (which subsequently turned to the speaker's 'mortal voice unchanged'), Proem IX indicates that the speaker's return to sound, begun in the second half of Proem VII, is now complete. This does not disavow the speaker's pleas for illumination in proems I and III, but it does argue for the more fundamental significance of hearing, the sense of obedience, also connected to the speaker's own, embodied song.

In all instances, whether they are sight- or sound-focused, Milton consistently returns to the epistemogenic quality of his poem: *Paradise Lost*, from its very beginning, is a poem of knowledge. This is clear from the speaker's plea for 'instruct[ion]' in Pro-

---

[300] On this see also the Conclusion below.

em I, and is taken up in the extended juxtaposition of corporeal and spiritual vision in Proem III. Both 'knowledge' and 'wisdom' are withheld from the blind speaker – a loss only to be redeemed – hopefully – through inner illumination by 'holy light.' In Proem VII, it is the speaker's Muse, Urania, who offers at least a chance of access to 'eternal Wisdom,' understood both as divine knowledge and knowledge of the divine. And in Proem IX, the speaker returns to his objective, stated in Proem I, to 'justify the ways of God to men' (i.e., to mediate and discursify such wisdom), which is now presented as his intention to celebrate, in song, a 'higher argument' superior to the subject matter of earlier epic poetry.

Considered in these terms, the four proems to *Paradise Lost* appear as consistent with some of the defining features of Milton's sensory discourse in his earlier and earliest poetry and prose. In their use of sensory-conceptual metaphor and evocation of sensescapes (the latter in Proem III in particular), they connect, for example, to the sensory discourse of the elegies (as well to that of *Paradise Lost* more generally, which is also concerned with the proper 'governing' of the senses and the tempering of the passions);[301] in their reflections on blindness, they bear comparison with a number of Milton's sonnets, as well as with *Samson Agonistes*. A new element in the sensory discourse of the proems, in contrast to the texts analysed in previous chapters, is that, at times, they address the actual functioning of sense perception (such as when the speaker of Proem III refers to the possible causes of his blindness) and integrate this more 'matter-of-fact' approach to the senses with the conceptual, mythological, and theological significances of the human sensorium.

In their constant awareness of the embodied quality of the speaker's voice, finally, the proems to *Paradise Lost* stand in the tradition of Milton's earlier poetry and prose. They combine a conception of the poetic text as the poet's vocal song, accompanied at times by other, more ideal voices (i.e., the Muse's, comparable to that of Philomela in Elegy V) with a conception, familiar from the prolusions, of the human voice as representative of the speaking subject's body – exposed to view (all the more so in the case of Samson or the blind speaker of *Paradise Lost*) and, possibly, to outside aggression. Among the texts analysed in this book, this aspect of Milton's sensory discourse is made most explicit in *Paradise Lost*, which opens with an invocation to the Muse to 'sing' with the speaker, and which, throughout, is presented as aiming for, in the words of Milton's poetological note on 'The Verse,' 'true musical delight.'

---

[301] See Jens Martin Gurr, 'The Senses and Human Nature in a Political Reading of *Paradise Lost*,' in: *The Five Senses in Medieval and Early Modern England*, eds Kern-Stähler/Busse/de Boer, 177–195.

Conclusion:
Trajectories in the Miltonic Sensorium

At the outset of this study in Chapter 1, four preliminary assumptions suggested possible approaches to the Miltonic sensorium. These concerned (1) the sensory-discursive continuity of Milton's poetry with his prose; (2) a particularly pronounced contiguity of different discourses in the early modern setting; (3) Milton's consistent (but consistently shifting) association of sensory discourse with the epistemic sphere; and (4) the resulting peculiarities (or 'eigen-sense') of Milton's investment in the senses. Over the preceding chapters, these simple assumptions have, to varying extents, been both vindicated and rendered problematic by the complexities of sensory discourse observed in action.

While there are demonstrable continuities between Milton's early poetry, his university prose dating from the same era, and the proems of *Paradise Lost* as samples of his later verse, there are indications that Milton was quite aware of the 'expected' role of sensory, and even more of sensuous, language (such as when he comments in Prolusion I that his subject seems 'better suited to a poetical exercise' than to an academic oration, or when the language of sensuous enjoyment appears in Proem III of *Paradise Lost* or in the tragic context of *Samson Agonistes* – apparently for purposes of dramatic heightening).

Likewise, the interconnection of Milton's sensory discourse with sensory components from various other (disciplinary) discourses – natural philosophy and proto-science, theology, Platonic and neo-Platonist philosophy – has also become apparent. However, the full extent and at times paradoxical configuration of these discursive adsorptions would certainly require (and merit) closer and more particular study before a fuller understanding of them could be gained. How may Milton's conflicting references to Galileo and astronomy, for example, be analysed more fully as components of the sensory-metaphorical discourse of *Paradise Lost* as a whole?

Milton's association of sensory discourse with epistemic matters was much in evidence in all of the analytical chapters. Still, some suggestive contrasts and possible developments should be pointed out. Milton's elegies – true to the broader classical understanding of the genre – emerged as both poems of immediate, individualised (sensory) experience (most prominently in Elegy VII) *and* as themselves vehicles of deliberation and thought (most prominently in Elegy V). This sensory-discursive profile resonates with their private, even intimate character (made formally explicit in Elegy I, a letter in verse to Milton's close friend Charles Diodati). In his prolusions, on the other hand, Milton, fulfilling the at times unpleasantly *public* role of orator,[1] repeatedly sub-

---

[1] Much later, Emily Dickinson would use 'public' in the manner of a dirty word: 'How dreary – to be – Somebody!/How public – like a Frog – …' Reconsider in this light Milton's disparaging

verts the generic expectation of an 'epistemogenic' academic lecture or debate by consciously reflecting on it or – as in the extravagant Prolusion VI – abandoning such expectations (almost) altogether. Here, as in most of the other texts discussed, Milton addresses the subject of a proper 'governing' of the senses, made lamentably (or epically) difficult by the persistent temptation of sensuality. The proper *application* of the five senses, meant to resolve this conflict, is a prominent point of interest in the sensory discourse of *Paradise Lost* and beyond, and would merit further study. In the proems to *Paradise Lost*, finally, the two perspectives collide: here, the representative, public form of the epic as a poem of knowledge dealing with 'great argument[s]' and matters of (the human) state; there, the intimacy, doubt (of knowledge, of the senses), and one-on-one addresses to the Muse, the Spirit, and 'holy light.' For all their uncertainty, however, the proems to Milton's epic represent a new addition to Miltonic sensory discourse – an aspect also present in *Samson Agonistes*, as well as in the sonnets and the mid-period prose –, namely, a concern for the process of *sense-perception itself*.[2] As I have suggested elsewhere, this concern seems fundamental to the sensory discourse of *Paradise Lost* as a whole, and should likewise be explored further (e.g., by reference to the distinct sensescapes of the poem, or to the relations between different classes of sensory agents among its characters).[3]

If, even in the absence of a sustained comparison between Milton's usage and the sensory-discursive habits of his contemporaries, some suggestions may be ventured as to his 'eigen-sense,' they should probably start from his affinity for certain (conceptual-) metaphorical complexes related to the senses. One is the imagery of towers, walls, and other *scopuli*, based in the conceptual-orientational metaphor VISION IS UP. As I have suggested, this is prominent in the early elegies, but it really occurs throughout Milton's writing life; much more could and should have been said about its relevance in *Paradise Lost*.[4] Another expresses, again and again in both Milton's poetry and prose, the notion that IDEAS ARE FOOD – which may equally be assimilated, savoured, misdigested or vomited as being unappetising. Another characteristic of Milton's sensory discourse –

---

parallel reference to (only?) the other 'speechifiers' (*oratorculi*) and the *ranuncula Seriphia* they resemble, discussed in Chapter 4.

[2] This sensory discourse of Milton's sonnets includes sustained references to music, as in Sonnet 13 ('To Mr H. Lawes, on his Airs'), as well as the blindness-centred sonnets 16 ('When I consider how my light is spent …', conventionally titled 'On His Blindness'), 18 ('To Mr Cyriack Skinner Upon his Blindness'), and 19 ('Methought I saw …'). As one example from the mid-period prose, consider Milton's playful insistence, in *The Doctrine and Discipline of Divorce* (1643/44), that Love is *not* (wholly) blind and, in particular, the astronomical *and* ophthalmological language in which this is phrased: 'Love, though not wholly blind, as Poets wrong him, yet having but one eye, as being born an Archer aiming, and that eye not the quickest in this dark region here below, which is not Loves proper sphere, […] often deceiv'd, imbraces and consorts him with these obvious and suborned striplings […], while they suttly keep themselves most on his blind side. But after a while, as his manner is, when soaring up into the high Towr of his *Apogaeum*, above the shadow of the earth, he darts out the direct rayes of his then most piercing eyesight upon the impostures …' (CPW 2: 255).

[3] See Gabel, 'Hierarchies of Vision.' This includes the sensescapes of heaven, hell, paradise, and others.

[4] For a first orientation, see the relevant passages in Dobranski, *Milton's Visual Imagination*, and especially the chapter on Milton in McKeown, *Fortification and Its Discontents*.

and one that connects more to its linguistic than to its conceptual side – is represented in this study by numerous individual observations regarding the idiosyncratic, often highly ambiguous use of individual lexical items referencing, more or less straightforwardly, the sensory sphere. In many cases, and by no means only with reference to the Latin poetry and prose, the readings suggested have borne out John Hale's contention that 'Milton's language' does not exist in the singular: indeed, Milton's wide-reaching linguistic training also informed his peculiar take on sensory discourse. In a number of passages in both the poetry and the prose, Milton displays an awareness, for example, of etymological and hence 'submerged' sensory meanings or metaphors – metaphors which, at the very least, are 'not dead but sleeping' (as Empson had it), and which are certainly a fully active component of discourse from the point of view of conceptual metaphor theory.[5]

Further research into all of these aspects would find ample material in Milton's remaining poetry and his polemical prose, as well as in his treatise *Of Education*, which I have touched on only briefly but which – addressed to the educational reformer Samuel Hartlib yet conspicuously ignoring Hartlib's friend Comenius – connects in significant ways to contemporary debates over the role of the senses in the (sensory) formation of children.[6] Even unlikely places such as Milton's rather matter-of-fact *History of Britain* (published in 1670, albeit begun much earlier) or his pastiche of travel narratives on Russia and East Asia, *A Brief History of Muscovia* (first published posthumously in 1682) are of considerable sensory-discursive interest when seen in the larger context of Milton's writings.[7] However, as with *Of Education*, a stronger contextualisation of Milton's sensory discourse *beyond* the confines of his own writings would be just as desirable.

With regard to all of the core aspects of sensory discourse derived from commonplace assumptions about poetic language, metaphor, and discourse, and presented more

---

[5] Empson, *Seven Types of Ambiguity*, 25. ('All languages are composed of dead metaphors as the soil of corpses, but English is perhaps uniquely full of metaphors of this sort, *which are not dead but sleeping*, and, while making a direct statement, colour it with an implied comparison.') Empson's ultimately 'mortalist' image – of supposedly dead metaphors waiting patiently for their resurrection – would have appealed to Milton, both the linguist and the theologian.)

[6] In *Of Education* (1644), Milton starts from the premise that 'our understanding cannot in this body found it selfe but on sensible things, nor arrive so cleerly to the knowledge of God and things invisible, as by orderly conning over the visible and inferior creature' arguing that 'the same method is necessarily to be follow'd in all discreet teaching' (CPW 2: 368–69). Education should begin 'with Arts most easie, and those be such as are most obvious to the sence' (CPW 2: 374). This approach obviously chimes with the idea that 'in contemplation of created things/By steps we may ascend to God' (*PL* 5.511; see also Chapter 5.2 above).

[7] Milton's account of Russian history, geography, nature, and culture was '[g]ather'd from the Writings of several Eye-witnesses,' as its title page and text proclaimed, a tradition 'established by Hakluyt and followed by Purchas' (CPW 8: 476). Throughout, Milton stresses the variety and great intensity of sense impressions confronting the traveller, from orthodox churches 'full of Images, and Tapers' to islands 'full of roses, violets and wild Rosemary,' and from 'noysom Fish' to 'Velvets, Damasks, Cloth of Gold and Tissue, [...] many sorts of Sugars. [... T]heir Markets smell odoriferously with Spices' (CPW 8: 477–78, 495, 504–5, 509). The last quotation, conspicuously, occurs not far from a reference to the 'but five Gates' built into the great Wall of China.

fully in Chapter 2 – namely, its use of (1) sensory language and (2) sensory metaphor (both linguistic and conceptual), its reference to (3) linguistic and extra-linguistic contexts and (4) the sphere of knowledge – the texts analysed have thus yielded ample and convincing evidence. Milton deploys these elements pointedly and with a degree of cross-generic and diachronic consistency, for illustrative as well as deliberative purposes. What underlies his use of sensory discourse in all of the texts discussed, however, is his conception of it as embodied, vocal speech. This, first traced in Chapter 2, not only serves to back up the claim of sensory discourse more generally to actually experiential, embodied reference; it also connects to Milton's ideas of the genres in which he was writing (elegy as threnody, epic as a 'song of knowledge'; prose as oratory, regardless of its actual enactment). In a culture in which 'knowledge about most things was, in fact, communicated in the form of speeches' held or printed, such a conception would, in any case, at the same time underline a writer's claim to epistemic authority posited by most sensory discourse.[8]

Inasmuch as Milton's sensory discourse has emerged as both embodied and abstract, both concrete and metaphorical, yet in all cases as a constructive and at times even essential element of his writing, it transcends earlier debates over the degrees of Milton's 'sensibility,' sensuousness, or even sensory perceptiveness, which I have outlined in Chapter 1. Rather, it seems to approximate the account given of the perceptual-cognitive dialectic by William Wordsworth, another latter-day Miltonian, in the lines prefixed to this study as an epigraph:

> For thus the senses and the intellect
> Shall each to each supply a mutual aid,
> Invigorate and sharpen and refine
> Each other with a power that knows no bound,
> And forms and feelings acting thus, and thus
> Reacting, they shall each acquire
> A living spirit and a character
> Till then unfelt, and each be multiplied
> With a variety that knows no end. (83–91)[9]

In the Miltonic sensorium, too, 'the senses' (i.e., perception, at times figured as sensation to affect a greater degree of immediacy) and 'the intellect' (i.e., perception reflected upon, and the metaphorical or conceptual structures derived from this) enter into a fruitful process of mutual interference. On one level, I have suggested by reference to the sensory-studies tradition, this 'intellect' really amounts to the 'hive mind' of a cultural moment in history, and its 'senses' to those of a collective sensorium. On another level, however, Wordsworth's description speaks to the constant negotiation in Milton's writing between perception and metaphor (does the sun only *look* 'like the God/Of this new world'?); between experience and concepts (as in the confrontation with Amor in Elegy VII); between the 'too little' of sensory deprivation (as in the case of blindness) and the

---

[8] Smith, *Acoustic World of Early Modern England*, 247–48.
[9] William Wordsworth, '[Not useless do I deem],' in: *Romanticism*, ed. Wu, 453–57, at 456.

'too much' of blind sensuality. These contrasts belong to the life world of the writer as much as they belong to the connotative world of his words. Different readings have tended to place Milton at one or the other extreme – most often at that of an overly intellectual sensory 'obtuseness' (Bagehot).[10] As the analyses presented in this study suggest, it is time to rediscover the potential of the Miltonic sensorium to 'invigorate and sharpen and refine' – in other words: its *productive* potential, in which illustrative and deliberative instances of sensory discourse are not mutually exclusive but rather inform and affect one another. Beyond the immediate scope of Milton's own writings, beyond even their reception and adaptation by Wordsworth and *his* contemporaries, the Miltonic sensorium thus emerges as a dynamic aggregate of experience and reflection, involved and implied in a chain of sensory-discursive exchanges which, indeed, 'knows no end.'

---

[10] One notable exception is Michael Clune's suggestion that, due to his interest in 'the difference between actual and virtual forms of perception' – and thus, in a sense, between perception and its conceptual abstraction –, Milton should be considered an exponent of a proto-Romantic sensibility. See, again, Clune, *Writing Against Time*, 154n20.

Epilogue
After-Images of the Miltonic Sensorium

In the nineteenth, twentieth, and twenty-first centuries, avant-garde film-makers, literary scholars, and cultural historians have not been the only ones inspired by the Miltonic sensorium. As an epilogue, I would like to consider three cases in which the sensory discourse of Milton's writings – and the sensory discourse of his poetry, specifically – has taken on an afterlife of its own. These are a sonnet by the Argentine poet, translator, and scholar, Jorge Luis Borges, first published in his 1964 collection *El otro, el mismo* ('The other, the same'); a 1826 painting by the French artist Eugène Delacroix; and finally another, more recent poem by the contemporary English poet (and translator from the Italian) Jamie McKendrick, first published in 2016. As this quodlibet of reception, reaction, and appropriation will suggest, the infinite variety of sensory-discursive encounters with the Miltonic sensorium to which I have just alluded at the end of my conclusion does include a variety of 'illustrative,' 'deliberative,' and, most of all, creative responses across centuries, countries, literary forms, and media.

Jorge Luis Borges, 'Una Rosa y Milton' (1964)

Una Rosa y Milton	A Rose and Milton
De las generaciones de las rosas	Of many generations of past roses
que en el fondo del tiempo se han perdido	That now are lost deep in the ground of time,
quiero que una se salve del olvido,	I'd love to see one saved from Lethe's slime,
una sin marca o signo entre las cosas	Pure and unmarked among those things *ou choses*
que fueron. El destino me depara	That are long gone. By destiny or grace
este don de nombrar por vez primera	(As their gift) I first name that nameless rose,
esa flor silenciosa, la postrera	Still undistinguished bloom, mine to disclose:
rosa que Milton acercó a su cara,	The last silent flower that Milton held close to his face,
sin verla. Oh tú bermeja o amarilla	Eyes sightless. O you of scarlet or of yellow chrome,
o blanca rosa de un jardín borrado,	Or white rose from a garden long since razed,
deja mágicamente tu pasado	Leave now, as if by magic, your deep past,
inmemorial y en este verso brilla,	Time out of mind, and shine here in my poem –
oro, sangre o marfil o tenebrosa	Like ivory, blood, or gold that gleams as twilight closes,
como en sus manos, invisible rosa.	Bloom as once in his hands, least visible of roses.

Jorge Luis Borges   tr. T. G.

In the case of Jorge Luis Borges (1899–1986) – 'decidedly a Miltonist,' according to John Shawcross –, the similarities to Milton indeed seem to be bordering on the epigonic.[1] As a poet, scholar, polyglot, Anglophile – his maternal grandmother was English –, public servant – director of Argentina's *Biblioteca Nacional*, no less –, and blind from middle age, Borges resembled his revered literary forebear in many respects (with the notable exceptions of his agnosticism and superior command of Old English). Borges returned to Milton throughout his writing life. As a young man, he had published an essay combining a Spanish translation of Milton's prefatory note on 'The Verse' of *Paradise Lost* with his own commentary and examples against rhyme, and in defence of blank verse.[2] He also returned to Milton again and again in his poetry, as Shawcross, Angelica Duran, and others have pointed out. Notably, this included references to Milton's sensory discourse. Thus, in his poem 'Del infierno y del cielo' ('Of Hell and Heaven,' 1942, later reprinted in *El otro, el mismo*), Borges refers to 'la visible tiniebla de Juan Milton' (16), giving a rendering in Spanish both of Milton's name and of his famous phrase from *PL* 1.63, 'darkness visible.' He had not yet gone blind when he wrote that line, but by 1954, when he was fifty-five years old (Milton had been forty-five), Borges's 'darkness,' too, had become 'visible.' Like Milton, Borges addressed his blindness in several of his poems, most famously, perhaps, in his 'Poema de los dones' ('A Poem of Gifts,' 1960), in which he undertakes a (sensory) theodicy of his own, reflecting on the circumstance that he had been made the custodian of an enormous library just around the time his blindness became total and he was abruptly shut off from all those 'books of knowledge fair':

> Nadie rebaje a lágrima o reproche
> esta declaración de la maestría
> de Dios, que con magnífica ironía
> me dio a la vez los libros y la noche …
>
> [Let no one's tears debase or slight
> This statement of God's mastery
> By which, with magnificent irony,
> I received both, books and night …][3]

---

[1] John T. Shawcross, '"Shedding sweet influence:" The Legacy of John Milton's Works,' in: Angelica Duran (ed.), *A Concise Companion to Milton* (Malden, Mass.: Blackwell, 2007), 25–42, at 37–38, quotation at 37. See also Angelica Duran, 'Three of Borges's Miltons,' *MS* 58 (2017), 183–200.
[2] Jorge Luis Borges, 'Milton y su condenación de la rima' [1925], in: Idem, *El tamaño de mi esperanza / El idioma de los argentinos* (Buenos Aires: Debolsillo, 2016), 91–95. At the conclusion of his essay, however, Borges remarks: 'I confess to the partiality of what I have written. The arguments in favour of rhyme are well known indeed; for this reason, I have had to emphasise those to the contrary' (tr. T. G.). Borges's poetic œuvre comprises both rhymed and unrhymed poems.
[3] All my quotations from Borges's poetry are taken from the following edition: Jorge Luis Borges, *Poesía completa*, 4th ed. (Buenos Aires: Delbolsillo, 2016 [2013]). The English translation of the lines from 'Poema de los dones' is based on that of Francisco González-Crussí, *The Five Senses* (New York: Kaplan, 2009), 44. Contrast Samson's reproach of light, discussed in Chapter 5.2 above.

In the following stanza, Borges points out that the responsible task of overseeing this 'city of books' has been given, of all contenders, to 'eyes without light, which can no better/Than read in the libraries of dreams/Such senseless paragraphs [los insensatos párrafos], no more,/As the dawns will cede to their zeal.'[4] Even though Milton is not named, the dawn setting, dream-like visitation, and attention to physiological detail seem quite familiar (Borges's reference to the labouring 'zeal' of his 'lightless eyes' most likely hints at the sleep phase of rapid eye movement, thought since the early 1950s to be responsible for most dreaming; the 'zeal[ous]'/rapid eye movement of the dreamer resembles that of a reader.)

In Borges's sonnet, 'Una rosa y Milton,' these two strands of his poetic work – one explicitly Miltonic, the other concerned with blindness – converge in a reflection on, or rather, a conjuration of 'la postrera/rosa que Milton acercó a su cara,/sin verla' – the last ever rose that Milton held close to his face without seeing it. This premise alone invokes a wealth of sensory-discursive connotations, ranging from the complex symbolism[5] and the conventional non-visual qualities of the rose – its scent, evoked by Milton holding it 'close to his face'; its thorns or other tactile qualities, suggested by the reference to 'his hands' in the last line – to Milton's own lament in the second proem to *Paradise Lost*:

> Thus with the year
> Seasons return, but not to me returns
> Day, or the sweet approach of even or morn,
> Or sight of vernal bloom, or summer's rose ...
> (*PL* 3.40–43)

Indeed, the whole sonnet – a poetic form intimately associated, in Milton's poetry, with his blindness – is rife with Miltonic echoes: there is the reference to an 'erased garden' ('un jardín borrado'); there is the address to a present yet absent abstract, reminiscent of Milton's invocations in the proems;[6] there is, finally, the slight echo, in the first line of the sonnet, of the very first line of *Paradise Lost* ('Of man's first disobedience ...'), rendered in Juan Escoiquiz's much-read translation of Milton's epic into Spanish – as *El Paraíso Perdido* (1812) – as 'Del primer hombre la disobediencia ...'[7] Sure enough, Escoiquiz, too, rhymes 'perdido' – a key term, obviously, of his *Paraíso Perdido* – with

---

[4] Paraphrase mine. Borges's 'insensatos' oscillates between a more or less neutral, sensory meaning ('unsensed') and a more strongly evaluative, more broadly cognitive one ('foolish').
[5] Borges appears to be playing on the Marian associations of the rose, in particular: his is 'sin marca o signo' – immaculate. But compare also the following phrases from Milton's blindness-and-dreaming-centred Sonnet 19 ('Methought I saw my late espousèd saint'): 'washed from spot of childbed taint' (5), 'Purification in the old Law' (6), 'vested all in white, pure as her mind' (9). A parallel passage in *Paradise Lost* (*PL* 4.706–717) associates the myth of Alcestis brought back from the grave (which forms the premise of the 'espousèd saint' sonnet) with 'espousèd Eve.'
[6] Compare Borges's address to the rose ('Oh tú bermeja o amarilla ...') with *PL* 1.6 as rendered by Escoiquiz: 'O tu! Verdad divina, y encendida/Unica Musa digna de mi canto ...'
[7] See Angelica Duran, '*Paradise Lost* in Spanish Translation and as World Literature,' in: Idem/Islam Issa/Jonathan R. Olson (eds), *Milton in Translation* (Oxford: Oxford University Press, 2017), 265–78.

'olvido.'[8] In Borges's sonnet, both words occur as part of a whole series of rhymes evoking a theme of loss: 'perdido,' 'olvido,' 'borrado,' 'passado.' Not insignificantly, however, – and, in a sense, just like Milton's epic – Borges's poem is about bringing back (to existence from extinction, to the present from the past, to memory from oblivion) and making whole again.

On a structural level, Borges's repeated use of run-on lines to create a drastic effect (as in '… que Milton acercó a su cara/*sin verla.*' – a typically Miltonic line break) and equivocation (red or yellow or white; gold or blood or ivory or shadowy) hark back to two of Milton's own favourite devices. The grand historical sweep of Borges's fourteen lines – including the deep past of 'many generations' ('en el fondo del tiempo') as well as the 'pasado/inmemorial' attributed to the rose – also gives the sonnet a flair distinctly reminiscent of the wide temporal expanse of *Paradise Lost*.

In Borges's original Spanish, the 'rosa' Milton is holding close to his face in the imaginary scene of the sonnet is inevitably gendered as female: *la rosa*. This, together with a number of other aspects of the poem, reinforces the impression that we are told of an encounter not between a man and an imaginary flower but between two persons, quite possibly lovers. Borges's poem, again, is a sonnet, and thus connected by association to the love-poem tradition of that genre. It is entitled not 'La rosa de Milton' – 'Milton's Rose' – but rather, 'Una rosa y Milton,' suggesting personification and a strong focus on the 'person' of the rose. Apart from Borges's Milton cradling the rose carefully 'in his [two] hands' and 'close to his face,' the love theme is supported by an ambiguity – admittedly hard to avoid – in the speaker's expression of his desire that *one* rose, at least, be saved from oblivion: 'quiero' ('I want'/'I love').

Still, for all the markers of romantic love in Borges's poem, there is also a dark undercurrent: its imaginary Milton *was* blind when he held the elusive rose which, in one of the several alternatives named, is characterised as 'tenebrosa' – 'shadowy', that is, 'dark' or 'gloomy.' Other elements of the poem's sensory discourse, too, are at least potentially negative: the rose is silent, and it is, ultimately, invisible. Nevertheless, it is ordered by Borges's poet-speaker to 'shine in this verse' (the speaker *knows* he is operating within a poem; this makes him a 'poet-speaker'). Milton's last rose is a rose of the mind, existing only through and in poetry. Borges himself addresses the creative power of the poetic speech act: 'El destino me depara/este don de *nombrar por vez primera/esa flor silenciosa* …' – the flower may be silent, but the poet is not. By the power vested in his 'destined' role of *agent évocateur* – as the speaker's self-image could be described –, he summons a rose that is supremely indeterminate into his (and our) presence: truly a feat of magic ('magicamente'). The rose is indeterminate, first, because it is 'sin marca o signo,' just one among many (the reverse of its purity); it is also hard to pinpoint in any historically definite sense (although surely *some* rose must have been the last Milton ever held close to his face?); and it carries all the colours, and hence, none (at that, the movement of Borges's enumeration from red through yellow to white underlines the rose's stronger association with unmarked purity than with carnal or bloody redness).

The rose of Borges's Milton is – or rather, it could be, and thus it is – all of these things at once. It is 'inmemorial' not only because it is supposedly old but also because,

---

[8] In a passage describing the devils' march toward oblivion in book 2, 'En un rincon del Reyno del olvido' – in some corner of the kingdom of oblivion.

ultimately, it only exists 'en este verso.' Its fictionality is the mirror-image of Milton's blindness: to him, it is invisible and thus indeterminate because he cannot see; to us, this indeterminacy is created by the art of the poet. Borges's poet-speaker is a creator and namer in the present – he 'is given this present of naming' *now* –, and he creates a paradoxical presence of the invisible, leading the poem as a whole to oscillate between presence and absence.[9] The discursive space in which this paradox plays out is, of course, the sensory discourse of the sonnet, and nowhere does this become clearer than in its final line, fraught with the tension between haptic materiality and invisible immateriality: '... como *en sus manos, invisible* rosa.'[10]

In being both concrete – 'as once *in his hands*' – and timeless, eternal, and abstract, Borges's rose (just like Milton's Amor in Elegy VII) is a symbol in the Coleridgean sense.[11] The strong sensory discourse of the sonnet, which involves all the senses except for taste, thus omits precisely the one sense opposed to the rose's purity (which is not a given if we recall the sensory discourse of *Paradise Lost*, where roses hover ambiguously between innocence and temptation).[12] All elements of the sonnet's sensory discourse considered – its references to roses and gardens, its invocation, its lexical and structural Miltonisms –, Borges arrives at a striking appropriation of the Miltonic sensorium in his homage to Milton.

Eugène Delacroix, 'Milton Dictating "Paradise Lost" to His Daughters' (1827/28?)

Miltonic sensory discourse has also left its traces in the iconographic tradition surrounding Milton, his life, and his work. This is particularly striking in the case of a painting by Eugène Delacroix (1798–1863), originally titled *Milton et ses filles ou Milton dictant le Paradis Perdu à ses filles* (i.e., 'Milton and his daughters or Milton dictating *Paradise Lost* to his daughters'). This scene was a standard of Milton iconography, and has been depicted dozens of times in paintings and engravings, most often in the eighteenth and nineteenth centuries. Typically, we see an earnest Milton, clad in 'Puritan' dress, sitting in a chair, gazing into space, while two of his three daughters sit by and jot down their

---

[9] Borges's description of the rose as 'bermeja' (literally, 'reddish,' but in some usages, 'matchless, unique') may additionally allude to the Isla Bermeja, a phantom island supposedly located in the Gulf of Mexico.

[10] The kind of haptic/manual tenderness suggested by Borges's description is reserved, in *Paradise Lost*, to Adam and Eve, who are repeatedly depicted as 'handed' (*PL* 4.739), most poignantly at their expulsion from Paradise: 'They *hand in hand* with wandering steps and slow,/Through Eden took their solitary way' (*PL* 12.648–49, emphasis added). See also Moshenska, *Feeling Pleasures*, 259, who points out that Milton's description of the first couple holding hands is actually quite unusual considering the iconographic tradition; his insistence on the point should thus be given particular attention.

[11] See, again, Wellek/Warren, *Theory of Literature*, 189, and Chapter 3.3 above.

[12] Contrast, for instance, *PL* 9.218 (Eve announces she will go to work on her own 'in yonder spring of roses') and *PL* 9.420–27 (Satan espies Eve 'veiled in a cloud of fragrance ... so thick the roses blushing round/About her glowed') with Adam's reaction to news of Eve's transgression at *PL* 9.888–93: '... soon as he heard/The fatal trespass done by Eve, amazed,/Astonied stood and blank ... / ... /From his slack hand the garland wreathed for Eve/Down dropped, and all the faded roses shed ...'

father's 'unpremeditated verse.' Milton and the composition of *Paradise* Lost have thus themselves become part of visual culture.

Remarkably enough, however, the strongest documentary-biographical piece of evidence for any such scene involving Milton's daughters does not mention writing at all. Instead, Milton's nephew Edward Phillips remembers the daughters' demanding regime of *reading* to their blind father:

> [Milton's two younger daughters] were Condemn'd to the performance of Reading, and exactly pronouncing of all the Languages of whatever Book he should at one time or other think fit to peruse; *Viz.* The *Hebrew* (and I think the *Syriac*), the *Greek*, the *Latin*, the *Italian*, *Spanish*, and *French*. All which sorts of Books to be confined to Read, without understanding one word, must needs be a Tryal of Patience, almost beyond endurance; yet it was endured by both for a long time; yet the irksomeness of this imployment could not always be concealed, but broke out more and more into expressions of uneasiness.[13]

'Exactly pronouncing ... all the Languages' Milton needed for his far-reaching studies – and not understanding a word of their very own 'performance of Reading' – Milton's daughters were reduced to mere voices. The writing, on the other hand, was done by a succession of (typically male) amanuenses, often former pupils of Milton's.[14] One possible incentive for conflating these two distinct aspects of Milton's work routine – apart from the fact, perhaps, that the poet dictating to his *daughters* instead of 'random strangers' made for a more stirring subject – might be the shared close similarity between the daughters' voicing 'performance of Reading, and exactly pronouncing' *and* the amanuenses' recording, on the one hand, and the scenes of night-time inspiration evoked in the proems of *Paradise Lost* itself, on the other. As Milton's 'heavenly Muse' is female and is characterised by her inspiring voice, she resembles his daughters' 'performance of Reading'; as she is associated with the composition and recording of the epic, she relates to the amanuenses. In the end, it appears only consistent to cast Milton's two younger daughters in the joint role of co-muses opposite their father.

In Delacroix's painting (Fig. 6), we see Milton slightly right of centre, dressed in the black-and-white habit of the stereotypical Puritan, seated in an upholstered chair by a table. Two of his daughters are seated to his right (i.e., in the left half of the painting). Their confrontation is clear: the daughters share the left half, while Milton himself

---

[13] Phillips quoted in *Early Lives*, ed. Darbishire, 77. See also the discussion by Lewalski, *Life of John Milton*, 407–409.

[14] See Lewalski, *Life of John Milton*, 320, 398, 415–16, 442, 448, 450. Cyriack Skinner records in his *Life* of Milton (traditionally attributed to Milton's nephew John Phillips, Edward's brother) that 'the Youths that hee instructed from time to time servd him often as Amanuenses, & some elderly persons were glad for the benefit of his learned Conversation, to perform that Office' (*Early Lives*, ed. Darbishire, 33). Again, there is no mention of Milton's daughters taking dictation from their father.

Fig. 6: Eugène Delacroix, *Milton Dictating 'Paradise Lost' to His Daughters* (1827/28). Source: Kunsthaus Zürich.

governs the right half of the painting. The poet's long hair contrasts, to some extent, with the severity of his clothing, as do the warm blanket on his knees, the red slippers on his feet, and the sumptuous carpet spread out over the table, on which a bouquet of flowers can be seen. Even at first glance, the scene can be characterised as markedly sensuous. Milton is turning his face from the daughter seated closer to him, who is taking his dictation, a look of eager expectation on her face (and, in particular, in her one visible eye, which is wide open and directed intently at her father); Milton's own eyes are closed and his head tilted slightly upwards in the typical posture of the blind seer.[15] More pronouncedly, however, it is turned to the side, as if he were listening intently to some sound source outside the image frame, at the same time exposing the poet's right ear to the beholder's view. Appropriately enough, the second daughter is seated off to the side of the image, holding a musical instrument suggestive of the poet's 'song.'

What moved Delacroix to paint this scene, and to paint it the way he did? Milton's own sensory discourse might be part of the answer. In the first half of the 1820s, two new editions of translations of *Paradise Lost* were published in France.[16] One of them included a French translation of one of the essays on Milton by Joseph Addison, whose works Delacroix is known to have been reading at the beginning of the decade; hence, perhaps, his interest in the subject now. Delacroix, who had spent some time in England, had, in any case, acquired a thorough familiarity with Milton's epic, which he read in the original.

Moreover, several pictorial precedents of the same scene could have been known to Delacroix in reproduction, among them Fuseli's treatment of the same subject (1793, Fig. 7) and another, quite different version by George Romney. The Belgian painter Henri Decaisne had even exhibited his painting *Milton* (showing the poet dictating to his daughters in an *outdoor* scene, see Fig. 8) at the same salon at which Delacroix had presented his *indoor* version. Despite their differences in setting, the two paintings share a number of parallels that make it appear likely – on chronological grounds – that Delacroix was, in fact, influenced by Decaisne's work.

Nevertheless, Delacroix's rendering of the much-depicted scene stands out for its conspicuous attention to the sensory sphere. According to the art historian and leading scholar of Delacroix, Lee Johnson, his version

> is outstanding for its *naturalism* and sensitive interpretation of the scene without dramatic exaggeration. Milton's blindness is not only expressed by his unseeing eyes, but implied in the suggestion of the senses he can still enjoy: touch, by the hand on the rich Turkish carpet covering the table; smell, by the flowers, hearing, by the mandolin held by his daughter. Unlike Fuseli, Delacroix conveys by purely pictorial means an idea of the work Milton is dictating, by placing on the wall a picture of the *Expulsion of Adam and Eve from Paradise*, derived from Raphael's fresco in the Vatican Loggia.[17]

---

[15] See Barasch, *Blindness*, 42–43, on the conflict between blindness/darkness and 'a drive toward light, vision, and desire for life' often expressed by this posture.

[16] See Lee Johnson, *The Paintings of Eugène Delacroix: A Critical Catalogue. 1816–1831. Volume I. Text* (Oxford: Clarendon, 1981), 123. For the following see Johnson's account where no more specific reference is given.

[17] Johnson, *Paintings of Eugène Delacroix*, 124.

Fig. 7: Henry Fuseli, *Milton Dictating to His Daughter* (1793).
   Source: Wikimedia Commons.

Fig. 8: L. Noel after H. Decaisne, *Milton* (1830?).
Source: Wikimedia Commons.

Johnson's list suggests that Delacroix – different in this respect from all other treatments of the subject I have seen – intended to convey, through the visual medium of painting, a multi-sensory impression of what Milton (and *Paradise Lost*) – were 'all about.' In other words: he wanted give a painted impression of Milton's sensory discourse.

That this is indeed an adequate description of Delacroix's pictorial agenda becomes even more likely if we consider the ways in which his representation conforms to the sensory discourse of *Paradise Lost* itself: Delacroix is not just following the conventional iconography of the senses (e.g., 'a stringed instrument stands for music and hence for hearing');[18] through his depiction, he is actively engaging with Miltonic sensory discourse. Apart from his close attention to the interplay of the senses in the moment of inspiration and dictation – Milton is listening to the Muse and gazing inwardly, as described in the proems; the writing daughter is listening and keeping an alert eye on her dictating father –,[19] Delacroix not only incorporates the sensory modes listed by Johnson, but also uses directed lighting to further emphasise particular aspects. Several elements of the composition stand out and/or appear to be emphasised by a ray of light entering the image frame from top right (Milton's 'holy light'?): the attentive face and eye of the writing daughter; the book at her feet (a finished volume of the poem?) and the one into which she is busy writing; Milton's forehead and hand; and a rose which appears to be sticking out from the bouquet on the table. As in Borges's sonnet, this rose may easily be identified with the 'summer's rose' mentioned in Proem III of *Paradise Lost*. Significantly, the writing daughter appears to be wearing another rose bloom for a brooch, so that Milton, seated between the table and his daughter, is framed on both sides by corresponding roses.

In addition to this combination of different sensory modes with several instances of 'Miltonically charged' sensory symbolism (e.g., the ray of light, the roses), Delacroix quite obviously alludes to the accounts given of Milton's habits of composition both in his early biographies and in *Paradise Lost* itself. As Lewalski paraphrases Aubrey's biographical sketch of Milton, he 'usually rose at four or five in the morning [and] liked first to have the Hebrew Bible read to him …'[20] The 'nightly visitation' of the Muse thus segued right into the morning duties of his daughters and amanuenses. Furthermore, according to his nephew and widow, Milton 'worked on *Paradise Lost* chiefly during the winter months': 'his Vein never happily flow'd, but from the *Autumnal Equinoctial* to the *Vernal* …'[21] Delacroix, who is perhaps also thinking of Milton's apprehension, stated in Proem IX, that too 'cold/[a] Climate' might 'damp [his] intended wing/Depressed' (*PL* 9.44–46), translates these elements of Milton's life world (*and* authorial self-representation) into a four-poster bed in the background, a substantial blanket on the poet's lap, and a pair of warm red slippers. In Delacroix's representation of the Miltonic sensorium, the sensorial is domestic – but at the same time it points to the more abstract

---

[18] For examples of this kind of iconography, see Carl Nordenfalk's essays, 'The Five Senses in Late Medieval and Renaissance Art' and 'The Five Senses in Flemish Art before 1600,' as well as Vinge, *The Five Senses*.
[19] 'Milton,' John Hale reminds us, 'composed out loud' (*Milton's Languages*, 132).
[20] Lewalski, *Life of John Milton,* 411; cf. *Early Lives,* ed. Darbishire, 6.
[21] Lewalski, *Life of John Milton*, 411; *Early Lives*, ed. Darbishire, 73. See also Lewalski, *Life of John Milton*, 448, and *Early Lives*, ed. Darbishire, 33.

realm of inspired hearing, inner vision, and sensory symbolism. This encapsulates, again, the twofold nature of sensory discourse as illustrative (or mundane) and deliberative (or transcendental).

At the exhibition at which Delacroix first presented *Milton Dictating 'Paradise Lost' to His Daughters*, 'the painting attracted little notice from the Salon reviewers. Those who did mention it were brief but complimentary.'[22] Perhaps the artist had been aiming a little too closely at a 'fit audience', familiar with the reference points of Miltonic sensory discourse.

Jamie McKendrick, 'Earscape' (2016)

For a third and final example of how Milton's sensory discourse has been taken up by later artists, I would like to turn briefly to the very recent past. In his poem 'Earscape,' whose title already suggests a conceptual proximity to sensory-studies notions such as 'sensescapes,' 'soundscapes,' or 'viewscapes,' the contemporary English poet Jamie McKendrick (b. 1955) superimposes Miltonic sensory discourse onto a slice of socio-economic history.

> *Earscape*
>
> Milton lost his sight in libertyes defence
> and I my hearing in oyles pursuit employed
> by factors who failed to plug our ears with down
> I was the fuse-and-dynamite boy who blew
> up bits of Derbyshire with blasts that lunged
> through the earth's crust barrelling out below
> to stun the blind mole in its burrow and
> bend the funicles of beetles antennae
> so now alone or in a crowd I hear
> the tinny thrum of protest from the earth
> a stridulating bug-eyed orchestra
> in the cellar of the battered dandelion
> and out in the air beyond our telescopes
> the admonition of a blackened star[23]
>
> *Jamie McKendrick*

Where Borges's sonnet had been focused primarily on the visual sphere, and Delacroix's painting had represented the interplay of hearing and vision in the moment of inspiration, McKendrick turns to hearing – though not without also referencing vision. In the opening lines of his poem, the allusion to Milton's Sonnet 22, dedicated 'To Mr Cyriack Skinner

---

[22] Johnson, *Paintings of Eugène Delacroix*, 126.
[23] Jamie McKendrick, *Anomaly* (London: Faber & Faber, 2018), 6. 'Earscape' was first published in the *London Review of Books* (21 April 2016). The reading 'beetles' in line 8 (no apostrophe) is given in all published versions of the poem.

Upon his Blindness' ('... these eyes .../Bereft of light their seeing have forgot ... / [I have] lost them overplied/*In liberty's defence*, my noble task ...'), as well as McKendrick's archaising orthography and inversions strike up a contrast between 'old language' – including some at least 'Miltonesque' usages such as 'in oyles pursuit employed' – and 'lived experience,' while at the same time establishing a connection to Milton's sensory discourse. Some of McKendrick's lines (fourteen lines, as in a sonnet) are perfectly regular blank verse, most feature drastic line-breaks; both aspects contribute to a distinct 'Miltonic feel' throughout the poem.

Apart from this, however, 'Earscape' is like a kaleidoscope in which fragments – blasting debris? – from different sources, Miltonic or otherwise, are reassembled. (Indeed, when McKendrick has his speaker recollect '[blowing]/up bits of Derbyshire,' he may also be thinking of Helen Darbishire, noted Milton scholar and editor not only of the *Early Lives* but also of what, for much of the twentieth century, was the most commonly referenced edition of Milton's poetry.) In the uppermost stratum of its polyphonic structure, 'Earscape' is the dramatic monologue, fittingly rendered in a somewhat wobbly kind of blank verse, of an early-twentieth-century 'fuse-and-dynamite boy' who has grown up, by all indications, to be a near-deaf poet. However, whereas Milton had sacrificed his vision for a 'noble' cause – namely, the defence of liberty –, the hearing-impaired speaker of McKendrick's poem was exploited for commercial gain in the extraction of fossil oil at the dawn of the petroleum age. In fact, McKendrick's reference is quite specific, as he is alluding to the circumstance that Britain's very first oilfield was, in fact, not located far out in the North Sea but onshore, in Derbyshire. Between 1911 and 1919, successive British governments aimed to reduce Britain's dependency on imported oil as a military-economic policy goal:

> In 1911, Winston Churchill was appointed First Lord of the Admiralty, and during his time in office he took the strategic decision to power British Naval ships with oil and phase out the use of coal. It was a strategic decision based upon improving the performance of the naval fleet. It worked and during the First World War the Royal Navy outperformed their German counterparts. However, Britain relied on importing oil from its colonies and dependencies with Trinidad and Persia supplying the lion's share. This made the UK vulnerable and as a consequence the search was on for an indigenous oil supply. The U.K. government issued a contract to drill 6 wells in Derbyshire, Staffordshire, and Scotland.
> ...
> The first well to be drilled was at Hardstoft in the parish of Tibshelf in the county of Derbyshire. 'Oil in quantity was struck in Hardstoft No 1 well of May 27th, 1919' ...[24]

This first oil field in Derbyshire is the one for which McKendrick's speaker lost his hearing. It was drilled as part of the British war effort in World War I. This military background resonates in the action of '[blowing]/up bits of Derbyshire with blasts/that

---

[24] Abstract for Jonathan Craig et al., 'Hardstoft – Britain's First Oil Field,' <http://www.searchanddiscovery.com/abstracts/html/2015/90216ace/abstracts/2099231.html> (last accessed 20 June 2019).

lunged/through the earth's crust,' which evokes the trench warfare of the Western front (and the poetry written about it by English poets). However, it also connects to McKendrick's ambiguous phrase, 'barrelling out below,' which alludes, at the same time, to the barrel of an artillery gun and the barrels into which the oil is filled. The 'cognates' of these images in Miltonic sensory discourse can be found in the combined mining, punning, and (artillery) warfare of the war in heaven in books 5 and 6 of *Paradise Lost*.

Milton only refers to 'ambrosial oils' in *Comus* (839),[25] but in *Paradise Lost*, both the 'bituminous lake where Sodom flamed' and the 'black bituminous gorge/Boil[ing] out from underground, the mouth of hell …' (which enables the construction of the Tower of Babel) are presented as places of negativity, obnoxious to the senses.[26] Much like the devils' sacrilegious digging in *Paradise Lost*, the blowing open of the first oil well recalled in 'Earscape' presents a kind of original sin, an irreparable transgression against nature. The present-day relevance of this becomes clear if we call to mind current debates in the United Kingdom about the more recent extraction method of hydraulic fracturing ('fracking'). As Derbyshire County Council, apparently not a disinterested party in the debate over fracking, explains on its web site,

> Derbyshire has a long and varied history of quarrying and mining. It has significant reserves of oil and gas from unconventional sources like coal bed methane and shale gas.
> … Fracking has never been carried out in Derbyshire but private companies licensed by the Oil and Gas Authority are investigating the potential for carrying out this process commercially in Derbyshire.
> The fracking process involves drilling deep into the ground and injecting water, sand and chemicals at high pressure to create tiny cracks or fractures. Shale gas can then flow up a well to the surface and be collected. …[27]

By addressing this controversial present-day topic via a 'historical detour' *and* connecting it to Miltonic sensory discourse, McKendrick places his poem squarely in the tradition focusing on Milton as, above all, a political writer and a champion of individual rights. It is not entirely coincidental, I think, that this is also the tradition which produced Blake's protest (in his epic poem, *Milton*!) against the 'dark Satanic Mills' of the Industrial Revolution, as well as Wordsworth's 'London 1802' ('Milton, thou shouldst be living at this hour,/England hath need of thee! She is a fen/Of stagnant waters …').[28] McKendrick's is a more indirect tone of admonition, but that his poem is indeed carried by an admonitory

---

[25] At Sabrina's transformation into a nymph: '… And through the porch and inlet of each sense/Dropped in ambrosial oils till she revived,/And underwent a quick immortal change …' By attributing life-giving powers to these oils, Milton inverts the Shakespearean echo of '… and in the porches of mine ears did pour …' (*Hamlet,* 1.5.63–64).
[26] *PL* 10.562, 12.41–42.
[27] Derbyshire County Council, 'Shale gas and hydraulic fracturing (fracking),' <https://www.derbyshire.gov.uk/environment/planning/planning-policy/minerals-waste-development-framework/shale-gas/shale-gas-and-hydraulic-fracturing-fracking.aspx> (last accessed 20 June 2019).
[28] Blake and Wordsworth both quoted from *Romanticism*, ed. Wu.

thrust is finally made explicit in its last line: the more impersonal, mute 'admonition of a blackened star' – a darkened view of the sun, seen 'beyond [the reach of] our telescopes' through the smoke-filled atmosphere – assumes the admonishing role once filled by the likes of Milton, Blake, or Wordsworth, poet-prophets appealing to the consciences of all who (still) have ears to hear. Seen in the context of these poetical-political lineages, McKendrick's dynamite boy figures as a (slightly) more modern version of the Blakean chimney sweep: exploited and broken by neglect (his ears could have been plugged), his hearing reduced to, at best, 'the tinny thrum of protest from the earth'.[29]

Apart from the strangely impersonal 'factors' (i.e., managers, but also 'circumstances') responsible for the speaker's impairment, the only other living beings in the poem are animals harmed – 'stunned,' 'ben[t]' – by the exploding dynamite. They both serve as sensory counterparts to the speaker: the 'blind mole in its burrow,' too, is pushing forward into the ground, but this is his natural habitat; his 'impairment' – his blindness – really is a form of adaptation and specialisation. Considering the reference to Milton's blindness in the first line – and contemporary attacks on Milton as a 'blind beetle' etc. – McKendrick's animal imagery should be seen as contributing to the distinctly Miltonic sensory discourse of his poem. In fact, the 'ben[t] funicles of beetles antennae' are about as far from the human sensorium as one can go without leaving the confines of sensory discourse altogether – as McKendrick demonstrates, sensory discourse may not only be botanical (instead of flowery); it may also be entomological (instead of immediately relatable).

In his multi-sensory references to 'a stridulating bug-eyed orchestra,'[30] McKendrick moves further in this direction of sensory alienation. These are strange senses – beetles' bug-eyes and antennae –, strange perceptions – their stridulating – McKendrick is evoking; Milton's blindness, by comparison, is readily accessible to the imagination. His punning on two obsolete meanings of 'crowd,' however, is downright Miltonic: one of them is sensory/auditory, the other refers to underground caverns – both, therefore, relate to earlier (sensory) references in the poem.[31]

Ultimately, the sensory discourse of 'Earscape' has more in common with the indignant Milton of the polemical prose – or perhaps with the sardonic descriptions and heavy punning of the war in heaven of *Paradise Lost* – than with the multi-sensory discourse of Milton's spring scenes, for example. In the eco-critical mode of his sensory discourse, McKendrick demonstrates that the senses – any senses, even the 'tinny thrum' filling the ears of the former dynamite boy and even the antennae of 'a stridulating bug-eyed orchestra' – are important in dealing with the lived-in environment (which becomes 'the Environment' only as it begins to collapse). Sensescapes are landscapes and vice versa,

---

[29] While an association of 'ear drum' is likely intended, there might be a further allusion here to Günter Grass's novel *The Tin Drum* and its stubborn boy-hero Oskar Matzerath, whom Grass, incidentally, characterises as *hellhörig* – 'keen-eared'.
[30] *OED*, 'stridulate, v.': 'to make a harsh, grating, shrill noise: said spec. of certain insects'; last attested 1895.
[31] *OED*, 'crowd, n.¹': 'an ancient Celtic musical instrument of the viol class, now obsolete … hence, a fiddle (still dialect); 'crowd, n.²': 'an underground vault, a crypt,' matching the 'cellar of the battered dandelion.'

whether they are filled with a variety of beautiful flowers or have only 'battered dandelion[s]' to offer.

'Earscape' is many things – a history poem, a political poem – but at bottom, it is a piece of war poetry: a poem about oil being needed for wars and about wars fought over oil; a poem about how the 'pity of war' (Wilfred Owen) exists in close parallel with the pity of getting pressed to ruin one's health, 'in oyles pursuit' or on account of some other 'factors.'

Drilling Deep: The After-Images and Echoes of Miltonic Sensory Discourse

Comparing Milton's own sensory discourse with the Miltonic sensory discourse of Borges and McKendrick, it is striking how the 'Other' of perception changes. In Milton, this clearly belongs in the realm of transcendence: God is the one who 'dazzles,' who causes Adam's senses to overload. In Borges, this elusiveness shifts toward history – his rose is transcendent, but it also comes from 'deep in time' ('el fondo del tiempo … inmemorial'). McKendrick's perspective is thoroughly historical, addressing the overlying strata of history and evolution within anthropocenic, geological, and, finally, cosmic timeframes. Is it really a coincidence that both poems considered in this epilogue use Miltonic sensory discourse to probe the past – in a temporal and even in the spatial sense of orientational metaphor, reaching for 'el fondo del tiempo' or drilling for oil? If this constitutes a kind of 'archaeology of the senses' along the lines suggested by Foucault, it could also be seen as a historicism they both share with Delacroix. Taking up the reception history introduced in the Prologue above, these three further examples of how the Miltonic sensorium has been appropriated by later artists suggest to me that there is simply something about the transitoriness of sense perception that makes us humans want to *delve into* its 'deep past' and explore the infinitely various historical expressions of the malleable, yet always recognisable, human sensorium.

Bibliography

Abbreviations

CPW	Milton, *Complete Prose Works* (Yale)
CW	Milton, *The Works* (Columbia)
ELH	*English Literary History*
ELR	*English Literary Renaissance*
Frisk	H. Frisk, *Griechisches etymologisches Wörterbuch* (3 vols, Heidelberg)
HALOT	Koehler–Baumgartner, *The Hebrew and Aramaic Lexicon of the Old Testament* (2 vols, Leiden)
HEI	*History of European Ideas*
JHI	*Journal of the History of Ideas*
JBL	*Journal of Biblical Literature*
KJV	King James Bible (Authorised Version)
KR	*The Kentucky Review*
LSJ	Liddell–Scott–Jones, *A Greek-English Lexicon* (Oxford)
M&L	*Mind & Language*
MLQ	*Modern Language Quarterly*
MQ	*Milton Quarterly*
MS	*Milton Studies*
ODNB	*Oxford Dictionary of National Biography*
OED	*Oxford English Dictionary* (on-line)
OLD	*Oxford Latin Dictionary* (1968 ed.)
PL	Milton, *Paradise Lost*
PR	Milton, *Paradise Regained*
PQ	*Philological Quarterly*
RBPH	*Revue belge de Philologie et d'Histoire*
R&R	*Renaissance and Reformation / Renaissance et Réforme*
SA	Milton, *Samson Agonistes*
SIP	*Studies in Philology*
SP	Milton, *Complete Shorter Poems* (2007)

Milton

Epistolarum Familiarum Liber Unus ... (London: Brabazon Aylmer, 'sub Signo Trium Columbarum,' 1674).
Complete Prose Works of John Milton, gen. ed. Don. M. Wolfe, 8 vols (New Haven, Conn.: Yale University Press, 1953–1982).
    Vol. 1: 1624–1642.
    Vol. 2: 1643–1648.
    Vol. 3: 1648–1649.
    Vol. 4,1: 1650–1655.
    Vol. 4,2: 1650–1655.
    Vol. 5,1: 1648?–1671.
    Vol. 5,2: 1649–1659.
    Vol. 6: c.1658–c.1660.
    Vol. 7: 1659–1660.
    Vol. 8: 1666–1682.
Complete Shorter Poems, ed. John Carey, 2nd ed. (Harlow: Longman, 1997 [1968]).
The Life Records of John Milton, ed. J. Milton French, 5 vols (New Brunswick, N. J.: Rutgers University Press, 1949–1958)
Paradise Lost, ed. Alastair Fowler, 2nd ed. (Harlow: Longman, 2007 [1968]).
Paradise Lost, ed. Jonathan Goldberg/Stephen Orgel (Oxford: Oxford University Press, 2004)
Poems of Mr. John Milton, both English and Latin, Compos'd at several times ... (London: Ruth Raworth for Humphrey Moseley, 1645)
A Variorum Commentary on the Poems of John Milton, vol. 1: The Latin and Greek Poems, ed. Douglas Bush (London: Routledge & Paul, 1970).
The Works of John Milton, gen. ed. Frank A. Patterson, 18 vols (New York: Columbia University Press, 1931–1940).

Other Primary References

Aristotle, *The 'Art' of Rhetoric*, tr. J. H. Freese (Cambridge, Mass.: Harvard University Press, 2006 [1926]).
Aristotle, *On the Soul. Parva Naturalia. On Breath*, tr. W. S. Hett (Cambridge, Mass.: Harvard University Press, 1957).
Aristotle, *Poetics*, ed. and tr. Stephen Halliwell (Cambridge, Mass.: Harvard University Press, 1999).
Bacon, Francis, *The Essayes or Counsels, Civill and Morall*, ed. Michael Kiernan (Oxford: Clarendon, 2000).
Bacon, Francis, *Sylva Sylvarum: or A Natural History, in Ten Centuries* (London: Printed by S. G. ... for Thomas Lee ..., 1677).
Borges, Jorge Luis, *Poesía completa*, 4th ed. (Buenos Aires: Delbolsillo, 2016 [2013)].
Browne, Thomas, *Pseudodoxia Epidemica: Books I–VII*, ed. Geoffrey Keynes (London: Faber & Faber, 1964).
Browne, Thomas, *Religio Medici and Other Works*, ed. L. C. Martin (Oxford: Clarendon, 1964).
Bunyan, John, *The Holy War, made by Shaddai upon Diabolus, for the Regaining of the Metropolis of the World, or, the Losing and Taking Again of the Town of Mansoul* (London: Printed for Dorman Newman, 1682).
Burton, Robert, *The Anatomy of Melancholy*, ed. Holbrook Jackson (London: Dent, 1977 [1621]).

Butler, Samuel, *Characters*, ed. Charles W. Daves (Cleveland, Ohio: P of Case Western U, 1970 [1659]).
Earle, John, *Micro-cosmographie: Or, A Peece of the World Discovered (1628)*, ed. and tr. Alexander Eilers (Würzburg: Königshausen & Neumann, 2018).
Evelyn, John, *The Diary of John Evelyn*, ed. E. S. de Beer (London: Oxford University Press, 1959).
[Iohn Florio,] *Queen Anna's New World of Words, or Dictionarie of the Italian and English tongues* ... (Melch. Bradwood for Edw. Blount and William Barrett, 1611)
The Great Cures and Strange Miracles, Performed by Mr. Valentine Gertrux [sic] ... (London: Printed for John Thomas, 1666).
Helen Darbishire (ed.), *The Early Lives of Milton* (London: Constable, 1965 [1932]).
Dingley, Robert, *The Spirituall Taste Described; and a Glimpse of Christ Discovered. In two Parts; grounded on Psal. 34.8. and Malac. 4.2.* (London: Matthew Simmons, 1649).
Donno, Elizabeth Story (ed.), *Andrew Marvell: The Critical Heritage* (London: Routledge, 1995 [1978]).
Hartley, L. P., *The Go-Between* (London: Hamilton, 1961).
Herbert of Cherbury, Edward Lord, *De Veritate*, ed. Günter Gawlick (Stuttgart: Frommann-Holzboog, 1966).
Hobbes, Thomas, *Hobbes's Leviathan: Reprinted from the Edition of 1651* (Oxford: Clarendon, 1958).
Hobbes, Thomas, *The English Works of Thomas Hobbes of Malmsbury*, ed. Sir William Molesworth (London: John Bohn, 1839–1845).
Hooke, Robert, *Micrographia: or some Physiological Descriptions of Minute Bodies made by Magnifying Glasses with Observations and Inquiries thereupon* (London: J. Martyn and J. Allestry, 1665).
Johnson, Samuel, *Lives of the English Poets*, 2 vols [London: Oxford University Press, 1961].
Johnson, Samuel, *A dictionary of the English language* ... 2 vols (London: W. Strahan for J. and P. Knapton, 1755).
Locke, John, *An Essay Concerning Human Understanding*, ed. Peter H. Nidditch (Oxford: Clarendon, 1979 [1975]).
Orphei Hymni, ed. Guilelmus Quandt (Berlin: Weidmann, 1962).
Mann, Thomas, *The Magic Mountain*, tr. John E. Woods (New York: Knopf, 1995 [1924]).
McKendrick, Jamie, *Anomaly* (London: Faber & Faber, 2018).
Ovid's 'Metamorphoses,' tr. Arthur Golding [1567] (Baltimore, Md.: Johns Hopkins University Press, 2002).
Parker, Samuel, *A Free and Impartial Censure of the Platonick Philosophie* ... (Oxford: W. Hall for Richard Davis, 1666).
Parkinson, John, *Paradisi in Sole Paradisus Terrestris. Or a Garden of All Sorts of Pleasant Flowers* ... (London, 1629).
Pepys, Samuel, *The Diary of Samuel Pepys*, ed. Robert Latham, 11 vols (London: Bell, 1971–1983).
Phillips, Edward, *The New World of English Words: Or, a General Dictionary: Containing the Interpretations of such words as are derived from other Languages* ... (London: E. Tyler for Nath. Brooke, 1658).
Plutarch, *Moralia, vol. IX: Table-talk, Books 7–9. Dialogue on Love*, trs E. L. Minar, F. H. Sandbach, W. C. Helmbold (Cambridge, Mass.: Harvard University Press, 1961).
Roberts, Lewes, *The Merchants Mappe of Commerce wherein, the universall manner and matter of trade, is compendiously handled* ... (London: R. O. for Ralph Mabb, 1638).
Shakespeare, William, *The Norton Shakespeare*, eds Stephen Greenblatt et al., 2nd ed. (New York: W. W. Norton, 2008).

Shawcross, John T. (ed.), *Milton: The Critical Heritage* (London: Routledge & Kegan Paul, 1970).
Sprat, Thomas, *The History of the Royal-Society of London, For the Improving of Natural Knowledge* (London: Printed by T. R. for J. Martyn, 1667).
The Transproser Rehears'd: or the Fifth Act of Mr. Bayes's Play. Being a Postscript to the Animadversions on the Preface to Bishop Bramhall's Vindication, &c. Shewing What Grounds there are of Fears and Jealousies of Popery. (Oxford: 'Printed for ... *Hugo Grotius*, and *Jacob Van Harmine*, on the North-side of the Lake-*Lemane*,' 1673).
Wood, Anthony à, *Athenæ Oxonienses: An Exact History of all the Writers and Bishops who Have their Education in the University of Oxford to which Are Added The Fasti or Annals of the Said University*, 4 vols (New York: Johnson Reprint Corporation, 1967 [1691–92]).
Wu, Duncan (ed.), *Romanticism: An Anthology*, 4th ed. (Chichester: Wiley-Blackwell, 2012).

Secondary References

Abrams, M. H., *The Mirror and the Lamp: Romantic Theory and the Critical Tradition* (New York: Norton, 1958).
Achinstein, Sharon, 'Milton's Spectre in the Restoration: Marvell, Dryden, and Literary Enthusiasm,' *HLQ* 59 (1996), 1–29.
Anderson, Judith H., *Light and Death: Figuration in Spenser, Kepler, Donne, Milton* (New York: Fordham University Press, 2017).
Atkinson, Niall, 'The Social Life of the Senses: Architecture, Food, and Manners,' in: *Cultural History of the Senses in the Renaissance*, ed. Roodenburg, 19–42.
Ausoni, Alberto, *Music in Art*, tr. Stephen Sartarelli (Los Angeles: J. Paul Getty Museum, 2009).
Avrahami, Yael, *The Senses of Scripture: Sensory Perception in the Hebrew Bible* (New York: T&T Clark, 2012).
Barasch, Moshe, *Blindness: The History of a Mental Image in Western Thought* (London: Routledge, 2001).
Barbara, Anna/Perliss, Anthony, *Invisible Architecture: Experiencing Places through the Sense of Smell* (Milan: Skira, 2006).
Beare, John I., *Greek Theories of Elementary Cognition from Alcmaeon to Aristotle* (Oxford: Clarendon Press, 2004 [1906]).
Benjamin, Walter, 'The Work of Art in the Age of Its Technological Reproducibility: Second Version' [1936], in: Id., *The Work of Art in the Age of Its Technological Reproducibility, and Other Writings on Media*, ed. Michael W. Jennings, Brigid Doherty, and Thomas Y. Levin (Cambridge, Mass.: Belknap Press of Harvard University Press, 2008), 19–55.
Berensmeyer, Ingo, *'Angles of Contingency:' Literarische Kultur im England des siebzehnten Jahrhunderts* (Tübingen: Niemeyer, 2007). Revised English edition: *Literary Culture in Early Modern England, 1630–1700: Angles of Contingency* (Berlin: De Gruyter, 2020).
Blackwell, Albert L., *The Sacred in Music* (Louisville, Ky.: Westminster John Knox Press, 1999).
Blakemore, Steven, '"With no middle flight": Poetic Pride and Satanic Hubris in *Paradise Lost*,' *KR* 5 (1985), 23–31
Blesser, Barry/Salter, Linda-Ruth, *Spaces Speak, Are You Listening? Experiencing Aural Architecture* (Cambridge, Mass.: MIT Press, 2007).
Bloch, Marc, *The Royal Touch: Sacred Monarchy and Scrofula in England and France*, tr. J. E. Anderson (London: Routledge & Kegan Paul, 1973 [1924]).
Blumenberg, Hans, *Die Lesbarkeit der Welt* (Frankfurt am Main: Suhrkamp, 1981).
Blumenberg, Hans, 'Light as a Metaphor for Truth: At the Preliminary Stage of Philosophical Concept Formation' [1957], in: David Michael Levin (ed.), *Modernity and the Hegemony of Vision* (Berkeley, Calif.: University of California Press, 1993), 30–62.

Borges, Jorge Luis, 'Milton y su condenación de la rima' [1925], in: Idem, *El tamaño de mi esperanza / El idioma de los argentinos* (Buenos Aires: Debolsillo, 2016), 91–95.

Boring, Edwin G., *Sensation and Perception in the History of Experimental Psychology* (New York: Appleton-Century-Crofts, 1942).

Boswell, Jackson Campbell, *Milton's Library: A Catalogue of The Remains of John Milton's Library and An Annotated Reconstruction of Milton's Library and Ancillary Readings* (New York: Garland Publishing, 1975).

Bowers, Fredson, 'Thomas Randolph's *Salting*,' *MP* 39 (1942), 275–280.

Briscoe, Robert, 'Vision, Action, and Make-Perceive,' *M&L* 23 (2008), 457–97.

Briscoe, Robert, 'Superimposed Mental Imagery: On the Uses of Make-Perceive,' in: Fiona Macpherson/Fabian Dorsch (eds), *Perceptual Memory and Perceptual Imagination* (Oxford: Oxford University Press, 2018), 161–85.

Broadbent, John B., *Some Graver Subject: An Essay on 'Paradise Lost'* (London: Chatto & Windus, 1960).

Brogan, Stephen, *The Royal Touch in Early Modern England: Politics, Medicine, and Sin* (Woodbridge: Boydell, 2015).

Brown, Eleanor Gertrude, *Milton's Blindness* (New York: Octagon, 1968 [1934]).

Burke, Peter, *Varieties of Cultural History* (Cambridge: Polity, 1997).

Burke, Peter, 'Context in Context,' *Common Knowledge* 8 (2002), 152–77.

Bush, Douglas, *English Literature in the Earlier Seventeenth Century, 1600–1660*, 2nd, rev. ed. (Oxford: Clarendon, 1962 [1945]).

Bynum, W. F./Porter, Roy (eds), *Medicine and the Five Senses* (Cambridge: Cambridge University Press, 1993).

Cable, Lana, 'Milton's Iconoclastic Truth,' in: *Politics, Poetics, and Hermeneutics in Milton's Prose*, eds Loewenstein/Turner, 135–151.

Cable, Lana, *Carnal Rhetoric: Milton's Iconoclasm and the Poetics of Desire* (Durham, N.C.: Duke University Press, 1995).

Campbell, Gordon/ Corns, Thomas N., *John Milton: Life, Work, and Thought* (Oxford: Oxford University Press, 2010)

Christie, John R. R., 'Introduction: Rhetoric and Writing in Early Modern Philosophy and Science,' in: Andrew E. Benjamin et al. (eds), *The Figural and the Literal: Problems of Language in the History of Science and Philosophy, 1630–1800* (Manchester: Manchester University Press, 1987), 1–9.

Clark, Stuart, *Vanities of the Eye: Vision in Early Modern European Culture* (Oxford: Oxford University Press, 2009 [2007]).

Classen, Constance, *Worlds of Sense: Exploring the Senses in History and Across Cultures* (London: Routledge, 1993).

Classen, Constance, *The Color of Angels: Cosmology, Gender, and the Aesthetic Imagination* (London: Routledge, 1998).

Classen, Constance (ed.), *The Book of Touch* (Oxford: Berg, 2005).

Classen, Constance, 'The Witch's Senses: Sensory Ideologies and Transgressive Femininities from the Renaissance to Modernity,' in: *Empire of the Senses*, ed. Howes, 70–84.

Classen, Constance, *The Deepest Sense: A Cultural History of Touch* (Urbana, Ill.: University of Illinois Press, 2012).

Classen, Constance, 'Feminine Tactics: Creating an Alternative Aesthetics in the Nineteenth and Twentieth Centuries,' in: *The Book of Touch*, ed. Classen, 228–39.

Clune, Michael W., *Writing Against Time* (Stanford, Calif.: Stanford University Press, 2013).

Cockayne, Emily, *Hubbub: Filth, Noise and Stench in England, 1600–1770* (New Haven, Conn.: Yale University Press, 2007).

Collinson, Patrick, *The Birthpangs of Protestant England: Religious and Cultural Change in the Sixteenth and Seventeenth Centuries* (London: Macmillan, 1988).

Condee, R. W., 'Ovid's Exile and Milton's Rustication,' *PQ* 37 (1958), 498–502.

Cook, Harold J., 'Medicine,' in Katharine Park/Lorraine Daston (eds), *The Cambridge History of Science, Vol. 3: Early Modern Science* (Cambridge: Cambridge University Press, 2008), 407–434.

Corbin, Alain, *The Foul and the Fragrant: Odour and the French Social Imagination*, tr. M. L. Kochan (Cambridge, Mass.: Harvard University Press, 1986 [1982]).

Corbin, Alain, 'A History and Anthropology of the Senses,' in: Idem, *Time, Desire and Horror: Towards a History of the Senses*, tr. Jean Birrell (Cambridge: Polity, 1995 [1991]), 181–195.

Corbin, Alain, *Village Bells: Sound and Meaning in the Nineteenth-Century French Countryside*, tr. Martin Thom (New York: Columbia University Press, 1998 [1994]).

Corns, Thomas N., *The Development of Milton's Prose Style* (Oxford: Oxford University Press, 1982).

Corns, Thomas N., *Milton's Language* (Oxford: Basil Blackwell, 1990).

Corns, Thomas N., 'Cultural and Genre Markers in Milton's *Paradise Lost*,' RBPH 69 (1991), 555-562.

Corns, Thomas N., 'Milton's English,' in: *A Companion to Milton*, ed. Thomas N. Corns (Malden, Mass.: Blackwell, 2003), 91–106.

Costello, William T., *The Scholastic Curriculum at Early Seventeenth-Century Cambridge* (Cambridge, Mass.: Harvard University Press, 1958).

Cox, Katherine, '"How cam'st thou speakable of mute": Satanic Acoustics in "Paradise Lost",' *MS* 57 (2016), 233–260.

Czarra, Fred, *Spices: A Global History* (London: Reaktion, 2009).

Danielson, Dennis, *Paradise Lost and the Cosmological Revolution* (Cambridge: Cambridge University Press, 2014).

Danius, Sara, *The Senses of Modernism: Technology, Perception, and Aesthetics* (Ithaca, N. Y.: Cornell University Press, 2002).

Day, Sean, 'Some Demographic and Socio-Cultural Aspects of Synesthesia,' in: Lynn C. Robertson/Noam Sagiv (eds), *Synesthesia: Perspectives from Cognitive Neuroscience* (New York: Oxford University Press, 2005), 11–33.

Debus, Allen G., *Man and Nature in the Renaissance* (Cambridge: Cambridge University Press, 1978).

Demaray, Hannah Disinger, 'Milton's "Perfect" Paradise and the Landscapes of Italy,' *Milton Quarterly* 8 (1974), 33–41.

di Cesare, Mario A. (ed.), *Milton in Italy: Contexts, Images, Contradictions* (Binghamton, N.Y.: ACMRS, 1991).

Dobranski, Stephen B., *The Cambridge Introduction to Milton* (Cambridge: Cambridge University Press, 2012).

Dobranski, Stephen B., *Milton's Visual Imagination: Imagery in 'Paradise Lost'* (Cambridge: Cambridge University Press, 2016).

Dugan, Holly, *The Ephemeral History of Perfume: Scent and Sense in Early Modern England* (Baltimore, Md.: Johns Hopkins University Press, 2011).

Duran, Angelica, 'The Blind Bard, According to John Milton and His Contemporaries,' *Mosaic* 46 (2013), 141–157.

Duran, Angelica, '*Paradise Lost* in Spanish Translation and as World Literature,' in: Idem/Issa, Islam/Olson, Jonathan R. (eds), *Milton in Translation* (Oxford: Oxford University Press, 2017), 265–78.

Duran, Angelica, 'Three of Borges's Miltons,' *MS* 58 (2017), 183–200.

Eagleton, Terry, *Ideology: An Introduction* (London: Verso, 1991).

Edwards, Karen, 'Milton's Reformed Animals: An Early Modern Bestiary: Introduction,' *MQ* 39 (2005), 121–131.

Edwards, Karen, 'Milton's Reformed Animals: An Early Modern Bestiary – A–C,' *MQ* 39 (2005), 183–292.

Edwards, Karen, 'Milton's Reformed Animals: An Early Modern Bestiary – D–F,' *MQ* 40 (2006), 99–187.

Edwards, Karen, 'Milton's Reformed Animals: An Early Modern Bestiary – L,' *MQ* 41 (2007), 223–251.

Edwards, Karen, 'Milton's Reformed Animals: An Early Modern Bestiary – P–R,' *MQ* 42 (2008), 253–308.
Edwards, Karen, 'Milton's Reformed Animals: An Early Modern Bestiary – S,' *MQ* 43 (2009), 89–141.
Edwards, 'Milton's Reformed Animals: An Early Modern Bestiary – T–Z,' *MQ* 43 (2009), 241–308.
Edwards, Karen L., *Milton and the Natural World: Science and Poetry in 'Paradise Lost'* (Cambridge: Cambridge University Press, 1999).
Eisenstein, Sergei, *The Film Sense* (London: Faber and Faber, 1968 [1942]).
Elias, Norbert, *The Civilizing Process: Sociogenetic and Psychogenetic Investigations*, tr. Edmund Jephcott (Oxford: Blackwell, 2000 [1939]).
Eliot, T. S., 'The Metaphysical Poets' [1921], in: Idem, *Selected Prose*, ed. Frank Kermode (New York: Harcourt Brace Jovanovich, 1988 [1975]), 59–67.
Eliot, T. S., 'Milton I' [1936], in: Idem, *Selected Prose*, ed. Kermode, 258–264.
Eliot, T. S., 'Milton II' [1947], in: Idem, *Selected Prose*, ed. Kermode, 265–274.
Eliot, T. S., 'Tradition and the Individual Talent' [1919], in: Idem, *Selected Prose*, ed. Kermode, 37–44.
Elmer, Peter, *The Miraculous Conformist: Valentine Greatrakes, the Body Politic, and the Politics of Healing in Restoration Britain* (Oxford: Oxford University Press, 2013).
Empson, William, *Seven Types of Ambiguity* (London: Hogarth Press, 1991 [1930]).
Empson, William, *The Structure of Complex Words* (Cambridge, Mass.: Harvard University Press, 1989 [1951]).
Encke, Julia, *Augenblicke der Gefahr: Der Krieg und die Sinne, 1914–1934* (Munich: Wilhelm Fink, 2006).
Evans, J. M[artin], *'Paradise Lost' and the Genesis Tradition* (Oxford: Clarendon, 1968).
Evans, J. Martin, *The Miltonic Moment* (Lexington, Ky.: University Press of Kentucky, 1998).
Evans, J. Martin, 'The Birth of the Author: Milton's Poetic Self-Construction,' *MS* 38 (2000), 47–65.
Fallon, Stephen M., 'The Metaphysics of Milton's Divorce Tracts,' in: *Politics, Poetics, and Hermeneutics in Milton's Prose*, eds Loewenstein/Turner, 69–83.
Fallon, Stephen M., *Milton Among the Philosophers: Poetry and Materialism in Seventeenth-Century England* (Ithaca, N. Y.: Cornell University Press, 1991).
Fallon, Stephen M., *Milton's Peculiar Grace: Self-Representation and Authority* (Ithaca, N. Y.: Cornell University Press, 2007).
Febvre, Lucien, *The Problem of Unbelief in the Sixteenth Century: The Religion of Rabelais*, tr. Beatrice Gottlieb (Cambridge, Mass.: Harvard University Press, 1982 [1947]).
Feingold, Mordechai, '"And Knowledge Shall Be Increased:" Millenarianism and the Advancement of Learning Revisited,' *The Seventeenth Century* 28 (2013), 363–393.
Fish, Stanley, 'Reasons That Imply Themselves: Imagery, Argument, and the Reader in Milton's *Reason of Church Government*,' in: Earl Miner (ed.), *Seventeenth-Century Imagery: Essays on Uses of Figurative Language from Donne to Farquhar* (Berkeley, Calif.: University of California Press, 1971), 83–102.
Foucault, Michel, *The Archaeology of Knowledge*, tr. A. M. Sheridan-Smith (London: Routledge, 2002 [1969]).
Fournier, Marian, *The Fabric of Life: Microscopy in the Seventeenth Century* (Baltimore: Johns Hopkins University Press, 1996).
Fowler, Alastair, *Kinds of Literature: An Introduction to the Theory of Genres and Modes* (Oxford: Clarendon, 1982).
Frank, Mortimer H., 'Milton's Knowledge of Music: Some Speculations,' in: *Milton and the Art of Sacred Song*, eds J. Max Patrick/Roger H. Sundell (Madison, Wisc.: University of Wisconsin P, 1979), 83–98.
Friedell, Egon, *A Cultural History of the Modern Age. Vol. 1: Renaissance and Reformation*. With a new introduction by Allan Janik (New Brunswick, N. J.: Transaction Publishers, 2008 [1930, orig. 1927]).
Friedman, Donald M., 'Comus and the Truth of the Ear,' in: *The Muses Common-Weale: Poetry and Politics in the Seventeenth-Century*, eds Claude J. Summers/Ted-Larry Pebworth (Columbia, Mo.: University of Missouri Press, 1988), 119–34.

Frye, Roland Mushat, *Milton's Imagery and the Visual Arts: Iconographic Tradition in the Epic Poems* (Princeton, N. J.: Princeton University Press, 1978).

Fryer, Louise, et al., 'Touching Words Is Not Enough: How Visual Experience Influences Haptic-auditory Associations in the "Bouba-Kiki" Effect,' *Cognition* 132 (2014), 164–173.

Gabel, Tobias, 'Hierarchies of Vision in John Milton's *Paradise Lost*,' in: *The Five Senses in Medieval and Early Modern England*, eds Kern-Stähler/Busse/de Boer, 117–134.

Gabel, Tobias, *Paradise Reframed: Milton, Dryden, and the Politics of Literary Adaptation, 1658–1679* (Heidelberg: Universitätsverlag Winter, 2016).

Garrison, John S., '"Overflowing Cups for Amorous Jove": Abundance and Attraction in Milton's Elegies,' in: David L. Orvis (ed.), *Queer Milton* (Cham: Palgrave Macmillan, 2018), 93–115.

Gavrilyuk, Paul/Coakley, Sarah (eds), *The Spiritual Senses: Perceiving God in Western Christianity* (Cambridge: Cambridge University Press, 2013 [2012]).

Geertz, Clifford, 'Thick Description: Toward an Interpretive Theory of Culture,' in: Idem, *The Interpretation of Cultures* (New York: Basic Books, 1973), 3–30.

Gerson, Lloyd P., *Aristotle and Other Platonists* (Ithaca, N. Y.: Cornell University Press, 2005).

Gifford, Don, *The Farther Shore: A Cultural History of Perception, 1798–1984* (London: Faber & Faber, 1990).

Gigante, Denise, *Taste: A Literary History* (New Haven, Conn.: Yale University Press, 2005).

Gilman, Ernest B., *Iconoclasm and Poetry in the English Reformation: Down Went Dagon* (Chicago: University of Chicago Press, 1986).

Ginzburg, Carlo, 'The High and the Low: The Theme of Forbidden Knowledge in the Sixteenth and Seventeenth Centuries,' in: Id., *Clues, Myths, and the Historical Method*, tr. John and Anne C. Tedeschi (Baltimore, Md.: Johns Hopkins University Press, 1986), 60–76.

Goldberg, Jonathan, *Writing Matter: From the Hands of the English Renaissance* (Stanford, Calif.: Stanford University Press, 1990).

Golinski, Jan V., 'Robert Boyle: Scepticism and Authority in Seventeenth-Century Chemical Discourse,' in: *The Figural and the Literal*, Benjamin et al. (eds), 58–82.

González-Crussí, Francisco, *The Five Senses* (New York: Kaplan, 2009).

Gouk, Penelope, *Music, Science, and Natural Magic in Seventeenth-Century England* (New Haven, Conn.: Yale University Press, 1999).

Greenfield, Concetta Carestia, 'S. M. Eisenstein's *Alexander Nevsky* and John Milton's *Paradise Lost*: A Structural Comparison,' *MQ* 9 (1975), 93–99.

Gurr, Andrew, 'Why Was the Globe Round?,' in: Idem, *Shakespeare's Workplace: Essays on Shakespearean Theatre* (Cambridge: Cambridge University Press, 2017), 167–180.

Gurr, Jens Martin, 'The Senses and Human Nature in a Political Reading of *Paradise Lost*,' in: *The Five Senses in Medieval and Early Modern England*, eds Kern-Stähler/Busse/de Boer, 177–195.

Hale, John K., *Milton's Languages: The Impact of Multilingualism on Style* (Cambridge: Cambridge University Press, 1997).

Hale, John K., 'Books and Book-Form in Milton,' *R&R* 23 (1999), 63–77.

Hammond, Paul, *Milton's Complex Words: Essays on the Conceptual Structure of 'Paradise Lost'* (Oxford: Oxford University Press, 2017).

Handley, Sasha, *Sleep in Early Modern England* (New Haven, Conn.: Yale University Press, 2016).

Harris, Neil, 'The Vallombrosa Simile and the Image of the Poet in *Paradise Lost*,' in: Mario A. Di Cesare (ed.), *Milton in Italy: Contexts, Images, Contradictions* (Binghamton, N. Y.: Medieval & Renaissance Texts & Studies, 1991), 71–96.

Hartman, Geoffrey, 'Adam on the Grass with Balsamum,' *ELH* 36 (1969), 168–192.

Harvey, E. Ruth, *The Inward Wits: Psychological Theory in the Middle Ages and the Renaissance* (London: Warburg Institute, 1975).

Heller-Roazen, Daniel, *The Fifth Hammer: Pythagoras and the Disharmony of the World* (Cambridge, Mass.: MIT Press, 2011).

Herbst, Seth, 'Sound and Matter: Milton, Music, and Monism,' in: *Milton, Materialism, and Embodiment*, eds Donovan/Festa, 37–55.

Heyd, Michael, 'Robert Burton's Sources on Enthusiasm and Melancholy: From a Medical Tradition to Religious Controversy,' *HEI* 5 (1984), 17–44.

Hill, Christopher, *Change and Continuity in Seventeenth-Century England* (London: Weidenfeld and Nicolson, 1974).

Hoffer, Peter Charles, *Sensory Worlds in Early America* (Baltimore, Md.: Johns Hopkins University Press, 2003).

Hollander, John, *The Untuning of the Sky: Ideas of Music in English Poetry, 1500–1700* (Princeton, N. J.: Princeton University Press, 1961).

Hollander, John, *Vision and Resonance: Two Senses of Poetic Form* (New Haven, Conn.: Yale University Press, 1985 [1975]).

Hollander, John, *The Substance of Shadow: A Darkening Trope in Poetic History* (Chicago: University of Chicago Press, 2016).

Howatson, M. C. (ed.), *The Oxford Companion to Classical Literature*, 2nd ed. (Oxford: Oxford University Press, 1989).

Howes, David (ed.), *The Varieties of Sensory Experience: A Sourcebook in the Anthropology of the Senses* (Toronto: University of Toronto Press, 1991).

Howes, David, *Sensual Relations: Engaging the Senses in Culture and Social Theory* (Ann Arbor, Mich.: University of Michigan Press, 2003).

Howes, David (ed.), *Empire of the Senses: The Sensual Culture Reader* (Oxford: Berg, 2005).

Howes, David, 'Introduction: Empires of the Senses,' in: *Empire of the Senses*, ed. Howes, 1–17.

Hull, John, 'Rainfall and the Blind Body,' in: *The Book of Touch*, ed. Constance Classen (Oxford: Berg, 2005), 324–327.

Hunt, Arnold, *The Art of Hearing: English Preachers and Their Audiences, 1590–1640* (Cambridge: Cambridge University Press, 2010).

Hutton, Ronald, *The Stations of the Sun: A History of the Ritual Year in Britain* (Oxford: Oxford University Press, 1996).

Ipgrave, Julia, *Adam in Seventeenth-Century Political Writing in England and New England* (London: Routledge, 2017).

Jacobus, Lee A., *Sudden Apprehension: Aspects of Knowledge in 'Paradise Lost'* (The Hague: Mouton, 1976).

Jardine, Lisa, *The Curious Life of Robert Hooke: The Man Who Measured London* (New York: HarperCollins, 2003).

Jervis, John, *Sensational Subjects: The Dramatization of Experience in the Modern World* (London: Bloomsbury, 2015).

Johns, Adrian, *The Nature of the Book: Print and Knowledge in the Making* (Chicago: University of Chicago Press, 1998).

Johnson, Lee, *The Paintings of Eugène Delacroix: A Critical Catalogue. 1816–1831. Volume I. Text* (Oxford: Clarendon, 1981).

Jones, Scott C., *Rumors of Wisdom: Job 28 as Poetry* (Berlin: De Gruyter, 2009).

Jones, Scott C., 'Corporeal Discourse in the Book of Job,' *JBL* 132 (2013), 845–863.

Jouanna, Jacques, *Greek Medicine from Hippocrates to Galen: Selected Papers*, tr. Neil Allies (Leiden: Brill, 2012).

Jütte, Robert, *A History of the Senses: From Antiquity to Cyberspace*, tr. James Lynn (Cambridge: Polity, 2005 [1998]).

Kennett, Frances, *History of Perfume* (London: Harrap, 1975).

Kermode, Frank, 'The Banquet of Sense,' in: Idem, *Shakespeare, Spenser, Donne: Renaissance Essays* (London: Routledge & Kegan Paul, 1971), 84–115.

Kern-Stähler, Annette/Busse, Beatrix/de Boer, Wietse (eds), *The Five Senses in Medieval and Early Modern England* (Leiden: Brill, 2016).

Kerrigan, John, 'Milton and the Nightingale,' *EC* 42 (1992), 107–22.

Keßler, Eckhard, 'The Intellective Soul,' in: *The Cambridge History of Renaissance Philosophy*, eds Charles B. Schmitt/Quentin Skinner (Cambridge: Cambridge University Press, 1988), 485–534.

Knott, Jr., John R., 'Symbolic Landscape in *Paradise Lost*,' *MS* 2 (1970), 37–58.
Koehler, G. Stanley, 'Milton on "Numbers," "Quantity," and Rime,' *SIP* 55 (1958), 201–217.
Kövecses, Zoltán, *Metaphor: A Practical Introduction* (Oxford: Oxford University Press, ²2010).
Kövecses, Zoltán, *Where Metaphors Come From: Reconsidering Context in Metaphor* (Oxford: Oxford University Press, 2015).
Kuhn, Thomas S., *The Copernican Revolution* (Cambridge, Mass.: Harvard University Press, 1976 [1957]).
Lakoff, George/Johnson, Mark, *Metaphors We Live By* (Chicago: University of Chicago Press, 1980).
Larson, Katherine R., *The Matter of Song in Early Modern England: Texts in and of the Air* (Oxford: Oxford University Press, 2019).
Laslett, Peter, *The World We Have Lost: Further Explored* (London: Methuen, 1983).
Leavis, F. R., *Revaluation* (Harmondsworth: Penguin, 1994 [1936]).
Leder, Drew, 'Visceral Perception,' in: *The Book of Touch*, ed. Classen, 335–41.
Le Huray, Peter, 'The fair musick that all creatures made,' in: *The Age of Milton: Backgrounds to Seventeenth-Century Literature*, eds C. A. Patrides/Raymond B. Waddington (Manchester: Manchester University Press, 1980), 241–272.
Leonard, John, *Naming in Paradise: Milton and the Language of Adam and Eve* (Oxford: Clarendon, 1990).
Leonard, John, *Faithful Labourers: A Reception History of 'Paradise Lost,' 1667–1970*, 2 vols (Oxford: Oxford University Press, 2013).
Lewalski, Barbara Kiefer, *Milton's Brief Epic: The Genre, Meaning, and Art of 'Paradise Regained'* (Providence, R. I.: Brown University Press, 1966).
Lewalski, Barbara Kiefer, *'Paradise Lost' and the Rhetoric of Literary Forms* (Princeton, N. J.: Princeton University Press, 1985).
Lewalski, Barbara Kiefer, 'The Genres of *Paradise Lost*,' in: Dennis Danielson (ed.), *The Cambridge Companion to Milton*, 2nd ed. (Cambridge: Cambridge University Press, 1999 [1989]), 113–128.
Lewalski, Barbara K[iefer], *The Life of John Milton: A Critical Biography* (Malden, Mass.: Blackwell, 2000).
Lewis, C. S., *The Discarded Image: An Introduction to Medieval and Renaissance Literature* (Cambridge: Cambridge University Press, 1964).
Lieb, Michael, '"Yet Once More:" The Formulaic Opening of *Lycidas*,' *MQ* 12 (1978), 23–28.
Loewenstein, David/Turner, James Grantham (eds), *Politics, Poetics, and Hermeneutics in Milton's Prose* (Cambridge: Cambridge University Press, 1990).
Lowenthal, David, *The Past is a Foreign Country: Revisited* (Cambridge: Cambridge University Press, 2015 [1985]).
Li, Chu-Tsing, *The Five Senses in Art: An Analysis of Its Development in Northern Europe* (PhD diss., State University of Iowa, 1955).
Lovejoy, Arthur O., *The Great Chain of Being: A Study in the History of an Idea* (Cambridge, Mass.: Harvard University Press, 1978 [1936]).
Lyotard, Jean-François, '*Veduta* on a Fragment of the "History" of Desire,' in: Idem, *Discourse, Figure*, trs Anthony Hudek/Mary Lydon (Minneapolis, Minn.: University of Minnesota Press, 2011 [1971]), 157–201.
Maier, Christl, *Daughter Zion, Mother Zion: Gender, Space, and the Sacred in Ancient Israel* (Minneapolis, Minn.: Fortress Press, 2008).
Mander, M. N. K., 'Milton and the Music of the Spheres,' *MQ* 24 (1990), 63–71.
Mandrou, Robert, *Introduction to Modern France, 1500–1640: An Essay in Historical Psychology*, tr. R. E. Hallmark (London: Edward Arnold, 1975 [1961]).
Marconi, Paolo, 'Una chiave per l'interpretazione dell'urbanistica rinascimentale: la cittadella come microcosmo,' *Quaderni dell'istituto di storia dell'architettura* 15 (1968), 53–94.
Marinelli, Peter V., *Pastoral* (London: Methuen, 1971).

Marjara, Harinder S., *Contemplation of Created Things: Science in 'Paradise Lost'* (Toronto: University of Toronto Press, 1992).
Marks, Lawrence E., *The Unity of the Senses: Interrelations among the Modalities* (New York: Academic Press, 1978).
Martin, Luther H./Sørensen, Jesper (eds), *Past Minds: Studies in Cognitive Historiography* (London: Routledge, 2011).
McCaffrey, Isabel, 'The Theme of *Paradise Lost* Book III,' in: Thomas Kranidas (ed.), *New Essays on 'Paradise Lost'* (Berkeley, Calif.: University of California Press, 1971 [1969]), 58–85.
McClary, Susan, *Desire and Pleasure in Seventeenth-Century Music* (Berkeley, Calif.: University of California Press, 2012).
McColley, Diane, *A Gust for Paradise: Milton's Eden and the Visual Arts* (Urbana, Ill.: University of Illinois Press, 1993).
McColley, Diane Kelsey *Poetry and Music in Seventeenth-Century England* (Cambridge: Cambridge University Press, 1997).
McInroy, Mark J., 'Origen of Alexandria,' in *Spiritual Senses*, eds Gavrilyuk/Coakley, 20–35.
McKeown, Adam N., *Fortification and Its Discontents from Shakespeare to Milton: Trouble in the Walled City* (New York: Routledge, 2019).
Miller, Paul Allen, '"What's Love Got to Do With It?": The Peculiar Story of Elegy in Rome,' in: *The Oxford Handbook of Elegy*, ed. Weisman, 46–66.
Milner, Matthew, *The Senses and the English Reformation* (Farnham: Ashgate, 2011).
Miner, Earl, 'Preface,' in: Idem (ed.), *Seventeenth-Century Imagery: Essays on Uses of Figurative Language from Donne to Farquhar* (Berkeley, Calif.: University of California Press, 1971), v–xiv.
Moshenska, Joe, *Feeling Pleasures: The Sense of Touch in Renaissance England* (Oxford: Oxford University Press, 2014).
Myers, David G./DeWall, C. Nathan, *Psychology*, 12th ed. (New York: Macmillan Worth, 2018).
Nicolson, Marjorie, 'Milton and the Telescope,' *ELH* 2 (1935), 1–32.
Nicolson, Marjorie Hope, *Mountain Gloom and Mountain Glory: The Development of the Aesthetics of the Infinite* (Seattle, Wash.: University of Washington Press, 1997 [1959]).
Nordenfalk, Carl, 'The Five Senses in Flemish Art before 1600,' in: *Netherlandish Mannerism*, ed. Görel Cavalli-Björkmann (Stockholm: Nationalmuseum, 1985), 135–154.
Nordenfalk, Carl, 'The Five Senses in Late Medieval and Renaissance Art,' *Journal of the Warburg and Courtauld Institutes* 48 (1985), 1–22.
O'Connor, Kari, *Pineapple: A Global History* (London: Reaktion, 2013).
Ogden, H. V. S., 'The Principles of Variety and Contrast in Seventeenth-Century Aesthetics, and Milton's Poetry,' *JHI* 10 (1949) 159–82.
Ong, Walter J., 'Logic and Rhetoric,' in: *A Milton Encyclopedia*, ed. William B. Hunter, vol. 5 (Lewisburg, Pa.: Bucknell University Press, 1979), 30–36.
Orgel, Stephen/Goldberg, Jonathan, 'Introduction,' in *Paradise Lost*, eds Goldberg/Orgel, vii–xxxiv.
Park, Katherine, 'The Organic Soul,' in: *Cambridge History of Renaissance Philosophy*, eds Schmitt/ Skinner, 464–484.
Partridge, Eric, *Origins: An Etymological Dictionary of Modern English* (London: Routledge, 2009 [1977]).
Partner, Jane, *Poetry and Vision in Early Modern England* (Cham: Palgrave Macmillan, 2018).
Pastoureau, Michel, *Couleurs, images, symboles: études d'histoire et d'anthropologie* (Paris: Léopard d'or, 1989).
Pastoureau, Michel, 'Une histoire des couleurs est-elle possible?', *Ethnologie française* 20 (1990), 368–77.
Pastoureau, Michel, *Green: The History of a Color*, tr. Jody Gladding (Princeton, N. J.: Princeton University Press, 2014 [2013]).

Pastoureau, *Red: The History of a Color*, tr. Jody Gladding (Princeton, N. J.: Princeton University Press, 2017 [2016]).
Patrides, C. A., 'Milton and Arianism,' *JHI* 25 (1964), 423–429.
Patrides, C. A., '*Paradise Lost* and the Theory of Accommodation,' in: W. B. Hunter/C. A. Patrides/J. H. Adamson (eds), *Bright Essence: Studies in Milton's Theology* (Salt Lake City, Utah: University of Utah Press, 1973 [1971]), 159–63.
Patterson, Annabel, *Milton's Words* (Oxford: Oxford University Press, 2009).
Pauschert, Uwe, *Joseph Glanvill und die Neue Wissenschaft des 17. Jahrhunderts* (Frankfurt: Peter Lang, 1994).
Peck, Linda Levy, *Consuming Splendor: Society and Culture in Seventeenth-Century England* (Cambridge: Cambridge University Press, 2005).
Pocock, J. G. A., *The Ancient Constitution and the Feudal Law: A Study of English Historical Thought in the Seventeenth Century* (Cambridge: Cambridge University Press, 1987 [1957])
Pocock, J. G. A., 'Languages and Their Implications: The Transformation of the Study of Political Thought,' in: Idem, *Politics, Language, and Time: Essays on Political Thought and History* (Chicago: University of Chicago Press, 1989 [1971]), 3–41.
Pocock, J. G. A., 'The Concept of a Language and the *metier d'historien*: Some Considerations on Practice (1987),' in: Idem, *Political Thought and History: Essays on Theory and Method* (Cambridge: Cambridge University Press, 2011), 87–105.
Pollak, Martha, *Cities at War in Early Modern Europe* (Cambridge: Cambridge University Press, 2010).
Poole, William, *Milton and the Making of 'Paradise Lost'* (Cambridge, Mass.: Harvard University Press, 2017).
Popkin, Richard, 'The Religious Background of Seventeenth-Century Philosophy,' in: *The Cambridge History of Seventeenth-Century Philosophy*, eds Daniel Garber/Michael Ayers, 2 vols (Cambridge: Cambridge University Press, 2003), I, 393–422.
Porter, Roy, *The Making of Geology: Earth Science in Britain, 1660–1815* (Cambridge: Cambridge University Press, 1977).
Prawdzik, Brendan, *Theatrical Milton: Politics and Poetics of the Staged Body* (Edinburgh: Edinburgh University Press, 2017).
Purrington, Robert D., *The First Professional Scientist: Robert Hooke and the Royal Society of London* (Basel: Birkhäuser, 2009), 81–91.
Quint, David, '"Things Invisible to Mortal Sight:" Light, Vision and the Unity of Book 3 of *Paradise Lost*,' *MLQ* 71 (2010), 229–69.
Rajan, Balachandra, 'Simple, Sensuous and Passionate,' *RES* 21 (1945), 289–301.
Ramachandran, V. S./Hubbard, Edward M., 'The Emergence of the Human Mind: Some Clues from Synesthesia,' in: *Synesthesia*, eds Robertson/Sagiv, 147–190.
Rath, Richard Cullen, *How Early America Sounded* (Ithaca, N.Y.: Cornell University Press, 2005).
Raymond, Joad, 'John Milton, European,' in: *The Oxford Handbook of Milton*, eds Nicholas McDowell/Nigel Smith (Oxford: Oxford University Press, 2009), 272–290.
Raymond, Joad, *Milton's Angels: The Early-Modern Imagination* (Oxford: Oxford University Press, 2010).
Revard, Stella P., *Milton and the Tangles of Neaera's Hair: The Making of the 1645 Poems* (Columbia, Mo.: University of Missouri Press, 1997).
Rice, Eugene F., *The Renaissance Idea of Wisdom* (Cambridge, Mass.: Harvard University Press, 1958).
Richek, Roslyn, 'Thomas Randolph's *Salting* (1627), Its Text, and John Milton's Sixth Prolusion as Another Salting,' *ELR* 12 (1982), 103–112.
Richek, Roslyn, 'Thom Randolfs Salting', *ELR* 12 (1982), 113–126.
Richek, Roslyn, 'Appendix: Milton's Salting,' *ELR* 12 (1982), 127–31.
Ricks, Christopher, *Milton's Grand Style* (Oxford: Clarendon, 1963).
Ricœur, Paul, *The Rule of Metaphor: Multi-Disciplinary Studies of the Creation of Meaning in Language*, tr. Robert Czerny (London: Routledge & Kegan Paul, 1978 [1975]).
Rivière, Janine, *Dreams in Early Modern England* (Abingdon: Routledge, 2017).

Roberts, Lissa, 'The Death of the Sensuous Chemist: The 'New' Chemistry and the Transformation of Sensuous Technology,' in *Empire of the Senses*, ed. Howes, 106–127.

Rogers, John H., *The Matter of Revolution: Science, Poetry, and Politics in the Age of Milton* (Ithaca, N. Y.: Cornell University Press, 1998 [1996]).

Roller, Lynn E., *In Search of God the Mother: The Cult of Anatolian Cybele* (Berkeley, Calif.: University of California Press, 1999).

Roodenburg, Herman (ed.), *A Cultural History of the Senses in the Renaissance* (London: Bloomsbury, 2014).

Roodenburg, Herman, 'Introduction: The Sensory Worlds of the Renaissance,' in: *Cultural History of the Senses in the Renaissance*, ed. Roodenburg, 2–17.

Røstvig, Maren-Sofie, *The Happy Man: Studies on the Metamorphoses of a Classical Ideal*, 2 vols (Oslo: Akademisk Forlag, 1954–58).

Roychoudhury, Suparna, *Phantasmatic Shakespeare: Imagination in the Age of Early Modern Science* (Ithaca, N. Y.: Cornell University Press, 2018).

Rudy, Gordon, *The Mystical Language of Sensation in the Later Middle Ages* (New York: Routledge, 2002).

Schivelbusch, Wolfgang, *Tastes of Paradise: A Social History of Spices, Stimulants and Intoxicants*, tr. David Jacobson (New York: Vintage, 1993 [1980]).

Schleusener-Eichholz, Gudrun, *Das Auge im Mittelalter*, 2 vols (Munich: Wilhelm Fink, 1985).

Schoenfeldt, Michael C., *Bodies and Selves in Early Modern England: Physiology and Inwardness in Spenser, Shakespeare, Herbert, and Milton* (Cambridge: Cambridge University Press, 1999).

Shapin, Steven, *Changing Tastes: How Things Tasted in the Early Modern Period and How They Taste Now* (Uppsala: Uppsalas Universitet, 2011).

Sharpe, Kevin/Zwicker, Steven N., 'Politics of Discourse: Introduction,' in: Sharpe/Zwicker (eds), *Politics of Discourse: The Literature and History of Seventeenth-Century England* (Berkeley, Calif.: University of California Press, 1987), 1–20.

Shawcross, John T., '"Shedding sweet influence:" The Legacy of John Milton's Works,' in: Angelica Duran (ed.), *A Concise Companion to Milton* (Malden, Mass.: Blackwell, 2007), 25–42.

Sherrow, Victoria, *Encyclopedia of Hair: A Cultural History* (Westport, Conn.: Greenwood Press, 2006).

Sherry, Beverley, 'The Legacy of T. S. Eliot to Milton Studies,' *Literature & Aesthetics* 18 (2008), 135–151.

Shohet, Lauren, 'The Fragrance of the Fall,' in: *Milton, Materialism, and Embodiment: One First Matter All*, eds Kevin J. Donovan/Thomas Festa (Pittsburgh, Pa.: Duquesne University Press, 2017), 19–36.

Shuger, Debora K., *The Christian Grand Style in the English Renaissance* (Princeton, N. J.: Princeton University Press, 1988).

Shumaker, Wayne, *Unpremeditated Verse: Feeling and Perception in 'Paradise Lost'* (Princeton, N. J.: Princeton University Press, 1967).

Silver, Sean B., 'Locke's Pineapple and the History of Taste,' *The Eighteenth Century* 49 (2008): 43–65.

Skinner, Quentin, 'Introduction: Seeing Things Their Way,' in: Idem, *Visions of Politics, Volume I: Regarding Method* (Cambridge: Cambridge University Press, 2002), 1–7.

Slepian, Michael L./Ambady, Nalini, 'Simulating Sensorimotor Metaphors: Novel Metaphors Influence Sensory Judgments,' *Cognition* 130 (2014), 309–314.

Smith, Bruce R., *The Acoustic World of Early Modern England: Attending to the O-Factor* (Chicago: University of Chicago Press, 1999).

Smith, Mark M., *Sensory History* (Oxford: Berg, 2007).

Smith, Simon, et al. (eds), *The Senses in Early Modern England, 1558–1660* (Manchester: Manchester University Press, 2015).

Spaeth, Sigmund G., *Milton's Knowledge of Music: Its Sources and Its Significance in His Works* (New York: Da Capo Press, 1973 [1913]).

Spitzer, Leo, *Classical and Christian Ideas of World Harmony: Prolegomena to an Interpretation of the Word 'Stimmung'* (Baltimore, Md.: Johns Hopkins University Press, 1963).

Spolsky, Ellen, 'Cognitive Literary Historicism: A Response to Adler and Gross,' *Poetics Today* 24 (2003).

Stanev, Hristomir A., *Sensory Experience and the Metropolis on the Jacobean Stage (1603–1625)* (Farnham: Ashgate, 2014).

Starr, G. Gabrielle, 'Multisensory Imagery,' in *Cognitive Cultural Studies*, ed. Zunshine, 275–291.

Stein, Arnold, *Answerable Style: Essays on 'Paradise Lost'* (Minneapolis, Minn.: University of Minnesota Press, 1953).

Steiner, George, *After Babel: Aspects of Language and Translation* (Oxford: Oxford University Press, 1977 [1975]).

Steiner, George, *Real Presences* (Chicago: University of Chicago Press, 1991 [1989]).

Stephenson, Bruce, *The Music of the Heavens: Kepler's Harmonic Astronomy* (Princeton, N. J.: Princeton University Press, 1994).

Sterne, Jonathan/ Akiyama, Mitchell, 'The Recording That Never Wanted to Be Heard and Other Stories of Sonification,' in: *The Oxford Handbook of Sound Studies*, eds Trevor Pinch and Karin Bijsterveld (New York: Oxford University Press, 2011), 544–560.

Stewart, Susan, *Poetry and the Fate of the Senses* (Chicago: University of Chicago Press, 2002).

Sundell, Roger H., 'The Singer and his Song in the Prologues of *Paradise Lost*,' in: John Max Patrick/Roger H. Sundell (eds), *Milton and the Art of Sacred Song* (Madison, Wisc.: University of Wisconsin Press, 1979), 65–80.

Svendsen, Kester, *Milton and Science* (Cambridge, Mass.: Harvard University Press, 1956).

Teeter, Louis, 'Scholarship and the Art of Criticism,' *ELH* 5 (1938).

Thirsk, Joan, *Food in Early Modern England: Phases, Fads, Fashions, 1500–1760* (London: Hambledon Continuum, 2006).

Thomas, Arvind, 'Milton and Table Manners,' *MQ* 40 (2006), 37–47.

Thomas, Keith, *Religion and the Decline of Magic* (Harmondsworth: Penguin, 1971).

Thomas, Keith, *Man and the Natural World: Changing Attitudes in England 1500–1800* (London: Allen Lane, 1983).

Tillyard, E. M. W., *The Elizabethan World Picture: A Study of the Idea of Order in the Age of Shakespeare, Donne and Milton* (New York: Vintage Books, 1959 [1942])

Tillyard, E. M. W., *Milton* (London: Chatto & Windus, 1961 [1930]).

Tullett, William, *Smell in Eighteenth-Century England: A Social Sense* (Oxford: Oxford University Press, 2019).

Tvordi, Jessica, 'The Comic Personas of Milton's *Prolusion VI*: Negotiating Masculine Identity Through Self-Directed Humor,' in: Albrecht Classen (ed.), *Laughter in the Middle Ages and Early Modern Times: Epistemology of a Fundamental Human Behavior, Its Meaning, and Consequences* (Berlin: De Gruyter, 2010), 715–34.

Veeser, H. Aram, 'Introduction,' in: *The New Historicism*, ed. H. Aram Veeser (New York: Routledge, 1989), ix–xvi.

Vinge, Louise, *The Five Senses: Studies in a Literary Tradition* (Lund: CWK Gleerup, 1975).

Wainwright, William J., 'Jonathan Edwards and His Puritan Predecessors,' in: *The Spiritual Senses*, eds Gavrilyuk/Coakley, 224–240.

von Maltzahn, Nicholas, *Milton's 'History of Britain:' Republican Historiography in the English Revolution* (Oxford: Oxford University Press, 1991).

von Maltzahn, Nicholas, 'Samuel Butler's Milton,' *SIP* 92 (1995), 482–495.

Wall, Wendy, *Recipes for Thought: Knowledge and Taste in the Early Modern Kitchen* (Philadelphia: University of Pennsylvania Press, 2016).

Wallace-Hadrill, Andrew, 'The Senses in the Marketplace: The Luxury Market and Eastern Trade in Imperial Rome,' in: Jerry Toner (ed.), *A Cultural History of the Senses in Antiquity* (London: Bloomsbury, 2014), 69–89.

Walker, Terry, *'Thou' and 'You' in Early Modern English Dialogues: Trials, Depositions, and Drama Comedy* (Amsterdam: John Benjamins, 2007).

Wallis, Patrick/Wright, Catherine, 'Evidence, Artisan Experience and Authority in Early Modern England,' in: Pamela H. Smith et al. (eds), *Ways of Making and Knowing: The Material Culture of Empirical Knowledge* (New York: Bard Graduate Center, 2017), 138–63.

Watson, Jackie, '"Dove-Like Looks' and 'Serpents Eyes:' Staging Visual Clues and Early Modern Aspiration,' in: *The Senses in Early Modern England*, eds Smith et al., 39–54.

Webster, Charles, *The Great Instauration: Science, Medicine and Reform, 1626–1660*, 2nd ed. (Oxford: Peter Lang, 2002 [1975]).

Webster, Erin, '"Presented with a Universal blanc:" The Physics of Vision in Milton's Invocation to Light,' *MS* 56 (2015), 233–271.

Webster, Erin, *The Curious Eye: Optics and Imaginative Literature in Seventeenth-Century England* (Oxford: Oxford University Press, 2020).

Weisman, Karen, 'Introduction,' in: Karen Weisman (ed.), *The Oxford Handbook of the Elegy* (Oxford: Oxford University Press, 2010), 1–12.

Welch, Evelyn, 'The Senses in the Marketplace: Sensory Knowledge in a Material World,' in: *Cultural History of the Senses in the Renaissance*, ed. Roodenburg, 61–86.

Wellek, René/Warren, Austin, *Theory of Literature*, 3rd ed. (Harmondsworth: Penguin, 1973 [1963]).

Wentersdorf, Karl P., 'The "Rout of Monsters" in *Comus*,' *MQ* 12 (1978), 119–25.

Wentersdorf, Karl P., 'Images of "Licence" in Milton's *Sonnet XII*,' *MQ* 13 (1979), 36–42.

Wheeler, Elizabeth Skerpan, 'Early Political Prose,' in: *A Companion to Milton*, ed. Thomas N. Corns (Malden, Mass.: Blackwell, 2003), 263–278.

Wille, Günther, *Akroasis: Der akustische Sinnesbereich in der griechischen Literatur bis zum Ende der klassischen Zeit*, 2 vols (Tübingen: Attempto, 2001 [1958]).

Williams, Raymond, 'Sensibility,' in: Idem, *Keywords: A Vocabulary of Culture and Society* [London: Fontana, 1976], 235–239.

Winn, James Anderson, *Unsuspected Eloquence: A History of the Relations between Poetry and Music* (New Haven, Conn.: Yale University Press, 1981).

Wnuk, Ewelina/Majid, Asifa, 'Revisiting the Limits of Language: The Odor Lexicon of Maniq,' *Cognition* 131 (2014), 125–138.

Woods, H., 'What Is "Milk of Sulphur?",' *British Medical Journal* 1 (1891), 670–1.

Woolf, Daniel, 'Speech, Text, and Time: The Sense of Hearing and the Sense of the Past in Renaissance England,' *Albion* 18 (1986), 159–193.

Zunshine, Lisa, 'Cognitive Historicism,' in: *Introduction to Cognitive Cultural Studies*, ed. Zunshine, 61–63.

Zunshine, Lisa (ed.), *Introduction to Cognitive Cultural Studies* (Baltimore, Md.: Johns Hopkins University Press, 2010).

On-line sources

Abstract for Jonathan Craig et al., 'Hardstoft – Britain's First Oil Field,' <http://www.searchanddiscovery.com/abstracts/html/2015/90216ace/abstracts/2099231.html> (last accessed 20 June 2019).

Derbyshire County Council, 'Shale gas and hydraulic fracturing (fracking),' <https://www.derbyshire.gov.uk/environment/planning/planning-policy/minerals-waste-development-framework/shale-gas/shale-gas-and-hydraulic-fracturing-fracking.aspx> (last accessed 20 June 2019).

Index

Abdiel 218n, 292n, 350
Abrams, M. H.
  The Mirror and the Lamp (1953) 47n, 128
accommodation 292n, 354
Achaemenids *see* Persia, ancient
Achilles 348, 360
Adam (*Paradise Lost*) 38, 52, 57n, 58 ,69, 82, 85n, 90n, 104, 117n, 137n, 141n, 143, 144n, 146n, 208, 227n, 244, 247, 252, 254, 256n, 258n, 260–6, 268, 277, 286–96, 308, 310–11, 314n, 320, 327, 330, 333, 337n, 342–54, 386
Addison, Joseph 378
Adonis 117, 306
Aegean 176n
Aeschines 228
Aesculapius 225
Africa 286
ages of life
  — childhood 152
  — youth 117, 124, 141, 146, 152–4, 157n, 161, 302, 309
  — maturity 152
  — old age 152
Alcestis 373n
alcohol 246
Alexander Nevsky (Eisenstein) 12n
allegory 43n, 51, 140, 148, 150, 154–5, 158, 166, 179–80, 206, 311
Alpheus 307–308
Alps 9
ambiguity 8, 27–28, 51, 63, 68, 78, 108n, 122, 125n, 148n, 181, 188–9, 191n, 207, 216n, 223, 225, 227, 264, 273n, 290n, 294, 300–302, 306n, 310, 315, 317, 335, 343, 346, 351–3, 359, 367, 374–5, 384
America
  — early European settlers in North America 43n, 201
  — Native Americans 181, 186
  see also Latin America
Amphiaraus 163
Amphion 203n, 221–2, 239n, 247, 262
Amsterdam 88
ancient history 19
angels
  — association with music 51, 208–209, 267–8, 343n, 358
  — cherubim 315n
  — fallen angels 51–54, 57–58, 84, 259, 263n, 264, 267, 268, 274, 287n, 294, 330n, 350n, 353, 357–9
animals 52n, 57n, 89, 103, 181–2, 188–9, 191, 201, 234–5, 243–4, 249, 267, 294, 385
  — adder 297
  — ass 235, 239
  — associated with lust, violence 89n, 149
  — beetle 297, 382, 385
  — bull 150n, 235–6
  — cow 236n
  — dog 235, 239
  — dolphin 147, 209–10, 249
  — elephant 236
  — goat 149n
  — boar 89n, 234–6, 240
  — fish 177n, 241–2, 245, 367n
  — frog 176–7, 199, 234, 365n
  — lion 89n, 194–5, 233n
  — lice 234, 236
  — mole 382, 385
  — phoenix 328–9
  — rhinoceros 236
  — shellfish 177n
  — snail 176–7
  — snake (serpent) 103–104, 166, 233, 266, 291, 297
  — swine 122, 239
  — toad 177n
  — wolf 88–89, 235
  — worms 312, 314
  see also bees, birds
Annales school 42
Anne (queen) 120n
anthropology 44, 62, 86, 105n, 210
Apelles 190
Apicius 234, 244–5
Arcady 192, 309
archery 122, 126–7, 131n, 136, 141n, 145, 155, 159–60, 163, 366n
Argentina 372
Arion 147–8, 209–210
Ariosto, Ludovico 360n
Aristophanes 234
Aristotle 28n, 71–73, 75, 79–80, 141n, 196, 205–211, 240, 244, 246, 284n, 285, 287n, 311n, 340n

Aristotle (continued)
  De anima 52n, 71, 173
  De Caelo 207n
  — 'intelligences' 207–208, 210
  Metaphysics 285
  Meteorologica 210
  Poetics 71
  Rhetoric 57n
  — theory of metaphor 71–74, 107
  — theory of perception 173n
Asia 186, 367
Asia Minor 186
astronomy 70, 104n, 115, 143n, 173, 196, 200, 256, 290, 296, 326, 328–9, 337, 365
Athamas 233
Athanasius of Alexandria 273n
Athens 53n, 92n, 132n, 220, 223, 260n
athletics 51, 59, 127, 356
  — fencing 356
  — running 53, 295
  — wrestling 356
Atlas (titan) 209
Attica 132, 346, 349
Aubrey, John 30n, 171n, 381
audio-visual media 10–13
auditory culture 43
  see also bells; music; musical instruments
aura 6, 217–9, 230
Aurora/Eos 130–32, 143, 186–7, 189, 198–9

Babel
  — confusion of tongues 267, 277–8,
  — Tower of Babel 384
Babington, Gervase 177n
Babylon 309n
Bacon, Francis 54–56, 182, 184–5, 195, 244, 289, 306, 315n
  Great Instauration (1620) 54, 55
  Historia Vitae et Mortis (1626) 244n
  Sylva Sylvarum (1626) 184–5, 195, 244, 306, 315n
  The Advancement of Learning (1640) 54, 56
Badminton (Glos.) 101
Bagehot, Walter 28–34, 369
  Literary Studies (1859) 28
bank (rising ground) 301–308, 310, 312
Barberini, Cardinal Francesco 19
Baroni, Leonora 151, 337n
Baroque culture 19
Basil the Great 203n
Battleship Potemkin (Eisenstein) 10n
beatus ille tradition 288

Beaufort, Duke of 101n
beauty 29–30, 71, 76, 80, 108, 117–124, 128n, 133–4, 143, 155, 157n, 158n, 161–66, 174, 185–6, 190–93, 205n, 227n, 265, 284n, 285n, 300, 308, 312, 352
bees 67, 132, 317 *see also* food: honey
Bellerophon 329–30, 337–8, 340, 342
bells 194, 307–308
Benjamin, Walter 6–10, 14, 42n
Bentham, Jeremy 101n
Bernini, Gian Lorenzo 136n
Bethlehem 290
Bible 18, 54, 57n, 58, 69, 74n, 82, 87, 88n, 211, 237, 239n, 254–6, 273, 281, 297n, 331n, 333n, 348, 354, 381
  — Book of Job 332–5, 340, 359
  — KJV/Autorised Version 203n, 302n, 318n, 320n, 332n, 334n
  — Vulgate 54n, 332n
  — Tremellius–Junius version 54n
  — Ecclesiasticus 54n
  — Flood 306n
  — Gen. 1:1 331n
  — Gen. 2:7 291n
  — Ex. 15:26 254
  — Ex. 16:31 58
  — Dtn. 28:28–29 281n
  — Isa. 45:9 291n
  — Dan. 12:4 54
  — Prov. 2:5 318
  — Prov. 8:24–25, 27, 30 332
  — Job 15:2 333n
  — Job 15:6–9 332
  — Job 28:22 334
  — Job 28:24a 334
  — Ps. 19:1–4 203
  — Ps. 34:8 318
  — Ps. 58:5 297
  — Matt. 15:14 299
  — Luke 1:76–79 302
  — John 1:1 282n, 331
  — John 1:8 282
  — John 4:14 274n
  — John 9:1–7 254
  — Rom. 1:20 320
  — Rom. 6:23 114n
  — Rom. 10:17 331n
  — Col. 1:15 282n
  — 1 Thess. 5:23 52n
  — Heb. 12:26 299n
  — Rev. 8:10–13 331
  — Rev. 21:6 274n, 307n
  — Rev. 21:16 120n

biology 3, 6, 38, 103
Bion 355n
birds 66–67, 137–38, 168, 180–82, 185–88, 190, 194, 200n, 201, 203n, 209–10, 234, 236, 245n, 267, 292–93, 334
— cock 65–66, 178, 180–82, 193–4
— eagle 328–29
— 'Irish birds' 234–36
— nightingale 65–66, 68, 128–30, 137n, 209, 309–310 *see also* Philomela
— lark 65–66, 129n, 209, 212
Blake, William 384–5
Milton (1804–10) 384
blindness
— attitudes towards 69, 108n, 255, 280, 299
— as punishment 255, 281, 298, 303
— congenital 255
— and old age 256, 273
— and work/duty 255, 304,
— healing of the blind 254–5, 298, 312
— iconography of 280–81
— in Milton's sonnets 366n, 382–3
— in *Paradise Lost* 255, 258, 269, 272, 298–300, 310, 312, 315–6, 319, 323–5, 328n, 338–40, 362–3
— in *Samson Agonistes* 301–317, 319
— of visionaries 284n, 296, 309
— temporary 127
— the blind leading the blind 85n, 299n
see also Milton, John: blindness
body 2, 40, 51–52, 57–60, 65n, 81, 85, 107, 134, 195, 206, 216, 220n, 222, 230, 232, 240, 244–6, 279n, 290–91, 298n, 303–304, 317, 322n, 333n, 340, 352, 357, 363, 367n
see also reductio ad corpus
Boeotia 233n
Boiardo, Matteo Maria 360n
Borges, Jorge Luis 371–5, 381–2, 386
— blindness 372–3,
'Del infierno y del cielo' 372
'Poema de los dones' 372
'Una rosa y Milton' 371–5
bouba-kiki effect 46n, 126n
Bowers, Fredson 237–8
Boyle, Robert 75, 100
Brant, Sebastian 216n
Ship of Fools (Das Narrenschiff, 1494) 216n
breath/breathing 6n, 66, 74n, 114, 117, 133–4, 137–8, 144, 184–5, 191, 194, 219, 224, 228–33, 242–3, 245n, 260n, 263–4, 301–307, 357–8
Browne, John (surgeon) 101n

Browne, Sir Thomas 71n, 236
Religio Medici (1642/43) 71n
Brueghel, Pieter, the Elder 85n
The Blind Leading the Blind (De parabel der blinden, 1568) 85n
Buckingham, George Villiers, Duke of 278n
The Rehearsal (1671) 278
Bunyan, John
The Holy War ... (1682) 311–2, *313*
Burton, Robert 235, 279–80
Butler, Charles
The Feminine Monarchy (1623) 317n
Butler, Samuel 280

Cadmus 210
Calliope 164, 339–40
Cambridge
— Cambridge University 18, 57, 114–5, 123, 169–70, 173, 202, 213–4, 216–7n, 225, 237, 303n
— Christ's College 18, 171
— Trinity College 237
Cambridge Platonists 76, 318, 321
Cambridgeshire 115
camera obscura 1
camera (lens) 1–2, 4–5, 8, 11, 14
Canidia 193
Carlyle, Thomas 54n
Castalian spring 126, 162n, 165, 300
Catholicism 71, 186, 331n
Cato 225
Catullus 116
Chapman, George 31
character writing 116, 280, 288–9, 295
Charles I
— execution of, 1649 17, 20, 90, 297
Charles II 101
— Restoration of, 1660 17, 297
— 'touching' for 'the King's Evil' 100
Charleton, Walter
Physiologia Epicuro-Gassendo-Charltoniana (1654) 27
Charon 179–80
Chaucer, Geoffrey 137n
chemistry 97–98
Christ/Jesus 53n, 158, 208, 254–6, 260n, 265n, 274, 282, 290, 298, 307, 309n, 318, 320–22
Christianity 35, 127, 180, 195, 203n, 208, 254–6, 258, 264, 274n, 281–2, 285–7, 296, 298n, 318, 320–21, 326–7, 335, 356, 358–60
— patience as a Christian virtue ix, 356–7, 359n, 361, 376
see also Catholicism; Protestantism

Christmas 281–2
church fathers 19
Church of England 35–36, 88, 231, 264n
Churchill, Sir Winston 383
Cicero 52n, 172, 204n, 205, 220, 223, 226, 229, 249
  De finibus bonorum et malorum 204n
Circe 122, 136, 145, 149n, 157n, 239
city/country 19, 21, 115–123, 128–9, 145–6, 160–61, 166, 214, 311
Civil War (England) 17, 20, 119n, 288
Classen, Constance 44–45
Cleombrotus 296n
Clio 115
Clytie 180, 182, 184–5
cognition 3, 46, 48–49, 62n, 103–104, 173, 279–80, 288
cognitive science 47n, 61, 68n
— cognitive historicism/cognitive cultural studies 41–49
Coke, Sir Edward 190
Cole, William 231n
  Adam in Eden (1657) 231n
  The Art of Simpling (1656) 231n
Coleridge, Samuel Taylor 27–28, 34, 129n, 158n, 332n, 375
  Kubla Khan (1797) 332n
  Principles of Genial Criticism (1814) 27, 34
College of Physicians 97–98
colours ('hues') 30n, 35, 37, 67, 158, 180, 185, 191, 265, 267n, 305–307, 360n, 374
— black 141n, 179, 187, 192, 198–9, 229, 274, 276, 280, 376, 382, 384–5 *for 'black bile' see also* melancholy
— blue 139
— green 29, 67–68, 124–5, 127, 131–2, 234, 288, 307–308, 332n
— purple 67, 148n, 306n, 308, 325, 338–9
— red 38, 117, 130–32, 148, 152, 182n, 291n, 374, 378, 381
— yellow 97, 124, 141n, 184, 228, 371, 374
Comenius, John Amos 367
Commonwealth and Protectorate 17, 20, 90–91
communication 3, 22, 52n, 61, 65, 80n, 126n, 171, 172, 228, 243n, 249, 263, 286, 303, 310–12, 333
conceptual metaphor 58–59, 79–90, 106–108, 120, 122, 135, 142, 145, 165, 167, 178–9, 200, 219, 225–7, 243, 245–7, 254, 258, 262, 285, 311, 323n, 328, 343–4, 352–3, 367
  A PLACE OF SENSUAL EXCESS IS A PARADISE 88
  BAD IS DOWN 142
  BETTER IS UP 81
  CHANGE IS MOVEMENT 262, 323
  CONSCIOUS(NESS) IS UP 81, 142n, 291n, 293
  DISCOURSE IS A FLOWING LIQUID 262
  EDUCATION IS A JOURNEY 81
  ELOQUENCE IS SWEETNESS 262
  EYES ARE LIMBS 81
  GOD IS A KING 82
  GOD IS UP 82, 258
  GOOD IS UP 142, 258
  HAPPY IS UP 81, 142n, 277n
  HARMONY IS UP 258
  HEIGHT IS VISIBILITY 120, 134–5
  IDEAS ARE FOOD 81, 83–84, 87, 174, 225–7, 230, 243, 245–7, 254, 309, 333, 343–4, 347, 349, 353, 357n, 366
  KNOWING IS SEEING 81, 178
  KNOWLEDGE IS LIGHT 175
  KNOWLEDGE IS UP 175, 256, 289n, 294
  LIFE IS A JOURNEY 80, 82n, 85n
  LIFE IS A PILGRIMAGE 81, 85n
  LIFE IS A SEA JOURNEY 80–81
  LIGHT IS UP 258, 275, 291n
  LOVE IS A JOURNEY 81
  LOVE IS CONQUEST 119, 121–2, 136, 145, 167
  LUST IS HUNGER 81
  MORE IS UP 81, 142n
  MOVEMENT IS A FLOW 262n
  OBJECTIONABLE HUMAN BEHAVIOUR IS ANIMAL BEHAVIOUR 89
  OBJECTIONABLE PEOPLE ARE ANIMALS 89
  PHYSICAL VISION IS KNOWLEDGE 87
  RATIONAL IS UP 81, 142n
  SEEING IS TOUCHING 81
  THE WILL IS DOWN 175
  THINKING IS LOOKING 81, 178, 351n
  TOUCH IS DOWN 142, 211, 291n, 293
  TRUTH IS LIGHT 311
  UNCONSCIOUSNESS IS DOWN 293
  UNDERSTANDING IS DIGESTING 84
  UNDERSTANDING IS REACHING A GOAL 84–85
  UNDERSTANDING IS TOUCHING 81
  UP/DOWN 135, 149, 167, 188, 219
  VISION IS HEIGHT 120, 135, 188, 191
  VISION IS UP 82, 120, 131, 142, 175, 188, 211, 258, 275, 289n, 293, 323, 366
  WIT IS SALT 242, 246
conscience 256, 385
contemplation 71n, 141n, 161, 173–4, 203, 217, 276, 285–91, 294–6, 311, 318–21, 329, 333n, 359, 367n
context 2, 5–10, 13–15, 17–18, 21–24, 34–38, 40–44, 47–48, 53, 60–61, 63–64, 68–70,

context (continued)
    79–94, 100–109, 131n, 135, 136, 142, 145, 150–53, 156, 159, 164, 166, 167n, 174n, 175, 177n, 186, 188–90, 196, 201–204, 207, 208n, 214, 222n, 223, 229, 231–2, 233n, 235, 248, 256–7, 260, 263–4, 278–9, 283n, 304, 315n, 318–9, 322, 332n, 337–8, 342–3, 345–7, 357, 367, 385
Corbin, Alain 42–43, 62
Corinth 126
cosmology 120, 143, 196–7, 202, 209, 274–5, 293n, 337n, 343, 357n
    — cosmic dance 210, 260
    — geocentrism 143n, 196n, 202
    — heliocentrism 104
    — Milton's cosmology 357n
country life 214, 288 *see also* city/country
criticism vs scholarship 34n, 36–41, 47–48, 59, 62
Cromwell, Oliver 17, 20, 349n
Cupid/Amor/Eros 117, 122, 131n, 137, 144–5, 149, 155–68, 211, 368, 375
curiosity 82, 143, 266, 344–5, 347
Cybele 135, 137–8, 149
Cyclops *see* Polyphemus (cyclops)
Cyprus 121, 133n

daguerreotype 1
Daphne 126, 159
Darbishire, Helen 383
Davenant, Sir William 283, 343
    Gondibert (1651) 283, 343
dawn 65–67, 124, 129–32, 148, 152, 154, 157–8, 167, 178, 180–82, 185–7, 198–200, 261, 267, 270–71, 298, 301–302, 308, 310, 338–9, 373, 381 *see also* Aurora/Eos; day; *Hymn to Dawn*; night
day 65–68, 96, 124, 129–30, 141n, 144n, 148, 151–4, 161, 169, 175–202, 209, 212, 215, 238, 248, 254–5, 271, 281, 290, 298, 301–305, 308, 310, 314–5, 317, 322, 324, 338, 373
    see also dawn; night
death 44–45, 67, 71n, 113, 114n, 116, 148, 152, 179, 188, 196, 198, 237, 260, 273, 291n, 302n, 308, 315, 330n, 334, 341, 347–8, 350, 354, 357
Decaisne, Henri 378, *380*
Delacroix, Eugène 21n, 371, 375–382, 386
    Milton et ses filles ou Milton dictant le Paradis Perdu à ses filles (1827/28?) *377*
delight and instruction 73, 136, 195
Delphi 126, 147
Demeter/Ceres 136, 137n, 146n, 149

Democritus 216
Demosthenes 220, 223, 239
Derbyshire 382–4 *see also* Darbishire, Helen
Descartes, René 52, 293, 296
Diana 131n, 145, 200
digestion 84, 225, 230–31, 237n, 243, 245n, 254, 343n, 357
    — 'concoction' 356–7
Dingley, Robert 103, 320–21
    Divine Opticks (1654) 103n
    The Spirituall Taste Described ... (1649) 320–21
Diodati, Charles 115, 123, 365
Dion Prusaeus 92n
discourse 10, 20–24, 51–61, 71–73, 79, 85–87, 89–94, 96, 98–102, 104–109, 128, 170, 122, 220–23, 226, 242, 262–4, 269, 273, 283–4, 319, 322, 335–6, 343–5, 347, 349, 353, 362, 365, 367
    see also sensory discourse
Donne, John 30, 147n, 282
    'The Bait' 147n
Downham, George 204
Dracontius 28n
dreams 126, 197, 265, 279–80, 284, 310n, 339, 373
    — dream visions 339
dryads 148–9
Dryden, John 120n, 278n, 288n, 293, 339n
    The State of Innocence (1674; printed 1677) 293
    'To His Sacred Majesty, A Panegyric on His Coronation' (1662) 339n
du Laurens, André 122n
    Discourse of the Preservation of Sight (1599) 122n
du Moulin, Pierre 88
    Regii Sanguinis Clamor ad Coelum adversus Parricidas Anglicanos (1652) 88
Dutch language 277n, 279n
Dutch Republic 18, 297

Earle, John 295
earth 69, 82n, 124–5, 132–5, 138–9, 141–5, 149, 167, 178–81, 185–8, 191, 194, 196n, 200, 202, 210, 244, 258, 265, 276, 295, 299n, 324, 327, 329, 331, 332n, 336–7, 345, 351, 366n, 382, 384 *see also* soil (earth, turf); Tellus (Earth)
Edwards, Jonathan 289n
Egypt 182, 328
Eisenstein, Sergei 10–15
    The Film Sense (1942) 10

ekphrasis 137, 349, 360
Electra 210
Eliot, T. S. 30–38, 41,
— 'dissociation of sensibility' 30
'The Metaphysical Poets' (1921) 30–31, 33
Eliphaz 333
emblems 43n
embodiment 22, 80, 149, 159, 211, 233n, 296, 328
— as process or event 53, 290, 303
— as created condition 53
— Incarnation 290
emotions 53, 75, 80, 86, 167–8, 193, 218, 267, 277, 317, 355
Empson, William 30, 352, 367
Engels, Friedrich 1
England ix, 10, 17–20, 36, 40n, 43n, 49, 70, 88, 90, 92n, 95–96, 98, 100, 109, 113n, 146n, 161, 182, 195, 202n, 225n, 230, 235, 238, 242, 264, 303n, 317n, 318–9, 355–6, 371–2, 378, 382, 384
English language 23, 52n, 54, 60n, 71n, 131n, 135n, 152n, 169n, 182n, 184, 228, 240, 242, 259, 260n, 277n, 284, 320n, 328n, 335, 367n
enthusiasm 278–83, 296, 322
epic 19–20, 51, 65, 170, 172, 196n, 251–2, 256–7, 259, 261, 266–9, 272, 283, 285, 293, 296, 301, 311–2, 315–6, 325, 330–31, 337–8, 340, 342, 346, 348–9, 353, 359–61, 362–3, 366, 373–4, 376, 378, 384
— epic simile 59, 73, 89, 267
— as a poem of knowledge 258, 269, 362, 368
— as song 90n, 164n, 254, 257, 258, 337, 342, 353
Epidaurus 255
episcopacy 20, 68, 74, 84, 114, 283
Erasmus 226, 232n
In Praise of Folly (1509) 226
Erebus 179–80
ethnology 38, 42, 44–46, 48
etymology 52–54, 60, 68n, 74n, 92, 131, 153, 159, 176, 216n, 217n, 230n, 262, 274n, 280, 328, 345n, 367
— *figura etymologica* 125, 176
— 'obedience' 92n, 254
— 'visit' 276–7
— pseudetymology 125
Eucharist 96–97
Euripides 301n
Phoenician Women 301n
Europe 17–18, 20, 45n, 49, 107n, 146n, 177, 184, 186, 190
Eurydice 164

Evelyn, John 136, 146n, 190n
Diary 136n, 146n, 190n
experience 2, 7, 9–10, 18–20, 31–34, 43, 47, 53, 59–61, 66, 68–69, 74n, 78, 80–81, 85–86, 95–96, 98, 104, 108, 114–6, 126–8, 148, 154–5, 158–60, 164, 166–8, 186, 189, 195, 197, 200–201, 215, 230, 232, 245, 248–9, 252, 288, 298–9, 308n, 310, 312, 316–20, 322–3, 336–8, 346, 350, 365, 368–9, 383
— witnessing 159, 166, 168
Eye-Salve for the English Army 299n

fancy *see* imagination ('fancy')
fate 51, 57, 206, 255, 322
fauns 149–50
Febvre, Lucien 42–43
feeling 28, 30–31, 37–38, 199, 215n, 218, 230, 294, 316–7, 319, 326n, 368, 375n
— ambiguity of the term 317n
figures of speech
— antonomasia 361
— epizeuxis 315
— pathetic paradox 315
— personification 119, 121, 135, 157, 180, 184, 199, 201, 374
film 1–5, 10–14, 163, 371
fire 97, 132, 138, 140, 142, 155–6, 163–4, 166, 233, 244, 274, 317n, 345–6
Florio, John 54
flowers 6n, 66–67, 70n, 124, 133–4, 137n, 146n, 153, 173, 180–87, 191, 201, 265, 276–8, 300, 302, 305–309, 378, 386
— *Calendula officinalis* (common marigold) *183*, 184
— 'Caltha' 180, 184–6
— *Caltha palustris* (marsh marigold) 184
— crocus 114, 146
— Eve's gardening in *Paradise Lost* 276–7
— heliotrope 180, 182, 191
— iris (*Lilium purpureum*) 306n
— of spring 124, 137, 153, 308
— rose, roses 31, 33, 66, 70–71, 114, 121, 133–4, 136, 140, 180, 182, 184–5, 271, 306–308, 310, 345, 367, 371, 373–5, 381, 386 *see also* rosewater
— violet 66, 96, 185, 308, 367n
— marigold 180, 182, *183*, 184
— scent of 31, 66, 173, 182, 184–5, 300, 309, 373
food 81, 83–84, 87, 174, 215n, 225–7, 230–2, 235, 240–47, 254, 307, 309, 321, 333, 341–353, 356–7, 366

food (continued)
— apples 237, 245, 307, 347
— beer 234, 240
— the forbidden fruit 59n, 253, 266, 288, 347, 352
— fruit 17, 58, 66, 147, 227, 231, 237, 253, 265–6, 276–7, 306n, 307, 343, 345, 348–51
— herbs 138, 225–6, 231n, 265, 345
— honey 58, 132n, 137, 141n, 146n, 223, 226n, 262, 308 *see also* bees
— leeks 229–32, 241, 245
— meat 231n, 236, 240, 243, 245
— mustard 225–6
— oil 226n
— pineapple 17, 48
— onions 229–232, 241, 245
— salt 96, 139, 140n, 141n, 203, 213–4, 218, 226–7, 237–43, 246–7
— salted fish 241–2, 245
— turnips 231–2
— vegetables 231–2, 245
— wine 64, 240n, 242, 322, 345–6
see also alcohol; gluttony; spices
Foucault, Michel 45n, 61, 64, 93–96, 98–109, 386
The Archaeology of Knowledge (1969) 61, 93
— discursive formations 22, 45n, 94, 98
— *énoncés / énonciations* 99
— subject positions 102
— system of dispersion 45n, 94
— surfaces of emergence 95
— field of memory 103
France 19, 194n, 238, 378
Friedell, Egon 1–10, 14, 46n
A Cultural History of the Modern Age (1927) 1–6
Fuseli, Henry 21n, 378, *379*

Galilei, Galileo 20, 69–71, 73, 87, 96, 99, 196, 201, 327–8, 365
— visited by Milton 20
— mentioned in *Paradise Lost* 20n, 69, 71, 73, 87, 201, 327–8
Ganymede 158–9, 307
gardening 88, 101n, 182, 276–7
Gaule, John 284, 296
Pys-mantia: The Mag-Astro-Mancer ... (1652) 284
Geertz, Clifford 62n
gems 138–9, 191, 193
Geneva 88
genres
— comedy (drama) 116
— dramatic monologue 383

— epic 19–20, 51, 65, 89–90, 170, 251–2, 254, 257–9, 261, 269, 283, 330, 337, 340, 342, 348, 353, 359–63, 366, 368, 384
— elegy 113–5, 123n, 131, 154, 166–8, 368
— georgic 309n, 342
— lyric poetry 65, 68, 124–6, 257, 310, 372–3
— pastoral 115, 116n, 124, 130–31, 143, 145, 147–9, 154, 166, 168, 193, 310, 342, 345, 355n
— prolusion 163–5, 172, 195, 206, 213–4, 245
— sonnet 252, 297, 363, 366, 373–4, 383
— threnody 114–5, 368
— tragedy (drama) 116, 359n
German language 7n, 24n, 93n, 254n, 277n, 279n, 328n
Glanvill, Joseph 100
gluttony 231, 235, 239, 245–7
God 57, 59, 70, 74, 82, 84, 87, 91–2, 149n, 174, 186n, 191, 195, 211, 219n, 242, 254–8, 263, 265–9, 271–8, 282n, 285–89, 291n, 293–7, 306n, 310n, 311, 314, 316, 318, 320–22, 327, 331–40, 342, 344, 347–9, 358–9, 361, 363, 367, 372, 386
— divine foreknowledge 51, 57, 286
— divine grace 58, 257n, 263, 276, 286, 320, 343, 347–8
— divine mercy 302n
— divine wisdom 84, 273, 286, 288, 291, 311–2, 324, 329–36, 340, 362–3
— GOD IS A KING 82, 264n
— pneumatology 319
— providence 51, 57, 82, 297
— Trinitarianism, Athanasian 273n, 282n
— Trinity 204n, 282, 319, 332
golden age 76, 132n, 150, 212n, 295
golden chain (Homer) 120, 206n
Golding, Arthur 266n
Grass, Günter 385n
The Tin Drum (1959) 385n
Greatrakes, Valentine 100–101
Greece, ancient 53, 118, 132n, 260n *see also* Athens
Greek language 53n, 54n, 93n, 113, 188, 200, 216n, 237n, 240n, 254n, 259, 272n, 320n, 326, 376
— Doric Greek 355, 358
— Milton's daughters reading to him 376
Greek terms and phrases
— *agapê* (unconditional love, charity) 117n
— *aisthêsis theia* ('divine sense') 318
— *atê* (delusion) 186, 298
— *aura* (soft breeze) 217, 219, 230

Greek terms and phrases (continued)
— *blephara* (eyelids) 187–9
— *blepein* (to look) 188n
— *diêgêsis/diêgêma* (narrative account) 54n
— *eikones* (lexical similes) 73
— *elegeia* (elegy) 113–4
— *erastês* (older male lover) 163n
— *erōs* (passionate love) 117n, 122n
— *ethos* (mood) 355
— *epignōsin theou* (knowledge of God) 318n
— *harmoniai* (musical modes) 355, 360
— *horân* (to see) 320n
— *idea* (class, group; idea, ideal) 279–80, 283–6
— *logos* (word, speech, reason ...) 57–58, 282n
— *mathêsis* (imparted knowledge) 74
— *mêden agan* ('nothing too much') 350
— *merops* (mortal; clear-voiced; bright-eyed) 188–9
— *metapherein* (to carry along, to use metaphors) 71
— *mêtêr oreia* ('Mountain Mother') 135n
— *morosophōs* (foolishly wise) 216, 247
— *nooumena* (things to be understood) 320
— *noûs/pneûma* (intellect/spirit) 51
— *ōdai* (songs) 53
— *ops* (voice; eyes, face) 188 *see also* Latin terms and phrases: *ops*
— *ouranos* (sky, heaven) 326
— *parabolê* (simile of 'proof') 73
— *phainomena* ('visible things') 320
— *phōs* (light) 126n
— *psuchê* (soul) 51
— *rhododaktylos Êōs* ('rose-fingered Eos') 132n, 298
— *skopein/skopelos* (to watch/a lookout place) 131
— *sōma* (body) 51n
— *sphingein* (to grip tightly) 230n
— *theōrein/theōria* ([to] behold/ing) 71n
— *ta aorata* ('invisible things') 320n
— *ta eirêmena* (things said, 'poetic forms') 72
— *thanatos* (death) 188
— *thnêtos* (mortal) 188–9
— *to agathon* (the Good) 284n
— *ton hêttō logon kreittō poiein* 57
guilds 96–98
Gunpowder Plot (1605) 113n, 186n

Hades (underworld) 163, 187, 198
Hades/Pluto 136, 187

Hakluyt, Richard 367n
Hall, Joseph 288–9, 295
  Characters of Virtues and Vices (1608) 288
happiness 81, 181, 211, 289, 294
  see also beatus ille tradition
Hardstoft (Derbs) 383
harmony 9n, 53, 206–209, 211, 221–2, 258, 260–61, 265, 268, 333, 335, 357–8
  concord/discord 203n, 206n, 267–8, 358
  'harmony of the spheres' 197, 202–13, 248, 315n *see also* Pythagoras
Harrison (apothecary) 97–98
Hartley, L. P. 45–46
Hartlib, Samuel 356, 367
Hawkins, Henry 182n
  Partheneia Sacra (1633) 182n
hearing 7, 38, 45, 66, 100, 107, 116, 137, 147, 152, 154, 164, 168, 171–3, 193, 195, 199, 200, 211-2, 223–4, 230, 242, 248, 254, 257, 264, 272, 289n, 311n, 315, 325, 331, 333–5, 338, 340, 342, 351, 361–2, 378, 381–5
  — more acute at night 193–5
  — deafness 100, 164, 210–11, 250, 297n, 362, 383
  — resonance 315n
Hebrew language 53n, 54n, 254n, 291n, 303, 309n, 326n, 328–9, 333–4, 376,
  — *genitivus hebraicus* 326n
  — Milton's daughters reading to him 376, 381
  — Hebrew roots 53n, 54n, 254n, 291n
  — Hebrew songs *see* psalms
Hebrew names, terms, and phrases
  — *adam* (to be red; man) 291n
  — *adamah* (red soil) 291n
  — *aph* (nose, nostrils; anger, wrath) 348
  — Belial (useless) 57
  — *binah* (understanding) 333–4
  — *chokhmah* (supreme wisdom) 333–4
  — *nephesh* ('living soul,' life-spirit) 53, 303
  — *samar* (to play and sing) 53n
  — *mismor* (psalm) 53n
  — *shuwt* (to run to and fro) 54n
  — *tishma* ('hast thou heard?') 333
  — *yada* (knowledge) 333
  — *yatzar* (to form, fashion; create) 291n
  — *yotzer* (potter) 291n
Helen of Troy 190, 193
Helicon 256, 325, 329
Helios 186
Heraclitus 176, 216n
Herbert, Edward, Lord Cherbury 30n
Hercules/Heracles 158, 163n

Hermogenes 205
Herodotus 118
heroism 309n, 359
Hesiod 178, 189n, 256n, 329n
Hesperides 309
Heydon, John 297
Hill, Christopher 34n, 49
Hippocrates 140–41
Hippocrene 329
history 1–9, 13–14, 17–19, 38–39, 41–49, 61–65, 71, 75, 85n, 89, 102, 105, 109, 114, 295, 299, 331, 367–8, 382, 384, 386
Hobbes, Thomas 75, 84–85, 215, 216n, 283, *Leviathan* (1651) 75
Holste, Lukas 19n
Homer 67, 73, 80, 89, 120n, 122, 132n, 198, 206n, 226, 252, 259–60, 270, 298–9, 309, 326, 348
 Iliad 348
 Odyssey 122, 348
honey *see* food: honey; *see also* bees
Hooke, Robert 76, 77, 99, 236
Horace 175n, 193n, 241, 288n
 Second Epode 288n
Hortensius 220, 239
Horton (Berks) 19n
Howes, David 44, 61–62, 86
Hull, John 32n
humour (comicality) 19, 68, 123n, 197–8, 207–214, 226–7, 231–2, 235, 240–41, 243, 245n, 247–50
 — 'salting' tradition 213–4, 237–40, 243, 246–7
 — comedy roast tradition 246n
 — serious jokes 250
 see also laughter; punning
humours, humoralism 45n, 140–42, 236, 247, 344n
 — black bile 141n, 179, 227n, 229, 280
 — blood 141
 — phlegm 141n
 — yellow bile 141n
Hylas 158–9, 163, 307
Hymen 145–6, 152, 185
Hymn to Dawn 187–9, 200

iconoclasm 39–40, 96–97
iconography 375, 381
 — of the five senses 43n, 311, 381
idolatry 35–36
Île de Ré expedition 238, 240–41
imagination ('fancy') 76, 130, 280, 283–4
Industrial Revolution 384
interiority 31
Ireland 100–101, 234, 236

iris (flower) *see* flowers
Iris 146n, 305–306 *see also* rainbows
irony 35, 88, 97n, 123, 139n, 215n, 219, 224, 262, 266–7, 269, 280, 292–4, 301, 305n, 307, 350n, 352, 355, 372
Italian language 19, 54, 259, 279n, 284n, 371, 376
Italy 19, 113n, 118, 124n, 190n, 337n

Jamaica 17
James I 184
James, William 44
Jerusalem, Heavenly (Zion) 120n
 — Mount Zion 300
 — 'Sion hill' 253, 260n, 300, 326n, 336
jewels 117, 119, 121n, 139, 179, 191n, 193
Job (Book of Job) 332–5, 340, 359n
John the Baptist 302n
Johnson, Samuel 27–28, 34, 335n
jokes *see* humour (comicality)
Jove/Zeus/Jupiter 117–8, 146n, 148, 150, 158, 210, 235
Juno 146n, 233n, 341, 348

Kepler, Johannes 202n, 296n
Kermode, Frank 43n
King, Edward 147n
kingship 17, 20, 82, 287n
knowledge
 — acquisition of 22, 168, 216, 227, 286, 288, 291, 294, 320
 — arcane knowledge 256–7, 354
 — experiential 64, 80–81, 114, 168, 249, 257, 294, 322, 351
 — first-hand experience 159
 — forbidden knowledge 347n, 354
 — of God 237, 256n, 286, 289n, 291, 294–5, 320, 322, 334–6, 340, 363
 — true and rational belief 206
 — wisdom 83–84, 91, 159, 216n, 217, 227, 243, 247, 271, 273, 286, 288, 291, 311–2, 320, 323–4, 329–36, 340–43, 350, 352, 362–3

lamentation 114, 167
Langland, William 204n
language
 — *parole/langue* 63
 — idioms (Pocock) 63–64
 — 'flowery' and 'botanical' language 71, 106, 385
 — 'poetic language' 64–65, 68, 70–71, 106, 367
Latin America 45n

Latin language 19–20, 22, 24, 54, 64, 68, 88, 113, 123–4, 155, 162, 169, 180, 202–202, 216n, 220n, 224, 227n, 228n, 240, 242, 244n, 254, 259–60, 272n, 276–7, 283, 290, 297, 339n, 345n, 367, 376
— Milton's daughters reading to him 376
— Latin elegy 123n, 365
Latin terms and phrases
— *actio in distans* 141
— *anima* (soul) 316n
— *aura* (soft breeze) 6, 139, 217, 219, 230 *see also* Benjamin, Walter
— *beatus ille* ('Happy Husbandman') 288
— *bos* (bull, ox; cow) 235–6
— *caecus* (blind) 187n
— *carmen* (song) 52n
— *cogitatio* (thought, 'reason') 316
— *comestor* (glutton, gourmand) 234
— *dies* (day) 178
— *discursus; discurrere/percurrere* (to run to and fro) 53–54
— *docere, delectare, movere* (to teach, delight, and move) 172, 176n, 216, 247, 249
— *Ens* (Being) 240
— *figura etymologica* 125, 176
— *fructus* (fruit; result) 227, 353n
— *furor* (frenzy, passion) 126–7, 164–5
— *gaudium* (joy) 180–1, 188
— *genus* (class, group) 73, 107n, 158n, 188, 285n
— *genus grande* (high style) 261
— *imaginatio* ('fancy') 316
— *ingenium* (ingenuity) 128, 222
— *labor* (toil) 215–6, 243, 245, 247, 302
— *lac sulphuris* ('milk of sulphur') 97–98
— *laetitia* (happiness) 180–1, 188, 217–8
— *liber naturae* (book of nature) 311n
— *lumina* ('lights'; eyes) 65–66, 117, 141–2, 162, 166
— *lux* (light) 162, 186, 314, 316
— *memoria* (memory) 316
— *mens* (mind) 316n
— *messes* (harvests) 134n, 345n
— *nugae* (trifles) 225–6
— *obaudire/oboedientia* (listen; obey) 254
— *oculi* (eyes) 162, 187
— *opinio* (opinion, belief) 206
— *ops* (power, resources) 138n *see also* Greek terms and phrases: *ops*
— *oratio/orator* (declaimed speech, prayer; orator) 176, 197, 248, 262
— *oratorculi* ('speechifiers') 176–7, 200, 248, 366n

— *otium in umbra* ('leisure in the shade') *see umbra*
— *percipere* (to pluck; to perceive) 227
— *pertransire* (to go beyond, travel) 54n
— *proceritas* (height, 'loftiness') 191
— *recta ratio* (right reason) 59, 92n
— *sal* (salt; wit) 226–7, 237, 240–41, 246
— *sapere* (to taste) 216n, 227n, 343n
— *sapientia* (wisdom; knowledge) 216n, 343n
— *scopulus* (crag) 131
— *sensim* (gradually) 151
— *somnium* (dream, vision) 339n
— *somnus* (sleep) 142, 339n
— *umbra* (shade; shadow) 140, 143n, 151–3
— *variatio delectat* (variety pleases) 215, 265, 268 *see also* perception: variety of sense objects
— *videre* (to see) 276, 283
— *videri* ('to be seen'; to seem) 138, 149, 161, 180n
— *visio beatifica* (beatific vision) 286, 289
— *voluptas* (pleasure) 215, 218, 243, 245–7, 302
laughter 216, 220, 228–33, 237n, 242–3, 247, 267n
Lawes, Henry 366n
Lawrence, Henry 345, 349
Lawrence (apothecary) 97
Leavis, F. R. 33–34
Leigh, Richard 278n
L'Estrange, Sir Roger 299n
No blinde guides (1660) 299n
Physician cure thy self (1660) 299n
Libya 181, 186
light 64n, 70n, 88, 117, 126, 127n, 131, 138, 140n, 145n, 148–9, 157, 161–2, 173–5, 179–82, 185–7, 190–94, 196–201, 219n, 254–6, 258, 270–75, 277–8, 280–84, 286–7, 290–92, 295–8, 300–304, 309, 311–2, 314–25, 330–31, 336, 338, 342, 346, 349, 353, 363, 366, 372–3, 378n, 381, 383
— inner light/illumination 253, 256–8, 272, 274, 278, 283, 296, 300, 315–6, 324, 330–31, 342, 363 *see also* vision: inner/spiritual vision
lightning 217–9
literary epistemology 22 *see also* epic: as a poem of knowledge; poetry: literary vehicle of knowledge
Lloyd, David 297
Locke, John 17, 75, 152n, 227n, 323n
An Essay Concerning Human Understanding (1689) 75n, 323n
— 'tabula rasa' 323n

logic 28, 52n, 58, 59n, 79, 175n, 203–205, 207, 213, 225–6, 368
— 'closed fist' metaphor 204n, 213
— 'thorns and brambles' metaphor 225–6
see also Milton: individual works, *The Art of Logic*
London 3, 18, 21, 66, 97, 99, 115–6, 119–21, 123, 134, 146n, 194n, 215, 234n, 384
— Tower of London 121
— fortifications of 119n, 121
— personification of 119
Long Parliament 91n
Longinus 205
love 71, 81, 91, 113–4, 116–9, 121–3, 126, 132, 136–7, 140, 145, 146n, 149, 152–60, 162–8, 179, 182, 201, 234–5, 283, 286, 310, 322, 366n, 374
— erotic 113, 117, 122–3, 131–3, 139, 153n, 158, 166, 181, 200, 234–5
— romantic 67–68, 117, 133, 135, 155, 181–2, 374
see also Cupid/Amor/Eros, Greek terms and phrases: *agapê*, *erōs*
Ludovisi, Cardinal Ludovico 136n
Lycaon 235, 240
Lyotard, Jean-François 60n

magic, sympathetic 182n
Mammon 139n, 211–2
Mann, Thomas 9–10, 14
   The Magic Mountain (1924) 9–10
manna 58, 83, 204n, 223, 346
marble 132n, 136n, 145–6
marriage 20, 117n, 132n, 145n, 146n, 179, 185, 210
Martial 189n
Marvell, Andrew 278–81, 283–4, 296
   The Rehearsal Transpros'd (1672/3) 278
Marx, Karl 1–2, 6–8, 42n, 47
Mary (mother of Jesus) 71, 373n
masque 38–39, 146, 191–2, 305
material (sensory) culture
— beds 65–67, 76, 131–2, 146n, 157, 169, 339, 381
— bells 194, 305n
— candles 186, 278n, 281, 317n
— 'rush-candles' (rushlights) 192–3
— telescope 99, 328, 382, 385
mathematics 98n, 205n, 326n
Matzerath, Oskar 385n
McKendrick, Jamie 371, 382–6
   'Earscape' (2016) 382–6

medicine 22n, 38, 64, 97, 99–100, 138, 228, 232, 255, 299n
— Galenic *see* Galen
— 'the King's Evil' (scrofula) 100
— Paracelsian *see* Paracelsus
— ophthalmology 299, 366n
melancholy 227n, 229, 279–80, 289 *see also* humours, humoralism
Mercury 223
Mesopotamia 182
metaphor 2, 4, 21, 39, 59, 115n, 120, 154, 161–2, 166, 184, 187, 199, 206n, 218, 224–5, 243, 246, 248, 249, 256n, 267, 284–5, 288n, 303, 338n, 340, 347, 349, 357
— of the body 40, 204n, 213
— sensory metaphor 71, 73, 90, 93, 106–107, 153, 173–5, 178, 285, 363, 365–8,
— orientational metaphor 142, 167, 188, 200n, 258, 275, 277, 279, 282, 291n, 293, 323, 386
— linguistic metaphor 61, 90, 106–108
— in Aristotle 71–74, 107
— in Ricoeur 72–73, 80n
— C17 attacks on 75–79
— target 80, 114n
— source 63, 71, 74n, 80, 107, 334
— 'dead' metaphors 80n, 204, 319, 367n
— Milton's 'pot simile' 84, 93, 172n
see also conceptual metaphor
metaphysical poetry 30–33
Mexico 45, 375n
Michael (*Paradise Lost*) 227n, 265n, 277, 306n, 349–52, 360
microcosm/macrocosm 191, 248, 279n, 281n, 294
Middle Ages 18n, 85, 175, 208, 235
military *see* warfare
Milton, John
— antitrinitarianism 282n
— blindness 20, 29, 31–32, 34n, 69, 89, 90n, 187, 252, 254–5, 282, 297, 375, 378, 385
— at Cambridge University 18–19, 57, 114–5, 123, 169–70, 173, 202, 213–4, 225n, 237
— daughters 21, 375–82
— 'fit audience' 261, 325, 339, 382
— iconography and image 171, 214n, 231n, 238–9, 375–378
— 'the Lady of Christ's' 171n, 214n, 231n, 238–9
— materialist/monist ontology 38–39, 53, 134n, 274n, 303n
— multilingualism 23n, 64n, 277n
— as a poet 28–35, 40, 133, 155, 251, 252,

Milton, John (continued)
255, 257–8, 269, 272, 283, 329, 340, 360–61, 363, 376
— as a polemicist 20, 23, 39, 89–90, 173, 297, 367, 385
— as a prose writer 21–24, 27, 34–36, 39–41, 65–69, 89–90, 106, 109, 169–70, 188–9, 202, 215n, 228, 240, 249–50, 253, 258, 261, 285n, 297, 331n, 355, 357n, 363, 365–8, 385
— as a religious thinker 35, 273n, 282, 285n, 286, 367n *see also* Chapter 5 more generally
— and science 20, 103–104, 172n, 201, 365
— travel on the Continent 19–20, 113n, 190n
— writing of *Paradise Lost* 20–21, 251, 378, 381

Milton, John, individual works
A Brief History of Moscovia (printed 1682) 18, 367
— 'Ad Leonoram Romae canentem' (1638/9) 151, 337n
— 'Ad Patrem' (1631/2?) 147n
Arcades (1629/30? or 1634?) 300n, 307n
Areopagitica (1644) 91–92, 170, 196n, 206n, 269, 355–7
At a Solemn Musick (1634) 59n
At a Vacation Exercise (1628?) 53n, 213, 228n, 240, 242
— 'Carmina Elegiaca' ('Elegiac Verses,' 1624?) 65–68, 71, 129n, 132, 134, 142, 156–8, 162n, 167, 169, 178n, 181, 184n, 193, 200, 339n
— 'Companion Poems' *see Il Penseroso; L'Allegro*
Complete Prose Works (Yale, 1953–1982) 30n, 34, 36–37, 40, 88n, 169n, 189
Comus ('A Masque …', 1637) 19, 23, 38, 53, 89n, 191–5, 201, 267n, 274n, 302n, 303, 305–306, 331n, 384
De Doctrina Christiana (found 1823, printed 1825) 273n, 282, 285–6
Defensio pro Populo Anglicano ('First Defence,' 1651) 88, 202n
Defensio Secunda ('Second Defence,' 1654) 34n, 88–90, 93, 177, 255–6, 298, 304
— 'De Idea Platonica quemadmodum Aristoteles intellexit' (1628?) 284n
— Elegy I 113, 115–124, 128n, 131n, 134–137, 139, 143–6, 153–5, 160–62, 165–6, 169n, 215, 365
— Elegy II 114
— Elegy III 114, 167
— Elegy V 65n, 115, 122n, 124–158, 160n, 162n, 165–7, 170n, 180n, 184–6, 200, 212n, 252, 256–7, 269, 291n, 300, 306, 309, 345, 363, 365
— Elegy VII 113, 155–167, 233, 365, 368, 375
History of Britain (1670) 57n, 367
— 'Ignavus satrapam …' ('Kings should not oversleep') 66n
Il Penseroso (1631?) 123n, 128n, 164n, 170, 194, 201, 283n, 289–91, 295, 305n
— 'In Obitum Praesulis Eliensis' ('On the Death of the Bishop of Ely,' 1626) 114
— 'In Obitum Procancellarii Medici' (1626) 274n
— 'In Quintum Novembris' (1626) 113n, 186n
L'Allegro (1631?) 65n, 146n, 170, 229, 345–6
Lycidas (1637) 19, 68, 89n, 115n, 147n, 215n, 231n, 299n, 307–308, 355
— 'Nativity Ode' ('On the Morning of Christ's Nativity,' 1629) 35, 208–209, 215n, 256n, 290
Of Reformation (1641) 27, 35–36, 40, 73, 84, 172n
Of Education (1644) 20, 27–28, 59n, 196n, 205, 355–6, 358, 367
Of True Religion (1673) 331n
— 'On the Death of a Fair Infant Dying of a Cough' (Winter 1625/6) 114n
Paradise Lost see individual main entry
Paradise Regained (1671) 126n, 132n, 260n, 307, 309n, 359n
Poems (1645) 20, 113, 155n
Poems (1673) 133
Pro Se Defensio (1655) 88
— Prolusion I 175–203, 212, 219, 237n, 248–9, 255n, 269
— Prolusion II 196–7, 200, 202–213, 248–9
— Prolusion III 171–5, 213, 226n
— Prolusion V 173, 175
— Prolusion VI 170–72, 176, 203, 213–50, 262, 269, 273n, 302, 310, 317, 340, 353n, 366
— Prolusion VII 172–5, 187n, 285
Samson Agonistes (1671) 21, 23, 40n, 299, 304–305, 312, 315–9, 338n, 359n, 363–6
— 'Song: On May Morning' (1629) 65, 116, 124, 142, 151, 156–7, 178n
— sonnets 23, 231n, 252, 297, 363n, 366
— 'Leonora' sonnets 151n, 337n
— Sonnet 1 68, 129–30, 310n
— Sonnet 4 284n
— Sonnet 12 177n, 235n, 239n
— Sonnet 13 366n
— Sonnet 16 36n
— Sonnet 17 345–7, 349, 351, 357n

Milton, John, individual works (continued)
— Sonnet 18 366n
— Sonnet 19 366n
— Sonnet 22 20, 256, 304, 382
The Art of Logic (*Artis logicae plenior institutio*, 1672) 52n, 59n, 72, 75n, 285n
— 'Theme on Early Rising' (1623–25?) 66, 68, 70, 132, 134, 142, 169, 250
The Readie and Easie Way to Establish a Free Commonwealth ... (1660) 34n, 204n
The Reason of Church-Government (1642) 39
— 'To Mr Cyriack Skinner Upon his Blindness' *see* sonnets: Sonnet 22
Milton, John, senior 18, 147n
Minotaur 150n
misogyny 122, 162
moderation/temperance 344, 350–51, 362
— tempering of the passions 356–7, 363
moon 69–70, 120n, 121, 130, 145n, 174, 192, 196, 210, 244, 274n, 314–5, 327–8
More (Morus), Alexander 88–89, 98, 177n
Morley, Thomas 268n
A Plaine and Easie Introduction to Practicall Musicke (1597) 268n
Moschus 355n
Moses 256–7, 309, 326, 331, 354
Mount Helicon 256, 325, 329
Mount Hymettus 132, 256
Mount Ida 132, 256
Mount Niphates 287
Mount Olympus 127, 148, 324, 326, 329–32
mountains 132n, 138, 153, 256–8, 300, 302, 325, 326n
multi-sensory settings, scenes etc. 6n, 9, 12, 68–69, 116n, 124, 134, 137–40, 146, 152, 158, 167, 181, 186, 189, 199–200, 228, 253, 276–7, 298, 302, 305–307, 310, 346, 381, 385
muse
— Nine Muses 115, 117–8, 126, 160n, 198–9, 201, 210, 215n, 224, 256, 300–301, 309n, 324–6, 329
— Milton's 'Heavenly Muse' *see* Urania
music 9, 18–19, 30n, 33, 35, 51–52, 59, 63–64, 68–69, 115, 146n, 147, 149, 154, 159, 169, 182n, 197, 203, 205n, 207–213, 221–2, 239n, 249–50, 257, 259–60, 262, 264, 267–9, 332n, 335, 337, 343n, 346, 355–8, 363, 366n, 378, 381, 385,
— ancient Greek modes (*harmoniai*) 355, 360
Dorian (or Doric) mode 260n, 355, 357, 358–9
Ionian mode 358
Lydian mode 358
Phrygian mode 355

— harmony 9n, 53, 212, 221–2, 258, 260–61, 265, 268, 333n, 335, 357n, 358 *see also* 'harmony of the spheres'
— madrigals 18, 356
— melody 67, 206–207, 209–210, 212, 268, 335
— musical education 18, 222, 268n, 356–7
— practical/audible music 203n
— and rhetoric 355
— of the soul 203n
— sphere music *see* 'harmony of the spheres'
see also musical instruments
musical instruments
— bass viol 222, 268n
— 'crowd' 385n
— guitar 356
— harp 51, 53n, 164n, 208, 221n, 261–2, 268, 309n, 325, 339, 340n
— lute 261–2, 346, 356
— lyre 147, 164n, 173, 209, 221–2, 239, 270, 272, 340n
— mandolin 378
— organ 229, 356
— syrinx (panpipe) 147
— theorbo 337n
— trumpet 115, 358
— violin 356
mythology, Greek/Roman 117, 121, 124, 127, 130, 133, 135–8, 140, 142–5, 148, 154–5, 160, 168, 178–82, 187, 189, 200–201, 210, 233n, 249, 299, 328, 363
Near East, ancient 118–20, 135
neo-Platonism 53, 279n, 284, 318, 340n, 365
— emanation 271
neurolinguistics 46, 61
new historicism 39
night 37n, 66–69, 73, 126, 129–31, 143–4, 147–8, 151–2, 157, 169, 175–80, 182, 186–7, 189–95, 197–203, 209, 215, 239, 248–50, 254–5, 262, 270–71, 285, 291, 300–304, 309–310, 314–5, 327, 338–9, 341–2, 361–2, 372, 376, 381
— activity/work 67, 190, 200–201, 255n, 300–301
— dusk 148–150, 152, 154, 157, 167, 267
— hearing, sharper at night 194–5
— night as blindness 255n
— nightly inspiration 199n
— sleep 45, 66–67, 81, 126, 137n, 140–43, 157–8, 167, 178–80, 187, 189–90, 195–8, 225, 280, 284, 292–3, 339, 367, 373
see also dawn; day
Noah 306n

North Sea 383
nourishment 83–84, 244, 247, 343–4, 349–50
nymphs 149–50, 158–9, 163n, 307n *see also* dryads

occultism 32, 279n
Oceanus 182
October (Eisenstein) 10n
Odysseus (Ulysses) 89, 93, 122
oil, petroleum, fossil oil 18n, 187, 383–6
— hydraulic fracturing ('fracking') 384
Olympic Games 59
Ong, Walter J. 52n, 75n
Ongee, Andaman Islanders 44–45, 49
ophthalmology 299, 366n
— cataract 299, 328n
— *gutta serena* 299
Ops 133, 135, 138n, 188
Origen of Alexandria 318n
Orion 160
Orpheus 164, 203n, 221–3, 239n, 247, 262, 272, 273n, 339–40, 342, 362
Orphism 187–8, 200 *see also Hymn to Dawn*
Overbury, Sir Thomas 116
Ovid 114, 118n, 120n, 123n, 132n, 135n, 136, 139n, 150n, 166, 184, 265n
   Metamorphoses 265–6n
Owen, Wilfred 386

pamphlets 20, 35–36, 90, 231, 278, 280, 283–4, 296–7, 299n
   A Just Complaint, or Loud Crie, Of All the Well-Affected Subjects (1643) 90
Pan/Faunus 149
Pandaemonium (*Paradise Lost*) 134n, 267
Paphos 121, 133n
Paradise Lost (Milton)
   — blind speaker 251, 297, 300–301, 309–310, 315–6, 323, 333, 338, 342, 362–3
   — book 1 211, 326, 354n, 358
   — book 2 51, 57, 92, 223, 264, 268, 330n, 360, 374n
   — book 3 82, 117n, 268, 271, 273, 275, 286, 291n, 296n, 298n, 353
   — book 4 143, 307, 360
   — book 5 52, 69, 83, 254, 262, 286, 291, 294, 298, 306, 329, 342, 344, 350, 354
   — book 6 11, 82, 208, 291, 349
   — book 7 82, 247, 276, 285–6, 350, 359
   — book 8 265, 350
   — book 9 37n, 90n, 233n, 254, 347–8, 351–4, 361
   — book 10 361
   — book 11 263, 306n, 348–9, 351
   — book 12 277, 362
   — Eve 28n, 38n, 58n, 69, 82–83, 85n, 117–8, 137n, 141n, 143, 146n, 252, 254, 261–3, 265–6, 268, 276–8, 287–8, 291, 293, 307, 308n, 310n, 330, 337n, 342–7, 350–53, 360, 373n, 375n, 378
   — Father 69, 127n, 256n, 268, 271, 273, 282, 285–6, 299n, 332, 348
   — mists and vapours 74n, 134n
   — proems 23, 251–3, 255n, 256, 258, 261, 271, 273, 282, 291, 301, 319, 322–3, 325, 329–31, 336, 338, 342, 353–4, 359, 361–3, 365–6, 373, 376, 381
   — sensescape of Chaos 191–2, 271, 275
   — sensescape of Heaven 212, 252, 271, 357, 366n
   — sensescape of Hell 53, 198n, 271, 273, 274–5n, 315n, 357, 366n
   — sensescape of Paradise 28, 116n, 253n, 346, 357, 366n
   — tree of knowledge 82, 254, 351
paradox 30, 79, 84n, 105, 123, 128, 137n, 143n, 145, 156, 160, 165, 210, 216, 257, 273, 282, 309, 314, 315, 317, 325, 365, 375
Paris 146n
Parker, Samuel 76, 278n
Parkinson, John *183*, 184, 300n
   Paradisi in Sole Paradisus Terrestris ... (1629) *183*, 184, 300n
Parnassus 126, 256, 309n
parody 54n, 126n, 170n, 172, 213, 225, 227, 232, 243, 248, 278, 293
passions 78, 84n, 135, 155, 163, 165, 167n, 172, 229, 233, 247, 249, 279, 341, 355–6, 363
Paul (apostle) 51, 114n, 318, 320, 331
Pegasus 329–30, 335, 337
Peneus 126
Pepys, Samuel 17–18, 95
perception 1, 3–8, 13–14, 18, 27–28, 31, 33–34, 40–41, 47–49, 52n, 53, 60–64, 67–72, 79, 85–86, 95–96, 99, 101, 103–104, 107–109, 126, 129, 134n, 147, 153–4, 157–9, 163, 165, 167–8, 173–5, 181, 184, 197, 199, 200, 208, 211–2, 215, 218–9, 225, 227, 230, 232, 240n, 247, 250, 253, 257, 264, 266, 279–80, 284, 288, 293–4, 298, 300, 302, 304, 309–311, 314, 318–22, 326, 330–34, 340, 351, 362–3, 366, 368–9, 385–6
— interoception 230n, 246
— 'make-perceive' 249–50
— sensory fatigue 216
— variety of sense objects 215, 242, 265–8, 367n, 368

Pericles 3
Persia (Iran) 383
Persia, ancient 118–9, 120n, 135, 181, 186, 234
Persius 189n, 211
Petrarch (Francesco Petrarca) 133, 347n
Phaeton 139–40
Phalereus 28n, 205
Phanes 179, 234
Philaras, Leonard 187
Phillips, Edward 254n, 257n, 349n, 376
Phillips, John 376n
Philomela 128–29, 137, 145, 147, 150, 153, 167, 168, 257, 363
philosophy 6, 17, 30n, 43, 57, 63, 69, 75–76, 79, 138, 175, 205–206, 215–6, 225–6, 243, 321
— academic 207
— atomism 143
— empiricism 22, 75, 179, 189, 323
— epistemology 22, 75, 101n, 173–4, 203, 285–6, 296n, 320, 333n, 353–4
— eudaimonism 351
— free will 57, 286
— Greek 53n, 204n
— metaphysics 75, 274, 284–5, 295, 298, 318
— natural philosophy 71n, 108, 210, 365
— ontology 53, 75
— Scholasticism 19, 57, 171, 173, 225, 285
— Stoicism 285
Phoebus (Apollo) 115, 117, 124, 126–7, 129–32, 136–45, 147–55, 159–61, 166–7, 173, 182, 185–6, 190, 198–200, 210, 215n, 260
photography 1–2, 4–6, 13n, 14
Phyllis 140n, 147–9, 169
pictura (of emblems) 43n
Pilgrim Fathers 17
pilgrimages, pilgrims 81, 85n
Pindar 53
pineapple 17, 48
Pirene 126, 300
planets 143–4, 196–7, 200, 202, 205n, 207, 260, 274n
plants 52, 102, 184, 191, 244, 276–7 *see also* flowers; trees
Plato 28n, 51, 53, 158, 173, 175, 196, 205–206, 210, 271, 274n, 278, 280, 283–91, 295–6, 318–21, 355–6, 360, 365
— ideas 173, 175, 196, 283–5, 295
Meno 285
The Republic 284, 287, 355
Timaeus 52n
pleasure 27–28, 65–67, 116, 120, 149, 151–2, 154, 163, 166, 172, 181n, 208, 215–8, 223–4, 227, 229n, 233–5, 243, 245–6, 249, 252, 302, 346–7, 352
Pliny the Elder 103n, 184, 315n
Plotinus 321
Plutarch 195n, 285n
Pluto *see* Hades/Pluto
Plymouth Rock 17
Pocock, J. G. A. 63–64
poetry 21–24, 29–30, 33–39, 47, 52, 59n, 63–65, 68–69, 71, 75, 78–79, 90, 126, 128, 151, 155, 159, 162, 166–8, 173, 175, 180, 185, 187, 189n, 200, 205, 208, 250–51, 259–61, 263, 269, 272–3, 284n, 296, 304–305, 308–310, 327n, 333–335, 345n, 348, 355, 359, 363, 365–7, 372–4, 383–4, 386
— function of 269
— inspiration 124–8, 136, 150, 165, 167, 199n, 223–4, 256–7, 261–3, 272, 274, 278, 296, 300, 310, 319, 323, 327, 329–30, 335–6, 338–9, 359, 361–2, 376, 381–2
— literary vehicle of knowledge 257–8, 269, 362, 366, 368
— moral dimension of 269
— pagan poetry 149, 272, 359–60
— poetic frenzy 126, 165n
— sacred poetry 268, 270, 273, 300, 309
— secular poetry 273, 335
Polyphemus (cyclops) 88–89
prelapsarian, postlapsarian 48, 58n, 89n, 211, 233n, 260–63, 266–8, 276–7, 286, 291n, 308n, 321, 326n, 342, 344–8, 351–2, 362
Primaudaye, Pierre de la 70n
prison 21, 197, 301–303, 305, 315, 338
prophecy 163, 204, 206, 256, 275, 302n, 309, 326, 378
Proserpina (Proserpine) 136–7, 145, 150, 153
Protagoras 57
Protestant Reformation 17, 27, 35–36, 40, 73, 84, 263
— nonconformism 241, 283, 296
providence 51, 57, 82, 253, 297
Prynne, William 231n
psychology 4, 38, 42, 47, 53, 68, 101, 126n, 195, 216n, 229, 280, 283, 303, 316, 355
— faculty psychology 19n, 101, 103n, 278, 280, 283n, 303n, 316
— Aristotelian 51–52, 173n, 240n
— human soul as a city/citadel 279, 311–2
— tripartite structure of body, soul, spirit 51–52, 59
— organic soul 52, 316n
— intellective soul 52, 59
— rational soul 52, 57

psychology (continued)
— Hebraic conception of the soul (*nephesh*) 53n, 303
Ptolemy 104n
punning 76, 88, 162, 192, 233, 237, 241–2, 244, 246, 287, 305, 330, 352, 353n, 384–5
Purchas, Samuel 367n
puritanism 30, 38, 39n, 121n, 161, 231, 264n, 284, 319–20, 375–6,
Pushkin, Alexander
Poltava (1828/29) 11
Pythagoras 196, 202, 205–207, 209–211, 260, 279n, 355
Pythian Games 51–53, 59

Quakers 100n
Quintilian
Institutio Oratoria 204n

rainbows 185n, 305–306 *see also* Iris
Ramus, Petrus 52n
Dialectic see Milton, *The Art of Logic*
Randolph, Thomas 214n, 237–40, 246
Raphael (*Paradise Lost*) 52, 58, 69–71, 82–84, 90n, 99n, 104, 141n, 208, 244, 247, 254, 264–5, 276, 288–9, 291, 294, 306n, 309n, 325, 327–9, 342–5, 347, 349, 351n, 352–4
Raphael (Raffaello Sanzio da Urbino) 378
recorded sound 1–2, 5n
reductio ad corpus 213, 243–6
Renaissance 19, 40n, 63n, 103, 124, 136, 149n, 175, 216n, 255n, 279n, 287n, 309n, 327n
— ideal of beauty 118
— literary practice 327
— Neoplatonism 340
Renaissance epic 19
Restoration 21, 100, 204, 237n, 255, 297, 338
rhetoric 28n, 39–40, 51–52, 57–58, 63, 75, 79, 84n, 88n, 91, 170–72, 175–9, 195, 197, 202–207, 213–6, 218, 220, 222–7, 229, 232, 235, 246–50, 259, 261–4, 268–9, 355, 368
— *genus grande* 205, 261
— Milton's *exordia* 172
— Milton's orator persona 213, 222, 239, 251
— 'open hand' metaphor 203, 249
— rhetorical decorum 175, 214, 232, 261
— speaker–hearer connection 171–2, 175, 197–200, 214, 216–220, 222, 224–5, 228, 230, 237, 241, 243–4, 247–8, 311
Rhodes 181, 186
— Colossus of Rhodes 186
Rhodope 164n, 325

rhyme 238, 253, 258–60, 281, 283, 309, 347n, 372–4
Richardson, Jonathan 379
Ricks, Christopher 33–34, 347
— 'the Milton controversy' 33–34, 36, 41
Riegl, Alois 8, 42n
right reason 57, 59, 92, 176
Roberts, Sir Lewes 95–96
The Merchants Mappe of Commerce (1638) 95
romanticism 28, 30, 47–48, 65, 128n, 279n, 360, 369n
Rome/Roman, ancient 3, 8, 19–20, 88, 91, 118, 120n, 136, 138, 146n, 149, 189, 223, 242, 244, 255n, 260
Rome 136n, 151, 186, 337n
— Tarpeian Rock 118, 120n
— Theatre of Pompey 118
Romney, George 378
rosewater 182n *see also* flowers: roses
Royal Society 76, 78, 100
Ruskin, John 68n
Russia 10, 17–18, 367

Salmasius, Claudius (Claude de Saumaise) 88–89, 297–8
Satan (*Paradise Lost*) 11, 51, 59n, 84n, 87, 103, 120n, 126n, 134n, 138, 177n, 252, 254, 258n, 260, 265–8, 271, 274n, 287–8, 291, 292n, 293, 296n, 298n, 310n, 330, 347n, 349–50, 352, 354n, 359–60, 375n
Satan (*Paradise Regained*) 53n, 158, 307
scholasticism 19, 57, 171, 173, 225, 285
science, modern 5–6, 13, 20, 22, 36, 47, 54, 63, 75n, 79, 103, 365
Scotland 88, 383
seasons 142, 152, 155, 266, 270, 300n, 308n, 310, 322, 336, 344–5, 373
— autumn 21, 136, 141n, 149, 237n, 267, 280n, 381
— spring 113, 116–7, 123n, 124–9, 136–7, 141–6, 148–55, 157, 162n, 165–7, 181–2, 185–6, 200–201, 257, 267–8, 300n, 302, 306, 308, 310, 385
— summer 6n, 141n, 146n, 213, 271, 305, 310, 373, 381
— winter 114n, 141–2n, 151–4, 175, 237n, 267, 280, 308n, 345–7, 381
Semele 139–40
Seneca 67n
De senectute 67n

sensation 1–5, 7, 10, 14, 27, 31, 46, 48, 59, 62, 86, 140, 157, 165, 219, 228, 230n, 250, 293, 323n, 345
senses/sensorium 1, 3, 6–8, 10, 14, 44, 48–49, 60–62, 85–86, 95–96, 101–102, 137, 153–4, 167, 317, 319, 321, 323, 352, 363, 385–6
— ambiguity of 'sense' 264, 373n
— as gates 311–2, 367n
— contact senses (touch, taste, smell) 211, 244, 296, 320–21
— distance senses (vision, hearing) 211, 248, 321
— hierarchy 42, 44, 66, 82, 101–102, 131, 142, 153, 191, 211, 232, 244, 258, 296, 314, 317, 325
— ideasthesia 136
— in the marketplace 95–96
— 'Miltonic sensorium' 15, 18, 21, 24, 27, 31n, 32, 34, 36–41, 107, 365, 368–9, 371, 375, 381, 386
— 'sense of knowledge' 107, 296, 311, 335
— sensory deprivation 136, 310, 315n, 338, 362, 368
— should be 'governed' 347, 349, 363, 366
— synaesthesia 47, 58, 68, 134, 136, 138, 140, 152–3, 167, 188, 200, 218–9, 221, 232, 307
— 'windows of the soul' 303
see also spiritual senses
sensescapes 3, 14, 28, 43, 116n, 166, 182, 190, 194, 253n, 271, 293, 308–309, 337, 346, 363, 366, 382, 385
— caves 145–6, 315n, 385
— circle/sphere 116n, 337
— cities 120, 145–7, 166, 190n, 215, 230n
see also Paradise Lost: *relevant subentries*
sensory discourse
— illustrative/descriptive mode 22, 61, 132, 152, 167–8, 174–5, 199, 248, 368–9, 371, 382
— deliberative/conceptual use 22, 132, 136, 144, 154, 156, 167–8, 174–5, 212, 232, 248, 282, 353, 368–9, 371, 382
— *discours sensible* (Lyotard) 60n
— 'sensory' 27–28, 36–37, 39, 71
— 'sensual' 27–28, 30, 35–37
— sensual temptation 29, 158, 161, 250, 254, 258n, 266, 307, 366, 375
— 'sensuous' 27–31, 33–37, 39, 41, 52–53, 58, 60, 65, 67, 69, 74, 92, 98, 106, 121–5, 128, 131, 133–4, 136–8, 145, 151–4, 158, 166–7, 181, 205, 215, 218, 223, 235, 246, 294–5, 298, 304–305, 307, 365, 378
— sensuous enjoyment 28, 67, 83, 123, 136, 149, 152n, 158, 265–6, 269, 294, 302, 304–305, 307, 309–312, 314, 343–4, 349, 351, 365
— as embodied/vocal speech 72, 89, 170, 199–200, 214, 221, 223, 242, 261–2, 268–9, 368
sensory receptivity 29, 32
sensuality 9, 28, 37, 104n, 123, 133–4, 149, 154, 184, 222, 239, 244–5, 247, 352, 366, 369
Seriphus 176–7
Serres, Michel 62n
sexuality 88–89, 131, 132n, 136, 141n, 145, 230n, 234n, 235–9, 247, 308n, 352
shade 115–6, 124, 139–40, 143, 149, 152–3, 157n, 301
shadow 6n, 124, 143, 151–3, 157n, 199, 302n, 341, 347, 366n, 374
Shakespeare, William 146n, 237n, 239n, 274n, 290n, 310n, 347n, 384n
A Midsummer Night's Dream 68, 239n, 280n
Hamlet 328, 384n
Romeo and Juliet 237n
Sonnet 73 274n
Sonnet 102 310n
The Tempest 146n
The Winter's Tale 290n
Twelfth Night 357n
silence 128–9, 193–5, 201, 210, 358
Simmons, Matthew 321n
Simmons, Samuel 258n, 321n
sin 95, 114n, 211–2, 235, 250, 254–6, 298, 341, 347, 384
— original sin 256, 384
Skinner, Cyriack 366n, 376n, 382–3
Skinner, Quentin 2
smell/scent 6n, 17, 31, 33, 38n, 44–45, 65–67, 70–71, 74n, 96–98, 114, 134, 137, 145–6, 152n, 173, 180, 182, 184–5, 187, 201, 211, 219n, 229–32, 241, 249, 265, 300n, 305–309, 319, 345, 348, 367n, 373, 378
Smith, Bromley 169, 184n, 188, 189n
Smith, John (philosopher) 321–2
Society of Apothecaries 97–100
Socrates 226, 284n
Sodom 384
soil (earth, turf) 66, 125–6, 130–31, 139n, 291n, 308, 358, 367n, 382
see also earth; Tellus (Earth)
Son (*Paradise Lost*) 268, 271, 273–4, 282, 286, 292n, 319, 347
song/singing 51–53, 58, 59, 65–68, 90; 114, 124–30, 134, 138n, 147–9, 151, 154, 157n, 160n, 164, 167–8, 180–82, 199, 203n, 206, 209, 216, 249, 252–4, 257–9, 261–4, 268–70,

song/singing (continued)
   300, 305, 309, 324–6, 330–2, 334–5, 337–42, 348, 353–5, 359–63, 368, 378
sophism 57, 170, 204, 223, 263n, 268
sorcery *see* witchcraft
South, Robert 297
Spain 17, 45n, 238, 259
Spanish language 371–4, 376
speech 54n, 58, 72, 75–76, 90–92, 104, 108, 114–5, 125, 135, 170–71, 175–8, 189, 197–8, 203n, 248, 263, 335n, 343
   — embodied 89, 199–200, 214, 220–21, 242, 249, 261–2, 268–9, 368
   — knowledge-oriented 169
Spenser, Edmund 360n
spices 17–18, 95, 134, 136, 185, 305, 367n
   — cinnamon 137, 153, 158, 305
   — cloves 17
   — nutmeg 18
   — pepper 17
   — saffron 145–6
spiritual senses 318–25, 340, 362–3
Sprat, Thomas 76, 78
   History of the Royal-Society (1667) 76
St Francis 287n
St Paul's School 18, 66
Staffordshire 383
stars 69, 117, 119–21, 138–9, 143–4, 147, 161, 179, 191–2, 196, 207–12, 274n, 287, 357n
   — 'influence' of 138, 144, 274n, 357n
Steele, Richard 171
Stone (apothecary) 98
Strike (Eisenstein) 10n
Styx 180, 274n
Suetonius 131n
sun/sunlight 66–67, 70, 104n, 115n, 121, 124, 126–7, 129–32, 135, 136, 138–45, 149, 152–3, 157, 161, 163, 166–7, 179–86, 188, 190–91, 196–8, 200–201, 203n, 231n, 237–8, 239n, 260, 265, 267, 270–71, 274–7, 279–80, 283–4, 286–7, 292–4, 296, 298, 300–301, 306, 309, 314–6, 322, 328, 332n, 336, 338n, 341, 368, 385
   — tactile quality of 142, 197, 201, 275, 292, 296
   — representing God 239n, 296
   — representing a king 275, 287
   — sensescape of 271
   — sunset 148, 186, 338n *see also* night: dusk
   — symbol of the eye/vision 136, 139–43, 158, 181, 190–91, 197, 200, 315, 338
sunrise *see* dawn

sweetness 83, 97–98, 116, 125–6, 140n, 141n, 261–2, 318, 321, 345
   — of discourse/speech 51–52, 58, 60, 73, 170, 223, 261–2, 263n, 343
   — smell of roses and violets 66–67, 96, 182, 184–6, 300n
   — of song/music 203n, 206–210, 221, 268
Switzerland 9
Sylvanus 148–9
symbol (Coleridge) 129n, 158n, 375
Syriac 376
Tantalus 240
Tasso, Torquato 360n
taste 17–18, 38n, 48, 58, 63–64, 68n, 73, 83–84, 95, 98, 134, 137, 141n, 142, 204n, 211, 216n, 223–7, 232n, 234, 237, 242, 244–5, 247, 253–4, 265, 293, 317n, 318, 320–22, 342, 343n, 344–9, 351–3, 361–2, 375
   — bitter 116, 141n, 165–6
   — salty 140n, 141n, 238, 246
   — sour 141n
   — sweet *see* sweetness
Teiresias 301n, 309n
telescope 69–70, 99, 328–9, 382, 385
Tellus (Earth) 124–5, 127, 132, 134–144, 146, 149–50, 152–5, 166–7, 180, 185, 190–91, 345
   see also earth; soil (earth, turf)
temperature 300
   — coolness 74, 139–40, 142–3, 152–3
   — heat 45, 140–44, 146n, 166, 184–6, 357n
   see also shade; shadow
temptation 29, 158, 161, 230, 250, 254, 258n, 260n, 266, 307, 366, 375
Tethys 139–40
Thamyris 270, 309
The Censure of the Rota upon Mr Miltons book ... 204
The German Ideology (Marx/Engels, 1846) 1
The Jazz Singer (1927) 1
The Transproser Rehears'd (1673) 278–84, 295–7, 299n, 318, 322
theatre 97n, 115–9, 123, 134, 136, 166, 259, 283
   — comedy 116
   — tragedy 116, 259, 359–62, 365
Thebes (Boeotia) 221n, 233n
Thebes (Egypt) 328
Theocritus 67, 355n
theology 22n, 38, 51, 57, 59n, 63, 71, 76, 102–108, 127n, 208, 209, 223, 241, 251, 254n, 257n, 271, 273n, 281–6, 295, 296n, 316, 318, 322, 326, 335, 363, 365, 367n
   — Arianism 273n, 282n
   — mortalism 367

theology (continued)
— socinianism 171
see also Bible; Catholicism; Christianity; Church of England; enthusiasm; God; puritanism
theophany 132, 153
Thirty Years' War 17
thunder 219
Tillyard, E. M. W. 33, 34n, 260n, 288n
Tillyard, Phyllis B. 169, 176n, 188n, 189n, 206n, 219n, 234n, 236n, 241
time 3–4, 7, 13–14, 34, 42, 46–47, 54, 152–4, 189–90, 212, 240n, 310, 331–2, 335–6, 371, 375, 386
— circularity of 124–31, 148
— historical 37–38, 42, 45–46, 48–49, 63, 65, 87, 95, 109, 168, 374
touch, tactile, tactility 32, 35, 37, 38n, 44, 66, 68, 74, 80n, 81, 96, 100–101, 107, 114, 125, 127, 131–4, 137–45, 149n, 150, 152–4, 156, 159–60, 166–7, 173, 175, 177n, 182, 184–7, 201, 204–205, 208–209, 211–3, 217–9, 221–4, 226n, 229, 234n, 236, 244, 249, 258n, 266, 275–7, 281, 291–3, 296–8, 300–301, 306, 308–309, 312, 314, 317–20, 333n, 336, 346, 358, 373, 378
— 'influence' (of the stars and sun) 138, 144, 192, 274n, 298n, 357n
— tactile healing ('touching') 100–101
towers 120, 134–5, 153, 161, 166–7, 277, 305, 366
travel 19–20, 54, 85n, 120, 136, 146n, 189, 192, 367
trees 133–5, 148, 150, 191, 222, 232n, 265–6, 348
— cypress 148–9
— elm 116–7
— pine 133–5
Trinidad 383
Troy 118–20, 135, 158, 190, 341
Tzotzil 45

Ulysses *see* Odysseus
Urania 148n, 253, 256, 270, 272, 275, 300, 315, 324–7, 329–32, 334–42, 353, 359, 361–3, 376
Uranus/Coelus 180
Uriel (*Paradise Lost*) 84n, 271

Venus (planet) 70, 196
Venus/Aphrodite (goddess) 114, 121–3, 133, 155–6, 159n, 160–63, 167, 190
verse 11–12, 33, 37, 41, 66–67, 70, 113–5, 189n, 237, 240, 256n, 262, 268, 339, 365, 374, 376
— blank verse 137n, 260n, 280–81, 297, 372, 383

— elegiac couplets 66, 113–5, 122, 150–51, 161n, 162n
— hexameter, dactylic 113, 150
— Milton's note on 'The Verse' 253, 258–61, 264, 269, 283, 337, 363, 372
— 'Miltonic half-line of derision'
— pentameter, dactylic 113, 150, 162n
— pentameter, iambic 238 *see also* verse: blank verse
— run-on lines 264, 312, 326, 351n, 374, 383
Vesta 145
Vienna Genesis 8
Vinge, Louise 43–44
Virgil 67, 88–89, 131n, 135n, 149n, 152n, 184, 259, 298, 309n
Aeneid 88, 348
Georgics 67n, 309n
vision (apparition) 2n, 124, 126–7, 146n, 148, 150, 175, 181, 202n, 227n, 256–7, 279–80, 284–6, 299n, 317, 327, 329–30, 336, 339–40, 351n, 361–2,
vision (sense of sight) 6, 14, 32, 37, 38n, 44, 64, 69–70, 87, 101n, 103n, 107, 116–7, 119–27, 131–2, 134–6, 138–46, 148, 152–4, 157–9, 161–7, 173–6, 179–80, 187–94, 197, 199–200, 211–2, 218–9, 223–5, 250n, 252, 255–6, 258, 265, 271, 273, 275–8, 280, 285–9, 291–3, 295–8, 300–306, 309–311, 314–5, 317–20, 323–30, 334–6, 338–40, 342, 353, 360–62, 378n, 382–3
— Adam's vision 314n
— angelic vision 69–71, 87, 99n, 327–8
— beatific vision 212, 282n, 289
— extramission theory of 303–304, 315
— eye 3–4, 6n, 20, 29, 31, 39–40, 53n, 69, 82, 95, 117–8, 121, 132n, 141, 148, 150, 161–2, 188, 191, 199, 208, 248, 255, 276, 287, 299, 301n, 305, 312, *313*, 316–7, 321, 327, 333n, 352, 354n, 366n, 367n, 373, 378, 381
— all-seeing eye of God 82, 87, 278, 286, 327, 334
— human vision 327, 329
— inner/spiritual vision 30, 256, 269, 272, 290, 296, 317–24, 327, 330, 338, 340, 363, 382
— visual-Platonic idiom 280, 284–5, 288, 295–6
see also blindness; conceptual metaphors
visual arts 2n, 4, 21n, 33, 43, 62–63, 136, 190, 340n, 371, 375–82
visual culture 43, 190, 376
voice 68, 88–92, 114, 131, 137n, 164, 171–2, 177–9, 187–9, 203n, 208–209, 213, 218–9, 221, 228–9, 234–5, 242, 251–5, 257, 260n, 262–3, 268, 270, 272, 287, 293, 307, 324–5,

voice (continued)
   330–32, 334–40, 342, 346, 353, 356, 359, 361–3, 376
   — embodied 13, 72, 89, 167–9, 172, 199–200, 214, 220–21, 223–4, 230, 232, 242, 249, 252, 253, 261–2, 268–9, 359, 362–3, 368

Wales 230
warfare 9, 11–12, 14n, 17–18, 82, 113, 119n, 120–22, 135, 145, 153, 156, 178, 240, 264, 278, 288, 291, 306n, 311–3, 325, 348, 352, 358, 383–4, 386
   — artillery 259–60, 384
   — fortifications 119–21, 134–6, 153, 161, 166–7, 221n, 277–9, 305, 311, 366
   — 'war in heaven' (*PL* 5 and 6) 11, 82, 264, 291, 325, 342n, 352, 358, 360, 384–5
water 139–142, 163n, 180, 194, 241, 244, 254, 270, 272, 274–7, 300, 302–303n, 305–306, 332n, 336, 384
   — dew 66, 131–2, 139–40, 180, 182n, 184, 223, 305–306
   — flowing water 262, 274, 300, 305
   — ocean 138–41, 189, 241, 305
   — 'water of life' 274, 319
   see also rainbows
West Indies 186
Wickhoff, Franz 8, 42n
William III 120n
Williams, Raymond 30n, 33
witchcraft 123, 136, 157n, 237, 284
Wolfe, Don M. 30n, 34–37, 40
Wood, Anthony à 237n
woods 3, 101, 128–30, 149–50, 164n, 191, 201n, 292, 325, 332n *see also* trees
Wordsworth, William 37n, 350n, 368–9, 384n, 385
   'London 1802' 384
   '[Not useless do I deem]' 368
World War, First 9, 383

Yeardly (apothecary) 98

Zeno of Elea 204n
Zephyrus 137, 158
Zeuxis 190
Zion *see* Jerusalem, Heavenly